The Quality Yearbook
2002

Other yearbooks available from McGraw-Hill

The 2002 ASTD Training and Performance Yearbook
   John A. Woods and James W. Cortada

The Supply Chain Yearbook, 2001 Edition
   John A. Woods and Edward J. Merien

The 2001-2002 ASTD Distance Learning Yearbook
   Karen Mantyla and John A. Woods

The Quality Yearbook 2002

James W. Cortada
John A. Woods

McGraw-Hill
New York Chicago San Francisco Lisbon London Madrid
Mexico City Milan New Delhi San Juan
Seoul Singapore Sydney Toronto

McGraw-Hill

A Division of The McGraw·Hill Companies

Copyright © 2002 by The McGraw-Hill Companies, Inc. All rights reserved. Printed in the United States of America. Except as permitted under the United States Copyright Act of 1976, no part of this publication may be reproduced or distributed in any form or by any means or stored in a data base or retrieval system, without the prior written permission of the publisher.

1 2 3 4 5 6 7 8 9 0 DOC/DOC 0 9 8 7 6 5 4 3 2 1

ISBN: 0-07-138079-5

The sponsoring editor for this book is Catherine Dassopoulos. The publisher is Jeffrey Krames. Design and production services were provided by CWL Publishing Enterprises, Madison, WI, www.cwlpub.com.

Printed and bound by R.R. Donnelley Company.

To order multiple copies of this book at a discount, call the McGraw-Hill Special Sales Department at 800-842-3075 or 212-904-5427.

Contents

	Preface	ix
	Acknowledgments	xii
PART ONE	**Background for Quality**	
	Introduction	1
	Classic in Quality	
	The Quality Management Maturity Grid, *Philip B. Crosby*	3
	Quality Perspectives	
	A Ticket to Ride, *Kristine Ellis*	14
	Quality—Why Do Organisations Still Continue to Get It Wrong? *B.G. Dale, A. van der Wiele, and A.R.T. Williams*	26
	Factors Related to Employee Perception of Their Leaders' Commitment to Implement Continuous Quality Improvement, *Lee Jones*	38
PART TWO	**Quality by Industry**	
	Introduction	55
	MANUFACTURING	
	The Counterintuitive Principles of the Toyota Production System, *Robert W. Hall*	57
	Building Blocks for Capital Projects, *Rohan Hoare and Gerhard Seiler*	67
	Performance Support on the Shop Floor *Jryki J.J. Kasvi and Matti Vartiainen*	74
	Improving Production Line Performance *Michael Umble, Van Gray, and Elisabeth Umble*	85
	Cost vs. Quality, *Doug Bartholomew*	96
	High-Performance Partnering by Self-Managed Teams in Manufacturing, *Joe Singer and Steve Duvall*	103
	SERVICES	
	The Effects of Satisfaction and Loyalty on Profits and Growth: Products Versus Services, *Bo Edvardsson, Michael D. Johnson, Anders Gustafsson, and Tore Strandvik*	116

Managing Customer Expectations in Professional
  Services, *Jukka Ojasalo* — 130
Customer Relationship Management Is Not an Option
  Kristin Anderson and Carol Kerr — 151

PART THREE Implementing Quality

Introduction — 175

QUALITY TRANSFORMATION

Planning/Strategy

Your Company Does Not Exist,
  Don Yates and Mark Davis — 163
Intellectual Capital Analysis as a Strategic Tool,
  Göran Roos, Alan Bainbridge, and Kristine Jacobsen — 171

Leadership

Become a Better Leader, *Kennard T. Wing* — 182
Leadership DNA: The Ford Motor Story,
  Stewart D. Friedman — 185
Developing Leaders: How Winning Companies Keep
  on Winning, *Robert M. Fulmer, Philip A. Gibbs,
  and Marshall Goldsmith* — 196

Cultural Transformation

Rethinking Empowerment: Why Is It So Hard
  to Achieve? *W. Alan Randolph* — 213
Lessons Learned from Innovative Organizations,
  Robin Cook — 231

Knowledge Management

Creating a Knowledge Culture, *Susanne Hauschild,
  Thomas Licht, and Wolfram Stein* — 235
Managing Customer Knowledge, *Eric Lesser,
  David Mundel, and Charles Wiecha* — 244
The Accidental Knowledge Manager, *Peter Dorfman* — 249
Infomediaries: For Knowledge, Look Within,
  Daniel Costello — 256

Voice of the Customer

How to Implement a Customer Satisfaction Program,
  *Earl Naumann, Donald W. Jackson, Jr.,
  and Mark S. Rosenbaum* — 262
Building a Solutions-Based Organization, *Steve Sheridan
  and Nick Bullinger* — 280
Keeping Customer Information Safe, *Peter Singer* — 289

Contents

Building Customer Relationships: Do Discount Cards Work? *Andrea McIlroy and Shirley Barnett*	293

Teams and Teamwork

Dare to Share, *Kristine Ellis*	308
Looking Before You Leap: Assessing the Jump to Teams in Knowledge-Based Work, *Rob Cross*	315
Does Teaming Pay Off? *Priscilla S. Wisner and Hollace A. Feist*	329

Learning Organizations

Focus-Pocus, *B. Joseph Pine II and James H. Gilmore*	339
Market Research for Quality in Small Business, *William L. Rhey and Frank M. Gryna*	342

QUALITY TOOLS AND TECHNIQUES

Process Management

Resolving the Process Paradox, *Robert A. Gardner*	355
Working by the Rules, *Emily Kay*	370
Know What Your Gages Are Measuring, *Gillian Babicz*	378
Should You Outsource Your Business Processes? *Christine Kirk*	383
Measurements for Business, *Philip Stein*	390
Improving In-Process Handling, *Steve Parsley*	396

Six Sigma

Six Sigma on Business Processes: Common Organizational Issues, *Doug Sanders and Cheryl Hild*	404
Reshaping Six Sigma at Honeywell, *Robert Green*	416
Six Sigma Beyond Manufacturing—a Concept for Robust Management, *Mustafa R. Yilmaz and Sangit Chatterjee*	424

E-Commerce

Catalyst for Collaboration, *John Teresko*	438
Developing Your Company's New E-Business, *Ava S. Butler*	443
Start Your Own Net Market, *Anne Field*	451
Creating a Customer-Friendly Website, *Angelo M. Donofrio*	456

FUNCTIONAL PROCESSES

Supply Chain Management

The Value Added Information Chain, *Susan L. Cisco and Karen V. Strong*	461
Dock-to-Shop Is Just-in-Time, *Maranda McBride, Sheilah Harrison, and Brian Clark*	478

Optimizing Economic Order Quantity (EOQ),
  Dave Piasecki — 485
Corporate Change and the Logistics Model,
  Jim Coker — 494

Information Technology
Fast Friends: Virtuality and Social Capital,
  Eric Lesser and Joseph Cothrel — 498
Through the Looking Glass: A Progress Report on the
  Enterprise Portal, *The Editors of
  Knowledge Management Magazine* — 511

Finance and Accounting
Improving Financial Performance Through Benchmarking
  and Best Practices, *Susan J. Leandri* — 522

STANDARDS AND ASSESSMENTS
ISO 9000 and Baldrige
ISO Quality Management Principles,
  ISO and Quality Systems Update Editors — 529
Does ISO 9000 Give a Quality Emphasis Advantage?
  Gavin Dick, Kevin Gallimore, and Jane C. Brown — 535
Fourteen Years of ISO 9000: Impact, Criticisms,
  Costs, and Benefits, *Thomas H. Stevenson
  and Frank C. Barnes* — 551
The State of Quality Auditing, *Greg Hutchins* — 564
Journey to the Baldrige, *Debbie Phillips-Donaldson* — 572

PART FOUR Quality References
Introduction — 585
Directory of Quality Resource Organizations — 587
Quality Resources Online 2002 — 607
A Quality Manager's Guide to the Internet,
  Vanessa R. Franco — 623
Directory of Magazines, Journals, and Newsletters
  That Cover Quality — 629
Calendar of Major Events, 2002 — 660
Index — 683

Preface

Our loyal readers of *The Quality Yearbook* will quickly realize that this year's edition is somewhat shorter than those of prior years. The length is a reflection of some findings and conclusions we have reached regarding the whole field of quality management practices that we would like to explain.

For nearly a decade with this yearbook, we have always sought out material that met several criteria that resulted in a publication that provided best practices, high-quality content, and clear writing, and that expanded our collective knowledge of new ways to be effective in the application of quality management. During the past decade we were able to pursue that objective because the field as a whole was still expanding and innovating, particularly in the early 1990s in the United States and in Western Europe. However, as the decade progressed, and as we reviewed thousands of articles and book chapters, it was becoming increasingly clear to us that the rate of innovation in new techniques and best practices was slowing. This should be of no surprise because the field rapidly matured in the late 1980s and early 1990s, with thousands of organizations adopting quality management practices and weaving these into the basic fabric of their activities and management processes. Since innovative practices were a major source of content for the yearbooks, as the rate of novelty decreased we began to find it increasingly difficult to provide as much new material as in prior years.

The second trend we noticed was the publication of many articles and books that essentially repeated concepts and best practices that had long been established and that were already very familiar to our readers. A decade ago we had committed to you that we would not be redundant in our choice of materials, with the one exception of some of the appendices describing organizations and quality publications. We honored that commitment. However, to maintain the original length of *The Quality Yearbook* would have required us to violate that principle. We decided that you would rather have a somewhat shorter volume that provided high-quality, fresh, and innovative material than a longer book with less outstanding content.

In no way are we suggesting that these two developments are negative; rather, they are further evidence that quality management practices are becoming such an integral part of how organizations operate today that differentiating quality management practices from normal business activities is increasingly difficult. In short, we think the quality advocates have won the war. Workers from CEOs to newly hired employees have embraced quality management across all industries and around the world. It is the way businesses and governments operate, and increasingly also in education. In many companies, for example, we have noticed that quality is so woven into the fabric of the enterprise that employees do not distinguish quality from what they do on a daily basis. In fact, over the past several years your two editors have held discussions around the question of whether or not to rename *The Quality Yearbook* simply *The Management Yearbook* or some variant of that theme because quality has become so mainstream.

We have, of course, continued to innovate in this yearbook, as we have over the years with earlier editions to reflect your changing interests, the ebb and flow of the topics covered in articles and books. That is why each year, while the basic format of the book remains more or less the same, some of the sub-sections evolve. These nine volumes together offer over seven thousand pages of material describing quality management practices as they have evolved and matured over the past decade. In looking at some of the earlier volumes, it is our observation that they remain fresh and relevant because they described quality practices that today are widely deployed. This is particularly the case with methodological pieces on training, communications, process management, SPC, measurements, and ISO 9000. The many Baldrige case studies represent examples of outstanding performance, as do the innumerable cases of implementation that we publish throughout each edition of the yearbook. Our decade-long emphasis on presenting case studies of actual implementations has resulted in this full set of yearbooks capturing organization-specific illustrations of a broad array of quality management practices, many of which were written by those who implemented them. This is a design strategy that has been continued in this issue of the yearbook.

Organization

The organization of *The Quality Yearbook* remains the same. As in previous editions, we have divided the book into four parts:

Part One, Background for Quality, continues the popular "Classics in Quality" section. This year we've included a chapter from Phil Crosby's seminal work, *Quality Is Free*. Since Crosby passed away this year, we thought this was a good way to honor his memory. Part One also includes a section called "Quality Perspectives" where we've included three articles selected to stimulate your thinking both about managing for quality and general issues in its implementation.

Part Two, Quality by Industry, covers quality management as implemented in manufacturing and services. In the manufacturing section, we've included six articles dealing with topics such as the Toyota Production System, the costs of quality in the automobile industry, and the use of self-managed teams on the floor at Harley-Davidson.

In the services section, we've included three articles that look at issues involved in delivering quality services, including a chapter from a new book on customer relationship management.

Part Three, Implementing Quality, presents the best articles and ideas from the past year on the theory and techniques of quality management. We have broken the readings into four categories:

Preface

1. Quality Transformation
2. Quality Tools and Techniques
3. Functional Processes
4. Standards and Assessments

Part Three is the longest part of the book and provides a wide spectrum of articles that explain the whys and hows of implementing quality, including many different examples from different companies and industries.

Part Four, Quality References, includes a wide variety of material to help you further your exploration of quality. Among the contents of this part, you'll find our completely updated directory of quality magazines, journals, and newsletters, now the most complete listing of such periodicals available. There is also our updated directory of World Wide Web sites that deal with quality issues. And there's a completely updated and annotated directory of organizations. You'll also find a calendar of events cataloging meetings and conferences of interest to quality managers in 2002.

What's New in the 2002 Edition?

We've included nearly 60 articles in this edition. We've included a new section, "E-Commerce," which looks at the Web and its use and management today. Process management and Six Sigma continue to get a good share of articles, because we think these are important topics to people working in quality. We have sought a balance between technical material and topics dealing with management issues, such as leadership, teams, communication, and training, because quality management is really an all-encompassing subject.

It is somewhat fashionable today to dismiss quality management as something companies have already tried, and it's not something in which people still have an interest. This may be the case, but the practices that emerge from the insights of Deming and many others have not been abandoned. In fact, they are accepted as standard procedures in the best-managed and most-admired companies. We don't have to call these practices "quality management." A better name might be "intelligent management" or "managing for excellence." Still, for the sake of convenience, we'll classify them as "quality management" for now. And while many of the articles in this book don't ever talk about quality in so many words, the practices they describe emerge from the systems view of organizations and the goals of process improvement and customer satisfaction. As we have heard it said, "I am not in quality, quality is in me." We take that approach to our selection of material for this book.

Our objective for *The Quality Yearbook* is to provide you with a tool for keeping up with the field of quality management. We expect these annual volumes to be the first place you look when you have a question about almost any subject in this field. We welcome your comments on what you like and suggestions you might have for improvement. Write us at jwcorta@us.ibm.com or jwoods@cwlpub.com. You can also visit our Web site at www.cwlpub.com.

Acknowledgments

This book has been a big undertaking for us, and we are indebted to many people who have played a role in its completion. At McGraw-Hill, Jeffrey Krames, publisher, and Catherine Dassopoulos, editor, have been an important part of our team.

At CWL Publishing Enterprises, we want to especially thank Robert Magnan and Nancy Woods for helping complete many of the tasks that have resulted in the book you hold in front of you. They are central members of our team.

We want to thank the editors, authors, and publishers of the magazines, journals, and books from which we drew the articles that make up the heart of this book. All were very forthcoming in supplying the permissions that allowed us to reprint the pieces you see here.

Finally, we want to thank those who have found the previous editions of this yearbook to be useful additions to their shelf of quality resources and thank those of you who are new buyers this year of the 2002 edition. You have made this the premier reference book on quality and management excellence. We look forward to serving your needs for many years in the future.

Jim Cortada
John Woods

PART ONE

Background for Quality

> The purpose of quality management is to set up a system and a management discipline that prevents defects from happening in the company's performance cycle.
> —Philip B. Crosby

This is a quote from the quality classic we have chosen to reprint in this 2002 edition of *The Quality Yearbook*. Phil Crosby was relentless in pushing for managing and improving operations so as to eliminate defects. Crosby passed away during 2001, and we thought reprinting a chapter from his first book, *Quality Is Free*, would be an appropriate way to start off this year. In this selection, he explains "The Quality Management Maturity Grid," a tool managers can use to learn where they stand on their company's quality journey.

We believe that quality is a journey, where we continuously learn from our experience and then, with discipline and commitment, continuously improve processes to reduce costs and deliver higher-quality outputs to customers. It includes proven techniques for doing this. Of course, names change. We now have Six Sigma management, for example (covered in this edition of the yearbook), but the foundation of every sound management approach finds its home in the principles expounded in quality management.

This is a book that's all about documenting and communicating practices that improve quality—quality for customers, quality for management, quality for employees, and quality for suppliers. Unlike some people who find Total Quality Management passé, we believe the practices usually included under this term are really the practices of the best-managed companies in the United States and around the world.

There are many nuances to TQM and different companies have put the tools, techniques, and cultural attitudes that are part of TQM (whether this term is used or not) into practice in different ways. This book provides lots of examples of these nuances. To set the stage for the rest of the book, we start with articles that fall into two areas: classics and quality perspectives.

Classic in Quality

It's been our practice in each edition of the yearbook to reprint articles and chapters from books that we consider to be "classics in quality." These are not necessarily taken directly from the literature on quality management. They demonstrate, rather, that the ideas of quality management have been on the minds of consultants and business managers for a long time. TQM has simply gathered these ideas into a coherent set of management practices.

As mentioned, for this edition, we reprint a chapter from Phil Crosby's *Quality Is Free*. This book was a major best-seller and was one of the books that raised managers' consciousness about the idea of quality and how you manage to achieve quality.

Quality Perspectives

The purpose of this section is to provide you with some thoughtful reflections on quality management by various respected business writers and consultants. We start with an article titled "A Ticket to Ride" by Kristine Ellis. It's a kind of review of several management perspectives, as reflected in popular books, such as *The One Minute Manager*, *In Search of Excellence*, *The Seven Habits of Highly Effective People*, and more. This is a thought-provoking piece. We believe that all the ideas in these books are consistent with the basic premises of TQM and the systems view of organizations and urge you to read the article from that view point.

Next we include "Quality—Why Do Some Organisations Still Continue to Get It Wrong?" from a British journal. It looks at why many companies don't seem to get this quality stuff and what can be done about it.

We conclude with a study done on employees' perceptions of their leaders' commitment to quality. It provides an interesting review of the relationship between employees and managers in organizations (in this case, a university) implementing quality management practices.

Classic in Quality

The Quality Management Maturity Grid

Philip B. Crosby

> *Phil Crosby is one of the real pioneers of quality management. He passed away in 2001, and we thought it would be appropriate to include a selection from his first book,* Quality Is Free, *as the classic in this edition of the yearbook. In this chapter, he describes what he calls the "Quality Management Maturity Grid," a tool to help managers understand where they and their organizations are on their quality journey.*

Management is the function responsible for establishing the purpose of an operation, determining measurable objectives, and taking the actions necessary to accomplish those objectives. Although management is usually thought of as having to do with chartered corporations or organizations, it operates elsewhere also.

Managing a family, for instance, is probably the most difficult of all jobs. It is clear that very few have been completely successful at that task. The small number of people who actually achieve their hoped-for potential could be explained as a matter of random success, considering the billions of individuals who have lived in the past and the billions who are living now. *Somebody* has to succeed!

The family suffers from three primary obstacles when it comes to management. The first is that the members of the organization are brought aboard without benefit of personal evaluation, psychological testing, or any of the other techniques that formal organizations use to screen employees. Thus, each member is an unknown quantity.

The second is that you are sort of stuck with the family group. If your three-year-old gives you a hard time, you can't fire her or toss her out in the snow. The neighbors will toss the child right back in. The hold that family managers have on their family personnel has an emotional and circumstantial base, and emotions and circumstances are changing all the time.

Third, the family managers, and in fact the family itself, are not trained for the job. They have no methods of measuring performance except in terms

---

Reprinted with permission of the publisher from *Quality Is Free: The Art of Making Quality Certain* by Philip B. Crosby, published by McGraw-Hill. Copyright © 1979 by Philip B. Crosby. All rights reserved.

of their own limited experience. They are required to provide financial means, security, and educational activities, often without having had the chance to learn by experience or practice. Once they do learn how to do the job, they are classified as obsolete and are forced to sit back, while not interfering, as the children take their turn at family management.

Families and business operations have a great deal in common. Both are people-oriented, and both have difficulty in measuring some important aspects of their progress. Family management measures everything against the manager's personal standards. Thus, approved activity is always several fads behind. The children like one kind of music, the adults like another.

Measurement becomes a matter of defining the "entitlements" and expectations of human existence. What are the members of each generation entitled to receive? What can they expect as their right from the family and what are they expected to contribute? As families grow more affluent through the years, the specifics change. Grandpa may have felt he was entitled to take the plow horse to school, riding with two siblings. Granddaughter may feel that each sixteen-year-old deserves her own car. Mother, who assumes her right to household conveniences, may also feel that she should receive unceasing adoration from each member of the group.

All individuals have developed some idea of the things society ought to provide for their physical and emotional well-being. A very few may have some idea of the things *they* should accomplish to attain those goals, or what they should give to others.

Families have difficulty setting goals, measuring performance, and accomplishing tasks. Like all human beings, they are also faced with difficulties of communication, difficulties that are compounded by emotional involvement.

> Quality management has always been looked at as a subjective operation, hard to define and measure.

Quality management has always been looked at as a subjective operation, hard to define and measure. That is because it has been relegated to the role of a results-oriented procedure rather than a planning operation. Just as the folklore of family management states that if you don't spoil children, and are sure to raise them with loving discipline, they will turn out to be good, so the folklore of business management states that if you have good in your heart, you will produce quality.

I have no desire to poke fun at these platitudes; they aren't all wrong. But you know from your own experience that it is a rare parent who doesn't feel that he or she has given a child the best possible upbringing under the circumstances. We kid ourselves into thinking that if our offspring had only listened more intently to us, things would have been better for them. Finally, however, no one knows any way to guarantee the best for their children, so parents take their chances and do the best they can.

However, quality management has just become too important to leave to chance. In this day of crushing taxation, mysterious methods of accounting, rollicking inflation, and unsettled politics, it may be that quality is the last

The Quality Management Maturity Grid

chance we have to make profits controllable. But if quality is to be a "first among equals," then management must have a way of measuring and controlling. You will not be surprised to know that I have developed just such a system.

Using the Quality Management Maturity Grid, even the manager who isn't professionally trained in the quality business can determine where the operation in question stands from a quality standpoint. All that is required is knowing what is going on. If the manager doesn't know that, then we are both in the wrong book.

For years I have been saying, every way I could think of, that quality is too important to leave to the professionals. Professionals must guide the program, but the execution of quality is the obligation and opportunity of the people who manage the operation.

However, I just didn't have enough objective evidence to convince everyone. Every step of achievement was done the hard way. We had to kill a mouse before they would give us a rat-catching license. Eventually, we worked our way up to a dragon a week. This method requires eight to ten years from the first conversation to a completely implemented quality program. It is never possible to assume that the program will continue to prosper. Every day requires the identification and destruction of new menaces. If you can't produce a dead dragon each week, your license may be revoked.

Robert Burns wished that we could be given the gift of seeing ourselves as others see us. Many of us echo that thought, probably because there is little chance of it happening. After all, our own version of ourselves is usually more flattering than that of others, and most people really don't want to know the truth about themselves.

Not many people really want to know the future, either, especially if it might hold disaster. Those who can predict the future have never been appreciated in their own times. History, mythology, and real life are full of situations where someone warned others of events about to happen—only to be scorned or ignored. Noah and the flood; Cassandra and the Trojan horse; Churchill and World War II; the list goes on and on.

People would rather handle the expected and mundane chores of today, like making a living. Typically, as individuals go through life, they collect a store of clichés and experiences that serve as a memory bank to draw on in handling situations as they arise. New thoughts or unfamiliar ideas must survive their encounter with this memory and experience library. Otherwise, they are cast aside as being unworthy.

It is this test of worthiness, this comparison with the past, that causes problems in the development and implementation of new thoughts and programs. Changing mind sets is the hardest of management jobs. It is also where the money and opportunity lie.

Take quality management in its truest sense as a "for instance." The purpose of it is to set up a system and a management discipline that prevents

> Using the Quality Management Maturity Grid, even the manager who isn't professionally trained in the quality business can determine where the operation in question stands from a quality standpoint.

defects from happening in the company's performance cycle. To accomplish this you have to act now on situations which may cause problems some time from now. Act now for reward later.

Management has to commit money this year to conduct quality testing so there won't be problems two years from now. A training program that costs a lot of time and money and may produce benefits must be established right away. Inspections and tests and corrective actions have to be accomplished before problems become big enough to become disasters.

Prevention like this is not hard to do—it is just hard to sell. It requires the ability to convince people that bad things will happen to them if they don't take early action. Most of us are unable, or unwilling, to accept such things intellectually, and are convinced only on the basis of experience.

But to wait until a failure is unassailable before learning from experience and only then advancing one more step is too much to expect of anyone. A career could be over before a person had the chance to experience each and every thing that can go wrong.

That is the frustrating part of it all. How can you bring the top operating people in your company, the ones with the money to spend or withhold, the ones who get to decide who does what—how can you bring them around to understanding quality management and all the things it can do for them?

Until the development of the Quality Management Maturity Grid, this conversion process was exclusively a function of the personal charm and convincing attitude of the quality management professional. If people liked and trusted the quality manager, things got done. However, even though good results produced evidence that the system worked, they did not necessarily guarantee the quality manager's right to increase efforts for prevention. It is a strange thing, this business of success not breeding more opportunity, but many management people have been frustrated by it.

In many cases, for instance, a value analysis job produces outstanding cost reductions, design improvement, and true profit growth. However, the next time such a study is proposed, it is met with blank stares. Success in these functional areas does not seem to provide a foundation on which to build further successes. Apparently, it is a matter of what particular effect is needed in the business at a particular time.

The need for long-range programs in quality can be deduced intellectually through the Grid. A manager of any operation can spend a few moments with the Grid, recognize familiar events, and pinpoint where the operation is at that moment. Then all that is necessary is to refer to the following stage of the Grid in order to know what actions need to be taken for improvement. And in the cases where an established program is now deteriorating, the Grid can be read backwards. You can see the last point at which you were successful and figure out how to get back there.

The grid is divided into five stages of maturity. Six management categories serve as the experience relations you must go through to complete the

The Quality Management Maturity Grid

matrix. By reading the experience condensed in each block, it is possible to identify your own situation.

All of this recognizing is done unemotionally and without anyone else knowing about it. Even if pride causes a little clouding of the exact status, it will usually only cloud to the extent of one stage, unless you are completely kidding yourself. That still means improvement is necessary. Said improvement can be recognized when it comes.

To become familiar with the Grid, it is necessary to recognize the content of each stage of maturity. Stories and case histories are utilized in the [rest of the book's chapters] to assist you in gaining this understanding. But you can know from just looking down the columns that the stages have a definite recognition pattern. I like to call the behavior at each level by its "stage" name.

Stage 1, *Uncertainty*, is indeed confused and uncommitted. Management has no knowledge of quality as a positive management tool. They speak regularly of their quality function in terms of being the policemen, or "gumshoes," whose job it is to catch the criminals in the act. Problems of nonconformance are considered the fault of not being tough enough on the "bad guys." Uncertainty learned management control from the Clint Eastwood movies.

Uncertainty casually places the quality function deep in the bowels of one of the operating departments: manufacturing, administration, operations, engineering, and so on. Inspection is sometimes a separate operation and is assigned to the production people so they "can have the tools to do the job."

These restrictions create the self-fulfilling prophecy that unsolved problems will always be around. Every problem is considered unique, even if it has been encountered before. Problems breed problems, and the lack of a disciplined method of openly attacking them breeds more problems. The result is emotion on the management level. The question becomes "who," rather than "what," caused the difficulty. Personalities are the predominate factor in problem attacking. This sometimes results in illogical firings and quittings as it becomes impossible to methodically examine a situation and solve whatever problems exist.

The cost of quality is not in the Uncertainty glossary, probably because local quality management doesn't know very much about it. However, anyone bringing up the subject will receive an audience if for no other reason than that it will be something no one has considered before. This is the key to starting some action in this type of company.

But quality improvement will never be part of a company in the age of Uncertainty. These companies are somewhat like alcoholics, whose number one symptom is emphatic denial that the condition exists. Therefore, improvement is not considered as an option. Uncertainty-age companies know they have problems but don't know why, although they do know it isn't because they aren't working hard. Everyone in Uncertainty works hard, and most are frustrated at the amount of brute force it takes to keep the operation moving.

> Stage 1, *Uncertainty*, is indeed confused and uncommitted. Management has no knowledge of quality as a positive management tool.

Stage 2, *Awakening*, is more pleasant, but no less frustrating. Here management is beginning to recognize that quality management can help, but is unwilling to devote the time and money to make it happen. If pressed into strengthening the quality operation, they will opt for putting one of the "gang" in that job. Selection is done on that basis because of the mistaken idea that the need for someone who understands the product or service is greater than the need for someone who understands professional quality management.

Awakening hasn't awakened enough to recognize that quality management takes more than understanding the technical aspects of a product or service. At this stage, however, inspection and testing are performed more often, and problems are identified earlier in the production cycle. This cuts rework costs a little while permitting some attention to resolving problems.

Chronic problems are listed and assigned to teams for action, although prime attention is still paid to keeping the product moving. In service companies the customer is cajoled more at this stage. Service problems are corrected quicker. But the basic problems are still not solved. Teams set up to attack problems accomplish quite a bit, but their scope is limited to the near future. Long-range solutions are not considered seriously.

An interesting thing happens when the cost of quality is calculated for the first time. The quality manager, having read a paper or attended a course, sits down with the comptroller to calculate this number. They assume the walls are coming down about them and they do a very detailed calculation, only to find that the cost of quality is very small. It may only be 3 percent of sales or less, which is the level that really well-run companies aspire to achieve. This often serves to convince everyone that things aren't as bad as they seem because "we can prove it by the number." However, as they will find out much later, they have been fooling themselves. They just don't include everything they are supposed to include.

Take inspection, for instance. In an Awakening company the inspection is conducted by a lot of different people in a lot of different areas. Because the quality department is so disorganized, when they are calculating inspection costs, they don't include the people who do adjustments and similar measurements on the production line. They don't include the burden on all inspection activities, and they probably don't include the inspectors who are working for manufacturing.

Awakening's warranty costs, for instance, include only the expense of replacing the product with a new unit. That is just the shop cost. How about all the correspondence? How about the repair time, the handling, the everything else? It is enough at this point to say that about one-sixth of what really exists will be calculated. That will be all they can find. But it is a start.

Awakening really comes to life when the magic of *motivation* has been sold. The idea is that if you hang up posters and have a contest, you will get people turned on to quality; then things will get better. The fact is that peo-

The Quality Management Maturity Grid

ple do enjoy entertainment and attention, and so they will respond for a few days. Then they tire of it and go back to what they were doing before.

So Awakening will put together a motivation package. They will make a few speeches and have a special lunch and even talk to the people. Immediately the results of this communication show themselves. Every measurement chart shows improvement. But it only lasts a little while—just long enough, in fact, for the employees to recognize that the effects of the effort are really short-term.

Realization of this usually causes Awakening to reevaluate the commitment to improvement, and may drive the company back into the Uncertainty stage. Complete regression is possible when the shock sets in. However, the employees of the company will usually offer encouragement and urge Awakening to continue stumbling along on the path of quality improvement. The employees have a much more practical view of things. They know instinctively that the company has to offer more constant quality in service and product alike or its very life will be threatened.

Such is the hard life of Awakening.

The stages of quality maturity do not provide individual guided tours like Scrooge's ghosts. They are easily identifiable, but they have no particular schedule. Lack of attention or a management change can quickly send Wisdom crashing to Awakening.

However, there is a moment when you can tell precisely when one stage is entered. *Enlightenment* appears with the decision to go ahead and really conduct a formal, regulation, card-carrying quality improvement program. With the establishment of a regular quality policy, and the admission that we cause our own problems, management enters the stage of Enlightenment.

In making this commitment it is necessary that Enlightenment establish its quality department as a balanced, well-organized, functioning unit. This group is to lead the crusade, and it must have the capabilities and resources to do so. All inspection and testing, quality engineering, data reporting, and similar activities must be included. And the department must have a quality education budget.

One of the most recognizable changes in the Enlightenment stage involves the approach to problem resolution. Facing problems openly, without searching for individuals to blame, produces a smoothly functioning system for solving those problems. Systems, of course, are only road maps; it is personal enthusiasm that makes them work or fail. When task teams are responsible for both resolving a current problem and preventing it in the future, they respond enthusiastically. Constant reassurance is necessary if people are expected to work into the future. They need to know you understand about gestation, birth, growth, and death.

The cost of quality will now get its first fair evaluation. Those who do the calculating will still miss a third of the costs, but they will develop a reasonable enough estimate to provide direction for cost eliminations. Nothing is

> *Enlightenment appears with the decision to go ahead and really conduct a formal, regulation, card-carrying quality improvement program.*

quite so effective as having cost data to show competing areas that one department has more effective methods of reducing costs than others.

And, of course, quality improvement is now headed up by an official quality improvement team, headed by someone other than the quality director. This team takes the time to understand the content and intent of each step before launching it. Their purpose is to establish a system and attitude that will last for a long time—one so well entrenched that it would take a hard-working quality reduction team to deactivate it.

Enlightenment still has problems and will have them for some time. But the quality team now feels confident that there is indeed a light at the end of the tunnel, not another train coming at them.

Wisdom is another matter altogether. Those involved deeply in this stage, and there aren't all that many of them, find themselves wondering why they used to have all those problems and why the quality department always lived in the other room. Things are basically quiet. Cost reductions are in effect; when problems appear, they are handled and they disappear. This is the point that every political administration strives to reach but usually does not because time runs out before it happens. Wisdom is the stage at which the company has the chance to make the changes permanent. Because of this, it may be the most critical of all the stages.

The quality manager usually receives a promotion, probably being made a vice president of the company. This can lull the manager into thinking about more exotic things than the constant pressure needed to maintain quality improvement. The reduction in management "noise" is in itself a temptation to reduce the efforts that brought the changes about.

Problem handling may be passed down to the lower levels of the organization, and checks on progress may be bypassed. This can cause the return of a "whodunit" type of organization. Incisive, in-depth reviews must continually be conducted on a "no mercy" basis. Relaxation of this practice is a sign of weakness.

Wisdom reports the cost of quality more accurately than any of the previous stages. The absolute number of dollars saved by paying attention to the cost of quality is usually far more than anyone expected. In many cases quality management has been thought of as just another measuring system with a clumsy title and definition. Now the company is finding that quality control is real, and people may expect too much too soon.

Wisdom is a great time to be running a company. Any task you want accomplished can be tackled successfully. The attitude, the systems, and the enthusiasm are all there waiting. As long as these three are not taken for granted, they will continue to produce.

You will know a *Certainty* company if you ever see one. It is all summed up in one sentence: "We know why we do not have problems with quality." What a delightful Buck-Rogers-in-the-twenty-fifth century comment! But it can be done; I know a few operations that have accomplished it.

Certainty considers quality management to be an absolutely vital part of company management. In fact the quality honcho is a member of the board of directors. In Certainty companies problem handling may become something of a lost art. Certainty's prevention system is such that very few significant problems ever actually occur. The cost of quality is down to where it consists almost entirely of the compensation for quality department members and the costs of proofing tests.

The quality improvement team is restructuring and recycling for the umpteenth time. Their most important project may be inviting all those who have served on the team at one time or another to come to a picnic during the summer.

It is a long, long way from Uncertainty to Certainty. But traveling that road is what the fun of management is all about.

The Grid as a Comparison Measurement

If you would like to use Grid measurement to compare different operations, keep in mind that the purpose of comparisons is to get those moving who aren't moving. It is not simply to report the results.

The company, division, or whatever should be rated by three individuals: the quality manager of the operation, the general manager of the operation, and a staff member who is not assigned to that location.

Have the individuals mark the Grid in the appropriate blocks. They should check the stage they think their operation is in for each of the six measurement categories. Let them know that you recognize that the evaluation is a subjective one, but that they are paid to be managers, and managers are mostly subjective. Award a point value for each stage according to its number. One point for an Uncertainty mark; two points for each Awakening mark; and so on. The maximum possible score is thirty. If someone comes up with thirty points, have an awards dinner and forget the whole thing.

If you handle the Grid right, you can use the comparison between the three individual raters to provide a motivation for becoming involved in improvement. You may be surprised to find that the general manager usually gives the company a lower rating than the quality manager. General managers have a better view of the herd.

The Grid is at its best when used to project a view of the company that all involved can accept. For this reason it is valuable in comparing the status of different companies or divisions. It also provides a continual source of direction concerning what needs to be done next. Managers may come to use the stages of maturity as a sort of verbal shorthand.

"We're just entering Enlightenment."

"We were Enlightened for a couple of years, then we got a new general manager who thinks quality is expensive. We'll have to drop back a stage or two until he gets educated."

> It is a long, long way from Uncertainty to Certainty. But traveling that road is what the fun of management is all about.

QUALITY MANAGEMENT MATURITY GRID Rater: _____			
Measurement Categories	Stage I. Uncertainty	Stage II. Awakening
Management understanding and attitude	No comprehension of quality as a management tool. Tend to blame quality department for "quality problems."	Recognizing that quality management may be of value but not willing to provide money or time to make it all happen.
Quality organization status	Quality is hidden in manufacturing or engineering departments. Inspection probably not part of organization. Emphasis on appraisal and sorting.	A stronger quality leader is appointed but main emphasis is still on appraisal and moving the product. Still part of manufacturing or other.
Problem handling	Problems are fought as they occur; no resolution; inadequate definition; lots of yelling and accusations.	Teams are set up to attack major problems. Long-range solutions are not solicited.
Cost of quality as % of sales	Reported: unknown Actual: 20%	Reported: 3% Actual: 18%
Quality improvement actions	No organized activities. No understanding of such activities.	Trying obvious "motivational" short-range efforts.
Summation of company quality posture	"We don't know why we have problems with quality."	"Is is absolutely necessary to always have problems with quality?"

Figure 1. **The Quality Management Maturity Grid**

The Quality Management Maturity Grid

Unit: _____		
Stage III. Enlightenment	**Stage IV. Wisdom**	**Stage V. Certainty**
While going through quality improvement program learn more about quality management, becoming supportive and helpful.	Participating. Understand absolutes of quality management. Recognize their personal role in continuing emphasis.	Consider quality management an essential part of company system.
Quality department reports to top management, all appraisal is incorporated and manager has role in management of company.	Quality manager is an officer of company; effective status reporting and preventive action. Involved with consumer affairs and special assignments.	Quality manager on board of directors. Prevention is main concern. Quality is a thought leader.
Corrective action communication established. Problems are faced openly and resolved in an orderly way.	Problems are identified early in their development. All functions are open to suggestions and improvement.	Except in the most unusual cases, problems are prevented.
Reported: 8% Actual: 12%	Reported: 6.5% Actual: 8%	Reported: 2.5% Actual: 2.5%
Implementation of the 14-step program with thorough understanding and establishment of each step.	Continuing the 14-step program and starting Make Certain.	Quality improvement is a normal and continued activity.
"Through management commitment and quality improvement we are identifying and resolving our problems."	"Defect prevention is a routine part of our operation."	"We know why we do not have problems with quality."

Figure 1. **The Quality Management Maturity Grid** (continued)

Philip B. Crosby was a business philosopher with more than 40 years of hands-on management experience. He taught management how to cause their organizations, their employees, their suppliers, and themselves to be successful. He published 14 books, all of which have been best sellers. His first business book, Quality Is Free *(from which this chapter is taken), has been credited with beginning the quality revolution in the United States and Europe. It has sold over 2.5 million copies and has been translated into 15 languages. His most recent book,* Quality & Me: Lessons of an Evolving Life, *was published in 1999. Chapter-by-chapter summaries of each book can be found under "Products" on the Web site ww.philipcrosby.com.*

Quality Perspectives

A Ticket to Ride

Kristine Ellis

Total Quality Management is deeply misunderstood by many—perhaps even by the author of this article. Most see it as a particular approach to managing using statistics and quality control. Deming and all who understand TQM would reject this. It is, rather, an understanding of the organization as a system and then managing in ways consistent with this understanding. This idea has many implications for how managers facilitate high performance and customer satisfaction. This article looks at several management trends over the past 20 years; the author includes TQM. We don't agree that TQM is a fad, but this article is still a useful review of these perspectives on sound management behaviors. However, we would contend that every one of these is a nuance on how to manage for quality. They are all consistent with what Deming and other pioneers recommended and take on more value when understood in that way.

It's no secret that training and organizational development initiatives come and go. Or that they come, go, and then come back again, sometimes with more influence the second time around. Organizational development is rife with these "magic bullets" which, for a while at least, move to the front seat in the hope they'll deliver everything from personal salvation to untold corporate riches.

At various times in the past few decades, corporations bought tickets on the rides of Total Quality Management and service excellence. They lined up for business concepts like Self-Managed Teams, the Learning Organization, Balanced Scorecards and Emotional Intelligence. And their managers took the guided tour to the "Seven Habits" and "One Minute Manager."

Without doubt, the carriers of these ideas—the people we most associate with a particular idea or movement—possess a common talent: the ability to tell and market a story that sets in motion a phenomenal wave of interest. Not everyone buys a ticket, of course. Those who've been around long enough are often slow to acknowledge the innovative and are frequently quick to condemn the glitzy repackaging of old ideas.

Reprinted with permission from the April 2001 issue of *Training* Magazine. Copyright 2001, Bill Communications, Minneapolis, MN. All rights reserved. Not for resale.

A Ticket to Ride

That said, every idea is a good idea if it has some value, whether it is drawn from a strain of other ideas or is the result of a eureka-type moment. It matters not whether it is old or new, ancient or modern. What gives credence to new proposals is the depth to which they permeate the corporate consciousness—rather than their position on *The New York Times* best-seller list.

The best of these "bullets," if you will, provide a common language and vision for promoting the fundamental purpose of an organization—they become almost magical, in a sense, when developed, implemented and nurtured properly. The worst prove to be little more than the prevailing flavor-of-the-month, often a stale one, that quickly fizzle and die. The staying power often depends on the temperament of those individuals or organizations latching onto the concept.

> Each new concept or trend can inform us of the larger picture, but these movements are just tools.

"Each new concept or trend can inform us of the larger picture, but these movements are just tools," says Geoffrey Bellman, a Seattle-based consultant and author of *The Beauty in the Beast: Breathing New Life into Organizations* (Berrett-Koehler, 2000). "The magic is not in the approach. It's in the embracing of a concept or movement," he explains. "Too often, the market embraces the 'how to' and forgets the 'why' part of the equation."

Those organizations or individuals that latch on to concept after concept need to step back and reflect on the pattern of their efforts, says Bellman. From that perspective, organizations can assess the latest magic bullet and determine how, if at all, it fits their larger purpose.

In that frame of mind, *Training* took a step back to look at how organizations have embraced some of the more well-known training and organizational development bullets of the past few decades and to see which, if any, hit the mark.

Total Quality Management

Who Fired the Bullet: W. Edwards Deming

The Bullet: So as to maximize the quality of the final product of an enterprise, organizations need a systematic method of managing people and processes.

Original Work: During World War II, Deming taught American industries how to use statistical methods to improve military products. In 1950 he published two groundbreaking books: *Some Theory of Sampling* (John Wiley and Sons) and *Elementary Principles of the Statistical Control of Quality* (Nippon Kagaku Gijutsu Renmei, now out of print). Deming helped guide the post-war recovery of Japanese industry and was so successful that by the mid- to late-70s, American industry began to take note of his ideas.

For the uninitiated, Total Quality Management may appear to have leapt out of the early 1980s to change the way America worked. With its focus on purpose and goals, customer needs, continuous process improvement and teamwork, TQM spurred talk of shifting paradigms and cultural overhauls. But it wasn't as out of the blue as some might think.

"I see it more as a defining moment," says team consultant Doug Peters, president of Douglas Peters & Associates, Mound, Minn. "People were already doing a lot around quality initiatives. The seductiveness of TQM was that it brought all of the pieces together and provided a clear process for implementation."

Today, those pieces are embedded in organizations throughout the world, while "TQM" is passé. "TQM was designed for the older, hierarchical organizations, so it's not as natural a fit in today's faster, leaner organizations," explains Peters.

> Like all big ideas, TQM requires hard work and unequivocal commitment from the top down. It fits, and sticks, in organizations willing to fully embrace it.

Like all big ideas, TQM requires hard work and unequivocal commitment from the top down. It fits, and sticks, in organizations willing to fully embrace it. "When you have forward-thinking management who are willing to trust and invest in their people and are willing to delegate, then you really see a company soar," says Dee Acree, a long-time consultant to both the public and private sectors, now based in Albuquerque. "Deming has a fantastic concept, but if you try to superimpose his ideas on an organization where the attitude is to hold onto power, it doesn't work."

As Acree says, when the commitment is there, the results are impressive. Consider 3M Company, St. Paul, Minn. In 1997, 3M Dental Products won the Malcolm Baldrige National Quality Award, the embodiment of Deming's principles. That same year, 3M Argentina won the country's national quality award, also based on Deming's principles. Both awards were direct results of 3M's Q90s program, introduced in 1990.

There wasn't an absolute edict from the top to adopt the Q90s quality criteria, according to Jean O'Connell, "so it stuck in areas where there was committed leadership from people who fundamentally believed that this was the right way to go," explains O'Connell, 3M's director of corporate quality. "In organizations where a leader focused on Q90s and continually asked that results be discussed in terms of the criteria, there was a significant amount of learning."

These days, O'Connell's focus is on the quality movement's latest golden child, Six Sigma, a priority initiative from 3M's new CEO, W. James McNerney Jr. Like TQM, the data-driven Six Sigma approach is a repackaging of existing quality improvement and statistical tools with a focus on results and accountability. Although moving to Six Sigma will require changes, such as a far greater emphasis on training, there's a continuity to the process, says O'Connell.

" The key to making the transition successful is our continuous improvement history that is embedded in 3M's culture," she says, "and building on it with Six Sigma rigor."

The One Minute Manager

Who Fired the Bullet: Ken Blanchard and Spencer Johnson

The Bullet: Management is a straightforward process that boils down to using three simple techniques.

Original Work: *The One Minute Manager* (William Morrow and Co., 1982) by Ken Blanchard and Spencer Johnson.

Just a titch more than 100 pages, with large type and ample white space, *The One Minute Manager* has, for 20 years, been boiling down management to three simple steps: one-minute goals, one-minute praisings, and one-minute reprimands. Enough said?

Not really. Obviously, good management requires more than that. But for the person new to supervising, the text offers some easy-to-grasp tools. "We offer it on a regular basis and people love the heck out of it," says Larry Fisher, assistant administrator of Human Resource Development Services for the State of Oklahoma, Oklahoma City. "It's a great motivator for a first-time manager, but you can't follow it to the letter," agrees executive coach Linda Dominguez of Executive Coaching and Resource Network, West Lake Village, Calif.

And there lies the weakness in this and many of the other magic bullets: people's inherent desire for instant solutions. "Reading *The One Minute Manager* and reading Senge's *The Fifth Discipline* are quite different experiences," says consultant Geoffrey Bellman. Senge's work has more concepts that would be far more useful, he says, *if* people had the time to digest them. But three concepts could hardly be made quicker and easier than in Ken Blanchard's and Spencer Johnson's little book.

Consultant Dee Acree has high regard for Blanchard but she considers *The One Minute Manager* trite. However, she has found much more value in his latest work, *Gung Ho!*, written in collaboration with Sheldon Bowles.

Based on another set of three principles, Gung *Ho!* uses the Spirit of the Squirrel, the Way of the Beaver and the Gift of the Goose to motivate employees by showing them their work is important, giving them control of how they do their jobs and providing encouragement.

The Native American context in the book is of particular significance for Acree as she works primarily with Native American owned and operated casinos.

And the work has been a peak experience for her. "They are investing the time, effort and money to get all of their people trained," she says. "They are not putting in a caste system where only upper and middle levels are trained. Everybody gets the same message, and then we do specialized training for specific roles. The result has been not just significant increases in profits, but a whole different attitude in the workplace."

Acree especially appreciates the focus on the worthiness of work. "If you want people to be motivated, they have to understand that their work is worth-

> Consultant Dee Acree has high regard for Blanchard but she considers *The One Minute Manager* trite.

while and helps make the world a better place ... that they are making a contribution," Acree says. "That is a fundamental thought that gets overlooked a great deal. *Gung Ho!* teaches caring and taking pride in what you're doing."

Service Excellence

Who Fired the Bullet: Tom Peters and Bob Waterman

The Bullet: The most successful organizations define who they are and their structure, then stick to what they know best. They also reward and nurture employee excellence and establish long-term client relationships built on trust, quality and value.

Original Work: *In Search of Excellence: Lessons from America's Best Run Companies* (Harper & Row, 1982) by Tom Peters and Bob Waterman, and *A Passion for Excellence: The Leadership Difference* (Random House, 1985) by Tom Peters and Nancy Austin.

Being customer focused moved from platitude to obsession in the early 1980s thanks, in part, to Tom Peters' *In Search of Excellence* and the follow-up tome, *A Passion for Excellence.* The two McKinsey consultants, Peters and Bob Waterman, focused on a number of features of excellence, but perhaps, above anything else, the authors' "secrets" of service most captured the business world's imagination. Despite the flurry, not all organizations made customer service a strategic initiative—as anyone who has spent frustrating minutes punching their way through phone menus can attest.

On the other hand, customer service is now the byword in any organization that serves the public, including government. "We now build customer service into most of the courses we run," says Larry Fisher, assistant administrator of Human Resource Development Services for the State of Oklahoma, Oklahoma City. "We are constantly reminding people who their customers are and getting them to think in terms of internal and external customers."

Of the 120 major state agencies that use his department's services, there are naturally varying degrees of commitment. The Tourism Department, for instance, has wholeheartedly taken up the "customer is first" cause, going so far as to put feedback cards in all of the hotel and motel rooms. On the other hand, the Corrections Department is still considering whether or not inmates are truly its "customers."

The customer service revolution has been around long enough now that its distortions are clear. For instance, it's good to give customers what they want, but that desire must be balanced with what they need and with what the organization can and should give long-term.

"Focusing on the immediate exchange with the customer is a double-edged sword," says Geoffrey Bellman, a consultant in Seattle. "Customers are naturally selfish, and that's important to realize if you want to retain them. But you also need to educate them, prepare them for what they want and help them see a broader view."

Myopic vision is not a problem at Fremont, Calif.-based The Men's Wearhouse, where Vice President of Training Shlomo Maor is passionate about focusing on the big picture. "Customer service is now a cliché," Maor says. "Every company that deals with the public has to say that they are committed to it, but what does it mean and how do they execute it? In the narrow sense, what they are talking about is having a friendly person in the store and a liberal exchange and refund policy."

At The Men's Wearhouse, the essence of customer service is customer loyalty. Take care of the immediate need but also save the customer the next trip to the store by finding out what else he needs. "That effort creates a type of relationship that will bring him back," Maor says. "It's an elaborate process—far different from cosmetic niceties."

Another vital characteristic of a truly customer-focused business, says Maor, is being honest in dealing with salespeople. It's imperative to set realistic expectations rather than pretending that it's possible to overcome all objections, another early tenet of the "*In Search of*" revolution.

"Anybody who has dealt with customers face to face knows that it's impossible to overcome 100 percent of customers' objections," Maor says. "When you communicate that unrealistic message to people in sales, you lose credibility. They know the reality. Then when you tell them something they should hear, they probably are not listening to you. You've lost them."

The Seven Habits

Who Fired the Bullet: Stephen Covey

The Bullet: Individual success comes from having an integrated, principles-based approach to solving personal and work problems, with an emphasis on building trust.

Original Work: *The Seven Habits of Highly Effective People* (Simon and Schuster, 1989).

People tend not to be on the fence when it comes to Stephen Covey and his *Seven Habits of Highly Effective People*. Dee Acree, a long-time consultant to both private and public sectors, considers him overrated. "I don't see anything original there, just really good marketing. I can provide the same concepts to my clients for a lot less money," says the Albuquerque training provider.

Greg Zobell, however, has a different take. "I've looked at a variety of approaches and this is the clearest and the most helpful I've found," says the assistant administrator of Desert Samaritan Medical Center, Banner Health System, Mesa, Ariz.

One of the big draws for Zobell is Covey's emphasis on building trust, which ties back to the philosophies purported by Deming in his 14 points, the foundation of TQM. "Deming taught us that we need to drive out fear and build in trust, but he never told us how to do that," Zobell says. "Covey does. *Seven Habits* provides a framework for people to understand how to be trustworthy, which subsequently evolves into trusting relationships, which evolve into an effective organization."

The Seven Habits are business-speak for core values: personal vision, leadership and management; interpersonal leadership; empathetic communication; creative cooperation; and balanced self-renewal. "These are well-distilled, briefly expressed life messages," says consultant Geoffrey Bellman. Covey—and other good marketers—is able to make his ideas accessible to people, helping them see the relationship between the concepts and the purpose of the organization, and more importantly, the relationship between the concepts and their life purposes.

That approach doesn't fly in some parts of the country or in some parts of the public sector. Larry Fisher, assistant administrator of Human Resource Development Services, runs into both working for state government in Oklahoma—in the heart of the Bible Belt. "The problem is that some of these concepts begin teaching behaviors and values," Fisher says. "With Emotional Intelligence courses, you start talking about how people think, and some people start getting nervous. It's the same thing with Stephen Covey's material."

Fisher started offering Emotional Intelligence courses several months ago and hasn't received much feedback either way. For those interested in Covey's courses, he refers them to the U.S. military. "The U.S. government spent a lot of time teaching the Seven Habits courses, so there are many certified trainers in our area and elsewhere," Fisher explains. "They'll do the training at a reasonable cost."

At Desert Samaritan and the other Arizona-based facilities of Banner Health, the Seven Habits material is widely used but not mandated across the board. Some managers request that all of their people take the training, but participation is primarily voluntary. "At Desert Samaritan, about 10 percent of the workforce has been through the training, but that represents about 85 percent of management," says Zobell. He does, however, expect interest to keep growing. "Bottom line, it makes a difference in people's lives."

The Learning Organization

Who Fired the Bullet: Peter Senge

The Bullet: Organizations that incorporate systems thinking for continuous learning are better able to respond to change and find opportunities for growth.

Original Work: *The Fifth Discipline: The Art and Practice of the Learning Organization* (Currency Doubleday, 1990) and *The Fifth Discipline Fieldbook* (Currency Doubleday, 1994).

Six years after *The Fifth Discipline* hit the best-seller lists, the principles of the learning organization have yet to be as widely embraced as, say, TQM and other magic bullets. In part, the hesitancy is caused by the complexity of Peter Senge's thesis.

"The concepts and ideas that are embraced are those that have technological tools that can be embraced quickly. Senge offers deeper concepts and less technology," explains consultant Geoffrey Bellman, adding that many organizations prefer Senge's second book, the *Fifth Discipline Fieldbook*, because it is "easier to grasp." Another challenge is people's tendency to see things differently, says consultant Doug Peters. "People in training and other functions have said for a long time that organizations have to stop every once in a while and take a look at what they're doing," he says. "That's fine in theory, but in large companies, people don't have the time to do that, they may not want to do it, and when they do do it, who is to say what it means? A lab person's view about a learning situation might be completely different that someone in manufacturing."

The real learning, says Peters, comes when there is time for each function to reach a common understanding of the learning taking place. "I have seldom seen organizations invest this amount of time," he adds, "so you end up with a few points on a flip chart that get filed and forgotten faster than you can say, 'just another management program.'"

That's not to say some companies haven't embraced the concept. At Guardian Life Insurance Co., the Fifth Discipline is incorporated into the company's management training with other concepts, but it is sporadically applied. "Some departments have taken more readily to it than others," says Karen Yong, learning solutions manager for the company's Spokane, Wash., operations center.

One aspect of Senge's discipline that has stuck far and wide is the use of the phrase "learning organization." But beware of those companies that just slap the name on an existing department and go on to the next big thing. Like the book itself, becoming a learning organization in the true sense of the word isn't that easy.

In Oklahoma, for instance, Larry Fisher, assistant administrator of the state's Human Resource Development Services, added a systems thinking course to the department's Certified Public Manager (CPM) program after using Senge's *Fifth Discipline Fieldbook* when teaching a graduate course at the University of Oklahoma. The CPM program is an intensive program requiring 300 hours of classes, four exams and four projects. "We had been talking about systems all along but not using that model," he explains. "After becoming familiar with it, I thought we really needed to bring it in so people would become aware of it."

Once part of the program, however, the model proved a difficult lesson. "People probably struggle with the systems thinking course in the CPM program more than anything else," Fisher says. "They tend to think linear and in

> Like the book itself, becoming a learning organization in the true sense of the word isn't that easy.

terms of legislative sessions. It's been a bit of push for some of them to grasp that what goes around literally does come around, and it will come back to meet you on the backside. So you better deal with it or you'll go down this trail again and again."

Fisher has incorporated some of Senge's videos but finds them "too theoretical" and lacking in actual "examples of doing," he says. "Frankly, they tend to be a bit dull." Fisher is now in the process of revising the two-day systems thinking course, keeping the content while reworking the exercises.

Balanced Scorecard

Who Fired the Bullet: Robert Kaplan and David Norton

The Bullet: Organizational success comes from harmonizing strategy across all four levels of the business: learning and development, customer relations, financial and operations.

Original Work: Concept introduced in a *Harvard Business Review* article in 1992; *The Balanced Scorecard: Translating Strategy into Action* (Harvard Business School Press, 1996).

> The Balanced Scorecard translates an organization's mission and strategy into measurable objectives.

It's probably not surprising that Guardian Life Insurance has embraced the Balanced Scorecard. It is, after all, a numbers-based organization. "Our management may be more receptive to understanding the need to balance all components than maybe any other type of organization," says Karen Yong, learning solutions manager for the Spokane, Wash., company. "We're not there yet, but at the managerial level, everyone understands that it needs to happen."

Introduced in 1992, the Balanced Scorecard translates an organization's mission and strategy into measurable objectives, typically breaking them into four perspectives: learning and development, customer relations, financial and operations. Consultant Geoffrey Bellman in Seattle sees the scorecard as a growing concept not yet peaked, and it pleases him. "What's appealing is the methodology. We make a scorecard and try to see that the various critical competencies and strategies of our business are balanced. It's a nice notion."

The scorecard approach has been embraced by a growing number of large corporations as a way to manage performance and strategy. Lucent Technologies, American Express, Halliburton and Eastman Kodak are just a few of the companies reported to be using it.

It also adapts to smaller-scale operations, says Dana Robinson, president of Partners in Charge, Pittsburgh. "We encourage our clients in human resources, organizational development and training departments to use the concept to figure out how to measure their own function," says Robinson, who coauthored *Performance Consulting: Moving Beyond Training* (Berrett-Koehler, 1996). "In training departments, for instance, a lot of what is measured is the number of courses and the number of people through the program. This is an important leg, but you want a multiple-legged stool."

The Balanced Scorecard format allows those other legs to include measurement of the efficiencies with which you accomplish that work, cycle time between request and solution, using the best modality to measure the quality of the program, and finally customer satisfaction—all of which can be monitored on a continual basis.

Self-Managed Teams

Who Fired the Bullet: Ricardo Semler

The Bullet: Teams that have the authority as well as the responsibility for specific outcomes can be more innovative and efficient.

Original Work: *Maverick: The Success Story Behind the World's Most Unusual Workplace* (Warner Books, 1994).

Since the State of Oklahoma began tracking the results of its quality efforts nine years ago, a significant chunk of change—more than $180 million—has been saved by "quality teams," most of which are leaderless. "Most of the teams are project-focused and not hierarchical," says Larry Fisher, assistant administrator of Human Resource Development Services for the state. "They see a problem and set about solving it or improving a process."

After organizations took up the TQM banner, performance teams became a way of life. Then, and now, most teams are cross-functional, but self-managed teams also gained a foothold, helped in part by books such as Ricardo Semler's *Maverick: The Success Story Behind the World's Most Unusual Workplace.* Semler gained notoriety when he let his employees take over the operation of his family's company in Brazil.

With self-managed teams, people within the same work area are jointly responsible and accountable for the determined outcome. In addition to delivering the product or service, they also take on duties otherwise handled by more supervisory roles, such as performance evaluations and hiring. "Particularly in some manufacturing environments, this concept is a good model because you can focus around a defined entity, like a manufacturing line," says team consultant Doug Peters in Mound, Minn. "Individual employees go from doing a specific task to keeping the line running at optimum performance. The concept spurred innovation and creativity, with less management."

The concept stumbles, however, when employees don't want the ownership and instead just want a job and a paycheck. Linda Dominguez, an executive coach with Executive Coaching and Resource Network, West Lake Village, Calif., has had good success solving this problem with self-managed teams. "People are held accountable, but they also have the authority within the team to change methods or procedures to make things work," she says. One of her clients responded to the ownership resistance among some employees by offering them other jobs. "Their choice was to accept the increased authority or change positions," she explains. "It worked well, and the self-managed team is still in place."

When self-managed teams don't work, it can also be due to a lack of true empowerment. "There are some negative connotations of the word 'team,' and it might be that it comes from 'empowered' teams in which people never felt fully empowered," says Carole Downing, vice president of Right Management Consulting, Wichita, Kan.

> When self-managed teams don't work, it can be due to a lack of true empowerment.

When Downing encounters resistance to her team approach, she simply avoids using the word "team" and concentrates on the advantages of interweaving consistent communication and accountability with the organization's goals and strategies. "I can come at it from a different viewpoint and make the case that it's just a better way of doing business," she says. "It's a methodology for streamlining and ensuring completion of tasks and also a way of communication."

It's on the latter front—communication—where many strategists and business people drop the ball, Downing says, and it's the most detrimental place to do so. But it's also the easiest to fix, she says. "It's just a matter of discipline. Do what you say you will do and be accountable."

No one sees the need for teams dropping off any time soon. For Peters' consulting business, temporary teams that can be formed and then dissolved when their purpose is complete offer organizations flexibility and speed. And Downing agrees: "I see a lot of companies going to a matrix or to a flatter organization, so they'll need teams even more."

Emotional Intelligence

Who Fired the Bullet: Daniel Goleman

The Bullet: IQ is too narrow a definition of a person's potential; people with emotional intelligence are more successful in all areas, including work.

Original Work: *Emotional Intelligence: Why It Can Matter More than IQ for Character, Health and Lifelong Achievement* (Bantam Books, 1995) and *Working with Emotional Intelligence* (Bantam Books, 1998).

Some trainers might have to dance around the words and even downplay the term "intelligence," but the concept of Emotional Intelligence seems to just keep gaining in acceptance.

Daniel Goleman's *Emotional Intelligence* hit the bookstores in 1995, just as the rush to the Web began. He defined Emotional Intelligence in terms of self-awareness, altruism, empathy, personal motivation and the ability to love and be loved. Although his thesis wasn't new—being rooted in earlier psychological studies of social intelligence—his timing was superb. People were ready to balance the growing focus on technology with a conversation about emotions.

Goleman's work, and in particular his second book, *Working with Emotional Intelligence*, proved to be an aha moment for executive coach Linda Dominguez of Executive Coaching and Resource Network. "The primary area I found myself working on with coaching executives and professionals had to do with fundamental issues of self-awareness," she says. "They were unaware of how their behavior mimics their emotions. I still see this every day, in both my executive coaching and my work with corporate teams."

But even in her home state of California, Dominguez still has to avoid calling it "EI" with some clients. For example, a municipality asked her to change the name of the Emotional Intelligence workshop she was going to conduct for law enforcement officials, fire fighters, and other city employees. The city leaders didn't want anything with the word "emotional" or even "intelligence" in it, she says. "There was concern that some attendees would find the terms threatening, feeling that they were going to be rated on an IQ scale. So we changed the name and called it coaching skills."

Guardian Life Insurance is just beginning to explore the option of bringing Emotional Intelligence into its core curriculum for senior managers, but learning solutions manager Karen Yong is also concerned with it appearing too soft. "In general, most of our managers do not appreciate going to touchy-feely classes; they like them to be more concrete," Yong says. "They know they need to understand more about the human aspect of management, but labeling it 'Emotional Intelligence' may not work."

In some arenas, however, everyone acknowledges that it's all about emotions. "Salespeople have to be emotionally intelligent," says Shlomo Maor of The Men's Wearhouse. "IQ is not as important as EI. You have to be able to delay your own gratification, empathize with the customer, be optimistic and understand, above all else, that emotions are contagious."

Kristine Ellis is a freelance writer for Training *in Helena, Montana.*

Quality—Why Do Organisations Still Continue to Get It Wrong?

B.G. Dale, A. van der Wiele, and A.R.T. Williams

This article explores, using five case histories, the reasons why organizations and their management remain immune to the need to improve the quality of their product and service offerings. There are a variety of reasons for this, and the authors also offer some potential countermeasures to this situation. In the final analysis, all of this reinforces the value of quality management and the intelligent application of its principles.

Quality has always been an issue in commercial dealings between different groupings and parties. The background to this is neatly summarised by Morrison (1994) along with the development of an identifiable quality assurance movement. It was the inroads made by the Japanese organisations into the markets traditionally dominated by the Americans and Europeans that first brought quality and its management to the attention of boardrooms in Western organisations. During the last two decades considerable attention has been focused on the issue of quality and much literature has been produced outlining how organisations should set about its improvement. In this time the subject has seen considerable development and the knowledge underpinning it has become widespread.

However, despite this increase in knowledge, the dissemination of material, and the associated publicity, there are still a number of organisations and their managements who appear to be immune to the quality events and developments which have taken place over this time frame. An inkling to the characteristics of this type of organisation is provided by Dale *et al.* (2000). In our experience these organisations tend to make a number of fundamental mistakes in the control, management and improvement of their product and service offerings. To those with a good working knowledge of quality management, the way in which these organisations treat their customers and the lack of basic application of quality technology to their business processes is staggering and bordering on the unbelievable. These organisations have no appreciation of the importance of customer satisfaction, service quality and service recovery, as outlined by researchers such as Grönroos (1984), Heskett *et al.*

Reprinted by permission of the publisher from *Managing Service Quality*, Vol. 11, No. 4, 2001. Copyright © 2001 by MCB University Press. All rights reserved.

(1994) and Horovitz (1990), and the impact on company profitability. The link between quality and business performance as portrayed by the "Baldrige Index" is missing in this class of organisations.

This paper opens by presenting five summary case histories of instances to which the authors have been subjected during the last 12 months and which provide suitable evidence that the organisations concerned fail to operate by a quality management ethos. These cases are based on personal experiences and are presented as examples of organisations who do not care about quality. The cases are presented in different styles and degrees of detail to reflect the various situations encountered as seen through the eyes of the customer. The commonalities underlying these respective cases are then identified and discussed. Following this an examination is conducted of the main causes of the factors identified along with potential countermeasures.

Case History 1: Transportyou

Transportyou is an organisation based in the UK and which is dedicated to the transportation of people along three major routes of track, resulting in a maximum journey of around 40 km taking around one hour. In this mode of transport they are in a monopoly position, but are in competition with bus travel and the motor car. The following are examples of inadequate quality behaviour evidenced in the last 12 months.

Transportyou has a no-smoking policy on their vehicles and 30 or so operating stations. Despite this publicised and clearly displayed policy, people smoke openly on the stations and on a few occasions on the vehicles. Four letters of complaint have been written by one of the authors to the company detailing this non-compliance together with a request that they should enforce the policy. The standard reply is that the central control room personnel, if they observe people smoking on a station, issue a warning over their passenger communication system. Despite a minimum of eight journeys per week by one of the authors and observing people smoking on the stations and considerable visible evidence of discarded cigarette ends on platforms and sometimes on the vehicles, no such communication has ever been heard.

Around 12 months ago Transportyou installed new ticketing machines on all their stations. For a period of approximately three months the ticketing machines malfunctioned. For example, they would not take paper money and deliver a ticket and it was often found that the machines were out of service. The problem is now less intense but still occurs on an intermittent basis. Transportyou has a policy that every passenger must have a valid ticket on boarding a vehicle and if their roving inspectors find a passenger who does not hold a ticket then they face a fine of £20. As a consequence of the non-functioning of the ticket machines, long queues of passengers frequently build up at a single machine, which is in working order; other passengers decide to take an alternative mode of transport.

> This paper opens by presenting five summary case histories which provide suitable evidence that the organisations concerned fail to operate by a quality management ethos.

The stations of Transportyou have begun to fall into a state of neglect with peeling paint, inadequate lighting and leaking roofs. This is at odds with the modern image of the vehicles used for passenger transportation.

It is six or so years since Transportyou came into operational service. One of the authors is a frequent traveller but he has never been subjected to any form of customer survey, neither does he know of any such survey ever being undertaken. This indicates that Transportyou is not interested in hearing "customer voices."

The key questions which are posed to the management of Transportyou are:

- Have you undertaken any form of customer care training for your staff?
- What problem-solving methodologies do you employ?
- What mechanisms do you have for the staff who have daily contact with customers to feed back their causes of concern and ideas for improvement?
- Have you identified the critical processes for your operations?
- Are you familiar with the basics of quality management?
- Have you any idea of the lost opportunity costs through your failure to deliver services which satisfy customers?
- Are managers managing the hardware of the organisation or are they managing the service to customers?

Case History 2: Computer House

Computer House is a large chain of shops for personal computers (PCs) and other electronic devices. The prices of PCs are changing at a rapid rate, so when deciding to buy a new computer for home use every effort is made through the advertisements of the PC shops to find the one which has the lowest prices for comparable specification machines within the range of interest.

The decision is taken by one of the authors to buy a machine and printer from Computer House late one Saturday afternoon and pay NFL 4,750. On the following Monday morning, Computer House is found to be distributing folders advertising exactly the same PC at a NFL 500 reduction in price. It took the customer about two hours to convince Computer House staff that they had to pay back the NFL reduction. The alternative is to bring back the PC and printer within seven days and get the money refunded; however, this would be a major inconvenience for both parties.

In this case, the staff at Computer House do not have any understanding of the way customers perceive the rules of the company; treated in this way they will not retain customers.

The key questions which are posed to the management of Computer House are:

- Is there any training for the employees and branch managers in relation to customer service?
- Are you aware of your actions on customer retention?
- Have you considered the effects of your discounting policies on customer buying behaviour?
- Are you aware of customer service facts such as: dissatisfied customers telling on average ten other people about the bad experience, customers are willing to pay to receive better service, etc.?

Case History 3: Software Inc.

Software Inc. is a supporting department of a university, focusing on giving support to students and staff with problems related to the use of PCs and software. The installation of software on home computing equipment to provide a link to the Internet seems to be easy in the special disk provided by Software Inc. In trying to install the software on the computer it takes some time to understand that the name of a server is needed. As a relatively inexperienced user of the PC the name of the server will not be known and it is necessary to contact the help desk of Software Inc. Despite this information it will be found that the software cannot be installed because "portal codes" are needed which have to be changed on the installation screens of the PC. So, back again to the help desk of Software Inc. to get the codes. In the meantime the installation is still a number of days off schedule. When an attempt is made to make the connection it will be found that a personal code/number is required. Back to the desk again to find out the code. If sufficient energy is put into all this searching for codes and names the machine will eventually work!

For example, a very simple scanner had to be connected to the PC. On the Internet site of Software Inc. installation manuals were found but not exactly for the type/number purchased and so a manual was taken for a comparable scanner. This did not work. After contacting Software Inc., it became clear that installation software could be downloaded from the Internet. However, this did not work. Contacting the help desk required an explanation on what had been done and what went wrong. This turned out to be far from easy. For example, when the expert says to turn off the computer, there is some uncertainty on what he/she means and to which switch the instruction applies. The type of help from the help desk is too general: try this and try that, and if it does not work get an expert to look at your PC and scanner. The scanner cost NFL 200 and it is expensive to seek advice from an expert at approximately NFL 200 per hour. So, an expert is sought within your own network, who is willing to help. After changing all kinds of installation screens and trying all kinds of ideas, the conclusion is to buy another scanner.

Technical experts assume too much technology knowledge from the users. They know what kind of codes and names are necessary to implement the software they are selling; however, this information is not given out in advance. The experts ask questions which are difficult to answer for the inexperienced user. They expect too much knowledge and give the users the feeling that they are stupid.

The key questions to the management team of Software Inc. are:

- Are you familiar with the service quality determinants and the quality gap model?
- Have you considered undertaking any form of customer satisfaction assessment?
- What is the degree of integration of your services?
- What is your policy on customer support?
- What kind of training has management organised for employees in relation to service quality?
- Have you considered applying some of the quality tools and techniques as part of a problem-solving methodology, to improve the services provided to customers?

Case History 4: Car Dealers

Car Dealers is a major regional dealer for one of the top branded German cars. Consider the case of a new car purchase. The car is selected, and at delivery minor defects are identified (i.e., a small inside sideboard around the backside window has to be replaced) and the installation of the safety box in the rear of the car. Car Dealers promises that the defects will be corrected as soon as possible. An appointment is made for the car to be returned to the garage. However, to travel from Car Dealers to the owner's place of work is difficult because of the lack of public transport. So, it takes some time to arrange this appointment for the car to be returned to have the faults rectified. Its collection proved to be a frustrating event:

- while repairing the inside sideboard, the mechanic has scratched the wooden panel on the inside of the door; and
- while placing the safety box in the rear of the car, the mechanic has cut the carpet in such a way that is not a precise fit.

This is explained to the service desk and they make excuses that these are just small mistakes about which you should not bother (i.e., the car does not drive any differently because of a very small scratch). After making clear that this is not acceptable, the manager is asked to join the discussion to find a solution. The explanation made by the manager is that new staff have been appointed and it is their policy to give the easiest jobs to the most inexperienced employee. The car has to be brought back again on another day and Car Dealers will place a new carpet in the rear. Because it is closing time, there is no other option than to return the car as suggested and go through the same process of arranging an appointment.

Car Dealers does not understand the importance of the quality service dimensions and is still looking to their products instead of their services as a major distinguishing factor. In the meantime, the customer concerned of course will never come back to Car Dealers.

The key questions which are posed to the management of Car Dealers are:

- What kind of introductory arrangements have been made for new employees?
- How does management monitor the work of new employees?
- Is management familiar with the service quality gap model?
- Does management recognise the difference between excuses and opportunities for improvement?

Case History 5: Cable Co.

Cable Co. (CC) is a new company established in response to the increased competitive situation in supplying digital services in the UK. One of the authors arranged with both British Telecom (BT) and CC that his telephone line and fax/Internet line and television would be transferred to CC on Thursday, 3 February 2000. The team charged with accomplishing this task arrived as agreed. After spending seven hours on the job they eventually left leaving the household:

- without television channels,
- unable to receive any incoming calls apart from those from CC,
- with one telephone extension not working.

One week later, the household was able for the first time to receive incoming calls and all extensions and the television are working.

The details below provide a blow-by-blow account written in personal terms of what happened in these six days. It is a sad tale of inefficiency, rudeness, and general incompetence.

Saturday, 5 February. There are still no incoming calls so the help line is contacted and a promise is made that the household will be on line during the afternoon. The specialist team was scheduled to arrive between 16.00 and 18.00. When the team did not appear at 19.30 the help line was contacted to ask where the specialists were. The response was they were in a traffic jam but could come later. The receptionist was told that this was convenient. The receptionist said that therefore it was the householder's fault that the specialists could not fix the telephone that day and the next possible appointment would be Wednesday, 9 February morning.

Monday, 7 February. The help line was contacted with a request to speak to someone in authority and discussion was held with a manager in the faults department on the phone. A promise that the household would be on line again by 16.30 at the latest. At 16.30 there was still no connection and the help line was contacted at 17.00 with a request to speak with a manager. The "manager" promised to send out a technician within the next two hours because, according to him, BT had connected us and there was therefore a fault somewhere in the house.

After nearly three hours, at 19.50, the help line was contacted again and a discussion was held with another manager. The discussion revealed that there was no technician booked for the address that evening but that someone would be sent out on Tuesday between 15.00 and 18.00.

Tuesday, 8 February. At 16.30 for the first time, someone from CC rang to check whether everything was now OK. They were told that the situation was exactly the same as it had been on the Thursday evening. The customer call representative therefore said she would send an "expert" who would put things right sometime after 18.00.

At 18.00 the "expert" arrived. He examined the situation and announced that the CC line had been switched on but that BT had not ported the line over to the CC network. The advice was that BT had to be contacted to get this fixed. The response was that this was offered on the previous Friday and had been told this was impossible. He said his instructions from his boss were that the householder should ring BT. The "expert" could not tell the householder the telephone number of BT, what department and who to contact. At which stage the householder said he could not ring BT under these conditions. The "expert" then rang his boss, who agreed that CC would continue to ring BT. The "expert" said this was a simple job and it just needed a new extension from the TV cable box. But the "expert" could, for some reason, not carry out the work himself. There was a team booked tomorrow (Wednesday) to do this.

At 19.30 a customer call representative rang from CC to ask if everything was sorted out. She was told that, despite the visits of six experts and/or specialists from various CC subcontractors, the situation was exactly the same as it had been at the beginning. A request was made to speak to a manager. Their manager, for the first time in the dealings with CC, apologised, was considerate and agreed that she personally would take responsibility for sorting out this mess.

She said she would ring BT immediately; the problem was now not in my house at all, but still with BT. She rang back after ten minutes to say that the BT man had put down the receiver on her. The manager promised to ring a BT manager she knew the next day and get something done. She provided her mobile phone number to call if needed. For the first time someone at CC was taking the initiative and keeping the householder informed as to what the trouble was and what was being done about it. The manager was also told about the telephone extension which still did not work and that there was a team coming to fix this the next day. She checked; there was no team booked. Despite this she promised she would send out a top engineer the next morning to sort this out.

Quality—Why Do Organisations Still Continue to Get It Wrong?

Wednesday, 9 February. At 09.00 the top engineer arrives. He is apologetic and efficient. He immediately diagnoses that the dead extension is in fact the main BT switch. No one else apparently had realised this. It will be simple: "We will run a cable from the TV box and put another telephone point in." He could not himself do this. He would call up another team. It was a simple 45-minute job. And he would stay until the new team arrived.

At 09.30 the manager who now owned the problem rang. She had spoken to her BT manager and things were being sorted out. At 10.30 the new team arrives and fixes the new telephone point in 15 minutes under the top engineer's careful guidance. At 11.00 the telephone rings. Incoming calls are on again.

Friday, 11 February. At 17.45 a ring at the doorbell. A gentleman from CC—"We are in this area next week. Would you like to be connected to CC cable telephone and television?"

In conversations with the various specialists and experts who visited, it became apparent that they felt poorly trained and always had to rely on being able to contact a supervisor if they came across any difficulty. Those who were themselves supervisors were continually interrupted as they attempted to carry out work by members of other teams asking their advice. One volunteered the information that once, when he went sick in the middle of the day, within one hour he had 62 messages waiting for him, although he had informed everyone he believed would contact him that he was leaving the job since he was ill. In general, the field staff with whom contact was made also felt that the customer call representatives had very little understanding of their jobs and therefore were continually promising customers things which were impossible to achieve.

Clearly neither field engineers nor customer services staff have access to any kind of database providing them with information about a customer's complaint or what has and is being done about it. The consequence of this is that every time a customer rings the help line, he or she gets a different operative who knows nothing of the background and the whole saga has yet once more to be repeated. Similarly with field engineers. Every time a different one/team arrives, they have received no previous information from their predecessors; they have no idea what their predecessors have tried in order to solve the problem and with what results. So every time the wheel has to be rediscovered.

The key questions which are posed to the management of Cable Co. are:

- How does organisational learning take place if at all?
- Should the organisation have been organised much more with a customer orientation?
- Are processes looked at from a customer point of view?
- How are customer complaints dealt with and their underlying causes identified and countermeasures put into place?

The Underlying Reasons for These Types of Quality Failures

The first thing to note is that all these companies are in the service sector. The authors (i.e., Dale *et al.* (1997)) have argued that service organisations, because of the simplicity of processes in comparison to manufacturing, should find it easy to get the basics of quality management into the organisation. Having made this point, service organisations are often not under the same pressures as manufacturing with respect to demanding customers and making cost reduction in their business processes. As a consequence, it is likely that the management of the organisations described in the paper will not be acquainted with the fundamentals of quality management. Because of the nature of the businesses the cash flow in the organisations is excellent, with little lag between the service undertaken and incoming monies. The companies also tend to be cash rich, leading to a lethargic approach to managing the businesses, with little drive to make improvements. The individual complaints made by customers from the public serve merely as an irritant and by themselves are not sufficiently strong, powerful or threatening to warrant a serious look at how they carry out their business and are improving customer service by eliminating the type of events described in the paper.

The organisations do not appear to be exposed to serious competition for their services and, as a consequence, can adapt a take-it-or-leave-it approach to their customers and are apparently willing to allow them to be inconvenienced and feel harshly treated. The delivery of services is not in line with advertisement material and the experiences suffered leave customers with a lack of confidence in the services offered.

In the businesses represented by the case study organisations there is a lack of a quality management heritage. They are all relatively new companies and have been concentrating on the operational and business issues with the mistaken belief that they will consider quality and its management at a later stage in the process. Quality management is therefore treated by senior management not as a priority and its responsibility is delegated to a lower level in the organisation.

The organisational structure and operation across multi-sites with a large number of interfaces presents a number of quality management challenges. The connections between customer service, service engineers and field operators and help desks appear to be particularly problematic. There is no evidence that the management teams have given sufficient intellectual thought to how challenges can be faced and met. Instead they have been ignored and the organisation has continued to operate in a detection type mode, with prevention activities given scant attention. There is also some evidence that the senior management teams of these organisations are transient in nature and thus there is a lack of stability in addressing the longer-term improvement concerns.

In addition to the inconvenience suffered by the individuals at the centre of these situations, there is also the knock-on effect to the organisations with whom the victims of these incompetencies have a relationship. There is what Taguchi (1986) terms "loss to society."

Potential Countermeasures to Reverse the Situations Encountered

The situations are reminiscent of what European manufacturing business was like in the 1970s and before the threat of the Japanese appeared. It beggars belief to find organisations still treating their customers with such utter disrespect. It causes one to question as to where their managements have been for the last three decades and to what type of education and training they have been subjected. It is almost as though the managements of these organisations have been immune to the quality evolution which has taken place over this time frame, along with appropriate dissemination routes.

Organisations by their very nature are not meant to change and it is essential that the organisations featured as case histories in this paper must be subjected to external and internal forces if they are to change the ways in which they behave toward their respective customers. Unfortunately, the voices of individual customers are not sufficiently powerful and it needs some concerted public and Government direction to provide the necessary pressure points for change.

The organisations have got to start employing some basic problem-solving methodology using the more simple tools and techniques to identify what is wrong with their business processes and providing the means to make improvements. They need to pick up the information on problems to allow them to improve customer service. The inspiration to do this can come from an internal change agent and/or suppliers who are more advanced in their quality management thinking.

> From a general manager's point of view, in this class of organisations, is improvement really worthwhile? We fear the answer all too often is no.

Summary

The evidence from these five case histories, from other experiences related by colleagues, and from the literature (Zemke and Bell, 1990; Capodagli and Jackson, 1998) indicates that customer satisfaction is not being treated seriously in many areas in the service sector.

From a general manager's point of view, in this class of organisations, is improvement really worthwhile? We fear the answer all too often is no. What is happening in these companies is obviously good business and they feel they have no need to improve. And the implication is clear: a quality professional working for service businesses such as those portrayed in this paper can resign without affecting company profitability. Their added value is nil. Why can the behaviour outlined in the cases be considered as good business?

Because the companies concerned have none of their resources on unimportant single customers.

What all our cases have in common is that the problems occur after purchase. They have already made the important sale and they are not going to sell us anything else for some time. In some of the cases outlined the customer has little option but to use their services. In others a repeat purchase is so far in the future that it is not worth salespeople providing the kind of after-sales service and service recovery which might lead to further sales.

But even if repeat purchase was not a reason to treat customers reasonably, surely, any quality manager would argue, all the companies concerned incurred unnecessary extra costs through their poor treatment of customers and by their disinterest in reasonable complaints. That is of course true. But we are professional quality people. We complain. We asked those who have dealings with the five companies whether they had similar complaints such as ours. The answer in every case was a surprising "Not very often." And yet, from our experiences, their key processes were so badly managed and controlled that the same problems must have occurred many times. Customers of these types of business apparently do not complain and so management will believe it is a waste of the companies' time and money to improve the processes.

There is a labor shortage in the service industry. Hours and conditions are often unattractive. So the industry has difficulty in attracting top-rate, keen permanent staff. So staff are often temporary and tend to move jobs more than in other sectors. Which in turn means new staff are untrained or over busy—and so the vicious circle of appalling customer service is reinforced. But labor in the service sector is cheap. Service businesses often pay poorly. If they wanted to improve customer service, retain staff and train them properly, they would have to pay them more. And if customers cannot or will not change their buying behaviour, how can spending extra money on extra pay, improving conditions, and introducing better training in order to improve staff possibly be cost-effective?

Some organisations as typically portrayed by these five cases will only take steps to improve if there is serious competition for their business. The important business is key and corporate customers and not single customers whose repeat purchases are either relatively small, a long way into the future, or guaranteed because of lack of competition. Improving customer satisfaction is impossible without top management commitment. Why should top managers of these organisations spend their valuable time trying to move their company in the direction of improved customer service when they can spend their efforts on new product or service development or on mergers and acquisitions?

In some circles quality is perceived as a faded star and a concept which has passed its sell-by date. However, the experiences outlined in this paper indicate that if the quality message is not heeded by organisations and other more quality-focused organisations enter the marketplace and the customer has a choice, then the business might not be as secure as it was in the past.

References

Capodagli, B., and Jackson, L. (1998), *The Disney Way; Harnessing the Management Secrets of Disney in Your Company*, McGraw-Hill, New York, NY, p. 60.

Dale, B.G., Williams, A.R.T., and van der Wiele, A. (2000), "Marginalisation of quality: is there a case to answer?" *The TQM Magazine*, Vol. 12, No. 4, pp. 266-74.

Dale, B.G., Williams, A.R.T., Barber, K.D., and van der Wiele, A., (1997), "Managing quality in manufacturing versus services: a comparative analysis," *Managing Service Quality*, Vol. 7, No. 5, pp. 242-7.

Grönroos, C. (1984), *Strategic Management and Marketing in the Service Sector*, Chartwell-Bratt, London.

Heskett, J.L., Jones, T.O., Loveman, G.W., Saiser, W.E., and Schlesinger, L.A. (1994), "Putting the service profit chain to work," *Harvard Business Review*, March-April, pp. 164-74.

Horovitz, J. (1990), *How to Win Customers*. Pitman, London.

Morrison, S.J., (1994), "Managing quality: a historical review," in Dale, B.G. (Ed.), *Managing Quality*, 2nd ed., Prentice-Hall, Hemel Hempstead, Ch. 2, pp. 41-79.

National Institute of Standards and Technology (2000), http://www.nist.gov/public-affairs/stockstudy.htm.

Taguchi, G. (1986), *Introduction to Quality Engineering*, Asian Productivity Organisation, New York, NY.

Zemke, R., and Bell, C.R. (1990), *Service Wisdom; Creating and Maintaining the Customer Service Edge*, 2nd ed., Lakewood Books, Minneapolis, MN, p. vii.

B.G. Dale is United Utilities Professor of Quality Management, Manchester School of Management, UMIST, UK. E-mail: Barrie.Dale@umist.ac.uk.

A. van der Wiele is Associate Professor at Rotterdam School of Economics, Erasmus University, Rotterdam, The Netherlands. E-mail: vanderwiele@few.eur.nl.

A.R.T. Williams is Professor, at Rotterdam School of Economics, Erasmus University, Rotterdam, The Netherlands. E-mail: williams@few.eur.nl.

Factors Related to Employee Perception of Their Leaders' Commitment to Implement Continuous Quality Improvement

Lee Jones

The purpose of this study was to investigate factors related to how frontline employees at a large Midwestern university perceive their leaders' commitment toward implementing continuous quality improvement on the job. The major findings of this study suggest that leaders within higher education will have to alter the way they manage to ensure that a climate is developed that will include the knowledge and skills of all employees within the organization.

There is growing unrest about the quality of higher education from local, state, and federal levels of government. Poorly prepared college graduates, uninformed professionals, outdated instructional methods, dysfunctional workflow processes, and leader unwillingness and inability to change are just a few of the challenges that higher education is experiencing. Other challenges include a major dispute over the mission of the university; meeting the needs of a more diverse student population; the mistrust that many external constituencies have of the university; and fiscal exigency (Cornesky et al. 1991). There is a major erosion of confidence in the leadership and the quality of higher education in this country. Respect for colleges and universities is in grave danger.

Universities are generally seen as large enterprises that have assets in excess of a billion dollars. The faculty and administrative staffs of America's universities are the largest group of intellectuals in any formal educational setting. Although universities spend millions of dollars for faculty and administrative salaries, universities are still an enigma and a paradox (Anderson and Meyerson 1992). Many within the university do not know where the university is headed. The problems within universities are not necessarily with faculty/staff salaries, but rather with the university's unwillingness to respond to the needs of society and leaders who are unable to respond to change.

In the past decade, higher education seemingly settled into a conglomerate of intellectual islands where the educational and social needs of a variety of students were met. During the beginning of the 1980s, higher education enjoyed what many in the academy called "fiscal flexibility" (Anderson and Meyerson 1992). The academy had the luxury of sincere collegiality and expanding budgets that resulted in an increase in academic and administrative departmental spending and a leisurely workplace. Universities had no real or pressing issues that threatened their future. In fact, many of the faculty and administrators saw the university as a safe haven where accountability for the academic and administrative performance was not an issue (Selin 1991). The university functioned practically without worry of major external influences.

Like many other profit and nonprofit organizations, higher education has been plagued with criticism about the lack of administrative and academic leadership to manage the academy, given the major transformation that is occurring (Lewis and Smith 1994). Problems with administrative leaders range from their inability to actually manage the changing organizational dynamics to operating a dysfunctional system that is based on fear. The lack of vision, insight, and administrative skill contributes to the lack of formal and informal management training (Martin 1994).

During the rapid growth of higher education in the 1960s and 1970s, unskilled or inefficient managers set the stage for long-term problems associated with strategic planning and development, fiscal management, and organizational development (Cornesky and Andrew 1992). Administrators without leadership qualities or visionary ability generally yield to their fear of the unknown when confronted with change. These and other problems with higher education's leadership affect how employees view the organization and the level of trust they have in their leaders' ability to manage them. Keith and Girling (1991) suggest that universities can no longer ignore the public's criticism of their leadership as a mere expression of "intellectual shallowness."

Deming (1986), Juran (1988), and Crosby (1990) have been a few of the leading pioneers and scholars in the quality movement. They offer theoretical foundations and many practical techniques on how the university can be transformed. Implementing the quality techniques offered by these scholars will lead to self-directed organizations that have: a defined mission; organized processes for implementing goals and objectives; value-driven leaders who believe in the human potential and who makes things happen; commitment to customer satisfaction; and the effective means for ensuring quality throughout the organization (Bonstingl 1993).

There are at least four major assumptions that are the basis for why uni-

> Administrators without leadership qualities or visionary ability generally yield to their fear of the unknown when confronted with change.

versities and public colleges must change and consider implementing continuous quality improvement initiatives (Lewis and Smith 1994). These are as follows:

1. Continuous quality improvement builds on the traditions of concern for quality that has characterized higher education in the United States and throughout the world.
2. Continuous quality improvement recognizes the need for the continuous development of the people who are a part of the higher education system, whether faculty, staff, or students.
3. Continuous quality improvement involves principles applicable to institutional administration and classroom teaching, thus bridging the gap between traditionally separate parts of the system.
4. Continuous quality improvement helps universities meet the challenges of the twenty-first century.

Overview of Management Philosophies

Many organizational development theorists have made significant contributions to the field of management and organizational development (McGregor 1985; Peters 1980; Taylor and Van Every 1993; Weber 1930). Many of these management philosophies continue to permeate today's governmental, business, and educational organizations and have played a unique role in shaping how they have operated over the years and how leaders have managed their employees. Emerging from the Industrial Revolution and the machine age, early twentieth-century scholars (Frederick Taylor, Max Weber, Henri Fayol, and others) tended to view their organizations as machines and their employees as cogs (Bolman and Deal 1987). For example, Weber's theory of organizational bureaucracy was developed from a mechanistic perspective. Weber used studies from sociology, religion, and economic life to develop how leaders should function within organizations. He was concerned with the relationship of authority figures and structure. His major contribution to the development of organizations was his theory of efficiency and why there is a need for structure. His contributions distinguished between authority and power. He defined power as "the chance for men to realize their own will in a communal action, even given the resistance of others who are participating in the action." He also stated that bureaucratic "legal authority" justifies the power that managers have over their employees. He believed that the legitimacy of the manager to give commands rests upon the rules that are rationally established by enactment, agreement, or imposition. Orders are given in the name of the impersonal norm rather than the name of personal authority.

Weber outlined three types of authority present in organizations: (1) charismatic, (2) traditional, and (3) rational-legal.

He described charismatic leaders as those whose characteristics and qualities set them apart from "ordinary people." An organization led by a charismatic leader is unstable, in that once the leader leaves his or her post, there is a split among the ranks. Most of the organizational employees begin to fight over who will reign as the next, new leader.

The traditional organizational leader succumbs to established norms, traditions, and rules. This leader inherits an organization with all its traditions and customs. The authority of a traditional leader takes on a bureaucratic nature, because the focus becomes one of structure, which is designed to achieve specific goals. This type of rationality suggests that to accomplish specific goals, every person in the organization contributes to the completion of the goals. The organization consists of rules, norms, and people who exercise "legal authority" to accomplish departmental goals. Weber strongly believed that the bureaucratic structure is an efficient system filled with coordination and control. It systematically shows the ability to calculate the consequences of actions.

In summary, Weber developed his theory of organizational development using historical concepts of capitalistic economic systems, which are based on the rational long-term calculation of economic gain. If economic gains occur, there is no need for long-term planning.

Background

Lewis (1993) cautioned universities against assuming that CQI can resolve all the functional issues universities face. If, however, universities approach the CQI process as a way of reviewing the critical processes and examine ways that will connect all of its "loose" parts to better serve the students—and ultimately make a measurable impact on society—then they will initiate a quality program that will be successful.

Universities adopting the principles of CQI are faced with the inevitable challenge of making significant organizational cultural changes. The American Society for Quality Control (1993) published a list of more than 100 colleges and universities that have begun to implement CQI within their organizations. This study found that most of these universities have focused their CQI techniques on employees' participation in decision making. This approach is typically implemented without the benefit of assessing the need to change the culture of the organization so that it can take full advantage of the experiences and skills of its human resources (Anderson and Meyerson 1992). Barriers to the successful implementation of CQI within the university fall in two categories.

1. Universities see themselves as participatory. Since they are structured both in a hierarchical and matrix form, they assume that faculty and staff input is present and effective.
2. Tradition and standard organizational culture determine the receptiveness

to and application of CQI (Bensimon, Neumann, and Birnbaum 1989).

Purpose and Significance of the Study

The purpose of this study was to investigate the factors related to how frontline employees within an Office of Business and Administration at a large state public institution perceive their managers' commitment toward implementing CQI on the job.

Of specific interest, the study explored the relationship between middle managers' perceived knowledge and skills of, and commitment toward, CQI and frontline employees' perception of their managers' commitment toward implementing CQI on the job.

The objectives and hypotheses for this study were as follows:

Objective 1. To describe the independent and dependent variables of the population.

Main independent variables
   a. Middle managers' perception of their own knowledge and skills of CQI
   b. Frontline employees' perception of their own knowledge and skills of CQI
   c. Middle managers' perception of their own commitment toward implementing CQI on the job

Extraneous variables
   d. Frontline employees' attitude toward their manager
   e. Frontline employees' attitude toward their job
   f. Frontline employees' length of time on the job
   g. Middle managers' length of time on the job

Main dependent variable
   a. Frontline employees' perception of middle managers' commitment toward implementing CQI on the job.

Objective 2. To investigate possible relationships among selected independent variables.
Ha. 1. There is a positive correlation between middle managers' perceptions of their knowledge and skills of CQI and their commitment toward implementing CQ1 on the job.

Objective 3. To investigate relationships among selected independent variables and the dependent variable.
Ha. 2. There is a positive correlation between frontline employees' perceptions of their own knowledge and skills of CQI and frontline employees' perceptions of their managers' commitment toward implementing CQI on the job.
Ha. 3. There is a positive correlation between middle managers' perceived knowledge and skills of CQI and frontline employees' perception of their middle managers' commitment toward implementing CQI on the job.

The Survey

The population of the study consisted of the employees and middle managers within the Office of Business and Administration at The Ohio State University. The Office of Business and Administration is a complex organization with over 1200 employees, including frontline employees, secretaries, shift supervisors, middle managers, department directors, assistant vice presidents, and a vice president. The mission of Business and Administration is as follows:

> All individuals of Business and Administration are committed to providing services, facilities, and technology to preserve and enrich a quality learning environment that advances education, scholarship, and public service.

The office is made up of the following university departments and areas: Property Management, Trademark and Licensing, Air Transportation, University Bookstore, Food Supply, Mail Services, Printing, Purchasing, Receiving, Reprographics, Stores, Traffic and Parking, Transportation, Travel Services, University Repair, Physical Facilities, Human Resource Management, Utilities, Building Services, Maintenance, Environmental Health and Safety, Engineering, Buildings and Grounds, University Architect, Wexner Security, university police, and telecommunications.

Business and Administration provided five-day classroom instruction to its 1250 employees over a two-year period. The purpose of this training program was to provide all employees with the tools necessary to implement CQI throughout the organization. The CQI training also addressed organizational culture issues and the importance of CQI. The training reviewed the CQI, university, and the Business and Administration mission statements and the six essential elements of CQI (commitment, communication, education, communication fact-based decision making, proactive approach, and continuous improvement).

Additionally, the office invested in a CQI library for its employees. More than 100 books, subscriptions, and articles were purchased. The library is made available to all employees within the office who desire an in-depth understanding of CQI and its theories. To encourage employees to explore the CQI principles, quarterly open forums were offered. These were designed to update employees on the new developments of CQI initiatives.

The target population was all frontline employees and middle managers within the Office of Business and Administration ($N = 1250$). The accessible population was frontline and middle managers who completed the "On the Job and Middle Management Instruments" ($n = 818$). The final number of respondents was 732 frontline employees and 86 middle managers within Business and Administration.

To achieve the objectives and hypotheses of the study, the "on-the-job (OTJ) and middle managers' instruments (MM)" were developed. Part 1 of the instrument consisted of three, 5-point Likert scale questions designed to collect information on frontline employees and middle managers' perception of their knowledge and skills of CQI. Part 2 of the instruments had five questions based on 5-point semantic differential scales used to measure employees' attitudes toward their jobs and their manager. Part 3 of the instrument was designed to measure employees' overall perception of their management commitment as well as report the number of years employees have been on the job. Both instruments were similar except the middle-management instrument contained 21 additional, open-ended questions. These questions allowed middle managers to respond, in detail, about their perceptions and knowledge of CQI. The scope of the two questionnaires is broader than the study; therefore, only those questions from the instruments that answer the objectives of the study were analyzed and scored.

The on-the-job instrument was administered to all frontline employees and was designed to measure employees' perceived knowledge and skills of CQI. The instrument also provides data on employees' attitudes toward their departments, the division, and their managers. Additionally, the instrument gathers information about employees' familiarity of CQI and other demographic information (that is, number of years on the job).

Content validity was determined by soliciting the support of the stakeholder panel. The stakeholder group is a panel of informed customers consisting of managers, frontline employees, and internal and external customers of Business and Administration. The stakeholder group's major functions were to identify evaluation questions, assess and draft instruments that will answer the questions, make decisions about data collection techniques, and review the pilot study data and recommend changes on instruments. The stakeholder team helped to develop the instrument. The first step consisted of generating all possible questions that the stakeholder team might want to ask on the instrument. A total of 94 different questions led to the next step. A synthesis of the trends helped guide the development of the final instrument. Finally, the research team developed proposed operational definitions for all the variables. The final instrument was much more comprehensive than needed for this study.

A panel of experts and a field test assessed the content of the final instrument. The panel consisted of experts in CQI and measurement. It was given a month to determine the completeness of the content and the appropriateness of the language used. The field test included a similar review by persons representing the proposed populations for the study. There were six individuals who reviewed the instrumentation for face validity and content validity. Results of the panel and field test were used to modify the instrumentation.

Data Collection

Data were collected from November 1994 to February 1995. The researchers who attended a special middle managers' meeting for each department within Business and Administration administered the instruments on site. The special meeting with the managers was divided into three parts. First, the managers were given a brief lecture on the purpose of the study. The managers were then given an opportunity to ask questions. Second, the middle managers were given 45 minutes to complete the instruments. The evaluation team was present during the entire time. After the instruments were completed, the managers were given a 10-minute break. Third, the managers were asked to identify one person in their areas, who was viewed as "trustworthy by their peers," to disseminate the on-the-job instruments. To ensure the possibility for a high response rate from frontline employees, the instruments were given to a peer within this group (not the supervisor) to monitor the completion. The designated person(s) within these departments was asked to collect the instruments from each person in his or her area or department. The names and phone numbers of each person responsible for disseminating the OTJ instruments were given to the evaluation team for future follow-up. The employees were given a total of two weeks to complete the instruments.

Completed instruments were collected on site. Employees did perceive the process to be confidential, and responded to the questions to the best of their abilities, leaving little concern that the collection process skewed the data. Ongoing follow-up for those who did not complete the instrument was achieved by communicating with the designated persons from each department. During the month of January 1995, the research team sent a follow-up memo to all managers reminding them to return instruments by the established deadline of February 28, 1995. Given the confidentiality of the instruments collected, there was not an identification code on the instruments. Thus, no follow-up with nonrespondents was conducted. The total number of instruments received from middle managers as of February 28, 1995, was 86. The total number of frontline employee instruments returned as of February 28, 1995, was 732.

For purposes of this study, middle managers and frontline employees groupings were used. All department heads and senior administrators were grouped as middle managers. All other employees within the department were grouped as frontline employees.

Classifications of the Respondents

Respondents were classified in two different ways: (1) middle managers or frontline employee: and (2) all employees were identified by one of six EEO codes. The EEO codes included the following:

- (00) = Employees who did not respond
- (01) = Executive, administrative, managerial (direct reports, associate vice presidents, directors)

- (02) = Faculty
- (03) = Professional, nonfaculty (managers and supervisors)
- (04) = Clerical and secretarial
- (05) = Technical and paraprofessional
- (06) = Skilled crafts
- (07) = Service and maintenance

Results of Objective 1: Description of Independent and Dependent Variables

Middle managers' perceived knowledge and skills of CQI. The middle managers' perceived knowledge was measured with a single Likert-type question on a scale of 1 to 5, where

1 = I really do not have any idea what CQI is.
2 = I have somewhat of an idea of what CQI is.
3 = I have a general understanding of CQI.
4 = I have a good idea of what CQI is.
5 = I have an excellent idea of what CQI is.

The higher the number, the greater the perceived knowledge. The scores on the middle managers perceived knowledge and skills of CQI are shown in Table 1.

The mean score for the managers' perceived knowledge and skills of CQI was also reported by department. The overall mean score of the middle managers perceived knowledge and skills of CQI was 4.23. The standard deviation was .63. Twenty-eight (33.3 percent) of the managers indicated they had an excellent perception of their knowledge and skill of CQI. Forty-seven had a good perception of their knowledge and skills of CQI. Nine of the managers perceived themselves to have a general understanding of CQI. Overall, the middle managers perceived themselves as having a good understanding of their knowledge and skills of CQI.

> Overall, the middle managers perceived themselves as having a good understanding of their knowledge and skills of CQI.

Frontline employees' perceptions of their knowledge and skills of CQI. Table 2 provides a summary of the frontline employees' perceptions of their own knowledge and skills of CQI. The mean of the frontline employees' perceived knowledge and skills of CQI was measured with a single Likert-type question as follows:

1 = I really do not have an idea of what CQI is.
2 = I have somewhat of an idea of what CQI is.
3 = I have a general idea of what CQI is.
4 = I have a good idea of what CQI is.
5 = I have an excellent idea of what CQI is.

The higher the number the greater the perceived knowledge of CQI. Of the 732 frontline employees who completed the instrument, 667 (91 percent)

Knowledge Level	Statements on CQI	n*	Percent	Cum. Percent
1	Do not have any idea of what CQI is.	0	0.00	0.00
2	Had somewhat of an idea of what CQI is.	0	0.00	0.00
3	Had a general understanding of CQI.	9	10.50	10.70
4	Had a good understanding of CQI.	47	54.70	66.70
5	Had an excellent understanding of CQI.	28	32.60	100.00
Unknown		2	2.30	
Total		86	100	

*n = Number of middle managers at the CQI knowledge level. Overall mean = 4.23 (on a scale of 1 to 5), SD = 0.63.

Table 1. **Middle managers' perceived knowledge and skills of continuous quality improvement**

Knowledge Level	Statements on CQI	n*	Percent	Cum. Percent
1	Do not have any idea of what CQI is.	58	7.9	8.7
2	Had somewhat of an idea of what CQI is.	97	13.3	23.2
3	Had a general understanding of CQI.	154	21	46.3
4	Had a good understanding of CQI.	240	32.8	82.3
5	Had an excellent understanding of CQI.	118	16.1	100.00
Unknown		65	8.9	
Total		732	100	

*n = Number of frontline employees at the CQI knowledge level. Overall mean = 3.39 (on a scale of 1 to 5), SD = 1.19.

Table 2. **Frontline employees' perceptions of their own knowledge and skills of CQI**

responded to this question. Sixty-five (9 percent) did not respond to this question. The mean score for frontline employees perception of their knowledge and skill of CQI was 3.394. The standard deviation was 1.19. Fifty-eight of the respondents felt they did not have an idea of what CQI is. Two-hundred forty (32.8 percent) respondents reported that they had a good understanding of CQI. Overall, frontline employees perceived that they had only a good understanding of their own knowledge and skill of CQI.

Middle managers' commitment toward implementing CQI on job. A 5-point Likert-type scale (1 = lowest level of commitment to 5 = highest level of commitment) was used to measure middle managers' commitment toward implementing CQI on the job. Table 3 provides an outline of the middle managers' commitment. The mean score of managers' commitment toward implementing CQI on the job was 4.31. The standard deviation was .802. Only three (3.5 percent) of the middle managers rated their commitment toward implementing CQI on the job a 1 or a 2. Forty-three (50 percent) managers rated their commitment either a 3 or a 4. Thirty-nine (45.3 percent) stated that they were very much committed to implementing CQI on the job. An overwhelming majority of the middle managers revealed that they are committed to implementing CQI on the job.

Extraneous variables: Frontline employees' attitude toward their managers. Several extraneous variables were described in the study. A 5-point semantic differential scale was used to measure employees' attitude toward their managers. Using the 5-point scale (1 through 5 for each pair), the frontline employees responded to the pairs of adjectives and marked where they thought their managers were on the continuum of each pair. Table 4 summarizes the frontline employees' attitude toward their managers. The adjectives were as follows: bad/good, unfair/fair, incomplete/complete, unable/able, hate/love, and unimportant/important.

The higher the number on each pair of adjectives, the more positive the attitude toward the concept. Of the 732 frontline employees who completed the instruments, 719 responded to this item. The mean score for frontline employees attitude toward their boss was 3.763. The standard deviation was .91.

Frontline employees' attitude toward the job. A 5-point semantic differential scale was used to measure employees' attitude toward their job. There were three questions that measured the employees' attitude. Questions 2, 4, and 10 from the "On the Job" instrument measured frontline employees' attitude toward their job. Question 2 was recorded to reflect consistency in scoring. The higher the number, the more positive the attitude toward their job. Question 4 measured employees' attitude toward the job using a 5-point semantic differential scale. Question 10 directly measured employees' attitude toward their job.

The overall mean score for frontline employees' attitude toward their job was 3.472, while the standard deviation was .762. The mean score on how

Level of Commitment	Frequency	Percent	Cum. Percent
1	1	1.20	1.20
2	2	2.30	3.50
3	6	7.00	10.60
4	37	43.0	54.10
5	39	45.9	100.00
Unknown	1	1.2	
Total	86	100	

Overall mean = 4.31 (on a scale of 1 = lowest level of commitment to 5 = highest level), SD = 0.80.

Table 3. **Middle managers' commitment toward implementing CQI in the job**

Attitude Measure: My boss is...	n	Mean	Standard Deviation
Bad/Good	707	3.78	1.12
Unfair/Fair	705	3.7	1.14
Incomplete/Complete	683	3.61	1.1
Unable/Able	691	3.9	1.05
Hate/Love	688	3.58	0.9
Unimportant/Important	692	3.93	1.01

Overall mean = 3.76, SD = 0.91.

Table 4. **Means and standard deviation of frontline employees' attitude toward their managers**

employees feel about co-workers' conflict was 3.84. Employees felt that for the most part (mean = 3.72) their bosses' words and actions match. The mean score on employee decision making was 3.13. Finally, employees felt that important information within the department was not shared with everyone.

Frontline perceptions of middle managers' commitment toward implementing CQI on the job. There were three questions that measured the frontline employees' perceptions of managers' commitment toward implementing CQI on the job. Question 3g was recorded to reflect consistency in scoring. The higher the number, the higher the perceived commitment.

To item 3g, "My boss would be supportive if employees followed the principles of CQI" (see Table 5), 711 frontline employees responded. On whether their boss would be supportive, 205 respondents were neutral. Sixty-one felt that their boss would not be supportive, and 153 felt that their boss would be supportive if they followed the principles of CQI. The overall mean was 3.4.

To question 3k, "Leadership in my department is committed to quality," 713 frontline employees responded. There were 273 who felt that their managers were committed to quality, while only 50 strongly disagreed that their managers were committed to quality. The mean for this variable was 3.4.

Finally, 668 frontline employees responded to question 22, "The level of commitment of my supervisor toward implementing CQI." There were 177 employees who agreed that their supervisors were committed to implementing CQI. Only 61 strongly felt that their managers did not have a strong commitment toward implementing CQI.

Overall, many employees took a neutral stance on whether their managers were committed to implementing CQI. As noted in Table 5, however, there were a large number who responded favorably regarding their managers' commitment. Additionally, very few employees responded unfavorably (strongly disagreed or disagreed) to their managers' commitment toward implementing CQI on the job.

> Overall, many employees took a neutral stance on whether their managers were committed to implementing CQI.

	Level of Commitment						
Statements	1	2	3	4	5	n*	Mean	SD
If employees wanted CQI principles, my boss wouldn't be encouraging.	61	97	205	195	153	711	3.4	1.2
Leadership in my department is committed to quality.	50	83	185	273	124	715	3.4	1.1
Level of commitment of my supervisor toward implementing CQI.	61	59	203	177	168	668	3.5	1.2

*Number of frontline employees

Table 5. **Means and standard deviations of frontline employees' perceptions of middle managers' level of commitment toward implementing CQI on the job**

Results of Objective 2: Relationships Between Selected Independent Variables

Davis' (1971) scale was used to determine the extent of the relationships between variables in the study. The statistical significance for this research was established *a priori* at an alpha level of .05.

Findings

Ha. 1. There is a positive relationship between middle managers' perceptions of knowledge and skills of CQI and their commitment toward implementing CQI on the job.

The findings of this study indicate that there was a statistically significant, positive relationship between middle managers' perceived knowledge and skills of CQI and their commitment toward implementing CQI on the job $(r = .51)$.

Test of the hypothesis. The research hypothesis was that there was a positive relationship between managers' perceptions of their knowledge and skills and their commitment toward implementing CQI on the job. This hypothesis was supported and found to be significant at alpha level .001. Therefore the hypothesis was accepted.

Results of Objective 3: Investigate Relationships Among Selected Independent Variables and the Dependent Variable

Ha. 2. There is a positive correlation between frontline employees' perceptions of their own knowledge and skills of CQI and frontline employees' perceptions of their managers commitment toward implementing CQI on the job.

The findings of this study indicate that there was a low, positive, statistically significant relationship between frontline employees' perception of their knowledge and skills of CQI and frontline employees' perception of their managers' commitment toward implementing CQI on the job $(r = .12)$.

Test of the hypothesis. The research hypothesis that there is a correlation between frontline employees' perception of their own knowledge and skills of CQI and frontline employees' perception of their managers' commitment toward implementing CQI on the job was supported and found to be significant at alpha level .001. Therefore, the hypothesis was accepted. Although there was a low, but significant relationship between frontline employees' perceptions of their own knowledge and skills of CQI and frontline employees' perceptions of their managers' commitment toward implementing CQI on the job, it is important to discuss the practical significance of this relationship. The nature of this low relationship between these two variables may suggest that, despite how frontline employees' perceive their own knowledge and skills of CQI, managers have to demonstrate their commitment when implementing CQI on the job.

Ha. 3 There is a positive correlation between middle managers' perceived knowledge and skills of CQI and frontline employees' perception of their middle managers' commitment toward implementing CQI on the job.

The findings of this study reject the hypothesis that there is a positive correlation between middle managers' perceived knowledge and skills of CQI and frontline employees' perceptions of their managers' commitment toward implementing CQI on the job $(r = -.060)$. There was no relationship between managers' perceived knowledge and employees' perception of management's commitment toward implementing CQI on the job.

> The findings indicate that there was a substantial, positive, statistical relationship between middle managers' perceived knowledge and skills of CQI and their commitment toward implementing CQI on the job.

Summary

Overall, employees within Business and Administration tend to have a positive attitude about their jobs and their managers. The findings indicate that there was a substantial, positive, statistical relationship between middle managers' perceived knowledge and skills of CQI and their commitment toward implementing CQI on the job $(r = .51)$. This relationship may suggest that managers who have positive perception of their knowledge and skills of CQI tend to be more committed to implementing CQI on the job.

The findings also indicate that there was a positive, low relationship between frontline employees' perception of their knowledge and skills of CQI and frontline employees' perceptions of their managers' commitment toward implementing CQI on the job $(r = .12)$. While this relationship is positive, the author questions the practical significance of this relationship. Despite frontline employees' perception of their own knowledge of CQI, they need to see their managers demonstrating their commitment toward implementing CQI on the job.

The findings rejected the notion that there was positive correlation between middle managers' perceived knowledge and skills of CQI and frontline employees' perceptions of their managers' commitment toward implementing CQI on the job $(r = -.060)$.

Recommendations for Practice

Although managers perceived themselves as having a high perception of their knowledge and skills of CQI, all managers need to manifest their knowledge and skills through committing themselves to the principles of CQI. Frontline employees need to know that their managers have the knowledge and skills of CQI, and employees need to see and feel the positive effects of their managers' knowledge and commitment.

Universities that are attempting to implement CQI throughout the campus, or in specific departments, must design their training activities so that managers' actual knowledge and skills are measured before and after the training. Managers who are cognizant of their knowledge and skills before the training would be in a better position to assess their management style relative to the CQI principles.

Similar to management CQI training, frontline employees within the Office of Business and Administration must feel that the CQI training is relevant to their roles. More important, frontline employees will need to be given an opportunity to demonstrate their knowledge and skills of CQI on the job. One way frontline employees can do this is to facilitate group class sessions.

While it is important to ensure that managers are first aware of the CQI principles, the next phase of training must match frontline employees with managers, to begin a departmental dialogue about how CQI fits within the current processes of individual departments. Placing managers and frontline employees in training where they deal with the realities of their work environments will assist in closing the huge gap that sometimes exists between managers and frontline employees.

Findings of this study show that a significant number of employees had either a good or excellent perception of their knowledge and skills. Each department within Business and Administration may implement cross-functional work teams that provide frontline employees with opportunities to demonstrate their knowledge and skills by actually facilitating a work team of which management is a part.

References

The American Society for Quality Control. 1993. Quality systems development: Managing implementation of CQI in *Proceedings* of *the Annual Quality Congress* (Las Vegas). Milwaukee: American Society for Quality Control.

Anderson, R., and J. Meyerson. 1992. *Productivity and higher education: improving the effectiveness of faculty, facilities, and financial resources.* Princeton, N.J.: Peterson's Guides.

Bensimon, M.E., A. Neumann, and R. Birnbaum. 1989. *Making sense of administrative leadership: The "L" word in higher education.* Washington, D.C.: ASHE-ERIC Higher Education Report 1.

Bolman, L.G., and T.G. Deal. 1987. *Reframing organizations: Artistry, choice, and leadership.* San Francisco: Jossey-Bass Publishers.

Bonstingl, J.J. 1993. *Schools of quality: An introduction to total quality management in education.* Alexandra, Va.: Association for Supervision and Curriculum Development.

Cornesky, R.A., and R. Andrew. 1992. *Using Deming to improve quality in colleges and universities.* Madison, Wisc.: Magna Publications.

Cornesky, R., S. McCool, L. Byrnes, and R. Weber. 1991. *Implementing total quality management in higher education.* Madison, Wisc.: Magna Publications.

Crosby, P.B. 1990. *Let's talk quality: 96 questions you always wanted to ask Phil Crosby.* New York: McGraw-Hill.

Davis, I.A. 1971. *Elementary survey analysis.* Englewood Cliffs, NJ: Prentice Hall.

Deming, W.E. 1986. *Out of the crisis.* Cambridge, Mass.: Massachusetts Institute of Technology, Center for Advanced Engineering Study.

Juran, J.M. 1988. *Juran planning for quality.* New York: The Free Press.

Keith, S., and R.H. Girling. 1991. *Education, management, and participation: New directions in educational administration.* Boston: Allyn and Bacon.

Lewis, J. Jr. 1993. *Leadership styles.* Arlington, Va.: American Association of School Administrators.

Lewis, R.G., and D.H. Smith. 1994. *Total quality in higher education.* Delray Beach, Fla.: St. Lucie Press.

Martin, B. 1994. *Developing quality schools: A handbook.* Toronto: Department of Educational Administration, Ontario Institute for Studies in Education.

McGregor, D. 1985. *The human side of enterprise: 25th anniversary printing.* New York: McGraw-Hill.

Peters, P. 1980. *The relationship of the satisfactoriness of North Dakota vocationally trained employees to selected factors of the employee, the supervisor, and the organization.* Unpublished doctoral dissertation, University of North Dakota.

Selin, D. March 1991. Distinguished Lecture Series. Ohio State University. Columbus, Ohio.

Taylor, J.R., and E.J. Van Every. 1993. *The vulnerable fortress: Bureaucratic organization and management in the information age.* Toronto: University of Toronto Press.

Weber, O.F. 1930. *Problems in public school administration: A plan and workbook* for *public school administrators.* New York & London: The Century Co.

Lee Jones is the associate dean for academic affairs and instruction and associate professor of educational leadership in the College of Education at Florida State University. E-mail him at ljones@coe.fsu.edu.

PART TWO

Quality by Industry

In Part Two we look at how quality management principles and practices are being implemented in different types of industries. Our breakdown of these categories is *manufacturing* and *services*.

In selecting articles, we have sought a balance between theory and practice, but with an emphasis on case studies and how-to. It's important to remember as you review what we've included here that the way organizations have implemented quality techniques in manufacturing might be applied in education or services and vice versa. So in reading these articles, don't just look for their application in their particular field. Look at them more broadly as a way to generate ideas you can use regardless of the sector you work in.

Here are some other highlights of Part Two:

Manufacturing

We start with a new review of how things are done at Toyota in "The Counterintuitive Principles of the Toyota Production System" by Robert Hall. Toyota just keeps getting better, and this article looks at how this company does it. See the table on page 61 that compares traditional intuitive management approaches with the Toyota way of doing things.

Next we look at how oil rig manufacturers learned something about their processes from VW and Sony, moving from customized plants to a series of standardized designs that customers can choose from.

Performance support is growing in importance in today's automated plants, and we've selected the article "Performance Support on the Shop Floor" to show how that's being done in some of the most forward-looking companies.

Then we include the article "Improving Production Line Performance." This looks at how to improve performance from the perspective of the theory of constraints. It's a useful review of techniques to enhance the efficiency and quality of production lines.

You'll next find an article from *Industry Week* called "Cost vs. Quality." It documents how the Big Three automakers are still learning that manufacturing for quality is always cheaper in the long run, and some of the problems still occurring that are getting in their way. We conclude the manufacturing section with a case study on how self-managed teams operate on the production line at Harley-Davidson. These teams work well, and this article explains in detail how management, working with the union, brought this about.

Services

The first article in this section is a study of the effect of satisfaction and loyalty on growth and profits in service-oriented firms and in product-oriented firms. It's a useful review of the value of delivering high-quality outputs as a foundation for growth—and the authors discover some interesting results in contrasting the two types of firms.

Next we include the piece "Managing Customer Expectations in Professional Services." The idea is that when these firms better manage what customers expect, they build better relationships with their customers to the mutual benefit of all concerned. The author includes some ideas on how to do this.

We end Part Two of the yearbook with an excerpt from a new book on customer relationship management called "Customer Relationship Management Is Not an Option" by Kristin Anderson and Carol Kerr. It provides a good introduction to this important concept of customer service.

Manufacturing

The Counterintuitive Principles of the Toyota Production System

Robert W. Hall

What makes the Toyota Production System different? What makes it successful? Understanding the answers to these questions is not necessarily intuitive, as this article by the editor-in-chief of Target, *the journal of the Association for Manufacturing Excellence, explains. The Toyota approach focuses on quality and continuous improvement—as all quality management does; they've just refined it a lot more than most of us.*

Business paradigms consist of basic, intuitive concepts: How to organize a company or enterprise. How it serves customers. What its objectives should be and who should set them. How work should be done, and how to design systems to insure that it's done. How people relate to each other at work.

Almost by definition, a business paradigm, once learned, translates into subconscious expectations at work. We no longer think twice about them. For instance, to buy something, we need a purchase order. Every process must leave an audit trail. Patterns of thought embedded in daily behavior and codified by law do not fade quickly.

No paradigm is internally consistent, but old ones are relatively predictable, so we hang onto them. When a new one is counterintuitive to an old one, we're apt to be spooked by the ghosts of the old ways, and revert to the familiar.

Learning the paradigm of the Toyota Production System (TPS), or Lean Manufacturing, generally starts with techniques: pull systems, 5S, setup time reduction, and the like. Some of these can be adopted without severely disrupting established business thinking. Those who persist start to see the paradigm beyond the techniques, a different pattern of thought about business, not just production, that leads to another step increase in performance. Perhaps this paradigm is also the gateway to the levels of performance needed in the 21st century.

To advance beyond easy imitation, everyone in a company has to think differently—*everyone*, from the board of directors to those doing hands-on work. All must struggle through counterintuitive fears, so the road to lean is filled with potholes. Whenever key people cannot get around a counterintuitive roadblock, progress stalls, stops, or reverses.

Although easy to understand, TPS process physics are of limited effect unless leaders understand the principles behind them. TPS principles affect everything, including relationships with employees, customers, and suppliers. They all interrelate, so they are not quickly learned, but are assimilated in due course.

The A-B-C Levels of TPS

For several years, the Toyota family companies and other leading Japanese practitioners of TPS have used the attainment classification system shown in Figure 1. A company, plant, or operating unit is classified based on an overall assessment of its prowess.

In its home Japanese setting, Figure 1 has stood the test of time. Figure 2 is a modification of it thought useful for discussing the categories from a Western view. The contrast between the two figures is mostly in defining A Class. Americans think of innovation as disruptive; TPS philosophers think that reaching for performance perfection leads to innovation by making it much easier to accomplish.

Most companies attempting TPS anywhere, including Japan, are C Class. B Class plants get attention. A Class is rare.

In C Class companies, TPS understanding has progressed little beyond

Class	Description
A+	Corporation has the ability to react and cope with all kinds of change.
A	Cost-conscious employees see everything as a potential cost or productivity problem and engage in furious problem solving.
B	TPS reveals problems and triggers kaizen to remove all kinds of waste.
C	A form of inventory system.

From Prof. Jinichiro Nakane and the working group of JAPICS, Waseda University, Tokyo.

Figure 1. **Levels of Toyota Production System attainment**

Class	Description
A	The company embodies TPS principles in all activities, including that with customers and suppliers, and uses them to be both innovative and flexible.
B	The principles, not just techniques, are in use. Disciplines are in place. Real process improvement takes place regularly and almost automatically.
C	The company copies techniques. Business has minimally changed.

Figure 2. **Levels of Toyota Production System attainment—modified format**

applying techniques. If led by a lone operations champion, the effort seldom penetrates much beyond the manufacturing function. Some suppliers may deliver materials in small lots in standard containers, but the effort to mutually improve with suppliers is limited.

On a C Class shop floor, primary process flows are usually visible. Detailed flows and item positions are not sharply defined. Clutter and backflows typically obscure evidence of quality problems or other problems that should glare like beacons.

Most telling, the operators do not have work instructions at hand, if needed, and observance of "standard work" isn't rigorous. Assembly workers, for instance, tend to "do it as it comes to them," oblivious to assuring quality outcomes by repeating a quality process time after time.

Inventory levels are not tightened to make everyone aware of problems, so improvement is sporadic, done only when opportunities or deviations come to management attention. Support personnel, like maintenance, don't realize that small improvement projects are also urgent. Because the staff directs significant process changes, they also bottleneck the improvement process. People may have to "work around" existing support systems, like scheduling, which no one "has time" to redesign. If attempted, visible control methods and standard work tend to decay.

Worse, when managers and staff remain far from process reality, they may buy a software package to manage a wasteful process, assuming that it is greatly improved thereby. In general, being C Class is simply falling short of B Class.

At the B level, improvement is built into daily processes. Processes aren't alternately improved, then run. All support functions and systems stay close to reality, promoting regular, autonomous process improvement. Trying an idea doesn't have to wait for a kaizen blitz. Back-up and support are readily available.

Support means focusing on workers and the work, not on the efficiency of the supporting department. For example, except for emergencies, maintenance schedules jobs to maximize *their* productivity, uninterrupted by tending to "trivial" problems. Some support personnel should be so close to the action that they can respond within less than a takt time if need be. (Unlike American plants forming self-directed work teams, Toyota never displaced foremen. Instead they are, in effect, first line support personnel—for training and for assistance with everything from cross-threaded screws to preparing engineering change requests and drawings.)

B Class companies understand that lean doesn't mean stripping an organization to 100 unsupported workers for every manager. The remote staff is lean: On-the-scene support eliminates the need for a superfluity of remote systems.

B Class staff and workers calculate and use takt time, observing it consistently in the performance of "standard work." That is, all experienced people can develop a set of instructions to perform error-free work within takt time themselves. If errors occur, they really do fix them on the spot, stopping the process if necessary. They regularly review their part of the process to see what can be changed to eliminate waste. If schedules call for a shift in the mix or type of work to be done, they may redo their own "standard work sheets, "thus becoming their own industrial engineer. Developing people to advance to B Class is not done swiftly because none of us are born with these disciplines.

B Class performance metrics dramatically improve over C Class. B Class plants are great tours because they pound hell out of any waste in sight, but they seldom go much beyond slaying the dragons of delivery productivity, quality, and cost.

A Class builds on process principles to extend its achievements. An A Class Toyota assembly plant will run four different platforms on one assembly line, for instance, and ramp up model changes fast—in a few days. The result is a variety of low-volume vehicles at a mass production cost.

To do this, the entire company and its suppliers must support each other to present new products to the customer quickly and flawlessly. Designing new platforms with high parts commonality certainly helps, for example. To work at the A Class level, most workers need ten years or more experience, so personnel are carefully selected to minimize turnover and to maximize cross training.

A Class plants, whether in fabrication or assembly, make technical complexity and model changes look simple. In the auto industry, the pace of technology is not extreme, but accelerating about as fast as car buyers can accept. However, auto technology is complex because of its variety, and if it isn't highly reliable, customers howl. To cope with the complexity, changes are being made, such as suppliers shipping more subassemblies rather than separate parts. At the A Class level, Toyota found that emphasizing process improvement to cope with constant change actually improved the traditional plant metrics on delivery quality, and productivity above B Class.

Can TPS apply to something like Electronic Manufacturing Service companies, where product life cycles swoosh like meteorites past the Starship Enterprise? By adopting the principles, absolutely. Those apply to any process,

The Counterintuitive Principles of the Toyota Production System

including product introduction. Techniques can rarely be copied exactly, but using the principles, techniques can be invented anew.

Intuitive Tradition	TPS Principles
Let everyone except a leader focus primarily on his own work.	Let all participants gain as broad and wide a view of a process as possible.
Develop a business plan for a financially defined unit. Work to achieve the plan, and to surpass competitors.	Envision ideal states for a total process and for each of its sub-processes. Lead everyone to work toward the ideals.
Design products, equipment, and technology separately. *Financially justify them*. Devise processes to link them.	Design products, equipment, and technology to fit an ideal process; process integration comes first.
A process is the sum of its parts.	Look for flows—relationships between parts of a process.
Management *controls* operations and directs process improvement. Vertical communication.	Management leads by "vision." Collaborate to operate processes and to improve them. Horizontal communication.
Create economies of scale.	Minimize information time lag between customers and suppliers. (Scope; speed.)
If it isn't broke, don't fix it. (No news is good news. We do most things right.)	Anticipate problems: First to prevent, then to correct. (Negative news has priority; act on it immediately.)
Manage by performance measures and exception reports.	Experience, observe, and confront reality constantly and immediately.
The concept of improvement is to make the local work easier.	Local process improvements should also improve total processes.
Staff-directed change or improvement. Refer problems to experts (often overloaded and often late).	Collaborative autonomy. "Autonomation." Limit the time to correct problems on the spot (the real reason for low inventories).
Don't sweat the small stuff.	Small steps of improvement add up.
Lead people with financial goals.	Lead people with process goals.
Being first with an innovation is more important than getting everything right.	Innovate fast *and* do it right.
Do whatever seems necessary to gain revenue or avoid loss.	Do what is needed when needed.
Rely on financial figures and key measurements for reward systems.	Compare performance to the ideal target. Example: Process value added ratios.
Directly guide improvement to increase revenue or to reduce cost.	Apply scientific logic to process improvement at the scene.
Develop technology and develop techniques. Develop people so that they can use them.	Develop and cross-train all associates to improve processes. In so doing, they master technology and technique.

Not included are such obvious contrasts as inventory considered as waste versus inventory considered as an asset. These 17 contrasting "principles" illustrate the difference between two comprehensive patterns of thought. However, each pattern of logic is a bundle of interrelated concepts feeding back on themselves, which isn't describable by a list. The lists are just a "starter kit" for thinking.

Figure 3. **Some "principles" of the Toyota Production System**

The "Principles"

These principles reinforce each other in non-linear fashion, so they are best learned experientially A Toyota sensei seldom talks about them until after people have experienced TPS techniques and "peopleware" practices. The underlying philosophies clarify by first learning to "live the system," then thinking deeply about it.

The "principles" listed in Figure 3 are a sample in no particular order. The best practitioners of the Toyota Production System remain students, becoming wiser but not dogmatic, as the long-retired UCLA basketball coach, John Wooden, admonished players, "It's the last ten percent you learn after you know it all that really counts."

When a paradigm changes, that ten percent stretches to nearly a hundred. Toyota is now reaching beyond A Class for a better way. The principles in Figure 3 might apply just as well to both the "greening" of processes and to processes tied together by Internet.

Crossing the paradigm divide is tough—both ways. Recently a young American, Scott Meza, who is learning TPS in Japan, visited his first plants in the United States, an eye-popping experience for him. Having seen neither a standard mass production paradigm nor a mixed system at work, he found it difficult to imagine how we got this way. We accept waste without seeing it.

But instinctively seeing shop floor waste leaves much more elsewhere. Often customers think that waste is good. Consider the advertising slogan of a local car dealer, "We stock 'em deep and sell 'em cheap." If his lot inventory dropped, customers would think he was not offering a full selection—or going out of business. This sales system is wasteful, but customers don't see it. Even leaders thoroughly in tune with TPS cannot buck traditions this pervasive. In the United States, Toyota's selling processes have to cater to customer expectations, too.

However wasteful the external business environment, one would think that we could exorcise the old ghosts lurking within companies like cost accounting and financial justifications. Although some accountants are now friendlier to TPS, the "justification" mentality still haunts us. For instance, training costs and improvement time for workers are hard to sustain. When financially pressed, it's hard to ignore the old spreadsheet logic that cutting such costs "just this once" will both fatten margins and cut overhead.

Experienced readers can easily add to the lists in Figure 3 by dredging up their own counterintuitive ghosts from confrontations past. Some spooks howl their presence. The more shadowy legacies subtly combine in our longstanding patterns of thought on the economics of running a company, or in our subconscious expectations of how leadership and control are supposed to work.

#1. Basic Notions of Economics Change

Many of our instincts about business in general, not just manufacturing, are

The Counterintuitive Principles of the Toyota Production System

legacies from the heyday of the industrial era. Until a few decades ago, the objective was to substitute machine energy and precision for manual energy and craft.

By these instincts, surely automation is an improvement, and once an equipment investment is made, we should wring the maximum from it. Run it as long as can be justified using ROI, capital budgets, big backlogs, and unit costs based on direct labor. This system may be weakening, but its ghosts linger on in areas that C Class companies seldom think about.

For example, if sales people, including field distributors, do not understand the processes' capability, they don't sell to it. They offer discounts for large-lot sales, all to be delivered the same day, whether important to a customer or not. Their bonuses depend on closing orders at reporting times, often at the end of accounting cycles. Staggering the close-out times is a simple fix, but since sales and accounting are usually far removed from "living TPS," it takes time for them to learn not to throw unnecessary variance into the system (a "principle" not listed in Figure 3).

TPS is a process-focused, "peopleware" system. Human development is the key, but employees can't literally be labeled an investment. The last time we did that, it was called slavery—a nasty ghost. When we try to interpret the new paradigm using the conventions of old ones, too many ghosts come with the conventions.

Regarding a manufacturing company as a consulting company makes the paradox more obvious. In a consulting company, ROI is not meaningful. Development of staff consultants and leading them to the right kinds of challenges is crucial. Margins and cash flow remain vital, but the concept of the processes underlying them changes.

With TPS, people doing the right thing by the customer at the right time make the difference. Experienced TPS leaders shoo off legacy ghosts and revolutionize how people are selected, trained, developed, assigned, and rewarded. They are not traditional bosses, but development directors, architects of a working environment for success.

> Experienced TPS leaders are not traditional bosses, but development directors, architects of a working environment for success.

Strong corrective action is still sometimes needed, so such leadership is not timid. However, TPS leaders mold the work environment by setting examples. The people doing the work are directly responsible for the process and for satisfying customers.

#2. Resisting the Urge to Control

Within Toyota, a TPS leader is often called sensei, or teacher, not a boss. The formal Toyota organization is a rigid hierarchy, but to work on process improvement, it breaks into informal groups without regard for rank. The president and a broom pusher could be in the same improvement group.

In Japan, Toyota has no teams as Americans think of them. Because Americans don't work in such a schizophrenic fashion, when Toyota opened plants in North America, they had to form teams (like everyone else) to break the instinct for hierarchical thinking.

In North American organizations, the problem is to resist the urge to control a process in detail. When the people doing the work "own" their process, and process flow is clear, primary responsibilities both for detailed work and for the integration of it are generally clear. When mistakes are made, the norm is for leaders and support personnel to assist the process owners to improve the process. Then issues can be addressed more rationally than by assigning blame—whether done by supervisory inquisition or in lunchroom scuttlebutt.

"Control freaks" who can't break this instinct can't make it in the Toyota Production System. Some can't help thinking that if I were in charge, micro managing, surely everything would be better. Others are lost without having a position on a status system ladder of "direct reports." No data have been collected, but on an informal basis, most lean manufacturing conversions have a ten to 15 percent casualty rate of staff, middle managers, and supervisors. Usually they take themselves out because they can't stand loss of status or abide the loss of detailed control.

> "Control freaks" who can't break this instinct can't make it in the Toyota Production System.

The problem isn't new. The received tradition is that managers are supposed to be *in charge*; peeved customers want to talk to the boss. However, business history is filled with stories of leaders who failed because they rose to a position in which they had to let others take operating responsibility, but they couldn't let go.

Over ten years ago, Allan Mogensen summed up how deeply this trait is embedded in memorable fashion. In the 1920s Mogensen developed a methodology called Work Simplification, which trained workers to improve processes and to develop their own work methods themselves. For the next 50 years, Mogensen tirelessly barnstormed the world pushing Work Simplification, pioneering a philosophy before its time. In company after company, it faded away after a year or two. The managements said, "We tried it and it didn't work."

Asked why this happened, a much wiser Mogensen in his late eighties responded, "The problem now is the same as the first day I went to work in 1916. The managers think that they should control a company in detail, and that the workers are only a bunch of ungrateful wretches."

TPS techniques are easy to try. The principles present a real challenge—us.

Where Next?

Technology advocates figure that human institutions simply evolve in response to changing technology. Exhibit A is that automobiles and other technology undeniably changed society during the 20th century. But that fact does not refute the possibility of creating an environment based on a different kind of "humanware." Toyota did it once, and would like to continue doing so.

But technology does set the stage for this drama, and the scenery changes rapidly. Broadband communication has now created a rush toward B2C and

The Counterintuitive Principles of the Toyota Production System

B2B. Supply chain software has burgeoned. Its purveyors advise buying a package for immediate advantage rather than trying to build a supplier-relations utopia first. Technique packages that do something like we always did, only faster, can be cost-justified, and we don't have to overcome that ugly problem in supplier relations called "distrust."

Within 25 years, we might use hydrogen-powered equipment, transmit CAD/CAM to make replacement parts at the point of use, and catalyze some kinds of parts to simply fabricate themselves. Much communication might be strictly computer-to-computer. (Our machines will be in touch and collaborate with yours.)

Interesting, but the "trust" problem is ignored. Perhaps the question to ask is why distrust is created. How can we inhibit its formation, or at least counteract its effects? (Forget utopia. TPS isn't utopia. The issue is how to get past our own limitations and do something never done before—low waste, collaborative networks.)

Toyota once did that on a smaller scale. The TPS was a human-centered innovation in process thinking. A much smaller Toyota wanted to achieve the benefits of technology without spending money. Without any breakthroughs in fundamental technology, the pioneers rethought and re-created, at the hands-on level, a different integrative process concept, simultaneously focusing on both the big picture and small detail. The techniques and the principles began to evolve.

TPS began as an in-plant revolution and evolved into a system of synchronized operations among suppliers. In time, the principles changed the new product development process. Using 21st century technology, Westerners are now trying to emulate some of Toyota's achievements that were observable in 1980 around Toyota City. But, hung up in old paradigms, they are doing so less successfully

Today, we're spanning a broader, more complex concept of operations covering more objectives (like environmental issues) and more geography than in 1960 or 1980. Our technologies are creating a powerful lifting force, but our old-paradigm guidance system has trouble leaving the launch pad.

Toyota and other Japanese companies of a similar bent are not sitting still. They are well aware, in general, of technology shifts. Initiatives are under way to develop a "post-TPS system," building on, modifying, or extending the principles that have evolved over the last 40 years—asking anew the big question of how to make an innovative, low-waste, human-oriented system function differently. But this effort probably cannot be successful if pioneered by one company alone. The expansion in operational scope and objectives is too great.

Some of the thinking is similar to that expressed in prior *Target* articles on "Distributed Excellence." Leap ahead and think of solving customer problems, not just selling artifacts. Everyone is really in the service business. Clean up our messes, environmentally and otherwise. (People crowded together seem to see that more easily than those who live in open spaces.)

Besides broadband, other technologies also have promise—nanotech, biotech, alternative energy, and more.

A new phase of this story is just beginning. There are no 10X advances to report. In fact, so wide is the gap that the advances may not even be interpretable by the measurements of the old paradigm. "Learning to see" may take on a new meaning—total process performance.

Robert W. Hall is editor-in-chief of Target *and a founding member of the Association for Manufacturing Excellence.*

Building Blocks for Capital Projects

Rohan Hoare and Gerhard Seiler

The makers of the New Beetle and the Walkman have a lot to teach the builders of oil rigs and chemicals plants. What can companies that specialize in large capital projects learn from Volkswagen and Sony, masters of mass production? That's what the authors of this article address. And if these processes can be transferred to oil rigs, it's likely they have relevance in every type of manufacturing operation.

Companies in the business of building large capital projects—power stations, chemicals plants, oil rigs, amusement parks, and the like—have long faced a quandary. The scale and highly specialized nature of such undertakings might seem to require heavily engineered custom treatment. Yet that approach, to the dismay of the contractor's shareholders, depends on large amounts of the contractor's capital.

Chemicals companies, for instance, produce their chemicals and gases in different volumes and proportions, and the capacities of their plants must correspond to the market's demand for these substances. Any builder of such plants wants to put them up as simply, quickly, and cheaply as possible, but the obvious way of doing so—using standardized parts, designs, and construction techniques—ignores variations in the needs of the purchasers. Is there any way to satisfy the relatively few (but individually significant) customers for the plants while containing capital expenditures, often the biggest item on a builder's balance sheet?

One manufacturer of chemicals plants has found a way to meet both sets of demands—and thus to create considerable value. It has done so by defying the instincts of many of its own engineers and borrowing a number of principles from a very different operating environment: mass production. Volkswagen, for example, produces noticeably different models (the New Beetle, the Golf, and the Audi TT) but uses the platform approach with standard models and components, thus achieving economies of scale. Likewise, Sony has produced more than 300 variants of its Walkman, all on a platform of standard motors, batteries, and assembly processes.

Applying that approach to low-volume capital projects might seem fantastic. Our manufacturer of chemicals plants, for example, generally builds

---

Reprinted by permission of the publisher from *The McKinsey Quarterly*, 2001, Number 2. Copyright © 2001 by McKinsey & Company. All rights reserved.

five to seven projects a year, usually with different outputs and sometimes on different continents. In a *decade,* a petroleum company might build just half a dozen oil rigs, each tailored to an oil field of unique size and chemical composition and each overseen by a separate project team that explores and develops the reserve and establishes the size and design of the oil rig for that particular field. Teams sometimes choose the contractor.

Yet "platforming" principles are being applied successfully even here. The companies involved treat a series of projects—sometimes lasting for five or ten years—as a portfolio, not as a series of individual schemes. The resulting shortened lead times, smaller inventories, and lower engineering, operating, and maintenance expenses are cutting the cost of the projects by as much as 30 percent, representing, in some cases, hundreds of millions of dollars. Furthermore, the uniform interfaces presented to operators promote safety by minimizing the risk of confusion.

Trading Precision for Strategic Freedom

Of course, platformed oil rigs, chemicals plants, and amusement parks are less finely tuned to a customer's requirements than a one-off model. But they improve efficiency in many ways. Since they embody lessons drawn directly from previous projects, they take less time to design. Companies can reap economies of scale by purchasing larger lot sizes of parts and materials, in fewer separate transactions, for projects that go up at roughly the same time. Fabrication is faster and less wasteful. And testing and certification are easier to perform. Indeed, a common design can halve the time and effort needed to design and build just about everything—except the platform itself, which must be made adaptable to a host of different circumstances (Exhibit 1).

Far from degrading a project's value, these savings often permit a developer to enhance it. One developer designed a single sophisticated—but standardized—motion system for the different attractions at all of its theme parks. The time and money saved by designing one system rather than many were used to create a unique theme for each attraction.

Platforming offers other advantages as well. The manufacturer of chemicals plants used to build custom designs, each with a specific output capacity. It now offers a series of standard plants whose output can be scaled up or down. Under the new system, a customer requiring a plant that can produce 2.5 million cubic feet of gas daily might be able to afford one capable of producing 3 million cubic feet—and of becoming operational in 50 or 60 percent of the time needed to construct its custom-built counterpart. Faster construction gives companies greater strategic freedom. A petroleum company that commissions a number of oil rigs with the same basic architecture, for example, can begin to have them built even before it has finished exploration. It can thus respond more quickly to an upturn in oil prices.

Moreover, the shorter the interval between the beginning and end of con-

> The manufacturer of chemicals plants used to build custom designs, each with a specific output capacity. It now offers a series of standard plants whose output can be scaled up or down.

Building Blocks for Capital Projects

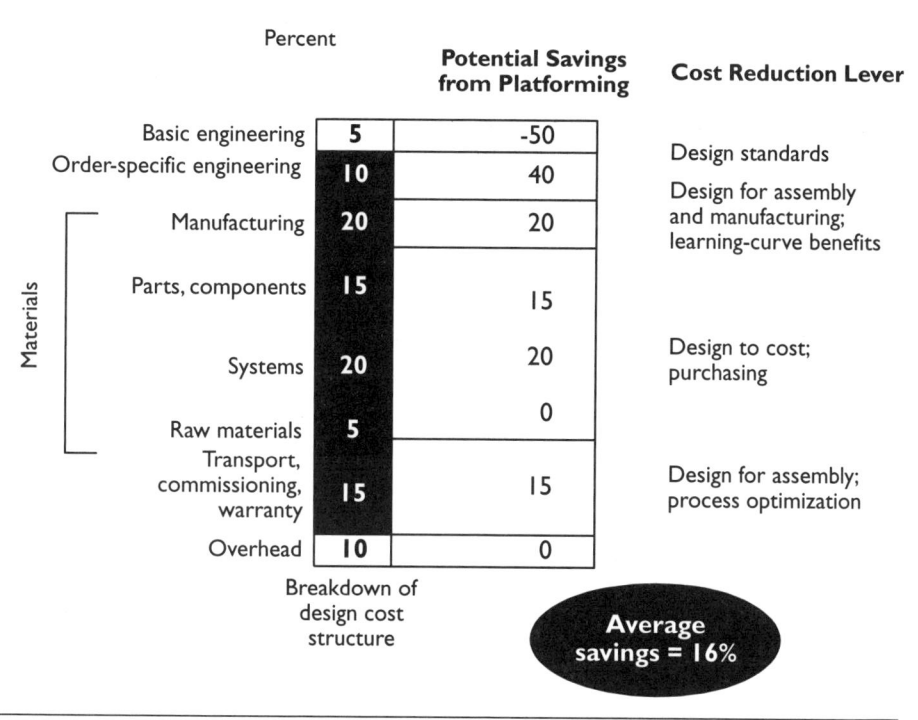

	Percent	Potential Savings from Platforming	Cost Reduction Lever
Basic engineering	5	-50	Design standards
Order-specific engineering	10	40	Design for assembly and manufacturing; learning-curve benefits
Manufacturing	20	20	
Parts, components (Materials)	15	15	Design to cost; purchasing
Systems (Materials)	20	20	
Raw materials (Materials)	5	0	
Transport, commissioning, warranty	15	15	Design for assembly; process optimization
Overhead	10	0	

Breakdown of design cost structure

Average savings = 16%

Exhibit 1. **A common design saves money**

struction, the less conjectural a company's projected capacity requirements will probably be. In cyclical industries in which supply, demand, and market prices fluctuate widely, the risk of getting estimates wrong is high, and it is even higher in exploration-based industries such as mining. Platforming makes it possible for companies not only to reach the market more quickly but also to adjust the scale of projects as they go up.

Designing and Building the Platform

Of course, platforming isn't appropriate for every kind of capital project. Its applicability depends on how many common elements can be identified in a series of projects and the probable impact on costs, risk, and time to market. One company, whose ten-year capital investment plans were based on its projections of the plant capacity it would require, concluded that platforming could reduce its costs by 10 to 15 percent (Exhibit 2). A feasibility study of this kind can be completed within weeks.

Once a company decides that a platform may be worthwhile, it must work out some basic design principles. The decision to give a car a front- or rear-wheel drive, for example, dictates the physical construction of the vehicle and the parts required to build it. One-size-fits-all solutions won't do: 15

Potential impact of capital
efficiency of platforming, percent [1]

Initial Project Portfolio Cost	100
Design Platforming[2]	8-10
Time to Market	3-8
Operability Improvements[3]	1-2
Surplus Cost of Standard Sizing	2-5
Final Portfolio Cost	**85-90**

Cost Savings = 10-15% +

1. Disguised example.
2. Includes materials, manufacturing, basic and order-specific engineering, and transport, commissioning, and warranty.
3. Includes plant uptime improvements, reduction in spare parts, and accelerated product ramp up.

Exhibit 2. **Analyze your portfolio to uncover savings**

years ago, for instance, General Motors built many of its Buicks, Cadillacs, Chevrolets, Oldsmobiles, and Pontiacs on common underpinnings (or platforms) to reduce costs by sharing parts, but GM failed to distinguish the individual models sufficiently to justify the price differentials among them. Flexibility can be even more important in capital projects, whose specifications can change during construction in response to shifts in market demand or the availability of resources.

Consider again the case of the manufacturer of chemicals plants. Their standardized layout, even with different capacity levels, helps experienced operators and maintenance personnel get up to speed on new projects quickly. Uniformity in component design and materials, meanwhile, helps ensure that plants located anywhere in the world are uniformly sound, despite local differences in skills and in the availability of equipment.

To promote these goals, the manufacturer has designed two kinds of module, both capable of being plugged in to the common platform, much as memory is added to computers. "Repetitive" modules have the same size and specifications, and they can be grouped together in varying numbers; "scalable" modules have common designs that come in different sizes.

One of the company's repetitive modules is a heat exchanger, which functions in a plant's cooling system rather like the radiator in an automobile. Because the company can install one or any number of identical modules, it succeeded, for example, in using two of them to meet the cooling requirements of a particular plant instead of custom-building a single larger module, as it would have done in the past. Although the plant built in this way had 10 to 20 percent more capacity than a custom-built plant would have, the design

Building Blocks for Capital Projects

and testing effort eliminated by using standard units more than offset the extra cost.

Repetitive modules can be applied to portfolios of idiosyncratic projects in very different industries. Companies in the petroleum industry, for example, once thought they had to custom-build the hulls that keep their oil rigs afloat, since each is a different size. But these companies now order and assemble repetitive flotation modules according to the buoyancy requirements of individual rigs. Construction can start before exploration is completed and before the petroleum company makes the final decisions about the rig's capacity or location.

Scalable modules are more complicated. A chemicals plant's distillation towers, for example, must operate under different pressures and therefore have to be constructed to different specifications as to heights, diameters, and tubing thicknesses. As a result, these towers can't be assembled from standard, repetitive modules without sacrificing production efficiency. The solution has been to develop a standard design that can easily be scaled up or down. Even though towers must be made one by one, money and time can be saved on design and engineering.

Often, scalable modules are intended to accommodate varying numbers of repetitive modules. The oil rig hull mentioned earlier is a scalable module using a common cylindrical design that varies in size. Upon this hull, the company stacks a series of modules, such as the power plant and the accommodations modules. The oil rig's galley, hospital, and recreation room are scalable modules; repetitive modules are used for the crew's quarters, bunkrooms, and offices, which are identical (Exhibit 3). The size of the power systems of the crew's quarters can vary because those systems are configured from standard, repetitive components such as turbines and compressors.

Modularization makes it possible for companies to cut their engineering and manufacturing costs, to simplify their outsourcing arrangements, and to eliminate redundant work processes and certification requirements. One designer of large capital machines reduced its manufacturing costs by 20 percent and its engineering costs by 40 percent when it shifted from job shop manufacturing processes to high-volume modularized ones.

> Repetitive modules can be applied to portfolios of idiosyncratic projects in very different industries.

Organizing the Platform

Typically, senior management starts to focus on capital projects only when they are late or go over budget. Leaders of companies that use platforms successfully, by contrast, focus on the *early* stages of platform design for a portfolio of projects, and they develop the sort of organization that can capture the greatest possible value from the platform.

It is easy to get things wrong. One company identified opportunities to standardize elements of a $1 billion project at a number of sites and thus to cut costs and construction time and to improve operations and maintenance.

Submodules, selected according to function, use a baseline standard → Submodules are constructed in batches for multiple facilities and then transported to installation site

Offices

4-person sleeping quarters

2-person sleeping quarters

Repetitive modules are installed singly or in combination with other identical units

Recreation room

Hospital

Scalable modules are customized with different specifications

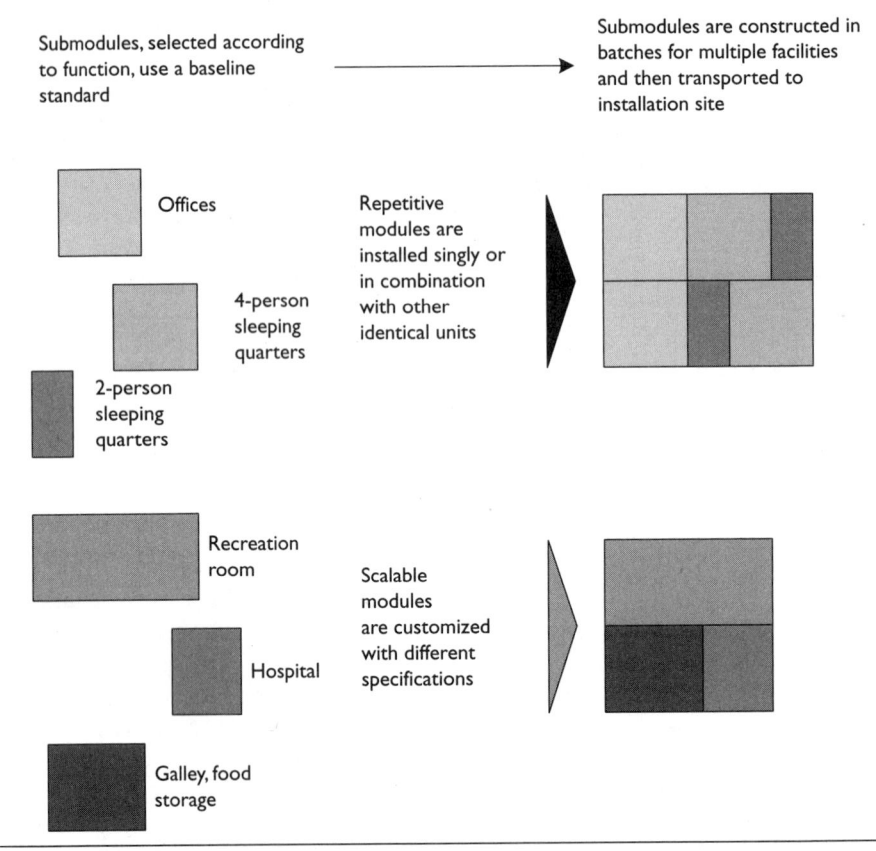

Galley, food storage

Exhibit 3. **Mix-and-match crew quarters**

In view of the overall project's size and the unique attributes of the separate sites, each construction job had its own project team. There was little central coordination among them, and ultimately their design choices diverged so much that the company had to scuttle the standardization plan. As often happens, the engineers resisted solutions that weren't optimal (and thus unique) for each job.

To avoid this problem, a cross-project team that enforces common designs—unless there is a convincing case for deviating from them—must oversee the project teams. The cross-project team should lead the project teams through a series of design choices, facilitating the flow of knowledge and best practice to the project teams, keeping a record of what was transmitted successfully, and coordinating and managing relationships with key contractors.

One petroleum company, for instance, appointed a highly respected business manager who had a technical background to head its standardization team. His role was not to second-guess the project team leaders but to come up with design ideas and to estimate their benefits. To promote standardization and to strengthen his own position, he made sure that senior people from each project were closely involved in the standardization team's work.

It is important to recognize the potential for conflict by defining roles clearly and establishing processes for resolving disputes before the design phase starts. The standardization leader at one company complained, "Months into the project, we're still looking for a way to resolve issues and move forward. As new project managers come on board, we have to start again at first principles."

Getting Contracting Right

Most companies that build large capital projects rely on contractors to do much of the work. Companies that experiment with platforming must get along well with contractors, because to make this approach work, a series of narrowly focused, project-based relationships with them must be replaced by relationships extending across an entire portfolio.

Platforming, moreover, can create value for the contractor as well as the client. The scalability of the design of the chemicals company's distillation towers gave the fabricator an opportunity to increase its labor productivity, to use its assets more efficiently, and to simplify its engineering processes. Indeed, before a client company signs construction contracts, it should identify the source of a project's economies, so that they don't flow mainly to the contractor. Yet the client must also offer the contractor incentives to operate efficiently. The chemicals plant company, for example, rewarded the fabricator of the towers for beating mutually agreed cost targets at various milestones in the project. As each stage was completed, the contractor's incentives rose.

Of course, it is essential to monitor the progress of projects and the compliance of builders with the terms of the contracts they sign. One way of ensuring compliance is to schedule each payout for the completion of a discrete phase of a project instead of paying the whole amount in a lump sum.

By managing projects as a portfolio—creating a solid platforming plan and strong organizational and contractor systems—the builders of capital projects can look forward to benefits formerly available only to mass manufacturers.

Rohan Hoare is an associate principal in McKinsey's Dallas office.

Gerhard Seiler is a consultant in McKinsey's Munich office.

The authors wish to thank Narendra Bhat for his contributions to this article.

Performance Support on the Shop Floor

Jyrki J.J. Kasvi and Matti Vartiainen

Work on the shop floor requires more and more knowledge. In fact, as the authors of this article note, "The traditional distinction between production work and knowledge work is becoming blurred." This article presents lessons learned from four shop floor performance support systems. These take advantage of new technology to keep information and provide workers with ready channels of communication when they need help.

Highly competitive global markets and the development of new technologies have brought about radical changes on the shop floor. While changes in the environment create new demands, new technologies and organizational forms bring new opportunities.

This period is creating new tasks and professions, but even the production of traditional products such as cars and mobile phones demands new tools, practices, skills, and knowledge. This revolution of working life comprises rapid changes in competency requirements. The traditional distinction between production work and knowledge work is becoming blurred.

New customer-focused production paradigms that stress quality, flexibility, and new technologies are just some of the factors that have increased competency requirements of shop floor work (Kasvi et al., 2000). Together, these factors often form an insurmountable proficiency overload. For example, in traditional line production people repeated frustratingly simple tasks over and over again, but on a high-tech assembly line it often happens that employees do not put together two similar products in a day.

What is more, they often assemble the products from scratch and manage the operation of their portion of the line by themselves. In these circumstances, people working on the shop floor cannot rely on memory alone.

As a result, management of operative knowledge has become crucial. When logistic chains were studied in the early 1990s, researchers found severe problems in the coordination of production processes that span production organizations. The reasons behind these problems centered on deficiencies in knowledge and communication management (Luhtala et al., 1994).

Knowledge has become an essential part of products and services, which have in many ways become knowledge products. Nevertheless, knowledge is not usually regarded with the same professionalism as the physical parts of a product. The quality outlays of deficient information are frequently neglected. For example, does your organization know:

- how much disruptions caused by deficient information cost?
- how much production of operative knowledge costs?
- what the lead and phase times of the "knowledge parts" of the products are?
- the reliability of the knowledge operations?

Multimedia on the Shop Floor

While studying computer-based training in the early 1990s researchers found that training was no longer sufficient (Kasvi et al., 1993). A new set of tools was acutely required to supplement training: tools that would deliver task-related knowledge directly to the work context, to the right person at the right place, at the right time, preferably in an easily digestible format. We were not aware of the electronic performance support system (EPSS) discussion initiated by Gloria Gery (1991) at the time, but she would most likely have recognized the resulting shop floor EPSSs or interactive task support systems as we preferred to call them.

The four shop floor support systems discussed here are all based on the same technological concept: assembly-line work sites are equipped with standard PC workstations that are connected to the infobase via a local area network. The workstations are used to deliver multimedia documents that consist of text, digitized pictures and speech, and occasionally video sequences and CAD drawings.

The multimedia documents are structured to reflect the hierarchical structure of assembly tasks supported. Tasks are divided into stages that are further divided into details.

For example, the assembly of a grounded extension cord might have a stage called "plug assembly" that consists of details called "lead connecting," "pull remover fixing," and "plug closing." If the assembly were to be supported, each stage and detail would have a multimedia screen of its own.

For an outside observer, a work task is a process that consists of the stage details, but to understand and to learn the task, the performer groups the details into higher-level units and stages with a meaning.

Multimedia was as fashionable in the early '90s as the Internet is now. Many multimedia systems were developed just because the technology was available. The question is: How do different combinations of text, pictures, sound, and video affect performance? To find the answer, the Helsinki University of Technology conducted a laboratory experiment with a product that consisted of Mekano blocks. The setting was based on the theories that

> A new set of tools was acutely required to supplement training: tools that would deliver task-related knowledge directly to the work context, to the right person at the right place, at the right time.

suggest that a human mind can process visual and auditory information in parallel. Thus cognitive processing of information presented with speech and pictures should be more efficient than processing of information that is presented with other media combinations.

The results were twofold (Repokari et al., 2000). People supported with speech and pictures completed the task faster than people who had text and pictures or only pictures. On the other hand, people that were supported with text and pictures made fewer errors than the others. Thus, media combination selection does seem to have an influence on the outcomes of the system.

Unfortunately, further studies conducted on the shop floor have not yet provided conclusive results as the shop floor environment presents too many restrictions and variables. Different media combinations have been observed to support assembly tasks adequately, but the differences have been lost to the noise. Nevertheless, observations indicate that different people use the media in different ways. While most seem to prefer digitized pictures as their primary medium, some are more text oriented. If a support system is to serve all its users, both groups should be taken into consideration.

The Four Cases

In all the cases discussed here, the tasks supported were complex complete build and assembly tasks. Lead times varied from 20 to 45 minutes. In all cases the number of orders varied rapidly, and people were often transferred from one task to another. What is more, products and manufacturing methods were revised often, sometimes daily.

In addition, management of paper-based support materials had in many cases proven cumbersome and impractical. As the number of product variations grew, the paper become harder to manage. In one case the actual paper was the problem, as the static electricity produced by paper damaged sensitive electronic components.

In the Direct Current (DC) drive case, the support system completely replaced paper documentation on the shop floor. Not even the assembly drawings that had been the most important source of information were needed.

In the DC drive case and the Information Support System case the need for support was underlined by a high number of product models and variants. For example, the theoretical number of ABB DC drive variants exceeds 1 million! In the other two cases, the products were so complex that even without a large number of variants, the tasks justifiably required support.

End Assembly of DC Drives

Our first realized support system was a prototype built in cooperation with the ABB Industry Ltd. Pitäjänmäki Power Electronics plant in 1994, and it has since been used to support end assembly of DC drives. The support system was used for three purposes: to orient new employees to their tasks, to support training by doing, and to support actual work task performance.

Initially the system was used extensively as people learned their tasks, but as people grew more proficient, the system was used less often. The use did not end, though, and even the most experienced employees used it regularly to check details of their tasks. The usage of the system changed correspondingly. While new employees followed the multimedia documents with discipline from one stage detail to the next, the old hands used the contents page of the documents as jump points to reach the details they needed.

As a result, the flexibility of production and the whole organization improved. It became possible to transfer people from one task to another in a moment's notice. Furthermore, a couple of years later the support system eased moving the whole line *and* the work practices to Germany. An influence on quality was observed when the system was down due to technical problems: the automatic testing system rejected more defective drives than when the system was up and running.

The problems focused on the maintenance of the information content. As the work methods were revised so often, the support documents did not always stay up to date. If, for example, the color of a part on the screen was different than the part at hand, people often thought that *they* had made a mistake and halted the work.

> Initially the system was used extensively as people learned their tasks, but as people grew more proficient, the system was used less often.

End Assembly of an Audio System

Our second case, the IMS support system (Interaktiv Montagestøtte), was created to support the end assembly of the Bang & Olufsen A/S CD player with a built-in tuner and amplifier, BeoSound 9000. There were no product variations to speak of, but the product was extremely complex. As a result of the design-oriented product philosophy of Bang & Olufsen, BeoSound 9000 includes a total of 23 circuit boards. No compromises have been made to facilitate manufacturability. In addition, new materials, methods, and tools were required.

What is more, as most of the products are made to order, employees are often transferred from one line to another. Need for support is aggravated by the seasonal nature of highest-end audio sales. Products like BeoSound 9000 sell much better in spring than in autumn. In addition to autumn holidays and longer work days in spring, the number of people in production grows from 350 to 480 in the spring season.

In addition to supporting task performance, the IMS system was designed to be used as a training tool and to support documentation of production methods. The idea was to create the information content during production method design. When applied in practice, this was found to be too cumbersome, as the methods change too fast during the planning phase. Instead, production testing was found to be the best time to author the first version of the support materials.

While the IMS system was tested in production, the employees working on the line started actively editing and commenting upon the information content of the system. Originally, editing the material was supposed to be restricted, but in the testing phase the lock had been left open. The people responsible for the work method design considered the material most useful. As a result, a liberal work method documentation scheme was adopted. After all, the people working on the line are the most experienced experts on their work methods.

According to a Bang & Olufsen study conducted in 1997, the IMS system was well suited for training new employees, who were able to practice without stress or embarrassment. Time needed for traditional training was reduced to one quarter, while the rest was replaced with learning by doing. This freed sorely needed planning resources as training of new tasks has traditionally been taken care of by product and task designers.

The IMS system was used for task support especially when assembly methods changed or people were uncertain of correct procedures. About half the shop floor employees kept the IMS system on while they were working. While the inexperienced employees followed the multimedia documents rigorously from stage detail to stage detail, the more experienced employees scanned the documents from stage to stage, only occasionally navigating to details in search of more detailed information. Even more experienced assemblers used the IMS system, but only when they were uncertain of something. The system was also used as a notepad: people kept one "page" on the screen to remind them of a detail they had had trouble with. In addition, the system was used to solve an obstinate quality problem. For a while, all the employees were required to use the system all the time and to go through every task stage detail.

Locating correct information from the system was considered easy and fast, but the quality of the still video pictures was considered poor. In addition, maintaining the information content was considered easier than before, as it was easy to do little revisions on the files in the server instead of copying and distributing paper file revisions to work sites. System users missed a function that would have correlated users and revisions and told the user which pieces of documentation had changed since the last time he or she had used the system. Another shortcoming was lack of connections to other software systems. Production managers would have liked to transfer information to and from the IMS system.

Task Supporter

While the systems used in the two previous cases had integrated authoring and reading functions into a single system, Task Supporter of Brainware Oy consisted of three subsystems for authoring, reading, and managing information content. The most important improvement of the system was reusability of the material: parts of existing multimedia documents could be copied to new documents. For example, a picture could be used in several Task Supporter documents.

If the picture was edited, the author was able to decide if the change was specific to one document or if the picture should be changed in all the documents that use it. The use of Task Supporter was studied in one company that had successfully implemented it. The complexity of the task supported was illustrated by the fact that the mere presence of the observer asking questions caused the employees to make several critical mistakes.

In addition to the Task Supporter system, three other sources of support were present:

- The product construction and the work environment had been designed to support assembly.
- Trainers' offices were next to the line and the employees were supposed to consult them when needed.
- The old paper documentation system was still operating.

This diversity caused problems as the information provided was not always in the same phase. While the trainers and supervisors usually informed the employees immediately of new revisions, it took several days before the paper documentation was updated and even more time before the multimedia documents were up to date. As a result, people did not always trust the Task Supporter system. Even the trainers were sometimes outdated. A training session was observed where the trainer, an engineer who had helped design the product, was several times corrected by the line workers. He had not been informed of the latest revisions.

Nevertheless, people were satisfied with the shop floor information environment. They noted, "Information works really well here. We are immediately told when there are changes coming. We can also go and tell, if we have new ideas to suggest. Things work better on our line than on the other lines."

Information Support System

The Information Support System (ISS) developed by Arrow Engineering Oy differs from the previously introduced systems in two ways. First, it does not organize task descriptions into task stages and stage details. Only stage details are addressed and given "pages" of their own. Second, ISS is designed to communicate with other shop floor software systems. So ISS knows which model is coming to the work-site next.

The introduction of an ISS was studied on a Finnish production line (Hailikari et al., 2000). The new line was the answer to the rapidly increasing demand for the products. New people were introduced to production all the time, and personnel turnover was almost nonexistent.

The employees interviewed considered ISS better and easier to use than the old paper documentation system. Instructions provided in the paper documents were considered badly organized and it was difficult to locate the information needed. In addition, the paper files were often in the way and not always where they were supposed to be.

On the other hand, some of the end users felt that they could have used more training. Some of the employees did not even know how to turn the computer on! Meanwhile, some of the end users felt that training would be a waste of time. This difference disturbed introduction of the system, as some of the people who would have benefited from further training were too shy to come forth and ask questions. In addition, not all of the employees trusted computers. This distrust was enhanced by the fact that ISS was often down during the implementation phase. Different fears were also associated with the system. People were afraid that the support system would automate task performance too much or reduce employees' ability to remember important things by themselves.

The author users of the system considered the multimedia documents easier and faster to update and maintain than paper-based documents. In the early 1990s, updating the support material took an average of 235 minutes. In the mid-1990s the introduction of a digital camera reduced the average time to 125 minutes, and in 1999 the introduction of the support system cut the time further to 91 minutes (Figure 1) (Koskinen et al., 2000).

Early '90s	Mid '90s (Digital Camera)	1999 (ISS)
Taking the photographs.	Taking the pictures with a digital camera.	Taking the pictures with a digital camera.
Writing and printing the new instructions and developing photographs.	Writing the new instructions and combining the digital photographs with PC editing tools.	Writing the new instructions and embedding the digital photographs with PC editing tools.
Clipping and gluing the printed instructions and photographs to the final format.		
Copying new instructions with a color copier.	Printing the new instructions.	
Distributing the new instructions to the assembly stations.	Distributing the new instructions to the assembly stations' paper booklets.	Putting the new instructions on the server.

Figure 1. **Maintaining support material has become more efficient with the introduction of new technologies (Koskinen et al., 2000)**

Lessons Learned

The implementation and efficient application of shop floor support has proven to be surprisingly challenging. For example, only about a quarter of the companies that had purchased the production license of Task Supporter actually used the system. One company even removed the system from production. The implementation problems were partly due to a turbulent economy: in several cases the plant in question had been sold and bought and the introduction of a new piece of software had been forgotten.

Once the support has been successfully implemented, there is surprisingly little resistance to change in spite of the fact that most of the end users have had very little experience in computer use. Mouse and keyboard are cumbersome, and in one case they were replaced with a bar code reader that the users were familiar with. In another case a foot pedal or a set of extra function keys was considered. The end users have almost unanimously considered computer-delivered support better than paper-based support arrangements.

According to our experiences, at least the following points have to be taken into consideration when shop floor support systems are designed:

- The goals of the system have to be well defined to have something to compare the results to. In addition, clear goals improve users' motivation to actually use the system.
- Interaction between developers and users of the system has to be intensive. Resistance to change and fears associated with new technologies have to be taken into account.
- Usability is paramount. For example, the novice users of the support system used in the DC drive production case required only 30 minutes of training (Nieminen et al., 1995).
- Authoring and managing the information content of the system has to be easy.
- The author and reader users of a support system require training.
- The authors of the content material have to know the tasks supported and their activity environment.
- The responsibilities have to be defined explicitly. In one case the person responsible for Task Supporter did not know about his responsibility for a year!
- A change agent is essential: in every successful case an agent dedicated to the support system was identified.
- The system has to be easy to tailor. As one production manager noted, "What do we do with a support system that takes half a year to tailor when we have to tailor our products and production on a daily basis?"
- The system must not be forgotten after implementation—but the system and its contents have to be maintained.

Discussion

In addition to delivering information, a shop floor support system should be used to support organizational learning. Actually a support system can be seen as the memory of a learning organization. To live up to the image, the system should support conceptualization and collection of the hands-on experiences of the employees. Unfortunately, mere technologies do not help if the organizational culture does not permit their application.

According to Nonaka's and Takeuchi's (1995) spiral of new knowledge development, individual and organizational learning are connected. To support this spiral, a support system has to address all the four transformations of tacit and explicit knowledge (Figure 2). Different tools are needed to support different transformations, and care should be taken to ensure that the

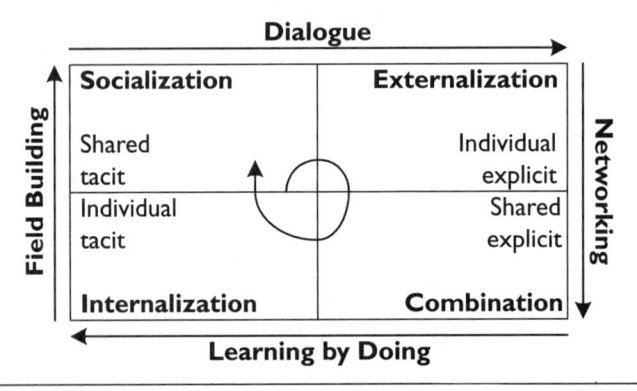

	Dialogue	
Field Building	Socialization Shared tacit Individual tacit	Externalization Individual explicit Shared explicit
	Internalization	Combination
	Learning by Doing	

Figure 2. **Designers of support systems should take Nonaka's and Takeuchi's (1995) spiral of new knowledge development into consideration. To foster individual and organizational learning, a support system is to support all the four transformations of tacit and explicit knowledge.**

tools applied on one part of the cycle do not disturb some other parts.

Until recently, the EPSS discussion has been based on definitions written in the early 1990s. There is a risk that if applied rigidly, these may lead to systems that disrupt the spiral of knowledge development (italics added by authors):

> An EPSS is the electronic infrastructure that captures, stores, and distributes individual and corporate knowledge assets throughout an organization to enable an individual to achieve a required level of performance in the fastest possible time and *with the minimum of support from other people* (Raybould, 1995).

> Those who have been able to see potential in EPS have also embraced its basic premise, that it is possible, and often desirable, *to enhance performance without necessarily promoting learning, to create expertise without necessarily creating an expert* (Rosenberg, 1995).

If social interaction is minimized with EPSS, as Raybould suggests, dialogue required for externalization of tacit knowledge may be diminished. If learning is minimized, as Rosenberg suggests, internalization of new knowledge may be influenced, as learning by doing does not happen. In our opinion, communication and information technologies are by name to be used to promote social interaction and learning, not to minimize them.

In addition, there are other, less tangible questions that should be taken into consideration:

- How does support affect mental workload of the end users? A system that is difficult to use may actually increase competency requirements of the task supported. In addition, a support system can be used to track and to time tasks, which may have counterproductive influences.
- How does support affect the work community? Knowledge is power even on the shop floor and a support system will certainly have an influence on those structures. Does support make knowledge more democratic, or does it actually impose new restrictions?
- How does support affect competency and creativity? A major part of our self-esteem is based on our craftsmanship in our respective fields. An interactive support system may be used to collect individual tricks of trade and socialize them for the whole organization. But where does that leave our self-esteem?

References

Gery, G. (1991). *Electronic performance support systems: How and why to remake the workplace through the strategic application of technology.* Tolland, MA: Gery Performance Press.

Hailikari, M., Repokari, L., Nieminen, M., Koskinen, T., Kasvi, J., Vartiainen, M., Pulkkis, A., & Kari, I. (2000). *Implementation of an information support system in assembly work: A case study.* Submitted for publication.

Kasvi, J.J.J., Pulkkis, A., Vartiainen, M., & Nieminen, M. (1993). Developing a hypermedia authoring system for task training and information arrangement on the shop floor. In V. Orpana & A. Lukka (Eds.), *Production Research 1993, Proceedings of the 12th International Conference on Production Research* (pp. 647-648). New York: Elsevier.

Kasvi, J.J.J., Vartiainen, M., Pulkkis, A., & Nieminen, M. (2000). The role of information support systems in the joint optimization of work systems. *Human Factors and Ergonomics in Manufacturing* 10 (2), 193–221.

Koskinen, T., Repokari, L., Nieminen, M., Hailikari, M., Kasvi, J.J.J., Vartiainen, M., Pulkkis, A., & Kari, I. (2000). *The evolvement of the information support's maintenance in assembly line during the 90's: A case study.* Submitted for publication.

Luhtala, M., Kilpinen, E., & Anttila, P. (1994). *LOGI managing make-to-order supply chains.* Helsinki University of Technology, Industrial Economics and Industrial Psychology, Report No 153. Otaniemi, Espoo, Finland.

Nieminen, M., Kasvi, J.J.J., Pulkkis, A., & Vartiainen, M. (1995). Interactive task support on the shop floor: Observations on the usability of the interactive task support system and differences in orientation and hands-on training use. In M.A.R. Kirby, A.J. Dix, & J.E. Finlay (Eds.), *Proceedings of the HCI'95 conference: People and computers X* (pp. 79-93). Cambridge, Great Britain: Cambridge University Press.

Nonaka, I., & Takeuchi, H. (1995). *The knowledge-creating company.* New York: Oxford University Press.

Raybould, B. (1995). Performance support engineering: An emerging development methodology for enabling organisational learning. *Performance Improvement Quarterly* 8 (1), 7–22.

Repokari, L., Nieminen, M., Hailikari, M., Kasvi, J., Vartiainen, M., Pulkkis, A., & Kari, I. (2000). *Different modalities in assembly support system user interface.* Submitted for publication.

Rosenberg, M.J. (1995). Performance technology, performance support, and the future of training. *Performance Improvement Quarterly* 8 (1), 94–99.

Jyrki J.J. Kasvi works as a researcher in the Helsinki University of Technology (HUT) Laboratory of Work Psychology and Leadership. He is focusing his attention on shop floor information environments: what kinds of knowledge are needed and how to answer to these needs. In addition, Kasvi has written several books and articles about computers, the information society, and computer games. He may be reached at jyrki.kasvi@hut.fi.

Matti Vartiainen is the professor of Learning Organization studies in the HUT Laboratory of Work Psychology and Leadership. In addition to learning organizations, his research activities focus on performance support, organizational innovations, product development, and reward systems. He may be reached at matti.vartiainen@hut.fi.

Improving Production Line Performance

Michael Umble, Van Gray, and Elisabeth Umble

This article examines production line performance from the perspective of the theory of constraints. It presents the advantages of the drum-buffer-rope strategy, a modified buffer approach that strips protection against breakdowns from non-constraint resources and concentrates all of the protection at the constraint. This is yet another specific tactic quality professionalis can use to improve processes and reduce defects.

Production lines rarely perform up to design expectations. Manufacturing managers, schedulers, and engineers constantly try to counteract the effects of equipment breakdowns, quality problems, line changeovers, and other problems that contribute to low productivity. This article explains how the theory of constraint's drum-buffer-rope (DBR) logistical system and buffer management concepts can be applied to production lines to significantly improve overall line productivity.

Causes of Poor Production Line Performance

In the TOC philosophy, a constraint is defined as anything that prevents the system from achieving higher performance, where performance is measured relative to the system's goal. In the real world, perfectly balanced production lines do not exist because of line dependencies, variability, and disruptions. Inevitably, production lines are characterized by resources that have differing finite capacities. And, in general, there is one resource that limits how much a single production line can produce. That resource is the constraint (bottleneck) for the line. All other resources are non-constraints that have some amount of extra "catch-up" capacity. Even though non-constraint resources occasionally stop working, the long-term output of the line is reduced only if the constraint is disrupted. Thus, the resource constraint is the key to achieving maximum line output.

Unplanned Disruptions

By design, most production line configurations provide for a limited amount of work-in-process inventory. Because of the high level of dependency

Reprinted from *IIE Solutions*, November 2000, with the permission of the Institute of Industrial Engineers, 25 Technology Park, Norcross, GA, 30092, 770-449-0461. Copyright © 2000.

between work stations, this leaves the production line extremely vulnerable to a variety of unplanned, random disruptions. A significant disruption at any station, or a series of disruptions working in combination, can create a domino effect that shuts down the line. These unplanned disruptions may create a loss of line output through three distinct mechanisms: breakage, starvation, and blockage.

Breakage refers to any disruption originating at the constraint resource. This directly causes a loss of constraint output and a corresponding loss of output for the entire system. *Starvation* occurs when one or more stations prior to the constraint experience disruptions, causing the constraint to run out of material. This results in down time at the constraint and a loss of system output. *Blockage* occurs when one or more stations after the constraint suffer disruptions, starting a chain reaction which sequentially causes upstream stations to stop working because there is no place to store any additional processed material. Eventually, the constraint work station will cease working because it has no place to off-load its completed units, resulting in a loss of system output.

Figure 1 shows a production line with the constraint operation (denoted as Station X) clearly identified. Figure 1 also indicates the relative location of stations along the production line where a disruption may lead to a loss of output because of breakage, starvation, or blockage.

> A production line changeover that requires set-ups is a disruption to the system that causes a loss of output.

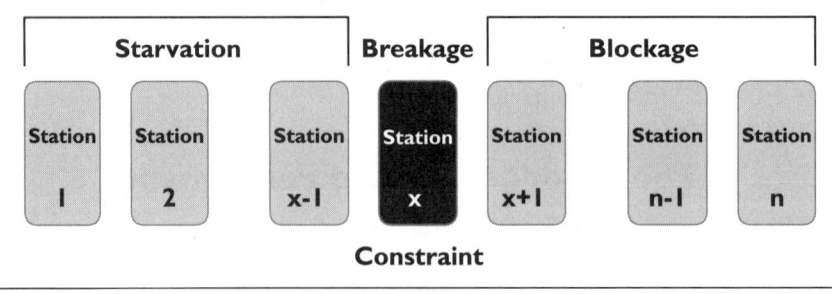

Figure 1. **Regions of the production line where work station disruptions may lead to starvation, breakage, and blockage**

Planned Disruptions: Line Changeovers

Production lines that produce more than one product often utilize equipment that requires set-ups. A production line changeover that requires set-ups is a disruption to the system that causes a loss of output. When a line changeover occurs, any required set-up time at the constraint resource results directly in a loss of productive capacity at the constraint and a loss of system output. In addition, set-ups at non-constraint resources create disruptions that may cause the constraint to suffer starvation or blockage. The result again is a loss of system output.

From a managerial perspective, there is a critical difference between set-

Improving Production Line Performance

ups and other categories of disruptions. Set-ups caused by line changeovers are (or should be) planned disruptions in the work flow.

The Production Line Simulation Model

Simulation was used to analyze the impact of different buffering strategies on an unbalanced production line that is subject to both unplanned disruptions and line changeovers. All simulation models assume a single production line that contains exactly one constraint resource and produces only one product type at a time. Of prime importance is the effect of unplanned disruptions and line changeovers on breakage, starvation, blockage, and ultimately, system output.

The production line to be simulated has 17 stations and is shown in Figure 2. Per-unit processing times at the various stations vary from two to 12 minutes. An alphanumeric grid is used to identify the various work stations and work-in-process storage areas. Station D4 has the longest processing time (12 minutes per unit) and is clearly the constraint resource. The stations B1 and D1 are part of a feeder line. The main line is protected from disruptions that occur on this feeder line by an inventory buffer at location E1.

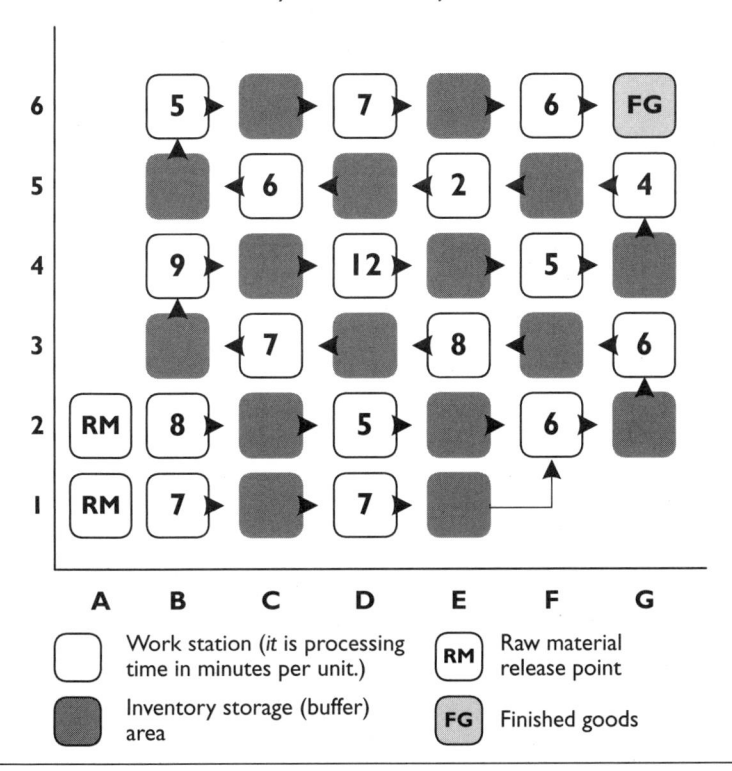

Figure 2. **A production line with 15 main line stations and two feeder line stations**

Two simulation models were used. The basic model is a dedicated production line that yields only one product. This eliminates the effects of line changeovers and allows us to focus on the effects of unplanned disruptions on the starvation and blockage mechanisms. In the second model, the production line produces different products in batches of 120 units at a time. In this model, the impact of line changeovers on starvation and blockage is emphasized. In order to isolate the effect of changeovers, the model assumes that the processing time required at a given work station is the same for any of the products processed at that station.

In both models, unplanned disruptions are randomly generated for all 17 work stations. The nature of the breakdowns is a function of two factors. First, breakdowns are randomly generated according to a uniform probability distribution. Once a breakdown occurs, then the duration of each breakdown is generated using a positively skewed discrete probability distribution with an average breakdown duration of five minutes and a maximum duration of 20 minutes. The end result is that each station will be in breakdown status about 6.5 percent of the time.

There is one exception to the typical pattern for station breakdowns. In order to illustrate an important point, the C3 station follows a different breakdown pattern. It breaks down only one-fourth as often, but the duration of each breakdown is a positively skewed distribution with an average duration of 20 minutes and a maximum duration of 60 minutes. Although station C3 has the same overall down time percentage as the other stations, the longer average duration creates the potential for a much more damaging disruption when a breakdown does occur. And since station C3 is located prior to the constraint, starvation should be expected to be a bigger problem than blockage. Station C3 is included in the model because many production lines include resources that wreak havoc when they break down.

Modeling Production Lines with No Changeovers

The production line environment with no line changeovers is simulated for 168 hours (seven 24-hour days). Since the constraint has a 12-minute-per-unit processing requirement, the constraint, and therefore the line, can produce no more than an average of five units per hour or 840 units per week. However, the simulation begins with no work-in-process in the system. Without initial work-in-process, it takes 97 minutes for the first unit of material to be fully processed, reducing maximum line output to 832 units. In addition, the expected breakdown rate of 6.5 percent at the constraint will further reduce expected constraint output by 54 units, yielding an adjusted expected maximum output of 778 units. However, even this level of output is seldom achieved in practice because of the disruptions that cause starvation and blockage.

The causes of lost output for the production system are recorded by classifying constraint down time as breakage, starvation, or blockage. (Note that if breakage at the constraint is generated while the constraint is already suffering from starvation or blockage, the down time is attributed to the previously existing starvation or blockage. This causes the recorded percentage of time that the constraint experiences breakage to be less than the expected 6.5 percent when starvation or blockage exists.) The quantity of work-in-process inventory in the main production line is also recorded at the end of each simulation run and averaged to estimate inventory levels.

The production line operation is simulated for 100 one-week periods. Three different line buffering strategies are modeled. In each of the three cases, the line is dedicated to one product and does not require set-ups.

Case 1: A Pure Pull System

The initial production line model mirrors a pure pull system that allows no excess work-in-process inventory on the line. That is, the maximum inventory at a storage location is one unit (except at E1, where 10 units are allowed to accumulate in order to de-couple the main line from disruptions on the feeder line). Each work station has permission to process material only if the buffer storage area it feeds is empty. As each unit of material completes processing at a station, it is moved to the inventory storage area for the next station, where the material waits until the next station can begin processing. This model will be quite vulnerable to the effects of starvation and blockage.

Case 2: An Unfocused Buffer Strategy

This model is the same environment as Case 1, except that the maximum inventory allowed to accumulate between stations is two units instead of one. This additional buffering is equally spread throughout the line and should reduce the impact of breakdowns before and after the constraint, resulting in less constraint time lost due to starvation and blockage. This case is also expected to increase production lead time and work-in-process inventory.

Case 3: A TOC Buffer Strategy

The TOC drum-buffer-rope approach recognizes that the key to increasing line productivity lies in concentrating protection at the constraint (D4). It is neither necessary nor desirable to provide protection for non-constraint stations since they have excess capacity and should not be fully utilized anyway. The buffering strategy must fully protect the constraint from the disruptions that occur elsewhere in the system and cause starvation and blockage. This is accomplished by establishing two types of buffers: a time buffer and a stock buffer.

A time buffer is located immediately in front of the constraint (at storage area C4 in the model) to protect the constraint from disruptions that occur prior to the constraint. This type of buffer allows a pre-determined amount of inventory to accumulate in front of the constraint. The term *time buffer* is appropriate because it is useful to think of the protection provided by this buffer in terms of time, not actual units of inventory. For example, if there are five units of inventory in the constraint's time buffer, this represents 60 minutes of processing time at the constraint. Therefore, this amount of buffer affords 60 minutes of protection against starvation-type disruptions at the constraint. In general, it would be useful to know the amount of protection provided by a buffer that contains different materials that require different processing times. For example, if a buffer contains two units of material that require 10 minutes of processing time per unit and eight units of a material that require 20 minutes of processing time per unit, then the buffer provides 180 minutes worth of protection. This is much more informative than simply noting that the buffer contains 10 units of inventory.

A space buffer is located immediately after the constraint (at storage area E4) to protect the constraint from disruptions that occur downstream from the constraint. A space buffer simply means that a designated amount of space will be made available to hold work processed by the constraint. Clearly, in the case of a time buffer, protection for the constraint takes the form of units of work actually sitting in the buffer storage area prior to the constraint. However, in the case of a space buffer, protection takes the form of empty space, which allows for the storage of the constraint's future output to guard against downstream disruptions. The positioning of time and space buffers relative to the constraint is illustrated in Figure 3.

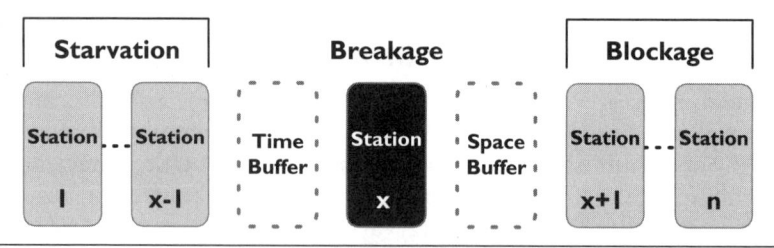

Figure 3. **Location of time and space buffers**

The TOC-based strategy for Case 3 is to allow time and space buffers of 12 units (144 minutes worth of work) immediately before and after the constraint. Except for these two buffers, the Case 3 environment is exactly the same as Case 1, with maximum inventory buffers of one unit on the main line. The TOC strategy is based on the rationale that it is not necessary to protect non-constraint resources with additional buffers because they should not be fully utilized anyway. The motivation is to increase system output by keeping non-constraint resource disruptions from causing starvation and blockage.

Simulation Results and Implications of Cases 1, 2, and 3

The results of 100 simulation runs for Cases 1, 2, and 3 are summarized in Figure 4. For each case, the results include the mean (μ) and standard deviation (σ) of total output as well as the mean percentage of time that the constraint was in production, breakage, starvation, and blockage modes. Also included is the mean number of units of inventory in the main line at the end of the simulation.

	Case 1		Case 2		Case 3	
Total Output	μ	σ	μ	σ	μ	σ
Total Output	653.57	21.34	710.50	19.28	753.18	16.98
Production (%)	78.84	2.56	85.71	2.28	90.94	2.00
Breakage (%)	5.55	1.31	6.18	1.56	6.27	1.56
Starvation (%)	12.11	2.27	6.54	1.79	2.65	1.48
Blockage (%)	3.50	1.54	1.56	1.11	0.24	0.33
Inventory units	9.91	1.36	17.16	2.01	18.83	4.05

Figure 4. **Simulation results for production line cases 1-3**

The average output increases from 653.57 units in Case 1 to 710.50 units in Case 2, an increase of 57 units of output. However, the average output of the TOC-based Case 3 is 753.18, an increase of 100 units from Case 1. Moreover, the inventory level for Case 3 is only slightly higher than for Case 2.

In Case 1, starvation is responsible for the biggest loss of productive capacity (12.11 percent) at the constraint. (Recall that the "troublemaker" resource, C3, is prior to the constraint.) The Case 2 strategy reduces the starvation percentage to 6.54 percent. But the starvation percentage for Case 3 drops dramatically to 2.65 percent. In Case 3, most of the starvation occurs because the model does not allow beginning inventory. Once the constraint time buffer is fully established, starvation rarely occurs.

Blockage accounts for a 3.5 percent loss of productive capacity in Case 1. This drops to 1.56 percent in Case 2, and an almost non-existent 0.24 percent in Case 3. Thus, the TOC-based strategy implemented in Case 3 virtually eliminates starvation and blockage! The only remaining significant source of lost production capacity for the constraint and the system as a whole are the breakdowns that occur at the constraint. That is, except for the starvation that occurs during the start-up period, the average output of Case 3 would nearly equal the design maximum of 778 units.

Modeling Production Lines with Changeovers

It is useful to determine the effects of the buffering strategies described above when line changeovers are required. To do this, the same basic production line layout described for Cases 1, 2, and 3 is used as a model for Cases 4 and 5. The primary differences are that the line produces more than one product and each line changeover requires set-ups. The model for Cases 4 and 5 assumes that batches of 120 units of each product are run before the line changes over to run a different product. Each line changeover requires a special crew to perform set-ups at each of the 17 stations. The set-up time at each station is randomly generated and averages one hour. But when a station is undergoing a set-up and a breakdown occurs at that station, this delays the set-up process and increases the actual set-up time. When a line changeover begins, the set-up crew works on one station at a time, starting with B1. The set-up begins as soon as B1 finishes processing the last unit of the previous batch. After B1, the set-up sequence is B2, D1, D2, F2, G3, E3, ... , F6.

In this model, down time at the constraint can be traced to four distinct causes:

1. Breakdowns at the constraint.
2. Constraint starvation, caused by unplanned breakdowns prior to the constraint.
3. Constraint blockage, caused by unplanned breakdowns after the constraint.
4. Constraint down time caused by set-ups at, before, or after the constraint.

Although set-ups before and after the constraint cause lost constraint time through the starvation and blockage mechanisms, this loss is categorized as caused by set-ups. Two cases involving line changeovers are modeled and simulated for 100 one-week periods. The cases compare the pure pull system with the TOC buffer strategy.

Case 4: Pure Pull System with Set-ups

This case is similar to Case 1. That is, one unit of inventory is allowed between stations. The difference is that this case allows for line changeovers and all set-ups are performed sequentially by the set-up crew.

Case 5: TOC Buffer Strategy with One Set-up Crew

This case is similar to Case 3. Time and space buffers of 12 units (144 minutes) are established immediately before and after the constraint, with maximum buffers of one unit allowed elsewhere on the main line. Like Case 4, this case utilizes a set-up crew to perform the set-ups required for the line changeover.

Simulation Results and Implications for Cases 4 and 5

The simulation results for Cases 4 and 5 are presented in Figure 5. The figure indicates the mean and standard deviation of total output and the percentage of time the constraint is producing product. Also shown is the percentage of time the constraint is not producing due to set-ups, breakage at the constraint, starvation, and blockage.

	Case 4		Case 5	
	μ	σ	μ	σ
Total Output	414.50	19.58	487.34	11.46
Production (%)	50.10	2.33	60.00	1.27
Setup (%)	37.04	1.06	33.95	1.44
Breakage (%)	3.65	1.06	4.50	1.22
Starvation (%)	6.85	1.76	0.80	0.94
Blockage (%)	2.35	1.36	0.73	0.59

Figure 5. **Simulation results for cases 4 and 5: production lines with changeovers**

As shown in Figure 5, the total output for Case 4 averages only 414.5 units with the constraint only utilizing 50 percent of its capacity. Significantly, the constraint loses 37 percent of its capacity to down time due to set-ups during the line changeover. On the other hand, the mean output for Case 5 rises to 487.34 units, an increase of more than 17 percent from the Case 4 average output. The TOC buffering strategy of Case 5 virtually eliminates starvation and blockage problems, while also decreasing the amount of constraint time lost to set-ups.

The time and space buffers provide significant protection for the constraint from the planned disruptions of the set-up process. When the set-up process begins, the flow of new product to the constraint is shut off from the constraint and the new product cannot be processed at the constraint until the constraint itself is set up. Establishing a time buffer in front of the constraint provides additional units of the previous product for the constraint to work on while set-ups are being performed at workstations prior to the constraint, thus enhancing system throughput. When the stations after the constraint are being set up, this disruption blocks the constraint from producing if the constraint is not allowed to off-load its output. To the degree that the output from the constraint can be temporarily stockpiled in a space buffer, once again, system throughput is enhanced. Clearly, sufficiently large time and space buffers at the constraint could virtually eliminate lost throughput due to set-ups at the non-constraint stations.

Set-up time at the constraint will always result in a loss of system output. But large enough time and space buffers can eliminate all other causes of lost output. However, permanent time and space buffers that are large enough to totally protect the constraint from starvation, blockage, and set-up disruptions would significantly increase the production lead time and generally result in increased inventory levels.

A practical solution that maximizes system output while minimizing system lead time and inventory is to adopt a modified buffer strategy that allows the buffers to increase and decrease as needed to provide the appropriate degree of protection. For example, when a line is operating normally, 144-minute buffers may be sufficient to protect against starvation and blockage due to breakage at individual stations. However, 144-minute buffers will not prevent down time at the constraint when the line undergoes a changeover. Thus, when a line changeover is imminent, the time buffer can be temporarily increased to the level necessary to eliminate the expected starvation that normally occurs from the changeover. Blockage at the constraint due to the changeover must be addressed by adjusting the space buffer. To eliminate blockage, appropriate temporary storage space must be made available for the constraint to off-load its output during the changeover period. After the changeover is complete, the buffers can return to their normal size. In practice, different products might require uniquely sized time and space buffers due to variable processing time, set-up times, and storage requirements.

Advantages of Drum-Buffer-Rope

There are two basic buffering strategies for protecting the throughput of the system. One strategy argues for spreading the allowable inventory throughout the system, which ultimately wastes protection on non-constraint resources. As demonstrated by the simulation results of Case 2, this approach generates significantly less than optimal performance. The other (DBR) strategy strips protection against breakdowns from non-constraint resources and concentrates all of the protection at the constraint—the resource that ultimately determines system performance. The simulation results of Case 3 indicate that this is an efficient mechanism for the protection of system throughput.

Strategies that attempt to establish buffers at some—but not all—resources are a combination of the above two pure strategies. The intent of such strategies is to provide some protection at non-constraints in an attempt to dampen disturbances that might eventually affect the constraint. Intuitively, compared to the DBR approach, such strategies would be inefficient in a constrained resource environment. Future research efforts could compare the efficiency of various multi-buffer strategies with the pure DBR strategy in a variety of environments.

In addition to the efficiency advantage, the DBR approach has two more advantages over more complex multiple-buffer strategies. One is that the DBR approach is relatively easy to devise and implement. The only key decision is the size of the time and space buffers at the constraint. Of course, like other buffering strategies, a deterministic solution for buffer size does not exist because of the dynamic interactions of the system. The recommended approach is to implement the time and space buffers, monitor how effectively the buffers are providing the needed protection, and adjust the buffer sizes accordingly.

A second advantage of DBR is better information that can be used to reinforce and enhance a process of continuous improvement. When attention is focused on one time buffer and one space buffer, it is easy to monitor the buffers and record instances when the buffers are depleted or nearly depleted due to various disruptions. Using a Pareto type analysis, the most significant sources of disruption can be identified. For example, in our model, lengthy breakdowns at C3 adversely affect system performance, either through lost output or by causing the constraint time buffer to be larger than otherwise necessary. Thus, the breakdown problem at C3 would become a prime candidate for an improvement project. As soon as the C3 breakdown problem is rectified, the time buffer can be reduced, thus reducing production lead time and system inventory. By repeatedly applying this process, high return improvement projects can be identified. With each improvement comes the benefit that system output can be maintained with less inventory.

For Further Reading

Goldratt, E.M., *The Haystack Syndrome: Sifting Information Out of the Data Ocean*, North River Press, 1990.

Katok, Elena, Tomas Serrander, and Mattias Wennstrom, "Throughput Improvement and Scrap Reduction in Aluminum Can Manufacturing," *Production and Inventory Management Journal*, 1999.

Srikanth, M.L., and Michael Umble, *Synchronous Management: Profit-Based Manufacturing for the 21st Century—Volume I*, Spectrum Publishing, 1997.

Michael Umble, Ph.D., is a professor of operations management at Baylor University. He is a certified fellow of APICS, a member of PMI, and a certified instructor with the Goldratt Institute.

Van Gray, Ph.D., is an associate professor of operations management at Baylor University. He is a former academic associate of the Goldratt Institute.

Elisabeth Umble, Ph.D., J.D., is an assistant professor of statistics at Texas A&M University. She is a member of IIE, ASQ, and the state bar of Texas.

Cost vs. Quality

Doug Bartholomew

Over and over we hear that the cost of quality is actually not a cost but an investment that yields great returns. However, it's a lesson that even the best companies have trouble understanding, as this article points out. The author examines the automotive industry and compares the Big Three approach with Toyota. The Big Three do not come off well. For more on Toyota, see the article in this yearbook, "The Counterintuitive Principles of the Toyota Production System."

What is the cost of quality? To Ford Motor Co. and Bridgestone/Firestone Inc., one of the costs of quality is the inestimable damage to both companies' reputations as wary consumers think twice about purchasing Ford Explorers or Bridgestone/Firestone tires.

What is the cost of quality? DaimlerChrysler AG may find out when results are in from its decision earlier this year to require suppliers to reduce costs by a fixed percentage. "Whether DaimlerChrysler's decision will have a quality impact is uncertain, but it may affect the quality of what they demand from suppliers," observes Joe Ivers, partner and executive director of quality and customer satisfaction research at J.D. Power & Associates, Agoura Hills, Calif.

Cost reductions alone need not translate to a lower-quality product. According to *IndustryWeek*'s 2000 Census of Manufacturers, which surveyed some 3,000 companies, manufacturers that were able to cut their costs by reducing scrap and waste tended to show more improvement in quality than those whose costs increased.

Manufacturers over the last 20 years have invested billions of dollars in various quality-improvement efforts. Among the most popular today are the principles of lean manufacturing as pioneered by Toyota Motor Corp. and the Six Sigma standards that help companies refine their quality efforts to achieve still greater improvements. In most cases, investments in these programs have been more than recovered by lower production costs, less scrap, fewer defects, and reduced warranty expense.

Even with these gains, the costs associated with badly designed, poorly made products continue to haunt the manufacturing community. "The cost of poor quality in terms of rework, scrap, and warranty expense is still a big number," says Bonnie Smith, director of the LeanSigma program at TBM Institute, a training and consulting firm in Durham, N.C. But most companies haven't got a clue as to what that cost is. "I've never walked into a plant where anybody knew the cost of quality," says Kevin Smith, president, Productivity Group, Div. Productivity Inc., Portland, Oreg. "It's amazing what design engineers don't know about manufacturing," says Jane Algee, producibility manager for the Comanche helicopter electro-optical sensor system program at Lockheed Martin Missiles and Fire Control in Orlando. Currently on a leave of absence in Tokyo, Algee, immediate past president of the Institute of Industrial Engineers, agrees that most product designers have little or no idea of the impact a poor design can have on both quality and cost. "It's eye-opening that a lot of these designers have been in industry over 30 years, yet they don't understand the cost of quality—how pinching a penny now can cost you a hundred times over in the future," Algee says. "It's kind of the American mistake."

Complicating matters, the rampant cost-cutting over the last two decades has caused manufacturers to take a hard look at just what level of durability and material quality they are willing to design into their products. Toyota, for instance, may have gone overboard with quality, some observers believe. "Toyota looked at their products and discovered their quality was too good," says Jeffrey Liker, professor of industrial and operations engineering at the University of Michigan, Ann Arbor. "They didn't need stainless steel parts in the engine area. They saved $100 billion by commonizing parts—using less expensive materials that perform the same function," says Liker, who wrote the book *Becoming Lean* (1998, Productivity Press).

While it's common for manufacturers to pay lip service to quality, it's clear to anyone who has ever bought a screwdriver that broke the first time it was used, discovered the rear-door lock on a brand-new SUV was defective, or had the transmission on a new car fail after less than 10,000 miles, that there is quality, and then there is *quality*. In sum, all products are not created equal.

Take the Bridgestone/Firestone-Ford controversy. Ford president and CEO Jacques Nasser has stated that Ford's research into its former supplier's tires indicates that "customer safety would be at risk" if Ford customers were to continue to ride on Bridgestone/Firestone tires. Likewise, John Lampe, chairman, president, and CEO of Firestone, says an expert hired by his firm concluded that the Ford Explorer could be unusually prone to skidding out of control in the event of a sudden tire failure, and that the vehicle's design, not the tires, put its occupants at risk. Despite the charges, both companies continue to claim their own products are safe.

The unusual public brouhaha raises serious concerns about the quality of two of America's foremost brands. During a recent Congressional investigation, Deputy Transportation Secretary Michael Jackson said the National Highway Traffic Safety Administration may investigate the Explorer's tendency to roll over. And U.S. Rep. John Dingell (D, Mich.) questioned whether Firestone had shaved the quality of its tires as part of cost-trimming efforts in the mid-1990s.

In what was perceived by some observers as an admission of poor quality in manufacturing at one of its plants, Bridgestone/Firestone in June announced plans to close its Decatur, Ill., tire facility, the main source of tires prone to suffer tread separations that led to more than 200 rollover fatalities, most of them involving Explorers. Executives said the decision to close the plant and idle close to 1,500 workers was not related to quality problems but rather to the need to reduce capacity.

That may be, but Ford's analysis of the tires that failed on its Explorers showed that an inordinate number that suffered tread separations were made at the Decatur plant, calling into question the quality procedures at the 59-year-old facility. The plant would have required substantial capital investment to upgrade. By closing it down, Bridgestone/Firestone will save more than $100 million a year. Sales of Bridgestone/Firestone replacement tires were down 50% in the first half of this year, compared with sales for the first six months of 2000, as wary consumers, concerned about quality, avoided the brand in droves.

Industry-wide, automotive manufacturers are notorious for cutting corners on their products to save a buck. For example, many motorists remember the days when all new cars came with a full-size spare tire. Today, most new cars come with a skinnier, cheaper wheel and tire combination that looks as if it belongs on a bicycle, not an automobile. These "donut" spares typically come stamped with a warning that they are not intended to be driven over 50 mph nor for more than 50 miles. By instituting this subtle change, auto manufacturers reaped huge savings on tens of millions of vehicles, because the smaller units cost less to make. Unfortunately, the switch—of which buyers were never informed—resulted in reduced quality for the consumer.

Clearly, careful attention to the design of a product—in terms of its manufacturability as well as its functionality and durability in the field—is critical. The flip side is poor design and engineering that, in the auto industry, leads to recalls and higher warranty costs for automakers.

"Warranty costs are huge in this industry," says Ivers of J.D. Power. "When not enough attention is paid to design in terms of manufacturability and engineering, you wind up with vehicles that need a lot of fixing." He cites the spate of problems owners had a few years ago with automobiles equipped with "T-tops"—sunroofs that leaked as a result of poor design that caused a lack of adequate weatherproofing.

Too Many Recalls

Recalls are common. Every month, automakers announce recalls to replace products or parts that fail. These include such things as fuel lines that rupture, components that melt due to proximity to a hot manifold, or electronic failures that may cause the vehicle to stop dead in traffic for no apparent reason. "Every auto executive in Detroit knows they're hurting because of quality," observes Martin Piszczalski, president of Sextant Research, an Ann Arbor, Mich., IT consulting firm.

DaimlerChrysler recently announced that 16,000 owners of its 2000 Mercedes-Benz M-Class vehicles should replace their rear-middle-seat belt anchor plate because it does not meet specifications. In the same week, Isuzu recalled 3,100 of its 2001 Rodeo Sport vehicles to replace fuel return hoses that crack and leak.

Last April (2001), an Alameda County, Calif., judge ordered Ford to replace defective ignition devices on an estimated two million 1983-1995 vehicles prone to stalling. A class-action suit charged that Ford had placed its thick-film-ignition module, which regulates electric current to the spark plugs, too close to the engine block where it was exposed to high temperatures, thus causing the module to fail.

Documents introduced in court showed that Ford confirmed the problem in its internal studies and could have moved the module to a cooler location at an added cost of $4 per vehicle. Ford denied the devices are defective, but the automaker has settled numerous other suits related to allegations of vehicles stalling. In August Ford reached a tentative settlement, agreeing to double the warranty protection to 100,000 miles on 5 million vehicles to cover the estimated $1 billion cost of fixing them.

In the last year or so, Ford has been plagued with quality problems, and CEO Nasser has publicly admitted the company's quality is "about average." Its Escape mini-SUV has suffered five product recalls. Overall, the automaker came in last among the top seven auto manufacturers in J.D. Power's latest ranking. Through its lean initiative, Ford this year plans to cut 4% out of the cost of making its vehicles, for about $800 million in savings. Perhaps most embarrassing for Ford was a pair of recalls the automaker announced earlier this year on its redesigned 2002 Explorer. The first was for over 50,000 vehicles built at the company's Louisville, Ky., plant, where a jagged edge along a section of the assembly line may have sliced tires. The second was for 56,000 new Explorers, built at both Louisville and a St. Louis plant, which may have loose rear-hatch windows that can shatter when shut.

Despite all these well-publicized slip-ups in quality, J.D. Power says overall quality of cars is improving. One reason for the apparent disparity may be that J.D. Power's annual survey of automobile owners focuses on their experience during the first three months of ownership of a new vehicle. It does not address durability or any problems that may arise when a vehicle has been owned for six months, a year, or five years.

In just the last three years the number of problems reported by new owners dropped from 176 per 100 vehicles in 1998 to 147 in 2001. "Things gone wrong, what we call TGWs, are evidence of a lack of quality," Ivers says.

Toyota and its Lexus luxury brand dominated the J.D. Power quality rankings for 2001, grabbing the top spots in seven of 16 different vehicle market segments. The Toyota Corolla ranked as the compact with the fewest complaints in the first three months of ownership. Similarly, the Toyota Avalon took first among premium midsize cars. Likewise, the Lexus ES 300 was the number-one-ranked entry luxury vehicle, while its big sister, the Lexus LS 430, rolled off with gold honors among premium luxury cars.

It comes as no surprise that the chief reason Ford, GM, and Chrysler continue to lose market share to Japanese and German automakers, analysts say, is the public's perception of the quality of American vehicles.

Quality Payback

To be sure, quality-improvement efforts are big in manufacturing today. For instance, Caterpillar Inc. is investing $20 million this year to train 2,700 employees in Six Sigma theory and practice. "It's a massive investment, and our goal this year is to at least break even on documented savings as a result," says Jim Owens, group president and executive office member.

"We see it as an investment in quality that will yield a return in terms of reduced reliability problems and improved warranty performance," Owens says. He is quick to point out that "the back-end cost of poor quality is only the tip of the iceberg. Quality affects the customer's buying decision in the future."

While some companies, such as DaimlerChrysler and Toyota, have ordered their suppliers to trim a fixed percentage of cost out of their operations, Owens says Caterpillar doesn't take that route. "I flinch when I hear blanket demands for cost reductions, as if those suppliers are going to take that out of their margins. We are cognizant that our suppliers are our partners who are committed to working with us to manage the cost of parts down." The bottom line, though, as Owens puts it, is, "Our quality is only as good as our supplier quality."

Caterpillar keeps close tabs on its certified suppliers in order to maintain quality. For instance, suppliers are prohibited from making changes in materials or processes without its concurrence. "The reason is that we have been burned a couple times when that happened," Owens says.

It's no secret that many manufacturers have succeeded in linking cost-cutting with quality improvement. Toyota, for instance, expects a 3% reduction in costs each year from its supplier firms, says Dan Cavanagh, plant manager at Dana Corp.'s automotive frame plant in Stockton, Calif. Producing 150,000 frames annually, the sprawling facility is a captive supplier to its sole customer, the General Motors-Toyota joint venture New United Motor Manufacturing Inc. (NUMMI) plant 60-plus miles away in Fremont, Calif. Workers at the plant, which performs 115 ft of welds on each 300-lb frame, are constantly looking for ways to improve quality and reduce costs. Each worker is expected to come up with three ideas per month, and in a recent month the average was 3.8, Cavanagh says.

In one work area, cycle time was reduced by 10 to 18 seconds by adding another welder, thereby reducing defects and eliminating a buildup of parts in that area. That one change led to both reduced costs and improved quality.

Unfortunately, it's a lot easier for managers under the gun to trim costs by exchanging one supplier's part for another's lower-priced one. After all, who's going to notice or care that a set of seals on a pump or valve came from a different manufacturer, or that substandard steel was used to make a part that otherwise would cost half again as much?

Toyota notices. "You shouldn't compromise quality for other issues, including cost-saving initiatives," says Ed Mantey, former chief engineer for the 2000 Avalon who is based at the Toyota Technical Center in Ann Arbor, Mich. "It's not a tradeoff—we want quality to increase and cost to come down. Toyota's reputation for quality differentiates our product from our competitors'."

Mantey says that when he ran the 2000 Avalon project, the company analyzed what buyers perceived were the strengths and weaknesses of the car's predecessor. "One thing people wanted us to improve was the front-door wind noise," he says.

In response, Toyota engineers completely redesigned the way the door was manufactured. Instead of what is known in the industry as a press-type door, they switched to a frame-type door. The first type of door is made from a one-piece stamping, while the latter requires that the steel section that forms the channel to hold the window glass be welded to the door's sheet metal.

The new type of door has a stiffer upper section that offers a better sealing surface for the weatherstripping that seals out wind and noise. Despite the need for welding, which is done both robotically and with hand-finishing, the frame-type door costs less to make. One reason is that with the press-type door, sections of metal have to be cut away for the guts of the door mechanism, and this metal becomes waste. The end result, says Mantey, is that "the customer gets better quality at lower cost."

Toyota also saved money without sacrificing quality by using local U.S.-made materials over those made in Japan. "We saved millions of dollars this way, and the part performance we found was at least equal or better to the original part but at a lower cost," Mantey adds.

Those within the auto industry are well aware of the tradeoffs that often occur between quality and cost, Mantey confides. "At one point a competitor said to me, 'It's less expensive to pay warranty claims than to overdesign the part.' All too often we have suppliers say to us, 'It's good enough for the Big Three, why isn't it good enough for you?'"

Mantey confirms that Toyota requires its suppliers to cut costs 2% to 3% each year. Even so, he says Toyota works with them to help them achieve these reductions while improving quality, as opposed to sacrificing it. He says one of the benefits of forcing suppliers to make such efforts is that "they don't keep cranking out the same parts year after year—they must continually improve them."

Mantey notes he just approved a supplier's request to use a new formula for electrodeposition coating on metal. "It's lower cost and gives better protection than the previous coating," he says. Toyota prohibits suppliers from arbitrarily changing processes or parts suppliers without seeking and obtaining approval from Toyota. "We do not allow them to compromise the quality of our vehicles for cost reductions," he says.

Supply-Chain Partnerships

Other industries are using similar approaches to improve quality while reining in costs. "We work with our supply chain, forming partnerships with the producers of component parts," says Brad Miller, senior manufacturing engineer at Medeco High Security Lock Co. in Salem, Va. Medeco's locks are sold only through locksmiths, primarily for commercial buildings such as government offices, banks, and convenience stores.

Medeco locks cost more than other brands. A typical deadbolt set alone costs $120, five or six times an average set. Because they come with antipick technology and security keys that cannot be duplicated at a hardware store, buyers feel the extra level of security is worth the price.

"If we are having trouble with a part, either dimensionally or functionally, instead of trying to accommodate a sloppy part, we'll visit the vendor to help them get back on track to provide a better part for us," says Miller. For instance, he recently had to visit a supplier to help the company redesign its process to correct a structural-integrity problem with its parts. Also, "We analyze our returns, which are really low, and attack those issues," he says. Not all manufacturers analyze their failures. "It's tricky to do that kind of analysis, and often what caused the failure is difficult to determine and it takes a lot of time," says Alice E. Smith, professor of industrial and systems engineering at Auburn University, Auburn, Ala. "And manufacturers often don't want to know."

But Miller believes even one product return a year should be cause for concern. "The biggest cost of poor quality is the image of the product and the company," he says. "Poor quality costs the company hugely in lost revenues."

That's the cost of quality.

Doug Bartholomew is senior technology editor for IndustryWeek. *Contact him at dbartholomew@industryweek.com.*

High-Performance Partnering by Self-Managed Teams in Manufacturing

Joe Singer and Steve Duvall

This article reports on the problems that Harley-Davidson was having with customer and employee dissatisfaction because it was unable to keep up with demand. The company introduced self-managed work teams, work system integration of design, and process implementation strategies. The article describes a high-performance work system infrastructure used to transform the manufacturing process from a traditional assembly line to self-managed team-based production. There are lots of lessons here.

In today's competitive environment, it is incomprehensible to ask your customer to wait as long as two years for a product with high visibility, one that also provides instant gratification. Yet that is exactly what was happening with the manufacture and sale of Harley-Davidson motorcycles. Due to its notoriety and the changing demographics of its customer base (i.e., a shift to baby boomers) over the past several years, the increased demand has far exceeded Harley-Davidson's production capabilities. As a result, customers had to wait anywhere from 16 to 24 months for their favorite motorcycle and employee productivity and satisfaction were declining due to feelings of powerlessness.

Such a situation would present a real engineering management dilemma for any organization, because while a backlog in demand and the ability to employ the advantage of economies of scale in the production process put you in an enviable position, the gap between supply and demand can create ample opportunity for competitors to penetrate the market and increase their share. Harley-Davidson has been trying, and continues, to protect its 55% worldwide market share.

Faced with constant pressure to improve performance, companies are closely examining their particular processes, patterns, structures, and practices and are turning to high-performance work systems as a critical approach to transforming their business strategy (Van Buren and Werner, 1996).

Reprinted with permission from *Engineering Management Journal*, Vol. 12, No. 4, December 2000. Copyright © 2000 the American Society for Engineering Management. All rights reserved.

To meet and anticipate the growing level of demand, increase its market share, and remain the number-one motorcycle manufacturer in the world, Harley-Davidson has undertaken several major engineering redesign and expansion projects. Most notable of these is the start-up of a new motorcycle manufacturing facility located in Kansas City, Mo., in 1998. The Kansas City facility was built in order to focus production on the sport motorcycle segment of Harley-Davidson's products, known as the Sportster models. These vehicles were previously produced at Harley-Davidson's York, Penn., factory and were fully transferred to Kansas City in the third quarter of 1998 when full production began.

In moving the Sportster production to the new Kansas City facility, the York facility was able to focus on increasing production of the cruiser and touring models. In turn, the Kansas City facility is able to specialize in sport motorcycle production and in the development of newly related products in order to increase its value added to customers.

The Kansas City expansion project, however, is about far more than just increasing production volumes and getting closer to the customer. This facility start-up has provided a tremendous opportunity for Harley-Davidson to enter a new era by creating an engineering management environment for a high-performance work organization (HPWO). Yeatts and Hyten (1998) describe an HPWO as having a guiding philosophy and culture incorporating a clear, engaging mission for each work team; supplier, customer, and union involvement; effortless availability of appropriate resources; and support systems that promote high-level (and creative) performance. Additional characteristics include a high level of cooperation, conflict resolution, and trust, built around team-centered decision-making processes and methods. Workflows are organized around key business processes, and people are grouped into self-managed work teams to continually improve and carry out their processes (Van Buren and Werner, 1996).

> This is an environment in which line supervisors do not exist and all employees are empowered to help make decisions that affect the manufacturing operations.

This is an environment in which line supervisors do not exist and all employees are empowered to help make decisions that affect the manufacturing operations. The HPWO is intended to utilize the talents, energy, and creativity of all employees in order to reduce operating costs, improve quality, and generate innovative new products (Lawler et al., 1998).

If, as Hans Thamhain (1996) predicts, today's technology-based companies gain their competitive advantage and economic benefits largely through innovation, then these added benefits should ultimately enhance Harley-Davidson's level of competitiveness in the global marketplace.

Strategic Partnering

Before the engineering management planning task force at Harley-Davidson selected the city where it would build its new factory, and before it even developed the HPWO structure, the company made a great effort to straighten out its relationships with its two unions—the International Association of Machinists and Aerospace Workers and the United Paperworkers International Union. Harley-Davidson has an excellent reputation for valuing its relationship with its employees, because the company places a heavy emphasis on the fact that its employees, whether union or salaried, are its first customer and greatest competitive advantage. Not surprisingly, it was extremely important for Harley-Davidson to solidify its relationship with its unions, since this new facility would operate within a team-based structure that is completely new to Harley-Davidson. de Leede and Stoker (1999) report that the use of self-managed teams in manufacturing has grown from 2% in 1986 to 32% in 1998 within the U.S. compared to only 8% in the European Economic Union. Manz and Stewart (1997) have predicted that this adoption rate will reach 45% in 2000.

In order to understand the uniqueness of the organizational changes at Harley-Davidson's Kansas City facility, one must be familiar with the background of the HPWO development. First, the transition to open partnering at Harley-Davidson began in 1994, when management and union leaders recognized that the motorcycle industry was rapidly changing and that in order to remain competitive, dramatic changes in employee relationships would have to take place. This effort led to what ultimately became known at Harley-Davidson as its Partnership Agreement (Exhibit 1). The foundations of this partnership agreement are its 23 elements of shared decision-making, or a master plan for increased joint consensus decision-making by June 2000 (Exhibit 2). With a clear understanding that business decisions were to become jointly determined by management and labor, the 23 elements were established to benchmark the cooperative level of decision-making in 1995 versus the level that would ultimately be achieved. The master responsibility list (Exhibit 2) is categorized according to policies, budgeting, production scheduling, strategic planning, and so forth. The purpose of this list is to clearly define the responsibilities of each of the groups within the operating structure and the guidelines ("fences") by which each of these activities is to be managed. This helps the work groups as they develop and determine their roles and the principles that should be considered as they carry out these responsibilities.

Harley-Davidson Motor Company, the United Paperworkers International Union (UPIU) and the International Association of Machinists and Aerospace Workers (IAM) have committed to jointly develop an independent, mutually beneficial partnership to more effectively accomplish the goals of Harley-Davidson and its stakeholders: employees, customers, shareholders, unions, suppliers, and the communities in which we function. We believe this will enhance the philosophies and policies for workplace change fundamental to the IAM and UPIU, as well as the Harley-Davidson, Inc. Business Process.

This partnership is based on a commitment to create a new era in labor-manage-

---

Exhibit 1. **Partnership agreement (continued on next page)**

ment relations. The key goals of the partnership are to improve quality, productivity, participation, flexibility and the financial performance of the Company while enhancing earning opportunities, long-term employment, job satisfaction and safety for employees.

The parties recognize that achieving this partnership will involve people in all parts of the organization in the information exchange, problem solving and decision-making processes to a far greater extent than in the past. The IAM, the UPIU, and Harley-Davidson recognize their collective responsibility to gain the establishment of a positive work environment which is beneficial to all.

We will develop, through shared decision-making, approaches to work focused on the development, production and timely distribution of products and services, including administrative support systems required to meet the current and future needs of our customers. These approaches to work will maximize the contribution of skills, knowledge, and information through the ongoing efforts and commitment of people to seek out, learn and apply competence in diverse disciplines.

This partnership will help us change together and make this change a benefit in taking actions required to accomplish our shared goals and objectives. We believe this will lead us to secure our employees'/members' future through increased market share, expanded workforces, better educated and trained workforces, increased profitability and overall return for shareholders, continued enhancement of wages and benefits—providing increased employment security for all employees.

This partnership we establish together enhances the probability for arriving at the realization of our vision of future work-life and a strong Harley-Davidson Motor Company.

/s/_____
President, International Association
of Machinists & Aerospace Workers

/s/_____
Chief Executive Officer
Harley-Davidson, Inc.

/s/_____
President, United Paperworkers
International Union

/s/_____
President
Harley-Davidson Motor Company

Exhibit 1. **continued**

Structuring Self-Managed Teamwork

Within the HPWO, various types of groups make up the Kansas City operating structure. A group is defined as a collection of people formed for a common purpose as determined by specific needs of the business and organized around key business processes (Van Buren and Werner, 1996). In order to bet-

No.	Master Responsibility Area	Goal	June 1995	June 2000
			Level of Involvement[a]	
1	Employee Participation	3	1	3
2	Education/training	3	some 1s, mostly 2s	2.5
3	Employee development	3	.5	2
4	Production scheduling	2	mostly 1s	2
5	Staffing levels up/down	3/1	1/1	3/2
6	Staffing hourly and jointly specified salaried positions	3	1	2
7	Subcontracting	3	.5	2
8	Technical integration	3	some 1s, mostly 2s	3
9	Defining customer value	3	mostly 1s	2.5
10	Work organization and product process improvement	3	mostly 1s	2.5
11	Quality standards	3	mostly 1s	3
12	Information sharing	3	1	3
13	Cost of product and process	3	1	2
14	Capital and operating budget	2-3 within approval	—[b]	2.5
15	Alternate sources of capital	3	1	2
16	Acquisitions/divestitures	2	1	2
17	Strategic business plan	3	1	3
18	Discipline/dismissal	3	1	3
19	Interplant transfers	3	2	3
20	Selection of resources	3	—	2
21	Design/location of new plant(s)	3	3	3
22	Internal communication strategy–regarding partnership	3	1	3
23	External public relations–regarding partnership	3	—	2.5

a. 1 = unilateral. 2 = unilateral with prior input. 3 = joint consensus and trust.
b. —, neither management nor labor at the plant level had any input on these issues.

Exhibit 2. **Summary of the 23 elements of shared decision-making**

ter understand the operating structure, it is important to clarify each group's responsibilities and roles.

The organizational structure of the facility has three distinct bodies—the plant leadership group (overall focus is plant-wide issues and operation objectives), the process operations group (overall focus is process-wide issues and strategies), and the natural work group (overall focus is daily operations and actions)—with unique and overlapping responsibilities (Exhibit 3). Their responsibilities and authorities are outlined in the master responsibility list.

Resource Groups

- Assembly PWG (NWG, NWG, NWG)
- Fabrication PWG (NWG, NWG, NWG)
- Powertrain PWG (NWG, NWG, NWG)
- Paint PWG (NWG, NWG, NWG)
- POG (Process Operations Group) at intersections
- PLG (Plant Leadership Group) at center

Key
PLG = Plant Leadership Group
POG = Process Operations Group
PWG = Process Work Group
NWG = Natural Work Group

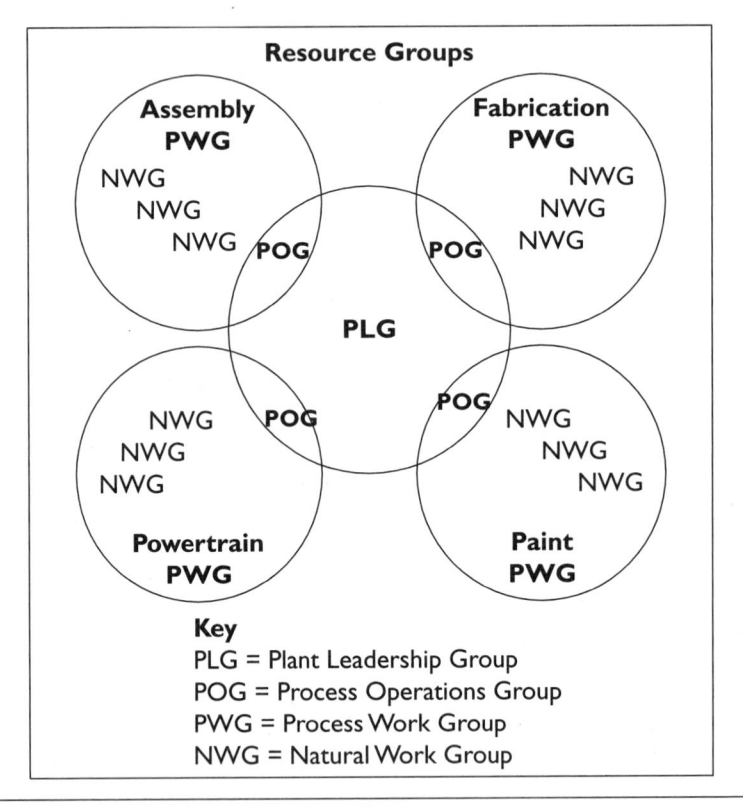

Exhibit 3. **Kansas City organization diagram**

All employment in the facility is team-based. Every employee throughout the organization belongs to a group or, at times, multiple groups.

The overall leadership of the Kansas City facility resides within the plant leadership group. The purpose of this group is to create a balanced perspective in the development and monitoring of the Kansas City facility's goals, objectives, and initiatives. Membership in the plant leadership group is intended to be as close as possible to a 50/50 split of union and salaried employees, based upon the partnering philosophy and shared decision-making process, and

High-Performance Partnering by Self-Managed Teams in Manufacturing

includes the following:

- General manager
- Presidents of both unions
- Four process leaders, one from each process work group
- Four team representatives, one from each process work group
- Finance process leader
- One maintenance team representative
- Process/product process leader

Of these, only five are permanent members: the general manager and each of the process leaders. The remaining representatives are on one-year assignments only. It should be noted that membership in this group is not indicative of a position of power; rather, its purpose is to ensure interdisciplinary representation and communication between all functional areas of the organization, so that when establishing policies and procedures, all non-plant leadership group members know that they are represented.

In addition to the establishment of plant-wide policies, this group focuses on such agenda items as quality goals, safety objectives, cost attainment goals, schedule and delivery objectives, and human resource policies, and on monitoring the effectiveness of self-managed team partnering throughout the organization. The plant leadership group is not in place to focus on solving day-to-day production-related issues. That responsibility lies within each of the process groups. As with the rest of the plant, the decision-making process utilized by the plant leadership group is consensus. In this setting, not even the general manager has the final word in decision-making; it is up to the entire group. There are some exceptions, originally identified and agreed upon as part of the master responsibilities list.

The Kansas City operating structure is practically void of a management structure. The only "management" is the general manager/vice-president; the process leaders replace what is typically called a department manager. The process leader's role is to guide, coach, and mentor and to ensure that the operating structure and guidelines are being adhered to and effectively practiced by those in his/her work area. This role can be challenging at times, because it is very easy to fall back upon the traditional command-and-control habits of a manager (i.e., making type 1 decisions versus obtaining consensus). In the event that this occurs, the work group members are quick to "push back" to the process leader and remind him/her of the expected behavior. This open discussion process helps ensure a checks-and-balance system between the self-managed teams and process leaders.

Process Self-Management

The process work groups, each comprising three natural work groups, are the core work units at the Kansas City facility. A process work group is similar to

> The Kansas City operating structure is practically void of a management structure. The only "management" is the general manager/vice-president; the process leaders replace what is typically called a department manager.

a department in a typical organization. The Kansas City facility has four primary process work groups: fabrication, paint, engine assembly, and power train assembly. All employees in a designated group report to the process leader (or self-managed team). All employees who support the process work group belong to a resource group (Exhibit 3).

The leader of each process work group is a member of the process operations group, which, in essence, acts as an extension of the plant leadership group for each specific process area. The process operations group is composed of the process leader, a union steward to represent the natural work groups, and one salaried employee who works in the process work group and reports directly to the process leader. The process operations group identifies action plans and strategies for the process work group that support the objectives established by the plant leadership group. Examples of such activities are training, quality objectives, budget tracking, and production objectives.

The natural work group is composed of all union employees who work directly within the group—these are the production employees who are manufacturing or assembling the vehicle. There are typically three natural work groups within a process area, and each of the natural work groups is established around a specific manufacturing operation or assembly function. In all cases, the teams have well-designed team boundaries with a responsibility for a complete unit of the production process, as opposed to the traditional Harley-Davidson manufacturing assembly where each worker adds a small part along the line. Aside from their primary responsibility for producing vehicles, the natural work groups also have to execute the goals and objectives established by their process operations group.

All salaried employees, who work full-time in the process work group, are permanent members of the resource group as long as they are assigned to the process work group. A typical resource group is made up of functional specialists, process engineers, and any employees with nontraditional union jobs who belong to a process work group. The resource group's primary purpose is to provide technical (servant leadership) support to the natural work groups and to focus on value-added improvements within their field of expertise. As an example, a resource group member may be the lead person in developing a new or improved technique, tool, or quality-enhancing manufacturing process. The resource group member may also work on resolving process issues that may be affecting product quality. They have to make their knowledge (value-added) contributions positive by transferring their technical skills/knowledge to the natural work groups.

Enhancing Team Implementation

Resource groups have the responsibility to provide support to the Kansas City operation, in the areas of maintenance, materials, human resources, information systems, finance, and product and process. Their ultimate responsibility is to act as a service organization to the natural work groups, to ensure that daily production is being supported by the skills, knowledge, and talent that they bring to the operations. They are considered technical experts within their area. The facility's cultural value is that "team-centered production is king," and the resource groups must make it their number-one priority to facilitate and service the process work groups.

The process leaders report to and are accountable to the general manager, and they receive their direction from a combination of the plant leadership group, the general manager, and the union presidents. All other salaried personnel report directly to a process leader. All functional leaders within the resource groups are indirectly accountable to the plant's general manager but report directly to the Harley-Davidson corporate office in Milwaukee, Wis. The purpose of this arrangement is to have the resource groups (such as information systems or human resources) continuously communicating with all the corporate-level counterparts to ensure that the Kansas City facility aligns itself with and operates within the overall corporate-wide strategies established for each of the resource groups. In contrast, the process work groups focus strictly on their operation within the Kansas City facility. One such focus is a corporate initiative to establish a value chain of common suppliers across all Harley-Davidson facilities. Within this model, it is the responsibility of the materials group to ensure that not only is the strategy being carried out but also that the Kansas City facility is simultaneously being fully supported from a supply standpoint. The resource groups have the ongoing challenge of finding the right balance between supporting the Kansas City operation and carrying out corporate strategies as they relate to their functional area.

Standards for Self-Management

No matter what the group assignment, there are certain operating standards that each group must follow to ensure that the plant's objectives are being met and that enhanced communication within and between work groups is a priority. For the natural work groups, each has a mandatory daily production meeting before and after each shift. These brief (15-minute) meetings are a time to share any concerns and ideas or to discuss any production-related issues that specifically affect their group operations (i.e., quality issues, part shortages, manning, etc.). The importance that Harley-Davidson places on ensuring that these meetings are held is demonstrated by the sacrifice of 30 minutes per day (15 minutes twice daily) of production time. At the plant leadership, process operations, process work, and resource group levels, a weekly meeting is mandatory. The intent of these meetings is to cover items such as group issues, calendars, scorecard measurements, and updates on each individual's activities. The meetings focus both on organizational structure and on enhancing the level of effective interaction and communication. Because each group has responsibilities that overlap with other functional areas, it is each individual's responsibility to share information with his/her home group.

What remains critically important about the entire team-based structure is that union and salaried employees are working hand in hand on a daily basis. The structure and the consensus decision-making requirement create an environment where it is natural for employees to involve the most informed people, union or salaried, whether it is decision-making or getting technical assistance from a resource group or process work group. There are other simple things that permeate this partnership in self-managed teaming. For example, when a new piece of capital equipment is being considered for purchase, there is always involvement from several members of a natural work group. It is not a situation where only an engineer and a purchasing representative make the decision. Natural work group members get involved in visiting the potential suppliers and in the selection process, negotiations, and equipment performance evaluations. They are encouraged and allowed to travel and participate in the entire process, just as a resource group member would. Another characteristic example is that there are no individual offices in the Kansas City facility. What exists is an open office environment with many "conversation" areas, where union and salaried personnel can work side by side. To further enhance the partnership, the general manager and two union presidents work in the same open cubicle.

> There are no individual offices in the Kansas City facility. What exists is an open office environment with many "conversation" areas, where union and salaried personnel can work side by side.

Enhancing Involvement

Another useful element of the operating process at Harley-Davidson is the inclusion of what are termed nontraditional interface positions. This job function can generally be described as a salaried-type position held by union members. As a result, within the organization we find union workers who work in functional service roles such as design, finance, purchasing, human resources, and engineering. The primary purpose, which supports the partnering objective, is to encourage shared understanding through involvement of union personnel wherever possible. These positions provide opportunities for union employees to represent all factory employees as plans are prepared and policy decisions are made. This is a purposeful approach, ensuring that the decisions and actions taken are more effective, because they represent the ideas of both the union and salaried workforce. The nontraditional jobs are posted the same as any other union full-time positions in the company, and those that are selected typically hold the positions for a year and then the process begins again. The benefit of a rotating position is in the continued use of the expertise of the union workforce and the continued education of these workers as a result of their involvement in different functions of the business.

A Balanced Scorecard

The entire operating system is not simply thrown "over the wall" for the employees to pick up and run with while still being expected to meet the plant objectives. First, there are measures known as scorecard items, which must be established by each group and are the basis for their performance. The plant leadership group's scorecard is the driving force behind all others; each group must create their scorecards to support that of the plant leadership group, which directly supports Harley-Davidson's corporate objectives. These scorecards contain balanced goals and measures, established for such items as customer satisfaction, quality, delivery, warranty, safety, training and development, and operating budgets. In lieu of supervisors, these scorecards act as self-motivators for performance. The high visibility of scorecard results forces individual team members to accept accountability for their team's performance. In addition to the monthly review of scorecard items, each group posts its results on a "mission control" or status board on a quarterly basis to announce to all that it is operating within the guidelines and group foundations. The group foundations represent agreed-upon behaviors and accepted norms focusing on meetings, team building, interpersonal communication, active listening, group expectations and behaviors, business focus, and roles and responsibilities. In the event of any deficiencies, the group is expected to develop an action plan to correct the problem.

Performance Results

Exhibit 2 presents data on the extent to which the goals set for the 1995 Partnership Agreement's 23 shared decision-making elements have been achieved. Substantial progress has been made in moving from a state of distrust characteristic of a unilateral command-and-control decision-making environment to a recharged labor-management environment characterized by joint consensus and team-building.

Manufacturing productivity has increased dramatically by 88%, with a 50% reduction in scrap and damaged components. Production costs declined between 30% and 45%, and dealer preparation work was halved.

Perhaps the greatest achievement in value added is related to satisfactions. As reported by Yeatts and Hyten (1998), there is overwhelming agreement that when management and unions are working cooperatively with full trust, self-managed work teams can make substantial improvements to traditional manufacturing processes. Employee satisfaction and "empowerment" at Harley-Davidson are at record levels, which may also explain why customer satisfaction with the Harley-Davidson Sportster has improved by 200%. The fact that a 16- to 24-month waiting period has been reduced to two weeks or less clearly has delighted all stakeholders.

Self-managed work teams at Harley-Davidson exhibit levels of quality improvements similar to those reported by Saturn Corp., IBM, and Texas Instruments (Elmuti, 1996). These results clearly point to the value of fully integrating total quality management into the structure of self-managed

Self-managed work teams at Harley-Davidson exhibit levels of quality improvements similar to those reported by Saturn Corp., IBM, and Texas Instruments.

teams to foster continuous improvement effects.

Conclusions

The spirit of genuine collaboration and cooperation between self-managed work teams and organizational management is a complex and multidimensional issue. The changes at Harley-Davidson represent a new process engineering management environment significantly different from what most of the employees are accustomed to or have experienced historically. These employees come from very diverse backgrounds, and most of their previous employers had a traditional hierarchical structure. Throughout the early stages of this effort, Harley-Davidson employees received extensive training on expectations and the skills and knowledge required to support this structure. This intense training will have to continue in order to make this operating (culture) environment successful. The challenge ahead will be for the organization to avoid falling back to traditional thinking and to continually reinforce the principles established by the partnership agreement between Harley-Davidson and the unions. As the company brings in new employees, they too will have to "fit" and be aligned with the operating culture. The plant leadership does have primary responsibility to keep the organization on track, but so do the empowered self-managed teams. Harley-Davidson's future depends upon a culture of self-managed teams aligned together for global competition.

Another challenge for Harley-Davidson is that of trying to transform its existing facilities (York, Penn.; Milwaukee, Wis.; Tomahawk, Wis.) so that they operate in the same manner as the Kansas City facility. Those facilities combined have more than 5,000 employees, so an enormous amount of time will be required to educate employees and align them with the HPWO objectives. This process is currently under way, although this situation is dramatically different from the Kansas City operation, where more than 95% of the employees are new to the Harley-Davidson organization. But Harley-Davidson is committed to seeing this transformation take place, and is not treating it as "just another program." It is well known throughout the organization that this transformation is imperative to the company's long-term competitiveness.

References

de Leede, Jan, and Janka I. Stoker, "Self-Managing Teams in Manufacturing Companies: Implications for the Engineering Function," *Engineering Management Journal, 11*:3 (September 1999), pp. 19-24.

Elmuti, Dean, "Sustaining High Performance Through Self-Managed Work Teams," *Industrial Management, 38*:2 (March-April 1996), pp. 4-11.

Lawler, Edward, Susan Mohrman, and Gerald E. Ledford, *Strategies for High-*

Performing Organizations, Jossey-Bass (1998).

Manz, Charles C., and Greg L. Stewart, "Attaining Flexible Stability by Integrating Total Quality Management and Socio-Technical Systems Theory," *Organization Science,* 8:1 (January-February 1997), pp. 59-70.

Thamhain, Hans J., "Enhancing Innovative Performance of Self-Directed Engineering Teams," *Engineering Management Journal,* 8:3 (September 1996), pp. 31-39.

Van Buren, Mark E., and Jon M. Werner, "High Performance Work Systems," *Business and Economics Review,* 12:4 (October-December 1996), pp. 15-22.

Yeatts, Donald E., and Charles Hyten, *High Performing Self-Managed Work Teams: A Comparison of Theory to Practice,* Sage Publishing, Inc. (1998).

Joe Singer, Ph.D., is a professor of business operations and analysis at the Henry W. Bloch School of Business and Public Administration, University of Missouri-Kansas City. He is a former president of the American Society for Engineering Management and the Small Business Institute Directors' Association. Contact him at 816-235-2320 or singer@umkc.edu.

Steve Duvall is a purchasing engineer responsible for procuring production equipment for the new Kansas City Harley-Davidson Motor Company manufacturing facility. He holds a B.S. degree in business administration from the University of Illinois and an M.B.A. from the University of Missouri-Kansas City.

Services

The Effects of Satisfaction and Loyalty on Profits and Growth: Products Versus Services

Bo Edvardsson, Michael D. Johnson, Anders Gustafsson, and Tore Strandvik

We all know that customer satisfaction and loyalty are important to the bottom line. But to what extent? The authors of this article found that loyalty has a positive effect for service firms but can actually have a negative effect for product firms. The research results indicate that product firms do not make money on loyalty but rather on customer satisfaction. This is a somewhat academic piece, but its message is clear and valuable.

This paper focuses on the similarities and differences between products and services with respect to the effects of satisfaction on firm performance. The differences between products and services have received significant research attention of late. That products outperform services on perceived quality and satisfaction, for example, is well documented (Fornell, 1992; Fornell & Johnson, 1993; Fornell et al., 1996; Johnson et al., 1999a, b). This difference is attributed to the co-production process that typifies the production and delivery of services. Because service production involves more of the human resources of the firm and customers themselves (Bateson & Hoffman, 1999; Edvardsson, 1997; Grönroos, 1990), it is more difficult to achieve predictably different quality levels. Products and services also demonstrate systematic differences in the relationship between perceived quality or satisfaction and productivity. Whereas changes in quality or satisfaction and productivity are positively related for more product-oriented firms, the relationship is negative for services (Anderson *et al.*, 1997; Huff *et al.*, 1996). Moreover, the interaction between satisfaction and productivity has a greater impact on financial performance for products (Anderson *et al.*, 1997).

Yet these studies have not examined how well the basic logic of the satisfaction-performance relationship operates in the context of goods versus services. According to this logic, satisfaction affects loyalty and retention, which in turn increases revenues and lowers operating costs to increase profitability (Johnson, 1998; Reichheld, 1996). In support of this argument, research using national satisfaction indices in both Sweden and the US shows that satisfaction has a significant positive impact on market value as well as accounting returns (Anderson *et al.*, 1994; Fornell *et al.*, 1995; Ittner & Larcker, 1996, 1998). But according to the satisfaction-performance logic, much of the effect of satisfaction on profits and sales growth is mediated by increased customer loyalty.

An interesting research question is whether this logic is more appropriate for services than products. As we shall argue, the satisfaction-loyalty-performance argument is more straightforward in a service context. One of the primary reasons is that the nature of production is fundamentally different in the two cases. Services are the result of a co-production process that involves the service firm, their employees and customers themselves and occur at a time and place of the customers' choosing. Because products are typically produced prior to sale, there are greater incentives to push inventories through price incentives. As a result, customers who are 'loyal' to a product should not be as profitable, on average, as customers who are loyal to a service.

> As we shall argue, the satisfaction-loyalty-performance argument is more straightforward in a service context.

We test this argument and related propositions using firm-level data from the Swedish Customer Satisfaction Index (Fornell, 1992) over a 3-year period (1995-97). Our results support the basic argument that the 'satisfaction logic' relating satisfaction to profitability is stronger for services than for products. In the following sections we overview the arguments relating satisfaction to profits and the nature of service versus product production. We then formulate a series of propositions and test them using the Swedish data. We end with a discussion of our findings and their managerial implications.

The Satisfaction-Loyalty-Performance Logic

The logic relating satisfaction and loyalty/retention to performance rests on the impact that satisfaction and loyalty have on different sources of customer-related costs and revenues. Satisfaction is defined here as a customer's overall evaluation of their purchase and consumption experience (Johnson & Fornell, 1991). Loyalty is a customer's predisposition to repurchase from the same firm again, while retention is whether the customer has actually repurchased from the firm. For purposes of our discussion and empirical study, we focus on loyalty as a proxy for retention. This allows us to use a large-scale database to test our predictions.

The logic argues that customer costs tend to be 'front-loaded' or occur early in a firm's relationship with a customer, while profits tend to be 'back-loaded' or accrue only after a customer is loyal for some time. Following Reichheld (1996) and Johnson (1998), these sources may be categorized into six factors that affect overall costs, revenues and resulting cash flows:

1. Acquisition costs. The costs of customer acquisition include incentive programmes, awareness advertising, prospecting costs, and the creation of internal customer accounts and records, all of which occur early in a firm's relationship with a customer. Low acceptance of, or response rates to, tactics designed to sign up new customers create significant expenses before customers generate any revenues.

2. Base revenues. Over each time period that a customer is satisfied and remains loyal, the firm receives base revenue from that customer. This base revenue is more evenly distributed the more frequent the purchase-consumption-repurchase cycle, such as the monthly rate on a phone bill.

3. Revenue growth. As customers remain satisfied and loyal, opportunities arise to generate increased revenues. This revenue growth comes from two general sources, the cross-selling of additional products or services and an increase in purchase volume or account penetration. For example, a satisfied insurance customer may increase the size of existing policies while also adding new policies to cover other insurance or financial needs.

4. Operating costs. While revenues should grow, operating costs related to the purchase-consumption-repurchase cycle should decrease. The more a firm gets to know customers, their habits, problems and preferences, the easier and less costly it should be to serve them. This would include knowing what types of problems tend to occur on customers' vehicles, how they like their meals prepared, or when they want their hotel room serviced.

5. Customer referrals or word-of-mouth. Firms that generate outstanding levels of satisfaction and loyalty generate customer referrals and positive word-of-mouth. The referrals and word-of-mouth, in turn, generate additional sales revenues from friends and family.

6. Price premiums. Existing customers tend to pay a price premium compared with newer customers. Satisfied, loyalty customers are more likely to be in a habitual or repeat purchase mode of behavior as opposed to a mercenary, problem-solving mode. As a result, they are less likely to take advantage of price discounts as through a coupon or a bonus for switching to a competitor.

The overall result is a per customer profit stream that increases over time. The more loyal the customer and the longer the customer is retained, the more sales and profits the customer generates. Reichheld (1996) reports such profit streams in a variety of service contexts, including the credit card, automobile insurance, automobile service, industrial distribution, industrial laundry service, advertising and life insurance industries.

Yet this performance logic rests on some key assumptions. First, a firm's customer base must have the opportunity to be loyal. While transient customers may generate positive or negative word-of-mouth, they will not generate direct repeat sales or cross-selling opportunities. Second, the costs of switching from one competitor to another must be low. When there are significant barriers to switching, customers may be hostages in that they are relatively dissatisfied but remain loyal (Johnson, 1998; Jones & Sasser, 1995). At least conceptually, however, these assumptions do not help us distinguish between products and services. But another assumption is that a high level of customer satisfaction creates loyalty. Put differently, loyalty is earned through high quality and satisfaction rather than being bought by, for example, a price promotion or other switching incentive. Based on the differences between product and service production (described later), we argue that loyalty is more likely to be earned for services and bought for products.

Two other assumptions further suggest that the satisfaction-performance logic is stronger for services. Customer referrals should have a greater impact on performance when the benefits of an offering are more intangible and difficult to communicate in the market-place. As services are inherently more intangible than products, customer referrals should make a greater contribution to service performance. Finally, the satisfaction-performance logic depends on the regularity of the purchase-consumption-repurchase cycle. For many services, it is a regular and oft repeated cycle (such as using and paying for phone services, bank services, gas-station services, insurance coverage, and so on). While the same is true for non-durable products (such as food products), this is not the case for major durable products (such as computers and automobiles).

> Customer referrals should have a greater impact on performance when the benefits of an offering are more intangible and difficult to communicate in the market-place.

Service Versus Product Production: Loyalty Earned Versus Loyalty Bought

A fundamental difference between services and products is in how they are produced and consumed (Bateson & Hoffman, 1999; Edvardsson, 1997; Grönroos, 1990). Services are activities that are typically produced in an interactive process in which the customers play an active role for the outcome. Some of these services are produced in interaction with the service company's employees (as with airline and hotel services), while in other cases the customer acts as 'sole producer' of the service (as with telecom services or ATM machines). Services are also produced, delivered, and consumed in time and space where processes overlap and the customer carries out core activities. A service company thus offers the prerequisites for a service, not the services *per se* (Edvardsson, 1997). By prerequisites for the service we mean the proposed offer; how this is to be realized in the form of process and resource structure. We view these prerequisites for the service as the end result of the service development process. In order to guarantee service quality, there has to be quality in all parts of the prerequisites for the service. It is the customer outcomes from this process, in the form of quality perceptions and satisfaction, which 'is the service' that drives customer loyalty and subsequent firm performance. Because of this co-production process, a service is only produced on an as needed basis. In this way, services represent an extreme form of 'just-in-time' production ('just as needed'). In contrast, products are the result of a sorting process that includes the separation and accumulation of parts or materials, the allocation of these materials into combinations that meet the needs of production units, and the ultimate production of the product (Johnson et al., 1999b; Reekie & Savitt, 1982). Importantly, these activities occur 'behind the scenes' from the customers' perspective. What emerges from the process is a heterogeneous supply of product offerings among which customers choose.

An important implication of these different production processes is that products are produced in advance of their purchase and consumption while services are not. For products, this creates opportunities and incentives to create 'loyalty' in more than one way. We distinguish here between loyalty earned and loyalty bought. Loyalty is 'earned' when customers receive high quality and are so satisfied with their purchase and consumption experience that they are inherently predisposed toward a particular firm or brand. Loyalty is 'bought' when customers are likely to buy again only because they receive some effective price discounting in, for example, the form of a coupon, trade promotion, or price deal. For products that are produced and inventoried, sales are generated both from those customers who are predisposed to purchase again (loyalists) and mercenaries that buy more on price (see Jones & Sasser, 1995). The problem is that while the mercenaries generate short-term sales, they involve lower margins and profits and do not necessarily generate future loyalty (Buzzel et al., 1990). For services that are produced as needed and not inventoried, the incentives to push inventories through a price mechanism and generate 'mercenary sales' should be significantly lower. As a result, loyalty to services should be more profitable.

Naturally, a firm's offering is probably composed of both product and service components. Yet certain industries remain primarily services while others are primarily products. We thus test our predictions using a sample of firms from industries that are commonly classified as products versus services. In the following section we formalize our predictions in the form of a conceptual model and series of propositions.

Conceptual Model and Propositions

Figure 1 depicts the model we use to contrast the effects of satisfaction and loyalty on firm performance. The ultimate endogenous constructs in the model are profits and revenue growth. Our previous discussion of the satisfaction-performance logic suggests that both of these performance measures should increase with satisfaction. The logic also suggests that the impact of satisfaction on performance should be at least partially mediated by customer loyalty. Accordingly, satisfaction should have a direct effect on profits and growth as well as an indirect effect via loyalty. The direct effect captures those contributions to revenues or cost reductions that are due directly to a positive consumption experience. Consider, for example, that once a product or service is purchased, operating costs decrease only if the customer is satisfied (independent of loyalty *per se*). Satisfied customers are less likely to demand product repairs or replacements or invoke service guarantees. Positive referrals and word-of-mouth are also a direct function of a positive purchase and consumption experience, not loyalty. The indirect effect of satisfaction via loyalty captures revenue growth and profitability due, for example, to repeat purchases, cross-selling and price premiums.

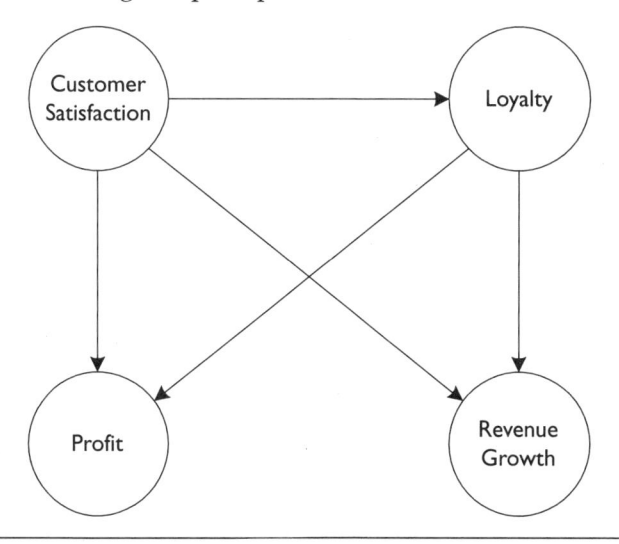

Figure 1. **Conceptual model linking satisfaction, loyalty, and performance**

Our discussion suggests systematic differences in model effects for products versus services. We have argued that the satisfaction-loyalty-performance logic is more consistent with service production, where loyalty is more likely to be earned, rather than with product production, where the potential to buy loyalty is greater. This suggests that the overall impact of satisfaction on both profits and revenue growth should be greater for services. If our arguments are correct, loyalty should mediate more of the overall effect from satisfaction to firm performance for services. These propositions are stated formally as follows:

- *Proposition 1:* Customer satisfaction and loyalty have a more positive overall impact on profitability for services than for products.

- *Proposition 2:* Customer satisfaction and loyalty have a more positive overall impact on revenue growth for services than for products.
- *Proposition 3:* The degree to which loyalty moderates the positive impact of satisfaction on both profitability and revenue growth is greater for services than for products.

Naturally, there are many other factors that affect profits and revenue growth that are not specified in our model. It will be important, therefore, to focus more on the relative differences between products and services to test our predictions. As described earlier, the positive effect of satisfaction on firm performance is well documented. There are no published studies to our knowledge that test the satisfaction-loyalty-performance logic for products versus services. However, an unpublished paper by Johnson and Hart (1998) examined the effects of satisfaction and loyalty on annualized market returns using a sample of product and service firms from the American Customer Satisfaction Index (ACSI) database. Their results are consistent with our predictions and are detailed in our Results section.

Empirical Study and Results

Two data sources were combined to estimate and contrast the model in Fig. 1 for products and services firms. The satisfaction and loyalty data used in the analysis originate from the Swedish Customer Satisfaction Index (SCSI). The SCSI was established in 1989 and was the first truly national customer satisfaction index for domestically purchased and consumed products and services (for details see Fornell, 1992). It has historically included approximately 130 companies from 32 of Sweden's largest industries. The data are collected through telephone interviews and the number of respondents for each company is 200-250. The financial data in our analysis originate from UC (translated from Swedish as the Information Bureau), which is Sweden's largest and leading business and credit information agency.

The companies and industries in the SCSI are categorized as competitive products, competitive services, or government and public agencies, as shown in Table 1. The classifications are based on standard industrial codes. Our focus is on the competitive product and service firms. There is generally no financial information available for governmental and public agencies. These agencies also enjoy significant monopoly status in the form of switching barriers when compared with firms in the more competitive industries. Our sample includes 61 cases of competitive product firms and 71 cases of competitive service firms from the SCSI. Each case is a separate company in a given year over the 3 years we have included (1995-97). However, most of the data are from 1995 and 1996. In 1997 the SCSI was forced to reduce the number of companies to half its normal size. This was because Sweden Post, the largest financial supporter and co-founder of the SCSI, could not continue its commitment due to large-scale restructuring and cost-cutting activities.

Competitive Products	Competitive Services and Retailers	Government and Public Agencies
Automobiles Food processing Newspapers Personal computers (business)	Airlines Banks (business) Banks (public) Clothing retailers Department stores Furniture retailers Gas-service stations Grocery stores Insurance (business) Insurance (life) Insurance (property) Mail order companies Shipping Travel (charter)	Broadcast TV Pharmacy Police Postal service (business) Postal service (public) Railroad Telecommunications (business) Telecommunications (public) Wine and spirits

Table 1. **Industries surveyed in the SCSI**

The satisfaction and loyalty constructs in the model are operationalized using the latent variable indices from the SCSI. These two latent variables are built as weighted-averages of multiple questions/indicators included in the SCSI survey (see Fornell, 1992, for details). The reason for working at a latent variable level is that the number of questions related to the areas has varied to some minor extent. The profit latent variable is operationalized for each firm using three reflective measures: reported profits (P1), profits before write-offs (P2) and return on capital employed (P3). Revenue growth is operationalized using a single measure of the total financial turnover for the firm.

Empirical estimation of the model in Fig. 1 was conducted using partial least squares (PLS). PLS estimation accommodates the network of cause and effect relationships in the model and latent variable estimation. PLS is essentially an iterative estimation procedure that integrates principal component analysis with multiple regression. Unlike covariance structure analysis (as via LISREL), the objective of PLS is to explain the ultimate dependent variables in the model (in this case financial performance). PLS is also well suited to small samples and skewed distributions. This motivates the use of PLS for estimation of the models represented in Fig. 2 (see Fornell & Cha, 1994, and Lohmöller, 1989, for detailed descriptions of PLS).

The estimation results are presented in Fig. 2. The results for product firms are to the left and the results for service firms are to the right. The figure includes the path coefficients or impact scores, the measurement loadings for latent variables and the R^2 values for the endogenous variables (loyalty, profit and growth). Recall that both satisfaction and loyalty constructs are measured

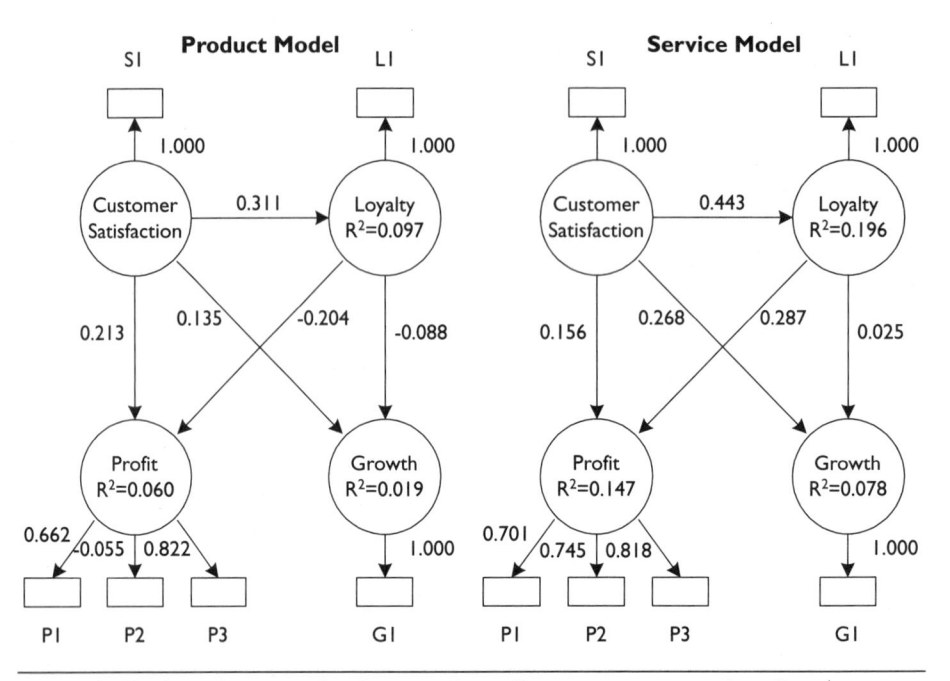

Figure 2. **Estimation results for product firms versus service firms**

using latent variables scores (multiple item indices) from the SCSI, while growth is measured using a single variable. Hence, the measurement loadings in these three cases are all equal to one. Jackknife estimates of the path coefficients show that all impacts are significant (at $p < 0.10$), with the exception of the impact of loyalty on growth for both models. Notice that while profitability for services is reflected highly in all three measures, profitability for products is a function of profit and return on capital employed (profit before write-offs is not systematically related to the other two profit measures).

Propositions 1 and 2 predict that the overall effect of satisfaction on profit and growth is greater for services than for products. Overall impact is calculated as the sum of the direct impact of satisfaction (e.g. 0.156 for the direct impact of satisfaction on profits for the service model) plus the indirect impact of satisfaction via loyalty (e.g. 0.443*0.287 for the indirect impact of satisfaction on profits for the service model). In support of proposition 1, satisfaction has a larger impact on profits for services (0.213) as compared with products (0.156). Likewise, in support of proposition 2, satisfaction has close to two times the total impact on revenue growth for services (0.268) compared with products (0.135).

The source of the effect is slightly different for the two performance measures. For profitability, the effect is driven by the significantly positive indirect effect of satisfaction on profits via loyalty for services compared with a negative effect for products. This is a rather stunning finding, that loyalty *per se* is not profitable for products, and is consistent with the notion that loyalty is more likely to be bought rather than earned. For revenue growth, the difference is driven primarily by the greater direct effect of satisfaction on revenue growth. The overall positive impacts that satisfaction has on the constructs in the model are not surprising in light of previous research using these data. Both the SCSI and the ACSI are significant predictors of loyalty (Fornell, 1992; Fornell et al., 1995) and, as cited earlier, are positively related to both financial and accounting returns. Yet the effect is clearly stronger for services.

Proposition 3 predicts that the larger total impacts for services are due to stronger satisfaction-loyalty-performance links. As noted, this proposition is clearly supported for profits. First, satisfaction has a larger effect on loyalty for services as compared with products (0.443 versus 0.311). Second, the impact of loyalty on profit is positive for services but negative for products (0.287 versus -0.204). Both of these findings are consistent with the notion that product loyalty is more likely to be bought while service loyalty is more likely to be earned. Thus, proposition 3 is clearly supported for profitability. The greater impact on revenue growth for services is, however, due more to the direct effect of satisfaction (0.268 for services versus 0.135 for products). This finding suggests that revenue growth comes primarily from such factors as customer referrals and word-of-mouth rather than customer loyalty *per se*.

Overall, our results support clear differences between products and services with respect to how satisfaction drives financial performance. The results are also consistent with the argument that loyalty for hardware can be bought, but services do not go on sale. Whereas product production creates inventories and incentives to move those inventories, services are only produced as needed. Ultimately, our results emphasize the importance of a positive purchase and consumption experience (satisfaction) as opposed to loyalty *per se* in driving firm performance.

Before moving to our discussion, we report on a similar contrast of product versus service firms by Johnson and Hart (1998) that corroborates our findings. These authors compared 49 service firms to 40 product firms from the ACSI survey whose 10-year annualized market returns are reported in the Fortune 500. In analyzing the Swedish data, we stacked observations from year to year to increase the sample size. In Johnson and Hart's study each firm was a single observation. Rather than stacking the data from year to year, the satisfaction and loyalty scores for 1994 through 1996 were used as multiple measures for satisfaction and loyalty respectively. Likewise, annualized market returns for 1995 and 1996 were used as multiple measures of market returns for each firm. The latent variable impact scores, shown in Fig. 3, are equally as dramatic as those in Fig. 2. (The measurement loadings are not shown in Fig. 3, but are all positive and significant.) While both the product and service firms showed a direct effect of satisfaction on market returns, there are three important differences between products and services that are consistent with our results. First, satisfaction has a greater positive impact on loyalty for services. Second, loyalty has a positive effect on profits for services but a negative effect for products. Third, the total effect of satisfaction on returns is much more positive for services (0.411) than for products (-0.078). This difference is even more striking than our results and suggests that the incentives for product firms to buy loyalty are even greater in the US compared with Sweden.

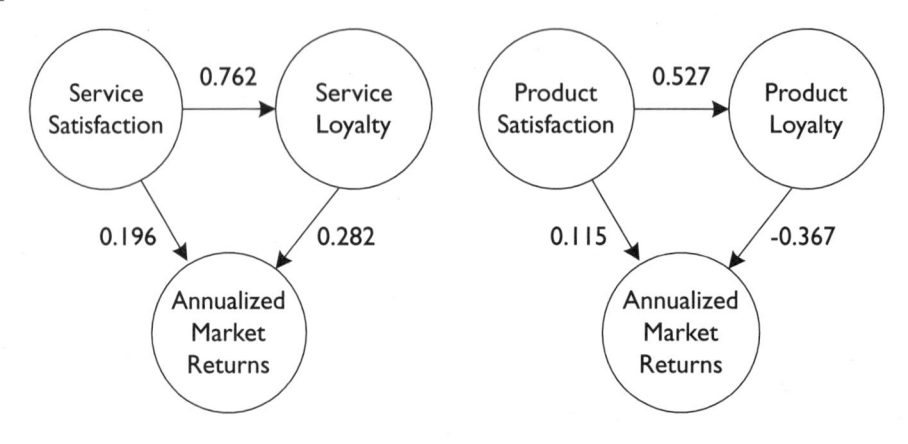

```
        0.762                              0.527
Service ──────▶ Service      Product ──────▶ Product
Satisfaction    Loyalty      Satisfaction    Loyalty
      \         /                  \         /
   0.196     0.282              0.115     -0.367
        ▶   ◀                        ▶   ◀
       Annualized                   Annualized
         Market                       Market
        Returns                      Returns
```

Figure 3. **Summary of results for services versus products from Johnson and Hart (1998)**

A recent example from the US highlights the phenomenon believed to be at the root of the problem. In 1998 General Motors created a 'Loyalty First' programme which amounted to nothing more than a price incentive to purchase its vehicles. All current GM owners were mailed coupons worth either US$500 or US$1000 toward the purchase of another GM vehicle. Within a week, GM dealers began to complain that, while the programme would generate sales, it would erode their profits and do little to generate long-term customer relationships. Indeed, competitors quickly announced that they would be happy to honor the GM coupons.

Discussion and Managerial Implications

The results from the study ought to be extremely important for product and service companies alike. As product quality, reliability and durability are getting more and more comparable across competitors (Johnson, 1998), product firms find themselves in the situation of having to distinguish themselves in other ways. Competing on price is a natural but dangerous option that ultimately lowers profitability. In contrast, competing more on services provides a platform for earning loyalty and increasing profitability.

We have argued that there are natural incentives to compete on price for products as opposed to services. A consideration of service quality and how it is communicated is another factor that probably creates a disincentive for services to compete on price. What a service company offers is often difficult for customers to assess and understand. Even if the service concept is clear and the prerequisites for a quality service are in place, the intangibility of service results in customers placing great emphasis on the trust they have in a service company. A low price has little or no effect unless the service quality is assured. Rather, a low price or 'extras' are more likely to give negative signals to customers regarding quality. Furthermore, positive word-of-mouth from someone the customer trusts increases the likelihood that the customer will prefer the service. In contrast, it may be much easier to assess product quality prior to purchase (as through test-drives, free samples, objective ratings from government agencies, or concrete warranties).

Both our results and those of Johnson and Hart show that for product firms, loyalty can have negative effects on firm performance. This is perhaps the most important finding from the two studies. It means that companies working with physical products, according to our data, do not make money on loyalty *per se*. Rather, they make money on customer satisfaction. Customer loyalty, as a behavioral intention, is a strong indicator of how people act in the future and it may very well be the case that customers actually come back to the same company again. What our data indicate, however, is that these customers do not necessarily spend more money with the company when they come back. Rather, they may just be getting a good deal. Satisfaction, on the other hand, cannot be bought in the same way as loyalty. One conclusion is that manufacturing companies should focus on increasing customer satisfaction rather than loyalty to improve their profitability. For services, according to our data, it is inherently difficult for firms to buy loyalty. Rather, they have to earn it.

One natural direction for future research is to explore differences among service firms themselves in terms of how they leverage the satisfaction-loyalty-performance logic. The research could even be extended to include different services offered by the same company where the differences may be even more pronounced. The role of the employees may thus be studied and understood more in-depth. However, this requires data, at a much lower level of aggregation than those available from the national satisfaction indices.

Another possibility is to compare results from even more European countries within, for example, the ECSI consortium. There is at least one other study that has been carried out along these lines (Johnson *et al.*, 1999b). This study included the three established national satisfaction surveys in Sweden, Germany and the US. The results reveal that across countries, satisfaction is highest for competitive products, lower for competitive services and retailers, and lower still for government and public agencies. Yet the pattern and significance of results vary uniquely by country. The results also support predictably lower levels of satisfaction in Sweden and Germany compared with the US and systematic changes in satisfaction in Sweden over time. Overall, the study supports the use of national indices for making meaningful comparisons of satisfaction on a broad scale. Again, however, richer data are needed to understand the nature of the cultural differences involved and their impact on satisfaction and loyalty.

Finally, it would be interesting to relate results from this type of study to the specific strategies that companies pursue with respect to their emphasis on generating short-run revenues (through cost-cutting or buying loyalty) as opposed to building long-term customer relationships.

References

Anderson, E.W., Fornell, C. & Lehmann, D.R. (1994) Customer satisfaction, market share, and profitability: findings from Sweden, *Journal of Marketing*, 58, pp. 53-66.

Anderson, E.W., Fornell, C. & Rust, R.T. (1997) Customer satisfaction, productivity and profitability: differences between goods and services, *Marketing Science*, 16, pp. 129-145.

Bateson, J.E.G. & Hoffman, K.D. (1999) *Managing Services Marketing: Text and Reading*, 4th Edn (Fort Worth, TX, Dryden Press).

Buzzel, R.D., Quelch, J.A. & Salmon, W.J. (1990) The costly bargain of trade promotion, *Harvard Business Review*, Reprint No. 90201.

Edvardsson, B. (1997) Quality in new service development: key concepts and a frame of reference, *International Journal of Production Economics*, 52, pp. 31-46.

Fornell, C. (1992) A national customer satisfaction barometer: the Swedish experience, *Journal of Marketing*, 56, pp. 6-21.

Fornell, C. & Cha, J. (1994) Partial least squares. In: R.P. Bagozzi (Ed.) *Advanced Methods of Marketing Research* (Cambridge, MA, Blackwell), pp. 52-78.

Fornell, C., Ittner, C.D. & Larcker, D.F. (1995) Understanding and using the American Customer Satisfaction Index (ACSI): assessing the financial impact of quality initiatives, *Proceedings of the Juran Institute's Conference on Managing for Total Quality* (Wilton, CT, Juran Institute).

Fornell, C., & Johnson, M.D. (1993) Differentiation as a basis for explaining customer satisfaction across industries, *Journal of Economic Psychology*, 14, pp. 681-696.

Fornell, C., Johnson, M.D., Anderson, E.W., Cha, J. & Bryant, B.E. (1996) The American Customer Satisfaction Index: nature, purpose and findings, *Journal of Marketing*, 60, pp. 7-18.

Grönroos, C. (1990) *Service Management and Marketing. Managing the Moments of Truth in Service Competition* (Lexington, Lexington Books).

Huff, L., Fornell, C. & Anderson, E.W. (1996) Quality and productivity: contradictory and complementary, *Quality Management Journal*, 4, pp. 22-39.

Ittner, C.D. & Larcker, D.F. (1996) Measuring the impact of quality initiatives on firm financial performance. In: S. Ghosh & D. Fedor (Eds) *Advances in the Management of Organizational Quality*, Vol. 1 (New York, JAI Press), pp. 1-37.

Ittner, C.D. & Larcker, D.F. (1998) Are non-financial measures leading indicators of financial performance? An analysis of customer satisfaction, Working Paper, Wharton School, University of Pennsylvania.

Johnson, M.D. (1998) *Customer Orientation and Market Action* (Upper Saddle River, NJ, Prentice Hall).

Johnson, M.D. & Fornell, C. (1991) A framework for comparing customer satisfaction across individuals and product categories, *Journal of Economic Psychology*, 12, pp. 267-286.

Johnson, M.D., Gustafsson, A. & Cha, J. (1999a) The evolution and future of national customer satisfaction indices, Karlstad, Sweden, Karlstad University, Research Report 98:14.

Johnson, M.D. & Hart, C. (1998) The essentials of loyalty management, Working Paper, Ann Arbor, University of Michigan Business School.

Johnson, M.D., Herrmann, A. & Gustafsson, A. (1999b) Customer satisfaction across industries, countries, and time: a test of Alderson's theory of market behavior, Working Paper, Ann Arbor, University of Michigan Business School.

Jones, T.O. & Sasser, W.E., Jr (1995) Why satisfied customers defect, *Harvard Business Review*, November-December, pp. 88-99.

Lohmöller, J.-B. (1989) *Latent Variable Path Modeling with Partial Least Squares* (Heidelberg, Physica).

Reekie, D. & Savitt, R. (1982) Marketing behavior and entrepreneurship: a synthesis of Alderson and Austrian economics, *European Journal of Marketing*, 16, pp. 55-66.

Reichhheld, F.F. (1996) *The loyalty effect—The hidden force behind growth, profits and lasting value* (Boston, Harvard Business School Press).

Note: The paper was presented at the workshop "Customer Satisfaction: Theory and Measurement" in Vienna, May 21-23, 1999.

Bo Edvardsson is President of the Service Research Center (CTF), Karlstad University, SE-651 88 Karlstad, Sweden. E-mail him at Bo.Edvardsson@kau.se.

Michael D. Johnson is The D. Maynard Phelps Collegiate Professor in Business Administration in the University of Michigan Business School, Ann Arbor, MI 48109-1234. E-mail him at mdjohn@umich.edu.

Anders Gustafsson is a researcher at the Service Research Center (CTF), Karlstad University, SE-651 88 Karlstad, Sweden. E-mail him at Anders.Gustafsson@kau.se.

Tore Strandvik is head of the Department of Marketing and Corporate Geography in the Center for Relationship Marketing and Service Management (CERS), Swedish School of Economics and Business Administration, Fin 00101 Helsinki, Finland. E-mail him at tore.strandvik@shh.fi.

Managing Customer Expectations in Professional Services

Jukka Ojasalo

This article examines three types of customer expectations in the professional services context: fuzzy, implicit, and unrealistic. The results of an empirical study suggest that making fuzzy expectations precise, implicit expectations explicit, and unrealistic expectations realistic will lead to long-term quality and customer satisfaction. While it's directly applied to professional services, the conclusions are relevant in any field.

The theory of disconfirmation has been used to explain the formation of customer perceived service quality and satisfaction. According to this theory, service quality and satisfaction result from how well the actual service performance, in other words the service process and outcome, matches the customer's expectations. Thus, expectations and their management are of great significance to perceived service quality and satisfaction. The idea of disconfirmation has its roots in Helson's (1948; 1964) adaptation-level theory, which suggests that states of satisfaction/dissatisfaction result from a comparison between one's perception of product performance and one's expectation level (see also Oliver and Linda, 1981). Several other studies have similarly described the basic mechanism behind the formation of satisfaction (Oliver, 1981; Oliver and Bearden, 1985; Oliver and DeSarbo, 1988; Swan and Martin, 1981; Swan and Trawick, 1981). According to widely accepted opinion in service research, customer perceived service quality results from how well customer expectations match actual experiences of the service (see e.g. Grönroos, 1982; Parasuraman *et al.*, 1988; Gummesson, 1991a).

This article first describes the nature of fuzzy, implicit, and unrealistic expectations. It then explains how systematic management of these expectations increases the likelihood of achieving long-lasting customer satisfaction. Next, it suggests a model which combines the different types of expectations and methods for managing them. After that, it explains how the findings and theories of this study relate to earlier theories and literature on the subject, and shows the contribution of the present study. Finally, managerial implications are discussed.

Reprinted with permission of the publisher from *Managing Service Quality*, Vol. 11, No. 3, 2001. Copyright © 2001 by MCB University Press. All rights reserved.

Earlier Findings on Expectations

Both CS/D (customer satisfaction/dissatisfaction) and service quality research have identified various kinds of expectations in the services context. Satisfaction theories also use the terms "comparison standard" and "expectation standard" instead of expectations (see Zeithaml *et al.*, 1993, p. 9). The function of comparison standards in satisfaction-generating disconfirmation equals the function of expectations in the formation of perceived service quality. Thus, comparison standards are also considered here. Table I shows expectations or comparison standards identified in the services context.

However, empirical research on service expectations has mostly been conducted outside professional services. Thus, there is a clear need to increase our understanding of expectations in this context (see table on next page).

Methodology

This article is based on an empirical study in which the quality of professional services was examined. The study was based on in-depth interviews and qualitative analysis (see e.g. Ackroyd and Hughes, 1981; Dey, 1993; Gummesson, 1991b; Marshall and Rossman, 1989; Taylor and Bogdan, 1984; Tesch, 1990).

The service examined in this study relates to management consulting, namely recruitment/executive search services. This service is used in situations where a problem can be solved by recruiting, although the competence area of these service providers is much broader and involves human resource management in general. The service consists of diagnosis, designing the optimal solution, executing the solution, and follow-up. The examined service included both the executive search (i.e. direct search or "head hunting"), and advertised search. In executive search, the candidates are sought and contacted directly by the service provider, and in advertised search this happens via newspapers or the Internet. Although this study had a special focus on recruitment services, the companies examined provided a large number of other management services and thus had extensive experience in professional services in general.

Seven highly experienced senior consultants from five different companies, their professional careers varying from 6 to 18 years, were interviewed in extensive multi-hour in-depth interviews which were tape recorded and transcribed. In service quality research, particularly in the case of consumer services, the data have often been obtained from customers, which often gives appropriate access to data. In the current study, however, a similar strategy would obviously not have been possible. Because of the confidential and sometimes even sensitive nature of the service in question, it was assumed that customers themselves would not always be open and frank in the tape-recorded interviews. In contrast, the consultants, who were not asked to expose the names of their clients, seemed to give particularly relevant and

Author	Expectations/comparison standards identified in the services context
Grönroos, 1982	• Expectations based on market communication, image (including former experiences), word-of-mouth and customer needs
Bitner, 1990	• Expectations based on pre-attitude and traditional marketing mix
Zeithaml, Parasuraman and Berry, 1990	• Expectations based on word-of-mouth, personal needs, past experiences and marketing communication
Bolton and Drew, 1991	• Expectations based on organizational attributes, engineering attributes, personal needs, word-of-mouth, and past experience
Boulding, Kalra, Staelin, and Zeithaml, 1993	• "Will" expectations, referring to what will happen in the next service encounter • "Should" expectations, referring to what should happen in the service encounter
Liljander and Strandvik, 1993	• Ideal standard, referring to the subjective norm • Industry standard, referring to the customer's perception of the brands in the market • Relationship standard, based on the overall experience a customer has of a particular service provider • Episode standard, referring to situationally adapted standards
Oliver, 1993	• Ideal expectations • Predictive expectations
Zeithaml, Berry, and Parasuraman, 1993	• Desired service, referring to the level of service the customer hopes to receive • Adequate service, referring to the level of service the customer will accept • Predicted service

Table 1. **Expectations and comparison standards identified in the services context**

credible data about the nature of customer expectations. In this study, service quality is understood in the traditional customer-oriented way in terms of the disconfirmation paradigm, however the data from the field came from the service providers.

The data were analyzed both between each interview and after they had all been conducted. The interview guides used included themes such as the role and dynamics of customer expertise as a buyer, problem solving methods and processes, formation of quality and satisfaction, overtime development of customer satisfaction, switching, development of trust and commitment, and customer uncertainty. For each interview, a different paper was drawn up which included various themes and open-ended questions for deeper discussion. These changes in the interview guide between different interviews were made based on the analysis of earlier interviews.

Many of the themes/open-ended questions had been discussed in earlier interviews but required additional data to deepen understanding, and some were totally new.

The list of themes represented the structured dimension in the interviews. However, the purpose was not to restrict the discussion to these themes, but rather to make sure that all of them were discussed. In each interview, several new and interesting themes emerged which were not on the list. This represented the unstructured dimension in the interviews, and such a dimension is particularly important when attempting to understand complex behavior in in-depth interviews (Fontana and Frey, 1994).

Altogether 413 open-ended questions/themes were raised by the interviewer (this does not include all the specifying questions, and often "one question" led to a set of questions posed in order to encourage the interviewee to discuss the theme as freely and broadly as possible). The interviewees also introduced various themes themselves, without being asked. The data were analyzed in terms of systematic coding and categorization of descriptions and statements given by the interviewees, as well as the formation of a synthesis which grasps these empirical evidences (Wolcott, 1994; Alasuutari, 1995; Silverman, 1995; Coffey and Atkinson, 1996).

Open Coding

The coding process included two phases: open and selective coding. In the open coding (Glaser, 1978, p. 56) or initial coding phase, the emphasis was on identifying and grouping phenomena related to expectations. During the interview process, discovering such phenomena, in other words identifying their existence, was of primary importance. Understanding their nature and making the preliminary conceptualization were also part of the process. The role of discovery dominated in the beginning of the interview phase, but then began to fade, as the role of understanding and conceptualization increased. All the emergent categories, the emergent relationships between them, notes, reports, illustrations and preliminary interpretations can be called the research diary or memo (Glaser, 1992). No further interviews were conducted once the saturation point of data had been reached. All the interviews were then transcribed and put into electronic form for further analysis.

Selective Coding

In selective coding (Glaser, 1978, p. 61) or focused coding, the purpose was to understand the nature of the phenomena and to conceptualize them. Once the data were transcribed, the analysis was done by repeatedly reading the transcription, by making notes regarding on which page and in which question (the questions were numbered) clues related to certain categories could be found. All the clues of a certain category were analyzed together. These categories were later either crystallized in the form of concepts or relationships between them, or they were abandoned due to a lack of or contradiction in clues, in which case the category just "died." An example of a crystallized category in this study is "fuzzy expectations" which is explained next.

Fuzzy, Implicit, and Unrealistic Expectations

Customers do not always have a clear understanding of what they want from the service provider. They may feel that something is wrong or deficient but do not know what it is. They wish for an improvement in their situation, but do not know what kind of improvement this should be. This kind of wish can be understood in terms of fuzzy expectations. Thus, customers have *fuzzy expectations* when they expect a change but do not have a precise picture of what this change should be. They may have a vague idea or ideas about the nature of the change which they most importantly would need, however they are not certain about it. If these expectations do not materialize, customers feel that the service was unsatisfactory, but they do not understand exactly why. *Precise expectations* are understood as reversals of fuzzy expectations.

Customer-switching behavior can sometimes also be explained within the context of the fuzzy expectations concept. Fuzzy expectations sometimes have a significant influence on why recruitment service customers abandon an existing relationship and switch to another service provider. Moreover, such customers may try several service providers without finding one that meets these fuzzy expectations.

Implicit expectations are associated with situations in which some characteristics or elements of the service are so self-evident that customers do not actively or consciously even think about them, or about the possibility that they will not materialize. The existence of implicit expectations becomes obvious when they are not met. For example, customers may expect the service provider to know them so well from earlier assignments that they feel there is hardly any need for the problem-definition phase at the beginning of the recruitment project. In this case, the implicit expectation becomes explicit, upon the customer's realization that the recruitment assignment cannot be ordered by phone, and time must be sacrificed for proper problem definition and solution design. This is a typical situation in which high long-term quality can be provided only at the expense of low short-term quality. *Short-term quality* generates satisfaction which emerges immediately, but does not last long, and *long-term quality* generates satisfaction which does not emerge instantly, but lasts a long time (Ojasalo, 1999a; Ojasalo, 2000a).

Explicit expectations are conscious assumptions or wishes about the service in the customer's mind. The customer pays explicit attention to whether these expectations are met and knows clearly what went wrong if they are not met. However, they are not necessarily expressed openly, at least not all of them.

Recruitment service customers may have *unrealistic expectations*. Such expectations are impossible or highly unlikely for any service provider, or the customers themselves, to meet. They typically involve defining the problem and designing the solution, and the execution of the solution or its effects. For example, customers may expect the service provider to find the type of person who does not exist. Unrealistic expectations towards the execution of the solution may be related to the schedule according to which the project should be undertaken, for example. Unrealistic expectations towards the effects of the solution can be illustrated as follows. A customer company has had a bad year and is close to bankruptcy. In a situation in which nothing further can be done, the customer company may think that the recruitment service can help in finding a new person to rescue the company from bankruptcy. Thus, the expected unrealistic effect of the new recruit is that the company will not go bankrupt.

The more realistic customer expectations are, the higher the possibility that they will be met in reality, and good customer-perceived service quality is more likely. Basically, a good match between expectations and experiences is more likely when expectations shift downwards and/or when the execution of the actual service which constitutes the experience shifts upwards. This study focuses on the first alternative later in terms of "calibrating expectations."

Realistic expectations are understood as reversals of unrealistic expectations. They refer to expectations which are likely to be fulfilled by a service provider, or by the customers themselves. Fuzzy, precise, implicit and explicit expectations can all be both realistic and unrealistic.

The customer's set of expectations may include all of the above-mentioned expectations at the same time, and their degree may vary (expectations can be more or less fuzzy, for instance). In other words, customer expectations may include fuzzy, precise, implicit, explicit, realistic, and unrealistic elements simultaneously.

Focusing Fuzzy Expectations

Focusing expectations refers to the service provider's efforts to make the customer's fuzzy expectations less fuzzy and more precise. This happens in a dialogue between the service provider and the customer. When the customer's expectations become more focused they are more precise and the customer is more convinced about the kind of change he is looking for and most importantly needs. In this process:

1. the service provider and the customer together explicitly recognize what problem should be solved; and

2. customer expectations focus on the solution to this problem.

For example, the structure of the customer's business may be causing various kinds of problems at the human resource level. However, the customer is not convinced that improving the business structure will more than anything else be the change that results in long-term satisfaction. Thus, the need to improve the structure of the business generates a fuzzy expectation and keeps it alive until it is met. In such an unclear situation, the customer may decide to see whether recruiting a new person or persons would bring about an improvement. If the fuzzy expectation is not identified, focused, and brought to the attention of the parties, a wrong problem will be solved. This means that the experience will not in the end match the fuzzy expectation. This naturally cannot lead to high long-term quality.

Together with the service provider, customers realize and become more convinced about what they need the most and what will satisfy them in the long run. As a consequence, expectations shift from what they were originally (fuzzy) towards a clear expectation of what service will correspond to their need. Thus, focusing fuzzy expectations involves a process of defining unclear problems and needs. By focusing fuzzy expectations, the service provider can avoid providing short-term quality at the expense of long-term quality, i.e. providing short-term satisfaction at the expense of long-term satisfaction.

Naturally, it may turn out that the revealed fuzzy expectation is something the professional cannot meet, in which case the service provider has the option, or obligation, of refusing the assignment. In such a case, a refusal also serves the service provider's long-term interest, since bad word-of-mouth would result from not solving the real problem. Thus, focusing fuzzy expectations serves both parties' best interests in the long run.

> Focusing fuzzy expectations always seems to increase the probability of a customer remaining satisfied in the long run and thus of higher long-term quality.

Focusing fuzzy expectations always seems to increase the probability of a customer remaining satisfied in the long run and thus of higher long-term quality. However, because this always requires the customer's time and may be perceived as annoying, it may, but does not necessarily have to, cause dissatisfaction in the short run.

Revealing Implicit Expectations

Customers may start to consider some service-related characteristics as self-evident facts during a customer relationship, especially after a long mutual history. This means that expectations may change from being explicit to implicit. Consequently, if the customer unconsciously starts to regard too many service-related features as self-evident facts, and thus has too many implicit expectations, the possibility of a mismatch between expectations and, experience increases. However, just as fuzzy expectations can be focused, implicit expectations can be revealed. Implicit expectations may become explicit, firstly, if the service provider purposely reveals them, and secondly, if they are not matched by experiences. However, in the latter case, the "accident" has already happened. Consequently, the implicit expectation which was not met at the time will probably not be a self-evident fact the next time.

The following situation illustrates how explicit expectations can become implicit, how unraveled implicit expectations can represent a potential risk for service quality, and how these expectations can be revealed by the service provider. In order to provide the recruitment service successfully, the professional must have sufficient information from the customer. The information the service provider needs to accomplish the assignment is an element of the service about which the customer may have implicit expectations. Basically, this information can be divided into two categories: general information related to the customer company, and case-specific information related to the particular assignment. It may be self-evident to the customer that the service provider knows or remembers all the company-related information from earlier assignments. This is not necessarily the case. The company may also have changed significantly since the previous assignment. Even though there may have been major changes in the customer company which the service provider should know about before starting to recruit a new person, the customer may take it as a self-evident fact that the service provider knows the new circumstances and not inform about it. In such a case, revealing implicit expectations is particularly useful. The customer may implicitly expect not to have to sacrifice time going through the same procedure again, with the service provider asking for all kinds of company-specific information. However, if this happens, then we have a situation where the customer's implicit expectations are not met.

Consequently, customer-perceived service quality concerning this part of the service is inferior and results in dissatisfaction. At this point, too, implicit expectations become explicit when the customer realizes that he or she does have to sacrifice time to provide the service provider with detailed information.

In the previous situation, if the service had met the customer's implicit expectations, short-term quality would obviously not have been low. However, if the new person had been recruited according to the old organization's requirements, he would probably be unsuitable for his job. Thus, long-term quality would have been low. On the other hand, if the service provider insists on having all the necessary information, short-term quality probably becomes low but the recruited person satisfies the present requirements of the customer's organization. Thus, long-term quality is high.

Revealing implicit expectations always seems to increase the probability of high customer satisfaction in the long run, in other words of high long-term quality. However, because this always requires the customer's time, it may, but does not necessarily have to, cause dissatisfaction in the short run.

Calibrating Unrealistic Expectations

Customers sometimes have expectations of a service which cannot be met by anyone, neither by a professional service provider, nor by the customers themselves. They often concern, firstly, defining the problem and designing the solution, secondly, executing the solution, and thirdly, the effects of the solution. Defining the problem and the solution refers largely to answering the questions "What is the (real) reason for the present problem?" and "How should the problem be solved?" When customers have expectations which are not fulfilled by the service, they will be disappointed, and when these expectations are unrealistic, disappointment cannot be avoided. However, if the unrealistic expectations can be made realistic, then it is possible to provide a service which satisfies the expectations.

When unrealistic expectations are calibrated and made realistic before or in the beginning of the service process, future disappointment can be avoided. Naturally, customers may still be disappointed and dissatisfied at the particular moment when they realize that their expectations are unrealistic (low short-term quality). However, if it turns out during a later phase of the assignment, when the customer has already sacrificed time, money and information, that the expectations were unrealistic, the disappointment is even greater. Thus, calibrating unrealistic expectations may sometimes, but not necessarily always, cause low short-term quality while avoiding low long-term quality.

> When unrealistic expectations are calibrated and made realistic before or in the beginning of the service process, future disappointment can be avoided.

Framework for Managing Customer Expectations

There is a clear need to approach customer expectations differently in professional services than in consumer services, as for example in a pick-up pizzeria service. Customer expectations regarding the latter are often more concrete and of a short-term nature. In professional services, the field of expectations is much more complex. In such a context it is necessary to analyze the different types of expectations and consider the relations between them, as well as the time aspect in the formation of satisfaction.

To summarize the concepts introduced above, customers have *fuzzy expectations* when they expect the service provider to deliver something but do not have a precise picture of what this would be. They feel the need for a change of some kind, but they do not have a clear understanding of what this change might be. In other words, they do perceive beforehand that something should be done, but they do not know what specifically. If the service rendered does not meet their fuzzy expectations, customers will still not know why they are not satisfied and the fuzzy expectations will remain fuzzy. Customers just feel that something is still missing. *Precise expectations* are understood as the opposite of fuzzy ones; customers know exactly what should be done. *Unrealistic expectations* are those which are impossible or highly unlikely for any service provider, or the customers themselves, to meet. *Implicit expectations* refer to situations in which some characteristics or elements of the service are so self-evident to customers that they do not actively or consciously even think about them, or about the possibility that they might not materialize. The existence of these expectations becomes obvious when they are not realized. They do not generate the feeling that something should be done. However, customers may state afterwards what was missing or what was inferior, if the service did not meet their implicit expectations. Implicit expectations cause negative surprise when they are not met, but when they are, they do not cause positive surprise. *Explicit expectations* are those which are consciously in the customer's mind in advance of the service experience, and which the customer actively and consciously assumes or hopes will become reality. The existence and degree of all these expectations is connected to short- and long-term quality.

Short-term quality generates satisfaction which emerges immediately, but does not last long, and *long-term quality* generates satisfaction which does not emerge instantly, but lasts a long time. Of these two, long-term quality is more important for relationship longevity (Ojasalo, 1999b).

The management of different expectations for long-term quality and satisfaction is suggested in Figure 1. Fuzzy expectations become precise, when they are systematically analyzed and focused by the service provider. In this case, the service provider will know exactly what to do and the customer what to expect. Implicit expectations become explicit when they are revealed beforehand by the service provider. As a result, the customer will avoid unpleasant surprises later. Unrealistic expectations can be calibrated to a realistic level by the service provider, allowing the goals of the service to be achieved later. All these methods of expectations management increase the likelihood of achieving long-term quality and customer satisfaction. However, managing expectations always requires customers to sacrifice time and share (confidential) information. Thus, expectations management may, but does not necessarily have to, cause annoyance and dissatisfaction in the short run.

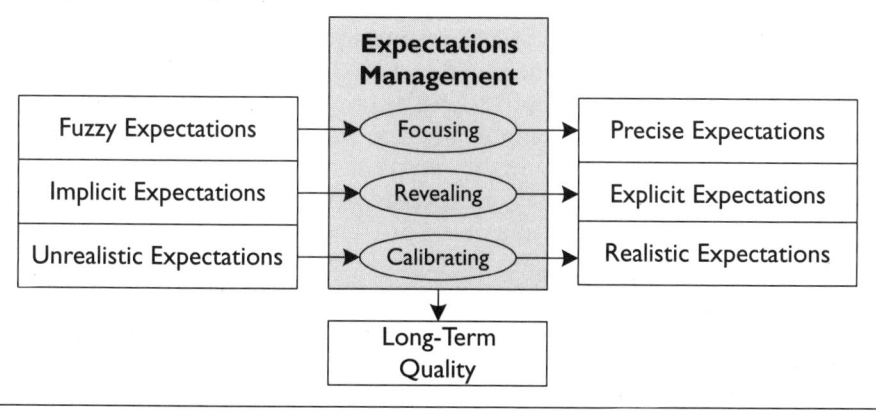

Figure 1. **A framework for managing customer expectations**

Discussion

This section explains how the findings and theories of this study relate to earlier theories and literature on the subject. It shows the gap between earlier knowledge and theories suggested here and puts forward the contribution of the present study.

Fuzzy Expectations

Evidences signaling the existence of fuzzy expectations have been discussed in the literature, especially in the case of professional services and professionalism. According to Wittreich (1966, p. 130):

> Indeed, often a client who wishes to purchase a professional service senses that he has a problem, but is uncertain as to what the specific nature of his problem really is.

Gummesson (1977; 1978) refers to customers of professional services who are aware of symptoms, but not of how the problem should be defined. Similarly, an International Labour Office (ILO) publication (Kuhr, 1996) gives a consistent view in concluding that it is not always obvious what the client's interest means and what the client really expects from the assignment in management consulting.

Gummesson (1993) gives a particularly interesting perspective on the fuzzy nature of customer-perceived service quality, as well as on its key antecedents. He sees service quality, as well as all its antecedents, as fuzzy entities which have a core of something essential, but are not clearly delimited and overlap one another. Similarly, Simonson (1993, p. 69) pays attention to how customers make choices, and concludes that "consumers' preferences are often fuzzy and imprecise."

The literature dealing with professional services and professionalism often refers to customers' inability to define their problem. Mitchell (1994), for example, considers the buyer of professional services much less able to pinpoint and define the nature of the problem. However, in terms of understanding service quality, this is clearly not sufficient. The reason for this is obvious. Service quality is understood as a gap between the customer's expectations and experiences (Grönroos, 1982), not as a gap in the customer's *ability*—good service quality cannot be the privilege of expert customers. Consequently, from a service quality point of view, there is a clear need also to consider situations, in terms of expectations, in which the customer does not have an exact comprehension of the problem. Gummesson's (1993) model responds to this need in bringing the idea of fuzzy logic into service research. Furthermore, what is reported in the current study deepens our knowledge by empirically distinguishing and defining a category of expectations termed fuzzy expectations, and positioning it among the other distinguished expectations—implicit and explicit—in a dynamic model.

> From a service quality point of view, there is a clear need also to consider situations, in terms of expectations, in which the customer does not have an exact comprehension of the problem.

Customer switching behavior and the dissolution of customer relationships have been approached largely in terms of transaction costs (Williamson, 1979), particularly in industrial marketing literature. Service literature has also examined switching, as well as relationship strength which is an integral concept in switching, and emphasized the role of service quality and satisfaction (Storbacka et al., 1994; Zeithaml et al., 1996), bonds (Liljander and Strandvik, 1995), and emotions (Roos, 1997). Expectations have a key role in the formation of perceived service quality. Consequently, they may naturally have a significant role in customer switching. However, in a switching context, earlier studies have paid little attention to the role of expectations which can be understood as fuzzy. In this respect, this study deepens our knowledge with its fuzzy expectations concept. It suggests that, in some cases, fuzzy expectations may be a major reason for customer switching, possibly also for continuous switching.

Implicit Expectations

Calonius (1980) argues that promises vary in explicitness. He uses the term "implied-in-fact promise" to refer to less explicit promises (Calonius 1992, p. 43). Similarly, Riddle (1986) refers to implicit and explicit service components. Zeithaml et al. (1993) refer to explicit and implicit *promises* as antecedents of expectations. By explicit service promises they (Zeithaml et al., 1993) mean personal and nonpersonal statements about the service given to customers by organizations. Explicit promises are made, for example, in advertising, personal selling, contracts and communication. By implicit service promises they (Zeithaml et al., 1993) mean service-related cues other than explicit promises that lead to inferences about what the service should and will be like. Implicit promises are made, for example, through price and tangibles associated with the service.

The similarity between the current concepts of explicit and implicit expectations and Zeithaml et al.'s explicit and implicit promises is that they both suggest that there are explicit and implicit factors involved in the customer evaluation process, which eventually result in perceived service quality. Yet, there are significant differences. Firstly, promises are not the same as expectations, but antecedents of them (see e.g. Zeithaml et al., 1993). Promises are received signals whereas expectations are the cognitive/affective effect of these signals. Secondly, promises do not always transfer directly into expectations. What is promised is not necessarily expected to happen. Customers may be aware that the promises made by the seller are false (Woodruff et al., 1991). Thirdly, explicit promises are not exclusively connected to explicit expectations, and implicit promises are not exclusively connected to implicit expectations. For example, implicit promises may arouse not only implicit, but also explicit expectations. The high price of the recruitment service, for instance, which is an implicit promise according to Zeithaml et al., may cause the customer to actively expect an ideal person to be found, even though the service provider has not given any such explicit promises. In such a case, an implicit promise awakens an explicit expectation.

The identification of explicit and implicit expectations is in line with Liljander and Strandvik's (1995) definition of quality at the episode and relationship levels, which also distinguishes explicit and implicit elements. Liljander and Strandvik (1995) see quality as the customer's cognitive evaluation of the service compared to, some explicit or implicit comparison standard. This study broadens the perspective by conceptualizing implicit and explicit expectations and by showing their potential short- and long-term effects.

Distinguishing implicit expectations from explicit ones deepens existing knowledge of the possible reasons behind inferior service quality. An implicit expectation has a negative impact on service quality when it is not met, but when it is met, it does not have a corresponding positive impact. In other words, implicit expectations can cause negative surprises, but not positive surprises. This concept makes it easier to understand various situations in which a customer is negatively surprised, in other words dissatisfied. Consequently, once the possibility of implicit expectations is acknowledged, it is possible to be prepared for them and to try to avoid their negative consequences.

Unrealistic Expectations

It seems that service quality research has paid little attention to unrealistic expectations. Yet, Grönroos (1990, p. 41) concludes that:

> If the expectations are unrealistic, the total perceived quality will be low, even if the experienced quality measured in some objective way is good.

This is in line with this study which also recognizes the danger of unrealistic expectations. Rau (1997, p. 31) also refers to situations in management consulting in which "the client has outlined an assignment that can be executed only in a fantasy world," and which consequently leads to dissatisfaction.

The nature of unrealistic expectations can be evaluated by viewing them against the traditional approach to perceived service quality in service research. Grönroos' (1988) and Zeithaml et al.'s (1990) models represent the traditional approach. Grönroos (1988; 1990; see also Grönroos, 1982) distinguishes four elements affecting expectations in his perceived service quality model: market communication, image, word-of-mouth, and customer needs. Earlier experiences are associated with image. Similarly, Zeithaml et al. (1990) list four factors affecting expectations: word-of-mouth, personal needs, past experiences, and marketing communication.

Of these four elements, customer needs are a natural trigger for expectations, but the significance of image and word-of-mouth was also apparent in the recruitment service. Of the elements cited by Grönroos (1988) and Zeithaml et al. (1990), the service provider's image and word-of-mouth have a higher potential to generate unrealistic expectations. In general, market communication obviously also has a high potential to cause unrealistic expectations. However, in the recruitment service, traditional marketing communication (advertising) has a lower potential to cause any kind of expectation simply because it is used so little.

The function of image is particularly interesting in the case of unrealistic expectations. In Grönroos' model (1988), image has a multiple function. On the one hand, it affects expectations, and on the other, it affects experiences. In the latter case it functions as a filter (Grönroos, 1990) which diminishes the consequences of negative characteristics in the service experience. Thus, image, when it is good, can have both a positive and a negative influence on perceived service quality. On the one hand, when experiences fail to live up to unrealistic expectations, a good image may compensate, leaving the customer more satisfied than he otherwise would be without the positive filter effect of the good image. On the other hand, it is possible that it is the good image in the first place that leads to unrealistic expectations, creating a situation in which these expectations cannot possibly be fulfilled.

This study broadens our knowledge of unrealistic expectations in services. It responds to the clear need to understand possible reasons behind unrealistic expectations, as well as their specific role in the process which results in quality perception.

Focusing Fuzzy Expectations

This study deepens our knowledge by paying attention to how significant an effect focusing fuzzy expectations, revealing implicit expectations and calibrating unrealistic ones or ignoring them can have on service quality. It also contributes by providing a dynamic model which connects these expectations and corresponding change activities to the concepts of short-term quality and long-term quality.

Fuzzy expectations increase the possibility that experiences will not meet expectations. However, this is not necessarily a threat to the service provider. On the contrary, if the service provider is aware of the possibility of fuzzy expectations and provides resources for dealing with them, then focusing them can provide a competitive advantage. According to Hamel and Prahalad (1991, p. 85):

> Some companies ask customers what they want. Market leaders know what customers want before customers know it themselves.

This makes sense particularly in the case of services in which the tendency to have fuzzy expectations is strong. Focusing fuzzy expectations to great extent involves identifying the particular need or problem to which the customer is primarily seeking a solution, but which he or she is unaware or uncertain of.

> Being proactive in consulting implies that the consultant thinks even of those needs and requirements of which a client has not been aware,

and helps the client to realize all his or her possibilities and needs (ILO publication, edited by Kubr, 1996, p. 489).

Fuzzy expectations focus towards a more precise solution when the needs and problems causing the customer's insecure feeling are defined in dialogue. Thus, the approach of this study contributes a fresh perspective to needs and problem definition by approaching it from an *expectations point of view*. Problem definition is something the service provider engages in and controls, but the dynamics of expectations are at work in the customer's mind during this process.

Revealing Implicit Expectations

Implicit expectations may have similar negative consequences as fuzzy ones. Ford and Rosson (1982) suggest that companies may allow their dealings with each other to become overly standardized and routine, causing the relationship to become "institutionalized" (Rosson, 1986, p. 57). Relationships evolve in various ways and customer expectations may also experience significant changes during relationships (Ojasalo, 2000b) and also the importance of different quality dimensions may vary (cf. Lehtinen et al., 1996). The presence of too many implicit expectations may well be associated with such situations. This study suggests that implicit expectations are typical, especially in relationships with a longer history.

Service quality research has paid little attention to revealing implicit expectations. Perhaps one reason for this is that it has not examined professional services to any great extent. In other than professional services, in everyday consumer services for instance, trying to reveal (or focus or calibrate) each customer's potential implicit (or fuzzy or unrealistic) expectations would simply be impossible. It would cost too much in relation to the price of the service, and require too much time and special expertise. In professional services, on the other hand, the costs of revealing expectations are often relatively small compared with the price, and particularly compared with the damage that may result from not revealing them. Moreover, unrevealed expectations may cause a much greater loss of time than the time spent revealing them. Professional service providers are often more competent at revealing expectations. Furthermore, it is also easier for smaller consulting firms to tailor the service to correspond with various revealed expectations than in highly standardized "service factories" (Schmenner, 1986, p. 24).

It should also be remembered that, with other than professional services, the customer often has more responsibility for the consequences of possible implicit expectations. In restaurants, for instance, it is the customer who has to remember to remind the waiter if he or she is allergic to grain. If the customer implicitly expects the waiter to remember to mention the allergy to the chef on the basis of previous visits and the waiter does not do this, the customer is largely responsible for the negative consequences. Restaurant customers should make sure that the waiter knows about any allergies. In contrast, in the case of professional services, it is the *service provider* who should make sure that the defined problem and the designed solution serve the best interests of the client, not only in the short term, but also and especially in the long term. For example, a doctor may prescribe penicillin for someone who is allergic to it and who implicitly expects the doctor to remember this from earlier treatment. In such a case, the doctor is more responsible for the consequences of the wrong solution.

Calibrating Unrealistic Expectations

Swan (1988) referred to lowering expectations as a means of increasing satisfaction. This view is in line with the arguments of this study concerning the consequences of calibrating unrealistic expectations. However, the difference is that this study sees lowering expectations as meaningful only when a customer has unrealistic expectations. Swan (1988), on the other hand, refers to situations in which the service provider purposely sets expectations at too low a level and thus ensures that the performance exceeds them. However, the view of this study is that customer expectations should neither be too high nor too low, but as realistic as possible. It should also be noted that customers sometimes have unrealistically low expectations as well. In such a case, calibrating expectations to a realistic level actually means shifting them upwards. Swan (1988) identified a major potential problem in how to lower expectations while keeping them high enough to encourage consumers to purchase the product on offer. Problems understandably emerge if the idea is to lower expectations to an artificially low level. The advantage of the interpretation offered in this study, which points out the importance of realistic expectations over expectations which are artificially manipulated to too low a level, is that customers are not lost by promising them too little. On the other hand, once expectations are calibrated realistically, customers are not disappointed either.

The idea of changing the customer's expectations before the service experience is also touched on by Brown and Swartz (1989), who refer to altering client expectations by educating the client to make expectations consistent with what the service provider is offering. Zeithaml and Bitner (1996) refer to communicating the realities in the industry to the customer. These views are in line with the views put forward in this study, suggesting that realistic expectations are preferable.

Managerial Implications

This study suggests that in the case of professional services—in which solutions require in-depth and accurate information, the stakes involved with service success/failure are often high, and the target is to create long-lasting customer relationships—expectations management pays off. Service research has paid surprisingly little attention to managing customer expectations. In the following, a series of measures are suggested for effective expectations management.

1. Keep in mind that customers may have several other expectations towards the service than just those expressed aloud to the service provider. All in all, the customer's set of expectations may include fuzzy, precise, implicit, explicit, unrealistic, and realistic expectations. Uncontrolled, these expectations may present a danger to long-lasting customer satisfaction. Sophisticated management of these expectations may, on the other hand, provide an opportunity to achieve long-lasting customer satisfaction, strong customer relationships, and competitive advantage.
2. Remember that the customer's satisfaction level with the service provided may vary significantly, and always consider customer satisfaction both in the short and long term. Short-term quality generates satisfaction which emerges immediately, but does not last long, and long-term quality generates satisfaction which does not emerge instantly, but lasts a long time. Often, customers do not know what satisfies them long term since they only see the symptoms, not the real underlying problem.
3. To realize effective expectations management focus fuzzy expectations, reveal implicit expectations, and calibrate unrealistic ones.
4. Use expectations management primarily to provide high long-term quality in order to create long-term customer relationships. The natural target of any service provider is to provide both high short-term and high long-term quality. However, this is not always possible in practice. If short- and long-term quality are an inevitable trade-off, then, from the relationship management point of view, it is a better alternative to provide long-term quality at the expense of short-term quality than vice versa.

Conclusions

This article explained an empirically grounded approach to managing customer expectations with the aim of achieving long-term quality and customer satisfaction in professional services. It explained the nature of three types of expectations typical in the professional services context: fuzzy, implicit, and unrealistic expectations. It also suggested methods of managing these expectations to facilitate long-term customer satisfaction and strong customer relationships. The article discussed how the findings and theories of this study relate to earlier theories and literature on the subject, and showed the contribution of the present study. Managerial implications of expectations management were finally discussed.

References

Ackroyd, S. and Hughes, J.A. (1981), *Data Collection in Context*, Longman, New York, NY.

Alasuutari, P. (1995), *Researching Culture. Qualitative Method and Cultural Studies*, Sage Publications, London.

Bitner, M.J. (1990), "Evaluating service encounters: the effects of physical surroundings and employee responses," *Journal of Marketing*, Vol. 54, April, pp. 69-82.

Bolton, R.N. and Drew, J.H. (1991), "A multistage model of customers' assessments of service quality and value," *Journal of Consumer Research*, Vol. 17, March, pp. 375-84.

Boulding, W., Kalra, A., Staelin, R. and Zeithaml, V.A. (1993), "A dynamic process model of service quality: from expectations to behavioral intentions," *Journal of Marketing Research*, February, pp. 7-27.

Brown, S.W. and Swartz, T.A. (1989), "A gap analysis of professional service quality," *Journal of Marketing*, April, pp. 92-8.

Calonius, H. (1980), "Behövs begreppet löfte?," *Marknadsvetande*, Vol. 1, pp. 9-13.

Calonius, H. (1992), "The promise concept," in Blomqvist, H.C., Grönroos, C. and Lindqvist, L-J. (Eds), *Ekonomi och marknadsföring, festskrift till Gösta Mickwitz*, The Swedish School of Economics and Business Administration, Helsinki.

Coffey, A. and Atkinson, P. (1996), *Making Sense of Qualitative Data*, Sage Publications, Beverly Hills, CA.

Dey, I. (1993), *Qualitative Data Analysis: A User-Friendly Guide for Social Scientists*, Routledge, London.

Fontana, A. and Frey, J.H. (1994), "Interviewing. The art of science," in Denzin, N.K. and Lincoln, Y.S. (Eds), *Handbook of Qualitative Research*, Sage Publications, Beverly Hills, CA.

Ford, D. and Rosson, P.J. (1982), "The relationship between export manufacturers and the overseas distributors," in Czinkota, M.R. and Tesar, G. (Eds), *Export Management*, Praeger Publishers, New York, pp. 257-75.

Glaser, B.G. (1978), *Theoretical Sensitivity*, The Sociology Press, CA.

Glaser, B.G. (1992), *Basics of Grounded Theory Analysis*, The Sociology Press, Mill Valley, CA.

Grönroos, C. (1982), *Strategic Management and Marketing in the Service Sector*, Swedish School of Economics and Business Administration, Helsinki.

Grönroos, C. (1988), "Service quality: the six criteria of good service quality," *Review of Business*, St. John's University, No. 3.

Grönroos, C. (1990), *Service Management and Marketing. Managing the Moments of Truth in Service Competition*, Lexington Books, MA.

Gummesson, E. (1977), *Marknadsföring och inköp av konsulttjänster*, Stockholms universitet/Marketing Technology Center, Akademilitteratur,

Stockholm.

Gummesson, E. (1978), "Toward a theory of professional service marketing," *Industrial Marketing Management*, Vol. 7, No. 2, pp. 89-95.

Gummesson, E. (1991a), *Kvalitetsstyrning i tjänste- och serviceverksamheter. Tolkning av fenomenet tjänstekvalitet och syntes av internationell forskning*, Högskolan i Karlstad, Karlstad.

Gummesson, E. (1991b), *Qualitative Methods in Management Research*, Sage Publications, Beverly Hills, CA.

Gummesson, E. (1993), *Quality Management in Service Organizations. An Interpretation of the Service Quality Phenomenon and a Synthesis of International Research*, ISQA, New York, NY.

Hamel, G. and Prahalad, C.K. (1991), "Corporate imagination and expeditionary marketing," *Harvard Business Review*, July-August, pp. 81-92.

Helson, H. (1948), "Adaptation-level as a basis for a quantitative theory of frame of reference," *Psychological Review*, Vol. 55, November, pp. 279-313.

Helson, H. (1964), *Adaptation Level Theory*, Harper & Row, New York, NY.

Kubr, M. (1996), (Ed.), *Management Consulting: A Guide to the Profession*, ILO, Geneva.

Lehtinen, U., Ojasalo, J. and Ojasalo, K. (1996), "On service quality models, service quality dimensions and customer perceptions," in Kunst, P. and Lemmink, J. (Eds), *Managing Service Quality*, Vol. 11, Paul Chapman Publishing, London.

Liljander, V. and Strandvik, T. (1993), "Different comparison standards as determinants of service quality," *Journal of Consumer Satisfaction, Dissatisfaction and Complaining Behavior*, Vol. 6, pp. 118-32.

Liljander, V. and Strandvik, T. (1995), "The nature of customer relationships," in Swartz, T.A., Bowen, D.E. and Brown, S.W. (Eds), *Advances in Services Marketing and Management*, Vol. 4, JAI Press, London, pp. 141-67.

Marshall, C. and Rossman, G.B. (1989), *Designing Qualitative Research*, Sage Publications, Beverly Hills, CA.

Mitchell, V-W. (1994), "Problems and risks in the purchasing of consultancy services," *The Service Industries Journal*, Vol. 14, No. 3, July, pp. 315-39.

Ojasalo, J. (1999a), *Quality Dynamics in Professional Services*, Swedish School of Economics and Business Administration, Helsinki.

Ojasalo, J. (1999b), "Customer relationship longevity and satisfaction sources in professional services," *Journal of the Economic Society of Finland*, Vol. 52, No. 3, pp. 145-54.

Ojasalo, J. (2000a), "Managing short- and long-term quality in professional business relationships," in Edvardsson, B., Brown, S.W., Johnston, R. and Scheuing, E.E. (Eds), *Service Quality in the New Economy: Interdisciplinary and International Dimensions*, ISQA International Service Quality Association Inc., New York, NY, pp. 47-56.

Ojasalo, J. (2000b), "The episodic, phase, and state approaches to customer relationships," in *Marketing in a Global Economy*, Francesca Van Gorp Cooley,

(Ed.), AMA American Marketing Association, Chicago, IL, pp. 363-70.

Oliver, R.L. (1981), "Measurement and evaluation of satisfaction process in retail settings," *Journal of Retailing*, Vol. 57, No. 3, pp. 25-48.

Oliver, R.L. (1993), "A conceptual model of service quality and service satisfaction: compatible goals, different concepts," in Swartz, T.A., Bowen, D.E. and Brown, S.T. (Eds), *Advances in Services Marketing and Management*, Vol. 2, JAI Press, Greenwich, CT, pp. 65-85.

Oliver, R.L. and Bearden, W.O. (1985), "Disconfirmation process and consumer evaluations in product usage," *Journal of Business Research*, No. 13, pp. 235-46.

Oliver, R.L. and DeSarbo, W.S. (1988), "Response determinants in satisfaction judgments," *Journal of Consumer Research*, Vol. 14, March, pp. 495-507.

Oliver, R.L. and Linda, G. (1981), "Effect of satisfaction and its antecedents on consumer preference and intention," in Monroe, K.B. (Ed.), *Advances in Consumer Research*, Vol. 7, pp. 88-93.

Parasuraman, A., Zeithaml, V.A. and Berry, L.L. (1988), "SERVQUAL: a multiple-item scale for measuring consumer perceptions of service quality," *Journal of Retailing*, Vol. 64, No. 1, pp. 12-40.

Rau, J. (1997), in the article by Kesner, I.F. and Fowler, S., "When consultants and clients clash," *Harvard Business Review*, November-December, pp. 22-38.

Riddle, D.I. (1986), *Service-Led Growth: The Role of the Service Sector in World Development*, Praeger Publishers, New York, NY.

Roos, I. (1997), *Customer Switching Behavior in Retailing*, Licentiate thesis, Swedish School of Economics and Business Administration, Helsinki.

Rosson, P.J. (1986), "Time passages: the changing nature of manufacturer-overseas distributor relations in exporting," *Industrial Marketing & Purchasing*, Vol. 1, No. 2, pp. 48-64.

Schmenner, R.W. (1986), "How can service business survive and prosper?," *Slogan Management Review*, Vol. 27, Spring, pp. 21-32.

Silverman, D. (1995), *Interpreting Qualitative Data: Methods for Analysing Talk, Text and Interaction*, Sage Publications, London.

Simonson, I. (1993), "Get closer to your customers by understanding how they make choices," *California Management Review*, Vol. 35, No. 4.

Storbacka, K., Strandvik, T. and Grönroos, C. (1994), "Managing customer relationships for profit: the dynamics of relationship quality," *International Journal of Service Industry Management*, Vol. 5, No. 5, pp. 21-38.

Swan, J.E. (1988), "Consumer satisfaction related to disconfirmation of expectations and product performance," *Journal of Consumer Satisfaction, Dissatisfaction and Complaining Behavior*, Vol. 1, pp. 2-9.

Swan, J.E. and Martin, W.S. (1981), "Testing comparison level and predictive expectations models of satisfaction," in Monroe, K.B. (Ed.), *Advances in Consumer Research*, Vol. 7, pp. 77-82.

Swan, J.E. and Trawick, I.F. (1981), "Disconfirmation of expectations and satisfaction with a retail service," *Journal of Retailing*, Vol. 57, No. 3, pp. 49-68.

Taylor, S.J. and Bogdan, R. (1984), *Introduction to Qualitative Research Methods. The Search for Meanings,* John Wiley & Sons, New York, NY.

Tesch, R. (1990), *Qualitative Research: Analysis Types & Software Tools,* Burgess Science Press, Basingstoke.

Williamson, O.E. (1979), "Transaction cost economics: the governance of contractual relations," *Journal of Law and Economics,* 22 October, pp. 232-62.

Wittreich, W.J. (1966), "How to buy/sell professional services," *Harvard Business Review,* March-April, pp. 127-38.

Wolcott, H.F. (1994), *Transforming Qualitative Data: Description, Analysis, and Interpretation,* Sage Publications, Beverly Hills, CA.

Woodruff, R.B., Clemons, S.D., Schumann, D.W., Gardial, S.F. and Burns, M.J. (1991), "The standards issue in CS/D research: a historical perspective," *Journal of Consumer Satisfaction, Dissatisfaction and Complaining Behavior,* Vol. 4, pp. 103-10.

Zeithaml, V.A. and Bitner, M.J. (1996), *Services Marketing,* McGraw-Hill, Singapore.

Zeithaml, V.A., Berry, L.L. and Parasuraman, A. (1993), "The nature and determinants of customer expectations of service," *Journal of the Academy of Marketing Science,* Vol. 21, No. 1, pp. 1-12.

Zeithaml, V.A., Berry, L.L. and Parasuraman, A. (1996), "The behavioral consequences of service quality," *Journal of Marketing,* Vol. 60, April, pp. 31-46.

Zeithaml, V.A., Parasuraman, A. and Berry, L.L. (1990), *Delivering Quality Service: Balancing Customer Perceptions and Expectations,* The Free Press, New York, NY.

Jukka Ojasalo is a Professor at the Swedish School of Economics and Business Administration, CERS Center for Relationship Marketing and Service Management, Helsinki, Finland. E-mail him at jukka.ojasalo@shh.fi.

Customer Relationship Management Is Not an Option

Kristin Anderson and Carol Kerr

Customer relationship management or CRM is an important topic these days. It is the logical extension of quality management's dictum of staying close to the customer and providing excellent service. This article is excerpted from the authors' new book on this subject that explains what CRM is about and how it can drive strategy. While many think CRM focuses on technology, the authors stress it is much more—it is strategic and vital to all organizations.

Peter Drucker said, "The purpose of a business is to create customers." Implied in his words and his work is the importance of *keeping* those same customers and of growing the depth of their relationship with you. After all, as research by Frederick Reichhold and Earl Sasser of the Harvard Business School shows, most customers are only profitable in the second year that they do business with you. That's right. Initially, new customers cost you money—money spent on advertising and marketing and money spent learning what they want and teaching them how best to do business with you.

Customer relationship management (CRM) can be the single strongest weapon you have as a manager to ensure that customers become and remain loyal. That's right! CRM is the single strongest weapon you have, even before your people. Sound like heresy? Let us explain what we mean.

Great employees are and always will be, the backbone of any business. But employee performance can be enhanced or hampered by the strategy you set and by the tools that you give employees to get the job done. Done right, CRM is both a strategy and a tool, a weapon, if you will. In your hands, and in the hands of your employees, CRM comes to life, keeping you and your team on course and able to anticipate the changing landscape of the marketplace. With CRM, loyal customers aren't a happy accident created when an exceptional customer service representative, salesperson or product developer intuits and responds to a customer need. Instead, you have at your fingertips the ultimate advantage—customer intelligence: data turned into information and information turned into a customer-satisfying action.

Reprinted with permission of the publisher from *Customer Relationship Management* by Kristin Anderson and Carol Kerr, A Briefcase Book. Copyright © 2002 by McGraw-Hill. All rights reserved.

Implementing CRM is nonnegotiable in today's business environment. Whether your customers are internal or external, consumers or businesses, whether they connect with you electronically or face to face, from across the globe or across town, CRM is your ticket to success.

Customer Relationship Management Defined

Customer Relationship Management is a comprehensive approach for creating, maintaining and expanding customer relationships. Let's take a closer look at what this definition implies.

First, consider the word "comprehensive." CRM does not belong just to sales and marketing. It is not the sole responsibility of the customer service group. Nor is it the brainchild of the information technology team. While any one of these areas may be the internal champion for CRM in your organization, in point of fact, CRM must be a way of doing business that touches all areas. When CRM is delegated to one area of an organization, such as IT, customer relationships *will* suffer. Likewise, when an area is left out of CRM planning, the organization puts at risk the very customer relationships it seeks to maintain.

The second key word in our definition is "approach." An approach, according to Webster, is "a way of treating or dealing with something." CRM is a way of thinking about and dealing with customer relationships. We might also use the word *strategy* here because, done well, CRM involves a clear plan. In fact,

Customer Relationship Management is a comprehensive approach for creating, maintaining and expanding customer relationships.

PATIENTS ARE CUSTOMERS, TOO

In the early 1990s Midwest Community Hospital (not its real name) recognized that managed care plans dictated where patients went for their first hospitalization. However, it was the quality of caring during their patient experience that determined whether or not individuals and families would choose MCH for their next healthcare need or move heaven and earth to have their managed care plan send them somewhere else. So, a "Guest Relations" program was launched to increase patient satisfaction and loyalty. It involved all patient contact areas, from the security personnel who patrolled the parking ramp, to the nurses and aides, to the facilities management team, to the kitchen and cafeteria staff. It forgot finance. Accounting staff, accustomed to dealing with impersonal policies and government-regulated DRG (diagnostic related groups) payment guidelines, took a clinical and impersonal approach to billing and collections. MCH found that all the good will created during the patient stay could be, and often was, undone when a patient or family member had an encounter with the finance group. MCH learned the hard way that managing customer relationships extends beyond traditional caregivers, and that to work, CRM must involve all areas.

Customer Relationship Management Is Not an Option 153

we believe that your CRM strategy can actually serve as a benchmark for every other strategy in your organization. Any organizational strategy that doesn't serve to create, maintain, or expand relationships with your target customers doesn't serve the organization.

Strategy sets the direction for your organization. And any strategy that gets in the way of customer relationships is going to send the organization in a wrong direction.

You can also consider this from a department or area level. Just as the larger organization has strategies—plans—for shareholder management, logistics, marketing, and the like, your department or area has its own set of strategies for employee retention, productivity, scheduling, and the like. Each of these strategies must support managing customer relationships. Sounds too logical to need to be mentioned. Yet it is all too easy to forget. For example, in times of extremely low unemployment, how tempting is it to keep a less than ideal employee just to have a more comfortable headcount? Or, consider the situation all too familiar to call center environments, where pressure to keep calls short goes head to head with taking the time necessary to create a positive customer experience.

> We believe that your CRM strategy can actually serve as a benchmark for every other strategy in your organization.

Now, let's look at the words, "creating, maintaining and expanding." CRM is about the entire customer cycle. When you implement your CRM strategy, you will capture and analyze data about your targeted customers and their targeted buying habits. From this wealth of information, you can understand and predict customer behavior. Marketing efforts, armed with this customer intelligence, are more successful at both finding brand new customers and cultivating a deeper share of wallet from current customers. Customer contacts, informed by detailed information about customer preferences, are more satisfying.

Are you a manager whose area doesn't deal with external customers? This part of the definition still applies. First, you and your team support and add value to the individuals in your organization who do come into direct contact with customers. Again and again, the research has proven that external customer satisfaction is directly proportional to employee satisfaction. That means that the quality of support given to internal customers predicts the quality of support that is given to external customers. Second, consider your internal customers as advocates for your department or area. For you and your team, CRM is about growing advocates and finding new ways to add value.

Finally, what do we mean by "customer relationships" in today's economy, where we do business with individuals and organizations whom we may never meet, may never want to meet, much less know in a person-to-person sense? CRM is about creating the feel of high touch in a high tech environment. Consider the success of Amazon.com. Both of us are frequent customers and neither of us has ever spoken to a human being during one of our service interactions. Yet, we each have a sense of relationship with Amazon. Why? Because the CRM tools that support Amazon's customer relationship strategy allow Amazon to:

- Add value to customer transactions by identifying related items with their "customers who bought this book also bought" feature, in much the same way that a retail clerk might suggest related items to complete a sale.
- Reinforce a sense of relationship by recognizing repeat shoppers and targeting them with thank you's ranging from thermal coffee cups to one-cent stamps to ease the transition to new postal rates.

In short, customers want to do business with organizations that understand what they want and need. Wherever you are in your organization, CRM is about managing relationships more effectively so you can drive down costs while at the same time increasing the viability of your product and service offerings.

Technology Does Not Equal Strategy

The past several years have witnessed an explosion in CRM tools, especially software applications. According to a recent report from Forrester Research (March 2001), 45% of firms are considering or piloting CRM projects while another 37% have installations under way or completed. These firms will spend tens of millions on CRM applications, often working with ten or more separate vendors.

Yet, the quality of customer service continues to decline. The American Customer Satisfaction Index, compiled by the University of Michigan's Business School, declined an average of 7.9% between 1994 and 2000. At the same time the number of on-line sites where consumers can post their customer service complaints for the entire world to see has risen dramatically.

What's going on here? If CRM is the powerful weapon we say it is, then why isn't service improving?

We believe the problem stems from confusing *technology* with *strategy*. In both large and small-scale efforts, it's not uncommon to see the term CRM used as shorthand for the technology that supports the strategy implementation. As you can see in Figure 1-1, your CRM strategy should drive your organizational structure, which should in turn drive choices around technology implementation. Yet, individuals and organizations become enamored of the technology applications and forget that they must start with a CRM strategy.

The language confusion doesn't help. Countless articles and reviews of CRM tools and technologies never mention strategy. They imply, or even come right out and say, that the only thing you need to do to have effective CRM is buy the right application. Yes, the right application is critical. But it is your CRM strategy that informs which application will be right for you.

A recent conversation with a new client vividly illustrated this point to us. Steve is the general manager for a new resort located in a remote setting. "What's your approach for customer relationship management?" we asked. "Well, we would like to buy a database management system," he said, naming

```
          Finance      Growth      Logistics
            Customer Relationship
             Management Strategy
       Shareholder
       Management                    Marketing
```

```
                      ⇩ Drives
```

```
       Policies                  Silo or Matrix
               Organizational
                 Structure
       Reporting     Measures      Controls
```

```
                      ⇩ Drives
```

```
                  Technology
                 Implementation
```

Figure 1. **CRM strategy drives structure and technology**

a particular application, "but right now our revenues just won't support the investment."

We tried again, "What's your strategy for making sure that guests who come to stay one time will want to come back? How do you ensure that every staff member works to create a bond with each guest?" "Well," he began, looking intent, "Everyone just does their best to be friendly and to make the guest feel welcome. We'll do more when we get the database in place."

Steve had fallen into the "CRM is technology" confusion. It's easy to do—and dangerous. Without a strategy to create, maintain, and expand guest relationships, Steve's resort may never have the revenue to invest in CRM tools—or even to stay in business.

Hotels, at least the good ones, have been managing guest relationships since long before the CRM tools we know today ever existed. So, fortunately for Steve, the seeds of a good CRM strategy were already in place. Front desk employees often asked guests if they were visiting for a special occasion. Information about anniversaries and birthdays was passed on to the restaurant, where complementary champagne or a special cake was provided. Sometimes, housekeeping took part and added special room decorations. However, because Steve was so focused on the high-tech solution he couldn't buy, he wasn't leveraging his hotel staff's natural approach to creating, maintaining and expanding guest relationships. There were a lot of "happy accidents" that resulted in happy guests. But there were even more missed opportunities.

The Power of CRM

The power of CRM comes from the clarity of your approach. Think for a moment about your personal planner and organizer. In a sense, it is your personal CRM tool. What do you use? A calendar with scribbled names, addresses, and a lot of Post-it™ notes? Or are you more organized, using a Franklin-Covey™ or DayTimer® binder? Perhaps you are the high-tech type, using the latest handheld personal digital assistant (PDA) to keep track of everything.

How well does your personal organizing system work for you?

We'd like to suggest that you can be as powerful with Post-it™ notes as with a Palm®, provided that you are clear about your intention and that you've chosen the right tool for you. We would guess, however, that a fair number of you are using (or at least carrying around) the organizer that someone else thought you should have. Maybe it's even the organizer that *you* thought you should have.

That's what happened to a good friend of ours. "I got a $500 PDA that I've never used, even after the first week of torturously loading in my loose data. I bought it because everybody else had one. They looked so organized and, well, kind of cool beaming things back and forth. I thought, if I get one then I'd look organized too. I'm still carrying it around...along with a calendar and a lot of Post-it™ notes."

Yet, another friend swears by her PDA, conscientiously entering every new name and phone number, religiously consulting its calendar before committing to meetings or projects, even using the portable keyboard to write reports and enter financial data.

A $500 PDA is a bargain if you use it, and an expensive toy if you don't. And the same is true of a $500,000 CRM tool.

To gain clarity about your CRM intention, think for a moment about your own customers, be they internal or external, consumers or business-to-business.

- What drives them to do business with you?
- If you manage an internal support area, ask yourself, given a realistic choice, would your customers choose to do business with you?
- In what ways do you need to enfold your customers in your business, so that you can better understand what they want and need—and more effectively provide it?
- What do your customers need and want to have happen during their encounters with you?
- What will drive your customers to continue to do business with you?
- What information about your customers will help you identify ways you can grow the amount of money they spend with you?

The answers to these questions will begin to clarify your CRM strategy.

Two examples from our consulting experience may help as you think about your own customers.

Consumer Product Contact Center. Sonjia manages a consumer product call center for a food manufacturing company. Her group responds to the 800# calls and e-mail requests offered by product users. Sonjia knows that her customers often choose these products because these are the brands their mothers and grandmothers used. She also knows that most of them don't even think about her or her group ... until they have a product question or concern. In the event there is a problem with a cake mix, cereal, or other product, the members of Sonjia's team need to obtain product codes from the customer. Beyond resolving problems and answering questions, the 800# call or e-mail contact is a great opportunity to reinforce customer loyalty and gather more information about this new generation of users. Therefore, Sonjia is clear that for her team CRM has to:

- Create a sense of relationship and reinforce brand loyalty with customers who seldom contact the company directly.
- Quickly and effectively turn around a product problem or concern.
- Gather product code information so that the potential impact of problems and concerns on other customers—those who don't make direct contact—can be assessed and corrections and improvements can be made.
- Allow customer contact representatives to demonstrate familiarity with an increasingly wide variety of products and packaging options.

Food Brokerage. Maurice owns and operates a food brokerage business, supplying fresh fruits and vegetables to area restaurants. He serves independent restaurants. The chef or souschef places biweekly, and even daily, orders. Chefs by nature aren't hesitant to tell delivery drivers when product quality is lacking. And if they are disappointed, they may well go to another supplier to get the items they want. Disappoint them too many times, and they may make a permanent supplier switch. Therefore, Maurice is clear that to add value CRM has to:

- Profile each restaurant and chef, so that both the brokers who place the bulk food orders and the drivers who make the deliveries know what fruits and vegetables each is likely to order in each season of the year.
- Track satisfaction with delivered merchandise, including refused shipments and those that were grudgingly accepted.
- Anticipate on-the-spot increases in orders, so that drivers can be prepared with extra asparagus, for example, when it looks particularly fresh and appetizing.
- Capture information about upcoming restaurant promotions and special events, in order to predict and accommodate changes.

The point to take away from all this is that the power of CRM lies in the clarity of your purpose. The intentions of Sonjia and Maurice are clear.

CRM Success Factors

While clear intention fuels the power of CRM, there are several other success factors to consider. We will focus on five of the most important here. Organizations that implement CRM with a strong return on investment share these characteristics.

1. Strong internal partnerships around the CRM strategy. We said earlier that CRM is a way of doing business that touches all areas of your organization. This means that you and your management peers need to form strong internal partnerships around CRM. If you and your organization are early on the road to CRM implementation, now is the time to bring your CRM needs to the table, and to be open to listening to the CRM needs of other areas. You may find that you have requirements that are, at least potentially, in conflict. Resist the temptation to go to war for what you need.

If your organization has gone off the partnership road with CRM, then now is the time to come back together and rebuild partnership with the area that is currently championing CRM. Let them know that you appreciate what they have done. Let them know what data you have to offer and help them understand how you plan to use the data you request from them.

2. Employees at all levels and all areas accurately collect information for the CRM system. Employees are most likely to comply appropriately with your CRM system when they understand what information is to be captured and why it is important. They are also more likely to trust and use CRM data when they know how and why it was collected.

3. CRM tools are customer- and employee-friendly. CRM tools should be integrated into your systems as seamlessly as possible, making them a natural part of the customer service interaction. A major manufacturer of specialty pet foods redesigned the pop-up screens for its toll-free consumer phone line. In the original design, the final pop-up screen prompted the representative to ask the caller's name and address. Yet, representatives had found that it was easier and felt more natural to ask, "What's your name?" and "Where are you calling from?" and "What's your pet's name?" at the start of the call.

4. Report out only the data you use, and use the data you report. Just because your CRM tool can run a report doesn't mean it should. Refer back to your CRM strategy, and then run the data you will actually use. And share that data with your team.

5. Don't go high-tech when low-tech will do. At Harley-Davidson, outside of Milwaukee, WI, during the summer they often leave open the big metal doors to the manufacturing facility to let in any breeze and the cooler evening air. Unfortunately, open doors occasionally let in other things, including skunks. A team met to consider the problem and possible solutions. After discussing the pros and cons of screens, half-doors, or keeping the doors shut, they came upon the ideal solution. When a skunk wanders in, just leave it alone and wait till it wanders back out. Skunks may be Harley fans, but they never stay long.

Organizations that successfully implement CRM look for the simplest solution when implementing their CRM strategy.

A low-tech solution that works for the people who actually use it is more effective than a high-tech solution that is cumbersome, costly and apt to be discarded or inconsistently implemented.

CRM Is Here to Stay

Lee Iacocca said, "The biggest problem facing American business today is that most managers have too much information. It dazzles them, and they don't know what to do with it all."

Isn't CRM just another management fad that adds to that problem? No. Done right, done well, your CRM strategy sets the agenda for what data you will collect, how that data will be translated into information, customer intelligence, and how that information will be shared across the organization.

We believe that the biggest problem facing business today is that most managers have too much data, and far too little relevant information.

When aggregate customer information is strategically collected and segmented, you can target new customer prospects. When customer preference information is easily accessible, you can craft superior service experiences—be they face-to-face, via telephone, or over the Internet. And when information about changing or additional customer needs is captured, you can expand the depth of the customer relationship.

CRM is the strongest weapon you have to create, maintain, and expand customer relationships, and it's here to stay.

CRM is the strongest weapon you have to create, maintain, and expand customer relationships, and it's here to stay.

Kristin Anderson is president of Say What? Consulting, a Minneapolis-based firm that works with individuals and organizations to assess existing customer service and communication practices, create and implement change plans, and improve service and communication effectiveness. She is co-author of several titles in the "Knock Your Socks Off" customer service series.

Carol Kerr is president of VisionResearch, an organization effectiveness consulting group working with high-tech, hospitality, and public sector organizations.

PART THREE

Implementing Quality

Part Three presents a large collection of articles that are the heart of this yearbook. They deal with the cultural, strategic, and tactical issues surrounding the implementation of management techniques that deliver high-quality outputs from smooth running processes. Reflecting what organizations have learned over the past several years, we have organized the material in this part into four logical groupings: *Quality Transformation, Quality Tools and Techniques, Functional Processes,* and *Standards and Assessments*. Within each of these groups you will find practical advice and techniques relevant to all types of organizations.

Quality Transformation

Quality management is not just a set of special techniques to add to your management repertoire. It requires a long-term commitment at the top and a disciplined, informed transformation of company culture. Managers must focus on supporting and developing the people who carry out the interrelated processes that characterize organizational work. This section includes articles dealing with *planning/strategy, leadership, cultural transformation, knowledge management, voice of the customer, teams and teamwork,* and *learning organizations*.

Our selection of articles is designed to give you a clear sense of the attitudes and practices that can help you make the transition to a culture that supports continuous improvement of processes and quality for customers.

Some articles in this section we'd like to call your attention to include, in planning/strategy, "Your Company Does Not Exist" by Don Yates and Mark Davis, which challenges basic assumptions about company boundaries and defining who and what your company is.

Moving on to leadership, we include the piece "Leadership DNA" by Stewart D. Friedman, which explains how Ford is implementing leadership develop into the fabric of the company. Despite some quality issues Ford has recently experienced, this is a very good look at the company's approach and commitment to developing leaders. In this section on leadership, we also have selected the *Sloan Management Review* article "Developing Leaders: How Winning Companies Keep on Winning," which documents how companies like Arthur Andersen, General Electric, Hewlett-Packard, Johnson & Johnson, and other keep new leaders in the pipeline.

Other articles look at why empowerment is so hard to achieve, how to create a knowledge culture, managing customer knowledge, a look at whether teaming pays off, and how to implement a customer satisfaction program. In general, we've looked for articles that provide things for you to think about and to do from diverse sources. We think you'll find all our selections useful.

Quality Tools and Techniques

We've divided this part of the book into three sections: *process management, Six Sigma*, and a new set of articles on *e-commerce*. The goal here is to give you practical ideas for making processes more efficient and effective. In the process management section, we've included six articles that give you a variety of perspectives on managing your processes. Here are some of the titles you'll find: "Resolving the Process Paradox" (a particularly good review of process management), "Should You Outsource Your Business Processes?" and "Improving In-Process Handling." Six Sigma is far more than a measure of process variation these days—it's a whole approach to managing to reduce defects in processes and in outputs. We've selected articles that explain this new approach. Finally, we include four articles that provide different views on e-commerce in terms of its value as a tool for facilitating connection with customers and beyond.

Functional Processes

How are quality management practices implemented in the functional process areas of organizations? This section of the yearbook is designed to answer that question. We highlight three areas this year: *supply chain management, information technology*, and *finance and accounting*. Some representative articles include "Dock-to-Shop Is Just-in-Time," "Optimizing Economic Order Quantity," "A Progress Report on the Enterprise Portal," and "Improving Financial Performance Through Benchmarking and Best Practices."

Standards and Assessments

This section concludes Part Three and combines material on ISO 9000 and the Baldrige criteria. We've selected pieces that summarize and explain the relation (or lack thereof) between quality and ISO certification and a review of several companies' journeys to the Baldrige.

Quality Transformation

PLANNING/STRATEGY

Your Company Does Not Exist

Don Yates and Mark Davis

We like articles like these because they challenge our assumptions, in this case about how to define an organization. Like the insights of Deming, which required looking at the organization as a system and not as a hierarchy, the ideas in this article make a similar request of the reader. We include it here because such changes affect how strategy is defined and communicated. The ideas described here may seem idealistic, but when implemented with commitment, they almost always enhance performance.

Pore over the bookshelves of CEOs and other senior managers, and you will often find miniature libraries on organization theory, many of them "leadership" books, from rip-offs of Sun Tzu's ancient classic, *The Art of War*, to highly popular books like those of Tom Peters. Pull these books off the shelf and flip through them. You'll often find them earmarked, with key passages highlighted or underlined for quotation in speeches.

It is staggering to count the sheer number of books and theories that have come up for their 15 minutes of fame: total quality management, management by objective, various forms of reengineering. Each has had its season as the rage of B-school electives and consultants' pitches. The best have deserved their wide currency, making tremendous contributions to our understanding of how organizations work and what they need to do better.

Still, not one of these models has become dominant. Not one has had staying power. After so many bright people have put forward so many well-thought-out programs, why is it that we still hunger for more? Why do senior

Republished with permission from *Journal of Business Strategy*, January/February 2001. Copyright © 2001 EC Media Group, Eleven Penn Plaza, New York, NY.

managers remain ready for the next big answer, as if they expect a unified field theory of management?

Perhaps the reason management and organization theorists have fallen short is that, for all their willingness to think anew, they have addressed the inadequacies of our governing paradigm without truly replacing it. They have been like early astronomers who resorted to all kinds of tweaks and nudges to explain why their models failed to predict the movements of the planets, and continued to hold this line even after the weight of evidence presented by Copernicus, Kepler, and Galileo. They find themselves in the position of the defenders of the status quo who could never quite bring themselves to pose such a disruptive question as whether or not Earth was the center of the solar system. But it is just this kind of disruption that history has shown us is necessary to sweep aside one paradigm to make room for another.

Perhaps we need a completely new way of looking at the organizational world. What might a new paradigm look like?

Perhaps, in a similar way, we need a completely new way of looking at the organizational world. What might a new paradigm look like? The best way to answer these questions is by beginning an open dialogue like the one initiated by Copernicus when he questioned the most fundamental beliefs of his day. We must ask disruptive questions about the most fundamental beliefs about organizations that make up our current worldview.

Three Disruptive Questions

Do companies really exist at all, or could the very idea of a company be considered a rhetorical fiction?

In other words, is it necessary to speak and think of a company as an entity that acts on its own as an individual?

Instead, could a company fairly be described as a force field made up of the relationships among the people who associate with each other under a common banner? After all, when the people who make up an organization go home at night, the company no more exists than a disbanded army. A company cannot imagine anything, cannot create anything, cannot sell anything. Only the individuals who make up the company can do these things.

This is a very elementary principle, but it is often such basics that get dismissed and overlooked.

And it is one that leads to a second disruptive question about another fundamental tenet of our times.

Do companies really exist to create profit?

No one can doubt that profit is a vital sign, one that confirms that an organization is satisfying external needs. This role of profit, vital as it is, has perhaps led us to exaggerate it. An organization must also respond to other things, especially to the needs of the people who make it up. After all, it is the people who comprise an organization who determine which activities to pursue, which "missions" to undertake—always with their own interests, dreams, and desires in mind.

This is seen more clearly when one traces any given company or organization back to its origins. To reduce it to the basics, an organization begins when a founder needs the help of others to get where he or she wants to go. These others join because they see their participation as getting them where they want to go—either because they are attracted to the founder's intent, or because they are offered inducements to come along. Every organization was first established to benefit the set of individuals who created it. No organization is an end in itself. They are all means.

This purpose for founding the organization—the fulfillment of the wants and needs of the members who make it up—remains its abiding purpose, whether it is acknowledged or not. However, for the members to fulfill their wants and needs, they must together, as an organization, successfully pursue the original intent that brought them together. They must achieve organizational results as a means to individual results.

Thus the first task of any organization is to serve the needs of the people who make it up and to honor their desires. The second task is to create a producing or servicing system that creates the results that will fulfill the organization's commitments to its customers. These two tasks are interdependent but distinct. The organization remains a tool to create for the founders and their colleagues what they really want (wealth, status, joy in the work itself). But to do so it must also succeed as a serving entity.

The challenge for the modern organization is to accomplish both tasks equally well. A company that can do both exceptionally well at the same time could be called an Extraordinary Organization.

In our everyday experience, we've all come across three other types of organizations. The most common is the Exploitive Organization, one that scores highly in serving the organization, but does poorly in serving the individuals within it. A second is the Egocentric Organization, one with high individual satisfaction, in which people are well rewarded, but the organization is poorly served (some of the more flamboyant S&Ls of the 1980s come to mind). A third kind of company, one which serves both individuals and the organization poorly, is simply Extinct.

The change programs of the past—total quality management, management by objective, quality circles—all focused on trying to improve these three faulty organizations by trying to perform one task, improving the results of the organization, without really working on the other task, meeting the needs and the wishes of the organization's people. The Quality of Work Life movement tried to improve on the people task, but did so primarily with a view toward serving the company. This too, falls short.

People must become the ends served by organizations, not the means to the ends of others. Corporate patriotism cannot motivate, liberate, or inspire people to take work "to the next level."

Questioning whether companies are real and whether they exist for profit leads us to ask possibly the most disruptive question of all—one that ques-

> This purpose for founding the organization—the fulfillment of the wants and needs of the members who make it up—remains its abiding purpose, whether it is acknowledged or not.

tions a belief that is fundamental to the way all organizations are run.

Is the belief that all authority in an organization must derive from a single source still supportable in an information age?

Since the first rumblings of the Industrial Revolution, organizations have been ruled through hierarchies. The paradigm of centralized power, as pervasive as it remains, may have reached its effective limits. Despite all the reinvention and reengineering, few proponents of change have questioned the need for command to emanate downward from the apex of an organizational pyramid to its base.

True, most of these proponents of change have envisioned flatter pyramids. That is, they would distribute power widely or push it down to lower levels. They applauded empowering the factory worker to pull the chain that stops the assembly line. They all stood in favor of delegating more power to teams dedicated to achieving specific results. But none has gone so far as to challenge the basic belief in hierarchy itself, to question the need for the whole structure of supervisors and the supervised.

Perhaps recent organizational theorists, for all their brilliance, have been like those medieval astronomers tweaking and nudging their models in vain. None have yet to consider what a new model of the organizational "Solar System" would look like if the planets themselves determined their own orbits and arranged their own positions.

The very idea that work could take place without central authority cascading down a given hierarchy is, of course, so very disruptive that it will most certainly be met with considerable resistance. After all, it took the church four centuries to accept Galileo; and he wasn't even threatening the control of every manager on earth.

These three questions, then, are certainly no less disruptive to our organizational status quo. Therefore, they require us to consider whether the time is right for them and whether an Extraordinary Organization built on new beliefs stemming from them is even feasible.

Machine Displaces Man, Man Displaces Machine

In our thinking today, the power-center of our productive universe is still the machine. It is around this focus that we think people and other resources must orbit. This remains true despite the fact that most people no longer work in factories but in the service sector. They are still expected to function as cogs in the machine, as Taylorite masses to be commanded and conducted down to their finest movements (or, in modern times, to their very thinking).

In the past, the machine at the center was the steam engine, the smelting furnace, and the production line. It had to be fed, stoked, and run by humans who were more or less interchangeable. What has changed is that the machine that organizes work today is, of course, the computer.

This is revolutionary, because the computer is the first machine to rely on the uniqueness of each individual who operates it and provides it with content.

This dependence on content—with all its nuance and need for context—makes the person, not the machine, the true center of the New Economy. In the past, when a factory worker left a job, he lost his connection to the machine. When a knowledge worker leaves a job today, it is the machine that loses the connection to the person, the operator who made the machine's output unique and valuable.

In some ways, we have come full circle to the time just before the Industrial Revolution when most people were basically independent actors. Before the advent of the big machine, most people were pretty much on their own, selling their wares in the marketplace. True, they had guilds and landlords to contend with. True, life could be nasty, brutish, and short. But at least many people could ply their craft or manage their farm as they saw best.

In the 21st century, the individual is once again a "free agent." Loyalty goes to one's self first, one's craft second, one's "employer" last. The high-tech knowledge workers of the 21st century carry their most valuable commodity inside their heads. Such workers will not hesitate to walk out the door if ignored or unappreciated. And when these workers leave, they will take valuable company assets with them, capital stock in the form of ideas and skills.

While the relationship of the individual to the organization has changed, our mindset has not. Work is more associative today than ever before. Most people still seek to fulfill their own goals by associating with others in a given organization. Yet this basic understanding, quite healthy for all parties, is often treated as a shameful secret, something to be buried or denied. In true Industrial Age fashion, people are still asked to enthusiastically pledge their loyalty to the organizational entity. We are still imbued with this false spirit of corporate patriotism, one that does everyone a disservice by obscuring the real reason people come together as an organization.

What is needed at the workplace is a more open learning environment, one where workers ascend the ladder by taking on new tasks and challenges. And the ladder they seek to ascend is not a ladder of status or of power, but of knowledge and skill. What is also needed is an environment in which people can become and act as fully interdependent equals. Only when they do will they be able to develop and put forth their full potential, which can carry them to the level of extraordinary. A hierarchical system is stuck in an everlasting parent/child world in which no one can ever reach that full potential.

One common objection to this approach, of course, is that a company without hierarchy is a company in which no one is in charge. This is the wrong way to look at it. Organized properly, a company without hierarchy is one in which everyone is in charge.

> Most people still seek to fulfill their own goals by associating with others in a given organization. Yet this basic understanding, quite healthy for all parties, is often treated as a shameful secret, something to be buried or denied.

The Extraordinary Organization

Can such organizations exist in the real worlds No organization currently appears to exhibit all aspects of zero hierarchy or of other attributes arising from new beliefs. However, taken together, the evidence is mounting that it is possible not only for Extraordinary Organizations to exist but also for them to substantially outperform the standard organization.

One London firm that exhibits a number of features of such new beliefs is an advertising agency called St. Lukes. It has a legal definition as a special kind of cooperative called a Qualifying Employee Shareholder Trust. Through it all members of the firm own shares of the company. Annual distributions are made with an equal number of shares going to each current member with at least one year of tenure. The people at St. Lukes adapted the acronym from this specie of legal corporation for their governing board, calling it the Quest. The Quest is a five-member council with two members elected, an outside attorney, and only two managers with seniority. A Treasury Committee, made up of virtually everyone in the agency who is charge of any kind of expenditure, debates and makes major financial decisions.

St. Lukes advertises its corporate mission thusly:

- Profit Is Like Health.
- You Need It, But It Is Not Something to Live for.
- The Treasury Monitors the Profit We Need.
- The Quest Monitors the Lives We Lead.

The Extraordinary Organization is equally adept at serving the needs of its individual members and the organization. St. Lukes does this because its members tap into the full intellectual and imaginative potential of every one of their colleagues. The people of St. Lukes provide the environment in which each member can fulfill his or her own wants and needs, discover latent abilities, and develop hidden talents. At the same it time, its democratic structure creates a pervasive sense of responsibility and accountability. The outcome? St. Lukes succeeds brilliantly, as an organization and as a place that bright people want to join, and rarely leave.

Another example of non-hierarchical thinking is organization members setting their own salaries. In his book, *Maverick*, Ricardo Semler tells how he did this in his company quite successfully. It has been done in the Silicon Valley in different ways. In one case it was done in an open meeting in which everyone was asked to select his or her own slice of the pie. In this case, the total chosen exceeded the budget, and the group decided to "pass the hat." Those who had more disposable income returned some of the raise they had just requested, leading to a new total that was right on target. Far from leading to contention, this second round left everyone satisfied because it was self-chosen rather than imposed. As incredible as it may seem to those raised under command-and-control models, in which salaries are assigned in private, the system of self-selected salaries works astonishingly well.

The idea of leaderless organizations, and attempts to create self-managed work teams, is not new. In 1969, Procter & Gamble created self-managed plants that were extremely successful. Educators a year earlier had adopted this approach, with the founding of the Sudbury Valley School in Framingham, Massachusetts, which has spawned imitators around the country. The school governs itself without a headmaster or principal. Each student and each staff member has one vote on school affairs carried out in the weekly "school meeting." Staff members return each year only if the school meeting elects them each spring. Students are "sovereign learners" who face no grades, no courses, no mandatory learning. Students from ages 4 to 19 mix with each other, exchange ideas, create projects, and generally follow their own path of inquiry all without direction from "above."

At first glance, this may sound like a throwback to the "free schools" and other excesses of the 1960s. In fact, Sudbury Valley is highly aligned with the needs of today's workplace. Fully 80% of its students go on to colleges and universities; all of them are learning the kind of self-discipline and free-form entrepreneurial thinking the New Economy requires.

Whether an ad agency in London or a school in Massachusetts, such Extraordinary Organizations function much like the human body, the ultimate example of an organization without hierarchy. We tend to think of the brain as understanding the body as a whole, like a CEO who runs a corporation. The biological truth is that for all the importance of the mind, there is no one "boss" in the human body. The heart knows when to pump, the skin knows when to open its pores or contract them, the glands know when to release a hormone.

Can organizations produce strong results from the collective work of individuals functioning without any central authority? The answer is yes, but only if six criteria are met. All members must:

- Understand that they are part of a system
- Know what the purpose of that system is
- Know what his or her part in the system is
- Be fully capable of doing one's part
- Be willing to execute one's part to the best of one's ability
- And do so in an environment of total communication.

The greatest danger is that in weathering a crisis, those building an Extraordinary Organization will be tempted to resort back to command-and-control.

The human body requires a feedback mechanism of neurons and hormones. So too does an EO require instantaneous communication, whether a formal system of well-defined meetings, an Intranet, or whatever combination of processes the members find effective.

To be fair, creating such an Extraordinary Organization is a difficult and sometimes risky venture. It requires a willingness to share ownership, in some cases equally, among all its members. Above all, such an EO requires abandoning some of the most deep-seated beliefs about leadership, hierarchy, and the very purpose of an organization.

The greatest danger is that in weathering a crisis, those building an EO will be tempted to resort back to command-and-control. If they resist this temptation and survive, the EO will be one that achieves no management hierarchy at all, just good solid self-management.

In exploring the Extraordinary Organization, firms are turning the old models upside down and inside out. They are quietly transforming the way organizations really work, effecting radical change with little fanfare or a place on the corporate bookshelf. Many who are doing it are not even aware that they are part of a larger trend. (Some even see themselves as small, freakish experiments.)

In time, however, the EO stands a good chance of long outliving some of the more heralded ideas and change programs of our times. Experiments with the principles underlying Extraordinary Organizations are bringing about quiet, steady change, promising to replace today's organizational model with something literally "beyond belief."

Don Yates, Ph.D., has been consulting with organizations for more than 25 years. He is the founder and principal of Yates and Associates, a consulting firm based in Portola Valley, California (www.yatesassociates.com).

Mark Davis is a consultant to Fortune 500 firms. He works with the White House Writers Group in Washington, D.C.

Intellectual Capital Analysis as a Strategic Tool

Göran Roos, Alan Bainbridge and Kristine Jacobsen

Carl Jung posited that for a healthy personality, there has to be merging of how others view us and how we view ourselves. The authors of this article come to a similar conclusion, that for strategy initiatives to be successful internal and external views of the organization must come together. They review what that means in different types of organizations, with special emphasis on intellectual capital as a vital component of strategic success.

What is strategy? Is it a thought, a statement that can be written on a piece of paper perhaps, stating a set of objectives and plans for achieving them? Is it more like an emotion, a matter of conviction, something we are all determined to do? Or is it something more political, the art of the possible, something on which the major players can agree and by which they can be guided?

Mintzberg (1987) has argued that strategy is a mixture of all three ideas. But most of the time, business leaders tend to conceive of strategy in terms of the rational model, a plan. On the other hand, they probably behave more in terms of the third idea, a political compromise, and we suspect that it is that concept which may be the best predictor of what actually happens in an organization. In fact, if you observe what happens in organizations, strategy is not as much a matter of intellect as a matter of fact. A firm's strategy should not be described by what managers say; it should be observed in terms of what actually happens. For example, a salesperson decides on whom to call today and what to say when they call. In both decisions, they may be only weakly guided by the officially articulated strategy. They may be far more influenced by what has recently happened on the account, what they believe the production people will actually deliver, and what will stand the best chance of increasing their commission *now* (perhaps irrespective of what the production people can deliver).

Under this view, strategy is an emergent property. It is not under management's direct control, rather it emerges from the combined behavior of the organization. People simply do things, but in calculating what to do they recognize what others in the organization are doing, or are likely to do, and adapt their own behavior accordingly.

Reprinted with permission from *Strategy & Leadership*, 24: 4, 2001. Copyright © 2001 MCB University Press Ltd. All rights reserved.

Thus, group behavior—an organization—emerges. Since people are aware of what has happened in the past, this group behavior tends to have some momentum and becomes difficult to change.

To make things more complicated, what people do is not necessarily the same thing as what they *say* they will do. It is often important to say the right thing, that is, those things people want to hear, and an important organizational skill is the ability to manage perceptions. Thus, there can be a kind of hypocrisy in the way people talk. What is said, or the way things are said, can change dramatically depending on the setting (public, private, formal, informal) and, of course, on who is present. What is said may change completely when presented with the real world ("I know what the strategy says, but do you want this order or not?"). In the worst case, managers can become seduced by words. The plan is discussed in terms that are strategically correct, but action is effected in the context of what can be done, and the two become completely disconnected.

So what can be done? In our view, it is important to recognize that strategy must be conceived in terms of three dimensions: the rational, the emotional, and the political. Moreover, we have to accept that making the right change cannot be neatly segmented into two independent questions: "What is the right change?" and "How do we make it happen?" These questions are two sides of the same coin and cannot be separated, which implies that strategy implementation cannot be separated from strategy formulation.

In what follows, we briefly review the external view of strategy: how a firm exists within its environment. This provides a predominantly rational analysis that is fundamental to strategy. But we also consider the resource-based view of strategy, particularly the integrative, dynamic view known as the intellectual capital approach. This provides a rich vehicle for engaging the emotional and political aspects of strategy and leads to deeper insights into implementation issues.

Approaches to Strategy

External Analysis

This view of strategy is an extension of microeconomics. It stresses that the firm must focus on raising industry profitability by purposefully modifying the industry structure to its own advantage. Perhaps the best-known exposition of this approach is found in Porter's (1980) book, *Competitive Strategy*, in which he describes his "5-forces" model.

This model encourages managers to look at four major, environmental, competitive forces: the relative negotiating power of suppliers and customers, the threat from substitute products, the threat from new entrants, and rivalry between existing players. It also considers more general harbingers of environmental change: political, macro-economic, social and technological developments. By discerning the changing balance of these forces, it is assumed that managers can elicit insights into what their organization should do. This was later extended into generic strategies of cost leader, differentiator and niche player in a never-ending game of stone, scissors, and paper (niche blunts differentiator, differentiator cuts low-cost producer, low-cost producer wraps niche).

Closely associated with the external-analysis school is the discipline of financial modeling: forecasting, sensitivity analysis, discounted cash flows, real options, and so on. It is not our purpose here to review or criticize all such approaches that provide insights into the dangers and opportunities the firm faces. However, understanding these approaches on their own is insufficient. They are not ends in themselves and, as Karl Marx said: "Our purpose is not to understand the world but to change it." Managers need to convert their understanding into action, and here the resource-based view tends to provide more traction.

The Resource-Based View

This view of strategy claims that differences in performance arise because successful firms possess valuable resources not held by other firms, thus allowing them to earn a form of monopoly rent (Wernerfelt, 1984). A clear example is a patent, which gives the patent-holder the right to earn monopoly profits for a specified period. However, there are many other examples. A brand confers a kind of monopoly (others cannot use the brand, although brand pirates may try). Special processes, access to certain customers, a monopoly of information, and status as a specified supplier are all examples of special resources that the company can exploit to create higher than normal returns.

Thus, competitive advantage is not so much the result of the dynamics of the industry in which the firm competes, but rather the processes of resource accumulation and deployment within the organization—in other words, how well the organization uses what it has.

These strategic resources must be relevant, i.e. they must ultimately impact the end products and services that create value for customers, which can be done only by lowering the customer's costs or increasing the customer's perceived value. They must also be rare and difficult to copy or substitute.

A particularly strong insight into such assets can be gained from the intellectual capital perspective of the firm, to which we now turn.

The Intellectual Capital Perspective of the Firm

The intellectual capital perspective was initially developed as a framework for analyzing the value contribution of intangible assets in an organization. The first major grounding of the work was published by Roos and Roos (1997) and in more theoretical detail by Chatzkel (2001) and Pike *et al.* (2001). This approach developed in parallel with work by Amit and Schoemaker (2001) and

> The resource-based view of strategy claims that differences in performance arise because successful firms possess valuable resources not held by other firms, thus allowing them to earn a form of monopoly rent.

shares many features with that view. It also draws on practical experience pioneered by Leif Edvinsson, director of Intellectual Capital at Skandia.

As with most emerging theories, there are many definitions of intellectual capital. But over the last few years, a consensus seems to have been formed of dividing intellectual resources into three different groups:

1. *Human capital,* comprising the competence, skills, and intellectual agility of the individual employees.
2. *Relationship capital,* which represents all the valuable relationships with customers, suppliers, and other relevant stakeholders.
3. *Organizational capital,* including processes, systems, structures, brands, intellectual property, and other intangibles that are owned by the firm but do not appear on its balance-sheet.

Exhibit 1 illustrates this generic, high-level framework or distinction tree. The resources that actually make up the categories are unique to each organization; only those resources that are important for creating value should be included in that organization's distinction tree.

> The presence of resources is not sufficient to create value. There is no correlation, for example, between the number of marketing experts in a firm and sales. The importance is in the way resources are deployed.

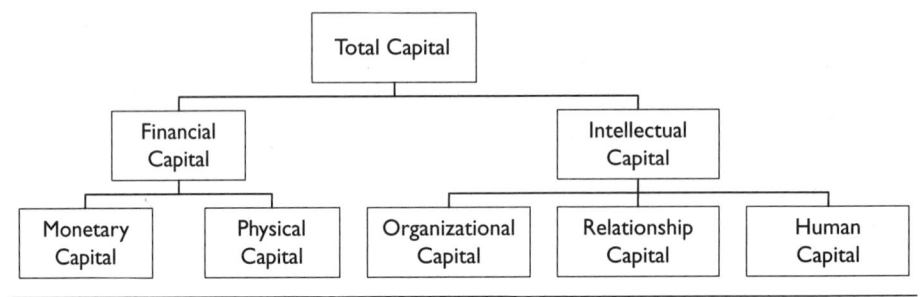

Exhibit 1. The distinction tree showing categories of intellectual capital

Total Capital
- Financial Capital
  - Monetary Capital
  - Physical Capital
- Intellectual Capital
  - Organizational Capital
  - Relationship Capital
  - Human Capital

The intellectual capital perspective, however, goes beyond the mere presence of a resource; it also considers the organization's ability to transform one resource into another. The presence of resources is not sufficient to create value. There is no correlation, for example, between the number of marketing experts in a firm and sales. The importance is in the way resources are deployed, which implies the transformation from one resource into another. Monetary value can, for example, be created through selling a process (organizational resources transformed into monetary resource), or new organizational capital can be created through formalizing knowledge into a process (human resources transformed into organizational resources). The impact of these transformations on value creation can be assessed and visualized through the intellectual capital approach with a "navigator," a model revealing all the value-creating resources (tangible and intangible), their transformations, and the relative importance of the resources and transformations for value creation (see Exhibit 2). (Note: The size of the circles reflects the impor-

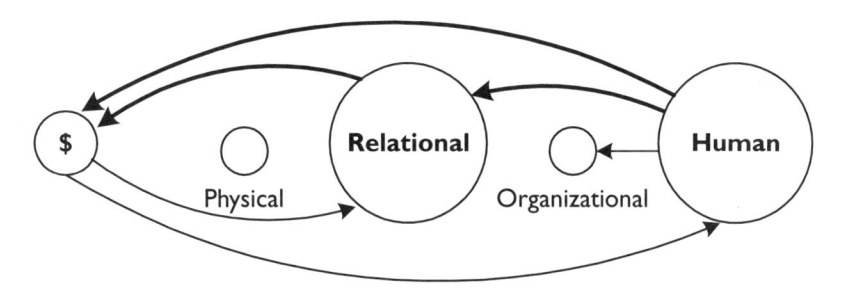

Exhibit 2. **The navigator for a people-centric organization**

tance of the resource. The transformation of one type of resource to another is shown by the connecting arrows. The thickness of the arrows represents the importance of the transformation.)

As an example, consider two firms operating in the professional service sector. They may be addressing quite similar markets, but the relative importance of their resources and the way they are deployed may be very different.

Company 1: People-Centered

Exhibit 2 shows a company that relies heavily on its human and relational resources. This company does need some monetary resources, but hardly any physical or structural resources. This is an organization focused around very knowledgeable and competent individuals who use these attributes to form personal relationships with their clients and to deliver value.

The firm hires only the best of the best (the people are, after all, its main competitive advantage). Its processes and procedures are very flexible, and training takes place through informal apprenticeship. Growth in this organization may be difficult, because it takes place through a kind of replication. This firm would probably be a partnership characterized by internal competition for clients and resources, but restrained by a partnership ethos and an emergent sense of "good manners." The quality of the product or service delivered may vary according to who is doing the job. Marketing and sales are also based on the individuals and are often a result of their personal prominence and reputation.

This organization survives and thrives thanks to low fixed costs and high billing rates and margin. Some of the money earned is used to sustain the relationships with clients, while some is used to maintain and develop the competence of the individual.

Company 2: Process-Oriented

Exhibit 3 visualizes a company operating in the same competitive space as the people-centered firm, but with a very different value-creating mechanism.

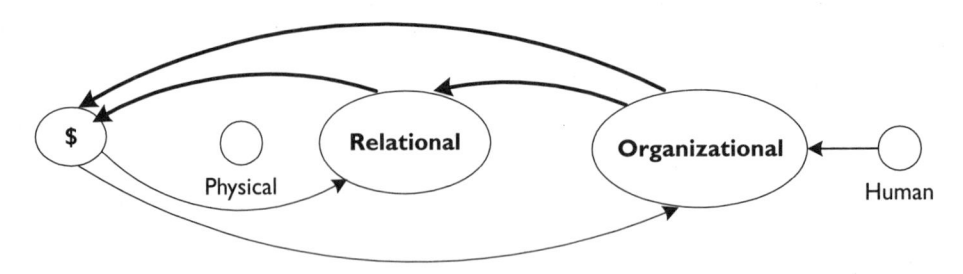

Exhibit 3. **The navigator for a process-oriented organization**

This company places a much larger emphasis on its structural resources and is less dependent on bright individuals. As this is also a professional service firm, the relationships with customers are obviously still very important. Human resources are relatively less important to value creation here compared with the people-centric organization. This does not mean that people are not important, but their relative importance is lower. The best people will be used to develop processes that are activated by less skilled employees.

This organization is characterized by organizational rather than personal relationships. The training and recruitment processes are more formal than in the people-centric organization. Product quality will be more standardized, and there will be a more system-focused approach. There will be more codification and rules, and the company may have higher fixed costs and lower margins than a people-centric firm; on the other hand, utilization may be higher.

Clearly these two organizations have different assets and philosophies. When presented with strategic alternatives, the relative merits of the different options may be quite different.

The Strategy Process

The proposed strategy process combines the best of both strategy approaches, and is represented by the diagram shown in Exhibit 4.

The Strategy Formulation Process

The main points about this process are the fusion between the external and internal analyses of the organization, and the role of the intellectual capital analysis in articulating the implications for the organization. At the end of the day, the only thing managers can control is the internal model of the organization itself. Therefore, they need to understand clearly what levers they can, and are prepared to, pull.

In practice, the development of strategic options will depend strongly on the context of a particular organization and may be triggered by a major change, probably in the environment but possibly from within (a change in

Intellectual Capital Analysis as a Strategic Tool

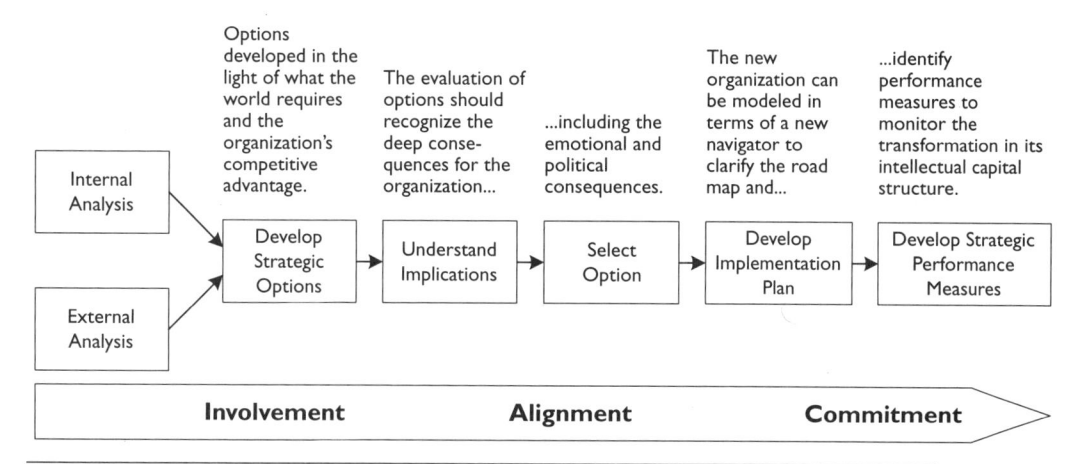

```
                    Options
                    developed in the                         The new
                    light of what the   The evaluation of    organization can    ...identify
                    world requires      options should       be modeled in       performance
                    and the             recognize the        terms of a new      measures to
                    organization's      deep conse-          navigator to        monitor the
                    competitive         quences for the      clarify the road    transformation in its
  Internal          advantage.          organization...      map and...          intellectual capital
  Analysis                              ...including the                         structure.
                                        emotional and
                      Develop           political                Develop         Develop Strategic
                      Strategic  →  Understand   →  Select  →  consequences.  →  Implementation  →  Performance
                      Options        Implications     Option       Plan             Measures
  External
  Analysis

              Involvement              Alignment              Commitment
```

Exhibit 4. **The strategy formulation process**

CEO, for example). However, we can categorize the dimensions of different options in the following ways:

- *Intent:* low-cost producer, differentiator, niche player.
- *Direction:* typically related to geography, products or services, customer segments and activities (degree of vertical integration or position in the value chain).
- *Means:* organic growth, alliance, acquisition, disposal, internal restructuring.

Even these few dimensions imply many possible potential options, and the problem is how to decide among them. Both strategic approaches are important.

Internal analysis informs managers on questions of whether the strategy is achievable. Do we have the requisite resources (human, relational, structural, physical, and monetary)? Can we deploy them effectively?

External analysis allows management to assess which option can survive. Essentially, the issue turns on determining whether a sufficient market exists: Is the world willing to give enough money to sustain the strategy? When considering intent, questions of demand elasticity become important, as do customer perceptions of value. With regard to direction, issues of market definition and size become important. The other crucial issue is to understand the capacity of others to react, particularly their reaction time. Ultimately, all competitive advantages are eroded: How long can the business earn monopoly rent? Is this enough time?

The issues are summarized in Exhibit 5.

However, in coming to an understanding of these issues, managers need to recognize the emotional and political implications: Are they willing to pay the price? What we find when undertaking this type of work is that executives

Strategic Dimension	Existence of Resources	Deployment of Resources	Willingness of Market to Pay
Intent	Do we have the assets that will enable us to earn a monopoly rent?	Can we deploy/ redeploy our resources appropriately?	Is there sufficient demand? How will other players react?
Direction			
Means			

Exhibit 5. **Analyzing strategic options**

are often not aligned on what this means. They often seem to have a shared opinion on what goes on in their external environment. They may agree on the right markets to attack and on the financial case, but they have different views on the relative importance of the different elements of capital, particularly intellectual capital. Moreover, they may disagree on the optimal deployment of this capital, which is not surprising, since these issues are likely to affect them personally.

Consider, for example, the professional service firms discussed earlier in this article. Both firms may recognize that their market offerings are becoming commoditized. They may both recognize that geographic expansion is important and that costs have to be reduced. Moreover, new developments in IT may make it easier to deliver solutions effectively over a wide area. From an external-analysis point of view, both firms come to the same conclusions.

For the people-centric firm, this could be a disaster. This firm lacks the structural capital to leverage its people. Its managers may recognize this and agree to develop better processes and more standardized methodologies. It all seems so easy and obvious, but people-centric firms lack the key human competence of proceeding in a methodical, disciplined manner, according to procedures laid down by someone else. Indeed, they lack the basic skills to design good procedures. They do not know how to recruit against formalized criteria. They cannot train people effectively in using formalized processes. They do not know how to present this formalized approach to clients. They do not know how to negotiate the contracts. They do not know what to do when the procedures do not seem to be working and quickly revert to type. They are unwilling to share their personal relationships and manage the client as a team.

All too often managers discover these issues after the strategy has been decided. Then, they may blame the problem on implementation difficulties. In our view, however, these issues are entirely predictable. This growth strategy is simply not viable in the people-centric firm. Moreover, when managers are faced with what the strategy truly means, they will reject it simply because they do not want it. Poor strategy is a source of grief!

Not everything favors the process-oriented firm, however. The people-centric firm may realize that the new IT developments provide opportunities for more creative and diverse opportunities for their clients. Their personal brilliance may allow them to generate more and better ideas. They may be very effective in personalizing solutions for clients. Their diversity allows them to conduct more experiments, and their personalized networks ensure that these are rapidly shared and improved without being stultified by procedures. They may be adept at forming alliances with similar firms in other regions. The whole process is oiled by the fact that employees and partners simply have more fun: they enjoy and thrive on the ambiguity and creative problem-solving "buzz." The process-oriented firm simply will not be able to react fast enough. Designing procedures and training people take time and money. Investment cases have to be made and weighed. Once again, when faced with what the strategy means, the managers of this firm may recoil in horror at the chaos it implies.

The problem is that these kinds of questions are often not raised, let alone answered, in debates on strategy. Managers lack the appropriate language and forums for discussion. Perhaps more importantly, they also often lack the will. Answering these kinds of questions—or, in the language of intellectual capital, designing the organization's navigator—requires managers to address fundamental issues of what their organization is and how it behaves. Distinction trees and navigators, therefore, raise important emotional and political questions. This means that they are difficult tools to use but, if used well, they can have very powerful effects.

The next step in the process is to plan the implementation. It is beyond the scope of this article to discuss implementation in detail, but it should be obvious that, by following the intellectual-capital approach, the issues of implementation become clearer. Moreover, since alignment on what implementation implies is an essential component of the strategy formalization process, many of the issues of resistance to change are dealt with early when they can do the least damage.

The final point in the process is a consideration of performance measurement. This is a crucial issue, because it allows managers to judge if they are on track.

Strategic Performance Measurement

Typically, organizations have good financial and operational measures (profits and through-put times, for example). They may also have some good external measures such as market share. However, they usually do not have good measures on their intellectual assets and how these assets are deployed. (For a deeper discussion on these issues see, for example, Pike and Roos (2001) and M'Pherson *et al.* (2001).)

If we again turn our attention to our two professional service firms, we see that what should be measured is very different in the two cases. For the people-centric firm, measures that reflect the importance of individual people in the organization and the relationships they have may be important (e.g., number of relationships per partner, number and size of jobs from new and old relationships, personal utilization, employee loyalty, and measures of personal influence within the firm). The process-oriented firm will have more measures reflecting the importance of structural resources and the business processes (process utilization, number of people trained in each process, processes development time, etc.).

These kinds of measures are important for a steady state but, when a strategic decision has been taken, it becomes more important to track progress toward the strategic objectives. It becomes difficult to generalize at this point. However, measures are again likely to be a blend of externally focused measures and a portfolio of measures tracking intellectual capital formation and deployment. For example, we hypothesized that both professional services firms may wish to extend their geographic reach. In the people-centric firm, a critical success factor may be the creation of strong personal networks between the chosen regions, and thus a key measure could be the number and duration of employee swaps between countries. For the process-oriented firm, however, the key measure may be the extent to which procedures have been harmonized and translated and the number of people trained.

Conclusion

We have argued a number of points in this article. First, successful strategy requires a fusion of the external and internal views of the firm. Second, the implementation of strategy is a political and emotive subject that cannot be divorced from the process of strategy formulation.

Strategy is meaningful only if it is backed up by commitment, not just at the executive level, but deeper in the organization. The tools and concepts of intellectual capital analysis are particularly useful in this regard. They allow managers to fathom the underlying model of how the organization works in practice and are, therefore, the core of the company's competitive advantage. They also force managers to address the difficult practical issues that make strategy meaningful.

Our final point is that the intellectual capital approach illuminates important performance measurement issues. The phrase "strategic performance measurement" is overused. In our view, this type of measurement indicates how well an organization is migrating toward its strategic intent. Measurements of intellectual capital formation and deployment tend to be lead indicators in this regard, and thus provide an indispensable addition to the CEO's performance dashboard.

References and Further Reading

Amit, R., and Schoemaker, P.J.H. (2001), "Strategic assets and organizational rents," *Strategic Management Journal*, Vol. 14, pp. 33-46.

Chatzkel, J. (2001), "A conversation with Göran Roos," an article accepted for the *Journal of Intellectual Capital* and accepted as a chapter in Chatzkel, J. (Ed.), *Conversations on Intellectual Capital*, published on the Internet.

M'Pherson, P.K., Pike, S., and Roos, G. (2001), "Strategic analysis adapted for IC networks and e-business networks," paper accepted for presentation at the Strategic Management Society's 21st Annual International Conference, October 21-24, San Francisco, CA.

Mintzberg, H. (1987), "The strategy concept I: five Ps for strategy," *California Management Review*, Vol. 30 No. 1, pp. 11-24.

Pike, S., and Roos, G. (2001), "Measuring and decision support in the knowledge society," paper presented at the 4th World Congress on Intellectual Capital, 22nd McMaster Business Conference, 2nd World Conference on E-Commerce, January 17-19, Hamilton, Canada.

Pike, S., Rylander, A., and Roos, G. (2001), "Intellectual capital management and disclosure," in Bontis, N. and Choo, C.W. (Eds.), *The Strategic Management of Intellectual Capital and Organizational Knowledge—A Selection of Readings*, Oxford University Press, New York, NY.

Porter, M.E. (1980), *Competitive Strategy*, The Free Press, New York, NY.

Roos, G., and Roos, J. (1997), "Measuring your company's intellectual performance," *Long Range Planning*, Vol. 30 No. 3, pp. 413-26.

Wernerfelt, B. (1984), "A resource-based view of the firm," *Strategic Management Journal*, Vol. 5, pp. 171-80.

Göran Roos is founder, chairman, and chief executive of Intellectual Capital Services (ICS) Ltd. (www.intcap.com). He holds chairs in strategy and intellectual capital at universities in Europe and Australia and has co-authored numerous books and articles on intellectual capital, strategy, and e-business.

Alan Bainbridge has 20 years' experience helping companies with strategic change and is KPMG secondee with IGS.

Kristine Jacobsen is a consultant with ICS and is the co-author of several book chapters and articles on strategy and intellectual capital.

Quality Transformation
LEADERSHIP

Become a Better Leader

Kennard T. Wing

There's lots to say about leadership, but not in this article, which is short and to the point. We include it as a kind of brief reminder of some of the basic skills of leading for quality. We believe that leadership skills such as those outlined here naturally emerge from people truly committed to implementing quality management. They are consistent with inspiring people to take responsibility for the quality of their work and their collaboration with others.

Think about the people who work in the unit you manage. Do they regularly create innovations that add value to the people you serve, increase productivity, and make it a better place to work ... or do they just maintain the status quo? Do they work together as a team ... or is it more an aggregate of individuals? Have they caught the vision of the cathedral they're creating ... or are they just laying bricks? If you're not satisfied with the answers to those questions, you could blame your people—or you could work on your own leadership skills.

But before you can improve, you need to know what leadership is. Sixty-five years ago, author Ordway Tead defined it as "the activity of influencing people to cooperate toward some goal which they come to find desirable." Dwight Eisenhower called it "the art of getting someone else to do something you want done *because he wants to do it* [italics added]." Note how the definition changes when the italicized words are omitted. It's the difference between leadership and manipulation.

How do you get there? Here are seven areas where most of us could improve:

Reprinted with permission from *Strategic Finance*, February 2001. Published by the Institute of Management Accountants, Montvale, NJ. www.imanet.org. Copyright © 2001. All rights reserved.

1. Walk your talk. Actions speak louder than words, so take a good, hard look at the example you're setting. Your people notice what time you come in, what time you leave, and how long you take for lunch and coffee. They know whether you take all the credit for what the unit accomplishes and whether you admit mistakes and take responsibility for screwups. They know exactly how susceptible you are to flattery and brownnosing. They see whether you take risks or avoid them. They hear if you bad-mouth others. It's unfair, but employees hold their bosses to higher standards than they hold themselves. For better or worse, your example is the strongest management tool you have.

2. Catch your people doing something right. It's easy to focus on flaws and mistakes. Some call it managing by exception. Unfortunately, the message your people get is, "Don't try anything new. Don't suggest anything new. Play safe." It's a recipe for an organization caught in suspended animation. Focus instead on finding contributions. Give yourself a quota of thanking at least one of your people each day for something specific they did. Can't find anything? Look harder. And don't forget to recognize people in front of their peers, too.

> Give yourself a quota of thanking at least one of your people each day for something specific they did. Can't find anything? Look harder.

3. Share your dream. Dare to dream about the future you want to create. Who can get excited about processing another invoice? Or making journal entries? People only get fired up when they are part of something larger than themselves. Worried your people won't buy in? Let them share in formulating the vision. There's no more powerful way. Then be optimistic and enthusiastic in communicating the vision. Enthusiasm is an infectious disease. Be a carrier. And don't worry about repeating yourself. Leaders need to do exactly that.

4. Grow people. Sometimes it seems there are only two kinds of bosses: the ones people will do only the minimum for and the ones people will do anything for. The biggest single difference between these bosses is what they believe about their people. The first kind believe their people are already in over their heads and treat them accordingly. The second kind assume their people are capable of much more than what they are currently doing. To be the second kind of boss, believe in your people more than they believe in themselves. Treat them with dignity and respect. Trust them. Give them important work at the edge of their skills and the discretion to decide how to do it. When they make mistakes (you want that, Silly), don't come down on them, but focus on learning for the future.

5. Celebrate victories. Everybody wants to be part of a winning team. Make sure your team gets a steady diet of victories. How? By breaking your dream into small bites. Then, as these small victories are achieved, take time to celebrate them together. There's no better way to solidify the team and refuel members' emotional commitment, which is the key to sustaining people through tough times.

> ### TEST YOUR LEADERSHIP QUOTIENT
>
> For each item, rate yourself from 1 to 5, where 1 means "almost never," 5 means "almost always."
>
> 1. Walk my talk   ____
> 2. Focus on contributions, not mistakes   ____
> 3. Share my dream   ____
> 4. Grow people   ____
> 5. Celebrate victories   ____
> 6. Build collaboration   ____
> 7. Am out in front   ____
>
> *Scoring:*
> 30-35: Great score! Now check it by letting your people rate you.
> 20-29: Average. Try focusing consciously every day for the next 30 days on improving *one* leadership skill.
> Below 20: Either you're just being modest, or consider reaching out for some help.

6. Build collaboration. Collaboration is the essence of every organization that's greater than the sum of its parts. Many aspects of management foster collaboration, while others inhibit collaboration. Does your performance appraisal process, as many do, create separate goals for each individual that are kept secret from everyone else? Instead, create team goals that are both public and shared. How often does your whole team get together in one room? Whether two people report to you or 2,000, create regular forums for face-to-face interaction. And don't lecture the troops. Promote open communication by spending more time listening than talking. Recognize that how you respond to early feedback will determine how much you'll get in the future—and what kind. Be aware that even healthy teams have disagreements and differences. Work to surface and resolve them, but even if you can't resolve them, get them out into the open. A wound exposed to the open air won't fester.

7. Get out in front. You can't lead by following your people. Get out in front by challenging the status quo. Steal ideas from other fields and industries. Experiment with new methods and approaches. Take risks. And don't forget to reward your subordinates who do the same, even when they fail.

Most people desperately want to be led, but they're fussy. They want the leader they follow to be worthy of their "followership." So give them what they want. Work on these seven areas, and be the leader you can be.

Kennard T. Wing, CMA, is a project director at the OMG Center for Collaborative Learning in Philadelphia. Pa., a nonprofit research and consulting organization focused on urban issues and urban institutions. You can reach him at Ken@omgcenter.org or (215) 732-2200.

Leadership DNA:
The Ford Motor Story

Stewart D. Friedman

Ford Motor Company has determined that leadership development is at the absolute center of all its efforts to succeed in the marketplace and as a corporate citizen. This article by the director of Ford's Leadership Development Center explains in detail why Ford has developed this center and how it works. It is a great example of how one company has made its commitment to people development and strategic success one and the same thing.

We live in extraordinary times. Not a day goes by when we don't hear or read about a new discovery, invention, or business initiative that will ultimately affect all of our lives. New media are transforming virtually every aspect of human action. On top of the digital revolution, add new business models, globalization, and new labor market dynamics (such as increased diversity and fresh attitudes about work and one's personal life) and you have a different world than business leaders have ever seen before.

The underlying structure of the global economy is shifting, bringing with it a bewildering array of unprecedented challenges that require a new kind of leadership. Developing the next generation of leaders at a time of momentous change is a monumental task. Yet, those of us in the field of leadership development must continue to ask fundamental questions:

- How can we accelerate the identification of candidates for leadership positions?
- What methods should we use to enable our people to become competitive in the new economy?
- How can we challenge our leaders to contribute to the transformation of our company?
- How can we accelerate the preparation of our best leaders for senior executive roles?
- How can we drive our company's vision deep into its culture?
- How can we create a new leadership mindset that invests in the developing leader as a whole person, capable of contributing not only at work, but also at home and in the community?

Ford Motor Company is facing those same questions; senior management

Reprinted with permission from *Training & Development*, March 2001. Copyright © 2001 by the American Society for Training & Development. All rights reserved.

has set the direction. In our 2000 Corporate Citizenship Report, chairman William Clay Ford Jr. writes:

> We see no conflict between business goals and social and environmental needs. I believe the distinction between a good company and a great one is this: A good company delivers excellent products and services; a great one delivers excellent products and services and strives to make the world a better place.

In the same report, our CEO Jacques Nasser observes:

> The transition from a traditional manufacturer to a 21st-century consumer company is critical for our long-term financial success. It requires a new mindset—one focused on connecting not only with our customers, but also with all of our stakeholders to make it work.

The DNA Revolution

Adopting a consumer mindset as well as one of environmental and social responsibility requires leadership.

Adopting a consumer mindset as well as one of environmental and social responsibility requires leadership. We need leaders who can make informed business decisions that will make our company better able to meet customer needs and increase shareholder value, as well as honor commitments to the world in which we live. Change like that is easy to talk about but difficult to implement. It will take nothing less than a massive shift in culture to create new leadership DNA. Nothing short of revolution will do.

And that is where our Leadership Development Center enters. Our vision is to be the center for the revolution, developing Ford Motor Company leaders to change the world. Our mission is to accelerate transformation to a consumer- and shareholder-driven business, to accelerate the identification and development of leadership talent, and to drive the company's mission, vision, and values deep into its culture.

How can we do that? We've developed a series of leadership programs centered around these core principles:

- Adopt a transformational mindset.
- Use action learning—learning by doing, leading, and teaching.
- Leverage the power of e-tools.
- Integrate work and life, what I call "total leadership."
- Generate business impact.

Let's examine the first two in depth and the others later on.

Adopt a Transformational Mindset

The chief way that Ford's Leadership Development Center is fomenting revolution is by creating transformational leaders—men and women who know how to get things done in ways that use the talents of their people for maximum business impact. Our leaders also learn to think "outside of the box" because our programs force them out of their comfort zones in everything from selecting a project to working with new people. Participants return to their positions enthused and ready to look at familiar challenges with fresh eyes and to try new ideas that deliver results.

We nurture the transformational mindset by consistently challenging participants to think of alternative possibilities. That push really begins before participants start the training. The workload of most programs isn't light, and the real work isn't done in the classroom but in the field of real business activity. Participants are expected to do work prior to the classroom phase—mainly, to choose a project and research feasibility. They must devise innovative ways to balance their usual workloads and assume responsibility for meeting program requirements. The challenge is to find ways to eliminate unnecessary tasks and obtain help. Many participants learn to empower their staff and to network with peers to delegate their day-to-day responsibilities. In itself, that is a significant opportunity for leadership lessons.

Transformational leadership at Ford is underscored, as reflected in our expected leadership behaviors, by these values: integrity, flawless execution, and the building of effective relationships with key stakeholders. In other words, while we're asking our people to think and behave differently, we are mindful of our company's culture and respectful of its rich cultural values.

Another aspect of the transformational mindset is the growing need to recognize the triple bottom line of financial success, environmental protection, and social responsibility. Our programs have community service aspects that serve to put our work as a company in the perspective of the larger social context in which we operate and to which we must contribute. There is a growing realization that a company such as ours (indeed, most companies for that matter) can't continue with traditional business models into the 21st century. We're actively incorporating renewable resource technologies and developing alternatives to the internal combustion engine, for example. Such bold actions require equally bold leaders to implement them. Success in the new century requires the transformational mindset, one found in our new leadership DNA.

> Our programs have community service aspects that serve to put our work as a company in the perspective of the larger social context in which we operate and to which we must contribute.

Use Action Learning

All of our programs feature action learning. Participants work individually or in teams with leaders at all levels on projects that challenge them to expand their creative abilities and refine their critical-thinking and execution skills—all in order to drive for improved business results.

Participants receive extensive feedback from multiple sources that enables them to improve and refine their leadership abilities. In addition, alumni of our programs serve as leader-teachers—a practice that helps participants and the instructor grow and develop new capacities for leadership. It's also a critical feature of our strategy to "spread the word."

Action learning creates business impact. The projects participants choose must have a business benefit in terms of customer satisfaction, cost reduction, or enhanced revenue. One of the most notable examples is the QIP—the Quantum Idea Project. It's the key to our New Business Leader program for first-time supervisors of salaried employees. The QIP, intended to drive revolutionary change at Ford, stretches an individual's capacity to think critically, innovate daringly, evaluate choices strategically, and support business objectives wisely. In the process, a manager begins to develop leadership skills that he or she can use every day.

The QIP process is organized according to key milestones, checkoffs, and evaluation processes inherent to a project. Biweekly, participants undergo a cycle of review that occurs in teams with a peer serving as co-strategist or advisor. Review also happens online on password-protected Websites. During these reviews, participants rate their projects as *green* (good to go), *yellow* (not quite sure), or *red* (stuck). Then, they receive feedback and support on how to maintain momentum and progress towards their goals.

Additionally, our programs instill a sense of accountability. Participants are evaluated on the outcome of their projects and how well they performed as leaders. For example, how did they interact with their peers? Did they network successfully? Did they learn new ways of doing things? Success as a leader depends on more than delivering results; it requires an ability to continually strengthen working alliances and a willingness to test new ideas. The feedback participants receive from multiple sources such as peers, clients, and supervisors adds to their sense of accountability. The feedback also becomes instructive in the development of a person's leadership style and capacity.

At present, the Leadership Development Center at Ford Motor Company offers nine programs—four core and five strategic change initiatives.

Four-Five Punch

At present, the Leadership Development Center at Ford Motor Company offers nine programs—four core and five strategic change initiatives. The four core programs play a significant role in the identification, selection, and development of Ford's next generation of leaders. For admission, candidates must be rated either as having high potential or recent high performance. The four core programs, targeted for specific leadership levels, are listed in ascending order:

1. *New Business Leader* teaches leadership through the pursuit of innovative ideas designed to transform the business. To date, participants have generated more than 600 QIPs (quantum idea projects), all of which aim for a specific business impact. Participants increase their leadership capacity by building skills in the 12 Ford leadership behaviors as they learn how to take their ideas from conception to implementation.

2. *Leadership for the New Economy* pioneers new ways to work. A primary goal is to enable leaders to deliver strong business results and enrich lives

by using new economy tools and by taking what I call a "total leadership" perspective—integrating work, home, community, and self. The lessons emerging from this program are accelerating transformation as participants teach others throughout the company about how they've changed the way work is done.

3. *Experienced Leader Challenge* demonstrates how to deliver improved business results in the form of cost reduction and revenue generation by working in cross-functional teams. Participants improve their leadership capacity by working in an environment that develops new business knowledge and that leverages the strengths of broad, cross-functional networks for specific results.

4. *Capstone* prepares people moving into positions of senior leadership. Capstone projects are strategic in nature and are designed to expand leadership capacity to the next level. Corporate officers are sponsors for projects, and senior leaders are involved in teaching, coaching, and evaluating participants.

The Leadership Development Center lends its support through strategic change initiatives, which by nature cut across vertical and horizontal boundaries. At present, there are five change initiative programs under way:

1. *Leadership for Consumer-Driven, Six-Sigma* complements the technical training of Black Belt candidates by teaching the leadership skills required for successful execution of Black Belt projects.

2. *Ford/Supplier BLI* fosters collaborative partnerships with Ford's key suppliers to improve understanding, increase efficiency, and lower costs.

3. *BLI 3 Flawless Execution* builds business leadership competencies in vehicle line, cross-functional teams responsible for designing, engineering, and developing new cars and trucks.

4. *New Leader Impact* rapidly integrates newly hired executives by cultivating networks throughout the company and by reinforcing their role as agents of change.

5. *Global Leadership Forum* brings Ford's top 300 executives together on a quarterly basis to focus on key business initiatives and to strengthen connections among the key players in our company.

> Graduates of our programs serve as leader-teachers, a practice that helps participants and the instructor grow and develop new capacities for leadership.

Those Who Can, Teach

Every program features extensive use of teachers. Graduates of our programs serve as leader-teachers, a practice that helps participants and the instructor grow and develop new capacities for leadership. The concept of leader-teacher isn't unique, but Ford places a high emphasis on teaching. The lesson begins at the top.

More than three years ago, CEO Jacques Nasser inaugurated the Business Leadership Initiative concept with himself as teacher. Now, thousands of managers are teaching other managers about everything from the basics of supervision to the intricacies of Six Sigma. Nowhere is the concept of leader-teacher more prevalent than in the *New Business Leader* program. The active participation of senior leaders in the Quantum Idea Project process is essential. Each QIP must have a senior leader sponsor who serves as a project mentor. The sponsor not only shepherds the project, but he or she also nurtures the leadership capacity of participants.

Another way that leader-teachers contribute is through feedback. Participants in all of our core programs receive extensive feedback from multiple sources to enable them to improve and refine their leadership abilities. The feedback is a two-way street; leader-teachers receive feedback on how they teach. That input is extremely valuable and gives them something to take back to the workplace.

Leader-teachers also create synergy throughout all of the action-learning programs. Graduates become teachers, sponsors, and mentors of participants. That creates cohesion in a spirit of revolutionary change and helps accelerate the transformational process that we're all engaged in.

The Power of E-Tools

If we're expecting people to work in the new economy, we need to give them tools to work more effectively. The global 24/7 reality makes working face-to-face often impossible; time zones and distance preclude it. Yet, we need people to work together. Thankfully, technology is making it possible.

> In our *Leadership for the New Economy* program, participants work in virtual spaces called "e-rooms" six weeks prior to commencement of the first residential (classroom) session.

The Internet and e-mail are the starting points; virtual collaboration is the next step. For example, in our *Leadership for the New Economy* program, participants work in virtual spaces called "e-rooms" six weeks prior to commencement of the first residential (classroom) session. They also begin working collaboratively in the e-room, using an online tool dedicated to their program sessions and monitored by faculty made up of Ford executives and outside faculty drawn from leading universities and consulting firms. Interestingly, the team set the standard in virtual collaboration, as the program was designed and delivered by people who functioned as a virtual team during most of the development.

Taking e-tools to the next step—as a learning exercise as well as a way to have fun—participants took part in an online auction conducted by AutoXchange (later Covisint), bidding on the opportunity to meet individually with outside experts from joint-venture partners and other companies that could offer useful insight and information on specific projects. Not only did the bidding process teach participants lessons about online auctions, but it also enabled them to expand their network of information and resources.

In using e-tools, participants invest time and energy trying out new ways of working that leverage synergies among work, home, and community, thus taking a total leadership approach. That might involve experimenting with telecommuting, flexible schedules, reduced face-time for internal meetings (while making more intelligent use of face-time for customers and other external stakeholders), and other new models for leadership.

To augment our e-leadership mindset, we launched a Web site devoted to leadership, with the intention to make it all things to all people at Ford who are interested in leadership. We consider it our virtual community for Ford leadership. Anyone at Ford can visit the site and learn how to gain insight into leadership best practices and get access to leadership materials, including self-nomination forms for admission to our programs. In addition, each program has e-rooms where participants can work independently or cooperatively on their projects.

Integrating Work and Life

We at Ford are pioneering a new dimension of leadership that seeks to integrate all aspects of a person's life. We call it "total leadership." Total leadership is similar to most leadership approaches in that it aims to achieve superior results. It's different from many prior leadership models because it starts with your life as a whole: your life at work, your life at home, and your life in the community. Total leadership recognizes that the stakeholder expectations in each of those domains can and do affect each other. Therefore, total leadership is about being a leader in all aspects of one's life.

> Boundaries between diverse domains of life are becoming more permeable and flexible, and leadership now must account for that emerging reality.

New technologies, specifically the e-tools, permit us to integrate stakeholder domains and even create synergies among them. No longer is business leadership confined to the work domain. Boundaries between diverse domains of life are becoming more permeable and flexible, and leadership now must account for that emerging reality. Leaders will have to leverage resources—financial and human capital, technology, new business models, and so forth—to gain synergies across diverse stakeholder domains: work, home, community, and self.

The total leadership perspective allows for a faster, more agile means to achieve superior business results in the 24/7, global, anytime-anywhere economy. More specifically, because it deemphasizes face-time and focuses on results both within and across domains, the total leadership perspective offers the potential for reduced workload and better results, in all aspects of life.

Business results increase in the short term because of

- increased motivation and commitment
- greater efficiencies in work processes
- reduced cycle times
- lower costs (from less travel, for example)
- enhanced customer focus through explicit emphasis on performance impact across the value chain

- more active engagement by business leaders in home and community life.

With employees having greater control in arranging their life circumstances, long-term business benefits accrue—including greater attraction and retention of top talent in the new labor market, less burnout and stress (potentially related to health-care costs), and decreased down-time from poorly managed connections between work and other aspects of life.

That's the good news, the opportunity. As pioneers facing the frontier of a new economy, the challenge for us is to develop the total leadership capacity necessary to bring the opportunity to reality. It requires understanding more about how to leverage the resources inherent in new-economy tools and models. That means learning how to

- capture synergies across domains of life so that total achievement in life is greater than just the sum of efforts applied at work, at home, in the community, and for one's self
- make more conscious and strategic choices about allocation of time and energy towards valued goals
- rethink the means by which work gets done in ways that force a results-driven focus
- reduce reliance on traditional work methods—face-time and co-location of resources—and use them more wisely
- innovate to better meet performance expectations of key stakeholders at work, at home, and in the community and those you hold for yourself
- aggressively cultivate networks and partnerships that provide the support needed for flexibility and agility in and across domains.

We believe our programs need to continue to develop total leadership capacity further to stay ahead of the curve in the rapidly evolving economic and social environments of business in the 21st century. It isn't a stretch to say that without a total leadership perspective, our company will not be able to compete successfully in the future. Total leadership is essential to Ford's new leadership DNA.

Generating Business Impact

All of the programs significantly impact business in two ways: financially and organizationally. Financially, each individual or team project must contribute to customer satisfaction, reduced costs, or increased incremental revenue. And we have some impressive statistics.

Participants in QIP programs have generated more than 600 projects, some with significant business impact such as tire recycling, vehicle customization, and new vehicle servicing models.

Leadership DNA: The Ford Motor Story

A recent *Ford Supplier/Business Leadership Initiative* program identified $300 in cost-reductions per vehicle, which is now in development. Three hundred dollars may not seem like much at first, but when you multiply it by thousands of vehicles, the savings is substantial.

Projects in the *Experienced Leader Challenge* program have identified more than $100 million in cost-savings and another $100 million in incremental revenue. Over the next three to five years, those numbers will likely climb to the billions in savings and earnings.

You can accurately declare that our leadership programs pay for themselves many times over. But that's only part of the story. The second business impact is the effect our programs are having on the organization. We're accelerating the process of creating leaders at every level by having emerging and experienced leaders work individually as well as collaboratively on projects of significant merit. We create synergies further among the programs that, in turn, further facilitate learning and speed the development of leadership capacities.

Bottom line: we are creating transformational leaders, men and women who know how to get things done in ways that use the talents of their people for maximum business impact. For that reason, I believe it's no exaggeration to say that the return on this organizational contribution is exponential. And in the new economy in which we face escalating customer demands, fluid market conditions, and global scale, exponential return is what is required.

> Success in the new economy, or any economy, will require men and women to adopt a transformational mindset.

Leadership development is an evolutionary process that changes as the needs of an organization change. Core principles, such as action learning or leader-teachers, may remain. But the what, why, and how of a program should change in response to emerging issues. As one who has taught leadership in an academic and now a corporate setting, I suggest these guidelines when creating a leadership development program:

Create a sense of urgency for leadership development. Leadership is not a nice-to-have; it's a must-do. Success in the new economy, or any economy, will require men and women to adopt a transformational mindset that enables them to anticipate change, develop strategies to meet new demands, and continue to maximize growth opportunities. In a nutshell, all of that requires leadership.

Our CEO, Jacques Nasser, is brilliant at conveying urgency. Despite years of record earnings, Nasser has been galvanizing Ford to transform itself as quickly as possible in an effort to become a 21st-century company capable of meeting escalating demands and adapting to the rules of the new economy.

Develop a brand for your leadership-development strategy. Every successful consumer product has a readily identifiable brand. Same goes for services. Brand, put simply, is the sum of the attributes, aspirations, and perceptions associated with a product or service. At the heart of successful brands is a sense of trust between the provider and the consumer. That's the kind of trust we're trying to foster with Ford employees whom we encourage to join our programs. Therefore, it makes good sense to develop a strong brand image around the kind of transformational leadership we're trying to create.

Our brand image revolves around creating a new leadership DNA. We even developed a logo (a double helix) and gradually began attributing to it positive characteristics of leadership at Ford. Over time, we believe our brand will become synonymous with the kind of transformational mindset Ford is creating.

Communicate the results of leadership-development activities. Communication is central to leadership, so why would it be any different for a leadership-development program? Tom Grant, program leader for *New Business Leader*, often talks about the time in the not-too-distant future when applicants to the program will exceed its capacity to deliver. Grant is no glutton for excess work, but he understands that when more people want to participate, we'll have achieved a measure of success.

Demand is tied directly to communications, so it's important to use all available means to communicate about your programs: Web site, e-mail, video, print materials. Be certain you also communicate your brand in everything you do. Make the logo and its associated images ubiquitous. But a word to the wise: keep senior leadership in the loop. Invite them to teach, and send them regular updates on what's going on in the programs. Solicit their feedback. Their active support is essential to the long-term health of your programs. Indeed, the Leadership Development Center at Ford isn't an HR initiative; it's owned by senior line management.

Celebrate achievements. Leadership programs should be targeted to achieve business results. When they do, publicize them. Let others in the organization know how the programs are affecting the bottom line. In this way, you can shift the perception of leadership development from a "cost" to a "revenue enhancer." More important, you will demonstrate that leadership development isn't something nice to have but a must-have that not only pays for itself, but also facilitates a mindset and culture that seek to build the business. Frankly, you can't put a price tag on that.

Promote your alumni as leaders of tomorrow. The ultimate measure of any leadership-development program is how well the alumni do. If graduates are moving up in the organization, it's an indication that the lessons of the leadership-development program are effective. As more graduates move up through our organization, the leadership message and example will become part of the culture and transformation process.

A leadership-development program can help its alumni achieve success in the organization in two ways.

One, alumni make terrific teachers. Keep bringing them back to your programs. They'll not only help your current participants, but they will also hone their own leadership skills.

Two, create an alumni association (similar to what universities do) to help grads of the leadership development programs network with each other and senior leaders. The success of a program depends on its alumni. The more you can do for them, the better you will do for your leadership development efforts and the organization as a whole.

Make no mistake: the Leadership Development Center is no charm school. It's more like an obstacle course devised by the Marines to bring out the best in Ford's leadership talent by pushing, prodding, and stretching for results.

David Murphy, our vice president of human resources, says, "We aim to be seen by Wall Street as the best-led company in the world, with leaders at all levels, building leadership capacity faster than any other corporation.

"We must become a company where leadership represents intellectual capital at such a level that it will out learn, out compete, and out lead all of the competition to ensure ongoing increases in shareholder value throughout the foreseeable future."

People who graduate from the Leadership Development Center gain improved customer focus, a renewed commitment to business results, and a greater understanding of their role in generating shareholder value. They become transformational leaders—ready, willing, and able to lead Ford Motor Company to meet future challenges. Perhaps the truest measure of our impact will be in the marketplace for talent when Ford is seen as *the* company to go to for the best leadership talent in the business world.

Stewart D. Friedman is the director of the Leadership Development Center at Ford Motor Company and co-author of Work and Family: Allies or Enemies? *(Oxford University Press, 2000).*

Developing Leaders: How Winning Companies Keep on Winning

Robert M. Fulmer, Philip A. Gibbs, and Marshall Goldsmith

How do Arthur Andersen, General Electric, Hewlett-Packard, Johnson & Johnson, Shell International, and The World Bank keep a steady stream of leaders moving up? This article shows how they focus on the five essentials of leadership development—assessment, alignment, action, anticipation, and awareness. In other words, leaders are sometimes born, but they are more often made, and these companies are taking action to make sure that happens.

Last June, as the business world watched expectantly, General Electric (GE) promoted three key executives (David Calhoun, Joseph Hogan and John Rice). Each would report to one of the three potential candidates to succeed CEO Jack Welch (James McNerney, Jeffrey Immelt and Robert Nardelli). Thus, if one of the latter moves into Welch's office, another seasoned GE professional will be ready to assume his role. Where do GE leaders come from? They do not spring up out of the earth overnight. For many years the company has worked hard to develop ongoing sources of leadership talent—not only to prepare for Welch's retirement next year, but also to enrich every level of the organization with strong leaders. When Ronald Reagan was spokesperson for GE, their slogan was "Progress is our most important product." Today the mantra could be "Leaders are our most important product."

Leaders who keep learning may be the ultimate source of sustainable competitive advantage. With that understanding, many companies are investing in leadership development (programs that help key executives learn leadership skills). As early as 1993, *Business Week* estimated that $17 billion was being spent annually on helping managers develop the thought processes and company-specific skills that could enable them to move up and lead their business areas. *Training* magazine estimates that in 1998 U.S. companies spent $60.7 billion on training.[1] But spending isn't the only commitment. World-class executives are investing significant amounts of their time per-

Reprinted from "Developing Leaders: How Winning Companies Keep on Winning" by Robert M. Fulmer, Philip A. Gibbs, and Marshall Goldsmith, *Sloan Management Review*, Fall 2000, by permission of publisher. Copyright © 2000 by Massachusetts Institute of Technology. All rights reserved.

sonally guiding and mentoring future leaders.[2] To them, leadership development is not a luxury but a strategic necessity.

What processes transform managers into strong leaders ready for strategic action? How do the best leadership-development organizations design, manage and deliver world-class programs?

In January 1998, the nonprofit research group American Productivity and Quality Center, based in Houston, the American Society for Training and Development, based in Alexandria, Virginia and author Robert Fulmer set out to find the answers. The group developed a study to investigate best practices in leadership development; in 1999, they expanded the study to explore the challenge of developing leaders at all levels of an organization.[3]

Thirty-five organizations participated as sponsors. (See the sidebar, "Benchmarking Methodology.") They sent representatives to a planning session, completed data-gathering surveys and attended or hosted on-site interviews. (See the sidebar, "Study Sponsors.") The consortium identified six companies as having a strong or innovative leadership-development process. Those six agreed to participate in the study as best-practice partners. (See the sidebar, "And the Winners Are ...") They were chosen because they exhibited commitment to developing leaders—but with marked diversity of approach, emphasis and culture.

The Strategic Perspective

Most significant: best-practice partners reported that they tied leadership development closely to business strategy and that they invested financial resources in it. CEOs did not support the programs out of a respect for education but from a conviction that such programs can assist in aligning functional areas with corporate strategy. Johnson & Johnson, for one, revised succession planning and performance-management systems to reflect the qualities anticipated by a leader-of-the-future exercise in a leadership-development conference.

Increasingly, programs that focus on developing future leaders are seen as a source of competitive advantage. GE's CEO, Jack Welch, described the company's Leadership Development Institute in Crotonville, New York, as a "staging ground for corporate revolutions." In fact, innovative ideas such as the Six Sigma quality-improvement program and GE's expansion into emerging economies have come from presentations made at leadership-development events. Tremendous growth, reductions in the number of GE employees worldwide and significant delayering of the organization in the 1980s and 1990s caused an enormous cultural shift. With fewer layers of management, individuals received fewer vertical promotions and hence fewer opportunities to practice being leaders. A new approach was called for. Today in the human-resource department's "Session C" meetings, senior executives assess key GE personnel. After an initial meeting in March, there are two or three addition-

> Best-practice partners reported that they tied leadership development closely to business strategy and that they invested financial resources in it.

> ## Benchmarking Methodology
>
> Benchmarking, the study's primary research methodology, involves identifying outstanding practices and processes from any organization anywhere in the world, learning from them and adapting them to a specific company's needs. Modeled on the human learning process, which also relies heavily on observation, benchmarking is the process by which organizations learn. The underlying rationale is that learning from best-practice cases is the most effective means of understanding the principles and the specifics of effective practices.
>
> In phase one, the group conducting the study reviewed the literature to identify leading companies in executive development; they talked with opinion leaders in management education, consulting and business; and they administered a survey to various people to identify their organizations' leadership-development support, specific innovative approaches and willingness to be best-practice partners. At the end of phase one, the study team had compiled a list of candidates for potential best-practice partners and a screening report. Sponsors met to review the initial report, select the final best-practice partners and discuss their objectives for the study.
>
> In phase two, representatives from the study sponsors visited best-practice partners for a day, seeking answers to detailed questions about the evolution, design, execution and successes of their leadership programs. The study sought to identify innovative practices and applicable quantitative data, such as budgets, program details and assessment criteria. The deliverables at the end of phase two were site-visit summaries, a two-day knowledge-transfer session (in which all the study sponsors and best-practice partners participated) and a final report.

al meetings and a wrap-up session in June or July to select employees who will attend the executive-development courses at Crotonville. At the end of the year, corporate leadership development, like all corporate functions, is measured by whether it was able to support GE initiatives. Steve Kerr, GE's chief learning officer, says jokingly, "Crotonville is GE's only unbudgeted and unmeasured cost center." Then he adds seriously, "Everyone would know if we weren't delivering strategic value."

Ralph Larsen, chairman and CEO of Johnson & Johnson, champions J&J's Executive Conference. Faithful to the company's decentralization tenets, he leaves the program's details to subordinates around the world but takes the time to suggest program themes.

At Arthur Andersen, the mission of the Partner Development Program (PDP) is "to help partners worldwide acquire and build the knowledge, skills and behaviors required to be valued and trusted business advisors in an ever-changing marketplace." To meet the needs of a business that continues to diversify and globalize, managers aim to keep the program closely linked with

STUDY SPONSORS

AARP	Lutheran Brotherhood
Aerojet	Medrad
Allstate Insurance	Nortel
American General	North American Coal
Ameritech	PDVSA-CIED
Amoco	Pharmacia & Upjohn
Buckman Laboratories	Shell International
Canadian Imperial Bank of Commerce	Smith & Nephew
	Sprint
Celanese	Thomas Cook Group
Chevron	The Timken Co.
Compaq Computer	U.S. Dept. of Treasury
Deere & Co.	U.S. Postal Service
Eastman Chemical	USA Group
Honda of America Manufacturing	USDA Graduate School
Johns Hopkins University Applied Physics Lab	Wachovia Corporation
	Warner-Lambert
Johnson & Johnson	Ziff-Davis
Lucent Technologies	

AND THE WINNERS ARE...

Best-Practice Partner Organizations

Arthur Andersen
General Electric Co.
Hewlett-Packard Co.
Johnson & Johnson
Shell International
The World Bank

Arthur Andersen's evolving business strategy.

Hewlett-Packard, under the leadership of CEO Carly Fiorina, is rushing to reclaim its status as a top high-tech innovator. Fiorina must convince the public and HP employees that HP is the hottest new company of the Internet era—without losing the old-time commitment to quality and integrity. Past HP glory led many excellent engineers to focus on what used to be important, instead of on the future. Once HP started to improve leadership development, the company could make better business decisions.

Today HP's senior executives actively participate in leadership development. Fiorina uses management meetings and leadership-development programs to articulate her vision of making the company "represent the next

> ## MAKING LEADERSHIP DEVELOPMENT STRATEGIC
>
> ### Five-Step Process, Best-Practice Programs
>
> #### Assessment
> - Andersen: Seeks quantifiable measures.
> - Shell: Looks for 25:1 ROI in its action-learning projects.
> - World Bank: Uses internal and external evaluation.
>
> #### Alignment
> - Johnson & Johnson: Ties 360-degree feedback to J&J's Standards of Leadership and succession plans.
> - General Electric: Uses a nine-block system (similar to competency ratings) and "Session C" meetings (where senior managers assess candidates for development).
> - Hewlett-Packard: Considers strategic needs for diversity and new leadership models.
>
> #### Action
> - General Electric: Uses programs called Work-Out and Change Acceleration Process.
> - Johnson & Johnson: Uses real-time business issues in its action learning for executive and midlevel managers.
>
> #### Anticipation
> - Shell: Uses forward-looking, hypothetical scenarios.
> - Johnson & Johnson: Uses a program called Creating Our Future.
>
> #### Awareness
> - Arthur Andersen: Is data-driven, uses feedback and surveys.
> - Shell: Uses committee of managing directors and Global Research Consortium (a group of transnational companies that sponsor research).

decade rather than the past one." Her predecessor, Lewis E. Platt, showed his support for leadership development by making personal appearances at all HP Accelerated Development Programs, opening and closing them with an opportunity for participants to have a dialogue with him. And Bob Wayman, HP's CFO, was the internal champion for a worldwide broadcast on closed-circuit television. During the broadcast, Wayman played an active role as facilitator of the panel discussion "Challenging the Growth Barrier." Senior HP executives have served as faculty in part of every core program. Fiorina's early commitment to communication with her management team has led to an expectation within the company that she will continue using leadership development as a "bully pulpit" for strategic change.

Cor Herkstroter, the former chairman of the Royal Dutch/Shell Group (which has dual headquarters in the Netherlands and the United Kingdom), once asked his top 50 to 60 leaders to suggest improvements in the company's financial performance. Shell's committee of managing directors decided that a new leadership-development process could be a catalyst for organizational change, and Shell's Leadership and Performance (LEAP) program was created. After the program showed measurable returns in the United States and elsewhere, Shell made it corporatewide.

When James Wolfensohn joined the World Bank as president in 1995, he created a mission statement that continued the bank's longstanding commitment to dispersing knowledge and financial resources but placed a stronger emphasis on the goal of reducing poverty worldwide. The new focus required change. Recognition of that need led to the Executive Development Program (EDP) for managers—a unique collaboration among Harvard Business School, the Kennedy School of Government, Stanford University, INSEAD and IESE (the graduate business school of the University of Navarra, Spain)—which offers five weeks of classroom training and a project to help the bank become more of a world leader.[4]

> The need for a process to build leadership skills has best-practice organizations looking both inside and outside their organizations for approaches that work.

The Five Critical Steps

Pronouncing a strategic vision is not enough to bring about change or to tie leadership development to the company's goals. Our data suggest that there are five critical steps to achieving those ends. (See the sidebar, "Making Leadership Development Strategic.") Examples of each step can be found in the corporate leadership programs of benchmark companies.

Awareness

The need for a process to build leadership skills has best-practice organizations looking both inside and outside their organizations for approaches that work. The foundation of such companies' leadership development is awareness—awareness of external challenges, emerging business opportunities and strategies, internal developmental needs and the ways other leading organizations handle development.

Arthur Andersen uses both internal and external data to determine the learning and development needs of the partners in the firm. Internal data come from client-satisfaction and employee-satisfaction surveys, upward communication and analysis of what the firm calls 450-degree feedback (360-degree feedback plus client evaluations).[5] Arthur Andersen wants to know how its partners are perceived in terms of their technical competence and their responsiveness to customers.

External data about new financial and managerial tools or about challenges in the business environment come from market research, business trends and leading-edge thinkers. The partner-development program also exploits the research Arthur Andersen does while serving clients—and the conversations on emerging trends partners routinely have with leading thinkers in management education and business practice. The PDP also makes use of the literature on new concepts in leadership development.

To ensure that its leadership-and-performance program does not simply react to the immediate needs of the business, Shell's LEAP team has an ongoing conversation with the committee of managing directors (representing all of Shell's geographic and functional areas) about corporate transformation. LEAP staff members negotiate an agreement with the executive of the business unit and the critical players who will go through the program. Together they create budgets for the team project and set time expectations and goals.

To gather external perspectives, Shell has joined the Global Research Consortium, a group of transnational companies that sponsors research. The consortium gives its members the opportunity to hear and discuss the latest on leadership and learning. Like other best-practice companies, Shell also works with consultants and professors to stay abreast of the latest in leadership research.

There is greater awareness today that best-practice organizations' corporate leadership-development function is specifically for strategic issues; more tactical management skills and business-specific challenges are usually left to business units. That seems to work well—corporate leadership efforts in best-practice organizations complement learning experiences within the business units and don't compete with them. Business operations are better equipped to handle their own management-skill training; corporate leadership programs concentrate on helping decision makers become more effective at using those skills.

> All the best-practice leadership programs tap leaders with extensive line experience.

All the best-practice leadership programs tap leaders with extensive line experience. At Arthur Andersen, Johnson & Johnson, and Shell, the heads of the leadership-development process have senior-level business experience. The use of business leaders is based on a belief that participation from executives will help ensure buy-in from the businesses and will keep the programs practical.

GE and Shell International bring in high-potential individuals on two-year rotational assignments to oversee leadership development. HP recruits key people from line positions for the same purpose. In addition to drawing on the business units, best-practice organizations access the experience of individuals in corporate education, human resources and academia. The director of GE's Crotonville center came from a university setting, and the head of World Bank's EDP has a background in corporate education.

Anticipation

Although business cases traditionally focus on the past and best-practice reviews focus on the present, the best leadership-development programs emphasize the future. Top leadership-development companies use anticipatory learning tools: focus groups that explore potential challenges or the impact of emerging technologies, decentralized strategic planning (planning that builds on many organizational levels' imagining of the future), analysis of future scenarios, and the Delphi method (successive rounds of composite predictions used to build awareness and consensus).[6]

Strategy guru Gary Hamel recommends decentralized planning because revolutions are beneficial and they "seldom start with the monarchy."[7] The participative and future-centered Merlin Process is an example of decentralized planning.[8] Managers imagine the organization a decade from the present and describe what it would look like if totally successful. In contrast to more conventional, top-down strategic planning, the Merlin Process has groups throughout the organization describe their ideal. The resulting presentations provide insight and input for senior executives and lead to more formal planning sessions.

From 1993 to 1996, J&J followed that pattern. During its second set of Executive Conferences, executives from around the world worked together for a week with outside consultants to create a vision for a decade later. Participants challenged conventional wisdom about the evolution of the health-care industry and focused on actions their divisions could take to create their future. J&J 2002, an extended scenario developed from future-focused interviews with more than 100 executives in six countries—and from published predictions about the future of health care projected multiple trends and discontinuities. Using a modified Delphi approach, participants assessed the probability and impact of 14 hypothetical developments. An integrative exercise called the Merlin Exercise was used to tie the various aspects of the program together. (A Merlin Process asks people to create a future vision of the company; the Merlin Exercise has participants apply course concepts to that vision.) Participant groups made formal presentations of the desired future to the CEO or the vice chairman.

The Merlin Exercise gets results. Upon being congratulated about a significant promotion to head a new J&J venture, one program graduate responded, "Well, it took almost a year, but I finally got our Merlin." The first step in the envisioned future had become a reality because of his commitment to the potential.

For some organizations, anticipation involves developing a list of the competencies that the company will need. (See the sidebar, "About Competencies.")

Action

Action, not knowledge, is the goal of best-practice leadership-development processes. Best-practice groups bring the world into the classroom, applying real-time business issues to skill development.[9] The answers to tough questions are not in the instructor's head; learners must discover them on the

> ### About Competencies
>
> A majority of the best-practice organizations have identified leadership competencies or at least have tried to define characteristics of successful leaders, but any discussion about competencies is generally controversial. Some even question whether competencies can be defined at all.
>
> Although not all the best-practice partners define competencies, each tries to pinpoint the characteristics of successful leaders within its particular organization. That is also true of the study sponsors, but the best-practice partners were more likely to have developed their competencies internally or with limited use of outside consultants rather than pursuing extensive, formal competency studies. The best-practice companies had more self-confidence about their ability to identify the key skills for leaders. And they made a point of keeping their competencies and developmental activities updated.
>
> Three-fourths of the organizations surveyed believe that once competencies are defined, they should be pursued consistently. Best-practice companies considered position, business unit and geographic location before deciding about which competencies would be considered essential. Johnson & Johnson sent a team around the world to make sure that what made a leader successful in the United States would translate to Europe and Asia. Although some of the wording for its competencies had to change, the behaviors were consistent. (continued on next page)

spot. And with program participants implementing their own recommendations, the learning experience benefits both the organization and the learner. Such action learning can be complicated and costly, however. That is why Arthur Andersen, for example, uses a modified approach that still includes prework and postwork. Before the course begins, the firm gives participants criteria for selecting a client with a business problem and a protocol for interviewing that client. Learners work in a team to develop client recommendations. After the course, the team must make a presentation to the actual client or the program sponsor.

At GE, Welch himself has been the one to choose the action-learning topics for each of the three annual business-management courses and for the annual executive-development course. Participants in both courses are highly motivated to carry out projects, important as they are to the company's direction.

Recommendations made by the participant teams are usually implemented. Students in one management course went to Russia and developed proposals for GE's operations there. A quality report from an individual in another course led to corporatewide adoption of the Six Sigma initiative, a quality-assurance program designed to eliminate defects from all products.

GE also supports what it calls the Change Acceleration Process (CAP), a

> (About Competencies, continued)
>
> Arthur Andersen defines a competency as a statement of the behaviors necessary to perform a job task. Although Arthur Andersen has no organizationwide set of competencies, the partner-development program has created its own list for company partners. It concentrates on nontechnical competencies that apply to all the service lines.
>
> The three broad categories of competencies are business development, personnel development and personal development. The common theme is leadership. The Partner Development Program group aims to develop an Arthur Andersen partner who
>
> - is a change agent
> - plans strategically
> - is globally aware
> - promotes advanced business and professional knowledge
> - is a marketer
> - is a trusted business adviser
> - provides valued integrated services
> - leads the team
> - develops people
> - builds relationships
> - is a skilled communicator
> - develops self
>
> Other companies have competencies geared to their particular business.

systematic attempt to turn managers into professional change agents by disseminating GE's accumulated knowledge about how to initiate, accelerate and secure change. If CAP is successful, says Welch, "people who are comfortable as coaches and facilitators will be the norm at GE. And the other people won't get promoted."[10]

At Johnson & Johnson, the purpose of the third group of Executive Conferences, which started in 1997, was to emphasize J&J's Standards of Leadership (a model developed by key executives working with McKinsey consultants) and to tie the standards to specific business issues through action learning. The principal session lasted five days, with prework and follow-up extending the experience. Before the core session, each operating unit discussed the business topic it would focus on.

Different J&J executives in the various businesses "sponsor" each conference session. Those who choose the topic are asked to pick one that can have significant or transformational impact. Past program topics have included top-line growth, product-development cycles, new-market entries and leadership development. Once the topic is defined, the executive sponsor chooses 50 to 130 program participants, who do additional preparation, such as gathering data and interviewing people in the company who might have some relevant insight.

Participants go through the program and return later for a day to report on implementation results. Typically, the process takes six to nine months. J&J's Executive-Conference approach includes work teams from the business area that is experiencing the problem being studied. The company's action-learning approach at the middle-management level, however, brings together high-potential individuals from all parts of J&J to tackle a more broad-based issue. The Executive-Conference issues aim more at organizational development, whereas middle-management programs focus more on development of individuals' skills.

Alignment

Because best-practice organizations recognize the importance of alignment between leadership development and other corporate functions, they often tie educational efforts to formal succession planning. At a few of our best-practice partners, the leadership-development function and the succession-planning function report to the same executive; other enterprises merely emphasize that a natural link exists.

At J&J, all development functions use 360-degree-feedback evaluations as a part of leadership development. Facilitators assess a multiple-choice, behavioral questionnaire, in which participants rate their performance in many areas and get ratings from supervisors, peers and subordinates. Plans may be made for participants to be coached later or to engage in activities to strengthen weak areas as part of the program, but the facilitators' assessments are not typically fed directly into succession planning.

Although the data were not conclusive, we believe the best companies are beginning to integrate and align assessment, development, feedback, coaching and succession planning. In the integrated model, leadership development becomes an important part of maintaining a steady flow of information throughout an organization and ensuring that top talent is tracked and continues to grow.

GE openly ties leadership development to succession planning. All employees are rated in a nine-block system for the annual Session C review. The review includes discussion about people's performance and their adherence to the values in GE's value statement. The system is an approximation of a typical competency model but was created quickly, simply and with GE self-confidence from a comment by Welch and elaboration by his HR team. It features a chart on which an employee's bottom-line performance is rated on one axis, with adherence to GE values on the other axis. Those who don't make their performance numbers but do adhere to GE values are given a chance to improve those numbers and get a higher rating. Those who make their numbers but don't demonstrate the GE values are rated low in the four-level model, which gauges promotion suitability. Those who do neither are rated lowest.

Senior managers spend most of their resources developing their best and brightest. They see that approach as delivering the most mileage: creating both role models and alignment on what is valued. Crotonville's leadership-development offerings are targeted at high-potential individuals, people the organization refers to as its "A Players." Each year the institute trains about 10,000 of GE's approximately 300,000 employees.

It is commonly said that, at GE, the corporate headquarters owns the top 500 people in the company and just rents them out to the businesses. To encourage the sharing of business talent, GE includes a negative variable in its performance appraisals for managers who hold back talented employees. Outstanding business performance and development of leaders go hand in hand.

Hewlett-Packard provides myriad opportunities for emerging leaders to develop and grow. Platt, the former CEO, recognized that many people who grew up with the founders were retiring and that their immediate successors looked a little too much like one another. He saw that as the company became more global, it would need more diversity of ethnicity and gender. Having a female CEO now may help change perceptions about who is leadership material. And HP's leadership-development process is clearly supportive of diversity goals, providing stretch assignments for the most promising people and making accelerated programs available for individual contributors and first-level managers.

Best-practice organizations use the goals of their leadership-development program as guides to putting the right people in the right programs. The goal of Shell's LEAP program is to create leaders at all levels, so the programs are open to anyone within the organization (although certain programs are targeted for those with the highest potential). GE and HP are more selective about entrance because they want to focus only on those individuals with the potential to move quickly through the ranks.

> Best-practice organizations use the goals of their leadership-development program as guides to putting the right people in the right programs.

Assessment

Best-practice organizations always assess the impact of their leadership-development process. To collect information on the perceived value, the best-practice partners use a number of tools and techniques. The Kirkpatrick Four-Level Model of Evaluation (participant reaction, knowledge acquired, behavioral change, business results) is typical.[11] Participants, human-resource-development staff, consultants and, in some instances, financial staff, do the assessments—the latter weighing program expenditures' return on investment. (See the sidebar, "An Executive Primer.")

Most best-practice partners use an assessment method called the Kirkpatrick levels to quantify the effect of leadership programs on business results. But both the study sponsors and best-practice partners use other met-

An Executive Primer

Five Steps Help Managers Get the Most from Leadership-Development Programs

Awareness—Make it a point to interview key executives about leadership development. Keep a record of your findings to use in succession planning and human-resource-development (HRD) initiatives. Insist that the head of HRD or your chief learning officer brief you on at least one conference per year that reflects the latest thinking on leadership development. Ask other key members of HRD to prepare short summaries of events they attend at corporate expense.

Anticipation—Start your meetings (with managers at all levels) with a request for the most significant trend or prediction that they think will affect your business. Ask them to summarize the most forward-thinking article, book or presentation to help you learn and to get colleagues thinking in anticipatory terms. Be sure that current challenges don't keep you from focusing on the future of your company. Define possible scenarios and how you would respond.

Action—Ask your HRD team members which business results have originated from your company's educational programs. Discuss the strategic initiatives that need their implementation assistance. Explore how you can use executive learning to make such initiatives happen more quickly and effectively.

Alignment—Look at your performance-management system (performance appraisals), your succession-planning profiles, your major education and development agendas and possibly a "competency model." Observe the consistency and alignment among the documents. Make sure they reflect a consistent set of terms, values and models. If they don't, work to align them more closely.

Assessment—Evaluate whether your leadership-development activities have been successful. Ask for evidence that programs reflect standards of success when you authorize a budget. (Shell doesn't consider a program valuable unless its returns are 25 times greater than its cost. Johnson & Johnson has feedback to assess observable performance change in key leaders.)

Overall—Think about how you want HRD, in general, and education, in particular, to support your strategic efforts. How must you change your human-resource profiles so that your company can become what you want it to be?

rics, too—including corporate performance, customer satisfaction and employee satisfaction. In general, best-practice partners were more aggressive than sponsors about measuring and evaluating program effectiveness.

Of all the best-practice organizations, Arthur Andersen is probably the most dedicated to assessment—and has reaped the benefits. The vast amounts of data the firm collects not only demonstrate the partner-development program's correlation with improved business results, but also show where the organization needs to head.

Although measurement is expensive and sometimes tricky, its benefits cannot be discounted. Arthur Andersen combines impact research with participants' course evaluations. Program attendees fill out evaluation forms before they take the class, immediately after the class is finished and three months later. The forms contain questions about the knowledge participants believe they have gained.

The impact research consists of comparing, course by course, partners who have attended PDP with those who have not. The results show that attendance increases both client satisfaction and per-hour billings. Impact research is done in a two-year cycle, with information gathered on partners a year before the program and a year after.

The use of both participant-satisfaction and impact-research measures helps provide a balanced set of results. Arthur Andersen found that one of its programs was not getting a high participant-satisfaction rating, but an impact analysis showed that the program was having a greater effect than any of PDP's other courses. (But, PDP staff members prefer to see both strong satisfaction and strong impact, so if partners have a low level of satisfaction the course will not be recommended.)

Regression analysis shows that course duration is an important factor in how satisfied participants are. The perception that a course is too long has a negative effect. (However, a belief that the program length is appropriate does not by itself improve overall satisfaction.)

Another key factor in determining satisfaction is whether program participants have similar levels of familiarity with the topic. What may be an exciting concept for one person could be old news to another. Arthur Andersen believes that moving to a problem-based course design will help it address different levels of participant knowledge.

To Shell's LEAP staff, a program adds value only if the team project generates revenues at least 25 times greater than the project's cost (a 25:1 ROI). During the initial contracting process, a LEAP staff member and the leader of the business unit determine the desired project outcomes, including financial targets. The business leader expresses his or her objectives in sending the candidate to the program; in many cases that defines the program and problem the team or individual will address.

You get what you pay for. Best-practice companies do consider costs, but their main focus is on the value the program can provide. When asked to rank the importance of various criteria in selecting an outside vendor, the companies put fees near the bottom of the list. Arthur Andersen invests approximately 6 percent of total revenues in education (more than $30 million). If

> Although measurement is expensive and sometimes tricky, its benefits cannot be discounted.

course offerings achieve their objective to improve business results, support is likely to continue.

Cost for each participant in the executive-development program at the World Bank is $22,000, which includes travel, lodging and business school fees for three modules and for the Grass-Roots Immersion Program (which gives managers one-week stints in a developing-country village or urban neighborhood so they can acquire a firsthand understanding of poverty). The cost is not charged back to the business groups but funded centrally through the bank's $12 million annual executive-education budget.

The New Strategic Reality of Leadership Development

Globalization, deregulation, e-commerce and rapid technological change are forcing companies to reevaluate the way they operate. Approaches that have worked for years are no longer effective. Development of leaders who think strategically is increasingly a source of sustainable competitive advantage. Hence observations of companies known for excellent leadership-development practices can be invaluable.

Leadership development has become too specialized to relegate to human-resource departments. In best-practice companies, top-level managers get involved. Without their support, leadership-development processes would founder. Of course, corporate leaders are more likely to offer support if programs are producing business results. By monitoring the effectiveness of the leadership-development processes, capitalizing on quick wins and communicating successes throughout the organization, the best-practice companies sustain a virtuous cycle.

Development groups such as Arthur Andersen's PDP and the one at GE's Crotonville site emphasize diligent crafting of programs, careful listening, constant monitoring and frequent communication. That helps senior executives understand how a leadership-development process can shape and disseminate an organization's culture, overcome resistance to change and achieve strategic goals.

At GE, the corporate leadership-development group endeavors to maintain buy-in. It interviews company leaders around the world on a regular basis to gauge future business needs and the characteristics future leaders should have. Additionally, the group at Crotonville identifies early adopters of a given development initiative and leverages their support.

Hewlett-Packard has garnered support for its leadership-development process by having both the CEO and senior managers participate in its programs. The executives serve as mentors, faculty and supporters in leadership-development design and programs.

Senior-level support for Johnson & Johnson's executive conferences is evi-

Leadership development has become too specialized to relegate to human-resource departments. In best-practice companies, top-level managers get involved.

denced by the fact that either the chairman or a member of the company's executive committee participates in each session, articulating J&J's credo and values—and the program's link to business success.

Although the best-practice firms differ in their emphasis on making leadership development strategic, the development program of each includes elements of the five critical steps:

- building awareness of external challenges, emerging strategies, organizational needs and what leading firms do to meet the needs;
- employing anticipatory learning tools to recognize potential external events, envision the future and focus on action the organization can take to create its own future;
- taking action by tying leadership-development programs to solving important, challenging business issues;
- aligning leadership development with performance assessment, feedback, coaching and succession planning; and
- assessing impact of the leadership-development process on individual behavioral changes and organizational success.

Most people, even if they have heard of the specific leadership-development practices of Johnson & Johnson or GE, have not grasped how to manage an integrated set of variables in order to achieve excellence in developing executives. Increasing the budget for education or changing the name of a training department to "corporate university" doesn't guarantee improved performance. Our study shows that, despite the diversity of approaches to leadership development in the best-practice companies, all share common goals: anticipating, supporting and aligning the organization's strategic initiatives with development, as well as gaining and sustaining competitive advantage. And increasingly, those companies choose an action-oriented, ongoing learning process closely linked to the strategic needs of the business.

References

1. "Industry Report 1998: Training Budgets," *Training*, October 1998, 47. See also: Jennifer Reingold, Mica Schneider and Kerry Capell, "Learning to Lead," *Business Week*, Oct. 18, 1999: 76.
2. John A. Byrne, "PepsiCo's New Formula," *Business Week*, April 10, 2000, 172; and Thomas A. Stewart, "How to Leave It All Behind," *Fortune*, Dec. 6, 1999, 345-348.
3. George Hollenbeck and Wesley Vestal, eds., *Developing Leaders at All Levels* (Houston: American Productivity & Quality Center, 1999); and Robert M. Fulmer, Joe Camillus and Justin McMorrow, eds., *Leadership Development: Building Executive Talent* (Houston: American Productivity & Quality Center and American Society for Training & Development, 1999).

4. Albert A. Vicere and Robert M. Fulmer, *Leadership by Design* (Boston: Harvard Business School Press, 1998), 218-223.
5. Arthur Andersen uses the term "450-degree feedback" to emphasize that feedback from clients is included in the process. Technically, 360-degree feedback is feedback from four quadrants of perspective: boss, subordinates, peers and customers. Respondents rate themselves.
6. For example, see: Michael A. Hammer and Steven A. Stanton, "The Power of Reflection," *Fortune*, Nov. 24, 1997, 291-295.
7. Gary Hamel, "Strategy as Revolution," *Harvard Business Review* 74 (July-August 1996): 69-81; and Gary Hamel, *Leading the Revolution* (Boston: Harvard Business School Press, 2000).
8. Robert M. Fulmer and S. Perret, "The Merlin Exercise: Future by Forecast or Future by Invention?" *Journal of Management Development* 12 (no. 6, 1993), 44-53.
9. For example, see: Stratford Sherman, "How Tomorrow's Leaders Are Learning Their Stuff," *Fortune*, Nov. 27, 1995, 90-98; and Thomas A. Stewart, "Telling Tales at BP Amoco," *Fortune*, June 7, 1999, 220-223.
10. "General Electric: The House That Jack Built," *The Economist*, Sept. 18, 1999, 23-27.
11. Donald L. Kirkpatrick, *Evaluating Training Programs: The Four Levels* (San Francisco: Berrett-Koehler, 1994).

Robert M. Fulmer is Distinguished Visiting Professor in the Graziadio School of Business, Pepperdine University. He is a co-author of Leadership by Design *(Harvard Business School Press, 1998) and* The Leadership Advantage *(AMACOM, 2000) and the author of* The New Management *(Prentice Hall, 1987). E-mail him at robert.fulmer@business.wm.edu.*

Philip A. Gibbs is a visiting professor at the College of William and Mary, where he teaches strategic management and mergers and acquisitions. E-mail him at philip.gibbs@business.wm.edu.

Marshall Goldsmith is co-founder of Keilty, Goldsmith & Co. He has collaborated on nine books, including The Leader of the Future *(Jossey-Bass, 1997),* The Leadership Advantage *(AMACOM, 2000), and* Coaching for Leadership *(Jossey-Bass, 2000). E-mail him at marshall@kgcnet.com.*

Quality Transformation

CULTURAL TRANSFORMATION

Rethinking Empowerment: Why Is It So Hard to Achieve?

W. Alan Randolph

You don't empower people, you acknowledge the power they have. However, in traditional hierarchical organizations, that's tough to do—just as it's tough to implement quality practices in a hierarchical organization as well. This article explores why organizations have such a tough time creating an empowering environment and the kinds of changes needed to actually have an empowered workforce. Of course, these are also the changes needed to successfully implement quality management.

To date, empowerment remains one of the most promising, yet mystifying, concepts in business. First introduced into the corporate world in the 1980s, it quickly became a buzzword with great promise. So far, however, it has had only selective impact. The attraction was simple to understand; senior managers covet employees who accept responsibility, take a proprietary interest in their work, and willingly work hard. At the same time, employees want to feel valued, involved in their jobs, and proud of their work.

The bottom-line is that managers and employees want very compatible outcomes—outcomes associated with empowerment. Why then, has it been so hard for most companies to find real empowerment? Why has the concept fallen into such disrepute? My research and experience in a wide variety of companies has taught me that the answer is at the same time simple and complex. It is time to rethink our understanding of this powerful tool.

Reprinted from *Organizational Dynamics*, Vol. 29, No. 2, W. Alan Randolph, "Rethinking Empowerment: Why Is It So Hard to Achieve?" copyright © 2000 with permission from Elsevier Science.

Not a Flawed Concept

The concept of empowerment is not flawed. Indeed, many companies in a variety of industries have successfully created cultures of empowerment. The list includes such well known companies as General Electric Co., Pacific Gas & Electric, Marriott Corp., and a variety of lesser-known companies like ABS Corporation in Virginia, Springfield Remanufacturing Corporation in Missouri, and Chesapeake Packaging Company in Maryland. Yes, empowerment can work and can work very well. But achieving it means turning inside out the assumptions about how managers and employees interact. Few managers and employees really understand empowerment, and they understand even less about how to shake free of their traditional, hierarchical mindsets and behavior patterns, and how to adopt a mindset and repertoire of behaviors consistent with empowerment. Whether we focus on managers or employees, the problem boils down to the need for massive change in people and organizational systems.

This paper will explore the core elements of empowerment and examine why people's ingrained assumptions about organizations make empowerment both difficult to comprehend and even harder to achieve. It will also focus on the complex interplay between organizational and human systems that must be changed if movement to empowerment is to occur. The creation of this new, very different culture will be broken down into three stages, and I will show how three interlocking tools build on a foundation of information flows to resolve the wide array of issues that arise at each stage of changing to empowerment.

Just What Is Empowerment?

My informal yet extensive research in a wide variety of companies indicates that most managers continue to define empowerment as "giving people the power to make decisions." Although relocating the locus of decision-making is a critical part of the empowerment process, that step alone is just another manifestation of the manager acting as director and controller. The manager still mandates the decisions people are allowed to make. This definition of empowerment also misses the essential point that people already possess a great deal of power—power that resides in their knowledge, experience, and internal motivation. To achieve real empowerment managers must embrace this wider concept and must focus on ways to "release the power within people to achieve astonishing results." Sounds simple, right? Well, not so fast! There are other players who can inhibit this release of power.

Employees, too, misunderstand empowerment. Many of them feel that empowerment means they will be given free rein to do as they please and the freedom to make all the key decisions about their jobs. Employees often fail to grasp that empowerment means sharing risks and responsibilities as the price for freedom to act, pride in their work, and ownership of their jobs. Indeed, empowerment entails much greater accountability for employees than in a hierarchical culture. But it is precisely this frightening increase in responsibility that creates a sense of engagement and fulfillment on the job. Empowerment is a strange combination of opportunity and risk.

In one retail food company, senior management became intrigued with the idea of "empowering their people." They held an all-company meeting and announced that they would begin to increase the decision-making options for people at all levels of the organization. As they did so, they were surprised to find that little if any change in people's behavior was noticeable. The middle managers were extremely concerned about losing control of the results for which they were held accountable; hence they withheld critical information from their employees. And the employees were scared to act for fear of making a mistake for which they might then be punished. Within two short months senior management decided empowerment would not work for them, and the idea was abandoned.

Needless to say, many other companies have given up, too. The journey to empowerment is a long and arduous trek, made especially difficult by misunderstandings of what empowerment really is. The journey requires managers and employees to challenge their most basic assumptions about how organizations should operate and how managers and employees should interact in pursuing organizational goals. Significant changes in individual and collective behaviors are essential. Simply announcing the destination will not be sufficient; neither will a traditional approach to organizational change. Fundamental changes in manager and employee skills, attitudes and relationships are needed. That means starting small, and adding leverage points that allow people to gradually grasp the purpose of empowerment, learn new attitudes, and develop new sets of skills. Getting to empowerment requires massive changes for everyone involved—a daunting task, indeed.

> Getting to empowerment requires massive changes for everyone involved—a daunting task, indeed.

Core Issues in Changing to Empowerment

To understand the magnitude of the changes that are needed to move to empowerment, it is helpful to focus first at the level of individuals, regardless of their organizational position. Chris Argyris has insightfully identified the two types of commitment on which progress toward empowerment turns. *External commitment* is consistent with old-style command and control (or hierarchical) forms of organization. It typifies the operating contract between managers and employees in hierarchical organizations. At every level of an organization built on *external commitment,* managers:

- Define tasks for employees at the level below.
- Specify the behaviors required to perform those tasks.
- Define performance goals for employees.

- Specify the priority of employee goals.

By contrast, *internal commitment* is more consistent with working in a culture of empowerment. It defines a qualitatively different operating contract between managers and employees, which requires a significant shift in the locus of responsibility. In an organization built on *internal commitment*, people engage in relationships, as follows:

- Individuals define their own tasks in the context of the company's vision and objectives, which are set by management.
- Individuals determine the behaviors and action plan required to perform their tasks.
- Managers and employees jointly define performance goals for individuals.
- Employees and managers specify the priority of individual goals and how they relate to company goals.

The vast difference between external commitment and internal commitment is made clear by these bullet points. The visible gulf in ownership, responsibility, and involvement makes it possible for us to understand just how difficult it is to change from a command-and-control culture to a world of empowerment.

Past History Blocks Change

Lest we jump to the conclusion that it would be far easier to create a culture of empowerment from scratch—by starting a new company—think again. Although it may be easier to create this new culture from the ground up, it is not at all simple. People are at the core of the process, and most people have a history of exposure to command-and-control thinking. Indeed, most of us are quite accustomed to operating in ways that are consistent with external commitment. The following questions have been and are all too familiar to each of us. "What do my parents want me to do? What does the school want me to do to get good grades? What does my boss want me to do?" Moreover, we have invested a lifetime in learning answers to these questions that meet the expectations of hierarchical thinking and assumptions. We are far less accustomed to dealing with the questions of internal commitment. "How do I want to contribute to the needs of my family? What do I want to learn from this school? How will I know I have learned something I can use? What do I need to do to help my company succeed?" These are the questions that arise when a corporate culture begins to support internal commitment. Managers and employees alike must learn to answer them if they are to operate successfully in a culture of empowerment.

To complicate things further, many of us possess hard-earned parenting, teaching, and managing skills that fulfill role expectations for leaders based

Rethinking Empowerment: Why Is It So Hard to Achieve?

on an assumption of external commitment. Indeed, we feel it is our responsibility as parents, teachers, or managers to tell people what to do, how to do it, and (sometimes) why it needs to be done. We feel as though it would almost be avoiding our responsibility to ask children, students, or employees such questions as, "What do you think needs to be done and why is it important? What do you think your goals should be? How do you think you should go about achieving your goals?"

I can recall a very interesting discussion in one of my consulting client organizations. As we worked hard to develop the skills and attitudes for a team-based culture, we kept encountering the same theme over and over again. No matter how much we discussed team decision-making, employees and managers could not get beyond the thought that eventually one person would have to make the final decision. They could imagine no way that a team could make a decision. Sure they could discuss options and provide input, but a final decision would have to be made by one person. At first I thought this might be unique to this engineering organization, but I have encountered this same phenomenon in numerous other settings.

Team decision-making and other aspects of an empowerment culture are part of a strange, new world for most of us. We have much to learn about how to operate there comfortably and effectively. Indeed, we have a long journey of learning ahead of us. We must learn new skills, new attitudes, new behaviors, new ways of relating, and even a new language.

An analogy might lead to further understanding the magnitude of the needed changes. Imagine you are a U.S. citizen working for a North American company. You learn that your company has been purchased by a Brazilian corporation, and starting next month your company is to operate according to Brazilian laws and customs, adhere to Brazilian cultural norms, and that henceforth, everyone must only communicate in Portuguese. You would likely feel a tremendous sense of "How will I ever do that? What does that really mean for me? And will I be able to make the changes that will be necessary to succeed in the new culture?" Moving to a culture of empowerment is a lot like this cultural shift. People may think the end result sounds interesting, even exciting, but they will have real concerns once they grasp the magnitude and difficulty of the long journey ahead.

The Language Differences

To gain a more in-depth understanding of the differences between the command-and-control, hierarchical culture, to which most people have become accustomed, and a new and different culture of empowerment, one need look no further than the languages used in the two cultures. The differences are not unlike the differences between, say, American English and Brazilian Portuguese. Consider the following lists of words, and compare them row by row:

Hierarchical Culture	Empowerment Culture
Planning	Visioning
Command and control	Partnering for performance
Monitoring	Self-monitoring
Individual responsiveness	Team responsibility
Pyramid structures	Cross-functional structures
Workflow processes	Projects
Managers	Coaches/team leaders
Employees	Team members
Participative management	Self-directed teams
Do as you are told	Own your own job
Compliance	Good judgment

As you compare the words in the two lists, the differences in attitude, norms, expectations, and associated behaviors become clear. For example, "planning" suggests that someone (usually the manager) knows where we are going and the best way to get there—we just have to follow the leader. "Visioning" suggests that someone points where we want to go (perhaps the manager again), but how we get there is left open for discussion and subject to the judgment of everyone involved. Further, "monitoring" suggests that someone (usually the manager) should check on each individual's performance and provide performance evaluations and feedback. "Self-monitoring" suggests that everyone possesses requisite goal clarity and measurement skills, as well as access to relevant data. Thus armed, they can check their own performance and make the behavior adjustments needed to stay on goal. And one more example, "Do as you are told" exemplifies the external commitment attitude in behavioral terms. Once you are told what to do, you can do it, but please do not use your intellect or judgment, and do not be too concerned about results—that is the manager's job. "Own your own job," on the other hand, exemplifies the internal commitment attitude. It suggests that, in a culture of empowerment, you care about results and use your intellect and judgment to decide how to achieve individual, team and company success.

This final example may best clarify the key distinction between a hierarchical culture and a culture of empowerment. In the former, individuals do what they are told—to a fault. Even when they know a task is not being done the best way, or that it may be altogether the wrong task, they may continue to do it in a spirit of malicious compliance. Why? Because that is what they are rewarded for, what they are expected to do, and what they have been conditioned to do over a lifetime of exposure to hierarchical management.

A colleague of mine once experienced an amazing incident in a bakery. The server behind the counter insisted that my colleague "take a number for better service," so that everyone could be served in the order in which they arrived. The only problem was that it was 5 a.m., and my colleague was the only customer in the store. Now, you may think this is strange and wonder

> Once you are told what to do, you can do it, but please do not use your intellect or judgment, and do not be too concerned about results—that is the manager's job.

how this server could be so dumb. But the fact is that the server had been so conditioned, so rewarded, and so trained to follow procedure (or risk severe reprimand) that he did so even though he knew better. In a way it was his way of following commands to a fault as a form of malicious compliance.

In a culture of empowerment, individuals respond very differently. They take the risk of challenging a task or procedure that they feel is not in the best interest of the organization. What compels them to act is a sense of pride in their jobs and a feeling of proprietary ownership of the results. They think about what makes sense in the situation and they act in ways that both serve the customer and achieve company goals and results. But where do we find such individuals, or better yet, how are individuals transformed into empowered people?

Empowered People

Some writers have suggested that, "Empowered people empower themselves." They argue that empowerment is not something managers do to their people. But that begs the question, "How do people empower themselves in a hierarchical culture?" Or more importantly, "How do they empower themselves when their life experiences have taught them how to operate in a hierarchical environment but not in an empowered culture?" My research in over 25 companies and with hundreds of people in those companies during the past 15 years suggests that it is futile to wait for people to become empowered in a command and control organization. They will not take the risks, and they will not be comfortable with the necessary levels of internal commitment. In short, they lack the skills, attitude, and behaviors needed to act empowered. My research also suggests that traditional change programs—comprised as they are of sequential steps that start with defining a vision of empowerment and planning a strategy to get there are not adequate to the task of driving the needed changes in people and systems.

> How do employees empower themselves when their life experiences have taught them how to operate in a hierarchical environment but not in an empowered culture?

In fact, to think of moving to empowerment as a sequential process of changing towards a new state is so badly flawed that it may doom the entire effort, despite everyone's good intentions. Applying sequential-change thinking to the journey to empowerment just does not acknowledge the scope and complexity of the challenge. An example may help illustrate what I mean.

People Do Not Change Easily

Several years ago I was involved as a consultant with a company that wanted to move to a team-based culture of involvement and empowerment. We were engaged in a year-long effort of training, behavioral change, and systems change. The process was well designed and orderly and appeared to be going smoothly. But one day after about six months and at the end of a training session, a veteran employee (20 years with the company) approached me and said, "This team stuff is really good and could make a significant difference, but you know, this too shall pass." I responded, "Excuse me, what do you mean?" He proceeded to explain that he had seen many great new ideas brought forth in the company, and that most of them started with a flash—only to die out after a few months, as the company embraced a new concept. He was essentially telling me that sequential-change processes that start with a big introduction usually fail when the going gets hard. He would just sit tight, not change and wait for the next idea. Beneath the surface, though, was another aspect that I saw in his face. He was scared to try to make the change, because he was not sure he could do it successfully. He had been relatively successful for 20 years in a hierarchical culture, and he could not imagine succeeding in such a radically new team culture. Both managers and employees and the supporting systems were failing to drive change in this organization.

A Complex and Endless Journey

This example is informative in helping us understand that the journey to empowerment is both complex and in many ways endless. Furthermore, it is strewn with multifaceted, counterintuitive, and nonlinear processes. The change demands that managers and employees unlearn old habits and assumptions that reinforce the hierarchy and inhibit empowerment. They must institute new habits and assumptions that allow the power within people to be released to achieve astonishing results. At the same time, many organizational systems, procedures, and operating methods must also change. And people throughout the organization must acquire the skills and desire to use the power they possess.

The bottom-line is that we do not need a better program to lead us toward empowerment. Nor can we expect management's announcement of the destination to mean that we are there. Instead, to make the fundamental and needed changes in the mindset and behaviors of individuals throughout the organization, and in their basic assumptions about working toward goals, requires an extensive and pervasive change effort. It means changing a complex, interacting set of systems, procedures, relationships, expectations, and consequences. The irony is that the needed change method is both extensive and simple. It is not a program, but rather an involved *process* of change, often employing counterintuitive techniques and evolving plans unique to each organization and its people. It means understanding and appreciating just how different empowerment is for everyone and then starting where people *are* in their current zone of comfort. The foundation for the process of change is information flow, but it involves two other interlocking elements and a gradual, persistent, and sensitive journey to empowerment.

So How Do We Achieve a Culture of Empowerment?

Research and experience have shown that when significant and fundamental changes are to be made in the behaviors of people in organizations, individuals manifest a variety of predictable concerns, sometimes directly but more often indirectly. To complete a process of changing to this strange culture of empowerment, it is essential to recognize, address, and readdress these concerns as they arise. Indeed, it is most helpful to understand that there are three distinct (but overlapping) major stages of concern that people experience as the process of changing to a culture of empowerment unfolds. These three major stages can be labeled as (1) *starting and orienting the process of change,* (2) *making changes and dealing with discouragement,* and (3) *adopting and refining empowerment to fit the organization.* Below I will discuss these stages and the issues that arise for people at each stage. I will also focus on three interlocking tools for empowerment that can be used in different ways, at each stage, to keep the process moving forward. These three tools are built upon a foundation of information flows and new structures for guiding the behaviors of people throughout the organization. The interlocking tools are *sharing information, creating autonomy through boundaries,* and *replacing the hierarchy with self-directed teams.* As I discuss the issues at each stage, I will show how these tools help address the relevant issues that arise.

Stage 1—Starting and Orienting the Process of Change

The long journey to empowerment begins with a need for *starting and orienting the process of change.* The challenge here is not to provide a big picture of the destination. Instead, it is to start taking some initial steps from where people are at present, and to have the steps founded initially in new forms of information sharing. Why information sharing first? At this stage individuals want answers to questions that relate primarily to *information* and *personal* concerns. Although it may seem logical to start with a clear vision of the empowered organization that is desired, such efforts fail to answer the initial questions on people's minds—questions that may not be explicitly stated, but are there just the same. People do not want to be told about a vision of empowerment and how it will benefit the company. Instead, they want answers to two types of preliminary questions:

Information Concerns: Why is the change needed? What is wrong with the way things are now? (Even if they do not like everything about how things are now, at least they understand them!) What is the change anyway? In short, people do not want to be *sold* on the change; they want to be told about it and learn why it is necessary.

Personal Concerns: How will the change impact me? What is in it for me? Will I win or lose by the change? How will I find the time to make the change?

> The long journey to empowerment begins with a need for *starting and orienting the process of change.*

People wonder if they have the skills and knowledge to make the change—they sense that it may not be all that easy.

Unless these initial concerns are addressed, they will continue to impede the journey to empowerment, by continually rising up and blocking progress. Fortunately, the three empowerment tools can help address these questions and get the process of change started.

The Experience of a Cable TV Company

At one cable TV company, senior management tried to start the movement to empowerment with a vision of a new type of organization, but the change process quickly broke down as people flooded management with a deluge of questions like the ones listed above. It became very clear that people lacked sufficient *information* to participate effectively in clarifying the vision and to give it meaning related to their jobs. They were more interested in why change was needed than in what the end result would be for the organization. Unless people can make sense of a new company vision as it relates to their jobs, it will be just another plaque on the wall. The tool that addresses this issue is not a better vision, but simply *sharing information* about the company and its performance, market share, profitability, measures of quality, waste rates, and so forth.

Senior managers in this company were, fortunately, good listeners and were not afraid to "open up the company books to employees." They began to hold company meetings and share information that had heretofore been only for their eyes. Gradually, they began to use their information technology system to make important unit and company information available to everyone on an "as-needed" basis. In other words, management started treating people throughout the organization like valued decision-makers. With this new information in hand, managers and employees could work together to understand why changes were needed, and what a new vision would mean to everyone. In other words, people were receiving answers to their questions of *information concerns*, which in turn helped them begin to act with responsibility and engagement.

Indeed, I have found that people without information cannot be empowered to act with responsibility; once they have information, they are almost compelled to act with responsibility. Sharing information seems to tap a natural desire in people to want to do a good job and to help make things better. With current information technology capabilities, there is no reason why anyone throughout an organization cannot have ready access to any information they need to do a better job.

Another powerful by-product of information sharing occurred in the cable TV companies. Opening up the books signaled to people that they were trusted and valued colleagues with management. This element is vital if empowerment is to be achieved. Information sharing kick-started the rebuilding and

> I have found that people without information cannot be empowered to act with responsibility; once they have information, they are almost compelled to act with responsibility.

Rethinking Empowerment: Why Is It So Hard to Achieve?

enhancing of trust throughout the organization. It allowed people to gain a clearer picture of the challenges facing the company and to discover how success would be based on a new and demanding sense of responsibility for everyone in the company.

At the same time, senior management feared they would lose control by sharing "their information" more broadly. There was tremendous anxiety for both managers and employees as the process of change began. But by starting slowly, sharing some new information—but not everything—and sharing in a public forum where it could be explained, everyone learned the power of information sharing to address their *information concerns*, build trust and responsibility, and alleviate senior management fears.

It Takes More Than Information Sharing

Although information sharing helps to kick-start the journey to empowerment, it alone cannot keep things moving. Indeed, the possession of information will stimulate questions of *personal concerns*. Though people may not openly express it, they have concerns about whether they will be able to operate successfully in the new culture of empowerment. They wonder whether they will be able to learn the language and skills needed to be effectively empowered. Without information people cannot assume responsibility; given information, they may want to be responsible, but realize they lack some needed skills and hence the confidence to change.

Enter the second interlocking tool for empowerment, *creating autonomy through boundaries*. But is not this somewhat counter-intuitive? Can you free people for empowerment by creating boundaries? Yes, but only if we remember, as pointed out earlier, that people are unfamiliar with the language, skills, and attitudes of responsibility that make empowerment possible. Senior management needs to set boundaries within which people can use the information they now are receiving to act with freedom and responsibility, gradually expanding the boundaries as people's competence and confidence to act empowered grows.

The use of clearly articulated goals is one example of setting boundaries. The sense of empowerment comes in leaving the action plan for individual employees to determine, perhaps in consultation with their managers or with peers. Setting boundaries also means providing skill training—for example, in how to read a budget, analyze an exceptions report, or run a meeting—in short, learning the skills needed to become empowered to act with responsibility. We must remember that people in the company probably have not had much experience with being empowered; they need time and guidance to develop the skills of empowerment. It is important to note, though, that boundaries are used differently in empowerment than in a hierarchy. In a culture of empowerment, boundaries define the domains within which people have autonomy and responsibility to operate; like rubber bands, they stretch

Enter the second interlocking tool for empowerment, creating autonomy through boundaries.

as people develop new skills. In a hierarchy, boundaries define what people cannot do; they operate more like barbed wire to keep people in limits.

Linking in the Third Tool for Empowerment

The third empowerment tool, *replacing the hierarchy with self-directed teams*, works in conjunction with the first two to speed up the journey to empowerment. To reach and operate in a culture of empowerment means developing and relying on teams to run the show. Why? Quite simply, because empowered teams are capable of much more than the sum of empowered individuals. Team members can help each other interpret and use the shared information more effectively; they can help each other clarify boundaries and make good decisions within the context of ever-expanding boundaries and responsibilities. But keep in mind that teams do not start off in an empowered mode. Indeed, they must develop the competencies and motivations to form self-directed teams that take on responsibility. During the first stage of the journey, teams are not yet ready for self-direction.

> To reach and operate in a culture of empowerment means developing and relying on teams to run the show.

In one manufacturing company, management combined the benefits of information sharing with team development by sharing information aggregated at the level of the teams. Essentially, they broke the company into team-level profit centers. Data were prepared to help the teams know their own productivity, waste percentage, quality measures and profitability. In monthly general company meetings, these data were shared for everyone to see. Teams could compare themselves to other teams and get ideas from others about how to improve their own results. Over time, the teams became quite comfortable with a new sense of responsibility, but not before they went through some times of discouragement.

Stage 2—Making Changes and Dealing with Discouragement

In time, and if the Stage 1 issues are reasonably well addressed, the journey will move into a second and disturbing stage, *making changes and dealing with discouragement*, a territory where people encounter yet more complicated issues and concerns. It is in this valley of discouragement that many managers and employees give up on empowerment and try to go back to their old way of doing things. They bemoan the decision to take the first steps toward empowerment, and now find themselves even more distrusting of each other. The issues people express in this stage will transition to a focus on *implementation* and *impact* concerns:

Implementation Concerns: What do I do now to become empowered? What must I do next? How do I manage all the details so I do it right? What happens if it does not work out as planned? Where do I go for help? How long will this change take? Are our difficulties typical? People want to have some clarity on how to move forward, as well as some empathy for how hard this change is. A strong fear of failure develops.

Impact Concerns: Is the effort really worth it? Is this change making a difference for the organization and me? Are we making any positive progress and how do we know? People want to know if their efforts are paying off, because change is so hard. But as a few people begin to recognize signs of progress, they will begin to sell each other on the value of empowerment. Slow and painful progress is being made, though many people do not yet see it.

At this stage, people throughout the organization need to be heard. To some extent, everyone, from top to bottom, is feeling confused and discouraged. They wonder why the change to empowerment is taking so long. Why is it so hard? Whose fault is it that this change is so difficult—surely not mine? Things probably seem worse than before, and a natural desire arises to return to the way things were.

The Feeling of Being Lost

Inevitably, during the second stage of the journey, people throughout the organization will feel a tremendous sense of being lost. We might compare this stage with sky diving for the first time. You and others have jumped from the plane and are in free fall. Now you begin to wonder where the ground is and whether the parachute will open. Perhaps equally important, you realize there is no going back! At this stage, people become very interested in the details of the empowerment process. Their *implementation concerns* are expressed in their desire to know what specific steps to take, how to manage all the details, and what to do when things do not go according to "plan." They sense the tremendous effort needed to make the journey to empowerment—perhaps for the first time realizing the true immensity of the task.

They will quite likely also feel a fear of failure, which they express by asking for detailed plans for action so they cannot be blamed for failure. There is a tendency to want to retreat to the old hierarchical model of doing what they are told to do. People throughout the organization are beginning to realize that empowerment means more freedom to operate, but also that it entails far more accountability than a command-and-control environment. In the old hierarchical culture, people were protected from responsibility as long as they did what they were told. In an empowered culture, their work and its results (positive or negative) are exposed for everyone to see. That is a scary proposition for most people.

During the discouraging stage of being lost and lacking the skills for empowered action, people need a great deal of guidance. They also need to find answers to their questions that relate to *implementation* and *impact concerns*. And some *information* and *personal concerns* continue to linger. The three interlocking tools for empowerment again prove useful for responding to these issues.

Information sharing can show people the impact of their efforts on business results. Seeing and understanding this impact provides incentive to keep moving forward. People can also use information to adjust their efforts, avoiding problems before they become too severe. In the manufacturing company mentioned before, the team-based information gradually began to reveal positive results. Competition among the teams served as an incentive for continuous improvement, and seeing their measures improve from month to month served as a powerful reward for their efforts to take on increased responsibility.

Before these feelings of success occur, the teams frequently feel a sense of frustration, which is based on the clear realization that they are not succeeding in all areas of responsibility. Oddly enough, this is the time to extend the boundaries of autonomy and to increase the expectations of teams. Rather than allowing people to succumb to their anxiety, the teams need to be pushed to use the information they now possess to set broader team goals that test and reward them for even more progress. Managers must help the teams continue *creating autonomy through boundaries* by working with them to set challenging but attainable goals. Then they must hold the teams accountable for results but leave it up to them to determine how to get the job done. In other words, let the *teams be a little more self-directed* and a little more responsible and autonomous.

Discouragement in an Information Services Company

In one information services company, as the teams encountered discouragement, management asked them to use the information at their disposal, which included the company's strategic business plan, to set three or four team goals and individual goals. Goals were subsequently clarified during meetings with managers. But the employees retained the primary responsibility for setting and achieving their individual and team goals. Initially, there was resistance to taking on this responsibility; employees neither felt they had the skills to set their own goals, nor did they want to be held accountable for the results. In time, team members helped each other, and the employees came to like the idea. They developed the sense of ownership and self-confidence that derives from being a valued contributor to their team and the company.

At this point in the journey, managers need to be prepared for some tough questions. People throughout the organization are gaining insight into empowerment and the way the company approaches issues. They are frustrated that things are not changing faster. They may see obstacles that are not yet on the radar screen for managers, and it is essential to listen and respond to their concerns, which may raise some very valid points. For example, people may ask why the performance management process evaluates individuals and evaluates them after the fact, when we are supposed to be focusing on a working partnership built around team effort. Indeed, performance management is one of the essential systems that needs to be changed to support the move toward empowerment. Almost all performance appraisal systems are, by design, at odds with a culture of empowerment. They rely on someone else monitoring and evaluating each person, rather than on self-monitoring and a partnership of evaluation between employee and manager. Hence they must be changed into a more collaborative, partnership process; this shift involves significant change in people's attitudes, as well as their learning new procedures and skills. They must also rely more heavily on information technology to make relevant information available for tracking and updating by both managers and employees.

Stage 3—Adopting and Refining Empowerment to Fit the Organization

Fortunately, for those organizations and individuals that stay the course and move past the stage of discouragement, there is a new, more productive organization wherein people begin to feel meaningful empowerment. This third stage of the journey, although not the final destination, is a giant step forward. People begin to feel a sense of competence and confidence to act in an empowered way at this stage of *adopting and refining empowerment to fit the organization*. Here, people want answers to *collaboration* and *refinement concerns*. They are ready to begin acting with power and with a greater sense of confidence, but they want to become partners in making empowerment a reality. Now they want answers to such questions as:

Collaboration Concerns: How do we get everyone involved in empowerment? How do we spread the word that empowerment is working? People are now focused on getting everyone on board with empowerment, because they are convinced it *is* making a difference for themselves and the organization.

Refinement Concerns: How can we make the changes even better? Can we improve on the original idea? People begin to focus on the proprietary position of continuous improvement on the job and in the organization. They want to use their knowledge, skills, experience, and motivation to achieve results.

At this stage, the desired culture of empowerment begins to come into focus, as people adopt internal commitment to their jobs and commit to regularly using the language, behaviors and skills required for empowerment. The organizational leadership has made significant progress in transforming the systems and procedures so that a culture of empowerment is both expected and better supported.

> At this stage, the desired culture of empowerment begins to come into focus, as people adopt internal commitment to their jobs and commit to regularly using the language, behaviors and skills required for empowerment.

Vital to Continue Working Toward Empowerment

It is vital to continue to work to get everyone involved in moving toward empowerment. Those who have begun to adopt the empowerment attitude and behaviors need to be encouraged to engage others who may be responding more slowly. People throughout the organization need to be encouraged to use their ideas to refine and improve the emerging culture of empowerment. They will see opportunities and obstacles that managers do not see, and they will have ideas for improvement that managers also do not see. It is a time for collaboration between team members and for team leaders with the teams. Empowerment is a new state of becoming, a dynamic equilibrium that releases the power of people, so they can achieve astonishing results and make refined use of their knowledge, experience, and motivation. People sprinkled throughout the organization have begun to experience the pleasure of being involved and engaged in their work. Employees and managers can now more actively work together as team members to continue the journey to a more full realization of empowerment.

With the culture of empowerment in sight, new ways can be found to share information in all directions in the organization, essentially bringing final destruction to the old hierarchical way of keeping people in the dark regarding vital operating information. *Information sharing* is the great equalizer, and full information sharing is vital to building and maintaining the responsibility and trust that are essential in a culture of empowerment. Teams and senior management must inform each other via collaborative sharing of information, because each has access to different types of information. And information technology systems can make information accessible to anyone in the organization, on demand.

> *Information sharing is the great equalizer, and full information sharing is vital to building and maintaining the responsibility and trust that are essential in a culture of empowerment.*

Achieving Empowerment in Retail Clothing

One retail clothing company built an information technology system that allowed a person anywhere in the organization, in any location, to have immediate access to whatever information they needed. Daily updates on sales and returns were made available so the information had a real-time quality. Anyone from top to bottom of the organization could access this information. The system also allowed people to input comments that facilitated organizational learning among departments and locations. The database allowed the associates to access the history of a client who walked in the door, so that more focused service could be offered. Over time, people have become very committed and sophisticated in using the information to enhance sales and customer service.

Building on such sophisticated and extensive use of information, the teams can expand and refine their responsibility for decision making. Relying more and more on an internalized vision and set of values as the *boundaries that create autonomy,* the remnants of the old hierarchy are demolished. For example, at Disney World, the cast members are so clear about company values that they can take responsible action without having to ask anyone for guidance or even refer to a company procedure manual. People know that the primary value is "concern for the safety of the guests." Second is "courtesy to the guests." When a cast member is assisting a guest with directions, and a safety alarm sounds on one of the rides, there is no hesitation about what to do. The cast member will quickly say, "I have to go," and will be off to assist with the safety problem.

At this stage of the journey, people are reaching the point where they feel capable of and willing to *replace the hierarchy with self-directed teams.* They have learned the skills and attitude of internal commitment needed to play a vital business role in an empowered organization. As team members, they have learned and are becoming comfortable with team decision-making, managing conflict, and holding themselves accountable for results. They are ready to release their power into the organization to achieve astonishing results. Everyone still needs encouragement, but it can come from anyone in the organization, as people increasingly operate like highly responsible and empowered team members.

The Final Step into a Culture of Empowerment

When managers and employees work together to deal with the issues encountered at the three stages, a culture of empowerment is achievable, but the journey is challenging and demanding. People throughout the organization must work long and hard to change their mindsets, assumptions, and behaviors, as well as the organizational systems that support a new culture. At long last, people become fluent in the language of empowerment. They now possess the skills and desire needed to act with responsibility and internal commitment. The organization and its leadership have made many changes to support empowerment, and managers have learned how to be partners with teams. They know a great deal about how to release the power within people to achieve astonishing results. Everyone has made the effort to achieve empowerment, because it makes good business sense in today's marketplace to engage people throughout the organization. People in all areas of the organization have learned the joys of being involved and engaged. They want to use their knowledge, experience, and motivation to achieve astonishing results for the company and to feel the sense of pride and ownership that comes with being empowered.

The journey to empowerment may never be fully realized, but people are now much closer to this new land. A significant transition has occurred in employees, managers, and organizational systems. People are no longer the same as they were in the culture of hierarchy. They are now full-fledged members of a culture of empowerment. They see the world and their own responsibilities and relationships in a totally new light, and they see ways to continue to grow toward even greater degrees of autonomy and responsibility.

Empowerment is achievable, but the journey is a challenge. Are you ready to start your own journey to the distant culture of empowerment? Are you ready and willing to lead your organization through the challenges in the valley of discouragement? Yes, empowerment is real, and it releases the power of people for astonishing results, but managers and employees alike have to choose to make the long, challenging and arduous journey of change! Hopefully, understanding the issues that must be faced along the way, and using the three interlocking tools to address the issues, will encourage you to lead the process of change.

W. Alan Randolph is professor of management in the Merrick School of Business, University of Baltimore. He is also a consulting partner with the Ken Blanchard Companies, Escondido, California. Recent books include The 3 Keys to Empowerment: Release the Power Within People for Astonishing Results, *with Ken Blanchard and John P. Carlos (Berrett-Koehler, 1999),* Empowerment Takes More Than a Minute, *with Ken Blanchard and John P. Carlos (Berrett- Koehler, 1996),* Getting the Job Done! Managing Project Teams and Task Forces for Success, *with Barry Z. Posner (Prentice-Hall, 1992). He recently published a 10-booklet discussion series titled* Power Up for Team Results, *with Ken Blanchard, John P. Carlos, and Peter B. Grazier (Berrett-Koehler, 2000). Randolph engages in consulting work on empowerment, performance management processes, project management, and self-directed teams.*

Lessons Learned from Innovative Organizations

Robin Cook

Sometimes it is useful to have a kind of "to do" list for making things happen. This short article is a "to do" list for creating a culture that facilitates quality management. It's based on an exploration of the lessons learned from studying successful organizations. There is nothing new here, but it is a good summary of what we know about successful cultures and yet again affirms the wisdom of the assumptions on which quality management is based.

Between January of 1998 and April of 1999, fifteen professionals from across the U.S., as well as from Canada and the U.K., came together to form the second class of the Innovation University Best Practices Fellowship. During five sessions, each in a different city, we visited or heard presentations from roughly 20 of the most innovative organizations in the world. This extraordinary opportunity to experience organizations such as Dell Computer, GSD&M, Nortel, Manco, Roberts Express, and Cirque du Soleil provided us with a wide variety of tremendous learning experiences. In this article, I will attempt to briefly outline some key lessons the Innovation University Fellows took away from the program.

Perhaps the most striking lesson we learned was just how much these disparate organizations had in common. Virtually every one of the organizations we visited displayed nine shared characteristics:

- Strong, clearly expressed *shared values*
- An appreciation of/for the *whole individual* and everything s/he can bring to the organization
- Cultures that encourage *openness* and *playfulness*
- *Celebrate successes* constantly
- A strong, clearly communicated sense of *history*
- Intense *customer focus*
- Clear focus on *trends*, even those that do not seem to directly effect current businesses
- *Cross-functional teams*

Reprinted with permission of the author from the Entrepreneurs' Help Page, http://www.tannedfeet.com/index.htm. Copyright © 2001 by Robin Cook. All rights reserved. The author wishes to credit Greg Fleet and Tim Mills for their contribution to this work.

Shared Values

The first common thread among the organizations we experienced was shared values. In every case, the organization went to great lengths to constantly express, reinforce, and build these values into its culture. In every case, it was clear that members of the organization made real efforts to live those values—they were not simply a plaque on a wall. GSD&M, an advertising agency in Austin, provided the best example of this. After going through an extensive values clarification process, they literally carved their core values in stone in the floor of the rotunda of their new offices.

In every case, the organization went to great lengths to constantly express, reinforce, and build these values into its culture.

Appreciate the Whole Individual

Every organization we visited demonstrated a clear understanding of the value each person brings to that organization and went to great lengths to encourage people to incorporate things from their "personal" lives into the professional setting. American Greetings encourages its workers to decorate their cubicles with personal artwork, whether it is directly related to work projects or not. New designs and art concepts have frequently resulted. At the Smithsonian Institution's Central Exhibit Design Facility, we were shown several examples of new techniques for construction of exhibits and displays that were adapted from extracurricular projects that employees were involved in. Manco told us about several new adhesive tape ideas that originated from their employees' hobbies.

Encourage Openness and Playfulness

Many of the organizations we saw practice open book management. All go to great lengths to encourage communication throughout all levels of the organization. Most recognize the value of random meetings and interactions and have designed their facilities to encourage such activities. eLab (now part of Sapient) here in Chicago included a "Napatorium," a "Leave-Me-Alone Room," and a room where each project was displayed for feedback from other teams and individuals in its offices. GSD&M designed its facility with numerous small meeting areas throughout, each with a unique, fun, playful décor, intended to facilitate random conversations. Manco (located in Cleveland) has regular events with fun, often family oriented themes, including a tradition of the company president swimming across an outdoor pond every January if the company meets or exceeds its financial targets. Many of the facilities we toured incorporated colorful, whimsical décor.

Celebrate Successes

Again, a practice common to every organization we saw. Both GSD&M and

Cirque du Soleil have prominent displays of awards throughout their building and GSD&M has a "brag board" at the main entrance. Roberts Express has ongoing employee, contractor, and customer appreciation activities. Manco has a regular schedule of company-wide events throughout the year to celebrate its accomplishments.

Clearly Communicate History

Dell Computer includes history lessons in its new employee orientation. Their practice of sending each new employee three boxes of materials and gifts prior to their official start date includes articles and other materials that prominently feature the company's history. American Greetings has displays of photos and artifacts throughout its offices showing the company's history and especially its origins. Cirque du Soleil designed its building to use materials that are intended to remind everyone there of the group's origins as street performers. Every organization we visited had cultural artifacts and teaching stories related to their shared histories.

Maintain Intense Customer Focus

In response to customer requests, Roberts Express has developed software for its call center that automatically routes incoming calls back to the original call taker, so that customers always speak with someone who is familiar with their shipment. GSD&M created dedicated, themed work spaces for their major accounts—an airport gate area for Southwest Airlines; a gas station motif for Penzoil; a giant, custom built, steel topped worktable for the Steel Industry; etc. Cirque du Soleil designed its entire building so that all workspaces have internal windows looking out into the training and rehearsal areas. Everyone, no matter what their function, can always look up and see what the end product is. Sterling Consulting created a sort of "customer ombudsman" position responsible for meeting with every client at the end of the engagement and evaluating the outcome. This person is charged with doing whatever is necessary to make things right should those outcomes not meet expectations.

Cirque du Soleil designed its building to use materials that are intended to remind everyone there of the group's origins as street performers.

Focus on Trends

American Greetings maintains several "trend rooms" which are changed every two to three months. On a rotating basis, employee teams are charged with identifying various color, motif, and other design trends that will directly or indirectly have an impact on their product lines. Nortel's Corporate Design Group is charged with constantly monitoring the cutting edge in technologies to find new ways to apply those trends to its products. While Dell Computer does not develop technologies themselves, they are constantly fine-tuning their production, inventory, and other systems to enable them to be the first to market with technology developed elsewhere.

Cross-Functional Teams

Nearly every organization we visited incorporated cross-functional teams and/or some form of cross-functional training as a regular, formal methodology. Perhaps the best example of this was the Nortel Corporate Design Group. CDG (since renamed, I believe) is Nortel's cutting edge, blue sky, five to eight year out technology design group. Each project in development was team based, teams, at a minimum, were composed of designers, engineers, and marketing people. One team that we met with was led by an employee with a doctorate in the behavioral sciences—certainly not what one would expect in a high-tech setting! The impact of this approach upon the products in development was simply extraordinary.

These represent the nine most striking common characteristics of the organizations we researched. All were in different industries. All had different business models and structures. Will implementing these concepts in your organization guarantee world-class innovation? Not necessarily ... but they will take you a long way down that road!

Robin Cook is a writer and consultant. Contact him at rnc@interaccess.com.

Quality Transformation
KNOWLEDGE MANAGEMENT

Creating a Knowledge Culture

Susanne Hauschild, Thomas Licht, and Wolfram Stein

> *When a company has a full commitment to quality management, it's easy to see the value of knowledge and its effective management for enhanced individual, team, and organizational performance. Integrating KM into the work of the organization requires more than lip service, as this article documents. It analyzes the differences between more and less successful companies and the role of knowledge management in the companies that are doing better.*

Ask a group of senior executives if they regard knowledge management as very important to the success of a company. Most will enthusiastically say that they do—a response befitting one of the trendiest topics in management circles.

Yet thinking that knowledge management is crucial and knowing what to do about it are very different. A McKinsey survey of 40 companies in Europe, Japan, and the United States showed that many executives think that knowledge management begins and ends with building sophisticated information technology systems.

Some companies go much further: they take the trouble to link all their information together and to build models that increase their profitability by improving processes, products, and customer relations. Such companies understand that true knowledge management requires them to develop ways of making workers aware of those links and goes beyond infrastructure to touch almost every aspect of a business.[1]

This article was originally published in *The McKinsey Quarterly*, 2001 Number 1, and can be found on the publication's Web site, www.mckinseyquarterly.com. Copyright © 2001 McKinsey & Company. All rights reserved. Reprinted by permission.

Because knowledge management is an increasingly essential component of innovation and value creation, we focused on two tasks—product development and order generation and fulfillment—as a way of identifying which companies in our survey were good knowledge managers. These tasks are the major contributors to the value a company generates. By using process performance and financial indicators, we categorized 15 companies as successful and 15 as less successful and then compared the two groups.[2] The successful companies cut throughput time by an average of almost 11 percent from 1995 to 1998, compared with an average of 1.6 percent at the less successful companies. Development time at the successful companies fell by 4.6 percent in the same period, compared with just 0.7 percent at the less successful ones.

We then compared the knowledge-management practices of the more and less successful companies to understand how those practices contribute to corporate success.[3] The survey's findings can be summarized simply: successful companies build a corporate environment that fosters a desire for knowledge among their employees and that ensures its continual application, distribution, and creation.

Creating a Desire for Knowledge

Less successful companies tend to take a top-down approach: pushing knowledge where it is needed. Successful companies, by contrast, reward employees for seeking, sharing, and creating knowledge. It requires effort to develop what we call "knowledge pull"—a grassroots desire among employees to tap into their company's intellectual resources. Creating databases or virtual team rooms isn't enough, since many employees resist using knowledge generated by other departments, for example. Worse still, many people believe that the hoarding of knowledge is power, a philosophy that may help individuals but hurts companies.

Partly to overcome barriers of this kind, successful companies tend to establish clear goals that promote knowledge pull by forcing employees to reach beyond themselves (Exhibit 1). Instead of wasting resources by avoiding knowledge that was "not invented here," employees at such companies use all available resources, including the corporate knowledge base, to improve their chances of reaching these goals. Almost all of the successful companies we analyzed set ambitious goals for product development and process innovation, while only 33 percent of the less successful companies did so for product development and only 27 percent for process innovation.

Other techniques used by successful companies include granting financial and other incentives to reward employees who pull knowledge from internal and external sources and who contribute their own knowledge to the corporate base. More than 70 percent of the successful companies surveyed, for example, had individual incentive systems linked to product development targets, compared with 27 percent of the less successful companies. Tying

Creating a Knowledge Culture

Percent of participants using specific techniques

■ Successful companies
□ Less successful companies

Set world-class standards for ...

	Product development	Process innovation	Product and process quality
Successful	93	87	87
Less successful	33	27	33

Offer employees incentives for ...

	Product development	Process improvement
Successful	73	60
Less successful	27	40

Encourage participative decision making in ...

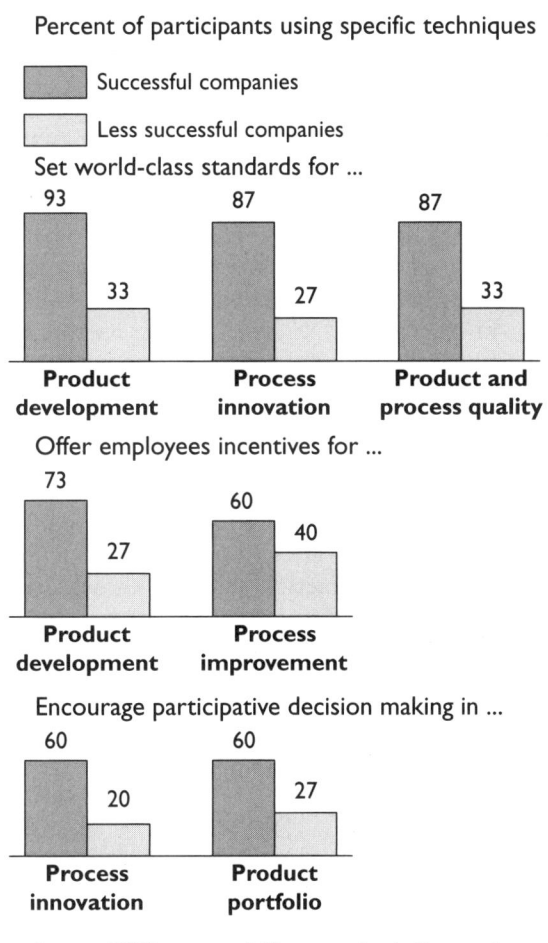

	Process innovation	Product portfolio
Successful	60	60
Less successful	20	27

Source: 2000 survey of 40 companies in Europe, Japan and the United States; McKinsey analysis.

Exhibit 1. **A lust for knowledge**

incentives to goals that employees can influence but not achieve on their own forces them to seek and to offer knowledge more broadly. At one U.S. high-tech firm, for instance, managers give employees cash incentives for filing patent applications, whether or not they are successful, to bring ideas out into the open and to discourage the hoarding of knowledge.

Financial incentives can go a long way toward creating this kind of knowledge pull, but unless they are developed carefully they could encourage the hoarding of knowledge and other counterproductive practices. (Linking an annual bonus solely to a sales rep's volume growth, for instance, could spark unhealthy competition within a company's sales force and, in extreme cases, foment rivalries that might damage overall performance.) Incentive plans can also include coveted office space and other obvious status symbols as well as an opportunity to travel and to receive more challenging assignments.

Incentive systems should promote a broad range of corporate objectives, and successful companies tend to include knowledge management among them. Instead of focusing narrowly on individual performance, such companies ensure that incentives uphold a balanced range of goals that might include financial success outside an employee's immediate unit, for when people benefit from the success of other units in their companies, they are encouraged to move away from the knowledge-is-power mind-set and to begin sharing what they know. Other approaches, such as research competitions with high-prestige, high-value prizes, are more direct ways to encourage the sharing of knowledge.

Although goals, incentives, and participation all play a significant role in aspects of corporate strategy other than knowledge management, successful companies tend to keep knowledge management in mind when crafting their overall strategies. The knowledge-pull mind-set can be created only if it becomes an integral part of corporate culture—a necessary first step before a company embarks on the more practical tasks of knowledge management.

Bringing Knowledge to Bear

Besides creating an environment that encourages knowledge pull, successful companies excel in applying, distributing, and creating knowledge—tasks that can't always be neatly separated. A technique that helps distribute knowledge, for example, could also facilitate its application in specific situations. Dividing the range of knowledge-management practices among these three tasks is partly a matter of convenience and partly an attempt to distinguish techniques by the speed with which they can improve corporate performance. The three categories also help to identify areas in which a company's overall knowledge-management effort should be improved.

Application

Every company is already sitting on a vast storehouse of knowledge, but much of it is underused. The application of knowledge that is already in hand is the fastest and most direct way of using knowledge to influence a company's bottom line (Exhibit 2). Furthermore, if companies fail to apply knowledge, its successful distribution and cultivation will have little impact.

Part of the problem is that "information" is generally a fact, whereas "knowledge," which focuses on linkages or relationships, is subjective. Each employee weighs knowledge against a different set of experiences and prejudices when deciding its meaning, value, and use. One global electronics company ran into problems of this sort when it tried to apply a technology being

Percent of participants using specific techniques

- ■ Successful companies
- □ Less successful companies

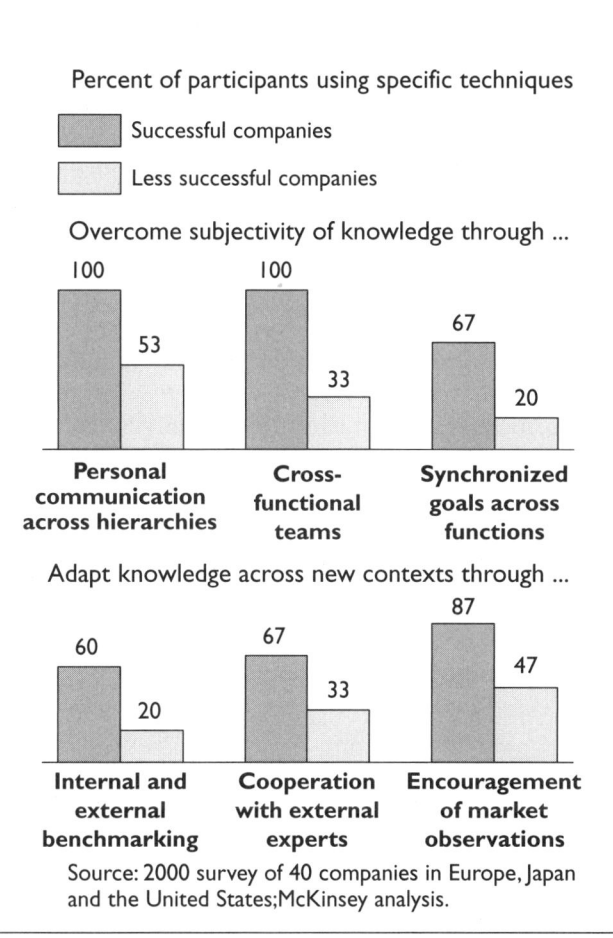

Overcome subjectivity of knowledge through ...

Technique	Successful	Less successful
Personal communication across hierarchies	100	53
Cross-functional teams	100	33
Synchronized goals across functions	67	20

Adapt knowledge across new contexts through ...

Technique	Successful	Less successful
Internal and external benchmarking	60	20
Cooperation with external experts	67	33
Encouragement of market observations	87	47

Source: 2000 survey of 40 companies in Europe, Japan and the United States; McKinsey analysis.

Exhibit 2. **Applying knowledge**

exploited at an overseas subsidiary to its traditional product line at home. A manager involved in the project explained that though the overseas team had described and explained the new method, differences in culture and business experience prevented it from being understood and implemented correctly. "We really had to bring the experts together in one team and arrange a personal work meeting, so that they could find a common basis to start from," the manager said. The information was there, but not the knowledge.

One way successful companies overcome this problem is to bring people together across functions and hierarchies. All of the best performers had cross-functional teams and frequent personal contacts among people at different levels, but only 33 percent of the less successful companies formed cross-functional teams and only 53 percent had cultures encouraging informal talks between managers and subordinates at all levels. It may sound obvious, but face-to-face meetings open the door to continued exchanges and can be an important way of creating a common understanding, particularly in multinational corporations whose teams are spread across the globe.

What is more, ideas can often be adapted to different processes or products, and successful companies actively try to apply knowledge to these new contexts. Some of the clearest examples of the way knowledge can be adapted come from companies that have searched far afield for new insights. To develop a more efficient luggage-handling system, for instance, one international airline studied how Indianapolis 500 car crews orchestrated pit stops during races. By applying these observations to a luggage-handling system, the company reduced downtime dramatically. In another case, a California construction company raised its rate of on-time cement deliveries to 95 percent, from 68 percent, by taking route-planning lessons from a local pizza delivery company.

Distribution

Techniques that benefit application often benefit distribution, since the two are closely linked. But application focuses on using knowledge for immediate effect, distribution on moving knowledge to where it can best be applied. Distribution relies heavily on good infrastructure to create electronic meeting places, on databases, and on other channels for spreading knowledge.

> Our survey showed that 67 percent of the successful companies used product development teams whose members rotated jobs, as compared with 27 percent of the less successful companies.

However, successful companies—even those with IT systems facilitating smooth and broad exchanges of data—know that the challenge goes beyond building information networks (Exhibit 3). Much of a corporation's most valuable knowledge is tacit—embedded in the minds of employees. Tacit knowledge is difficult to manage, but successful companies have figured out ways to manage it. One global capital-goods company assigned product developers to the shop floor to supervise the production of the modules they had designed. This program opened up lines of communication between assembly-line employees and developers, thus giving the developers better insight into production problems, establishing continuing relations between the two groups, and encouraging the exchange of tacit knowledge between them. Within five years, the program, together with other measures, had cut production costs by 15 percent and throughput time by 80 percent.

Our survey showed that 67 percent of the successful companies used product development teams whose members rotated jobs, as compared with 27 percent of the less successful companies. Since personal meetings seem to be the best way of sharing tacit knowledge, 93 percent of the successful companies locate development teams in the same facilities used by groups with which they work closely, such as supplier teams. Only 33 percent of the less successful companies take this approach.

Despite the general agreement on the benefits of IT infrastructure, less successful companies were far behind their successful counterparts in creating data networks accessible across functions. Only 7 percent of the less successful companies had created regularly updated procurement databases that

Percent of participants using specific techniques

■ Successful companies
□ Less successful companies

Capture tacit knowledge management ...

	Successful	Less successful
Co-location of teams or departments	93	33
Job rotation	67	27
Use of intranet to identify internal experts	53	7

Create networks through ...

	Successful	Less successful
Regular training with internal and external experts	73	20
Networking with external partners	93	20
Cross-functional databases	87	7

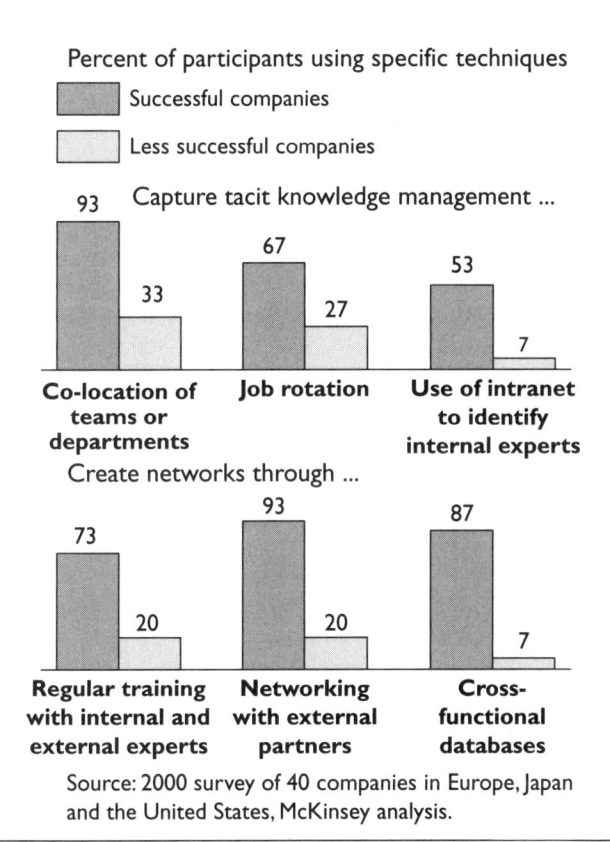

Source: 2000 survey of 40 companies in Europe, Japan and the United States, McKinsey analysis.

Exhibit 3. **Distributing knowledge**

could be read by product developers, for example, compared with 87 percent of the successful companies. In addition, there were sharp differences in the ways companies encouraged personal networking. The survey also revealed wide gaps in the use of training by internal and external experts (73 percent for successful companies versus 20 percent for less successful ones) and in creating strong networks with external partners (93 percent versus 20 percent). Both are effective ways of distributing internally and externally generated knowledge throughout a company.

Creation

Of all the tasks involved in managing knowledge, its creation is the most slippery, because creativity is cultivated rather than ordained. To remain vital, companies need new knowledge: ways of making paperwork run more smoothly, say, or developing new products or services. New knowledge, moreover, is a necessary raw material for innovation, another strategic goal that partly overlaps with knowledge management. As Georg Von Krogh has observed, "Knowledge creation is the key source of innovation in any company."[4] Innovation and the creation of knowledge—both closely tied to new products and services—can often be sparked by similar techniques (Exhibit 4).

Percent of participants using specific techniques

■ Successful companies
□ Less successful companies

Encourage innovation and spontaneity through ...

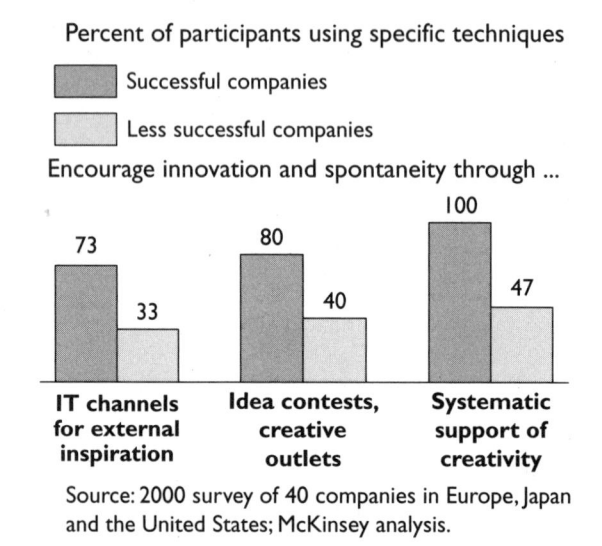

IT channels for external inspiration	Idea contests, creative outlets	Systematic support of creativity
73 / 33	80 / 40	100 / 47

Source: 2000 survey of 40 companies in Europe, Japan and the United States; McKinsey analysis.

Exhibit 4. **Creating knowledge**

Our survey showed that successful companies often tried to foster creativity by making the jobs of employees more interesting—for instance, by allowing employees to participate in projects not directly linked to their usual work. Eighty percent of the successful companies, as compared with only 40 percent of the less successful ones, had programs to encourage creativity, such as idea contests and opportunities to work on diverse projects. Means of access (such as fast Internet connections) to a wide range of external stimuli were available at 73 percent of the successful companies but at only 33 percent of the less successful ones.

Sometimes even bald-faced gimmicks work. One global electronics company developed a so-called virtual Hollywood and asked "directors" (employees) to present "scripts" (improvement ideas) to "investors" (general managers) who would choose the ones to "produce" (implement). The project promoted out-of-the-box thinking and in the first year generated submissions from 200 teams addressing process improvement and product development.

Successful companies understand that knowledge management and information technology are not synonymous. These companies' knowledge-management programs, far from being special, one-off projects, are long-term efforts that involve all aspects of the business and dovetail with other strategic decisions.

Among the techniques we examined, many of those that distinguish successful companies from their less successful counterparts could be described as attempts to do things faster, cheaper, and better. In today's changing economy, the key to faster, cheaper, and better is to bring the full force of a company's knowledge to bear on the effort. Knowledge—not land, labor, and capital—is now the lifeblood of a corporation.

Notes:

1. Knowledge management is the focus of a large and expanding body of literature. The books that helped us analyze the findings of our survey included Kazuo Ichijo, Ikujiro Nonaka, and Georg von Krogh, *Enabling Knowledge Creation: How to Unlock the Mystery of Tacit Knowledge and Release the Power of Innovation*, New York: Oxford University Press, 2000; and Thomas H. Davenport and Laurence Prusak, *Working Knowledge: How Organizations Manage What They Know*, Boston, Massachusetts: Harvard Business School Press, 1998.
2. Ten moderately successful companies were intentionally left out to get a significant differentiation.
3. The companies we examined covered a wide spectrum of industries: automotive, capital goods, and high technology. We also looked at a handful of companies, from other industries, that were specifically chosen because of their reputation for good knowledge management. Successful techniques, we found, worked across industry categories.
4. Georg von Krogh, "Care in knowledge creation," *California Management Review*, spring 1998, Volume 40, Number 3, pp. 133–53.

Susanne Hauschild is a consultant in McKinsey's Vienna office, and Thomas Licht is a consultant and Wolfram Stein is a principal in the Munich office.

Managing Customer Knowledge

Eric Lesser, David Mundel, and Charles Wiecha

> *If you're going to practice quality management, you have to listen to the voice of the customer. Knowledge management has methods to do that, and this article explains how to capture and store data, develop information from the data, diffuse this knowledge across organizational units, and incorporate it into business processes. Businesses that successfully manage customer knowledge can build customer loyalty and react faster to marketplace trends.*

Nearly every business leader will tell you that having and using knowledge about customers is critical to the success of their enterprise. Yet roughly half of the large companies Forrester Research surveyed reported that they do not plan to use customer information in designing or implementing marketing or customer service processes. In product development, nine out of 10 companies reported that they do not have plans to use customer information to improve the results of this process.

Why are so few companies using customer data? First, because it can be difficult to acquire the right data. Capturing large quantities of sales receipt data is inexpensive, but it is rarely helpful in building useful knowledge. In contrast, recording shopper behavior through personal observation and video is costly, but can be much more valuable.

Customer data gathering is also complicated because the data needed by one business unit or process is often generated in another area of the organization or even by a third party (for example, by intermediaries between the manufacturer and the ultimate consumer). Moreover, knowledge developed by one business unit may be available to, but still unused by, another because individuals in the receiving unit don't have confidence in the source.

And data gathering is just the start—there's also the problem of transforming all the data collected into useful information, which requires strong analytical skills, and then transferring it across organizational boundaries.

Then there are the problems of the customers themselves. Customers aren't easily pigeonholed. New and existing customers, former customers, current customers who also buy from competitors, and potential customers who have only bought from competitors may value product and service attributes differently. Customers are also complex. They make purchase and use

Republished with permission of the publisher from the *Journal of Business Strategy*, November/December 2000. Copyright © 2000 by EC Media Group, Eleven Penn Plaza, New York, NY 10001. All rights reserved.

decisions based on complicated decision-making processes and structures. And what customers want, need, and value varies over time.

In short, lack of time, resources, and focus can limit a company's ability to make the critical transformation from data to insight. But there are strategies that are useful in bridging these gaps, including: using extended dialogues between customers and organizations; fostering internal communities designed to share knowledge across organizational boundaries; enabling knowledge to be used at the point of customer contact; and providing leadership support for customer knowledge activities.

Deriving Value from Customer Knowledge

The arguments in favor of using customer knowledge are hard to dispute:

- Today, when competitors can easily observe and copy each others' successes, customer knowledge, which can neither be readily observed nor easily copied, is an important contributor to success.
- In a world where customers can make instantaneous comparisons between similar products, the ability to target offerings to specific customer requirements becomes more and more important.
- An enterprise can achieve "first mover advantage" by offering new or improved products and services that better serve customer wants and needs.
- Companies can better compete in highly price-sensitive marketplaces by focusing on product and service parameters customers value most and eliminating unnecessary features that reduce profit margins and increase customer frustration.
- If an organization knows patterns of customer demand, it can reduce inventory requirements and unused manufacturing or service capacities.

Customer knowledge creates value when companies incorporate it into planning and operating activities. Traditionally, firms have focused customer knowledge management efforts on supporting enterprise customer sales and marketing processes, such as direct mail campaigns, catalogs, and telephone solicitations. Customer knowledge provides guidance and direction to these processes by improving the enterprise's understanding of the factors that influence customer decision making, leading to more effective marketing and sales strategies.

In addition, customer knowledge can improve service and support by enabling enterprises to reuse "best practice" solutions that have worked in one situation to solve similar problems for other customers. Customer knowledge can also help an organization predict which sorts of services and support offerings customers are likely to want or need, and to develop more effective strategies for meeting these needs before they are even articulated.

Customer knowledge creates value when companies incorporate it into planning and operating activities.

Customer knowledge can also enhance product and service development, product manufacturing, service delivery, and fulfillment. Product and service developers can be more successful in creating customer value and developing successful offerings if they understand unfulfilled and evolving customer wants and needs. Manufacturers can create efficiency improvements by fine-tuning operating processes to the patterns of customer demand.

Improving the Availability and Use of Customer Knowledge

Our research has identified four approaches that can expand the availability and use of customer knowledge:

- Creating and nurturing enterprise-led "customer knowledge development dialogues,"
- Creating and operating enterprise-wide "customer knowledge communities,"
- Facilitating the capture of knowledge-relevant data and the use of customer knowledge at the point of customer contact, and
- Demonstrating enterprise leadership commitment to customer knowledge.

The importance of customer knowledge and the problems that impede its development suggest a role for enterprise-led customer knowledge development dialogues.

The importance of customer knowledge and the problems that impede its development suggest a role for enterprise-led customer knowledge development dialogues—probing, collaborative, and purposeful explorations of customers. These dialogues must focus not solely on the results of purchasing and use decisions, but instead on developing an understanding of customer values and what drives their decisions and actions. Because customers don't easily articulate these values—and may not even understand them—dialogues need to involve an array of questioning, probing, and observing and cover a complex set of customer behaviors and motivations. Because customers change over time, these dialogues must be ongoing.

Customer dialogues must be both guided and structured. Guidance is required so that data and information gathering is focused on relevant customer knowledge needs. Structure ensures that the context and meaning of the data and information are clear, especially to users who may not be directly involved in the dialogue process. It also provides the means for organizing the data, information, and insights from a variety of sources.

Because customer diversity increases the need to understand multiple customer segments, companies need to involve carefully chosen sets of diverse customers in customer knowledge development dialogues. They should ensure that the chosen dialogue channel, mechanism, or media does not bias the sample of involved customers.

One example of successful customer knowledge development dialogues is the Jeep jamboree, one of several customer events DaimlerChrysler sponsors. At these events, which are held at different locations across the U.S. and attract enthusiasts from all around the country, Jeep employs engineers and ethnographic researchers to build a better understanding of Jeep owners' relationships with their vehicles. In addition to observing drivers in a variety of skill-related events, Jeep employees connect with customers through both informal conversations and semi-structured roundtables. Through these discussions and observations, Jeep engineers get feedback on changes to existing models and suggestions for future models.

A second potential customer knowledge management strategy is the formation of enterprise-wide, customer knowledge communities (CKCs) within the company itself. CKCs help the firm organize and unify its approach to understanding customers and facilitate the transfer and use of this knowledge across organizational boundaries. They operate much like the communities of practice Etienne Wenger and Bill Snyder recently described in the *Harvard Business Review*. They focus on developing member capabilities, building and exchanging knowledge, and creating shared languages, models, and cultures directed toward understanding customers.

Typically, these communities focus on a single customer, or customer segment. For example, IBM builds communities focused on its major accounts. Using a collaborative virtual workspace called the CustomerRoom, individuals from different divisions within IBM exchange knowledge about particular accounts, including customer contacts, upcoming proposals, and research opportunities that can address emerging customer needs.

> Using a collaborative virtual workspace called the CustomerRoom, individuals from different divisions within IBM exchange knowledge about particular accounts.

A third important strategy focuses on facilitating both data gathering and the use of customer knowledge at the point of customer contact. Customer service representatives and customers alike have less time to devote to each other. Making it easier for customer support services (including representative-driven and self-service models) to access and use structured data, information, and experiential knowledge is one mechanism for responding to these time pressures.

For example, one financial services organization experimented with information technology to support outbound call centers that focused on potential customer defections. Using a combination of customer activity information and customized solutions to address customer dissatisfaction, these systems enable customer service representatives to make real-time offers that can entice profitable customers back to the company.

A fourth important customer knowledge management strategy focuses on enterprise leadership. Increasing an enterprise's customer focus and investing the resources and attention needed to initiate and maintain customer knowledge development dialogues and customer knowledge communities requires leadership attention. Leaders need to exhibit their commitment to creating a customer-focused operation; demonstrating their conviction that improving the enterprise's customer knowledge is key to implementing successful performance changes. For example, Jim Rodgers, vice president of marketing at Ford's Lincoln-Mercury division, actively participates in, and encourages other employees to monitor, customer-related chat rooms, such as those hosted by Edmunds.com.

The Payoff

Managing customer knowledge requires that organizations undertake a range of knowledge creation activities including acquiring, capturing, and storing data, developing information by combining data, context, and theory, and creating knowledge and understanding based on this information. Organizations must then be able to take this knowledge, diffuse it across organizational units, and incorporate it into day-to-day business processes to realize its full value.

None of this is easy, but creating, sharing and using knowledge about customer wants and values can be a vital contributor to organizational success. Businesses that successfully manage customer knowledge can react faster to marketplace trends, increase brand loyalty, and facilitate the purchase and use of their products and services. Through customer knowledge activities, organizations can truly understand their most valued resource.

Eric Lesser is an executive consultant with the IBM Institute for Knowledge Management. He recently co-edited Knowledge and Communities *(Butterworth-Heinemann, 2000) and edited* Knowledge and Social Capital *(Butterworth-Heinemann, 2000).*

David Mundel is a research consultant. He is co-author of an IBM white paper, Managing Customer Knowledge *(2000).*

Charles Wiecha is a researcher with IBM Research and Adjunct Assistant Professor in the Engineering and Public Policy Department at Carnegie Mellon University. He is co-author of an IBM white paper, Managing Customer Knowledge *(2000).*

The Accidental Knowledge Manager

Peter Dorfman

Knowledge management, like quality management, requires, as we all know by now, the commitment of top management. This article looks at some of the unforeseen effects that happen when a KM initiative is not well thought out. Unless everyone understands the value-creating nature of knowledge management, as with quality management (and the two actually go together), there are going to be problems.

A corporate knowledge management initiative can have many unforeseen effects on management and staff. At one site, knowledge workers will welcome the effort, anticipating the benefits and pitching in as both users of and contributors to the knowledge pool. Yet at another site in the same company, the KM project may meet with skepticism and confusion.

At one large retailer that launched its KM program three years ago, the response was a quiet revolt. "We were plotting its downfall," recalls a veteran of that experience in the IT department's help desk group. "We agreed among ourselves not to use the tool or submit content to it. I eventually began to soften, but my buddies were actively trying to sabotage the project."

It's not hard to see why this company prefers to remain anonymous. What could produce such a hostile response to a progressive management initiative? In this case, the primary problem was stunningly bad communication. Relations between the support team and management already had been deteriorating for some time before the project began. Consultants began showing up for closed-door meetings with executives. By the time management asked the support staff to work with the consultants, rumors were flying. "We sincerely thought management had a plan to get rid of tech support," the former staffer says. "We felt they were going to take our knowledge and then dump us."

The KM project was eventually accepted, but a number of the covert saboteurs, who under different circumstances might have been essential contributors to the project, left the company, taking their knowledge with them.

Reprinted by permission of the publisher from *Knowledge Management*, February 2001. Copyright © 2001 by Freedom Technology Media Group. All rights reserved.

Blueprint for Failure

This unfortunate example is extreme but not unique. In many organizations, top managers conceive a KM project, then drop its execution into the laps of supervisors and knowledge workers who are at best incompletely trained for it. Like the help desk agents, those people become accidental knowledge managers (AKMs), to borrow the title from Anne Tyler's novel *The Accidental Tourist*, about a popular travel writer whose secret of success paradoxically is that he hates to travel.

Too often, KM projects are imposed on people who have other jobs to do and whose performance is measured against objectives unrelated to their new responsibilities in authoring and using knowledge. KM essentially just happens to them. They are expected to fashion their own roles in the initiative and are given little or no guidance, training or documentation. They may be saddled with sketchy expectations, undocumented processes and no benchmarks against which to measure success. As a result, knowledge workers resist the initiative. They worry that if they spend time managing knowledge, their careers will suffer.

Most supervisors recognize that their direct reports are right to be concerned. And they know that when their people underperform, the supervisors' own performance measurements may be negatively affected. When more conventional employee performance metrics fall off, they tend to back away from enforcing the knowledge authoring mandate. When this happens, the knowledge workers are happier, but KM objectives stop being met.

Even the best-intentioned executive or management team can inadvertently create accidental knowledge managers. To take the accidents out of a knowledge management initiative, they need to understand what their worthy idea will put folks through. For either audience, here are some ways. Some examples follow from KM projects in customer support, but the issues they depict could arise in any business environment where people are hired for other skills but asked to take on these new responsibilities.

Clarifying the Aims

Although it's unlikely that management's objective in developing a KM project is to reduce headcount, the intention may well be to get more out of people while they're there. It also may be to enable the organization to cope more gracefully when people leave on their own. Customer support agents, for example, remain in any one position for an average of little more than a year. Management wants the rest of the team not to have to relearn everything that a particular agent knows after he or she moves on. In this field, other typical motives for KM initiatives include increasing customer satisfaction with services, enabling staff to handle a wider range of issues, shortening the durations of calls and reducing the escalation rates of problems. The rationale for

> Too often, KM projects are imposed on people who have other jobs to do and whose performance is measured against objectives unrelated to their new responsibilities in authoring and using knowledge.

each of these objectives is straightforward. Each can be measured in some way, and each has an obvious bearing on quality of service, customer satisfaction and team productivity. But these goals aren't self-evident, and management has to articulate them to the people expected to achieve them.

A key tool for communicating this message is the mission statement, strategic plan or project charter. If the initiative doesn't have such a document, whoever has overall responsibility for the initiative must make sure that it is created. All significant players in the initiative should help to draft it.

Next, get key participants to look at the objectives through the lens of their own experience. The accidental knowledge manager often is the first to spot a mismatch between reality and expectation; goals that make sense in the abstract may be absurd in practice. Take, for example, the notion of shortening the durations of calls. An agent who has extensive, pertinent knowledge at hand can retrieve the answers to many questions in seconds, deliver them to the caller and move on—or so the theory goes. In fact, answering the question may be only the first step in a lengthy discussion of how to execute the solution. A quick answer satisfies the customer, but it often leads to longer transactions, not shorter ones, as emboldened customers try to find out what else the agent knows.

If an AKM can't bring issues like this to the attention of the project leaders, the organization has problems that will hobble any knowledge initiative. In fact, one of the most common stumbling blocks to successful knowledge management is poor vertical communication. Peers may interact comfortably with each other, but invisible walls exist between managers and their subordinates or between Tier One and Tier Two analysts in tiered service organizations. These kinds of barriers erode confidence and spawn negative rumors.

Pay for What You Get

Not every organization succeeds in balancing the productivity objectives for KM with the requirements of knowledge workers' core jobs. If people are going to devote time to knowledge authoring, that time has to come from something they're doing now, such as managing cases or talking to customers.

Over time, capturing and sharing knowledge should make your staff more productive and make it easier for them to manage their time. In the short run, however, time conflicts will be a daily issue, so leaders must empower their people to document these clashes and to make the case for different ways to accommodate both the knowledge initiative and their main responsibilities. If they become willing to step up and be agents of change, it will show the organization at large that your team has an important role in managing the company's intangible assets.

You can't always be democratic about this. If you need heroic contributions to make the initiative successful, be firm. But be clear about what is expected and what the incentives for and benefits of success will be.

Many knowledge workers have the potential to rise through a series of increasingly responsible and lucrative jobs. Still, if you are asking them to contribute to a knowledge base from which their peers and successors can extract and use their collective wisdom, resistance is natural. In response, it makes sense to point out that you are simply trying to deal with losing them eventually.

You are making significant demands on these accidental knowledge managers, and they deserve some kind of specific recognition for this. Recognition frequently takes the form of incentives, which can be intangible rewards such as comp time for extraordinary hours spent in authoring knowledge or the privilege of reserving "protected time" away from the regular demands of the job to spend contributing to the knowledge base. Tangible incentives for contributions at some specific level of diligence can be attractive items such as dinners or music CDs as well as cash.

Such incentives do not necessarily have to be lavish. Darrell Johnson, customer support manager at Cutler-Hammer, a Pittsburgh-based electrical components manufacturer, has administered incentive programs for knowledge authors and administrators. He suggests that incentives be awarded for well-understood reasons and as publicly as possible.

Incentives work best when they are tied directly to the accomplishment of specific objectives, but more general rewards can also provide motivation. Every KM project is really a succession of phases, ideally punctuated by small, recognized, interim successes. Celebrate these successes. At the end of the first phase of a recent initiative at Enterprise Rent-A-Car (see the sidebar "Driving Smart"), consultants noted that the knowledge workers involved had often kidded about being involved in a "battle" and having collected "war stories." During a convivial wrap-up meeting, their supervisors handed the participants military-style medals and certificates identifying them as "knowledge management veterans."

Knowledge management is still a new discipline. The leader of a project may be as naive about it as the knowledge workers who are drafted into it. By recognizing that they have become accidental knowledge managers, participants can identify the mismatches between the demands of the new project and the way their conventional work is managed and evaluated. Along the way, they help to put drifting knowledge initiatives back on a productive course.

Driving Smart

One company that has had success in avoiding knowledge management accidents is Enterprise Rent-A-Car. Based in St. Louis, the company employs some 40,000 people, operates over 4,500 rental branch offices in the United States, Canada, the United Kingdom, Ireland and Germany, and has a fleet of more than 500,000 vehicles.

Its field support department provides support for technology-related problems to all Enterprise employees worldwide. Deanna Harris, assistant

The Accidental Knowledge Manager

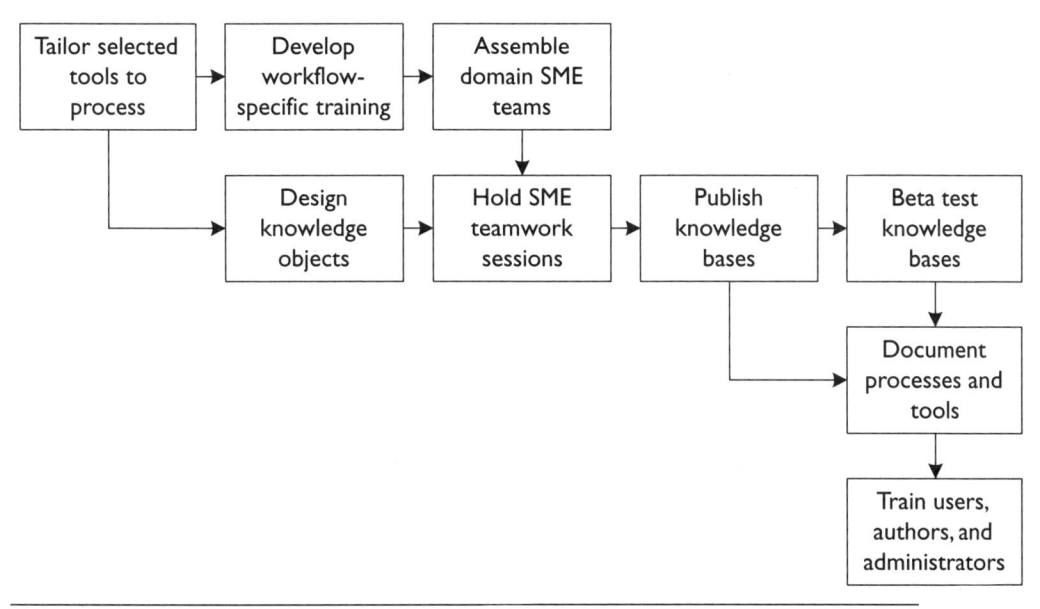

Figure 1. **Knowledge management workflow—this chart can make it clear that people at all levels of the organization are expected to contribute**

vice president for technical support, who has run the department for six years, began KM efforts three years ago. "We understood the value of capturing and sharing knowledge," she says. "Support people were needlessly reinventing solutions to old problems. We knew we could reduce our overall costs and improve operational efficiency by removing the need for these redundant efforts."

At the start, Harris found that employees wanted tangible evidence of the value of the initiative. "From the beginning we needed to get everyone together and develop a KM solution as a team," she says. "You have to break it down to specifics, phases and tactics and show people exactly what's in this for them."

As in most organizations, there was trepidation about change. Some customer support analysts (CSAs) feared that management was attempting to change their mission from being a help desk to being merely a call center, where they were expected to read solutions from cue cards and pass along anything complex to more experienced technicians. "Our biggest challenge with this initiative was buy-in: to get the people to believe, to participate and to share their knowledge," Harris recalls.

Aided by a team of employees and consultants from LaBounty & Associates Inc., she worked to open lines of communication about the real direction of the KM implementation. Harris chose Todd Kreuger, then manager of quality assurance in the field support department, to drive the effort. Kreuger and the consultants developed a program to give everyone in field support a personal stake in the success of the project. They identified five core domains, tightly defined areas of technology for which field support teams were responsible. They built a team to generate knowledge for each domain, making sure that each team was built around a subject matter expert (SME) from the engineering group and included members from all three tiers of the service organization. The process included two days of intensive communication among all group members.

Each team sequestered itself to discuss the basic diagnostic logic that a typical Tier One CSA would use to troubleshoot a problem in a particular domain. Each team created flow charts of this logic and from them built decision trees to represent the knowledge.

For each class of problems, a team had to capture the knowledge a CSA would need, to take the most effective steps to resolve an issue for Enterprise employees in rental branches. But the interactions among team members also demonstrated what was going to be required of the SMEs to generate that content. It illustrated, for example, the need for style conventions. And it showed team members at all levels the key role that Tier One analysts would play in identifying new issues or revisions to be documented in the knowledge base.

In short, this team experience eliminated ambiguities in the roles of employees in the processes of knowledge creation, administration and publishing. Management's objectives became clear, and knowledge contribution has now become a recognized part of the job at all levels of field support.

A defining moment came when the team members—both those who were to author the knowledge and those who were to use it to assist customers—saw the pilot knowledge bases go "live" for the first time. They were able to see the results of what had been an intensive manual process in the form of a software solution; they could follow the diagnostic steps of the tool, arrive at valid solutions and see their own logic accurately reflected in the system. As a result, trust developed rapidly in both the knowledge base and the team implementing it.

Now knowledge authors who submit solutions create a "ticket," just as they do when a field support customer reports a problem. They can track what happens to their submissions from the day they are created until they become generally available.

This is classic bottom-up knowledge management; the KM team developed the system, but the authors have the ownership required for it to work. There is a clear understanding between the CSAs, their supervisors and management as to when analysts can block out time to work on authoring content, so there is no conflict with their phone time. "It has been a tedious three years, but the benefits of KM to our customers, to

ACCIDENTAL KNOWLEDGE MANAGERS SPEAK UP

KnowledgeFarm has conducted an informal survey of technical professionals who view themselves as accidental knowledge managers. Among the 47 respondents, 63 percent said they were involved in their company's internal help desk, external support or IS management. As for their status in the company, 41 percent identified themselves as a team or project manager, 21 percent as a support analyst and 10 percent as executive management. The remaining 28 percent included consultants, engineers and others.

Virtually all respondents viewed themselves as important players in their KM projects: 34 percent said they run the project day-to-day, 24 percent developed the strategy for KM, another 24 percent initiated the project and 10 said the project depends on their participation. The remaining 8 percent make significant decisions or participate regularly in the KM effort. (Percentages have been rounded off to the nearest whole number.)

Among other things, respondents also commented on their outlook, their sense of job satisfaction and security, and the ultimate outcome of the project. Of particular interest, given the "accidental" origins of their involvement in the project, are the respondents' personal feelings of satisfaction, accomplishment and frustration, as revealed below.

Nearly half of all respondents felt personal pride in the project but 13 percent found it frustrating or threatening.

Personal Impact of KM
The KM project has represented a major personal accomplishment: **48%**
The KM project has made the job more satisfying: **17%**
KM has made it easier to succeed in the job: **14%**
KM has resulted in significant frustration: **10%**
Impact of KM has been neutral: **8%**
KM has been a threat to job security: **3%**

When the project created stress, almost half of respondents traced its source to indifferent management or poor planning.

Sources of Stress for Participants
Low management support: **24%**
Undocumented processes: **24%**
Bad tool choice: **7%**
Poor training: **7%**
Lack of IS support: **7%**
Lack of incentives to participate: **7%**
Lack of interest among clients: **3%**
Unrealistic expectations: **3%**
No stress experienced: **18%**

Peter Dorfman is founder and president of KnowledgeFarm, a KM consultancy in Lebanon, NJ.

Infomediaries: For Knowledge, Look Within

Daniel Costello

Middlemen spring up in every field when they can add value to a process (although they sometimes outlast their value). This article explains a particular type of intermediary: one who facilitates the sharing and exchange of knowledge people need, to do their jobs and make improvements. What do these people do and how do they do it? These are questions this article addresses.

The disjunction between company employees and company knowledge hasn't always been so acute. A business is, after all, a community of sorts, and every community has librarians, chroniclers, sages and gossips. But as the speed of business has accelerated, the tolerance for delay in getting information has shrunk almost to the vanishing point.

This demand for immediate access to relevant knowledge has given rise to a new business role: the internal infomediary, who creates or manages systems to connect employees with the knowledge they need. Infomediaries may bear any of a range of titles and may not be designated on the org chart as knowledge controllers; what matters is what they do. "Their responsibility is to keep their finger on the pulse of the knowledge flowing around the organization," says Stacie Capshaw, senior analyst with the Delphi Group in Boston.

Not long ago, the trend in enterprise information flow was toward disintermediation. The promise of new technologies such as intranets, collaborative groupware, workflow management and search tools was that people would gain direct access to the knowledge sources they needed, bypassing traditional conduits and intermediate layers (or "middlemen") within an organization.

But direct access by everyone to everything hasn't proven to be a panacea. "You can get a lot of information off of the Internet," says David Bender, executive director of the Special Libraries Association in Washington, D.C., "but how you're going to distill that information so that you can use it becomes a problem." Bender argues that even if the right information is found but not in an easily usable form, the employee is likely to bypass it and go on.

What users need is a knowledge infomediary: someone who knows what the company does, where knowledge resides within it and in what forms that knowledge may be valuable in contributing to the bottom line. "Anyone who

Reprinted by permission of the publisher from *Knowledge Management*, September 2000. Copyright © 2000 by Freedom Technology Media Group. All rights reserved.

Infomediaries: For Knowledge, Look Within

can take and analyze, evaluate, package and disseminate information in this useful fashion is going to give somebody a business advantage," says Bender.

These working knowledge partnerships represent a step forward. "If you look at the evolution of information professionals, some time ago it was, just in case you need this information, we have it available. Then it went to just in time; we would give it to you whenever you needed but not have it always available. Then it became just for you. Now it has become just with you,'" says Bender. Instead of merely providing an infrastructure for tapping into knowledge, infomediaries work proactively to understand the informational needs of individuals and cooperate with them to achieve business goals.

Infomediaries are not necessarily limited to chief learning or knowledge officers or formal members of a knowledge management team. IBM's Institute for Knowledge Management (IKM) in Cambridge, Mass., recently examined this emerging role. "We looked at 13 or 14 different jobs, and they had diverse names, diverse industries and diverse kinds of surface descriptions: 'learning supporter' at GM, 'knowledge steward' at Arthur D. Little, 'relationship manager' at IBM and so on," says Joseph Horvath, a senior consultant and research manager at IKM.

> Infomediaries are not necessarily limited to chief learning or knowledge officers or formal members of a knowledge management team.

```
┌───────────┐     ┌───────────┐     ┌───────────┐
│ Knowledge │ ←→  │ Knowledge │ ←→  │ Knowledge │
│  Seekers  │     │Infomediary│     │  Sources  │
└───────────┘     └───────────┘     └───────────┘
```

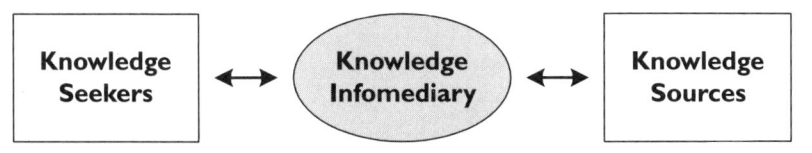

Figure 1. **Infomediaries connect knowledge seekers with the sources they need**

Three Kinds of Help

The researchers did identify common denominators that help clarify what the occupants of these various positions do. "It boils down to three categories that we call stewards, brokers and researchers," says Horvath. By understanding these segments, companies can begin to understand how to identify the appropriate infomediary for their organization.

The primary infomediary role of a *knowledge steward*, explains Horvath, is to collect, analyze and organize tacit knowledge held by individuals within an organization, which may be a team, a department or a whole company. Rather than working one-on-one to fill individual needs for information, stewards act as observers—watching what people are doing and interviewing individuals—to uncover and translate tacit knowledge into explicit knowledge. A steward might, for example, interview a sales representative after he or she completes a large deal to develop a best practices story from which others can learn. Stewards also act as evangelists to market the value of knowledge sharing and encourage everyone to contribute information and utilize the KM systems. In this sense, the chief knowledge officer is an executive-level steward.

Many companies have found that they can't just throw technology at the problem of capturing and sharing information and expect people to use the system. Instead, it takes a commitment to making sure the content in the KM system stays current and relevant. Horvath points out that if you develop a collection of lessons learned or best practices, somebody should have responsibility, even part-time, to manage and nurture that repository. "When usage starts to drop off, that person can remind and cajole users and make sure that the content stays fresh and gets routed to the people who have the necessary expertise to evaluate its quality," he says.

Rather than focusing on capturing or codifying knowledge, *knowledge brokers* have a more direct connection to knowledge seekers and project teams. "The dominant function is establishing connections between individuals to achieve the transfer of tacit knowledge one-to-one," says Horvath. In other words, brokers connect individuals so they learn from each other, converting tacit knowledge into value for the company. Approachability, credibility, experience within the company, personal networking skills and responsiveness characterize successful knowledge brokers. For example, a broker might be a partner at a consulting firm who responds informally to inquiries from consultants within the firm about a given area of practice with suggestions or pointers to sources of information and instances of best practices.

Brokers facilitate information sharing to accomplish specific business goals. For example, at Viant Corp., a digital business consulting firm based in Boston, knowledge brokers are half of a combined "high-tech, high-touch" approach to knowledge management. "The high-tech component is a knowledge management system and processes," says Chris Newell, Viant's chief knowledge officer. "The high-touch component is these roles we call project catalysts." Rather than waiting passively for someone to come to them, project catalysts are integrated with business teams. This role was designed for active, experienced people who work with teams throughout a project's life cycle. They help with everything from identifying skills and expertise a team already has or may need when launching a new project through ensuring that knowledge is captured and deposited in a knowledge repository.

The third major infomediary role is the *knowledge researcher*, whose primary function, according to Horvath, is to search for, retrieve and deliver explicit knowledge residing primarily outside the business. This role tends to mix knowledge of the business with research and retrieval skills. A good knowledge researcher exhibits the desire to help others, strong online search capabilities, knowledge of the industry and general intellectual curiosity. This area features corporate librarians and records managers, although there are some differences between the two as they apply to knowledge intermediation.

Records management, explains Delphi's Capshaw, typically looks at how we categorize information and how we build taxonomies to classify records. Librarians tend to focus on "requirements analysis" as well as search and retrieval. They are trained to help someone figure out what they need (as

Type of Knowledge Infomediary	What does the infomediary do?	How is knowledge converted?	How does the intermediary interact with the knowledge seeker?	How the intermediary interact with the knowledge source?
Steward	Capture knowledge	Tacit to explicit	Indirect request	Internal
Broker	Connect people	Tacit to tacit	Direct request	Internal
Researcher	Search, retrieve, transfer	Explicit for transfer	Direct request	Internal, external

Figure 2. **Infomediary roles can be classified into three major types: steward, broker, and researcher, according to IBM's Institute for Knowledge Management**

opposed to what they might be asking for), where the information is and how to present it in the most useful package.

Able to Change

A successful infomediary also adapts to changing environments and evolving needs. "When you look at the profile of someone who is working effectively as a knowledge leader, regardless of what their background is, it's the ability to become a chameleon," says Capshaw. An infomediary may have to fill multiple functions in a single day. For instance, in one meeting he or she may discuss the records management needs of a particular team, but in another present an IT perspective. At another time, the infomediary might have to talk about how the company evaluates and acquires external publications. So even though many infomediaries come from areas of specialization, they have to be able to generalize and maintain an overview perspective.

The Delphi Group recently found that successful infomediaries have been with their organization at least 10 years and exhibit a passion for knowledge management. "If you think about it, it takes a fairly extroverted person, day-in and day-out, to be talking to people about knowledge," says Capshaw. "You have to find somebody who has the subject matter expertise as well as the personality to do a good job at this. It's almost a knowledge management marketing function." For that reason, she says, few knowledge leaders are hired from the outside. Even when these jobs are advertised, they're more likely to be filled from within the organization.

It can be difficult to attract good people to this role. To begin with, those with expertise are in demand. Some people won't want to go into roles that they perceive as having no status. They may wonder whether this new role in the corporation is an advance or leads to a career dead-end and whether there is a path out if problems arise. A scientist, for example, might see no advantage in being pulled from his or her core competencies in the lab to spend part of the day helping others advance their own research.

Viant tries to promote acceptance of the infomediary role. It begins by choosing knowledge catalysts who are respected, fairly senior individuals who convey status to this role. Second, their tenure is temporary. "We do it by rotation. We don't want them to come in and stay in this enterprise role," says Newell. The short term not only makes the position more palatable for senior executives, it builds an understanding and acceptance of what infomediaries do when more people experience this role.

Facilitating Technology

The proliferation of internal portals is enabling direct access to many types of information. While the self-service model may appear to obviate the need for intermediation, the two actually are complementary. A well-designed knowledge portal can support and enhance the human role by providing easy, timely answers to routine or standardized information. At the same time, the infomediary is skilled at ensuring that these tools provide what the knowledge employees need. As part of a team developing a knowledge-base portal, infomediaries can draw upon their expertise and resources to facilitate the collection, categorization, repackaging and presentation of relevant knowledge.

In reality, though, such portals are limited. Most knowledge doesn't lend itself to being codified in technology. "We believe that when we finish building or rebuilding a system—even if it's the most advanced system you could imagine, with expertise location capability and incredible searching ability—80 percent of the knowledge is still tacit," says Viant's Newell.

In this murky environment, human infomediaries can shine. They make the connections to tacit knowledge and can set up formal as well as informal channels to translate it into explicit knowledge. They collect, evaluate and repackage tacit knowledge to give everyone access, and they facilitate the transfer of experiences and insights directly between individuals. "They have knowledge mostly in their heads about where there are similarities across the organization—not only where it is, but who is more inclined to share it," says Capshaw.

Determining Value

To date, estimates of return on investment (ROI) in knowledge intermediaries have been nebulous. Historically, information technology has gotten the upper hand with management because its costs and ROI are easier to identify. As knowledge infomediaries find a higher profile, their value should become easier to quantify.

Capshaw notes that libraries and records centers have struggled to maintain their budgets as IT is introduced, but that situation may change. "In this information age, I think people are acknowledging there is more to it than sticking a Web browser on your desktop," she says. "There is usually a curve organizations go through of Why do we need intermediaries? We have the Web. We have Yahoo. We have Alta Vista. We can do our own searching. Then the organization usually comes full circle and says, What are we doing? We are not paying engineers to surf the Web all day."

Businesses are beginning to discover that the next point on this curve is internal infomediaries. They perform a variety of functions, such as acting as a knowledge steward, broker or researcher, and possess a range of skills from personal networking, listening and trustworthiness to online search, content management and experience with the firm. But common among all infomediaries is the ability to connect employees with the knowledge they need, whether that knowledge resides in another person, an internal knowledge repository or a database far away.

Daniel Costello writes about business and technology from Santa Monica, Calif.

Quality Transformation

VOICE OF THE CUSTOMER

How to Implement a Customer Satisfaction Program

Earl Naumann, Donald W. Jackson, Jr., and Mark S. Rosenbaum

Managers recognize that customer satisfaction is critical—yet many customer satisfaction initiatives accomplish nothing. The authors of this tactical article contend that an effective customer satisfaction program must be based on an understanding of customer value. They outline the factors to be considered in implementing a customer satisfaction program and then present a hypothetical case study that shows how these factors can be used.

Customer satisfaction is undoubtedly one of the top strategic issues in the new decade. It has been a major topic of discussion in American boardrooms since the 1980s, yet the exact formula for creating an effective customer satisfaction program is still murky. Given that customer satisfaction is positively related to loyalty, which in turn leads to increased profitability, market share, and growth, the importance of developing an effective program is critical.

To try and clear up this murkiness, researchers have explored the failures of many customer satisfaction programs. According to a study conducted by Arthur D. Little and McKinsey (Duffin 1993), fewer than one-third of all customer satisfaction initiatives accomplished anything, and two-thirds of them ground to a halt. Ahire (1996) cites the major reasons for these failures as lack of top management commitment, unrealistic expectations about the time

Reprinted with permission from *Business Horizons*, January-February 2001. Copyright © 2000 by The Board of Trustees at Indiana University, Kelley School of Business. All rights reserved.

frame and cost of implementing them, over- or under-reliance on statistical methods, and the failure to develop and sustain a quality-oriented corporate culture.

A major problem with most customer satisfaction programs is that they begin with an attempt by the marketing research department to send customers an "off-the-shelf" survey, or one from another company, to probe their attitudes about customer service. Although this seems to be an easy and inexpensive method, the results are generally less than satisfactory. Each firm should take the initiative to develop its own measurement program based on its needs and the needs of its customers. Only then will survey results be useful to management and lead to future improvements.

An effective customer satisfaction program must be based on an understanding of *customer value*—from the customer's perspective, the ratio of the expected benefits of a product or service to the expected outlays. Because customers can seldom determine the benefits or outlays objectively, their expectations and perceptions of them become critical. These expectations and perceptions can be separated into two groups: *hygiene factors* and *satisfiers*. Hygiene factors are mandatory for satisfying customers, whereas satisfiers are enhancing factors—the "extras." A McDonald's customer may indicate that cleanliness is a hygiene factor, but that the children's play area is a satisfier. As a result, high satisfaction levels can be achieved when hygiene factors meet customer expectations and satisfiers are delivered at levels that *exceed* those expectations. (For a discussion of these two factors in creating customer value, be sure to read "One More Time: How Do You Satisfy Customers?" by Earl Naumann and Donald W. Jackson, Jr., in the May-June 1999 issue of *Business Horizons*.)

> An effective customer satisfaction program must be based on an understanding of *customer value*—from the customer's perspective.

How does a firm foster satisfaction for its customers? Figure 1 outlines the various factors to be considered in implementing a customer satisfaction program. It attempts to correct for the potential problem of focusing solely on customers, striving instead for the goal of maximizing customer value. The following analysis is based on this proposed model. The order in which each factor is reviewed is not important. However, all the factors are important in developing an effective customer satisfaction program.

Figure 1. **Factors influencing a customer satisfaction program**

Senior Management Support

Senior management has a critical role in the success or failure of any customer satisfaction program. The impetus to develop the program must begin there. No firm can truly satisfy its customers unless top management acts as the chief satisfier, paving the way for all business units and employees to join the bandwagon. Unfortunately, top management's enthusiasm tends to dwindle when the expected benefits of implementing the program are not realized in the short term.

> Most programs of any kind fail due to the lag between the philosophy and actual results.

Most programs of any kind fail due to the lag between the philosophy and actual results. During the hiatus between implementation and review, both management and workers become frustrated and lose interest. Top management also tends to leave employees out of the program design process, which explains the common lack of employee support.

To prove that the upper echelons "walk the talk," senior managers may consider linking everyone's compensation, including their own, to customer satisfaction. Before resorting to this method, however, they need to ensure that everyone in the firm has training and support. Overall, senior management must play various roles in creating a customer service program: implementing the initiative, supporting that initiative for the long run, and continually encouraging employee teams to contribute their efforts and ideas.

Customer Information

Companies that build a customer orientation by placing customers' interests first, while still including those of all other stakeholders, tend to perform better than companies that do not. But who are a firm's customers?

To develop a customer satisfaction program, the term "customer" must be well defined. In addition to the traditional consumer, there are three groups of customers that are often neglected in customer satisfaction programs: internal customers, channel members in consumer markets, and buying center members in business-to-business markets. In some companies or divisions, intracompany transfers may constitute a large portion of sales, so generating satisfaction among these internal customers is very important.

As power has shifted more clearly to consumers, channel intermediaries (particularly those close to the consumer) have gained power as well. Because of the diversity of brands competing for shelf space, retailers play more of a gatekeeper role than ever before. Ensuring that they remain satisfied is obviously important. However, channels may also include brokers, wholesalers, and distribution centers, each of whom may have different decision criteria. A good customer satisfaction program will include at least the most important of these types of channel customers.

Business-to-business marketing often implies satisfying the purchasing manager. However, the power to formulate purchase decisions is dispersed

How to Implement a Customer Satisfaction Program

among various individuals in most firms. In a high-tech industry, people from such departments as engineering, production, purchasing, quality assurance, and research and development may be involved in the purchase decision process. Because each department evaluates suppliers differently, an effective customer satisfaction program needs to pursue the multiple views normally found in the buying decision.

How does a company obtain information from all of its customers? The first step is to gather it from customer contact personnel, account data, warranty cards, and/or service records. Although such internally generated information is somewhat biased, it normally reveals general customer issues and is readily available at little or no additional cost.

The second step is to search for high-quality information on customers' priorities and their degree of satisfaction with the current state of processes. Examples of this approach include soliciting customer feedback on a company Web site, installing toll-free hotlines to customer service, and analyzing shifts in purchasing through secondary market research.

Another important step that yields information is simply to talk to customers. This will help alleviate problems often associated with using one survey instrument to solicit feedback from all customer segments. It can also help customers focus on the entire relationship instead of just the last transaction. Customers are rarely completely honest with companies during face-to-face evaluations, however; often they tend to be overly complimentary. So the goal should be to discover everything that is important to them rather than solicit straightforward opinions about their satisfaction with the company. In particular, this discovery should include their perceptions of not only product quality but also service quality and price. And customer viewpoints should transcend the entire life of the product, not just right after the purchase transaction.

Once the company has obtained customer information, it must determine the importance of various criteria. Although management input is critical in such an assessment, we recommend using customer input as well. During open-ended interviews, customers can be asked to define critical incidents—situations in which they were either very satisfied or very dissatisfied. The onus is on management to sift through these responses and identify the common key threads that yield satisfaction. Management should focus on closing performance gaps before trying to exceed customer expectations. Other ways of determining the relative importance of criteria are to have customers use a rating scale, a rank ordering, or a forced allocation technique.

A strategic option every company should consider is to share customer satisfaction data with the customers. Currently, most firms overlook the opportunity to provide such feedback. One company that does not miss that opportunity is the Kenmar Corporation. And not only does Kenmar use customer feedback to achieve a competitive advantage, it also involves its customers in collecting service problems. Any time the company receives a low

A strategic option every company should consider is to share customer satisfaction data with the customers.

score on a survey question, it initiates an action plan. After gaining management approval, the plan is sent to the unsatisfied customer for final approval.

The most common weakness at this point is to include only current customers in the discovery process. Ideally, both former and potential customers should also be included. Customers often leave not because of price concerns but because of service issues, so former customers may offer a plethora of needed service information. They can normally provide a detailed statement of the strengths and weaknesses of a particular firm, while potential customers are a good source of overall industry perceptions and trends. The objective is to obtain an initial view of appropriate benchmark criteria—that is, how the firm stacks up against the competition.

> When gathering customer information, it is often helpful to sort the responses into three categories: requirements, expectations, and wants.

When gathering information, it is often helpful to sort the responses into three categories: requirements, expectations, and wants. Requirements are those product and service attributes that customers must possess. If a company buys a copy machine and needs delivery in a week, that becomes a requirement. In contrast, expectations are product or service quality standards that the product *should* possess, such as ease of use or a warranty. The wants—sometimes referred to as "delighters" or "exciters"—are those things customers would like to have but do not really expect, such as unusually outstanding service.

A word of caution here: while it is often possible to distinguish between requirements, expectations, and wants at any one point in time, customer views may change. An expectation this year may be a requirement next year. The rate of change among categories is determined largely by the products or services offered by the competition. Customer expectations are not static, so company performance must keep up.

Measuring satisfaction must be a continuous process that infuses the voice of the customer into the firm's decision process. There are three reasons for this. First, very few firms ever achieve 100 percent customer satisfaction. But by striving for it, a company will continuously improve, along with employee morale and satisfaction. Second, because customers' views are constantly changing, if a customer satisfaction program presents only one-shot glimpses of those views, the customers may drift away. If their needs are dynamic and the firm is static, gaps will emerge. The third reason involves competition. Although some competitors may not change, many will. If a firm is not engaging in competitive benchmarking on a continual basis, competition may overtake it. The firm may be improving, but at a slower rate than its competitors. The results will be competitive vulnerability followed by poorer financial performance.

Benchmarking

Benchmarking—the process of comparing performance to some standard—has emerged in leading-edge companies as an informational tool to support continuous improvement and competitive advantage. There are typically three benchmarking standards.

The first is a comparison with an internal performance base, such as a past performance indicator. A key reason for exerting a great deal of effort in the initial customer satisfaction survey is to provide a reliable base for future comparison.

The second standard, an industry-wide comparison, includes two types. The first occurs when a firm, such as J.D. Power & Associates, gathers and disseminates information about the various competitors in an industry. However, the data are seldom in a form consistent with a firm's internal historical customer satisfaction data, so comparisons are more difficult. These surveys do provide a beneficial basis for comparison and can raise issues that may have been overlooked in internal surveys.

Another industry-wide comparison type of standard involves a number of competitors or a trade association jointly funding a study that compares the performance of each company with an industry average. The cost to each firm is usually low because several firms are helping to defray it. The company data are proprietary, while the overall averages are shared among the participants. The specific questions can be modified somewhat to fit a participating firm's needs. Thus, this standard is normally more detailed and useful than the more generic type.

The third and most useful benchmark standard is against key competitors. A firm needs to identify those competitors in its industry and gather information from their customers as well as its own. A detailed profile of competitive strengths and weaknesses can be combined with relative importance ratings, allowing the firm to pinpoint critical deficiencies and develop detailed action plans to correct any shortcomings.

Some firms have taken this type of benchmarking a step further. Instead of just developing a benchmark on competitors, they identify the best firm in any industry at a particular activity. L.L. Bean may be benchmarked for telephone order processing or customer service. American Express may be benchmarked for billing and payment transactions. Regardless of how the external benchmarking is conducted, it provides a measure of reality. Although an internal survey of current customers may reveal information, competitive benchmarks reveal potential threats and weaknesses vis-à-vis the company and its external environment.

In the quest for competitive advantage, it may not always be best to copy the very best. It may be better to use "best value benchmarking" rather than best practices. Best value is the solution that produces the most beneficial practices for the least expenditure of money and time. For example, says Rayner (1996), best practices might call for cutting delivery time by 60 percent, but achieving this might require spending $1 million on new equipment and take two years to implement. On the other hand, the best value solution might cost $40,000, take two months to implement, and improve delivery time by 30 percent.

In the quest for competitive advantage, it may not always be best to copy the very best.

Although benchmarking can offer tremendous benefits, it also involves some common pitfalls that can impair the process. Schuster (1997) lists these as unclear definitions, unfair comparisons, and analyzing the wrong variables. Unclear definitions arise when benchmarking participants are measuring unequal variables. If a company is benchmarking a competitor on revenues, its billing system must be similar to that of the other company; otherwise it may be reacting to a false reading. Unfair comparisons occur when a company opts to benchmark with the wrong partner. A 200-bed hospital based in Tallahassee would be foolish to benchmark with a 1,000-bed hospital located in Boston. Benchmarking partners should be alike in terms of key factors, including geographical region. Finally, a company can analyze the wrong variables when it benchmarks nebulous data or data that are not critical for overall competitiveness. A hospital may opt to benchmark a competitor on departmental costs, even though costs per patient per day or per admission would more easily reveal differences that the hospital could target for improvement.

Employee Input and Action

A company does not increase its customer value simply by meeting expectations; it has to exceed them. However, the only way employees will put forth the extra effort required to exceed customer expectations is when they believe management is focused on their well-being. Any customer service initiative, says McCarthy (1997), that does not take into account employees—who they are, how they are trained, how they are treated, how aware they are of their customers' needs, and how easy (or difficult) the culture and working environment are—is doomed from the start. Kaplan and Norton (1996) corroborated this finding by discovering a positive correlation between employee morale and customer satisfaction.

A fundamental method for obtaining employee input is for management to create empowered employee teams. Although the concept is not novel, truly empowered teams are still few and far between. With their direction established by senior management and their efforts guided by business needs, empowered teams can be used to improve customer satisfaction, increase employee productivity, raise quality, and lower overall corporate costs.

The real purpose of a customer satisfaction program is to generate detailed action plans. If a company chooses not to practice continual improvement and does not make any changes to increase customer satisfaction based on credible data, then senior management has missed a key opportunity. When the results of a customer satisfaction lead to positive changes in the firm, the process is worthwhile. The real litmus test of such a program is to provide direction for organizational change and improvement. Action plans should logically flow from the data. Because many of the issues that affect customer satisfaction span functional boundaries, firms must establish cross-functional teams to develop and implement action plans.

The question is how to bring employee input into a customer satisfaction program. Insights into different methods include encouraging teamwork, so firms should use teams to contribute to the effort. The employees who interact with the customers should assist with developing the program. Management should encourage employee suggestions, respond to them, and reward those employees who solicit improvements. Employees must receive the proper tools (including the latest technology) for making fundamental customer service decisions. In the case of service breakdowns, they must be empowered to solve the customers' problems. Firms also need to ensure through training that employees know how to handle various customer service issues and understand which tools to use in various situations. Their roles must be clear. Finally, management needs to support employee customer satisfaction initiatives at all levels, providing incentives for employees to deliver outstanding quality service.

Obviously, the above list is not exhaustive and companies can implement other methods to ensure that employee input is being incorporated into the customer satisfaction program. The bottom line on employee input is that management must solicit and implement the views of all employees in developing the program.

Financial Evaluation

The process of developing an effective program to satisfy customers is far from simple. But companies should experience positive financial benefits in the long run. As customer satisfaction grows, revenue grows, through positive word of mouth, greater customer loyalty and retention, fewer lost sales and referrals, and customers' willingness to pay price premiums.

However, these revenue increases must be balanced against implementation costs, which include maintaining a customer service department, training expenses, personnel costs, and market research costs. There are also costs associated with returns, warranties, customer accommodations, and so on. Parenthetically, many firms actually try to reduce these latter costs by "doing it right the first time."

The objective for a company is to find the level of customer satisfaction at which the higher revenues outweigh the costs by the maximum amount. The exact point at which customer satisfaction-related profits are maximized is difficult to determine. However, if a firm is at a 95 percent level of satisfaction and the cost of achieving the extra 5 percent may greatly outweigh the benefits, it should probably not try to shoot for the 100 percent satisfaction level.

The Wonder Corporation

Using a hypothetical firm, we can illustrate the process by which an effective customer satisfaction program can be developed. "The Wonder Corporation" is a traditional, top-down, hierarchically managed company that currently manufactures six different product groupings, one of which is Product A. This product is considered a cash cow, accounting for both 30 percent of sales and 30 percent of the company's profits.

Although Wonder maintained a solid rapport with its current customer base, a rapidly changing market was beginning to take a toll on Product A's sales performance. Given the company's solid history and extensive customer base, senior management decided to initiate a customer satisfaction program in the Product A division. It believed that Wonder could survive well into the 21st century if it could maintain that base and keep its customers from defecting.

Senior Management Support

Wonder's management realized its first challenge in developing an effective customer satisfaction program was the need to involve the entire company. In the past, programs had often been initiated that quickly dampened enthusiasm among management and employees. To demonstrate that this program was more than another halfhearted effort, senior managers decided to walk the talk of customer satisfaction and began to devote several hours a day to promoting the program in various ways. Several actively participated in employee quality groups and customer satisfaction training. Many spent time with the employees in Customer Service and performed some of their duties to gain a better understanding of the needs of the current customer base.

Many senior managers also took part in Wonder's customer satisfaction program for employees. Both Customer Service employees and salespeople received specific training on handling customer complaints, including communication and interpersonal skill enhancement well as technical and product knowledge training. Wonder also had a special training session for its functional managers so that all would realize their respective roles in the customer satisfaction effort.

Cross-functional teams were instituted whose main responsibility was to customer service problems and develop solutions. These teams spanned functional boundaries and were empowered to implement their recommendations within certain budgetary limitations. Senior management also implemented programs to recognize the accomplishments of the quality groups. One program tied satisfaction measures to group bonuses; another rewarded individual efforts.

Front-line employees were actively encouraged to report customer satisfaction information via an internal network system. When they made suggestions, senior management promptly acknowledged them and regularly informed employees about their status. Regardless of whether a suggestion was implemented, the suggestion program was supported by recognition and personnel rewards. In addition, management ensured front-line supervisor support by making both the number and quality of employee suggestions a significant part of a supervisor's performance evaluation.

Senior management decided to share customer satisfaction information with all employees by making the data visible in many places. Surprisingly, this very simple move proved to be a powerful message to employees that Wonder was committed to the program. Finally, in addition to measuring customer satisfaction, management also measured how satisfied employees were with their jobs, compensation, and benefits.

Customer Information

Once senior management at Wonder decided to initiate the customer satisfaction program, both in-depth interviews and focus groups were conducted using contact employees, current customers, previous customers, and even some competitors' customers. From these sources, a list of more than 40 attributes that help satisfy customers was generated. Realizing it could take three or four questions to measure a specific attribute accurately, the list was pared down to 22, using statistical techniques (such as factor analysis) and several focus group interactions. The reduced list of 22 is shown in the sidebar below. Various attributes encompassed common value-added processes that could be grouped together, since a solution to one issue could affect others. Although the argument could be made that each attribute is somehow related to every other one, the most dominant relationships drove the grouping process. Both senior and functional-level management collaborated to group the attributes into seven categories, shown in Figure 2. To communicate customer satisfaction results, Wonder used simple graphic presentations, believing that the simpler the findings could be presented, the more likely everyone would continue to support the process.

The most shocking finding of this stage was the number of variables that influenced customer satisfaction. Wonder had commenced a quality improve-

REDUCED LIST OF SPECIFIC SATISFIERS

Durability	Complaint Resolution
Appearance	Telephone Response
Reliability	Information Accuracy
Shipment Timeliness	Invoice Accuracy
Shipment Damage	Invoice Timeliness
Driver Courtesy	Inquiry Responsiveness
Rep's Accessibility	Total Cost of Use
Rep's Knowledge	Market Price
Reliability, Follow-up	Supply Costs
Structural Designs	Productivity
Sample Timeliness	
Technical Quality	*Source: Naumann* (1995)

Specific Attribute	Summary Characteristic
Durability, Appearance, Reliability	Product Quality
Shipment Timeliness, Shipment Damage, Driver Courtesy	Transportation and Delivery
Rep's Accessibility, Rep's Knowledge, Reliability, Follow-up	Sales
Structural Designs, Sample Timeliness, Technical Quality	Design
Complaint Resolution, Telephone Response, Information Accuracy	Customer Service
Invoice Accuracy, Invoice Timeliness, Inquiry Responsiveness	Invoice and Administration
Total Cost of Use, Market Price, Supply Costs, Productivity	Value

Source: *Naumann (1995)*

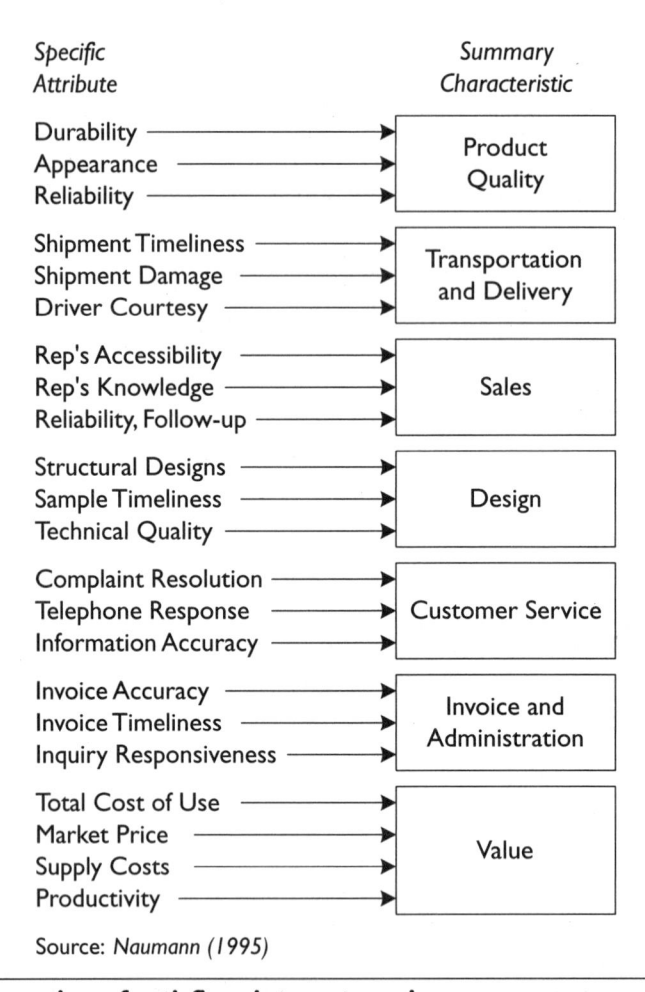

Figure 2. **Grouping of satisfiers into categories**

ment program several years earlier and had completed significant strides in raising product quality. So senior management was chagrined to find that that was only one of seven broad characteristics that concerned customers. In retrospect, management realized it had fallen into a common quality trap, focusing on conformance to specifications it had developed rather than on conformance to customer expectations.

A customer satisfaction model for Product A is presented in Figure 3. This model captured most of the cause-and-effect relationships for the product, although some attributes could be further decomposed. At this point, a questionnaire was developed for a telephone survey. Because Product A is a component subassembly sold to about 150 customers, all customer firms were included in the research. In each firm, three or four functional areas were

How to Implement a Customer Satisfaction Program

Specific Attribute → *Summary Characteristic*

- Durability, Appearance, Reliability → Product Quality
- Shipment Timeliness, Shipment Damage, Driver Courtesy → Transportation and Delivery
- Rep's Accessibility, Rep's Knowledge, Reliability, Follow-up → Sales
- Structural Designs, Sample Timeliness, Technical Quality → Design
- Complaint Resolution, Telephone Response, Information Accuracy → Customer Service
- Invoice Accuracy, Invoice Timeliness, Inquiry Responsiveness → Invoice and Administration
- Total Cost of Use, Market Price, Supply Costs, Productivity → Value

Summary Characteristics → Overall Customer Satisfaction → Financial Performance (Sales, Market Share, Profit, Etc.)

Source: Adapted from Naumann (1995)

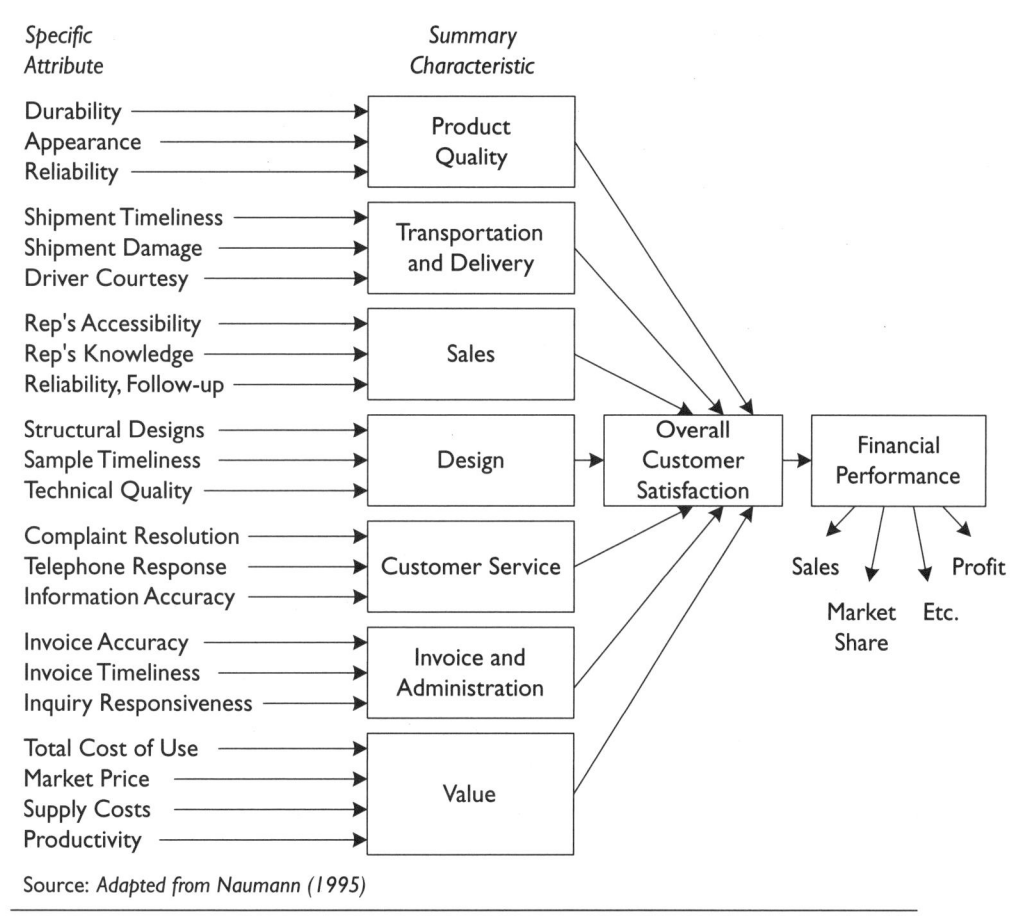

Figure 3. **Wonder Corporation customer satisfaction model**

involved in the purchase decision and post-purchase use of the product, so each of those areas was included, for a sample of 500 current customers. Two hundred past customers and an equal number of competitors' customers were also surveyed.

The questionnaire had three parts: (1) demographic data; (2) determining the relative importance of each attribute; and (3) measuring Wonder's performance on each attribute. Present and past customers were asked to rate Wonder's actual performance. For the competitors' customers, a disguised approach was used. Those respondents were asked to assess the top four firms in the industry, one of which was Wonder Corporation. If the respondents had no actual experience with a particular firm, they were asked to present their perceptions of what they thought the firm was like. Initially, respondents were asked to allocate points based on the relative importance of each of the seven broad categories. Then, for each category, they were asked to rate the relative importance of each attribute. Wonder's performance was measured using a seven-point scale, with 1 representing very poor performance and 7 representing very good.

Once the performance evaluations and importance ratings from current and previous customers were collected, the overall mean value was plotted for the sample of each characteristic by combining the results into a performance/importance grid (Figure 4). Wonder's executives were delighted to notice that their quality improvement efforts had not been misdirected. Both product quality and design were essential to customers, and Product A was viewed as reasonably good in both characteristics, though there was certainly room for improvement. More troubling were the sales and value characteristics. Both areas were reasonably important to customers, but performance was much weaker than expected. Customer service was apparently a little less important than sales and value, but its performance was also subpar. These three characteristics held some very clear potential for improving customer satisfaction. Because transportation was contracted out to a trucking firm, the problems in shipment timeliness and transit damage would require a joint effort to resolve. The new automated billing system was apparently working well; customers rated performance on this characteristic fairly high.

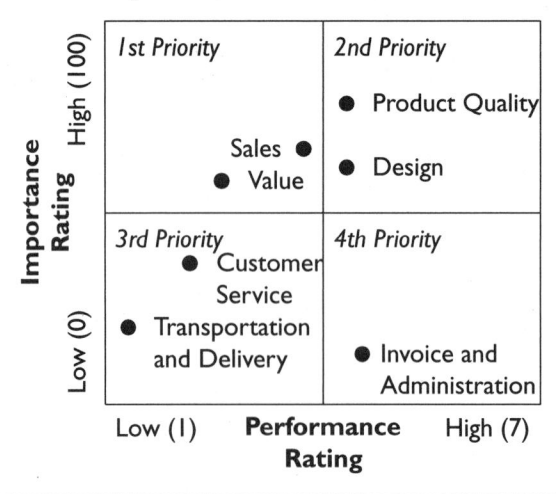

Figure 4. **Wonder Corporation performance/importance grid**

Benchmarking

The data from current and past customers provided a good internal benchmark against which to compare subsequent performance, but Wonder also needed to know its competitive position. Table 1 combines the relative importance of each attribute with the competitive data. Realizing that Wonder's performance could be compared to each of its other three key competitors, executives decided to compare it to the industry average as well.

Characteristic	Mean Importance Weight	Mean Competitive Difference	Strategic Weight	Priority
1. Product Quality	25	+1.0	+25.0	7
2. Transportation and Delivery	6	-1.4	-8.4	4
3. Sales	19	-0.5	-9.5	3
4. Design	18	+1.2	+21.6	6
5. Customer Service	12	-1.2	-14.4	2
6. Invoice and Administration	4	+2.3	+9.2	5
7. Value	16	-1.0	-16.0	1

Source: *Naumann (1995)*

Table 1. **Competitive benchmarking**

From the 200 responses from competitors' customers, they randomly selected 50 for each of the three competitors, as well as 50 from Wonder's current customers. These 200 responses constituted the industry average, or the external benchmark.

Column 1 of Table 1 contains each of the broad characteristics. Column 2 gives the mean importance of each category based on a 100-point forced allocation scale. Column 3 is the difference between Product A's performance rating and the industry average. For example, as measured on a seven-point scale, Wonder's rating of 5.0 was 1.0 higher than the industry average of 4.0. A positive sign denotes that Product A was better than the industry average; a negative sign means it was below the average. Column 4, the strategic weight, is obtained by multiplying the importance times the competitive difference to yield managerially actionable data. Column 5 establishes the priority for action; the most negative numbers are the highest priorities because they are the greatest strategic weaknesses. The higher the strategic weight, the more likely it is viewed as an area of competitive strength.

Employee Input and Action

For each category, cross-functional teams were established to develop and implement action plans. When resources were needed, they were allocated on the basis of the priorities established in Table 1. However, because importance ratings and competitive position were also gathered for each of the 22 attributes, every cross-functional team broke the data down further. Figure 5 shows the results from the product quality team. As shown by the mean portion of the 100-point allocation, the most important product quality attribute was reliability, followed by durability and appearance. However, a vulnerable competitive position made appearance a priority issue.

Characteristics	Importance Weight	Competitive Difference	Strategic Weight	Priority
1. Durability	30	1.1	+33	3
2. Appearance	20	-1.1	-22	1
3. Reliability	50	-0.3	-15	2

Source: *Adapted from Naumann (1995)*

Figure 5. **Product quality characteristics**

Figure 6 shows how the product quality team assigned responsibility for its area. Because Product A contained components purchased from Suppliers A and B, outside suppliers were important to improving appearance. Inside Wonder, the engineer most involved with appearance was designated the team champion responsible for coordinating the efforts of production, quality assurance, and Supplier A. Although developing the action plan was a team effort, final responsibility rested with the team champion.

By this time, Wonder was not quite a year into its customer satisfaction program for Product A. The process had been trying at times, but employees were becoming believers. There were 22 teams functioning and progress had been completed in every attribute, although successes were harder to obtain

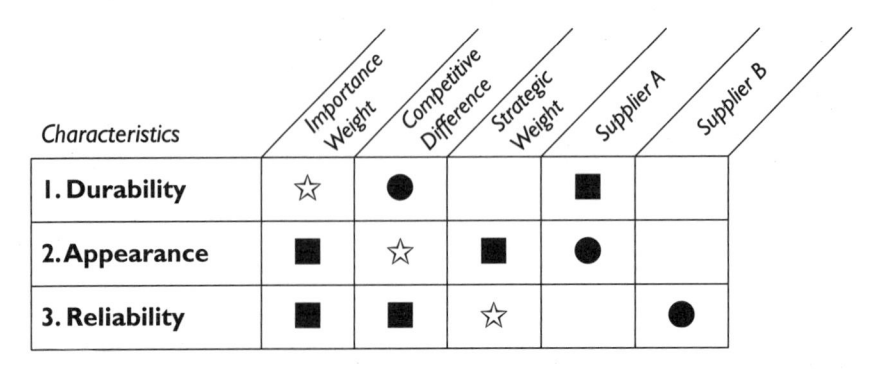

Characteristics	Importance Weight	Competitive Difference	Strategic Weight	Supplier A	Supplier B
1. Durability	☆	●		■	
2. Appearance	■	☆	■	●	
3. Reliability	■	■	☆		●

☆ High Involvement---The Champion
● Moderate Involvement---Team Member
■ Low Involvement---Team Member

Source: *Adapted from Naumann (1995)*

Figure 6. **Assignment of responsibilities for product quality**

in some areas than in others. While the aggregate customer satisfaction score comprising three overall measures was a relatively crude measure, current external benchmark data (Figure 7) demonstrated that Wonder had overtaken

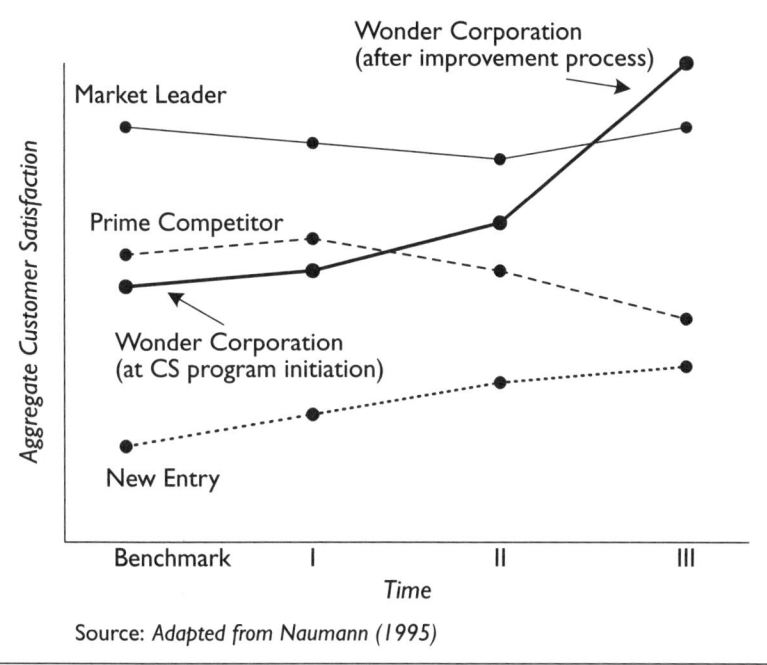

Figure 7. **Aggregate competitive customer satisfaction measures**

the market leader in overall customer satisfaction.

Financial Evaluation

To examine the relationship between customer satisfaction scores and corporate financial performance for Product A, Wonder tracks such metrics as the product's profitability, market share, and margins. The company has developed a business unit-specific model for Product A that links various measures to customer satisfaction. Using a model similar to Figure 3, it derives the attributes that affected customer satisfaction. To improve performance on these attributes, management has found it necessary to invest human and financial resources. Going back to the model, it assesses whether it would be better to make a capital expenditure to improve the reliability of the product or invest in a sales training program to increase the knowledge of the salespeople.

These decisions can be seen from a perspective similar to return on investment. For instance, management calculated it would take a $1 million capital expenditure to increase customer satisfaction one percentage point, which would account for a 1 percent increase in market share. On the other hand, training salespeople would require a $200,000 investment that would increase customer satisfaction .8 of a percentage point, translating to a .5 percent increase in market share. Clearly, although the capital expenditure results in higher market share, the relative return on the sales training was much higher and the resultant savings could be invested elsewhere in the satisfaction program.

The customer satisfaction program at the Wonder Corporation is not perfect. However, it has continued to evolve and improve. The bottom line is the positive results it has shown and the fact that senior management continues to support the program. In fact, senior managers decided to embark on the challenge of extending it to the company's five other product divisions. Moreover, they have initiated a program whereby employees or organizational groups who exceed expectations are awarded bonuses, recognition, and other incentives for outstanding customer service. Most important, the quality teams did not disband after the first year. Senior management believed that challenges associated with customer satisfaction would always arise. Thus, team input on resolving those challenges has proved to be essential, especially on complicated matters that incorporate many issues.

One can say that there is no real conclusion to any customer satisfaction program. Over time, every program can be improved and enhanced. The decision criteria may change, as may the relative importance of each criterion. Large changes may make benchmarking difficult, but most changes require small refinements, such as fine-tuning instruments. If care is taken in the discovery phase of developing a customer satisfaction program, subsequent changes should be minor. Nevertheless, the questions should always be asked: Is there a better way to do this? And if so, is it worth the cost?

References

S.L. Ahire, "TQM Age Versus Quality: An Empirical Investigation," *Production & Inventory Management Journal*, First Quarter 1996, pp. 18-20.

R. Deshpande, J.U. Farley, and F.E. Webster, Jr., "Corporate Culture, Customer Orientation, and Innovativeness in Japanese Firms: A Quadrad Analysis," *Journal of Marketing*, January 1993, pp. 23-37.

M. Duffin, "If Something's Worth Doing," *TQM Magazine*, August 1993, pp. 7-9.

R.S. Kaplan and D.P. Norton, "Using the Balanced Scorecard as a Strategic Management System," *Harvard Business Review*, January-February 1996, pp. 75-85.

C. Loew, "How Teams Transform Corporate Cultures," *Technical Training*, March-April 1999, pp. 32-35.

D.G. McCarthy, *The Loyalty Link: How Loyal Employees Create Loyal*

Customers (New York: Wiley, 1997).

E. Naumann, *Creating Customer Value: The Path to Sustainable Competitive Advantage* (Cincinnati: Thomson Executive Press, 1995).

E. Naumann and K. Giel, *Customer Satisfaction Measurement and Management. A Practitioner's Guide* (Cincinnati: Thomson Executive Press, 1995).

E. Naumann and D.W Jackson, Jr., "One More Time: How Do You Satisfy Customers?" *Business Horizons,* May-June 1999, pp. 71-76.

B. Rayner, "The Devil's in the Details," *Electronic Business Today,* November 1996, pp. 57-63.

K. Schuster, "Benchmarking: How Do You Measure Up?" *Food Management,* August 1997, pp. 42-49.

D. Spehar, "Use Customer Input for Improvement and Corrective Action Plans," *Quality Progress,* August 1999, p. 112.

Earl Naumann is the president of Naumann and Associates in Boise, Idaho, consultants in customer value, customer satisfaction measurement, and customer loyalty. E-mail him at enaumann@naumann.com.

Donald W. Jackson, Jr., is a professor of marketing at Arizona State University, Tempe, Arizona. E-mail him at Donald.Jackson@asu.edu.

Mark S. Rosenbaum is a doctoral student in marketing at Arizona State University.

Building a Solutions-Based Organization

Steve Sheridan and Nick Bullinger

It's conventional wisdom (or at least it should be) that customers don't buy products but solutions to problems. Why, then, do so many companies still think and operate as if they are selling products? That issue is the foundation of this article, which explains the difference between product-based and solutions-based organizations and explains how companies that want to listen and then respond to the voice of the customer can become solutions-based.

"We need to become a customer-focused, high-value, solutions provider!" the CEO thundered. With that, the eyes of every member of the senior staff turned on the senior VP for sales, P.J. Harris. Believing the CEO was absolutely right, Harris immediately set the sales staff to work on "customer solutions."

P.J.'s sales people, serving as the customer's advocate, worked diligently across multiple functions and business units to assemble the unique combination of product and service components that could solve a customer's problems. And some of them became successful as solutions providers. Those who had the most experience, the closest links to customers, and the strongest internal network—not to mention the personal fortitude to spend time serving as customer advocates—devised and sold solutions that thrilled their customers.

In the following quarter, however, P.J.'s numbers drifted lower. Because it took so much time to assemble each solution, the best sales people tended to work on fewer accounts. The rest of the staff lost business, either because they couldn't supply solutions as quickly as their customers wanted or because they never fully grasped the changes required to become a true solutions provider. P.J.'s people simply weren't winning on a consistent basis, and their customer relationships weren't generating the value they could.

Many executives can readily sympathize with P.J. Harris. They're finding that making the shift from a product-centric to a solutions-oriented organization can shake the organization to its very roots. At the same time, they realize that it's essential that their company be something more than a vendor with a product.

Republished with permission from *Journal of Business Strategy*, January/February 2001. Copyright © 2001 EC Media Group, Eleven Penn Plaza, New York, NY.

The good news is that it's not necessary to embark on a major reorganization in order to become a solutions-based organization. Marketing, product development, and sales can lead the charge, as long as the ultimate goal is to align the entire organization with the solutions strategy.

That realignment can take place over time, as the company addresses the six success factors that provide the foundation for developing a solutions-based organization: (1) drive solutions design from an understanding of customers' needs and patterns of their business issues; (2) augment internal capabilities by partnering to provide complete solutions; (3) create a solutions-development process that breaks through autonomous product units; (4) evolve the sales approach to reflect the differences between selling products and selling solutions; (5) create lower-cost channels to continue to drive product revenue; and (6) focus on the organization dimensions most critical to creating a solutions-ready environment.

> The good news is that it's not necessary to embark on a major reorganization in order to become a solutions-based organization.

Know the Customer's Business as Well as You Know Your Own

Yet another market study won't help a company develop effective solutions. Solutions design must reflect an understanding of customers' needs and of the patterns of their business issues. Therefore, companies must study their customers' entire enterprise rather than focus on specific product lines (see Figure 1).

There are several approaches to building robust needs-gathering capabilities. Many firms have adopted technology-driven processes (e.g., customer rela-

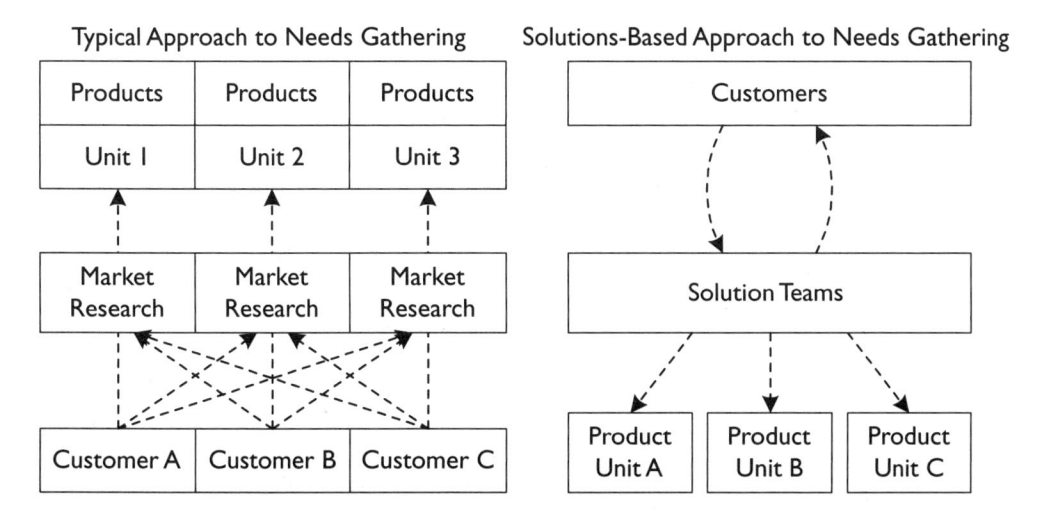

Figure 1. **Needs gathering, typical vs. solution-based**

tionship management systems) that continually bring the customer "closer" to the marketing organization. These technologies can be extremely powerful.

Technology is not a panacea, however. Some firms have found it more effective to move marketing "closer" to the customer by adding marketing professionals to sales teams. If this isn't possible, the company must, at a minimum, ensure that marketing actively participates in account-planning sessions.

Whatever approach a company takes, the goal is to guide solutions definition by continually gathering information and communicating it to the marketing organization.

Find Partners Who Can Help You Provide Complete Solutions

If a company has been bold in defining its solutions opportunity, it is unlikely that it will have the resources to supply all of the required solutions components.

If a company has been bold in defining its solutions opportunity, it is unlikely that it will have the resources to supply all of the required solutions components (e.g., products, services, financing). Inevitably, it must create partnerships that fill these gaps. However, the partner selection process is fraught with pitfalls. It's all too easy to create a patchwork of responses to a large customer's business requirements or to enter into too many partnerships. Either misstep can produce an unwieldy morass of relationships and service agreements that dilute the organization's focus.

The process of finding the "right" solutions partners—partners that will provide lasting strategic benefit—takes as much thought as evaluating a major acquisition opportunity. The process has five vital steps:

- The company must begin by clearly and carefully defining its technology, skill, capability, or knowledge gaps.
- It must develop screening criteria that address not only those gaps, but also whether the potential partners' strategic and operating principles are compatible with its own.
- It must avoid a sunk-cost mindset by developing a risk-adjusted business case for the partnership opportunity and a means to measure performance against these expectations.
- It should state explicitly the advantages the new partnership provides the customer and each participating vendor.
- It must develop and agree to explicit service level agreements.

These five steps take a significant investment of time, effort, and perhaps even money. But the alternative—addressing solutions gaps by hastily selecting among the known candidates—is a shortsighted approach that often fails to deliver optimal value not only to the company but also to its customers.

Break Through Autonomous Product Units

When individual product units are designed around a product-development process, decision makers typically focus on maximizing value to the unit rather than to the company as a whole. This mindset can stop solutions-development processes in their tracks.

Combating the problem doesn't require a mass reorganization of product development, however. In fact, mass reorganization can significantly disrupt the company. A better choice is to "overlay" a solutions-development capability on top of existing product-development capabilities.

Establishing solutions teams comprised of the right people with the appropriate level of decision-making authority is key to the overlay process. Effective solutions demand the company's best thinking, and they must also serve the individual product units' interests. Therefore, team members should come from multiple product units. Members should have authority to define the value proposition, determine the pricing strategy, and select alliance partners. Solutions teams that lack decision-making authority spend more time brokering decisions across product units than on bringing solutions to market.

The success of the overlay process also depends on visible support of the company's top leaders. Strong support from the top will reinforce the teams' decision-making authority and demonstrate commitment to the solutions orientation. And the company's executive compensation plan must reflect that commitment. If it is heavily weighted toward overall company performance, rather than individual product unit performance, managers' budgeting decisions and development priorities will reflect the solutions orientation.

Establishing solutions teams comprised of the right people with the appropriate level of decision-making authority is key.

Make Sure Your Sales People Sell Solutions, Not Products

In a traditional product-selling environment, the customer is responsible for everything from defining the problem and the purchase requirements to identifying appropriate suppliers and determining how their products should be integrated. The supplier simply responds to the request for proposal or purchase order and fulfills the order.

In contrast, a solutions provider is a business partner that helps customers at every stage of the process, from initial opportunity identification to post-implementation support (see Figure 2). This means sales people must perform a new set of activities, such as helping the customer "sell" the effort internally, and the company must redesign the sales process and sales management approach to reinforce the new set of key activities.

Typical Product Sales Process

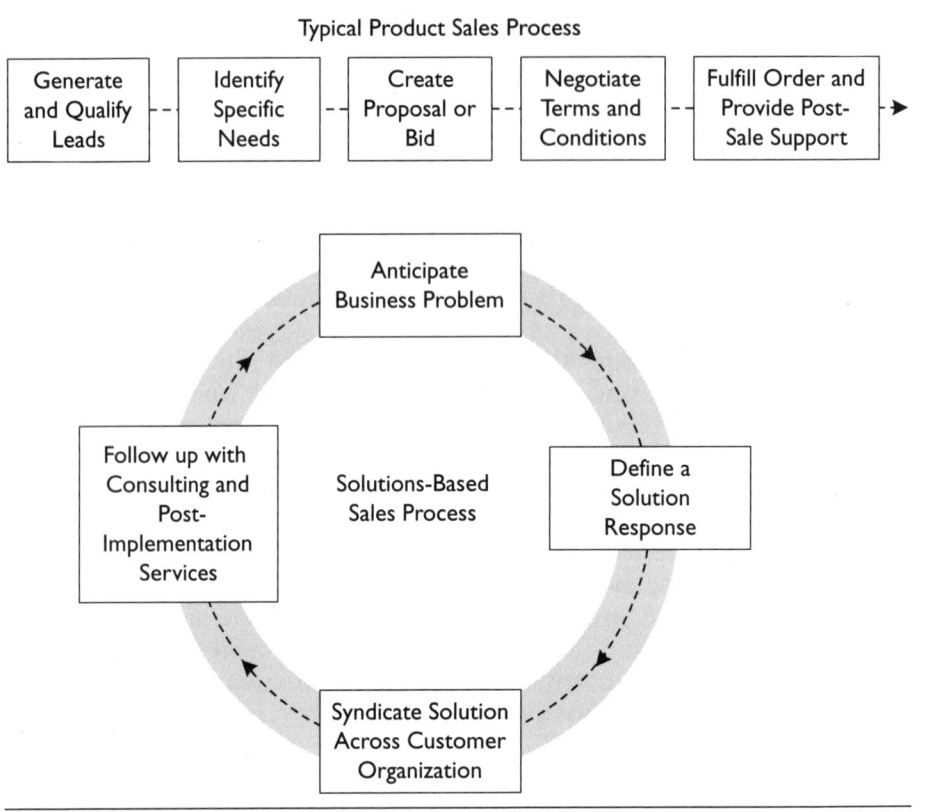

Generate and Qualify Leads --- Identify Specific Needs --- Create Proposal or Bid --- Negotiate Terms and Conditions --- Fulfill Order and Provide Post-Sale Support →

Solutions-Based Sales Process (cycle):
- Anticipate Business Problem
- Define a Solution Response
- Syndicate Solution Across Customer Organization
- Follow up with Consulting and Post-Implementation Services

Figure 2. **The new sales process vs. the typical sales process**

Create Lower-Cost Channels to Continue to Drive Product Revenue

When companies redirect sales efforts to selling solutions, sales people may devote less attention to pure product sales. This can be a mistake. Purchasers of large-scale solutions often need replacements and upgrades of the components of the larger solutions. Companies have found that by supplementing a solutions sales force with lower-cost and broader-reaching channels for product sales, they can grow not only solutions revenue, but also product revenue from new and existing customers.

Companies can also use these lower-cost channels to supplement the direct sales force. When customers order products through lower-cost channels, the company can keep the overall price of the product lower and encourage the direct sales force to focus on helping the customer solve high-priority business issues.

The two primary channels for continuing or even accelerating product sales are building a network of distributors and building a Web-based sales capability. Either alternative has dramatic implications for the organization. Companies must address such questions as: How is intimacy maintained with important customers? What new processes need to be put in place to support the channel? What are the implications for order fulfillment and customer service?

Create a Solutions-Ready Environment

The organization dimensions most critical to creating a solutions-ready environment are: (1) knowledge-building, not training; (2) management processes and leadership, not just structure.

In a solutions environment, it is important to be adaptable and nimble, because the sales process for a solution is much less predictable than the sales process for a product. In fact, effectively creating, selling, and supporting solutions requires a new, more flexible set of competencies within the marketing, sales, and service organizations than traditional sales. Sales associates must be able to identify and understand customer needs, match appropriate solutions to those needs, and justify the business case for making a greater investment in a solution.

These skills are more effectively taught through sharing and application of knowledge than through traditional classroom training. Each marketing, sales, and service professional need not be an expert in all aspects of a solution, but all of them must know how to bring to bear the collective intelligence of the organization on each decision and customer interaction. They must have access to real-time information for the specific situation, in order to have the greatest impact on performance (see Figure 3).

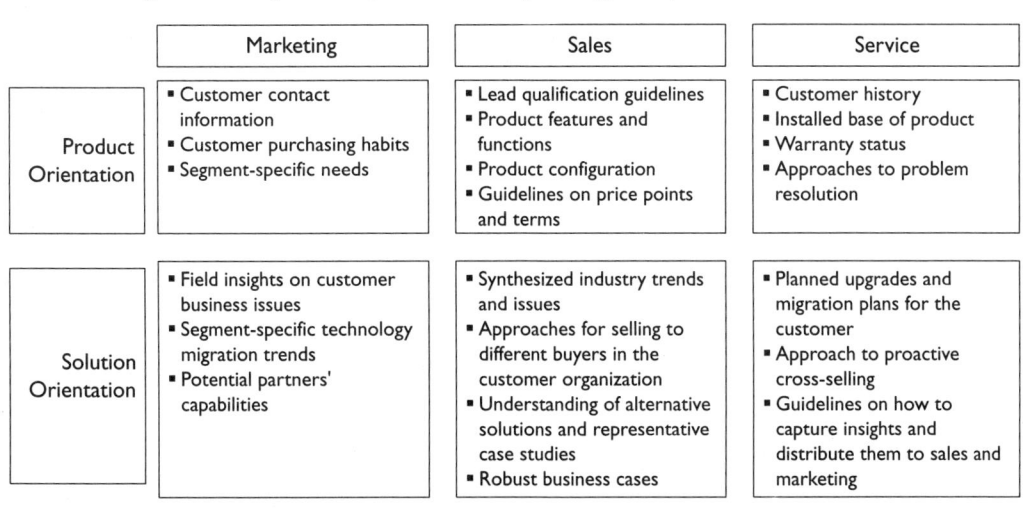

	Marketing	Sales	Service
Product Orientation	• Customer contact information • Customer purchasing habits • Segment-specific needs	• Lead qualification guidelines • Product features and functions • Product configuration • Guidelines on price points and terms	• Customer history • Installed base of product • Warranty status • Approaches to problem resolution
Solution Orientation	• Field insights on customer business issues • Segment-specific technology migration trends • Potential partners' capabilities	• Synthesized industry trends and issues • Approaches for selling to different buyers in the customer organization • Understanding of alternative solutions and representative case studies • Robust business cases	• Planned upgrades and migration plans for the customer • Approach to proactive cross-selling • Guidelines on how to capture insights and distribute them to sales and marketing

Figure 3. **Needs gathering**

Traditional product companies can also increase their solutions orientation by building effective management processes and leadership. In particular, management must be able to measure performance for particular solutions. Measurements by product line will be of little help to executives trying to make decisions at a solutions level. And financial measures alone are not enough. Managers also need to track specific measures of competency levels within marketing, sales, and service and specific metrics associated with alliances or partnerships.

In addition, for each solution there will be multiple initiatives under way, ranging from solutions definition to partner selection to knowledge building. It is critical that managers have an effective way to manage and integrate the various initiatives, both within an individual solution and across the entire solutions portfolio. Once effective management processes are in place, the leadership team can provide the guidance the organization needs and can accurately assess the organization's solutions capability.

Take Big Steps, One at a Time

Moving to a solutions-based organization is not easy. Each critical success factor is a major undertaking in and of itself. Each must be approached holistically, with an understanding of what levers (e.g., incentives, skills, process) will effect the greatest change. Because implementing a drawn-out transformation program can drain resources and dramatically increase the risk of failure, the more successful companies attack one or two solutions competencies at a time. The challenge is to identify which factor will be the most effective catalyst for accelerating the organization's development of solutions capabilities (see Figure 4).

The migration to solutions is not an all-or-nothing venture. Today, many successful companies are building on existing product excellence and developing complementary services and products to deliver a "one-stop" response to customer business issues. Companies that can find ways to accelerate this migration to a solutions focus will realize the promise of improved margins, stronger customer relationships, and additional means of competitive differentiation. For many companies with a strong product heritage that are looking for a way to reposition themselves in the market, building a solutions-based organization may be just the solution they are looking for.

ANATOMY OF A SOLUTIONS-BASED ORGANIZATION

Providing a solution requires more than simply cross-selling products or wrapping products with services and financing capabilities. Real solutions address a customer's business issue or imperative. They are comprised of all the necessary products and services that will improve a customer's business performance. They are not restricted by a company's internal capabilities or driven by a product unit's latest innovation.

Building a Solutions-Based Organization

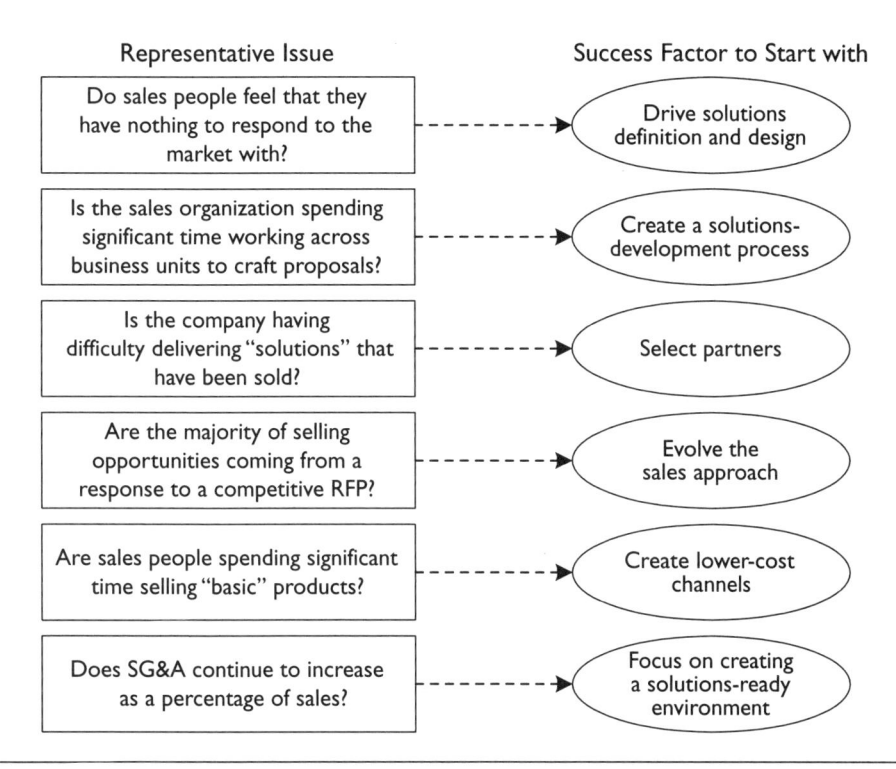

Representative Issue	Success Factor to Start with
Do sales people feel that they have nothing to respond to the market with?	Drive solutions definition and design
Is the sales organization spending significant time working across business units to craft proposals?	Create a solutions-development process
Is the company having difficulty delivering "solutions" that have been sold?	Select partners
Are the majority of selling opportunities coming from a response to a competitive RFP?	Evolve the sales approach
Are sales people spending significant time selling "basic" products?	Create lower-cost channels
Does SG&A continue to increase as a percentage of sales?	Focus on creating a solutions-ready environment

Figure 4. **Success factors**

The most successful solutions providers are those that have bolder vision of their role—a vision that aspires to directly improve the customer's business performance. They look beyond analyzing their own value chains to understanding the customers' value chains. When they understand the sources of value that drive customers' profitability and competitive position, these solutions providers can craft solutions that visibly add value, solutions that leverage their unique capabilities to meet customer needs. If they lack all the necessary capabilities and cannot develop them internally, they acquire them from another company through an alliance, partnership, or acquisition.

The boldest solutions providers move beyond the traditional role of vendor and become their customers' business partners. This partnership ultimately allows the solutions provider to help the customer set strategic direction and budget priorities.

Successful solutions providers realize that there is a correlation between customer loyalty and successful delivery of solutions. And they realize that the companies that think and act the most boldly will be the most successful.

Steve Sheridan is President and Nick Bullinger is director of BridgeStrategy, headquartered in Chicago, with offices in San Francisco and Stamford, Connecticut. BridgeStrategy is a management consulting firm that helps Fortune 1000 and start-up companies develop and rapidly implement solutions-based and customer-driven business and technology strategies. For more information, visit www.bridgestrategy.com.

Keeping Customer Information Safe

Peter Singer

Listening to the voice of the customer includes keeping customer confidences. As more and more companies are transacting business over the Internet and as privacy concerns increase, companies must become more sophisticated about security systems to keep their customers' information safe. This article reports on what measures some of those companies are taking and the results.

Increasingly, e-commerce customers will trust their personal information only to online businesses that promise to guard those digital assets. Smart companies realize this and are taking steps to protect customers' data.

According to IDC, a Framingham, Mass.-based IT research firm, the worldwide market for Internet security products increased 32 percent to roughly $4 billion from 1998 to 1999.

Many of these products were purchased to help the 90 percent of large corporations and government agencies that had detected computer security breaches in the previous 12 months, according to a 2000 survey conducted by the Computer Security Institute, a San Francisco-based organization of security professionals.

However, companies must do more than spend money. "Sometimes, e-businesses are so eager to get up and running that they skip some key steps," says Mike Bilger, Memphis, Tenn.-based managing principal for IBM Global Services' Security and Privacy Services. "The development process has to include measures to detect viruses and hackers, as well as to educate employees about security."

Companies also need to consider their model, adds IDC analyst Chris Christiansen. Business-to-consumer enterprises need to look at privacy, confidentiality and ID theft, he says, while business-to-business operations should think about a much higher level of authentication (because money and intellectual property are involved) and granular authorization (providing customers, partners, suppliers and employees with selected access to data, content and applications).

Reprinted with permission from *Beyond Computing*, November/December 2000. Copyright © 2000 IBM Corporation. All rights reserved.

Multilayer for Multinational

Ruesch International, a Washington, D.C.-based financial institution, specializes in cross-border payments of about $8 to $10 billion a year, as well as related services, for its more than 30,000 clients. Initially, it conducted all business via phone, fax and mail. Today, however, about 15 percent of its customers execute their payments using RueschLINK, an Internet-based system that facilitates quick transactions.

"Our biggest concern was security," recalls Ron Szoc, senior vice president and chief information officer. "Our business clients place tremendous trust in us."

Szoc chose Baltimore Technologies' CyberTrust, which offers privilege-based user access, data confidentiality, audit trails and user-authenticated binding transactions.

RueschLINK with digital certificates was introduced in May 1999. A Ruesch customer applies for a one-year certificate, which is downloaded to the desktop of an authorized employee. The digital certificate is linked to only one PC and browser. CyberTrust hosts the certificate site.

Ruesch customers need a certificate for access beyond the initial screen. Each employee receives a personal ID and password plus the corporate ID, and individual permission is needed for each transaction type. Individuals receive access to certain functions, are assigned a limit on how much they can commit, and can click only on permitted browser buttons. The connection closes if there isn't any activity for 20 minutes.

"We're in competition with banks, so we have to do whatever we can to gain a competitive edge," Szoc explains. "Having a successful security system in place has generated great customer feedback, and we're emphasizing this when we market our services." The company feels that its clients are confident doing business with RueschLINK thanks to its advanced security.

Virtual Wall Street

Quote.com, in Mountain View, Calif., was an early provider of Internet-based investment services—such as transaction capabilities, news and research—for some 40,000 online investors who trust the company with sensitive financial data.

Early security consisted of network-level security (filtering within routers and switches to protect the site from areas not within the public domain) and secured socket layer encryption (a set of protocols that use a private key to send documents). "At the time, we thought our security was good," says Kaj Pedersen, vice president, engineering, "but we later realized that we needed newer technology to make unauthorized entry to customer accounts virtually impossible."

Pedersen chose Sanctum's AppShield. It responds to unauthorized behav-

> **PLAY IT SAFE**
>
> Regardless of the tools used to ensure the security of customer information, there are certain steps businesses should take, according to Mark Savage, a security consultant with Andersen Consulting in Atlanta.
>
> - Don't rely solely on technology; management control and intervention are also required.
> - Align security policies with business strategies, since policies drive programs.
> - Carefully evaluate what level of security is required and determine whether it adds value to the enterprise.
> - Keeping security management in-house will give you full control, but be aware that finding and training quality security staff in a tight labor market is difficult.
> - Outsourcing security is an option, but be sure to get a strong service-level agreement to compensate for the lack of control over out-of-house staff.

ior anywhere on a site and blocks online application manipulation. "We saw this as a strategic advantage within the financial space that enables us to protect our customers," he explains.

Running in Quote.com's Windows NT environment on Compaq servers, AppShield handles about 450 million page views per month. It ensures that a Quote.com client is able to perform only those functions for which he or she has signed up. For example, some clients can only view information, while others can also conduct transactions.

AppShield's Policy Recognition Engine analyzes each page and creates a dynamic security policy based on the HTML. Its Adaptive Reduction Technology enforces the intended security policy. It analyzes incoming requests based on the policy for a specific page—whether a sell order can be executed, for instance—and passes authorized requests to the server. It blocks hacking attempts, rejecting illegal requests and generating a notification to a management log.

"Quote.com was a going concern when we decided to install AppShield in the spring of 1999," says Pedersen, "so it was critical that we be able to install it quickly and with no discernible disruption of customer service. While we expected some delays, we were pleased that adding this critical level of security was invisible to our clients."

There had been attempts at unauthorized entry, but none since installation, Pedersen says. "The success of our customer data security program gives us a real competitive advantage." Page views, he reports, are running about 15 million a day, up from three to four million a year ago.

Credit Union Vault

Eastern Corporate Federal Credit Union (EasCorp), based in Woburn, Mass., acts as a credit union for credit unions, providing short-term loans, handling excess deposits and processing checks for its 325 member credit unions in the Northeast. Three years ago, EasCorp migrated many of its business functions to the Web. Members could then retrieve copies of checks for research purposes, check account balances, locate payment notices, and download electronic transactions. This greatly increased the need for enhanced security.

"Because our members would be able to use this open forum to obtain that information, we needed to establish a system of member authentication," explains Chris Smith, vice president, computer information systems.

EasCorp selected RSA's Keon digital certificate management solution, which protects EasCorp's Internet application, issues digital certificates, and simplifies user sign-on and system security administration. The certificates work with multiple applications, eliminating the need to issue a different certificate for each one. EasCorp runs a mix of Windows NT on Dell PowerEdge servers and UNIX on NCR servers.

"The certificate is loaded onto the authorized user's hard drive, so access is associated with only that terminal," Smith reports. "When validated, the stored user profile opens a second set of 'doors' that grants the level of permission associated with the profile." The certificate contains the individual's name and the routing number of the financial institution they work for. These identify the user and index an SQL server database containing an "authorization profile" that provides details about which applications the individual can access.

Besides the enhanced security, the system offers improved manageability over traditional user ID/passwords, says Smith. Since certificates are tied directly to the authentication mechanism already in place, there is no need to memorize new user IDs or passwords. Also, a certificate can be marked as non-exportable, which ties it to a particular machine.

As businesses move from a paper world to a digital one, they will have to become more sophisticated about security systems to keep their customers' information safe.

Peter Singer is a freelance writer based in New York who specializes in business and IT-related stories, He also has experience as a corporate communications practitioner for a major high-technology company.

Building Customer Relationships: Do Discount Cards Work?

Andrea McIlroy and Shirley Barnett

Here we have a case study from New Zealand on how discount cards work to enhance customer loyalty and generate extra business. Do they add value for customers? Do they affect the relationship between the company and those it serves. What these researchers found reinforces what we might expect—the cards do have meaning to customers, but they are no substitute for good customer service and quality products.

Relationship marketing focuses on getting and keeping customers. It has developed from the traditional view of marketing that focused on single, discrete transactions. Relationship marketing is concerned with customer loyalty because of the benefits of retaining customers, and the activities involved in it are aimed at developing long-term, cost-effective links between an organisation and its customers. Enhancing relationships with customers means treating them fairly, enhancing your core service by adding extra value and, perhaps most important, providing a highly customised service for each individual. While ensuring that existing customers are satisfied with the service, many managers are also developing loyalty schemes in an effort to entice customers away from their competitors.

Customer retention has a direct impact on profitability and past research has claimed that it can be five times more expensive to obtain a new customer than to retain one (Haywood, 1989, cited in Reid and Reid, 1993). Naturally, then, considerable time and money is being spent in many organisations to develop strategies to retain customers.

Competition in the hospitality industry is intense, and this is increasingly evident as customers seek hotels and restaurants that offer the best value for money. However, cost is only one of the factors that influences customer choice. Recommendations from friends, past positive experiences and a close relationship can all lead to customers returning to a particular hotel or restaurant.

In times of economic downturn it is particularly important that strategies which can entice customers to return are used so that organisations can compete effectively and increase revenue. Hospitality providers should consider using relationship marketing, even in times of high occupancy, in an attempt to foster long-term customer relationships. However, there is an inherent problem in relationship marketing in terms of the Pareto rule. Typically about 80 percent of revenue comes from only 20 percent of customers. It should therefore make sense to concentrate most marketing resources on this 20 percent, but the problem for managers is that the most financially rewarding 20 percent are not necessarily the loyal customers (Dowling and Uncles, 1997).

The focus of this paper is relationship marketing and the theory discussed is supported by a New Zealand hotel case study. The following discussion will outline relationship marketing and the three central principles of loyalty and satisfaction, profitability and retention. These principles are closely interwoven in relationship marketing but in order to examine and discuss them they are presented separately. The final part of this paper presents a case study of one New Zealand hotel which developed and sold a discount card in an attempt to develop loyalty with their customers.

Relationship Marketing

Relationship marketing has emerged as an important topic in both academic and practitioner discussion and literature. The basis of relationship marketing is customer loyalty because retaining customers over their life will contribute to enhanced profitability. This implies that companies have to learn continuously about their customers' needs and expectations which are ever changing and often unpredictable. Customer relationships can then be enhanced by offering increased value which companies are able to derive from their learning (Morris et al., 1999). However, relationship marketing is not a new concept and as long ago as 1982, the quality guru, W. Edwards Deming, commented:

> Profit in business comes from repeat customers, customers that boast about your product and service, and that bring friends with them (cited in Lowenstein, 1995, p. 9).

Traditionally, marketing has overemphasised the attraction of new customers, but today, well-managed organisations work hard to retain their existing customers and increase the amount that existing customers spend with them. On average it costs a firm five to six times as much to attract a new customer as it does to implement retention strategies to hold an existing one (Lovelock and Wright, 1999). The costs of attracting new customers include advertising and promotion, but loyal customers also act as word of mouth advertisers and will generally spend more.

As well as improving profitability, relationship marketing is aimed at developing long-term, cost-effective links between an organisation and its customers. A variety of strategies can be used to maintain and enhance relationships. These include treating customers fairly, offering service augmentations and ensuring the service is customised for the needs of each individual customer. For example, hotels are beginning to customise service, and regular guests are given the same room, their table is booked for dinner at their regular time and newspapers can be ordered and delivered.

Nevertheless, it is important to remember that not all customer relationships are worth keeping. If an organisation changes its strategy or customers change their behaviour they may no longer fit the firm's profile. Further analysis of customer relationships may show that some are no longer profitable because they cost more to maintain than the revenues they generate.

Just as investors need to dispose of poor investments and banks may have to write off bad loans, each service firm needs to regularly evaluate its customer portfolio and consider terminating unsuccessful relationships (Lovelock and Wright, 1999, p. 114).

Before an organisation can begin to develop a relationship marketing strategy, it is important that three underlying principles are understood: loyalty, profitability and retention. These are discussed in the following sections.

Loyalty

> The key to the successful adoption of relationship marketing lies in the building of client loyalty in dynamic business environments (Morris *et al.*, 1999).

Before a relationship with a customer can develop, loyalty must be present. Loyalty is an old-fashioned term that has traditionally been used to describe fidelity and allegiance to a country, cause or individual. In a business context loyalty has come to describe a customer's commitment to do business with a particular organisation, purchasing their goods and services repeatedly, and recommending the services and products to friends and associates.

> ... loyalty occurs when the customer feels so strongly that you can best meet his or her relevant needs that your competition is virtually excluded from the consideration set and the customer buys almost exclusively from you—referring to you as "their restaurant" or "their hotel" (Shoemaker and Lewis, 1999, p. 349).

A loyal customer can mean a consistent source of revenue over a period of many years. However, this loyalty cannot be taken for granted. It will continue only as long as the customer feels they are receiving better value than they would obtain from another supplier. There is always the risk that a customer will defect when a competitor offers better value or a wider range of value added options. Dowling and Uncles (1997), suggest that:

> ... loyalty programmes must enhance the overall value of the product or service and motivate loyal buyers to make their next purchase.

There are many examples of programmes that attempt to build customer loyalty and retention, including frequent flyer programmes used by airlines and frequent stayer programmes, which are used by hotels. Typically, these schemes give returning customers inducements to encourage repeat business at the same supplier.

Loyalty programmes are often set up to encourage customers to enter lasting relationships with an organisation by rewarding them for patronage. Managers also hope to gain higher profits through extended product usage and cross selling, to retain and grow high-value customers, and to defend their market position in the face of a competitor loyalty scheme.

It is important that loyalty-based marketing should not be confused with short-term price promotions, which seek to generate momentary bursts in sales. Loyalty schemes should be carefully focused to identify customers who are likely prospects for long-term relationships.

Short-term price promotions are typified by the proliferation of loyalty schemes and discount cards and managers often believe that loyalty can be bought by this kind of inducement. However, while such initiatives can have a dramatic effect on sales, it is questionable whether, in isolation, they can maintain solid long-term customer support. Godfrey Rooke, chairman of Hong Kong DMA, commented that:

> Most people think issuing cards will make customers automatically loyal ... it won't. People tend to buy just to get a discount which is detrimental to many businesses as it affects retail margins (Australian Banking & Finance, 1999, p. 4).

Satisfaction

An important concept to consider when developing a customer loyalty programme is customer satisfaction. Satisfaction is a measure of how well a customer's expectations are met while customer loyalty is a measure of how likely a customer is to repurchase and engage in relationship activities. Loyalty is vulnerable because even if customers are satisfied with the service they will continue to defect if they believe they can get better value, convenience or quality elsewhere.

Conventional wisdom of business, academia, and the consulting community is that customer satisfaction is a necessary element and cornerstone of total quality, and that, if satisfied, the customer will remain loyal. This is a myth, and potential drawback, of having a total customer satisfaction focus (Lowenstein, 1995, p. 10).

Therefore, customer satisfaction is not an accurate indicator of customer loyalty. Satisfaction is a necessary but not a sufficient condition for loyalty. A customer travelling away from home may be very satisfied with a hotel in which they stay, but they will not necessarily stay in the same hotel when they visit that area again. Other variables impact on the customer's choice, including price, location and convenience. Loyalty is established when the customer makes a commitment to the brand and returns to the same hotel whenever they are in the area. In other words, we can have satisfaction without loyalty, but it is hard to have loyalty without satisfaction (Shoemaker and Lewis, 1999). While there is no guarantee that a satisfied customer will return it is almost certain that a dissatisfied customer will not return (Dube et al., 1994).

There is a link between customer retention and satisfaction, loyalty and profitability and this is illustrated by Orr (1995), who states that the best way to get the repeat business that you need to be profitable is by:

> ... loyal programs, frequent-buyer clubs, plain ole' [sic] good service and fair prices.

The principle of profitability underpins relationship marketing.

Profitability

Traditionally, marketing has emphasized the need to attract new customers. However, organisations today recognise that profitability has more to do with retaining existing (profitable) customers and increasing their spending than trying to attract new customers (Richards, 1998). The longer a customer stays with a company, the more profitable they become. They use more of a company's services over time and are usually willing to try new products. Loyal customers may also be willing to pay more to "stay in a hotel they know or go to a doctor they trust than to take the chance on a less expensive competitor" (Reichheld and Sasser, cited in Lovelock, 1992, p. 252). In addition:

> ... repeat patrons are less expensive to target. They are easily accessible: names, address and other relevant data are known (Haywood, 1989, cited in Reid and Reid, 1993, pp. 5-6).

Retaining customers means that you can reduce your marketing costs, therefore increasing profits.

Repeat customers also act as a marketing resource by recommending the service to friends and colleagues and positively supporting the services and products offered. They are a great source of word-of-mouth advertising. These customers may tell up to ten people about the service to which they feel loyalty:

> ... and almost 20 percent claim that they would go out of their way to mention their favorite hotel when discussing hotels with friends or colleagues (Bowen and Shoemaker, 1998, cited in Shoemaker and Lewis, 1999, p. 349).

Hotels which address this problem of customer retention are going to be more profitable in the long term. It is common for an organisation to lose 15 percent of its customers every year, however:

> It is estimated that companies can boost profits by almost 100 percent by retaining just 5 percent more of their customers (Reichheld and Sasser, cited in Lovelock 1992, p. 251).

This leads us to the last principle to be discussed, customer retention.

Customer Retention

Customer retention is the crux of relationship marketing. If an organisation is not able to keep customers and build long-term relationships, it will continue to operate with discrete one-off transactions.

> Discussions of retention marketing seem to be dominated by frequent flyer points and customer discounts. But research shows that what really drives repurchase is high-quality customer service and well-managed, strategically delivered formal and informal communications (Vavra and Pruden, 1998, p. 50).

Customers do not remain with an organisation just because of the discounts offered or the loyalty programme that is available. The service provided must also meet the expectations of the customer. An organisation building customer retention should:

> ... enable customers to receive what they want, when they want it (just-in-time), a perfect delivery each and every time with the desired levels of service that appeal to the consumer (Morris *et al.*, 1999).

A desired outcome of providing quality in all transactions is customer retention. While there is no guarantee of a satisfied customer's repeat visit, it is nearly certain that a dissatisfied customer will not return. Managers must understand customer perceptions and expectations of quality. Research has indicated that assessments of quality and satisfaction are critical in the process by which a consumer develops a positive attitude towards a particular experience, makes a repeat purchase and develops brand loyalty (Webster, 1991, cited in Ayala *et al.*, 1996). However, mistakes do occur within an organisation, but:

> ... it is fundamental and essential to commit to service recovery (Tse, 1996, p. 303).

Service recovery is about turning around a bad service experience and retaining the customer after something very annoying has happened:

> In simple terms, it's the special effort customers expect you to put forth when things have gone wrong for them (Zemke, 1998, p. 279).

The following case study of a New Zealand hotel illustrates some of the points discussed in the literature.

Case Study

Background

The research reported here was conducted in Palmerston North, New Zealand. Palmerston North is a provincial city, situated in the middle of New

Zealand, with a fairly homogeneous population of approximately 75,000 people. Known as the "Knowledge City," it is the site of a large multi-campus university that is also the major national provider of tertiary level distance education. There are also two other tertiary education providers in the city. Together these institutions account for approximately 15 percent of the population, and much of the commercial activity in the city is related to this education focus.

Palmerston North is not a major destination for international visitors to New Zealand, but it does host a large number of conferences each year and there are numerous conference facilities available. It also has the highest per capita number of restaurants in New Zealand and there is intense competition for the limited disposable income of the local population.

The hotel that took part in this research is one of an international chain of hotels. It has 154 guestrooms, a brasserie and bar, a family restaurant, a health club and extensive conference and banqueting facilities. This is one of the larger hotels in Palmerston North and its occupancy rate, currently 50-55 percent, is on a par with the competition. The business development manager believes that if it were not for the revenue from the other facilities, the hotel would struggle to remain open on accommodation revenue alone.

Currently, the customer profile of the hotel is 60 percent business and 40 percent tourism or event driven, and the average room stay is just over 1.3 nights. The hotel estimates that about 20 percent of current business is from repeat customers, but no specific information is available about this.

Corporate marketing programmes initiated by head office have not always worked in the hotel, so local marketing initiatives have been launched in Palmerston North. These have been aimed at increasing bar and restaurant revenue and have been targeted at the business market. They include a "Business Roundtable Dinner," which is an opportunity for lone business customers to meet, dine and network with others staying in the hotel, and a "Business After Five" happy hour, hosted by the general manager once a fortnight for hotel guests and local business people to meet and network.

The hotel has undertaken some specific events marketing to improve its weekend occupancy rates and this seems to have been successful. Follow-up letters are sent to the event organisers asking for direct feedback on their stay, and these are also used as a way of encouraging customer loyalty. Again, there is no specific information available from the hotel about the impact of this initiative on customer loyalty.

The latest marketing push has come from the introduction of a Gold Card, which is aimed to increase local awareness of the hotel by encouraging new customers and enticing past customers to return. A reputable firm based in Auckland markets this card, and it claims that customer loyalty and retention is enhanced by the purchase of it. It is also claimed that the card will encourage repeat visits from customers.

The card, which costs NZ $39.50, provides a variety of discounts and "two for one" deals at the hotel in Palmerston North, including the brasserie, the bar, the family restaurant, the health club, the conference centre and various special occasion offers. Accommodation deals are available locally and from other hotels in the chain throughout NZ. Sales of the card began in September 1999 and at the time of the research 700 had been sold.

In this exploratory research, the aim was to investigate whether the Gold Card promotion is likely to lead to customer loyalty and build customer retention. In order to investigate this, a mail survey was sent to all customers on the hotel Gold Card database.

Data Analysis and Discussion

In November 1999, a four-page questionnaire was sent to the 700 customers identified by the hotel as having bought the card at the time of the mailout. These customers were asked to respond by 10 December and 186 usable responses were received, giving a response rate of 27 percent. Of these 186 respondents, 56 percent were female and 44 percent were male.

No information was available about the areas of the city targeted by the card sellers. As the card was sold at a householder's door and the benefits and costs of services were explained, it can reasonably be assumed that only people who thought they could afford the card and the services for which benefits were offered would purchase it.

Of the respondents, 78 percent were 50 years or younger, and 62 percent reported a household income of up to $60,000 (see Tables I and II). The majority of respondents—64 percent—were living in adult-only households while 36 percent lived in households with children.

Table III summarises information about respondents' reasons for purchasing the card and their reactions to some of its features. The vast majority had purchased the card for personal rather than business use although some had obviously purchased it for both (statements 2 and 3). The data also show that two-thirds of purchasers were new customers of the hotel, that most of them believed that the card offered a good range of benefits and that it represented good value for money (statements 1, 5 and 6). This motivation for purchase would probably be particularly strong for the 32 respondents from households with children where the combined income was up to $45,000, as an extra $39.50 from the weekly budget is quite a substantial amount. Many comments made by respondents in respect of the family restaurant also tended to reinforce the notion that people had purchased the card because it was perceived to be good value for money. Comments included:

... good value for money.
... the ... is a great family restaurant with value for money meals.
... excellent service, good value for money.

One-third of respondents said they purchased the card because of persuasive

Age	Percentage
Under 20	2
21-30	26
31-40	26
41-50	24
51-60	10
Over 60	11
No response	1

Table I. **Respondent age**

Income (NZ$)	Percentage
Under 29,999	16
30,000-45,000	27
45,001-60,000	19
60,001-75,000	9
75,001-90,000	9
Over 90,000	13
No response	7

Table II. **Combined household income**

sellers (statement 4). While this might be a pleasing result for the hotel and particularly for the firm that markets the card, it should be tempered with comments made elsewhere in the questionnaire—12 people felt that the seller had misrepresented the card; a further nine commented that they had not read the small print carefully and felt "ripped off." Some specific comments included:

> The seller told me you get two meals for the price of one but that is not entirely true ... The seller told us we could use the gym at any time but that was not entirely true, there is limited usage. I think the idea of a card is great but I am disappointed in the way it was sold to mc.

> The main reason I bought the card was because of the gym and spa facilities. I was led to believe by the seller that the gym was much bigger than it actually is. At times when I have attempted to use the spa, I have been unable to because of cleaning, etc. I believe I was misled by the seller and would not buy another card.

These results tend to suggest an emphasis on transaction rather than relationship marketing, with a focus on the single sale rather than customer retention (Morgan, 1996). They also suggest that the customer perceived the relationship to be unequal and not the win-win scenario which is characteristic of relationship marketing (Gummesson, 1995).

No.	Statement	Yes (Percent)	No (Percent)	No reply (Percent)
(1)	Customer of hotel before card purchased	33	66	1
(2)	Card purchased for personal use	96	3	1
(3)	Card purchased for business use	16	79	5
(4)	Card purchased because of persuasive sellers	32	64	4
(5)	Card purchased because of good range of benefits offered	88	9	3
(6)	Card purchased because good value for the money	90	6	4
(7)	Would recommend that others purchase card	62	31	7
(8)	Would purchase another card if promotion run in future	57	39	4
(9)	Would be prepared to pay more for a card that could be used in any of the hotels in the chain	17	78	5
(10)	Card should be valid for six months from date of purchase	74	18	8
(11)	Would pay more for a card which was valid for one year from date of purchase	37	58	5
(12)	Would prefer a card the size of a credit card	74	19	7

Table III. **Card purchase and features**

Even though one-third responded that they purchased the card because of persuasive sellers, almost two-thirds of the respondents would recommend that others purchase the card (statement 7). This reinforces the idea that customers saw the card as providing a good range of benefits and good value for money. This is further supported by the fact that just over half of the respondents would purchase another card if a similar promotion were run in the future (statement 8).

It is interesting that only 17 percent of the respondents said they would pay more for a card that could be used in any of the hotels in the chain (statement 9). This indicates that the purchasers of the card were more interested in the local facilities like the brasserie, bar, family restaurant and health club than they were in the "away from home" facilities like accommodation.

Statements 10 and 11 are interesting, with three-quarters of respondents being prepared to purchase a card that is valid for six months from the date of purchase. However, only just over one-third were prepared to pay more for a card that was valid for one year from the date of purchase.

On a more general note, 74 percent of respondents thought that the card should be the size of a credit card (statement 12). The current card is slightly larger and therefore difficult to fit into a wallet or a credit card holder.

The customer loyalty and satisfaction, profitability and retention link has been widely discussed (see for example Shoemaker and Lewis, 1999; Morgan 1996; Morris et al., 1999; Gummesson, 1995) and this discussion has been further explored in the first part of this paper. In order to establish whether the purchase of this card might lead to customer loyalty and retention, respondents were asked about the various services used and their intention to use the services after the card expired.

Table IV shows the percentage of the sample who had used the various services since purchasing the card and the percentages who answered "yes" to the following question: "If you did not have a Gold Card, would you still use the following services?" The percentage of respondents using the services was fairly low, except for the family restaurant, which tends to reinforce the notion that customers primarily bought the card to get "cheap deals." As a customer retention strategy its success is therefore doubtful. The conference venue hire and special occasion benefits had, in fact, each been used by only five respondents and only 9 percent (n = 17) had used the accommodation benefits. There was no way of telling whether accommodation had been used in Palmerston North or at other hotels in the chain.

Service	Current Usage (Percent)	Use Again (Percent)
Bar	25	17
Brasserie	32	26
Family restaurant	53	57
Health club	24	8
Accommodation	n/a	n/a
Conference venue	n/a	n/a
Special occasion	n/a	n/a

Table IV. **Current use of service and intention to use service again**

A total of 25 percent of respondents had used the bar; however, only 17 percent indicated that they would use the service after the card expired. There were a number of comments from respondents that referred to their dissatisfaction with the service provided in the bar.

> The bartender was unfriendly and rude—after ordering a glass of wine at "$6" a glass he barely filled it past half way and when questioned just turned his back.

> Why I marked ... bar low was because of the inexperienced bar persons and having to wait *so long*.

Customers are unlikely to return or become loyal if they are dissatisfied with the service provided (Dube et al., 1994). Comments from respondents indicate this may be the case in this instance.

A higher number, 32 percent, had used the brasserie and 26 percent indicated that they would use it again. These results are no doubt partly attributable to the extremely competitive nature of the hospitality market in Palmerston North. Some reasons for not using the brasserie in the future are listed below:

> I enjoy the food at the Brasserie but the prices are quite high without the card.

> Probably [use again] although all depends on $$$. Brasserie was good ... no complaints.

> Would most likely continue to use the Brasserie, much competition in PN, perhaps other places would be first choice.

The results for the family restaurant were more positive—53 percent of respondents had used it, and 57 percent said that they would continue to use it after the card expired. This anomaly suggests that some customers were already users of this service before they purchased the card and would continue to be loyal customers:

> I will still use the family restaurant because it is an excellent place to take children.

> Yes I will continue at the family restaurant because it offers a good family meal.

Many of the comments made about the family restaurant tended to emphasise the value for money and family-friendly nature of the facility. In total there were 27 positive comments and only two negative comments about it. Positive comments included "good value," "affordable, speedy service," "good family meals," "accommodates children," "friendly staff" and "good service."

The health club had been used by 24 percent of respondents. Significantly, only 8 percent said they would use the facility without the card. While the gymnasium/health club market in Palmerston North is relatively competitive, many of the current providers are often heavily used at peak times. The hotel has a facility that is under-utilised and could therefore be very attractive to new customers. However, the benefits offered by the card did not prove attractive to a number of respondents. For example, several people commented on the fact that they could not use the health club after 5 p.m.—a prime time for many workers to go to the gym. Others commented about equipment not working and the shortage of towels and filtered water.

It is significant that over 70 percent of those who used the brasserie, the bar, the family restaurant and the health club were either very satisfied or satisfied with the service. However, the percentages of those indicating that they would use the service again were relatively low, except for the family restaurant (see Table IV). This highlights the point that satisfaction is not an accurate indicator of customer loyalty.

Summary

The overall picture is not a positive one in terms of building customer loyalty. Even with the most popular service, the family restaurant, there were a relatively high number of respondents, 23 percent, who said that they would not use it without the card. The card used in this promotion offered price discounts, traditionally a transaction marketing tool (Morgan, 1996). However, "creating brand relationships is the ultimate goal of loyalty programmes" (Shoemaker and Lewis, 1999, p. 351). The relationship needs to have a long-term focus and offer ongoing value to the customer which establishes the brand as the customer's preferred supplier. In order to do this, the hotel would need to consider moving to strategies such as bundled promotions and frequency programmes (Shoemaker and Lewis, 1999) which have been shown to develop customer loyalty, build customer retention and increase profitability. Currently, the customers of the hotel who purchased a card and responded to the questionnaire, exhibit the characteristics of Morgan's "mercenaries" (1996, p. 31). They have high satisfaction, low to medium loyalty and low commitment to the company. These customers tend to shop around on the basis of price, impulse or fashion. In order to succeed, loyalty programmes need to develop "loyalists" (Morgan, 1996, p. 31)—customers who have high satisfaction, high loyalty and who will stay and be supportive of the company. Committed customers who are loyal to the brand do not respond to the lure of competitors.

Conclusion

The focus of this paper has been on relationship marketing and the principles of loyalty and satisfaction, profitability and customer retention. Generally speaking, as the relationship between the customer and the service provider gets closer, satisfaction and loyalty levels of the customer rise (Colgate, 1999).

In order to build such a relationship, managers must ensure that customers are fairly treated, that their needs and expectations have been met, that value has been added to core services and that each customer receives a customised service. Every effort should also be made to target those customers who are the most profitable.

The hotel described in the case study has attempted to build customer loyalty and therefore retention by selling a discount card in Palmerston North. The main finding from the research was that a discount card does not appear to increase customer loyalty and that many customers buy the card because they perceive it to be good value for money. This is supported by the fact that few of the respondents to the survey stated that they would remain customers of the hotel once the card had expired.

References

Australian Banking & Finance (1999), "Loyalty programs questioned," Vol. 8 No. 10, June, p. 4. Retrieved 31 January 2000 from Expanded Academic online database on the World Wide Web: http://web4.infotrac.galegroup.com.

Ayala, G., Staros, E.V. and West, J.J. (1996), "Marketing quality in the hotel sector," in Olsen, M.D., Teare, R. and Gummesson, E. (Eds), *Service Quality in Hospitality Organisations*, Cassell, London, pp. 259-77.

Colgate, M. (1999), "Customer satisfaction and loyalty—how New Zealand banks need to improve," *University of Auckland Business Review*, Vol. 1 No. 1, pp. 36-48.

Dowling, G.R. and Uncles, M. (1997), "Do customer loyalty programs really work?" *Sloan Management Review*, Vol. 38 No. 4, pp. 71-82. Retrieved 14 December 1999 from ABI online database.

Dube, L., Renaghan, L.M. and Miller, J.M. (1994), "Measuring customer satisfaction for strategic management," *Cornell Hotel and Restaurant Administration Quarterly*, Vol. 35 No. 1, February, pp. 39-47.

Gummesson, E. (1995), "Relationship marketing," In Glynn, W.J. and Barnes, J.G. (Eds), *Understanding Services Management*, John Wiley & Sons, Chichester, pp. 244-68.

Lovelock, C. and Wright, L. (1999), *Principles of Service Marketing and Management*, Prentice-Hall, Englewood Cliffs, NJ.

Lowenstein, M.W. (1995), *Customer Retention: An Integrated Process for Keeping Your Best Customers*, ASQC, Milwaukee, WI.

Morgan, A. (1996), "Relationship marketing," *Admap*, No. 366, pp. 28-33.

Morris, D.S., Barnes, B.R. and Lynch, J.E. (1999), "Relationship marketing needs total quality management," *Total Quality Management*, July, p. S659. Retrieved 31 January 2000 from Expanded Academic online database on the World Wide Web: http://web4.infotrac.galegroup.com.

Orr, A. (1995), "Customers for life," *Zip/Target Marketing*, Vol. 18 No. 3, March, pp. 20-1. Retrieved 10 January 2000 from ABI online database.

Reichheld, F.F. and Sasser, W.E. Jr. (1990), "Zero defections: quality comes to services," in Lovelock, C.H. (1992), *Managing Services: Marketing, Operations and Human Resources*, 2nd ed., Prentice-Hall, Englewood Cliffs, NJ, pp. 250-8.

Reid L.J. and Reid, S.D. (1993), "Communicating tourism supplier services: building repeat visitor relationships," *Communication and Channel Systems in Tourism Marketing*, pp. 3-19.

Richards, T. (1998), "Buying loyalty versus building commitment. Developing the optimum retention strategy," *Marketing and Research Today*, Vol. 26 No. 1, February, pp. 43-51.

Shoemaker, S. and Lewis, R.C. (1999), "Customer loyalty: the future of hospitality marketing," *International Journal of Hospitality Management*, Vol. 18 No. 4, pp. 345-70.

Tse, E.C.-Y. (1996), "Towards a strategic quality framework for hospitality firms," in Olsen, M.D., Teare, R. and Gummesson, E. (Eds), *Service Quality in Hospitality Organisations*, Cassell, London, pp. 299-311.

Vavra, T.G. and Pruden, D.R. (1998), "Customer retention and the stages of service after the sale," in Zemke, R. and Woods, J.A. (Eds), *Best Practices in Customer Service*, American Management Association, New York, NY, pp. 38-51.

Zemke, R. (1998), Service recovery: turning oops! into opportunity," in Zemke, R. and Woods, J.A. (Eds), *Best Practices in Customer Service*, American Management Association, New York, NY, pp. 279-88.

Andrea McIlroy is a Senior Lecturer in the Department of Management Systems, College of Business, Massey University, Palmerston North, New Zealand. She is a co-author of Competitive Customer Service *(Wellington, NZ: Brookers, 1999). E-mail her at A.McIlroy@massey.ac.nz.*

Shirley Barnett is a Lecturer in the Department of Management Systems, College of Business, Massey University, Palmerston North, New Zealand. She is a co-author of Competitive Customer Service. *E-mail her at S.J.Barnett@massey.ac.nz.*

Quality Transformation

TEAMS AND TEAMWORK

Dare to Share

Kristine Ellis

This article bridges two subjects: teamwork and collaboration and knowledge management. It is about facilitating the cooperation and collaboration necessary for a good knowledge management system to be put into place. The essence of teamwork is a sharing of information and collaboration to achieve shared goals and maximize the strengths of individuals and the group. Understanding the sharing to make this happen is described here.

Put a group of retail marketing people together with a group of engineers who design battlefield command and control systems, and what do you have? A model for knowledge sharing, says David Snowden, director of IBM Global Services' Institute for Knowledge Management, Wiltshire, United Kingdom. These seemingly disparate groups "face a very similar challenge—large amounts of uncertain incoming data," he explains.

The unlikely coalition was formed after a major United Kingdom retailer requested Snowden's help in improving sales. He gave the group 10 weeks to come up with 10 marketing ideas that wouldn't cost the retailer any financial investment but that would produce measurable results within the year.

Then he got the company's CEO to promise dire consequences should the marketing people fail in completing the frontline objectives. "It was a very good group, and I would have no compunction about doing it again because we picked people we knew were going to solve the problem," Snowden explains. The marketers were carefully selected for their organizational connections and natural tendencies to collaborate and seek out knowledge. But once they were in the group, Snowden wanted to disrupt their presumptions about their own expertise. Pairing them with another group of undeniable, if unsettling, experts shook them up and got them thinking differently.

Snowden also wanted to quickly build trust, hence the pressure from the CEO. "If you put people together under extreme pressure, they will naturally

Reprinted with permission from the February 2001 issue of *TRAINING* Magazine. Copyright 2001. Bill Communications, Minneapolis, MN. All rights reserved. Not for resale.

trust each other," he says. "This group trusted each other completely for the period of that assignment and for quite a long time afterwards."

It's difficult to discuss knowledge sharing or knowledge management without talking about trust. While knowledge management technology is giving companies more sophisticated and easier ways to break barriers, knowledge sharing still depends on people. And most people won't risk sharing what they know without a good reason or a feeling of trust. As a result, knowledge management-savvy organizations must create cultures conducive to sharing even as they build their knowledge management infrastructures.

Giving to Get Back

When Buckman Laboratories, Memphis, Tenn., launched its enterprisewide knowledge network in 1992, CEO Bob Buckman would personally e-mail salespeople who didn't contribute each week. "He would ask them what we could do to help them use the system, then he'd sign it, BOB," says Melissie Rumizen, knowledge strategist and Webmaster of Buckman's Knowledge Nurture Internet site. "It was very effective."

One of the keys to Buckman's success in knowledge management, says Rumizen, is that the system has always been easy to use. Initially the Buckman Information Manager, as the network was called, was a CompuServe application, integrating e-mail and forum access with mainframe access. Renamed K'Netix–The Buckman Knowledge Network in 1994, the system evolved, moving from CompuServe to Microsoft Outlook Express via the Internet in 1998. Buckman also removed its mainframe system that year, and K'Netix is now powered by ERP, UNIX and some Windows NT server applications.

From the users' perspective, the system's evolution hasn't strayed from the priorities of reliability and ease of use. "Time is still a factor," Rumizen says. "People always have too much to do, and contributing to the system is an additional task. So we've tried to make it less of an add-on and more just part of everyone's work."

As a pioneer of knowledge management, Buckman Labs broke new ground in identifying and solving some of its challenges. For example, those reluctant salespeople had been hired specifically for their independence. As a global company, Buckman needed people who could make decisions and solve problems on their own. That still holds true today—the company employs about 1,300 people in 90 countries—but psychological testing of potential hires now includes gauging their willingness to collaborate.

Buckman also has informal areas on the system. In the electronic break room, for example, people play word games, exchange recipes and even pass on insights about customers. "It's important because it gives us a place to have fun and make the social connections that enable knowledge sharing. It strengthens the 'we,'" Rumizen says.

Companies that don't want to spend the years Buckman has to create a

Psychological testing of potential hires now includes gauging their willingness to collaborate.

sharing culture often try to jump-start their knowledge management programs with incentives and reward programs. But knowledge management pros Wendi Bukowitz and Ruth Williams strongly caution against this type of motivation. "We were talking with one of our human resource partners who suggested giving people frequent flyer miles in exchange for [information] contributions," says Bukowitz, director of intellectual asset management for PricewaterhouseCoopers, Chicago. "It has been done, but what ends up happening is that as soon as the rewards go away, so do the contributions."

A better tactic involves taking steps to ensure a fair return on their investment of time and knowledge. "Reciprocity is very much central to the concept of knowledge management, says Williams, another director in Bukowitz's division. "It's a credit-based system, not a cash transaction. People give with the understanding that they will get something back."

Sometimes it's a matter of recognition. Bukowitz and Williams recommend that organizations establish explicit intellectual asset policies that require attribution to be embedded into the document to give the contributor the recognition he or she deserves.

Feedback is another important return on the investment that can be dealt with through policy. "One of the reasons people don't contribute is because they feel they are just dropping their knowledge into a big, black hole," Bukowitz explains. "Does anybody care that it's there? Does anybody use it? It's really very meaningful to people to know when their contribution is used. So putting feedback mechanisms into the system is important."

Trusting the Messenger

In addition to trusting that the knowledge they share won't just be swallowed up by the organization, people also need to trust that the knowledge they receive is accurate. "With online communities, everyone has a role to play," Williams adds. "For some, the role is contribution, and for others it's more of a learning role. There's nothing wrong with that."

For those whose role is learning, knowledge management's most valuable feature is that it gives access to the *people* with the knowledge rather than just the knowledge, says Tom Brailsford, manager of knowledge leadership for Hallmark Cards' Consumer Research Division, Kansas City, Mo. In addition to organizing knowledge management efforts within his own division, he facilitates about 25 other knowledge management efforts throughout the company.

One of the projects with which he is consulting involves peer-elected subject matter experts. "The members of the online community will nominate the subject matter experts," he says, adding that the resulting status can help drive participation. "We're hoping that people will participate because they need to know the knowledge being shared, but also because they need to be recognized by their peers as knowledge people and contributors to the knowl-

GET ON BOARD

With the knowledge management (KM) train roaring down the tracks, it's time for training and human resource professionals to jump into the role of engineer, according to Dede Bonner, president, New Century Management, a consulting and learning services firm in Leesburg, Va. "It sure beats watching the train go by or getting run over," she adds.

If anything, HR has been slow to get on board. "HR is the keeper of the culture, and yet, to a large extent, the profession has ignored knowledge management," says David Owens, CKO for the St. Paul Companies, St. Paul, Minn. "It's time for them to become much more involved."

Bonner has several KM recommendations:

- **Move Beyond the Traditional Definition of HR.** Rather than viewing HR as a collection of functions such as training, recruitment and staffing, adopt a more strategic focus. Redefine training and learning as true business imperatives that are critical to the financial success of the organization.
- **Take the Lead in Building Trust.** Start with a complete and honest assessment of the organization's current trust issues, including how trustworthy staff and management consider HR to be. Examine the company's history of trust-making and trust-breaking events. For example, if an HR group was instrumental in a downsizing that reduced the staff by 20 percent, there's a strong possibility that it will have to work harder to change its organization's culture than an HR group without this history.
- **Leverage the Concept of Continuous Learning.** As acceptance of the concept grows, employees are no longer feeling forced to go to training and are more likely to be self-motivated to learn. Training professionals simply need to match delivery methods with preferred learning styles and skill needs.

KM offers HR what Bonner calls a "golden opportunity" to move into the executive boardroom. In fact, her ideal training professional or HR director of the future is the CEO. "My ideal vision is that it's a blended position," she says, "and that the knowledge of the people will finally be recognized as the organization's greatest asset."

edge domain."

On the knowledge management spectrum, Hallmark is far removed from organizations like Buckman Labs, for which knowledge management is a top-down initiative. "It's very much a grassroots effort here," Brailsford says.

Hallmark's Consumer Research Division instigated the effort a few years ago, when Brailsford and others realized that they were sitting on vast amounts of data. In addition to that explicit knowledge, they were concerned about sharing the tacit knowledge researchers were carrying in their heads. "It made sense for us to first organize what we know as a division, and then to share it, which led to a whole host of cultural issues," he says.

Hallmark underwent a major reorganization in 2000, triggering a big influx of personnel. The new faces have helped change the culture, Brailsford says—and they've made it very clear how organizational barriers get in the way of knowledge transfer. "We've gotten a lot better at knowledge sharing, but we still don't have a lot of the tools we need to facilitate it."

Although knowledge management isn't a CEO initiative, it is now part of the company's conversation. Last year Hallmark announced its goal to triple its business by 2010. Brailsford and many of his coworkers believe that more effective use of the company's knowledge is paramount to achieving that growth.

Getting the Message

There's little doubt of the value placed on knowledge management at the St. Paul Companies, St. Paul, Minn. The company's executives and senior managers convey the message both inside and outside the company. Knowledge is a key resource and it needs to be harvested, just like any other resource.

"Our approach is top-down messages and bottom-up activity," says David Owens, CKO and vice president of The St. Paul University (SPU), the company's learning organization. Over the last few years, that combination has created an environment of trust, he says.

SPU is the embodiment of the company's belief that learning and knowledge management are two sides of the same coin. "Whereas some companies will take a jaded training department and call it a university, hoping that magically it will become a better operation, we've set up a university made up of 14 colleges," Owens explains. "Each is led by one of our top executives, which is a very public statement about the importance of learning and sharing."

When employees sign up for an SPU course, they are in actuality signing onto a learning community. They get access to the Web site that gives them course content, contact to the instructor or facilitator, and instructions for any pre-work required. Depending on the class, there might be classroom learning in which employees meet face to face. And there is always post-course work that involves the company's Knowledge Exchange, an element of the company intranet.

"For instance, a leadership development program might give them two weeks to find examples of leadership in the company and then require that they write stories about the examples and post them on the Knowledge Exchange," Owens explains.

Owens is a firm believer in using storytelling as a technique for sharing knowledge. Stories about the St. Paul Company's history and tradition are posted on the Intranet to communicate the company's core values, and he and others in SPU constantly encourage their executives to tell more stories and talk a little less about stock price in their speeches and presentations. "Instead of just giving us data, put it into a story. It can be a one-liner, even," he says. Or it can be a major presentation, if the teller is adept and the story powerful. Last year, St. Paul Companies brought in astronaut Jim Lovell who told the story of the flawed Apollo 13 mission. The lives of the astronauts were saved and the mission salvaged because the people on the ground could share their knowledge with those in space.

Deflating the Trust Issue

Storytelling works because human society is complex rather than complicated. That distinction is crucial, says Snowden, whose company, IBM Global Services, has applied for a patent on its storytelling techniques. "With a complex system, the whole is always different than the sum of its parts, whereas with something that's complicated, the whole and the sum of its parts are always the same," he says. "Human society never stays static long enough for you to adopt a reductionist or purely analytical technique."

Given human complexity, you can't mandate trust—so effective knowledge management systems either have naturally occurring trust groups or they eliminate the need for trust altogether. Storytelling can do this by using "disruptive metaphors," says Snowden, that move people into a "metaphorical setting."

He often tells the story of how John Harrison, a carpenter and clock maker, developed an accurate method to measure longitude on ship in the 18th century, as explained in the book *Longitude* by Dava Sobel (Walker & Co., 1995). Even Galileo and Sir Isaac Newton were stumped because seamen determined longitude by knowing exactly the time aboard ship and simultaneously the time at a reference place of known longitude—quite a feat when their pendulum clocks were knocked cuckoo by rolling waves. The common, but clever, carpenter designed a clock that kept accurate time onboard, thus keeping ships on course. It took 70 years for the scientific community to trust Harrison's invention and admit he was right.

Ask a group of executives to give five examples of how they've treated their employees like the astronomers treated the clock maker, and they'll share their experiences. But if asked for five examples of when, through ignorance, they ignored the creative talents of their subordinates, their reaction would be quite different.

"If you move people into a metaphorical space, they can say things they wouldn't otherwise say," Snowden says. "You won't own up to a major failure around people you don't trust, but in a metaphorical space, you can own up to it in a different way."

Another thing companies can do, he says, is assign people to small groups and give them collective responsibility for knowledge sharing, rather than requiring each of them to contribute individually. If they are asked to meet a few times a year and contribute three pieces of knowledge every time they meet, they'll start sharing what they know and even developing new knowledge.

"The key is to stop trying to institutionalize trust, and step back and look at three or four simple things that can be done," Snowden says. "Once completed, they will give rise to the highly complex behaviors we are trying to achieve."

In the long term, Snowden hopes that knowledge sharing becomes so pervasive an element in an organization that there is no need for knowledge management officers. "One of the best knowledge people I know is a librarian," he says. "She has a great knowledge exchange going on by getting older employees to tell stories to younger employees, and she can't do anything unless she can persuade somebody to do it. So everything she does is sustainable, it doesn't depend on somebody on top telling people to do it."

St. Paul Companies' Owens agrees with the need for sustainability. "Knowledge management in general is more of a cult now than a religion. You have evangelists in some companies, and once they leave, the whole thing dies because it is dependent on one person or group. That's why we're building knowledge sharing into the very nature of work, so it doesn't matter who is here."

Kristine Ellis is a freelance writer in Helena, Mont. edit@trainingmag.com.

Looking Before You Leap: Assessing the Jump to Teams in Knowledge-Based Work

Rob Cross

While cooperation is always necessary in any type of work, setting up formal teams may not be, especially in knowledge work. Sometimes the costs versus the benefits are too high. The author suggests that managers consider other approaches than teams in that case. He also has some excellent tables summarizing the changes required to successfully move from a functionally-based organization to one based on teams.

We live in exciting but unsettling times. In an economy in which knowledge is becoming more and more central to wealth, effective management practices can yield success more rapidly than at any other time in history. Yet although this environment offers many opportunities, it also poses great challenges to traditional organizational principles dating to Max Weber and Frederick Taylor. Rigid bureaucracies impede the flow of information across functional and hierarchical boundaries. Excessive specialization fragments work processes, making it difficult to integrate expert knowledge and respond nimbly to environmental demands. As a result, many companies have turned to team-based structures to improve collaboration across departmental boundaries, integrate specialized functional and technical knowledge, and increase responsiveness to demanding stakeholders.

With minimal fixed asset or geographic constraints in knowledge-based work, team-based designs often seem a natural and easy solution for improving collaboration and productivity. However, experience has proven the transition to teams a difficult one, requiring infrastructure realignment and the development of appropriate cultural values and leadership skills. Drains on productivity and employee morale can occur if the design is inconsistent with a firm's strategy, information and performance management systems, leader-

Reprinted with permission from *Business Horizons*, September-October 2000. Copyright © 2000 by the Board of Trustees at Indiana University, Kelley School of Business. All rights reserved.

ship style, or employee skill base. Moreover, altering any of these elements to support the design usually requires great time and cost to develop, implement, and administer.

Many management texts and consultants begin with the assumption that teams are imperative. But we believe executives should consider alternative means of enhancing collaboration if the net benefit of switching to teams is minimal. Organizational design mechanisms such as cross-department performance measures and integration roles can effectively unite disparate specialties in core work processes when teams would be too costly. And several concurrent technological advancements in connectivity, video, and groupware are rapidly making electronic communication media sufficiently interactive and contextually based to support dispersed collaboration of specialists. Executives making the jump to team-based designs too soon may find they have invested significant resources to establish technologies, control systems, incentive schemes, and reporting structures that do not offer an optimal way of organizing.

> We believe executives should consider alternative means of enhancing collaboration if the net benefit of switching to teams is minimal.

There are important benefits and costs that executives must analyze in the decision to switch to teams. Experience has shown this to be an important analysis for two reasons. First, depending on a firm's operating model and infrastructure, the costs often exceed the anticipated benefits. Alternative technical and organizational design mechanisms can facilitate necessary collaboration more efficiently than a full transition to teams. Second, when teams *are* viable, analysis helps ensure that the firm is maximizing their value and targeting important "barriers" in implementing them. Defining the anticipated benefits and obstacles of a team-based structure can provide critical guidance to intervention and design decisions emerging in the turmoil of implementation. This ensures strategic alignment rather than piecemeal solutions as problems emerge.

The Potential Value of Teams

Will a team structure really work for you? Can it follow through on its potential to improve your firm's collaboration, knowledge integration, and responsiveness? The framework in Figure 1 outlines several questions managers can use in sorting out the benefits and costs of teams to their organizations. We begin with the benefits.

Do customers value a breadth of expertise in their transactions with a company? Cross-functional teams can both enhance revenue and create switching costs by expanding the breadth of products and services offered to a customer. Two regional banks the author has worked with are finding that a team-based approach allows greater coordination of marketing efforts and more efficient use of employees who bring highly specialized industry and product knowledge to bear on their customers' problems. For example, each has found that corporate lending teams with leasing or cash management experience can be highly effective in marketing a breadth of specialized products to a client. Uniting these specialists to provide an integrated solution to a customer's problems often reveals otherwise missed opportunities and helps establish the banks as full-service financial advisors. Though this had been a stated goal of both institutions for years, it was not until they reorganized into industry-focused teams and gave the specialists responsibility for greater account penetration that integrated financial solutions emerged.

Value Propositions of Teams
- Does the market value a breadth of expertise at the customer interface?
- Does the market value innovation spurred by integrating cross-functional perspectives?
- Do customers value responsiveness and flexibility?
- Can teams yield efficiencies in important work processes?

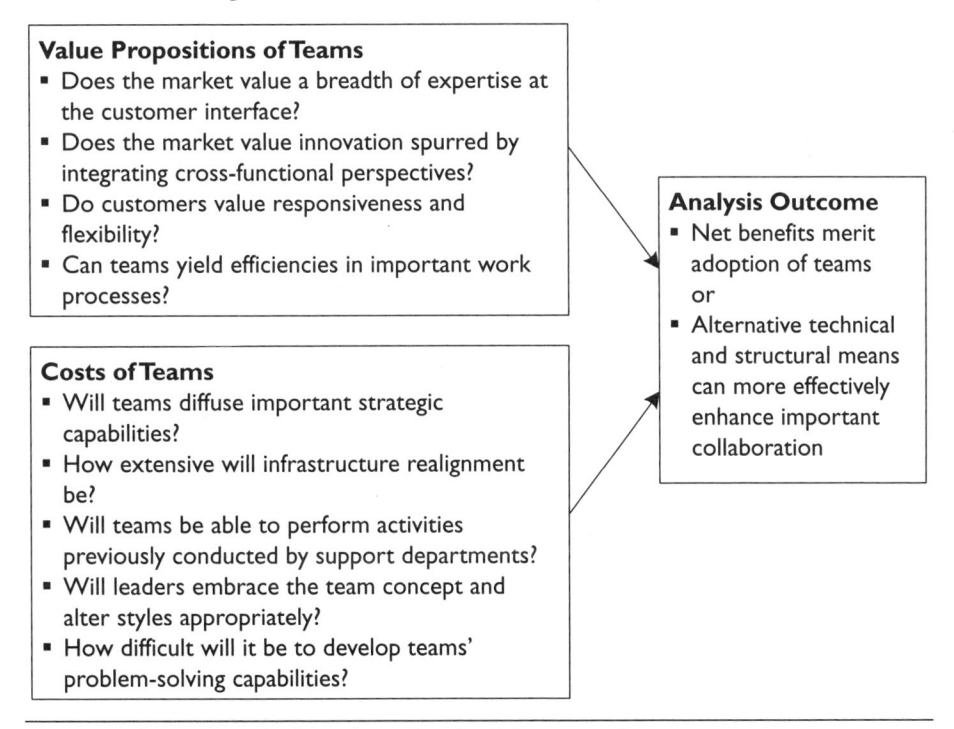

Costs of Teams
- Will teams diffuse important strategic capabilities?
- How extensive will infrastructure realignment be?
- Will teams be able to perform activities previously conducted by support departments?
- Will leaders embrace the team concept and alter styles appropriately?
- How difficult will it be to develop teams' problem-solving capabilities?

Analysis Outcome
- Net benefits merit adoption of teams
or
- Alternative technical and structural means can more effectively enhance important collaboration

Figure 1. **Questions informing the decision to adopt teams**

Expanding a relationship with an existing customer is almost always more profitable than marketing to new clients. Executives often firmly believe that additional products or services can be sold to existing customers. However, customers are often reticent to expand relationships with one specific firm—offering strategic, political, efficiency, or quality arguments for their actions. Though difficult to quantify, a company anticipating additional revenue from the transition to teams should critically evaluate the potential of such a windfall. Does the firm have the reputation and client contacts to make additional offerings viable? What strategic, economic, and political reasons might preclude customers from expanding a relationship with the firm? What is the profitability of these additional offerings in various bundles?

Researching such questions helps ground the value from expanded client relationships that a specific team configuration can yield.

Do customers value innovation spurred by integrating cross-functional perspectives? Innovation is crucial to success in today's dynamic business environment. The growing complexity of problems, the proliferation of formally educated specialties, and the pace at which knowledge becomes obsolete often requires innovation efforts to span disciplinary boundaries. Teams can be effective mechanisms for collecting information and analyzing decisions from several different perspectives when developing integrated services or products. As a result, more and more permanent teams are responsible for new product development and continued product extensions in areas ranging from applied R&D to software development to professional services.

One global consulting firm establishes accountability for innovation by forming cross-disciplinary teams of strategy, information technology (IT), and organizational design specialists. On a quarterly basis, the teams report to an advisory board on the integration of external best practices and internal client projects into cross-disciplinary systems.

Of course, innovation generally does not come free. It requires specific incentive schemes to motivate creativity, as well as organizational investments to screen and bring new ideas to market. Executives anticipating more innovation from teams should critically examine the form of innovation desired and its alignment with strategic objectives. For instance, a specific operating model will likely place more emphasis on innovation in either product/service offerings or process efficiencies. Once important forms of innovation are identified, market research or process analysis can help define the value teams may offer via greater innovation. Though such an analysis will not yield pinpoint accuracy, it can help ground potential team value better than considering innovation abstractly as an unquestionable reason to adopt a team-based structure.

Do customers value responsiveness and flexibility? Switching to a team-based design often improves decision making by uniting relevant knowledge specialists from important points in a company's core work process. Teams can be appropriate when specific expertise is commonly sought to resolve client issues. Alternatively, they may also be appropriate when specific relationships are profitable enough to warrant the potential inefficiencies of uniting cross-disciplinary functions. Ideally, teams in these situations apply better-informed and timely decision making to important but ill-defined customer problems.

A company pursuing teams to enhance such flexibility and responsiveness should actively assess its customer base in order to understand the strategic and economic value teams can provide. In many situations, team flexibility and responsiveness yield quantifiable benefits of customer loyalty that go unrecognized. In such time-sensitive environments as investment banking, responsiveness can give customers value that techniques such as conjoint analysis can help quantify. However, such "loyalty" and pricing benefits will likely not be capitalized on unless specifically targeted and then supported with relevant performance metrics and technology.

Can teams yield efficiencies in core work processes? Teaming can also remove functional barriers from core work processes. One national mortgage provider recently switched to a team-based structure to minimize inefficiencies from cross-functional hand-offs. Over the years, this firm had evolved into a functional structure with large staffs specializing in origination, processing, and underwriting housed in separate buildings in various parts of the country. High-level process maps of work activities and estimates of time spent on each task were used to determine non- value-added costs and other collateral expenses resulting from these departmental boundaries. An in-depth analysis pointed out that cycle times and costs could be saved by establishing regional centers with teams composed of mortgage originators, processors, and underwriters.

Non-value-added activities can be reduced in a team-based structure if fewer cross-functional hand-offs are involved in the work flow. Team structures capitalizing on this form of value can often be found in repetitive work environments requiring ongoing, smooth integration of various knowledge specialists—areas such as insurance claim processing, retail lending, and patient care teams in hospitals. Mapping these processes can help determine whether the benefits of organizing around the work flow outweigh those of maintaining functional specialization. A rough estimate of efficiencies gained by a team-based design can then be calculated by multiplying total compensation by the non-value-added time that would be eliminated.

> A transition to teams can have a critical yet often unrecognized side effect over time—the loss of key capabilities developed in the functional environment.

Potential Costs of Teams

After considering the benefits of switching to a team-based design, executives should conduct a candid evaluation of the potential costs such a transition would entail. A series of fairly straightforward questions can help identify both the hard-dollar investments and the productivity losses likely to accompany a team-based structure.

Will teams diffuse important organizational capabilities? A transition to teams can have a critical yet often unrecognized side effect over time—the loss of key capabilities developed in the functional environment. One commercial lending institution learned this lesson painfully. After switching to a team-based structure, the bank enjoyed greater collaboration between lending, analysis, and servicing functions that seemed to yield both internal efficiencies and greater depth and breadth of client relationships. Yet two years into the process senior managers became concerned with mounting credit losses. Their conclusion was that the depth of functional skills in analyzing increasingly complex transactions had dissipated after the transition to teams. Further, information systems had been switched to support the needs of the teams, distracting attention from overall portfolio concentrations. In changing to teams, dilution of organizational capabilities can happen in at least two unique ways. First, technical specialization, the hallmark of the functional firm, can be lost in the transition. In the above bank example, a critical capability that dissipated in the new team-based environment was risk management. This decline in credit quality was not noticed immediately but over a longer period of time, suddenly manifesting itself in high credit losses for the institution.

Second, infrastructure such as information or performance management systems may shift over time to support team operations and distract a company from its core business. As performance metrics become more and more customized to the unique operations of teams, a firm's primary business proposition can become diluted. Managers considering teams should either be comfortable with these costs over time or be aware of the additional infrastructure investments necessary to avoid diluting important capabilities.

How extensive will infrastructure realignment be? Many change efforts falter because of poor implementation or a lack of fit between a firm's social and technical architecture. Depending on the existing infrastructure, a team-based design may require a fundamental realignment of the firm's structure, information, and performance management systems. When a firm must alter itself to support teams, associated costs arise.

First is the cost of developing and administering new performance management, information, and human resource systems—especially if they must be maintained in parallel with systems of areas that are retaining a functional structure. Second is the cost of confusion during transition. Team-based firms demand fundamentally different behaviors from both employees and management on such critical issues as decision making, interpersonal relations, and goal setting. Establishing effective performance metrics, incentive plans, and information systems to support new ways of working is more difficult than executives often realize. This results in a good bit of confusion; forward progression moves in fits and starts.

In one successful transition to a team-based structure, a software development firm had the luxury of both time and financial resources to implement a holistic redesign over a one-year period. The effort met the market, operational, and efficiency goals set out by senior management; yet, as outlined in Figure 2, it required significant changes to almost all aspects of the firm's operations. Understandably, many companies lack the resources or executive support for such holistic efforts. However, at least two structural changes are critical to support teams (and thus entail development and implementation costs contingent on existing infrastructure).

First, ensuring that teams have the appropriate information to make decisions is critical but too often overlooked. To plan for both short-term and long-term success, teams often need different forms of information than firms have

Design Elements	Functional Structure	Team Structure
Strategic planning process	• Primarily a convergent strategy process; executive team responsible for strategic decisions	• Primarily divergent process; teams charged with crafting strategic plans to serve unique markets
Structure	• Functional structure without specific customer focus • Coordination of interdepartmental issues handled largely at executive level	• Cross-functional team structure with skills to serve specific markets • Coordination largely handled in individual teams; specific integration roles created to coordinate among teams
Process	• Little standardization of content or scope of documentation	• Increased standardization of content and scope of documentation
Performance Management	• Financially based statements providing budgetary information to functional heads • Functionally oriented goals based largely on financial budget information • Goals set by functional heads providing a targeted volume goal to individual employees • Individual performance assessment based exclusively on superior's assessment of individual performance	• Team-based P&Ls and balance sheets with conventions unique to each team • Balanced performance measures monitored at the team level • Team goals negotiated between teams and senior management; individual goals a function of team goal distribution • Individual performance assessment based on team leader and 360° evaluations
Incentives	• Incentive schemes based largely on attainment of individual goals	• Incentive pools funded based on team performance and distributed based on attainment of balanced scorecard goals
Development	• Development goals focused on building a depth of skills around functional needs • No focus on interpersonal skills	• Cross-training rewarded as part of balanced scorecard goals • Development goals focused on acquisition of interpersonal skills
Technology	• Functional departments rely heavily on unique technologies to perform duties	• Team-based design emphasizes collaborative technologies (Groupware)

Figure 2. **Shift in infrastructure to ensure strategic alignment**

traditionally provided. However, switching GAAP and operational information systems from a functional to a team-based focus is difficult and time-consuming. Performance management systems must move from departmental budgets to some form of team-based financial and operational measures relevant for each team's unique stakeholders. Designing and implementing these systems often requires considerable time and effort from newly formed teams, support departments such as accounting and IT, and executive decision makers. As a result, both hard and soft costs are incurred contingent on the firm's existing information systems and the skills of its support departments.

Second, switching effectively to a team-based structure requires that performance management systems regard teamwork and contribution to the team as more important than in most individually focused appraisal systems. Often this results in a transition from a tenure or grade-based system to a salary scheme that rewards for skills or knowledge contributed to the team as a unit. In addition to base pay schemes, team-based organizations often use bonuses that focus on team performance. Again, both hard and soft costs accompany this transition. The time and money consumed in redesigning performance management systems often far exceed expectations. Moreover, enormous drains on productivity frequently result as employees comfortable with an individualistic reward system suddenly find a portion of their pay "at risk" based on the performance of others.

Will leaders embrace the team concept and alter styles appropriately? Many leaders have developed an authoritarian notion of leadership that is inconsistent with a team environment. Executives often struggle with a weakened ability to lead by mandate in the team-based structure. One senior manager captured these thoughts in the following statement:

> I struggled to find my niche in the team structure. At first I thought it was going to be great because the teams would be making so many of the tactical decisions that I didn't enjoy or sometimes even feel were appropriate for me to make. However, I quickly came to realize that decision making constituted the bulk of my job in the old structure and it was tough to let go of. I can personally recount several situations early on when I was more authoritative than I should have been with the teams—largely because I did not know how else to contribute.

Effective leaders in team-based structures help teams become self-sustaining and self-monitoring units. They must be able to articulate a goal and motivate employees toward it, yet often remain neutral on the means of attaining that goal. Such skills develop slowly and with effort on the part of executives. Training can facilitate this process, but there will be some who suffer through the transition and cling to traditional leadership styles. Depending on the prevalence and position of these people, huge productivity drains can occur as former functional leaders and newly formed teams battle for influence. Senior management often discounts this problem by claiming that all employees will have to get "on board" with the team philosophy or leave. However, particularly in today's job market, it is often a very difficult proposition to replace a skilled but authoritarian leader Underground power struggles may freeze firms in the transition to teams such that they cannot leverage either the efficiency or depth of expertise in a functional structure or the flexibility and improved decision making anticipated from the team-based design. Though impossible to quantify precisely, it is important for executives considering teams to be aware of the kind and extent of productivity loss they may face given their existing personnel.

Can teams perform activities previously performed by support departments? To be accountable, a team must be as self-contained as possible to control the factors affecting its ability to deliver results. Often this requires a methodical, months-long transfer of responsibilities in tandem with a plan to ensure that appropriate skills are in place to handle the new duties. A common problem is overburdening teams with too many, often novel, tasks. Newly formed teams often find that coordination and planning work previously handled at the executive level migrates lower, while new tasks emerge, such as role definition and budget analysis. Leaders often recognize the magnitude of this work and thus overestimate the ability of teams to take on new forms of work as they become self-managing.

Specific tasks and a transition plan should be established early to ensure that no responsibilities slip through the cracks and the team is not unduly burdened. For instance, who will handle recruiting for the team? If it is to handle recruit evaluations, it must be skilled in the firm's specific interviewing techniques in order to ensure some level of consistency among employees. Shifting such duties consumes time and resources from the team, support functions, and senior management. More important, the balance of power is shifted away from both leadership and support areas. Political problems in such transitions can make this an arduous process, depending on the influence of affected stakeholders.

How difficult will it be to develop teams' problem-solving capabilities? In most knowledge-intensive firms, a team is only as effective as its ability to jointly share relevant data and opinions and then converge on a plan of action. Essential dialogue skills of active listening, inquiry, and advocacy often need to be introduced and practiced before they are used effectively in group settings. Core teamwork skills such as dialogue and active listening—hardly new concepts—take on added importance in team-based firms, where cross-functional groups make increasingly important decisions. Groups with different backgrounds and experiences can produce better overall solutions, but only if the problem-solving sessions are constructive and do not revert to defensive routines that inhibit learning.

Problem solving also faces challenges stemming from educational or career specialization and preferred cognitive styles. Specialization leads to

> To be accountable, a team must be as self-contained as possible to control the factors affecting its ability to deliver results.

expertise based on prior success, which molds a certain mindset for looking at the world and approaching problems. Product development and brand management teams often encounter this problem. Each functional specialty comes with its own interests and tools (market segmentation, discounted cash flows, capacity planning) and tends to push its own approach without considering others' viewpoints. It is important in such a scenario to help team members consider problems outside the mindset of the specific tool they may bring. However, although easy to diagnose, remedying such a problem is often time-consuming, involving training and interventions in team development, group problem-solving techniques, and meeting facilitation.

Supporting Important Collaboration

> Executives should consider alternative means of enhancing collaboration if the net benefit of a transition to teams is minimal.

Executives should consider alternative means of enhancing collaboration if the net benefit of a transition to teams is minimal. One alternative structure attracting the attention of practitioners today is the *community of practice*—an informal group of people who interact with one another regularly on related issues and challenges. Though generally not visible on any organization chart, communities of practice often play a critical role in sharing knowledge and solving problems. They aid collaboration in such diverse settings as professional services, R&D, and manufacturing. In many cases, they comprise effective forums for people with specialized knowledge to collaborate and learn from one another. At other times, they provide the means of developing strategic capabilities or technologies and facilitating change.

Communities of practice differ notably from conventional organization units, such as teams or task forces. The latter have a task orientation, are often launched for a specific purpose, have formal requirements for membership, and are usually responsible for some type of final deliverable. The former, on the other hand, are usually more fluid in their membership. Participation can range from highly dedicated, committed individuals to more peripheral players who tap into community activities on an as-needed basis. By easing the transfer of relevant practices, reusing explicit knowledge assets, and refreshing knowledge bases, communities can have an impact on efficiency, effectiveness, and the ability to innovate.

Communities of practice can be foundational to a firm's strategy. The World Bank has developed and supported them for some time now, on both a technical and organizational front. It currently has over 100 such communities and a continually rising rate of participation in them. As the Bank supplements its emphasis on lending money with providing development expertise, these communities will contribute more and more to its strategic direction. And they are very effective vehicles for collaboration and knowledge transfer in helping participants solve problems quickly. At Buckman Labs, members of communities of practice from around the world routinely respond to inquiries within a 24-hour time frame. It is common to hear of stories in which people posed questions on critical business issues to a community and received responses from all over the world in time to solve a critical operational problem or win a specific piece of business.

These critical collaborations do not require physical collocation. Many firms have recently begun to leverage on-line communities of practice to allow people to engage relevant experts with a problem. At Sun Microsystems, the popular Java software product has been widely adopted for World Wide Web applications and has made major inroads into corporate computing. Sun's Java Center Organization is a professional service group that works with customers on the design and implementation of Java application systems. Because Java is so new, and because of the rapid pace of development in the software industry in general, people working on advanced Java applications have a great need to share knowledge and code in solving problems efficiently. Because the Java Center Organization is a global community spanning 24 time zones that needs virtual tools to promote collaboration, it has turned to on-line community-building as a critical piece of its business strategy. It consists of about 150 core members and more than 1,000 others who either work with the Java Center or take advantage of their solutions and knowledge. Mailing lists are used for announcements, news, and requests for information. Web sites on SunWeb, the company intranet, are used for information of more enduring interest and to highlight or whiteboard during conference calls and e-mail discussions.

Identifying points at which collaboration among specialists in a firm yields benefits can often be done simply by mapping key knowledge processes such as strategy formulation, new product development, or core work processes. Despite the complexity and specialization of knowledge work, at a high level the work processes can usually be boiled down to a series of activities entailing information collection, analysis, collaborative decision making, and dissemination. Mapping specific knowledge processes in detail allows management to identify essential activities in the value chain where improving collaboration can yield efficiency and customer service benefits without necessarily incurring the costs of a team-based design. Product development teams often use functional specialists early on to define specifications, then periodically for design reviews (key points in the development process), rather than have them become permanent team members. The important point is to assess critically what forms of collaboration need to occur, then consider suitable means of promoting this collaboration if teams are ineffective.

Very often, structural and technical means can be used to enhance collaboration among parties without physically housing them together. From a technical perspective, the use of groupware, video conferencing, a bulletin board, or Internet access can facilitate interactive information sharing and collaboration on new marketing prospects, product development, or knowledge base maintenance. One major petroleum company has begun to reap unanticipated benefits from its investment in video-conferencing. The technology was initially put in place to virtually bring engineering expertise to remote problems such as deep sea drilling platforms. However, perhaps a more important side benefit is the working relationships that geographically dispersed employees are forming. Executives have indicated that employees are more likely to leverage expertise outside their local office—a welcome event in this engineering culture that once had a significant "not invented here" value system.

Providing a technical foundation, however, does not necessarily guarantee that employees will use it (at least not as intended). It is equally important to find ways of measuring both individuals and teams on their contributions to the firm's overall intellectual capacity. One software development company created knowledge centers around certain technologies on which individuals or groups were held accountable for keeping the company up to date. Consulting firms and some law firms are adopting similar approaches to managing and disseminating knowledge in key strategic competencies.

Human resource policies can also enhance collaboration through innovative performance and career management systems focused on managing organizational knowledge. The goal is to develop employees with T-shaped skill sets—a deep technical understanding of a specialty combined with an understanding of upstream and downstream activities in a core process. Not only can these people network effectively throughout a firm to make things happen, they are also better equipped to be part of cross-functional problem-solving teams or future general managers. Says Leonard-Barton (1995), they can "shape their knowledge to fit the problem at hand rather than insist that the problem appear in a particular recognizable form."

As we move further into a knowledge-based economy, traditional organizational principles are growing ineffective. Many executives, grasping for solutions to improve collaboration and innovation, often reach for team-based organizational structures as a natural cure for all ills. To be sure, cross-functional teams can be effective in bridging functional and hierarchical boundaries and integrating specialized sources of knowledge. Far too often, however, executives seem to base these important decisions on sports or civic metaphors more reflective of an appealing notion of teamwork than on a keen understanding of the potential benefits and costs.

Teams should not be adopted based on a belief that enhanced collaboration and teamwork will necessarily ensue with little effort or cost. Rather, it is important to assess such a transition objectively both to make sure it is an appropriate organizational solution and to guide intervention and organizational design efforts in implementing the teams. An ill-informed decision to make the switch can be costly as well as surprising to resource-constrained executives who, in abandoning efforts they should not have undertaken, end up causing more harm than good.

References

D. Ancona and D. Caldwell, "Demography and Design: Predictors of New Product Development Team Performance," *Organization Science*, August 1992, pp. 321-341.

C. Argyris, *Knowledge for Action: A Guide to Overcoming Barriers to Organizational Change* (San Francisco: Jossey-Bass, 1993).

C. Argyris and D. Schon, *Organizational Learning II: Theory, Method and Practice* (Reading, MA: Addison-Wesley, 1996).

J.S. Brown and P. Duguid, "Organizational Learning and Communities-of-Practice: Toward a Unified View of Working, Learning and Innovation," *Organization Science*, February 1991, pp. 40-57.

R. Cross, A. Yan, and M. Louis, "Boundary Activities in 'Boundaryless' Organizations: A Case Study of a Transformation to a Team-Based Structure," *Human Relations*, June 2000, pp. 841-868.

T. Davenport, *Process Innovation: Reengineering Work through Information Technology* (Boston: Harvard Business School Press, 1993).

T. Davenport and L. Prusak, *Working Knowledge* (Boston: Harvard Business School Press, 1998).

D. Denison, S. Hart, and J. Kahn, "From Chimneys to Cross-Functional Teams: Developing and Validating a Diagnostic Model," *Academy of Management Journal*, August 1996, pp. 1,005-1,023.

A. Donnellon, *Team Talk: The Power of Language in Team Dynamics* (Boston: Harvard Business School Press, 1996).

D. Dougherty, "Interpretive Barriers to Successful Product Innovation in Large Firms," *Organization Science*, May 1992, pp. 179-202.

P.F. Drucker, *Post-Capitalist Society* (New York: Harper Business, 1993).

A. Edmondson, "Psychological Safety and Learning Behavior in Work Teams," *Administrative Science Quarterly*, June 1999, pp. 350-383.

K. Fisher and M. Fisher, *The Distributed Mind* (New York: AMACOM, 1998).

J. Galbraith, *Designing Organizations* (San Francisco: Jossey-Bass, 1995).

J. Katzenbach and D. Smith, *The Wisdom of Teams* (New York: Harper Business, 1994).

J. Lave and E. Wenger, *Situated Learning* (Cambridge: Cambridge University Press, 1991).

D. Leonard-Barton, *Wellsprings of Knowledge: Building and Sustaining the Sources of Innovation* (Boston: Harvard Business School Press, 1995).

D. Mankin, S. Cohen, and T. Bikson, *Teams and Technology: Fulfilling the Promise of the New Organization* (Boston: Harvard Business School Press, 1996).

R. Miles and C. Snow, *Fit, Failure and the Hall of Fame* (New York: Free Press, 1994).

S. Mohrman, S. Cohen, and A. Mohrman, *Designing Team-Based Organizations: New Forms for Knowledge Work* (San Francisco: Jossey-Bass, 1995).

D. Nadler, M. Gerstein, et al., *Organizational Architecture: Designs for Changing Organizations* (San Francisco: Jossey-Bass, 1992).

I. Nonaka and H. Takeuchi, *The Knowledge-Creating Company* (Oxford: Oxford University Press, 1995).

J.E. Orr, "Sharing Knowledge, Celebrating Identity," in D. Middleton and D. Edwards (eds.), *Collective Remembering* (Newbury Park, CA: Sage, 1990), 169-189.

E. Schein, "How Can Organizations Learn Faster? The Challenge of Entering the Green Room," *Sloan Management Review*, Winter 1993, pp. 85-92.

E. Schein, "Three Cultures of Management: The Key to Organizational Learning," *Sloan Management Review*, Fall 1996, pp. 9-20.

P. Senge, *The Fifth Discipline* (New York: Doubleday Currency, 1990).

M. Treacy and F. Wiersema, *The Discipline of Market Leaders* (New York: Addison-Wesley, 1995).

E. Wenger, *Communities of Practice* (Cambridge: Cambridge University Press, 1998).

E. Wenger and W. Snyder, "Communities of Practice: The Organizational Frontier," *Harvard Business Review*, January-February 2000, pp. 139-145.

Rob Cross is a research manager at IBM's Institute for Knowledge Management in Cambridge, Massachusetts, and a lecturer in the Organizational Behavior Department, School of Management, Boston University. A previous version of this article was presented at the 1999 International Conference on Work Teams, where it was selected for a Best Paper award.

Does Teaming Pay Off?

Priscilla S. Wisner and Hollace A. Feist

This article looks, from a variety of perspectives, at the differences teaming has made at Bell Atlantic in terms of the company's ability to lower costs, improve quality, and improve its overall strategic performance. What the authors document is that the creation of teams has paid off big time. Sometimes it may seem too much work to establish teams. As this article demonstrates, the effort is well worth it.

Work teams have been lauded as one of the major business innovations of the 1990s, helping companies to achieve productivity and service breakthroughs. During the past decade, there has been an explosion in work team implementation, in companies both large and small, at management levels and employee levels, and in both manufacturing and service companies. One reason for this is that a team structure supports emerging business practices such as total quality management, lean production, business process reengineering, and creating flatter and more decentralized organizational structures.

Popular belief is that teams increase corporate value by positively impacting employee satisfaction, quality, and productivity. Yet few research studies have established a clear connection between teaming and performance, and even fewer have quantitatively assessed the impact of teaming on corporate performance. Before investing extensive time and financial resources to implement work teams, managers need to know if the investment pays off. At a minimum, they need to measure the impact of the change on key corporate success factors and where possible link those impacts to corporate value.

Bell Atlantic Corporation conducted an extensive research study on the payoffs of teaming. In particular, it carefully traced the implementation of teaming to monitor and record teaming's impact on three key success factors:

- productivity,
- service quality, and
- employee satisfaction.

Furthermore, Bell Atlantic found that the increase in productivity directly impacted company revenue providing a link between implementing work

Reprinted with permission from *Strategic Finance*, February 2001. Copyright © 2001 and published by the Institute of Management Accountants, Montvale, NJ, www.imanet.org. All rights reserved.

teams and increasing corporate value. The short answer to the question "Does teaming pay off?" is a resounding "yes." We'll describe the implementation and measurement of the teaming impact at Bell Atlantic and share some of the lessons and insights that benefit financial managers charged with strategically evaluating the impact of teaming in their organizations.

Critical Issues at Bell Atlantic

The short answer to the question "Does teaming pay off?" is a resounding "yes."

Created in 1984 when the U.S. government forced telecommunications giant AT&T to deregulate, Bell Atlantic Corporation had as its mission to provide comprehensive telephone services to business and residential customers in the mid-Atlantic region of the U.S. (Last year Bell Atlantic merged with GTE, and the company is now known as Verizon. The incidents in this article pertain to Bell Atlantic.) From the company's inception, Bell Atlantic management faced numerous business challenges, including a changing regulatory environment, exploding competition for phone and communications services, and an increase in product offerings as a result of changing technologies.

A teaming strategy was adopted to support Bell Atlantic's three primary strategic initiatives—shareholder value, customer satisfaction, and employee commitment. At Bell Atlantic, three drivers of corporate value are employee productivity, service quality, and employee satisfaction.

- Productivity improvement creates value for Bell Atlantic by increasing revenues and by minimizing personnel costs through increased efficiency.
- Service quality at Bell Atlantic has strong customer satisfaction implications, as service quality is measured during an employee's contact time with the customer. Bell Atlantic is also regulated by the government and is required to report a number of customer service metrics.
- Employee satisfaction is a key metric because the work process in the call centers is labor intensive, and Bell Atlantic management is very concerned about maintaining good labor relations. Any change in the work environment that leads to employee dissatisfaction has strong potential to negatively impact employee commitment and productivity and also customer satisfaction. Conversely, Bell Atlantic management believes that the benefits of employee satisfaction are improved employee commitment (lower turnover), improved productivity, and enhanced customer satisfaction.

Implementing Teams

Bell Atlantic operated 45 consumer call centers, staffed with about 6,000 sales consultants, that provided sales and service support to residential customers.

10 Critical Factors that Make Teams Work

Our analysis of teaming shows that it absolutely pays off in terms of delivering value to the employee, to the customer, and to the organization. But it requires commitment throughout the organization and an investment in people, systems, and process changes. Below are some of the lessons we learned from our experience at Bell Atlantic.

- **Champion.** Teaming needs a senior leader who demonstrates teaming behaviors in both good times and bad. Is this leader willing to share power, information, decision making, and responsibility with all levels in the business?
- **Systems assessment.** You need to assess the systems necessary to support a successful teaming implementation: communication, performance measurement, performance feedback, continuous improvement of work process, financial, training, availability of nonproductive meeting time.
- **Road map.** You should develop a "road map" for successful team implementation. That means communicate a high-level plan of action that outlines pre-implementation, implementation, post-implementation, and ongoing teaming processes.
- **Long-term view.** You should view a teaming strategy as a continuous journey, not a program that can be started and stopped at a whim. If a company views teaming as a "flavor of the month" program, it can destroy employee trust in management.
- **Comprehensive training.** You need to develop a comprehensive training process and invest in the time necessary to train all team members. Teaming education is critical to the team's success.
- **Select a management team.** The leader must be prepared to change management team members because not everyone on the management team can or will support his/her teaming vision. The leader should help members of the management team to self-assess their belief systems, then encourage change if necessary. The management team selection process should be consistent with teaming strategy.
- **"Walk the talk."** Team leaders must be prepared to demonstrate desired teaming behaviors through their own actions and words. That means communicate with the teams frequently, listen, and share both the good and the bad news. It also means empower teams to make decisions on meaningful areas of the business.
- **Boundary management.** It's critical that teams understand boundaries, restrictions, and desired outcomes before they're empowered. Once you empower teams to make a decision, you can't take back this empowerment.
- **Recognition.** You must recognize performance at every opportunity.

> Keys to success in recognition include an open process—making awards in public, not private; timing—recognizing someone promptly after they've made the effort you want to recognize; size and frequency—big enough, often enough; personalized—the awarder may matter.
> - **Identify key success factors**. You need to develop baseline measures of key results before teaming is implemented and continue to measure results throughout the implementation and ongoing. Tie evaluation criteria to strategic objectives of the company. Demonstrate that teaming produces measurable financial gains to the company. Be prepared for negative impact to some key results during the initial implementation, and determine whether or not these negative results are due to teaming or other factors; don't overreact to negative results by stopping the implementation.

Call centers were converted to a team structure over the course of a two-year period, and at the time of the study about half the call centers had implemented teaming.

The basic job function of the sales consultant remained the same in both the teamed and the nonteamed offices, but the organizational structure for the teamed offices changed. These changes included:

- An office committee made up of sales consultants and an assistant manager who helped to identify, coordinate, and communicate team needs;
- Physically grouping team members together and changing furniture to remove high walls;
- Training focused on team processes, cooperative communication, and problem-solving skills;
- Weekly team meetings to discuss results, solve problems, or to cross-train team members; and
- A performance feedback system that related individual results, team results, and summary data about other teams' performance, creating an environment of acknowledgment and learning that many sales consultants lauded. The feedback system also helped to identify "best practice" sales consultants, who were then asked to share their skills with other team members.

Bottom Line: The Evaluation of Teaming

The call center evaluation project used data from three call centers both before and after teams were implemented. The teamed group consisted of 53 sales consultants from two call centers with the same manager. The nonteamed group was 84 sales consultants in a single call center that was scheduled to begin team implementation about a year later.

Does Teaming Pay Off

Bell Atlantic human resource, business unit, and call center managers helped to identify and select key performance metrics. In addition to observations and feedback we gathered from meeting with Bell Atlantic managers and sales consultants, we used a wide variety of data spanning a 15-month period to evaluate the impact of teaming:

- Multiple measures of productivity that Bell Atlantic routinely records for all call center transactions:
  - average call length,
  - call conversion ratio (percentage of calls that included a sale),
  - products-sold rate (products sold per online hour), and
  - strategic revenues generated (revenues related to key product sales);
- Service quality data recorded by call center and Bell Atlantic quality assurance managers;
- Two employee surveys, one measuring employee satisfaction and the other measuring employees' perceptions of the teamed work environment.

Productivity improvement. When we compared productivity changes for the teamed employees with productivity changes for the nonteamed employees, we found a clear result: Teaming improves productivity. The teamed sales consultants outperformed the nonteamed sales consultants in three of the four productivity measures—average call length, call conversion ratio, and products-sold rate (see Figure 1, p. 319). While both groups had increases in average call length, the increase for the teamed employees was slightly less, indicating that they were increasing efficiency of their call time. Even more important, the results show that they were doing a better job converting calls to sales and selling more products. These results have had a direct financial impact for Bell Atlantic—increased efficiency at handling calls impacts costs through reduced headcount, while the improvement in selling skills and sales results will favorably impact revenues.

When we compared productivity changes for the teamed employees with productivity changes for the nonteamed employees, we found a clear result: Teaming improves productivity.

The increase in the products-sold rate is the most telling measure of the revenue impact of teaming. Our analysis shows that a teamed sales consultant, on average, would generate over $21,000 per year in sales revenues more than a nonteamed sales consultant (see box just below).

POTENTIAL IMPACT ON REVENUES

Additional products sold by teamed employees: 44.4 per month
Annualized difference: 532.8 per year
Average annualized product revenue: $40
Incremental revenue per teamed employee: $21,312
Potential revenue gain to Bell Atlantic: $127,872,000

> ### WHEN EMPLOYEES LEARN
>
> Implementing teams promises paybacks in terms of employee productivity, quality, and satisfaction. But do teams pay off? Organizational theory maintains that teams are an effective mechanism to link corporate objectives with improved organizational performance, and company stories in the popular business press assert that implementing work teams creates value for an organization.
>
> Teams are thought to perform better than individuals because the members combine their complementary skills and experience to facilitate real-time problem solving. Teaming is also believed to promote cross-training and more effective learning patterns, making it possible for companies to react with more speed and flexibility in today's competitive environment. Teams have been described as a "win-win" situation for the organization and the employee because teams are a more effective working method for the organization and enhance job fulfillment for the employee.
>
> Teaming is also seen as a key driver of improving quality, creating an environment where learning and best practices among team members are shared routinely, as well as fostering employee participation and empowerment. Work teams also empower workers by transferring control from managers to employees. Employees that are more involved in their job decisions are more likely to be satisfied with their jobs and committed to the organization.
>
> Numerous studies have measured the impact of teaming on productivity, quality, and employee satisfaction, but the results of these studies create an unclear picture of the impact of teaming on performance. Some studies have found a positive impact of teaming, many have found no impact related to teaming, and a few have even reported negative impacts. The confusion in outcomes is compounded or perhaps caused by the methods used to evaluate the outcomes. Due to the nature of field study research, most researchers don't have adequate performance data from before an organizational change occurs as well as after the change takes place. Most companies don't have a control group of employees available to compare with a treatment group of employees. Often research is done using survey data of employees' perceptions rather than organizational measures. And most research projects are short term, making it difficult to assess the longer-term impact of the organizational change.
> (Continued on next page)

Multiplying the average gain of $21,312 times the 6,000 Bell Atlantic sales consultants, the potential revenue gain from teaming is over $127 million! Although the organizational development and implementation costs related to teaming weren't available for this project, the total costs are certainly a fraction of the revenue gains. This analysis demonstrates that team-

Does Teaming Pay Off

> (Quick Review of Team Research, continued)
> Bell Atlantic's study is unique in that the research took place as the change was happening. Multiple measures of productivity, service quality, and employee satisfaction data were available for employees working in teams ("teamed" group) and for those not working in teams ("nonteamed" group). The data were collected prior to the teaming changeover and again nine months after. Most of the performance data used were data that Bell Atlantic routinely collected and audited for each employee. These strong research design factors lend credibility to the findings in this study and increase confidence that the positive impacts found for the performance outcomes actually do relate to the teaming implementation.

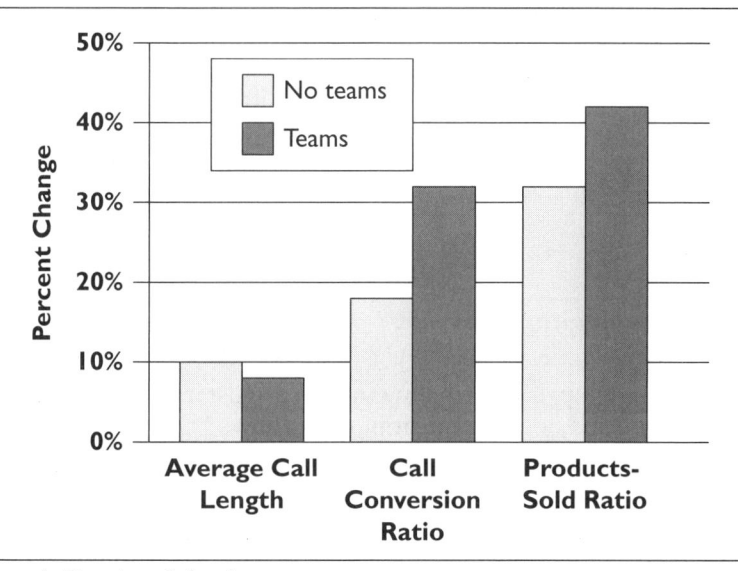

Figure 1. **Productivity improvement**

ing, through its impact on productivity, strongly impacts corporate value.

Bell Atlantic's strategic initiatives include shareholder value, customer satisfaction, and employee commitment. As important as the productivity impact is to creating shareholder value, it's imperative to Bell Atlantic that the teaming strategy also support customer and employee objectives.

Service quality improvement. Sales consultants are rated on 13 service quality criteria for each customer call. Examples are demonstrating job knowledge, treating the customer with courtesy, completing paperwork accurately, and thanking the customer for calling Bell Atlantic. Sales consultants' calls are monitored on average four to six times each month, and a monthly service quality score is tabulated for each sales consultant. Prior to teaming, the average score for the teamed offices was just under 88, but this score increased to over 91 after the company implemented teaming and continued to increase throughout the year (see Figure 2). We couldn't compare the teamed employees' service quality scores with the nonteamed employees' scores for this evaluation, but business unit data showed that the teamed offices improved more at service quality than did the nonteamed office.

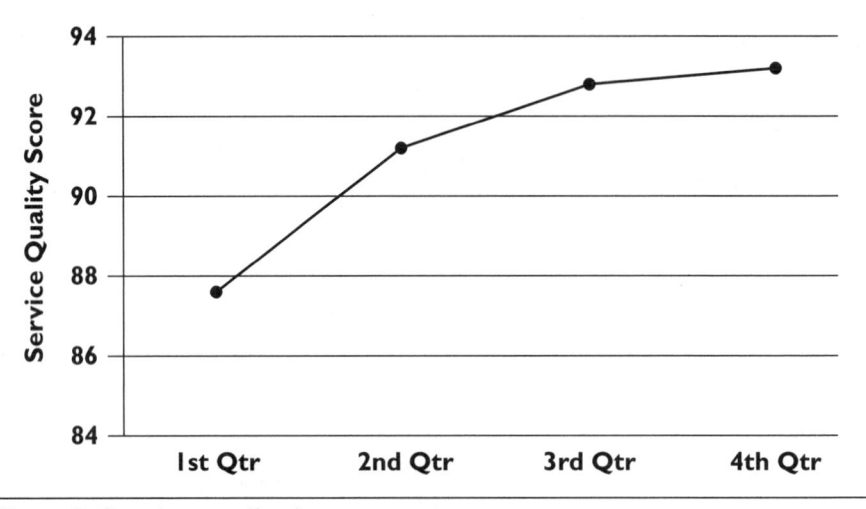

Figure 2. **Service quality improvement**

Employee satisfaction improvement. An employee satisfaction survey administered to the teamed and nonteamed employees showed that employee satisfaction increased in both offices. But the teamed sales consultants demonstrated much greater gains in satisfaction (21% to 16%), supporting the conclusion that teaming positively impacts employee satisfaction. The manager of the teamed offices noted that the employees became much more involved in contributing to the work environment after the team structure was implemented. Here are some examples:

- The number of employee suggestions increased,
- Employees participated more in meetings,
- Employees took more initiative in identifying and solving problems, and
- Some employees volunteered to take on additional assignments in the office.

What Made a Difference?

We wanted to better understand how teaming impacted the employees' work environment, so we asked the employees' opinions about changes in their work roles after teaming was implemented. The overwhelming response was that employees have strong positive reactions to the teaming implementation and structure. As shown in the box below, most teamed employees say they feel more involved, accountable, knowledgeable, enthusiastic, and empowered. These characteristics drive employee behavior and impact how an employee feels about the company and treats the customer. And they ultimately impact productivity and profitability.

Sales consultants also reported several positive aspects of the team structure:

1. Common goals were created by the joint decision-making process;
2. Employees could work together to solve problems;
3. The decision-making process was much more realtime;
4. The team structure promoted cross-training;
5. The physical proximity between team members increased learning since team members could observe how their colleagues handled customer calls; and
6. They could turn to others on their team for help with sales tools and techniques.

As you can see, the impact of teaming at Bell Atlantic was significant and important. At the time of this study, Bell Atlantic management was debating whether or not work teams were an effective organizational structure to align operations with strategic objectives. The business unit and call center managers were enthusiastic about the team structure but needed to justify the investment in time and financial resources to upper management. After receiving the results of this study, management implemented teaming throughout the remaining call centers, and now it has been implemented throughout the Bell Atlantic organization.

TEAMING'S IMPACT ON EMPLOYEES

Two-thirds or more of the teamed employees agreed with the following statements:

Since I began working on my team at Bell Atlantic...

- I feel more encouraged to come up with new and better ways of doing things.
- I am held more accountable for my productivity.
- I have a better understanding of how to increase customer satisfaction.
- I am more willing to put forth extra effort toward my job.
- I feel more empowered to achieve team goals.
- the members of my team cooperate better to get the job done.

Linking to Corporate Value

Strategic cost management isn't just about measuring the costs associated with operations. It's about measuring and managing the drivers of corporate value. Creating corporate value requires managers to align a company's strategy with the systems and structures needed to carry out that strategy and to create a set of financial and nonfinancial performance metrics that measures progress toward corporate objectives. Ultimately, the financial executive must be able to answer the question: Does this initiative create corporate value? Does it pay off?

We found that teaming pays off through improving productivity, quality, and employee satisfaction. Increased productivity can lead to lower operating costs and increased revenues. Improving service quality leads to improved customer satisfaction, which means the company benefits through increased market share, customer loyalty, additional revenues, and reduced transaction costs. Investment in practices that enhance employees' quality of work life promises paybacks such as improved employee satisfaction, more commitment, and less turnover.

What benefits has your company derived through teaming?

Priscilla S. Wisner, CMA, Ph.D., is an assistant professor of world business at The American Graduate School of International Management in Glendale, Ariz. You can reach her at (602) 978-7153 or wisnerp@t-bird.edu.

Hollace A. Feist is a former Bell Atlantic manager with 25 years of telecommunications and business management experience. Now she's a consultant in Jacksonville, Fla.

Quality Transformation

LEARNING ORGANIZATIONS

Focus-Pocus

B. Joseph Pine II and James H. Gilmore

This article puts a particular twist on the idea of the learning organization in terms of how it learns about customers and their needs. Written by authors who specialize in mass customization, they suggest that focus groups (and similar information gathering approaches) will not tell you what you really need to know. They suggest instead a more active approach characterized by capturing information learned from everyday customer interactions.

Focus groups have lost their focus. Once a cutting-edge technique for probing the psyche of the public, they've outlived their usefulness. They are like a tired magician performing the same tricks week after week in the Catskills. Call 'em focus-pocus groups, for after a company has conducted hundreds of focus-group interviews, its likelihood of uncovering a truly fresh perspective is almost non-existent. It isn't enough to hear what people say they want. You have to find a way for people to show what they want, and that won't happen in the stilted environment in which focus groups occur.

Because innovation is more important in today's economy than ever before, the guidance from focus groups can be downright dangerous. Most focus groups simply confirm to companies that what they are doing is right—give or take a tweak—and discourage them from striking off in a new direction. For fundamentally, people answer the questions asked of them. All too often, the answers provided are as much a function of the thinking from which the questions are generated as they are an indication of true desires.

What is needed is a whole new approach to exploring possibilities and identifying what customers really could use, especially if the intent is to gain true insight for potential new offerings. Here are three critical principles, each one challenging a deep-seated tenet of traditional focus-group methodologies.

This article originally appeared in the April/May 2001 issue of *Context*. Copyright © 2001, DiamondCluster International Inc. Used with permission. All rights reserved.

Search for Uniqueness, Not Commonality

With focus groups, companies bring a number of customers together and strive to determine how they are all alike. They search for commonality, in the hope of finding some large, homogeneous need that can be served by a standard offering. Fuhgedaboutit!

Markets are no more. The lowest common denominator is a math concept, not a doctrine of human behavior. Customers are unique. Period.

So, instead of a focus group, companies should conduct a de-focus group. Get a bunch of customers together to find out how they vary in their wants and needs. Delineate dimensions of common uniqueness—those areas where customers most differ in their individual needs—and then design your offerings to eliminate the sacrifice each customer encounters along those dimensions when he buys a standard offering.

Japanese eyewear retailer Paris Miki Inc. used such an approach when it created the computerized Mikissimes Design System. The company went to its store by the Louvre in Paris to test out the system, watching how customers responded to its suggestions for mass-customized eyewear. Eyebrow shape was found to be one key area of common uniqueness. Every customer's eyebrows differed in shape, but each one looked best when the top edge of the company's rimless glasses matched that exact shape.

Stop Talking and Start Watching

With focus groups, the medium is the mistake. Having participants talk about what they want inherently limits the prospects of uncovering new opportunities. It is the using of a good or service that defines the customer experience, so you have to observe customers in action to understand their unarticulated needs.

Recently, when a flight attendant asked what one of us wanted to drink, she heard "nothing, thanks" in response. The woman in the adjacent seat also declined. It wasn't that we weren't thirsty; on the contrary, we each brought a plastic bottle of soda onboard and secured it in the seat pocket in front of us. Why? We wanted to use our laptop computers without risking a beverage spill. If airlines treated flights as their learning laboratories—having flight attendants observe customer behavior to gather insight—they would quickly see the opportunity to serve resealable containers in lieu of open cups. They might also install cup holders or perhaps have future aircraft designed with two tray tables for each passenger—one for food and one at a separate level for laptop computers and other personal items.

Don't Periodically Withdraw; Do Research Every Day

Companies today make only a periodic investment in focus groups, usually when in the throes of product development. But when products are mass customized, such development occurs with every customer interaction. So, rather than withdraw to the confines of conference rooms with surveillance mirrors for what-if scenarios, engage individual customers every day in live, continuous, point-of-interaction research into the design of the companies' offerings.

When Ritz-Carlton employees observe the behavior of each guest and write down personal desires on Guest Preference Pads, they're engaging in such daily research. For some preferences, such as for hypoallergenic pillows on the bed or contemporary jazz on the radio, the hotel has the capability to readily fill those needs. Other personal desires, while easily ascertained, are more intractable to fulfill efficiently on a chainwide basis. Think mango-flavored iced tea or customized check-in times. What about sending clean shirts overnight to the guest's next destination? These kinds of interactions yield significant design decisions: Do we ignore this desire, or maybe perform it just this once? Perhaps we remember it, but fulfill it only on an ad hoc basis—or do we go all out and create a system for its efficient delivery for whoever wants it? But even these decisions, while complex, create rich opportunities for formulating new offerings.

USAA, the worldwide insurer and financial-services company serving predominantly clients in the military, shows how. It has a system called ECHO, for Every Contact Has Opportunity. Through it, employees capture spontaneous feedback about the often very specific wants and needs of its members. "Action agents" then review what they learned to instigate changes in USAA's programs, procedures, and offerings. Among many other enhancements, agents quickly fixed a glitch in a voice-response unit, enabled members to make convenient payments with credit cards rather than only checks, and created an insurance offering to cover high-tech hearing aids for the company's increasingly aging member base. USAA proves that systematically monitoring every customer contact indeed has opportunity.

In any company, mining such a base of information will yield far more value than any focus group could possibly provide. It's not magic; it's performing daily research into the differences of individual customers by studying their behavior and then responding. As Yogi Berra once put it, "You can observe a lot just by watching."

B. Joseph Pine II and James H. Gilmore are co-authors of The Experience Economy: Work Is Theatre & Every Business a Stage. *They can be reached at pine&gilmore@customization.com.*

> Rather than withdraw to the confines of conference rooms with surveillance mirrors for what-if scenarios, engage individual customers every day in live, continuous, point-of-interaction research into the design of the companies' offerings.

Market Research for Quality in Small Business

William L. Rhey and Frank M. Gryna

This article also focuses on learning about customers, but if the Pine and Gilmore piece that proceeds it takes the "hip" approach, this one is more traditional and looks at why small businesses need to be more systematically study their customers and the best methods to do that. Frank Gryna has worked on books with Joe Juran and knows of what he speaks with regard to quality and its implementation.

Small businesses cannot afford the luxury of resting on their haunches. In order to survive they must consistently delight customers through the highest quality products and services.

Capturing the voice of the customer through market research is essential to every organization, regardless of how many customers it serves or how many people it employs. This article focuses on market research in the small business sector—research that determines a firm's quality standing in the marketplace and helps plan for product quality in the future. We will explain the concept and benefits of market research for quality and present the results of a study we conducted involving four small firms. Based on the information gathered from this study, we provide recommendations on conducting market research for quality in small manufacturing and service firms.

Three Areas of Market Research for Quality

The American Marketing Association defines marketing research as "the function which links the consumer, customer and public to the marketer through information—information used to identify and define marketing opportunities and problems; generate, refine and evaluate marketing actions; monitor marketing performance; and improve the understanding of marketing as a process."[1] As applied to the quality of goods and services, market research is the systematic collection, recording and analysis of data concerning quality as viewed by the customer. Market research for quality provides the facts needed by management to make short-term decisions and developing long-range strategies for quality.

From *Quality Progress*, January 2001. Copyright © 2001 by the American Society for Quality. Reprinted with permission.

While small organizations typically do not have the resources, time and skills to do extensive market research, an external set of eyes (the customer) is necessary to alert management to the eccentricity and whimsy of the marketplace. It is imperative to retain this customer focus when planning for quality, integrating the voice of the customer into each of three areas of market research.

The three areas of market research that are necessary for planning for quality are:

1. Measuring current customer satisfaction. Information from several sources indicates that a strong relationship exists between financial performance and customer satisfaction,[2] making satisfaction measurement particularly important.

To properly measure current customer satisfaction, we need to translate the term "quality" into specific attributes that customers say are important. These attributes should not be restricted to characteristics of core and auxiliary products, but should include quality attributes for the full life cycle of the customer/client relationship—from the customer's initial contact with a salesperson to customer service after the sale.

We also need to learn the relative importance of these attributes to the customer and how the firm compares to the competition where these attributes are concerned. Finally, customers must be asked if they would purchase from the company again or recommend it to friends.

2. Determining customer needs for product development. In order to successfully develop future products, we must understand customers' needs. Too often, however, we do not differentiate between stated needs and real needs. A customer may state the need for a clothes dryer, for example, but the real need is to remove moisture from clothes. Once we understand the real vs. stated need, we are much more equipped to meet customer requirements.

Sometimes, customer needs are hidden until the customer switches to a competitor. But to create and retain customers, we must identify and meet any hidden needs.

As is the case in measuring satisfaction, several facets are involved in determining customers' needs. These include both short-term needs to modify current products and long-term needs to integrate quality into product development. We must ask customers what their needs are, methodically study how customers presently use the product and analyze customers' systems of use in order to identify hidden needs.

3. Analyzing customer retention and loyalty. Researching customer retention and loyalty starts with the distinction between customer satisfaction and customer loyalty. Customer satisfaction concerns what customers say—their opinions about a product. Customer loyalty addresses what customers do—their buying decisions.

> To properly measure current customer satisfaction, we need to translate the term "quality" into specific attributes that customers say are important.

> ## QUESTIONS FOR SMALL-BUSINESS STUDY
>
> ### Customer Satisfaction
> - How do you measure customer satisfaction?
> - How do you determine what are the important factors for a customer to buy from you?
> - What level of detail do you use in determining customer satisfaction?
> - Is satisfaction measurement a regular activity, or do you measure primarily when complaints are high?
> - In planning the acquisition of customer feedback information, do you obtain input from your managers on what type of information they need?
> - Is customer feedback information disseminated to your managers and work force in a way that stimulates action?
> - Do you ask customers if they would buy from you again?
> - What obstacles prevent you from doing thorough customer satisfaction measurement?
>
> ### Customer Needs and New Product Development
> - What role does customer feedback play in new product development?
> - Do you document customer feedback, that is, use focus groups, assign salespeople to obtain feedback or use other methods to obtain feedback?
> - Can you point to examples of changes you have made in a product or service as a result of customer feedback?
> - What obstacles prevent you from obtaining thorough customer feedback?
>
> ### Customer Retention
> - Do you follow up on lost customers to determine the reasons for the customer defections? If yes, do you document and create a database and then generalize on the learnings?
> - Do you measure the customer retention rate?
> - Is there a benchmark in your industry for the customer retention rate?
> - How do you use information on lost customers to make changes in the product, service or other aspects of customer interactions?
> - Do you have a policy for recapturing lost customers?
> - What obstacles prevent you from obtaining thorough information on lost customers?

High levels of customer satisfaction don't always yield high levels of customer loyalty. A satisfied customer may buy from your company but may also buy from competitors. A loyal customer will buy primarily (or exclusively) from your company. Research dealing with retention and loyalty should also

	Bank	**Insurance Co.**	**Home Builder**	**Brass and Aluminum**
Customer Satisfaction Feedback Issues					
Rely on intentional but informal feedback?	Yes. Managers talk with customers informally.	Yes. Reps are constantly asking questions.	Yes. Ongoing during construction.	Yes. On sales visits; part of the job.
Value formal feedback system?	Yes. Appointments set to interview clients.	Moderately. Postcard survey but not regularly done. No regular formal reports.	Yes. During construction, at closing. Periodically up to one year after closing.	No. Sales rep. contact is key.
Do top management and employees who need feedback receive results?	Yes.	Yes. Meetings, discussions, committees and sales department offer feedback.	Yes. Feedback from interviews, surveys and focus groups distributed internally.	Yes. Sometimes employees go to customer to understand usage.
Attempt to get feedback on repeat purchase intentions?	No, but monitor retention.	Informally but intentionally with policy renewals.	Ask if they would recommend builder to friends.	Informally. Standard salesperson procedure.
Obstacles to obtaining feedback.	Employees wish to avoid confrontation. Lack of time.	Expense.	Sales people reluctant to detail reasons for lost sales; hard to reach customers at home.	Clients with large purchases have complex buying processes.
Customer Needs and New Product Development Feedback Issues					
Are questions asked for new product development?	Formal surveys done for needs in new areas.	Yes. Customers have a choice of many products.	Not enough. Some questioning of realtor groups in new areas.	Yes, it's a part of the salesperson's job.
Has customer feedback led to product changes?	Yes. Several products and services.	Yes. E-mail and voice mail capability.	Yes. From realtor and customer feedback.	Yes.
Obstacles to obtaining feedback.	Time commitments from customers and employees.		Time and money.	None, unless they don't tell us.
Customer Retention and Loyalty					
Formal method to assess issues of lost customers?	Yes. Daily report on closed accounts and reasons for closure; no formal policy for recovery.	Yes. Renewals provide retention measure; no formal feedback system; no formal recovery system; retention over 90%.	Seek to assess lost potential customers through reports of salespeople; no quality information on why customers buy elsewhere.	No formal system; yearly assessment of clients by salespeople and managers; very low rate of customer defection.
Obstacles to obtaining feedback.	Being overcome.	Few if any.	Not a priority.	None.

Reprinted with permission of the companies surveyed.

Table 1. **Market research use by firms surveyed**

identify the reasons for customer defections.

Many managers believe they have all the necessary data concerning these three areas. But customers aren't always asked the right questions, leaving gaps in the research. To make matters worse, customer feedback is seldom obtained in an objective manner due to a lack of resources, time and skill.

A Study of Four Small Businesses

When selecting the small businesses for our study, we followed the definition of the U.S. Government Small Business Administration (SBA). The SBA defines small businesses as those with fewer than 250 employees, so we looked for companies having 50 to 125 employees.

Four small businesses in the Tampa Bay, FL, area participated in our study: two from the manufacturing sector and two from the service sector. Each of the selected businesses has a market niche and has proven profitable in the recent past.

Inland Homes, a residential home builder with about 100 employees was the first subject, followed by Tampa Brass and Aluminum, a castings and machining company employing 50. Our third subject was Jones and Hawkins Insurance, an insurance broker with 60 employees. Terrace Bank, a privately owned community bank with 112 employees, was the final company we researched.

We visited each firm twice, meeting with one or more people from management (usually including the owner or president). The first visit outlined the purpose of the research project and presented managers with a list of specific questions to be asked on the second visit. See sidebar "Questions for Small-Business Study," for the list of questions.

Table 1 shows our findings on how these small businesses conduct market research in each of the three areas—current customer satisfaction, customer needs for product development, and customer retention and loyalty

It's important to note that while a number of traditional methods for conducting market research are available to small businesses, our recommendations are based on the results of our study (see sidebar "General Concepts of Market Research for Small Business"). Eight traditional methods of research are summarized in Table 2, and complete descriptions can be found in the books *On Great Service*,[3] *Marketing Research*[4] and *Marketing Research Methodological Foundations*.[5]

Measuring Current Customer Satisfaction

The first area our study addressed concerned customer satisfaction measurement. All four companies said they consistently and intensely obtained informal input by speaking with customers one-on-one. Several of the companies made sure face-to-face contact occurred regularly—having someone stand in the middle of the bank lobby once a week, for example, asking customers for feedback. One company met with focus groups and used questionnaires for individual customers. That company obtained specific feedback by asking: "If you could make one change in the product we sold you, what would it be?"

Features of Data Collection Methods				
Method	Expense	Internal or External	Recommended Frequency	Recommended Sample Size
Market surveys.	Shared expense; will vary with partnership; $500 to $5,000.	External; trade group; university initiative.	Not more than annually. Generally every two or three years.	Generally over 400.
Post-transaction interviews.	Moderate, $0 to $15 per interview.	Can be either.	Continuously to annually.	Varies by survey design.
Focus groups.	$1,500 to $3,000 per group.	Can be either. External recommended in most cases.	Varies by purpose and design. Quarterly to annually.	Eight to 14 respondents in a group.
Mystery shoppers.	$50 to $100 per transaction; varies with time commitment.	Can be either. External recommended in most cases.	Weekly, monthly or quarterly depending on size and nature of business.	Varies with nature of business.
Employee reports, surveys and interviews.	Employee's time.	Either or both.	Continuously for defection or lost business. Periodically for surveys.	Proportionate to size of department or customer service force.
Complaint boxes.	Minimal; materials and employee time to publish and assess.	Internal.	Continuously.	Uncontrolled.
Customer advisory groups.	$100 to $1,000 per group session; or annual cost which varies with size of panel.	Internal.	Periodically; monthly, quarterly or semiannually.	Varies with design; focus group size more than 100.
Specialized segment surveys (new, lost, competitors or specialized).	$5,000 to $10,000.	External.	Periodically; semiannually to annually.	Varies with size of group, intention and design; anywhere from 20 to more than 200.

Table 2. **Summary of survey methods**

Recommendations. While we strongly recommend that small businesses use the customer voice to learn what customers think, it's important to collect the correct data in enough detail to make short- and long-range decisions. Our research indicated that contact with individual customers was often done by upper management, usually the president or owner, or someone who directly reports to the president or owner. This helped assure that the right questions were asked and that the responses were disseminated to those who could take action.

Remember, a key to measuring customer satisfaction is uncovering which product or service attributes are important to the customer. The management group (not just the marketing department) should consider the question: What marketplace research information is needed to learn what customers think of our product? The answer(s) to this question will identify the product attributes or features to be explored and will consider both the relative importance of the attributes and their quality relative to the competition. Such a discussion provides good input for planning the research and helps assure that management takes action on any results the research yields.

Be sure to identify the product attributes that collectively define satisfaction. Terms like "customer satisfaction" and "quality" are too foggy. Our study identified examples such as the accuracy of a transaction at a bank or the workmanship in a residential home.

Managers, employees and a sample of customers should be asked (in preliminary research) what attributes they think constitute high quality. Trade journals may identify standard measures for the industry and can be a good place to start, but all users of market research results must have input in the research design to assure that the content and depth of the results meet their needs.

After collecting this input, finalize the list of attributes using a larger sample of customers. Remember that the list of attributes should not be limited to attributes of the product, but should span the entire cycle of customer contact from initial contact with a salesperson through use and servicing of the product. In one industrial product, for example, quality was determined to have six attributes: reliable performance, efficient operation, durability/life, ease of inspection and maintenance, ease of wiring and installation, and product service.[6]

You can use a generic template of attributes. For example, in the area of customer service, the SERVQUAL model[7] identifies five dimensions: tangibles, reliability, responsiveness, assurance and empathy. After defining these terms, it presents customers with 22 statements that examine the difference between customer expectations and perceptions. These statements can be customized for each product or company.

Once the list of attributes is defined, it is useful to ask customers the relative importance of the attributes. Determining their importance enables the company to concentrate its actions on those attributes having the highest return.

Many believe that data on quality from customers are incomplete unless they include a comparison to the competition. Comparing attributes to the competition typically offers a few surprises—low ratings for certain attributes of a product, for instance. Obtaining data on competitor quality involves a variety of methods. Testing in a laboratory and testing under usage conditions are popular methods for physical products. Other methods include directly asking customers for ratings on competitors, using mystery shoppers and organizing focus groups.

Ideally, data about competitors should focus on each product attribute. When a noncustomer purchases from a competitor, it is useful to ask an open-ended question such as: What are the chief reasons you bought from company X?

As might be expected, the companies we studied said that time and resources were obstacles to performing research. An additional problem was that customers and employees wanted to avoid negative or confrontational discussions. To combat these problems, consider using quality related data already available. Some possibilities include data on declines in sales, customer complaints, salespersons' reports and spare part sales. Other existing data, such as government reports, reports from independent laboratories, data from trade associations and trade literature, can easily be collected—often from the Internet.

Market research for quality takes time, resources and special skills—all of which are in short supply where small businesses are concerned. Therefore, it is understandable that such research can only be done occasionally. An occasional survey is better than no survey at all. Periodic surveys provide data for analysis of trends and other matters. If time is a large constraint, consider asking a local university for help when designing and conducting research.

You can also save time by sampling. Surveying a carefully designed sample of customers in depth is more useful than surveying large, hastily organized groups.

Determining Customer Needs for Product Development

The second area of our study looked at obtaining and applying customer feedback to the development of new products. All four companies provided examples of product changes made as a result of customer feedback. Sometimes, the changes were not made until sales declined, suggesting that proactive research could have prevented lost sales. In other cases, formal research (questionnaires, focus groups) was conducted before embarking on new geographical markets, influencing how the product was designed for the new area.

Recommendations. Many organizations learn basic customer needs and use that information in new product development. But organizations striving for superiority probe customer needs much more deeply. This not only means a tremendous focus on customer needs, but involves matters such as sharing responsibility for customer results, tailoring product solutions for individual (rather than group) needs, and developing the trust to share the operating information and practices of other service chain partnerships. Such an approach requires time and effort. It also means carefully choosing customers (and rejecting others) who have the technical capability and culture to yield significant economic and other benefits.[8]

Many organizations learn basic customer needs and use that information in new product development. But organizations striving for superiority probe customer needs much more deeply.

To start, assemble a group of upper management employees who are involved in the development of new products. This group addresses one question: What marketplace information is needed to identify present and future customer needs? Simple places to look for answers include trade publications, trade shows and the customer environment.

Of the eight data collection methods described in Table 2, focus groups, employee research and reporting, customer advisory groups and special customer surveys can be particularly helpful when identifying customer needs. However, to achieve superiority, additional means must be considered. Understanding the needs of the customer requires listening to the voice of the customer by conducting special studies and analyzing the present use of the product.

Multiattribute customer satisfaction studies, including those involving data on competitors, are an important source of information on customer needs. Such studies should include both satisfaction ratings and importance ratings on various attributes.

To analyze the product's current use, we must learn firsthand about customer problems—from the initial receipt of the product to the product's final disposition. We must conduct research beyond product warranties as the customer desires product performance during the product's entire life, not just the warranty period.

This means visiting the site where the customer is using the product and intensely observing how the product is handled. These visits provide information about conditions of field use, problems reported by the customer, remedial steps taken (or considered) by the customer to improve the product and needs for which the customer sees no present solution. We also learn those problems not reported by the customer such as the costs of operating and maintaining the product and technical services required to support it.

We must identify every need—even those the customer forgets. Customers may have certain problems about which they do not complain because they do not associate the problems with the product. Two of the companies we studied presented customers with a written list of product options to remind customers of any needs the customers might have. Identifying such needs and problems leads to remedies and, thus, additional sales.

In addition, consider compiling the characteristics of key customers (and noncustomers) into a database. Keeping these profiles helps to identify obvious and not so obvious needs.

Information on the needs of people who are not customers is often a major gap. This information is needed to learn why they are not customers and what it would take to obtain their business. Be sure to include a sample of this group in your research.

Market Research for Quality in Small Business

> **GENERAL CONCEPTS OF MARKET RESEARCH**
>
> The following general concepts are based on the information supplied by the four companies we researched:
>
> - Owners and managers of small businesses have more contact with customers than their counterparts in large companies.
> - Although customer views on quality are most useful when compared to customer views on the competitors' products, little information is gathered on quality relative to the competition.
> - Market research tends to concentrate on current customers, neglecting to address the views of noncustomers—prospective future customers.
> - When designing market research, you should ask operating managers what questions need answers in order to improve operations.
> - Even though managers have taken formal steps to obtain feedback where customer retention and loyalty are concerned, they are only partially aware of the market research techniques available.

Analyzing Customer Retention and Loyalty

The questions our study asked about customer retention and loyalty looked at measuring retention rate, industry benchmarks on retention rate, the reasons for losing customers, using information on lost customers to make changes, recapturing lost customers and obstacles in obtaining information.

For two of the organizations, data on customer retention are automatically and continuously compiled. At the insurance company, yearly renewal rates on policies provide a measure of retention. At the bank, a daily report on closed accounts (with customers' reasons for closing) supplies data for measuring retention. In some cases, industry benchmarks are available for use. In one of the organizations we studied, the equivalent of a retention measure is the referral rate—the percentage of customers who say they would refer friends to the company.

Two organizations reported difficulty when researching why customers took their purchasing power to the competition. The companies said they had a hard time convincing employees to ask customers about buying a competing product because both employees and customers wanted to avoid confrontational discussions.

Recommendations. Acceptable levels of customer satisfaction do not guarantee acceptable sales figures. In some industries, more than 90% of customers report that they are "satisfied" or "very satisfied." Meanwhile, repurchase rates are only about 35%.[9] Therefore, we can see that while researching customer satisfaction is important, the research is incomplete unless we investigate customers' loyalty and intention to repurchase.

When compiling your research, consider asking customers one or more of the following:

- Would you purchase from us again?
- Have you recommended our product to a friend?
- What could we do to assure that you purchase from us again?

Such questions could be asked as part of periodic market research using any of the eight methods listed in Table 2. Market surveys, focus groups, customer advisory groups and special customer surveys, however, are particularly useful for retention and loyalty research.

Although retention data is typically available within the company, it alone is not sufficient. Multiattribute studies on quality relative to the competition must be completed as they provide reasons for customer defections, triggering preventive action that internal data cannot.

A further indication of loyalty is whether the customer would purchase other products and services the company offers. Information on what share of "the customer's wallet" is spent with a company is a dramatic measure of loyalty. Research on customer satisfaction and loyalty, therefore, should include questions such as:

- Are you aware that we sell other products?
- Have you bought other products from our company? If not, why not?

Market research information on quality relative to competition is important to understanding loyalty. Data must be captured as to why customers switch their purchases to the competition as these defections represent a significant economic loss. For some industries, a decrease in defection rates of five percentage points can increase profits by 25% to 100%.[10]

One company we studied reported that customers were more likely to give frank responses in a questionnaire when they were asked about taking their business elsewhere. But it can be difficult to use a questionnaire to determine the exact reason customers go to a competitor (experience suggests that customers often camouflage their answers). To better decipher the reason, consider your data on customer satisfaction, particularly if data on the competition are available.

Instead of the questionnaire, you may want to consider using focus groups of defecting customers. Focus groups can provide valuable, in-depth information that a questionnaire cannot. In this instance, be sure to ask group members for specifics when discussing their reasons for switching, and use an experienced leader to guide the group.

About 75% of the dissatisfied customers who complain will switch to a competitor.

But potential customer defections can be identified and eliminated by using data on customer complaints. Analyze these data for types of complaints and their frequencies, and design a system to make sure complaints are addressed and problems solved.

Turning Research into Action

The results of market research for quality must be linked to company operations in order to achieve high customer satisfaction and loyalty and minimize customer defections. Some action steps include:

- Communicate the research results to line managers, making sure they understand the results and take the appropriate actions. One company we studied sought information about new customers but did not document it. The research simply remained with the employee collecting the feedback. To prevent information from sitting in filing cabinets, those who conduct the research should explain the results to the operating managers.
- Analyze the results, identify areas requiring investigation and action, and assign responsibility for follow-up.
- Incorporate research results into strategic planning and budgeting processes. Market research results may lead to a conclusion to take action on product design, operations or service.
- Track and distribute information on customer retention and loyalty, reasons for defections and the percentage of customers who purchase more than one product from the company.
- Consider complaints as early indicators of potential customer defections, and have a policy and a plan for addressing complaints and recapturing lost customers.

Market Research and Small Business

Small businesses should not be deluded into thinking that they can't perform market research for quality because of a lack of time or resources. Market research methods can be reduced in scope and complexity to be cost effective. Research, even if it's rudimentary, should be part of the cycle of planning that all small businesses go through.

Market research seeks objective customer insight in the interest of quality service to consumers. And as the quality of goods and services remains a high priority in U.S. business, organizations have no choice but to integrate that customer insight when planning for quality. Clearly, the more an organization—small business or large corporation—understands its customer, the greater chance that organization has for a successful future.

References

1. Peter D. Bennett, ed., *Dictionary of Marketing Terms* (Chicago: American Marketing Association, 1988).
2. Michael J. Ryan, "Linking Quality, Customer Satisfaction and Financial Performance," *Proceedings of the 10th Annual Customer Satisfaction and*

Quality Measurement Conference (Chicago: American Marketing Association and ASQ, 1998).
3. Leonard L. Berry, *On Great Service* (New York: Free Press, 1995).
4. David A. Aaker, V. Kumar and George S. Day, *Marketing Research*, fifth edition (New York: John Wiley and Sons, 1995).
5. Gilbert A. Churchill, Jr., *Marketing Research Methodological Foundations*, fifth edition (Chicago: Dryden Press, 1991).
6. Frank M. Gryna, *Quality Planning and Analysis*, fourth edition (New York: McGraw Hill, 2001).
7. Valerie A. Zeithaml, A. Parasuraman and Leonard L. Berry, *Delivering Quality Service* (New York: Free Press, 1990).
8 Fred Wiersema, *Customer Intimacy* (Santa Monica, CA: Knowledge Exchange, 1996).
9. Frederick F. Reichheld, *The Loyalty Effect* (Boston: Harvard Business School Press, 1996).
10. Ibid.

Bibliography

Anton, Jon, *Customer Relationship Management* (Englewood Cliffs, NJ: Prentice-Hall, 1996).

Bultmann, Charles, "How To Define Customer Needs and Expectations: An Overview," *Customer Satisfaction Measurement Conference Notes* (Atlanta: ASQ and American Marketing Association, 1989). As originally written by Tom F. Gillett, "New Ways of Understanding Customers' Service Needs."

Goodman, John A., "Measuring and Quantifying the Market Impact of Consumer Problems," a report for the St. Petersburg-Tampa Section of ASQ, 1991.

Rust, Roland T., Anthony J. Zahorik and Timothy L. Keiningham, *Return on Quality* (Chicago: Probus Publishing, 1994).

Scanlan, Philip M., "Integrating Quality and Customer Satisfaction Measurement," *Customer Satisfaction Measurement Conference Notes* (Atlanta: ASQ and American Marketing Association, 1989).

William L. Rhey is an associate professor of marketing at the University of Tampa, FL. He earned a doctorate in marketing from the University of Mississippi in Oxford.

Frank M. Gryna is a distinguished professor of management at the University of Tampa, FL. He is also a professor of industrial engineering emeritus at Bradley University in Peoria, IL. Gryna earned his doctorate in industrial engineering from the University of Iowa in Iowa City.

Quality Tools and Techniques

PROCESS MANAGEMENT

Resolving the Process Paradox

Robert A. Gardner

This may be one of the best and most useful articles in the yearbook. It succinctly captures a number of important concepts dealing with process management and improvement—including whether it's smarter to outsource certain processes rather than improve them. It systematically leads you through how to understand your processes, identify those most critical and that have the highest payoff for improving, and how to institutionalize improvement as standard operating procedure.

Continuous process improvement (CPI) is an essential business strategy in competitive markets because:

- Customer loyalty is driven by delivered value.
- Delivered value is created by business processes.
- Sustained success in competitive markets requires a business to continuously improve its delivered value.
- To continuously improve value creation ability, a business must continuously improve its value creating process.

Although processes have always guided our actions and determined business results, the process movement is fairly new to the general business community. The movement is, however, gaining wider acceptance as more business leaders recognize the relevance of processes.

From *Quality Progress*, March 2001. Copyright © 2001 by the American Society for Quality. Reprinted with permission.

The promises of the movement, such as quantum improvements in quality, productivity and cycle times, are certainly appealing and promote high expectations for those embracing its tools and techniques. Unfortunately, the results being produced in many organizations do not match the promises of the practitioners or the expectations of business leaders.

In *Process Edge: Creating Value Where It Counts*, Peter Keen describes companies that experienced a measurable decline while they were making dramatic improvements to their processes.[1] He calls this the process paradox. The problem, says Keen, is that companies tend to focus improvement efforts on processes that do not substantially affect the capabilities that create value, and value creation is the sustenance of business.

Value is an economic concept that considers the cost to attain a benefit and the cost of the benefit itself. Process improvement frequently requires significant investments of time and financial resources to identify and implement improvements. Clearly, you should carefully consider if process improvement is the most appropriate value enabling strategy before making these investments. When both sides of the value equation are considered, it may actually make more sense to leave a process alone, or to outsource it, rather than to improve it.

Resolving the process paradox involves looking at how you select processes for improvement and how you select strategies for improving those processes.

Targeting Processes for Improvement

All processes are not created equal. Quantum improvements in unimportant processes will generally produce insignificant business results, while small improvements in important processes may produce significant improvements in business results. If you are to produce meaningful results with your process improvement efforts, you must target the right processes in ways that increase their ability to create or enable value.

To target your processes you have to answer these three questions:

1. What are your processes?
2. Which processes are most important to the organization?
3. How well are these processes performing?

Senior managers will typically not know the correct answers to these questions. When this happens, process improvement becomes a matter of ready, shoot, then aim. It is essential for organizations to address these fundamental questions before launching major improvement interventions.

Selecting Process Improvement Strategies

The Maslow maxim, "He that is good with a hammer tends to think everything is a nail," also applies in the process improvement world. It is not uncommon to see respected practitioners apply a single strategy or methodology to a wide variety of process problems. However, all process problems cannot be addressed via a single tool. Instead, tools should be selected and deployed as required to systematically advance the capability of processes in response to the unique business needs and priorities of the enterprise. This requires a toolbox, not a hammer.

Meaningful Process Improvement

This strategy for launching a system of process improvement in an organization is designed to avoid the pitfalls of the process paradox and to promote process improvement investments that yield meaningful results. The strategy is comprised of four phases (see Figure 1). Phase 1, data collection, collects the information and data needed for process targeting, while Phase 2, targeting processes, uses the information and data from Phase 1 to make and deploy the targeting decisions. These two phases are performed only once.

Phases 3 and 4 comprise the activities needed to establish a system of ongoing process management and improvement. The key difference between Phases 3 and 4 is that Phase 3 deals with enterprise management responsibilities, while Phase 4 deals with process owner responsibilities. Both of these phases are ongoing.

The strategy is built on several founding principles. The principles of process relevance and process performance are combined to establish a method for targeting processes. The principle of process maturity is used to provide a systematic approach to selecting improvement strategies for targeted processes. Although the strategy recognizes the absolute necessity of process performance metrics, it does not call directly for metrics development. Instead, it uses a maturity continuum to drive the development, deployment and utilization of performance metrics as processes are ready for them.

Attending to the processes of the enterprise should be a primary responsibility of management. Without effective management oversight and direction, the chances of falling victim to the process paradox are greatly increased, and Phase 3 seeks to address these needs.

Phase 1: Data Collection

1.1 Identify the value creation streams. The first step is to identify the value creation stream(s) for the enterprise. The value creation stream is comprised of the key activities that are required to take a product or service from initial concept to the hands of the end customer (see Figure 2).[2]

Value can only be defined by the end customer and is meaningful only when it's defined in terms of specific products and/or services. Product and service information can be coupled with customer defined value information to construct a value proposition, a document that describes the benefits and

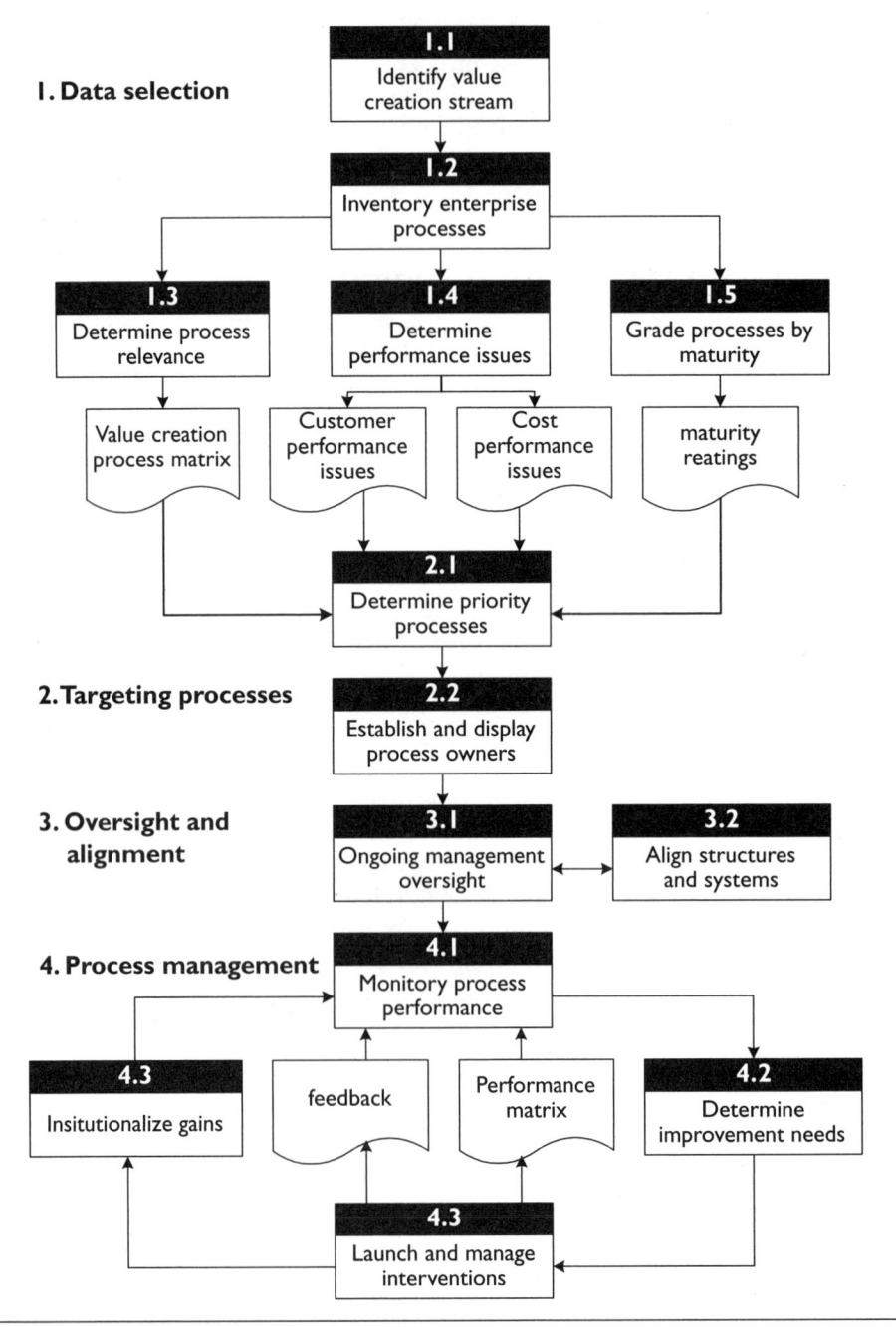

Figure 1. **Process portfolio management**

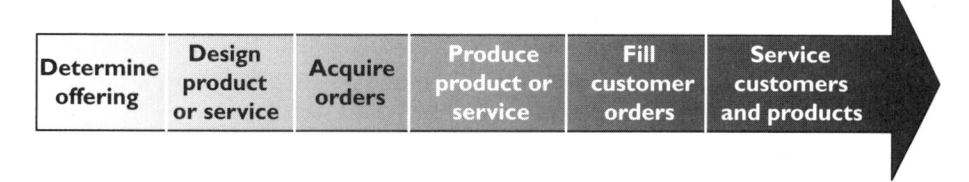

| Determine offering | Design product or service | Acquire orders | Produce product or service | Fill customer orders | Service customers and products |

Figure 2. **Value creation stream**

pricing arrangements of products and services that will attract customers and support the enterprise's financial goals.[3] The value proposition is essential for evaluating the value contributions of work processes and for aligning internal structures, systems and measurements.

1.2 Inventory enterprise processes. The next step is to inventory the business, management and support processes operating within the enterprise. One approach to identifying business processes begins by tracing the material and information flows that occur between the business enterprise and the outside world.[4] The material and informational entities contained in these flows are either produced or consumed by processes. For each process discovered, it is helpful to identify the state of each entity as it passes between the enterprise and the outside world. For example, a customer order or entity might have the states of received, booked, released, picked, packed, shipped and billed as it passes back and forth. Each of these state changes is produced by a process.

When the inventory has been completed, it's time to begin developing the process portfolio for the enterprise. The following items may be included initially:

- **Name:** Use verb/object construction, for example "develop product" or "fill orders."
- **Purpose:** The overall, unique purpose of the process, including primary products produced and value adding transformations involved.
- **Boundaries:** Differentiate the process from its environment, primarily in terms of key customer/supplier interfaces.
- **Interdependencies:** Describe the key interdependent relationships between the process and other processes.

The following items may be added to the portfolio as they are determined:

- **Owner:** The individual(s) responsible for process design and performance.
- **Performance goals:** Should focus primarily on the value proposition, business drivers and committed outcomes.
- **Operational metrics:** The measurements and related standards used to manage process performance.
- **Performance management:** The methods used to manage process performance.

> One approach to identifying business processes begins by tracing the material and information flows that occur between the business enterprise and the outside world.

- **Feedback mechanisms:** The key customer satisfaction and complaint management methods.

The Dimensions of Process Performance Measurement

Process performance is evaluated along three dimensions:[5]

1. **Effectiveness:** The extent to which the outputs of a process meet the needs and expectations of its customers. Effectiveness is synonymous with quality and exists primarily for the customer.
2. **Efficiency:** The extent to which resources are minimized and waste eliminated in the pursuit of effectiveness. Efficiency is primarily for the benefit of the enterprise.
3. **Adaptability:** The ability of a process to accommodate change. Adaptability is not change control—it is the ability of a process to know when external conditions have changed and to dynamically reconfigure itself to handle those changes without sacrificing effectiveness or efficiency. A highly adaptive process behaves like an organism, not like a machine model.

These dimensions are used throughout the rest of this article to build a framework for classifying the maturity of processes and for guiding the systematic development of process metrics.

1.3 Determine process relevance. Relevance is used to describe the importance of processes to the enterprise along two dimensions: relevance to value creation and relevance to strategy. Processes higher in relevance will receive greater scrutiny in Phase 2, targeting processes.

Processes can be classified along the value creation dimension by using the following three categories:

1. **Value creating:** Processes that directly determine or contribute to value creation, such as product design, product production and customer service.
2. **Value enabling:** Processes that do not directly contribute to value creation but are essential to enabling the processes that do, such as analyzing market conditions and managing inventory.
3. **Supporting:** Processes that neither create nor enable value but are necessary to support the apparatus of the enterprise, such as human resource development and financial accounting.

Value creating processes typically relate to the core competency of the enterprise and are mission critical. They are also the processes that are seen and experienced by external customers. At the other end of the scale, supporting processes tend to be fairly standardized and are frequent candidates for outsourcing.

Resolving the Process Paradox

The value creation process matrix is a useful tool for displaying value creation relevance information pictorially. It can also highlight the interdependencies between processes while visually positioning them based on their role in the value creation chain. Figure 3 provides a simplified example of the way the processes in a manufacturing organization might be positioned using this tool.

	Determine offering	Design product or service	Acquire orders	Produce product or service	Fill customer orders	Service customers and products
Value creating processes	Acquire customer feedback Acquire market data		Acquire customer orders Receive orders			Service customers
Value enabling processes	Market analysis	Plan requirements		Maintain inventory Manufacture product	Fill orders Distribute statements	Maintain customer account
Infrastructure support processes	Manage vendors Develop human resources		Financial accounting Check credit	Plan production		Process payments

(Process relevance ↑ ; Value creation stream →)

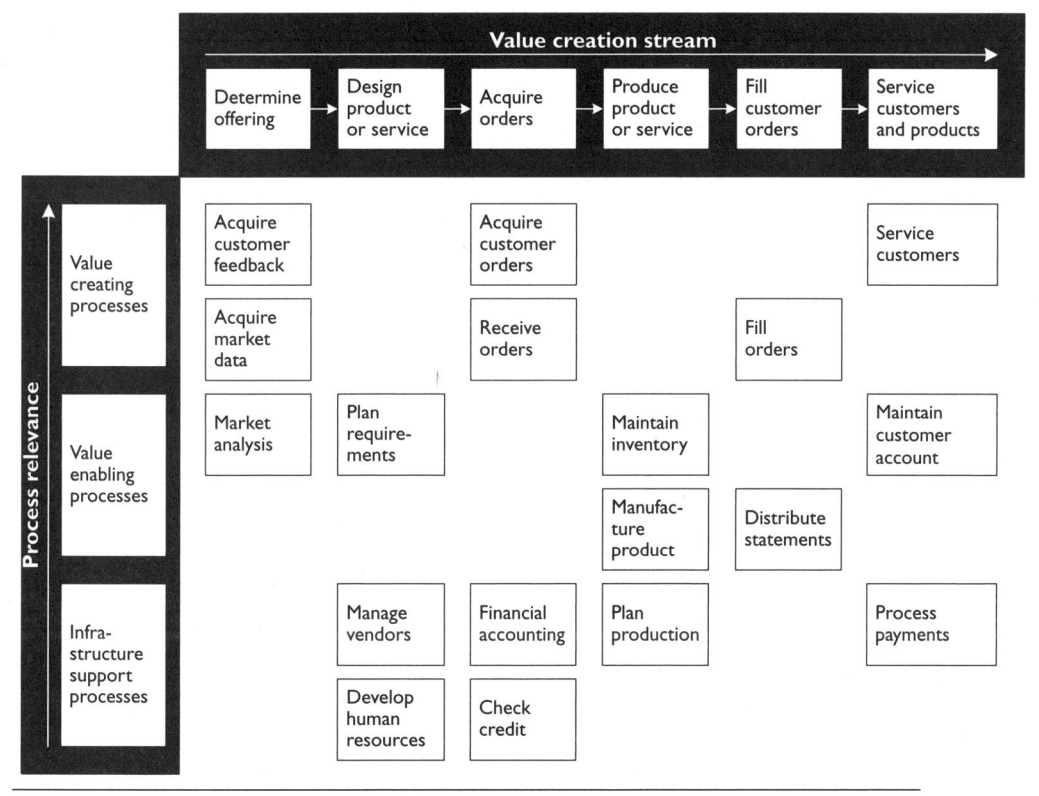

Figure 3. **Value creation process matrix**

The second dimension, strategic relevance, simply classifies processes in terms of their importance to the long-term strategies of the enterprise. By combining the dimensions of value creation and strategic relevance, you are in a better position to know which processes are important to sustaining the competitive ability of the enterprise.

1.4 Determine performance issues. Process performance issues are the second input used in Phase 2, targeting processes. These may surface while you are evaluating process performance along two dimensions:

1. The customer performance dimension (a measure of effectiveness) allows you to determine the presence and nature of any customer issues concerning the products and services they are receiving. A variety of methods

may be used to gather this information, including surveys, interviews, focus groups and complaints, but you should try to avoid relying on a single data collection tool.

Measuring customer perceptions involves more than just measuring satisfaction—it involves determining the specific product and service dimensions that are causing customer issues. This helps to identify the specific processes that are driving these issues and provides a foundation for developing process effectiveness measurements later.

2. The cost performance dimension (a measure of efficiency) allows you to evaluate the operating costs of key processes. Activity-based costing (ABC) is the best tool to use here. The principles underlying ABC are simple: Products and services are produced via work activities, these activities consume resources and resource consumption incurs costs. The Consortium for Advanced Manufacturers-International Cross (see Figure 4) illustrates these linkages and the cost views they provide. By determining the costs incurred by resource consuming activities, you can evaluate costs along both the product view (the vertical axis) and the process view (the horizontal axis).[6]

1.5 Grade processes by maturity. The process maturity continuum is offered as a simple way to evaluate the maturity of a process and to guide the selection of process improvement strategies. The continuum uses a series of crite-

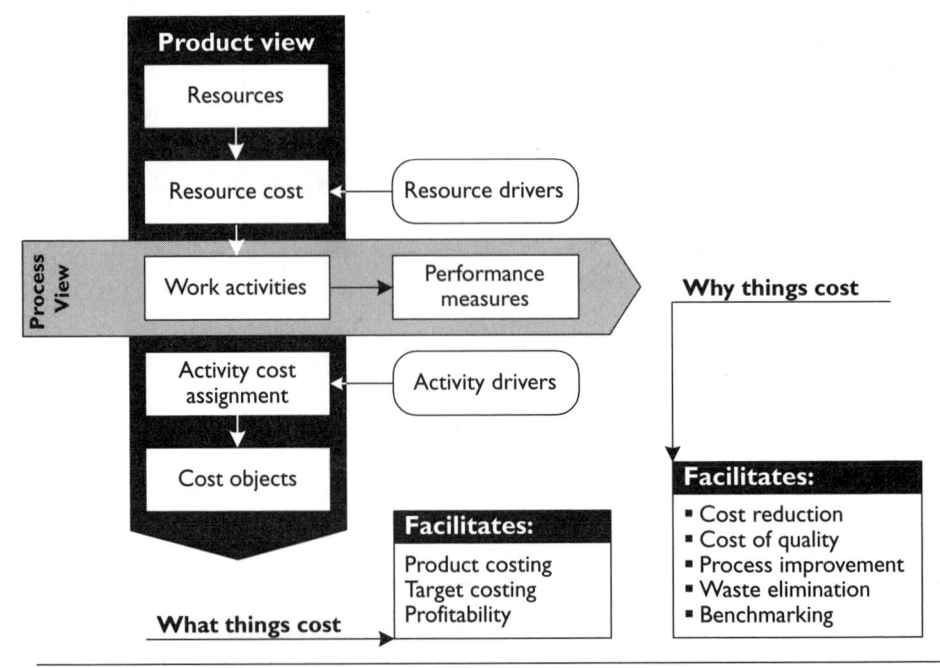

Figure 4. **Multiple cost views of activity-based costing/activity-based management** (Consortium for Advanced Manufacturers—International Cross)

ria to ascertain the relative maturity of processes along a six-level scale (see Figure 5).[7,8] Each level is defined in terms of process management practices, such as standardization, measurement and corrective action, and performance outcomes, such as customer satisfaction, process capability and efficiency.

As processes move up the maturity scale, they demonstrate higher levels of effectiveness (quality), efficiency (resource utilization) and adaptability. Each level is inclusive of the lower levels and necessitates a different set of improve-

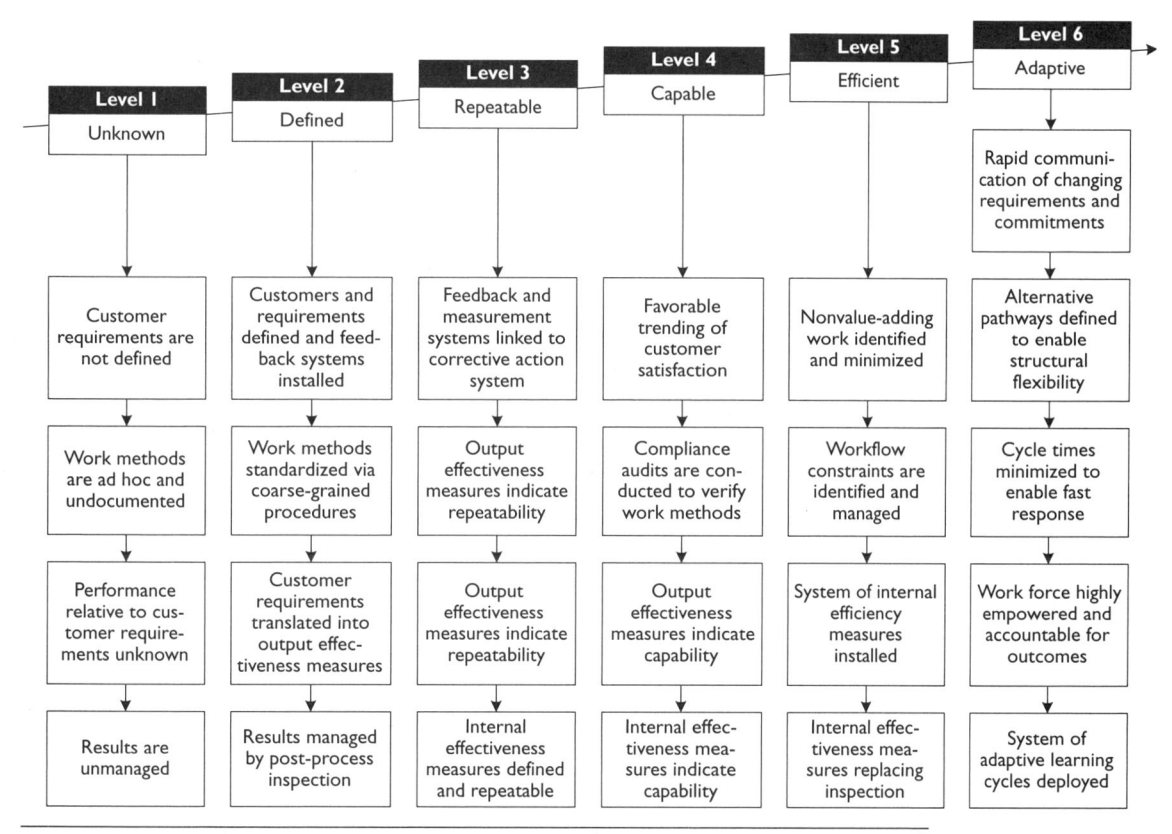

Level 1 Unknown	Level 2 Defined	Level 3 Repeatable	Level 4 Capable	Level 5 Efficient	Level 6 Adaptive
					Rapid communication of changing requirements and commitments
Customer requirements are not defined	Customers and requirements defined and feedback systems installed	Feedback and measurement systems linked to corrective action system	Favorable trending of customer satisfaction	Nonvalue-adding work identified and minimized	Alternative pathways defined to enable structural flexibility
Work methods are ad hoc and undocumented	Work methods standardized via coarse-grained procedures	Output effectiveness measures indicate repeatability	Compliance audits are conducted to verify work methods	Workflow constraints are identified and managed	Cycle times minimized to enable fast response
Performance relative to customer requirements unknown	Customer requirements translated into output effectiveness measures	Output effectiveness measures indicate repeatability	Output effectiveness measures indicate capability	System of internal efficiency measures installed	Work force highly empowered and accountable for outcomes
Results are unmanaged	Results managed by post-process inspection	Internal effectiveness measures defined and repeatable	Internal effectiveness measures indicate capability	Internal effectiveness measures replacing inspection	System of adaptive learning cycles deployed

Figure 5. **The process maturity continuum**

ment strategies to enable the performance characteristics associated with it.

The continuum provides a useful framework for guiding process improvement work because it provides the basis for comparing processes, recognizes the progression of characteristics needed to build good processes and shapes the selection of improvement strategies.

Phase 2: Targeting Processes

2.1 Determine priority processes and strategies. Use the process relevance, performance and maturity information that was developed in Phase 1 to identify the processes requiring immediate attention (your priority processes). Processes that are high in relevance and low in performance are first priority. These processes are also candidates for the more aggressive value enabling strategies, such as redesign or reengineering. For example, the "acquire customer orders" process in Figure 3 is highly relevant since it is a value creating process. If the customer performance or cost performance data from Step 1.4 indicate significant performance issues with the process, the process will take high priority.

Processes at the intermediate stages of relevance or performance are second-level priority processes and may be tackled via incremental value enabling strategies, such as CPI. Processes at the lowest level of relevance may be candidates for outsourcing if they are poor performers or for potential products if they are high performers.

> Targets establish the basis for accountability and help determine the process improvement strategies that may be selected.

Managers should set performance targets for the priority processes. These targets should define the performance characteristics, the performance levels for those characteristics and any time frames that are appropriate. Targets establish the basis for accountability and help determine the process improvement strategies that may be selected.

2.2 Establish and deploy process owners. Traditionally, the emphasis of management has been on the main hierarchical work unit, the department. However, business processes frequently cut across organizational boundaries, leaving departments with only a snapshot view of the overall process. As a result, no one is held responsible for the end-to-end processes.

Enter the process owner. The process owner is not concerned with assuring the performance of departmental tasks, but with the successful realization of a complete end-to-end process.[9] The process owner has responsibility for the design of the process, its documentation and performance measurements, and for training process performers in its structure and conduct. This is not an operational or full-time role; it is a role that is primarily concerned with the capability of the process, not the daily performance of work.

Phase 3: Ongoing Oversight and Alignment

3.1 Management oversight of priority processes. By this point, the organization's management has determined the priority processes, defined the process owners and established performance objectives. Although the delegation work has been completed, final accountability must still reside with the organization's managers. To this end, the managers must regularly monitor the performance of priority processes, support the process interventions that are under way and hold people accountable for results.

3.2 Align organizational structures and systems. As process management practices and performance improvements are deployed, it is sometimes necessary to align the organizational structures and systems with the core business processes. This requires the support and authority of senior management. Without strong senior management support and leadership, it is difficult to deploy significant change across organizational boundaries.

Phase 4: Manage and Improve Processes

Phase 4 is an iterative system of process management and improvement that mirrors the plan, do, check, act cycle (see Figure 1). The keystone to this phase is performance measurement and monitoring. Put simply, without ongoing measurement and monitoring, you don't have process management, and without process management, you can't sustain process improvement. The process owner has primary responsibility for this phase.

4.1 Monitor process performance. The process owner regularly monitors and evaluates process performance results. Although there may be few performance metrics initially, the maturity continuum and improvement cycles will correct these deficiencies over time.

4.2 Determine improvement needs. Improvement needs are determined based on the relevance, performance and maturity of processes. However, when you are dealing with immature processes, the maturity continuum will play a stronger role in this determination since performance metrics will be relatively scarce. As mentioned previously, the maturity continuum provides specific guidance for developing process performance metrics. For example, Level 2 emphasizes the development and deployment of customer feedback and output effectiveness measurements. Thereafter, Level 3 adds internal effectiveness measures, and Level 4 adds efficiency measures as needed.

As performance measurements, standards and practices are implemented, they become essential tools for managing process performance. However, the maturity continuum still provides the framework for advancing the capability of processes.

4.3 Launch and manage interventions. Process owners should select and dispatch performance improvement interventions based on business priorities and process performance levels. They should also evaluate the improvements resulting from these interventions via performance measurement data and categorize the results based on the attained maturity levels.

The selection of the improvement strategy is an important decision that should consider both the degree of improvement required and the current maturity level of the problem process. Generally, there are three classes of performance improvement interventions:

1. Problem solving: Problem solving is normally dispatched to resolve oper-

Improvement needs are determined based on the relevance, performance and maturity of processes.

ational problems. It is also used in the early stages of maturity to identify and remove the causes of process variation. The distinguishing feature of this tool is the use of root cause analysis and iterative hypothesis testing. By itself, problem solving is not a strategy for advancing the capability of processes; it is a tool that repairs components that have broken.
2. CPI: This is a strategy for incrementally advancing the capability of processes. It should be used when near-term improvement needs are small and risks need to be avoided. Here the emphasis is on analyzing process data and generating and evaluating improvements. Common incremental techniques include standardization, variation reduction, cycle time reduction, waste elimination and constraint management.
3. Process innovation: Innovation should be used when the amount of improvement required is large. The risks and effort associated with innovation are higher than with the incremental approaches. Process redesign and enterprise reengineering are the principle techniques in this group. Both strategies seek quantum gains in performance.

A Process Improvement Reference Guide

Figure 6 connects improvement strategies and tools with process maturity levels. As the diagram illustrates, the transition from each level to the next requires fairly specific strategies that are unique to that level. The diagram provides a simple road map for systematically advancing the capability of processes by applying tools as they are appropriate. It is clearly an incremental tool.

To use this guide, you must first know the current maturity level of the problem process. If, for example, you want to advance a process from Level 3 to Level 4, you would probably want to adopt variation management as your strategy. The methods you would use to address variation management are statistical process control and problem solving. The tools and techniques you would use might include process input management, internal control points management or error proofing.

4.4 Institutionalize gains. Improvements must be institutionalized and leveraged to realize their full potential.

Institutionalizing improvements: There are several prerequisites to promoting an effective transition from the drawing board to the front lines, including:

1. A complete and properly executed rollout plan.
2. A clear system of accountabilities.
3. Enforcement of accountabilities.

All three are essential—and none can compensate for the absence of another. Although process improvement teams can address the first two, only senior management can cause the third to happen.

Resolving the Process Paradox

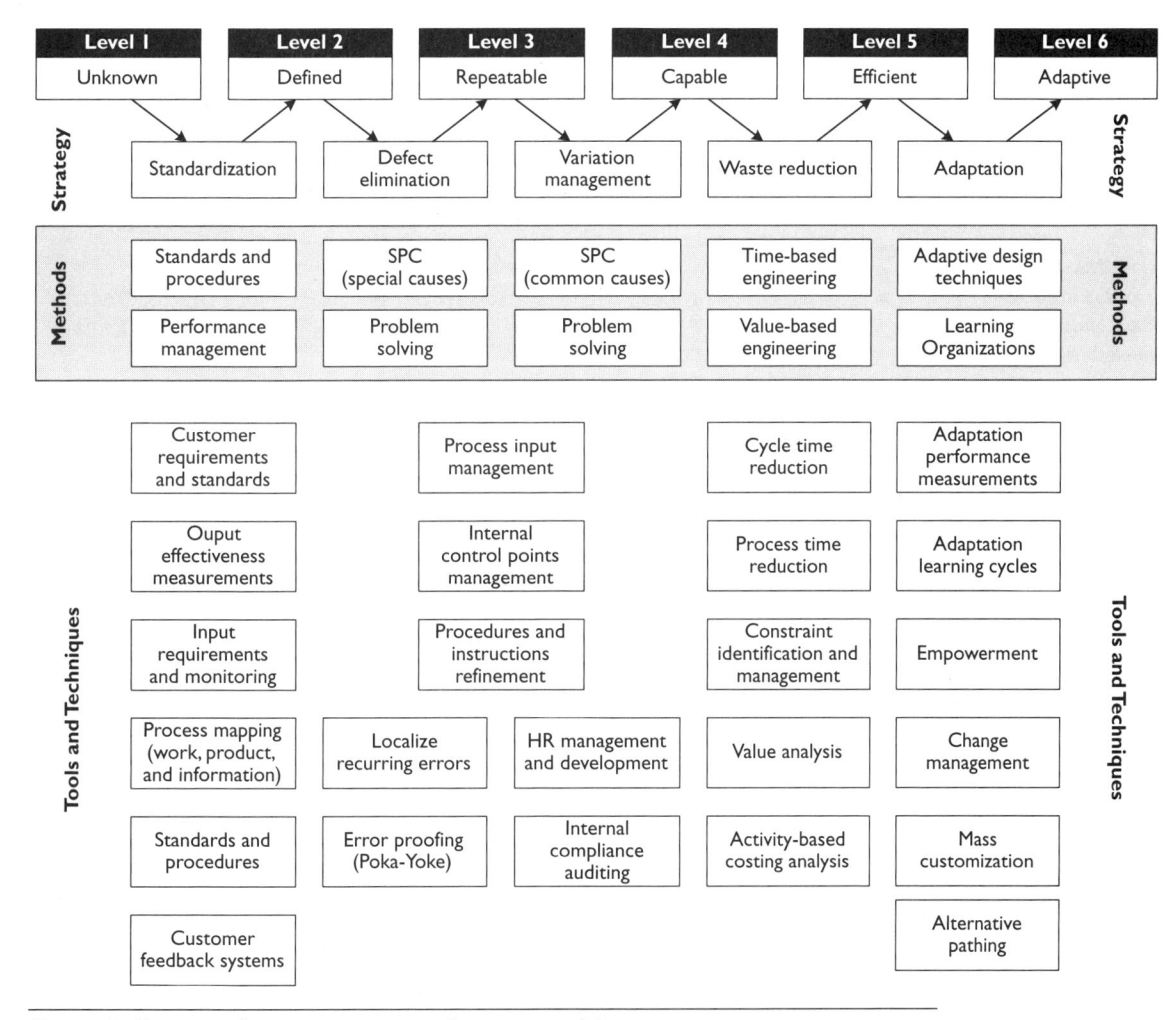

	Level 1	Level 2	Level 3	Level 4	Level 5	Level 6
	Unknown	Defined	Repeatable	Capable	Efficient	Adaptive
Strategy		Standardization	Defect elimination	Variation management	Waste reduction	Adaptation
Methods		Standards and procedures	SPC (special causes)	SPC (common causes)	Time-based engineering	Adaptive design techniques
		Performance management	Problem solving	Problem solving	Value-based engineering	Learning Organizations
Tools and Techniques		Customer requirements and standards	Process input management		Cycle time reduction	Adaptation performance measurements
		Ouput effectiveness measurements	Internal control points management		Process time reduction	Adaptation learning cycles
		Input requirements and monitoring	Procedures and instructions refinement		Constraint identification and management	Empowerment
		Process mapping (work, product, and information)	Localize recurring errors	HR management and development	Value analysis	Change management
		Standards and procedures	Error proofing (Poka-Yoke)	Internal compliance auditing	Activity-based costing analysis	Mass customization
		Customer feedback systems				Alternative pathing

Figure 6. **Process improvement reference guide**

Leveraging improvements: Leveraging improvements across an enterprise presents its own set of challenges, including:

1. Determining where the improvements may offer benefits.
2. Determining how to sell the improvements.
3. Transferring the skills and knowledge required to deploy the improvements.

Here again, senior management involvement is essential to making improvements happen.

Resolve the Paradox

By using this strategy and the tools it embraces, business managers will be able to know what their processes are, which are most important to the enterprise, how well the important processes are performing and what tools should be used to advance key processes along the maturity continuum. This knowledge helps resolve the process paradox as well as satisfy the following critical success factors:

- Continuous process improvement must be viewed as a management system, not as a series of disconnected projects that simply pick low hanging fruit.
- Process improvement must be applied to whole processes, not just to process components. Working on components in isolation risks suboptimization.
- Process improvement must be deployed against strategically relevant processes and performance issues, or it won't be viewed as viable or important.
- Process capability must be systematically built on the foundations described in the process maturity continuum. Without these foundations, you are more likely to have a house of cards than capable processes.
- Process improvement requires more than the support of senior managers. Managers must participate in very specific ways. If we fail to integrate the roles of management into our processes and supporting management systems, these roles likely won't be fulfilled.

Obviously, this strategy is not a quick hitter approach. The road to good health and capable processes requires identifying and systematically addressing priorities. This strategy seeks to begin at the beginning and build the required foundations along the way. In the end, this is the fastest and surest way to meaningful results.

References

1. Peter G.W. Keen, *Process Edge: Creating Value Where It Counts* (Watertown, MA: Harvard Business School Press, 1997).
2. James P. Womack and Daniel T. Jones, *Lean Thinking* (New York: Simon & Schuster, 1996).
3. Frank Ostroff, *The Horizontal Organization* (New York: Oxford University Press, 1999).
4. Raymond L. Manganelli and Mark M. Klein, *The Reengineering Handbook* (New York: American Management Association, 1996).
5. Gabriel A. Pall, *The Process Centered Enterprise* (Boca Raton, FL: St. Lucie Press, 1999).

6. Gary Cokins, *Activity-Based Cost Management: Making It Work* (New York: McGraw-Hill, 1996).
7. Software Engineering Institute, Capability Maturity Model for Software, Version 1.1 (Pittsburgh: Carnegie Mellon University, 1993).
8. H. James Harrington, *Business Process Improvement* (New York: McGraw-Hill, 1991).
9. Michael Hammer, *Beyond Reengineering* (New York: Harper Collins, 1996).

Robert A. Gardner is director of quality assurance for Compris Technologies in Kennesaw, GA. He earned a master's degree in government (survey research methodology) from Western Kentucky University in Bowling Green. Gardner is an ASQ certified quality manager.

Working by the Rules

Emily Kay

This is a kind of "raise our consciousness" article about the rules, spoken and unspoken, that govern how people operate in organizations. These rules have to do with tradition but they also have to do with the knowledge of employees. This article suggests that organizations need to make these "rules" explicit to create standardization across the organization. This, of course, makes improvement much easier.

Do you know how your business operates on the nitty-gritty level of the procedural rules that guide its employees' minute-to-minute actions? You should. When it comes to competitive positioning, the devil is in the details. But those details usually aren't easy to get at; typically they're stored in the heads of business unit employees or in the legacy computer code that controls business processes.

Process information—in the form of thousands of detailed rules that govern how customers are treated, how transactions occur, how product offerings are priced and how employees are compensated—can be just as strategic a corporate asset as content knowledge. It's also just as inaccessible. If, however, you were able to extract those business rules from their hiding places, centralize them and ensure they were in standard form, you'd be able to change them throughout the enterprise, whenever and as quickly as change was needed.

Automate or Fall Behind

Recently one health insurer undertook just such a task. To shorten the underwriting process, improve the accuracy of underwriting decisions and potentially save millions of dollars, Blue Cross Blue Shield of North Carolina (BCB-SNC) deployed a knowledge management system of which business rules are a central element. The company, which offers both managed care and traditional health insurance services for both groups and individuals, set out five years ago to define its underwriting rules, centralize them and make them accessible to employees. The need for the system was obvious, according to Sue Ryan, who was hired in 1995 to help build the system. Under the old sys-

Reprinted by permission of the publisher from *Knowledge Management*, November 2000. Copyright © 2000 by Freedom Technology Media Group. All rights reserved.

tem, any three trained medical underwriters reviewing the same health insurance application might have come up with three different assessments of the likely cost of insuring that individual or group. Today, BCBSNC underwriters use a rules-based system that "takes away that subjectivity and is very consistent," says Ryan, who now is the company's manager of underwriting services in Durham, N.C.

BCBSNC is hardly alone in recognizing the need to automate the management of its business rules: the policies and procedures that define, limit or drive daily business activity. But as part of a knowledge management strategy, the systematizing of business rules is still in its infancy.

Every business operates by rules, whether or not they are formalized or recorded. But when those rules are known only to veteran employees or are buried in code, they cannot easily be shared. "Business rules are about capturing what your experts know and disseminating it to people who don't have that expertise," says Tod Loofbourrow, president and CEO of Authoria Inc., a software vendor in Waltham, Mass.

Modern business rules systems are based on rules engines, which convert business logic expressed in application code into rules logic stated in English and stored in a separate database. The goal is to rationalize a business's rules, eliminate conflicting versions used by different sites or business units and put them in a form in which they can be administered by business unit employees without the hands-on involvement of IT specialists. Using these new tools, line-of-business users never see what the rules engine sees, only the English-like representation of the rule, which they can query. For example, a user might say, "Show me all the rules about a certain type of auto insurance policy." When permitted, users can also define or modify rules.

A system that allowed a business unit executive, for example, to change almost instantly the commission structure on a line of the company's products—rather than having to put in a request to IS that might take days or weeks to satisfy—would allow that unit to respond quickly to a competitor's move. Being able to include new products in existing sales, invoicing, service and support rules could speed time-to-market of those new products by weeks.

These systems play a key role in protecting the integrity of both processes and data. Whenever business users access corporate data, such a system will check the business rules associated with it and ensure that no data gets stored that violates those rules in some way. A rule can be as seemingly trivial as the number of decimal places required for numbers or as clearly important as the qualifications for a category of preferred customer status.

Without such systems in place, the policies and practices that have been coded directly into the program logic of applications that run business processes are difficult to support and change. "The problem is that these atomic units of knowledge—business logic—are not accessible," says Ron Ross, a principal with Business Rule Solutions LLC, a consulting firm in Houston. "The logic is either buried in legacy systems or exists as tacit knowledge in the heads of a

Every business operates by rules, whether or not they are formalized or recorded.

few key workers, in memos, procedure manuals and help messages. It's not coordinated, orchestrated or managed, so you can't reapply it effectively." It is, in other words, unmanaged knowledge.

Business Rules and KM

Business rules and knowledge management are inextricably linked. In fact, business rules should be a core component of any organization's knowledge management strategy, says May Abraham, a knowledge-based decision-support systems specialist with a financial institution in New York that declined to be named. "Business rules are a central aspect of knowledge management functions," she says. "A knowledge management practice allows the company to identify and organize the rules in a repository, which facilitates change and development in a fast-moving business environment."

To Russ Capone, vice president of individual financial services in the financial systems department of the Prudential Insurance Co. of America in Newark, N.J., business rules are essential to knowledge management strategies. "A knowledge management strategy will enable businesses to quickly respond to change, be more efficient and better meet the needs of customers," says Capone. "Business rules are the specific details behind that strategy; it's getting down to the whats, the hows and the whys."

Fannie Mae, the Washington, D.C.-based financial services company and mortgage market maker, uses business rules to share corporate knowledge, according to Colleen McClintock. Now a business rules product manager with Ilog Inc., a software vendor in Mountain View, Calif., she served for several years as a consultant to Fannie Mae. Using its homegrown knowledge acquisition and rule management assistance (KARMA) system, which was built using the Ilog Rules for C++ rules engine software, Fannie Mae can describe, in its own business rules language, policies about loan purchasing and underwriting. A point-and-click interface enables business users to define new rules and modify existing ones. The system automatically generates code for the rules engine.

KARMA serves several departments within Fannie Mae. "The marketing department uses the tool to define new and special programs and new loan products," says McClintock. "The credit policy department uses the same tool to define restrictions to manage risks, and the mortgage operations department uses the tool to resolve loans that don't pass policy checks."

Implementation Challenges

In a typical organization that has grown over time, says Abraham, the business rules that define its operations are embedded in overlapping systems and an array of people, processes and procedures. One of the principal challenges for such a company is to figure out how to get business unit employees across the organization to apply the same business rules consistently. That effort is ongoing at Fannie Mae, according to McClintock; the company is still in the process of deploying KARMA company-wide. Although Fannie Mae began its business rules project in the mid-1990s, only about 25 employees in the marketing, credit policy and mortgage operations units currently use it.

It has taken so long because of the plethora of software languages in use. "The process of making more applications share the same business policies takes time," McClintock says. Consolidating knowledge by implementing consistent business rules strategies across applications written in Cobol, Fortran and other languages is, in her words, "a huge undertaking."

Eventually, Fannie Mae expects to allow its lending institutional partners to use KARMA to define their own rules. Brokerage firms, for example, could have company-specific rules governing their ability to purchase jumbo loans. Using Fannie Mae's rules tool, these lenders could define and manage those rules themselves, says McClintock.

As well as the problem of incompatible IT platforms, another major stumbling block for large enterprises is the logistics of delivery. For example, Weyerhauser Co., a forest products company in Federal Way, Wash., wanted to build a knowledge base for its employee service center (ESC). The project involved figuring out how to provide personalized information about human resources (HR) policies and plans to its 50,000 geographically dispersed employees.

"We're looking at an application to let us target information to specific group employees so they would get one answer consistently," says Ralph Horner, Weyerhauser's ESC process manager. Toward that end, his group launched a corporate knowledge base in only five months using Authoria HR, a Web-based tool that uses links to Weyerhauser's PeopleSoft HR system and separate rules and data repositories to build in real time a personalized Web page for each employee. With the application in place, HR workers can quickly and easily answer employees' questions about benefits and policies. An added benefit is that HR staffers can maintain the rules base, since the user interface is based on a Q-and-A format and doesn't expose business unit employees to the underlying C++ code.

Not everyone at Weyerhauser was happy about the standardization of HR business rules, which included consolidating the HR function into a single organization instead of having several HR entities specific to the business units. The centralization effort involved changes in service delivery and the elimination of some HR positions.

"You get challenged because people have ownership of what they're doing," says Horner. "The change management process means changing or eliminating the way they do processes that they had developed." But rules-based personalization can give employees a sense of being better cared for, thus increasing loyalty as well as lowering call center and HR personnel costs.

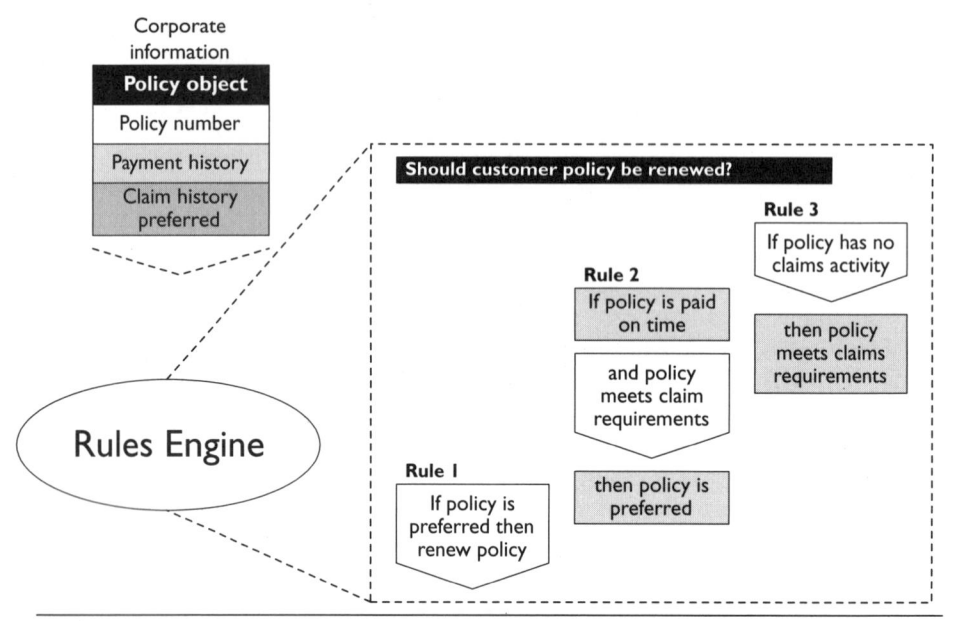

Figure 1. **A rules engine can help companies to automate and coordinate their business rules, as in this example from the insurance industry**

Playing by the Rules

Ideally, organizations would like to eliminate a costly link in the chain of business rules by giving line-of-business workers direct access to the rules, without IT department involvement. Some companies believe that the natural-language qualities of rules descriptions will enable nonprogrammers to build business process applications without drawing upon IT resources, but a number of practitioners deny that it will ever happen. "This is a naive impression, because rule specification itself is dominated by strict syntactical structure," says David Loshin, president of Knowledge Integrity Inc., a consulting firm in West Hempstead, N.Y. "Even if it is not called programming, the skill and experience required match that of a programmer."

Even if complete user independence isn't feasible, some companies have managed to slash their IT involvement. Despite KARMA's intuitive, English-like language, Fannie Mae employees still must rely on a trained business analyst to maintain the system and ensure that the rules are defined correctly. Still, no programmer intervention is needed to change rules or define new ones. Business users can perform such tasks, thus shortening the whole process. (For more on this process, see the sidebar, "Launching a New Business Rule.")

That facility, says Ilog's McClintock, translates into a competitive advantage. In the past, it would take up to nine months to implement a new product or program. Businesspeople would have to specify its terms, an analyst

> ## LESSONS LEARNED
>
> Business managers and consultants who have implemented business rules systems offer some battle-tested suggestions on setting your priorities.
>
> ### Plan Ahead
>
> Wherever possible, standardize policies, processes and plans across the company before deploying technological solutions. "The more standard you are, the less complex the effort and the less work you have to do to implement [technology]," says Ralph Horner, employee service center process manager with Weyerhauser Co. in Federal Way, Wash.
>
> "Think before you code," says Barbara van Halle, founder of Knowledge Partners Inc. in Flander, N.J. "Set yourself up to capture rules and manage them before you hire your Java programmer."
>
> ### Consider Culture
>
> Taking a knowledge approach to business rules is more an organizational and political challenge than a technical one. "One of the biggest roadblocks to moving toward a knowledge-oriented organization is the underlying theme of data ownership and the lack of a data-ownership policy," says David Loshin, president of Knowledge Integrity Inc. in West Hempstead, N.Y. "Someone who creates data or manages access might claim they own it. People become protective of their turf."
>
> ### Start Small
>
> Don't attempt to externalize all your business rules. "We started off with a few projects," says May Abraham, a knowledge-based decision-support systems specialist with a New York financial institution. "We didn't attack all the rules, just the most complex and hardest to maintain."
>
> ### Base It on Business
>
> Business rules should come from business objectives rather than IT system requirements. "You'll get better-quality rules, you can trace the rules better, and you'll have a business link," says Abraham.
>
> A related benefit is that it's far more expensive to use programmers to maintain business rules than to make business analysts responsible for a business rules repository. Furthermore, IT staffers designing business rule applications need the same level of business understanding that knowledge workers have, says David Plotkin, senior data administrator with Longs Drug Stores Inc. in Walnut Creek, Calif.

would have to decide how to implement it and a programmer would have to code it; only then could testing and migration begin. The new process, which shifts much of the responsibility for defining new policies and programs from the IT department to business workers, takes only days. "Applications can change at the speed of business," says McClintock.

Blue Cross Blue Shield of North Carolina used Aion, rules-based development software from Computer Associates International Inc., to build its automated medical underwriting system (AMUS). This solution enabled the health insurer to eliminate or redeploy eight underwriters and 15 support personnel and replace them with four underwriting processors. "We don't need highly skilled professional underwriters [for routine underwriting projects now]," says Ryan.

AMUS' rules-based decision-making engine stores underwriting rules in English, so underwriters can make changes to the rules as needed. The engine links to an IBM IMS database server and BCBSNC's proprietary systems for rate quoting, policy writing and risk management. The rules engine determines whether to underwrite applicants after assessing their eligibility and medical risks.

In addition to reducing staff size, the business rules-based system has enabled BCBSNC to reduce the time its small group health unit takes to make an underwriting decision from a week to a day. The company also has improved the accuracy of underwriting decisions and brings in additional revenue by selling the system to other Blue Cross companies.

"Our operating environment is constantly changing, with changes to goals, strategies, products, markets, staff, law and regulatory requirements taking place frequently," says Abraham. "Rules must be understandable, easily related to their business context, quickly and easily updated for required changes, and remain the property of the business."

Flexible systems also bode well for the future. "The ability to change the system later is where the big payback is," says Barbara van Halle, founder of Knowledge Partners Inc., a consulting firm in Flander, N.J. An organization gains a competitive advantage from, she says, "speed of delivery, the ability to change quickly and the opportunity to externalize and publish the rules behind the system. That's what knowledge management is about."

An organization must be able to modify its policies, processes and operations on short notice to stay competitive. Identifying, capturing and sharing its business rules is critical to operating with more coordination and efficiency and boosting the bottom line. Allowing business unit workers to manage business rules accelerates the speed with which corporations can respond to fast-changing market conditions.

LAUNCHING A NEW BUSINESS RULE

The process for launching a new business rule can be rather involved, according to Colleen McClintock, business rules product manager with Ilog Inc. in Mountain View, Calif. However, the result—the formalization of a company's rules and the subsequent ease of modification—is likely to be worth the effort.

> At Fannie Mae, for example, according to McClintock, a business user in credit policy or marketing might define a rule using a point-and-click interface. Once the policy is validated, a business analyst will generate the code. In Fannie Mae's case, there's a button on the application that says "generate"; clicking on it generates executable code that the rules engine understands.
>
> McClintock says that when the rule definition process begins, the rule has "new" status. Once business users define it, its status is "complete." After it goes through the business validation process, its status changes to "validated." Then it goes to the business analyst, who runs it through the test environment to make sure that it doesn't violate other existing rules or policies. If testing is successful, it moves through the normal migration process into production and gets "implemented" status.
>
> 1. The appropriate department (such as credit or marketing) defines the policy.
> 2. It goes through an internal validation process, in which other business users must approve the policy before the organization accepts it.
> 3. After business people sign off on it, the rule goes into a testing phase.
> 4. If it behaves as expected, it moves into production.

Emily Kay writes about technology as a principal with Choice Communications, an editorial consulting firm in Chelmsford, Mass.

Know What Your Gages Are Measuring

Gillian Babicz

A key aspect of executing and maintaining the integrity of process on the shop floor is the use of gages to check work and make sure the correct outputs are being delivered. To make sure this happens, gages must be properly calibrated. ISO standards call for such calibration. This article explores some of the issues involved with gage calibration from a variety of perspectives with examples from different types of operations.

Calibration is the comparison of a standard of a known uncertainty to another measurement tool of unknown certainty to detect, correlate, report or eliminate by adjustment any deviation from required performance specifications.

Today, many assume that because a piece of test equipment is working correctly, it must be calibrated and accurate. Only if the equipment has traceable calibration records can this be the case. But how can one be certain that equipment does indeed have traceable records when hundreds, if not thousands, of gages must be calibrated on a regular basis?

The frequency of the calibration depends on tolerance requirements of the job, amount of use and conditions under which the gages are used. But do hard and fast rules apply?

"Though ISO 17025, General Requirements for the Competence of Testing and Calibration Laboratories, clearly states that, 'a calibration certificate shall not contain any recommendation on the recalibration interval,' the best source for establishing calibration intervals is still the equipment manufacturer. Through the use of data collection within their calibration labs, manufacturers are best equipped to adapt experience data from similar applications," said Kevin Shannon, quality manager at DeFelsko Corp. (Ogdensburg, NY).

Richard Pirret, marketing manager of Fluke Process Tools (Everett, WA), agrees that the best place to go when looking for calibration interval recommendations is the manufacturer. But, not all manufacturers will give recommendations. Sometimes the most practical way to determine intervals is from experience. "A pressure transmitter that's critical to the performance of the plant, might be looked at every 90 days or half year. As [a company] develops more confidence in that measurement tool or family of tools, they can relax that. They might move calibration out to 1 year—they might move it out to 2 years. They can adjust the calibration intervals so it more appropriately matches their experience," said Pirret.

Linda Bogaski, vice president of JBL Systems (Macomb, MI), said if a measurement tool's calibration interval is 60 days, but the tool has been sitting on the shelf the entire 60 days or has only been used 5 days, it could be "a waste of money" to calibrate the tool.

One must also consider how variation in the measurement result could affect the product or processes it is intended to measure, said Shannon. "Critical applications should always safeguard their processes by minimizing the calibration interval," he said.

Often it's the management instrumentation packages, or software packages, that look at a measurement tool's history and record how it has behaved over time, whether it's in or out of tolerance and if it's out of tolerance, by how much.

"If measurement tools were found quite within tolerance, that's an indication that you can stretch the calibration interval of that device or that class of device. Software allows you to look at behaviors of classes of measurement tools over time and adjust your approach to them accordingly," said Pirret.

A Software Solution

Although software is not necessary to keep track of gage history, the pencil and paper method is only as good as its limitations and makes it difficult to retrieve information. Papers might be misplaced, remain unchanged or someone may walk off with the files containing the calibration records. It would be difficult with a manual system to track all the measurement tools used by manufacturers.

A software-based system allows information to be recorded, tracked and retrieved in an effective and efficient manner. Software facilitates searches, particularly those relating to historical data, such as purchase date, past passes or failures, and last calibration.

"If an individual has the time to establish a manual tracking and filing system, it may be sufficient for a small company. However, when considering the

TECH TIPS

- A paper and pencil gage calibration tracking system is limited in its use by manufacturing operations that require hundreds or thousands of measurement tools.
- Calibration intervals can be shortened or lengthened, depending on the operator's comfort level with the tool.
- Software tracks the gage's history and information is easily retrievable.

demands of today's industry and the availability of custom designed software applications it is hard to imagine a cost-effective manual system," said Shannon. Many gage tracking software packages are available for less than $500.

The software program a company chooses depends on its particular needs, but a list of features for a software package includes:

- Identify the measurement tool by make, model and serial number.
- Identify the measurement tool's place in the process.
- Determine the measurement tool's physical location at a given moment.
- List the measurement tool's appropriate ranges.
- List the measurement tool's specifications, including accuracies and certainties, or acceptable tolerances.
- Identify a correct calibration procedure.
- Track the date and time that the measurement tools were checked and record any adjustments.
- Identify the technician who checked the measurement tool.
- List the types of errors that might be found, a list of parameters having to do with the performance of that particular measurement tool.
- Gage repeatability and reproducibility.
- List the standards to which the measurement tool is traceable.
- Show a picture of the measurement tool so someone new to the process will know to calibrate the correct gage.

Today, many programs generate an e-mail reminder that flags the equipment due for calibration. Reports can be generated by department, equipment or date. Records can be maintained and updated on a continual basis.

But who should have access to these records is in debate. Some will argue that only the metrology manager, or person in charge of calibration, should have access to the information. Others contend that all employees using gages should have at least read-only access. A database should contain the gage's entire history. "For a critical measurement, you wouldn't want to use a gage that's on its last legs," said Bogaski.

Once a gage has been calibrated, a calibration label should be attached. At a minimum, these labels should include an identification number, date of last calibration, identifying marks for the person placing the gage in service and the date of the next calibration. Additional information, if room allows, includes a description of the gage, status of the gage—repaired, limited use, pass or fail—and how it's been used.

The rigors of the shop floor can cause labels to fall off or become unreadable. "Any label damaged so that it may affect the readability of its contents must be replaced. It is helpful to maintain a database of all calibration information to facilitate the recreation of label information as required," said Shannon. Laminating labels and using labels with strong adhesives can help reduce label degradation.

Calibration Intervals

So why must gages be calibrated at regular intervals? A variety of conditions make gages move out of tolerance. Here are a few:

- Time. The general drift of any device over time.
- Frequency of use.
- Misuse and abuse, including using the wrong gage for a job or dropping it.
- Environmental conditions, such as temperature, vibration and chemical pollutants.
- Internal contamination, such as things that coagulate and clog the measurement tool, particularly in pressure instrumentation.

Even though rugged gages address these problems, they tend to be heavier and more awkward to handle than nonrugged gages, resulting in less use by operators.

Lab vs. Workstation

Some will contest that keeping the measurement tool in its original environment during calibration will yield more accurate results, but others argue that the readings are more accurate in a lab environment.

"We contend that you want your measurement tools calibrated in situ. Calibrate them onsite because they're in the temperature environment, and they're in the vibration environment. They're in the environment in which they're actually going to be working," said Pirret. Also, taking that measurement tool out of a process to calibrate in a lab, may not only be a difficult physical process, but it disrupts the workflow, and other accommodations must be made to continue the process, whether it's installing a replacement or shutting the machine down.

Others will argue that the lab is the better place to perform the calibrations. Bogaski said a lab provides better conditions and eliminates interference with the machine's operator. It's difficult to do the calibration if the operator is standing over your shoulder, waiting for the calibration to be done so he can get back to work.

Bottom Line

Management commitment and employee training are vital to gage management programs, but it goes beyond these requirements. "An effective calibration program needs to have the ability to correctly capture gage performance history, record it and provide access to that data in the future," said Pirret.

Bogaski said gage control is a recurring problem that weakens metrology programs. "The people in charge of gages are given the responsibility but not

> ## TEST REPORTS AND CALIBRATION CERTIFICATES
>
> Each test report or calibration certificate shall include at least the following information, unless the laboratory has valid reasons for not doing so:
> - Title, i.e., Test Report of Calibration Certificate.
> - Name and address of laboratory and location where the tests and calibrations were carried out, if different from the address of the laboratory.
> - Unique identification of the test report or calibration certificate, such as the serial number, and on each page an identification in order to ensure that the page is recognized as part of the test report or calibration certificate, and a clear identification on the end of the test report or calibration certificate.
> - Name and address of the client.
> - Identification of the calibration method used.
> - Description, condition and unambiguous identification of the items tested or calibrated.
> - Date of receipt of test or calibration items where critical to the validity and application of the results and dates of performance of the test or calibration.
> - Test Reports and Calibration Certificates
> - Reference to sampling plan and procedures used by the laboratory or other bodies where these are relevant to the validity or application of the results.
> - Test or calibration results with, where appropriate, the units of measurement.
> - The names, functions and signatures, or equivalent identification, of the persons authorizing the test report or calibration certificate.
> - Where relevant, a statement to the effect that the results relate only to the items tested or calibrated.
>
> Source: ISO 17025

the authority to do their jobs." Gages are passed from person to person within the plant, and the measurement tools are not returned to the person in charge to record its usage.

Shannon said, "An effective gage calibration program requires a well-thought out system, with a competent and conscientious individual responsible for its implementation and maintenance. Individuals calibrating and using equipment must be aware of the critical role that correctly calibrated equipment plays in product verification."

Gillian Babicz is associate editor of Quality *magazine.*

Should You Outsource Your Business Processes?

Christine Kirk

In many organizations, it may make sense to outsource a number of business processes, especially in the accounting area. This article explains why that is true and provides some directions for how to effectively choose processes for outsourcing and how to transition in-house operations to companies that specialize in these functions. It includes a useful sidebar that explains the things to look for in selecting a business processes provider.

Many of the *Fortune* 100 have been among the leaders in outsourcing some of their business processes because they've been in the best position to see the benefits they could derive from it. They've had to concentrate a great deal of capital and human resources in developing their own business processes, like the finance and accounting systems needed to manage far-flung corporate operations. Having learned what it takes to do best-in-class business processing, huge corporations often recognize that outsourcing these functions can be an important part of their strategies—expediting long-needed changes and improving their competitive advantage in a tightening marketplace. It's predicted that by 2003 almost half the companies that are implementing enterprise systems, integrated software, and technology will turn this work over to outsourcers (*Digital System Report*, Spring 2000).

But business process outsourcing can work for any size company, especially companies with sales of $250 million and more. The sooner they recognize it, the better off these companies will be from a strategic and competitive standpoint. That's because BPO isn't just a convenience—it's a competitive weapon.

How It Started

Business process outsourcing began to emerge in the mid-1990s, but it erupted in the last year or two with the growth of the Internet and the recognition that noncore yet critical processes can, and often should, be handled offsite by contractors. Companies that in the 1980s and early 1990s were consolidating services—like accounting—in one location are now realizing that they can

Reprinted with permission from *Strategic Finance*, January 2001. Copyright © 2001 by the Institute of Management Accountants, Montvale NJ, www.imanet.org.

take the next step. They can hand off responsibility for these services to a single provider who also services other companies and thereby garner the advantages of economies of scale.

A good BPO provider frees financial and other executives from having to recruit and retain qualified back-office personnel and provide them with sophisticated technology. As a result, executives gain the freedom and flexibility to concentrate on what they do best. BPO is, in this sense, liberating and strategically valuable. Geoffrey Moore, in his latest book, *Living on the Fault Line*, says it's critical that a company focus its management's time and talent on those functions that will directly differentiate company offerings. Not to do so confines valuable executives to maintenance tasks that don't add to shareholder value. To quote him, "Any behavior that can raise your stock price is core—everything else is context." So, unless the CFO's time—spent on solving finance department personnel issues or attending myriad meetings regarding his or her department's process improvement goals—is actually increasing shareholder value, it isn't time well spent.

Outsourcing can also be strategically valuable in the quality of the information it provides. A good provider—because of its wide experience with a variety of clients and because business processes are its single focus—can offer better information that's more focused and more timely. In short, a good BPO provider can offer corporate decision makers timely and accurate information. This includes delivery of the company's key performance indicators—as determined by the executives who need them—when and wherever they need them. And this might mean access to the information while they're on business in Asia or visiting grandma over the holidays.

For many middle-market companies, getting the right information at the right time has become increasingly challenging.

- For some it's the challenge faced with exponential growth, which requires rapid scalability. And when this growth is due to the acquisition of or merger with another company, whose accounting is likely to be on a different platform, the conversion process to a single system can be lengthy and expensive.
- For others it's the difficulty of receiving real-time financial information, which can be an impossibility when simply closing the books is a painful 10- to 15-day process of gathering information from disparate departments. In a world where timely decision making is critical to a company's strategic management, a comprehensive and accurate company picture is essential to sustaining that competitive edge.
- Many now have international operations that present them with problems that are difficult and expensive to address, like the challenges with multiple-currency reporting and varying accounting practices between countries. These added complications must be addressed by having a common platform on which to communicate between countries and their various business units.

- Others lack the capital resources to keep up with the rapid technological changes in business processes.

Outsourcing lets these companies replace the sunk-cost model with a rental model, just as companies did when they stopped buying automobiles for select employees and started leasing them. The result? Costs become optimal and predictable. One of the best examples is technology. Smaller companies especially don't have the money to invest in constantly upgrading computers and other equipment. But they don't have to do so anymore because the technology the BPO provider offers is continuously updated.

How the Process Works

Here's the model that we and a few other companies are developing to make all this work.

The provider starts by working with the client to determine what information the client needs to manage the business and make informed decisions. Does the client want to gather information on a regional basis, by business line, or both? Does the client want information about margins? Cash flow? Aging of customer receivables? Does the client want revenue figures by product, client, geography, or all three? What are the other important metrics? And are the client's processes up-to-date and efficient? The BPO provider uses best practices to design business processes that will capture the necessary information.

In any industry, perhaps as much as 80% of the business processes can be considered standard. That means a BPO provider can come to its clients with a proven blueprint for the majority of their processes. Expertise of that sort enables the BPO provider to offer not only superior insight and speed of implementation, but also its proven process methodology and software expertise.

The remaining 20% of business processes usually need to be customized. Again, the BPO provider's wide expertise enables it to design processes quickly and cost effectively, and, at the same time, to be best in class. For example, this may include technologies like imaging and workflow in high-volume transaction processing environments or special project accounting functionality provided to clients with many consultants in the field.

In partnership with a systems integrator, the BPO provider works with its client to design the accounting systems and the software to make the processes work. By working this way, the BPO provider can serve as the client contact while the integrator stays behind the scenes. This involves a combination of enterprise software integration as well as the customization necessary for the client to meet their reporting needs. The specifics will vary from customer to customer and industry to industry.

Then the BPO provider partners with an Application Service Provider (ASP) to host the hardware and the software needed to make the processes

> Outsourcing lets these companies replace the sunk-cost model with a rental model, just as companies did when they stopped buying automobiles for select employees and started leasing them.

work. It's the ASP's responsibility to ensure that the data lines and software are operating 24/7, removing the burden of both ownership and maintenance from the client. Some clients communicate with their ASPs over secure data lines, but most are shifting to the Internet because it's cheaper and more convenient.

Once the processes and the technology are in place, it's time to take a look at staffing. A full-service outsourcing company provides the processors who handle accounts payable, accounts receivable, payroll, general ledger accounting, fixed assets, preparation of financial statements, and other processes.

These individuals usually work at a shared services center, located wherever prices for real estate and skilled labor dictate. They don't have to be near the client. Some may be former employees of the client who have moved over to the BPO provider's payroll. All are experienced financial and accounting professionals, attracted to the BPO provider in part because its core competency is in their area of expertise. The draw here is that outsourcing can lead to better opportunities for financial professionals because they can move from the company's back office to the BPO's front office—and they get all the associated benefits of being a contributor to their company's core focus.

But the BPO provider may not require as many employees to handle the future-state accounting functions as the company employed—due to processing efficiencies, workflow, technology, economies of scale, etc. But a people-focused BPO provider can, and should, make the transition process a pleasant one for both those who are hired by the BPO provider and for those who aren't. The steps usually involve: 1) offering temporary contracts to all employees to allow for an effective transitional period, 2) interviewing the company's current accounting professionals (to determine the stellar performers whose cultural values match those of the BPO provider), and 3) offering permanent employment and/or relocation packages to the employees selected and willing. For those employees who aren't offered permanent employment contracts, the BPO provider should provide outplacement services, which may include employment counseling, job placement services, and a severance package. Employee satisfaction is vital to the successful outsourcing relationship and shouldn't be overlooked or undervalued.

In the shared service center environment, these employees perform similar services for more than one client—an approach that creates still more economies of scale. And even though it may seem otherwise, each client receives personal service. Your BPO provider should offer tools to enable the client decision makers access to a dedicated account manager. Another option, in addition to the use of pagers, e-mails, and phones, is the use of a customized Web-based BPO information portal that provides the client immediate access to the account information they need.

An additional benefit with this new model is that companies who opt to outsource some of their processes can be based anywhere in the world and can have numerous office locations. Web-enabled products with multinational,

THINGS TO CONSIDER IN CHOOSING A BPO PROVIDER

Look for knowledge and experience:
- Select a provider with knowledge of more than a single enterprise resource planning (ERP) system so that recommendations are unbiased and can best match your company's particular industry.
- Plan ahead—be sure your selection criteria include scalability. Can your provider support your growth and deliver acquisition support?

Establish key performance indicators:
- Your company's key performance indicators (as determined by you) should be a part of the BPO provider's service delivery and should be timely, accurate, and easily accessible.

Select a company sponsor:
- Pick an internal sponsor or project manager to serve as a liaison to your BPO provider. This point person should have the knowledge to execute the necessary tasks and the support from inside the organization to do so. Don't let internal politics undermine the progress.

Determine reasonable timelines:
- Establish reasonable expectations. If you force a rushed, unrealistic transition, you both may be dissatisfied with the outcomes.

Avoid scope creep:
- Maintain a focused vision of your project's purpose. When an enterprisewide system is being implemented, new functionality is discovered. Your company can derail the project's timelines by asking for additional features or processes that are outside the project's original scope.

Forestall micromanagement:
- Once you've done your due diligence and identified the outcomes you expect, allow your BPO provider to determine what processes to use to deliver those outcomes. Their expertise is in improving processes, so don't tie their hands or fail to make use of their experience.

Consider cultural issues:
- Evaluate the BPO provider's corporate culture against your own. Often, many of your employees may end up on the payroll of the BPO provider. Corporate collisions have damaged many otherwise beneficial partnerships.
- Look for a BPO provider who maximizes teams in their company's organizational structure. Teams that are tailored to each phase of the implementation and transition take advantages of synergy, creativity, and a multitude of skill packages.

> **Value your people:**
> - Keep your people informed through each phase of the transition, and encourage two-way communication. Work out a deal that's fair and compassionate (whether they are outplaced or outsourced), and select a BPO provider that demands the same.

multi-language, and multi-currency capabilities can be accessed by anyone with proper security, anywhere.

How to Get the Most from Outsourcing

Business process outsourcing may sound good, but there are three critical issues every company needs to deal with if they want it to succeed. You'll need to:

Contract with a provider where the BPO is a strategic part of the business. As the market for business process outsourcing expands, so will the number of companies offering it. But many of them won't have BPO as a core competency. They have merely forced internal scope creep to take advantage of a larger market share, which means a client has requested additional services beyond the scope of the provider's core expertise. These companies won't offer the kind of cutting-edge expertise that comes from focusing on BPO and gaining from experiences with a wide range of clients. They're the equivalent of hiring a general practitioner for your quadruple bypass.

Plan to give your BPO partner in-depth expected outcomes, but don't expect to tell them how to go about accomplishing these goals. Let them do what they do well.

View your relationship with the BPO as a true partnership in which they are advising you. You have selected your BPO provider. You have established a Service Level Agreement. Now remember, this is a partnership, not merely a vendor/supplier relationship. Plan to give your BPO partner in-depth expected outcomes, but don't expect to tell them how to go about accomplishing these goals. Let them do what they do well. Also, encourage your company to implement the recommended internal process improvements that will allow efficiency improvements for the BPO provider. In order to achieve optimal efficiency the client must cooperate and make adjustments that will benefit the overall implementation. In other words, you must "Help them to help you." Not only will this effort reward your bottom line, but it will give you a competitive edge in strategic decision making. An example might be that your BPO provider is encouraging the use of paperless invoice approvals using imaging and workflow, but your department heads are used to approving hard copies that are routed via interoffice mail. This streamlining and automation can create efficiencies that will allow advantages like up-to-the-minute information for the client who is calling about the status of an invoice as well as improving the company's cash management.

Pay special attention to the human dimension in moving to an outside provider. Inevitably, any shift to an outsourcer produces employee concern. That's true even if the BPO provider hires many of the same people who had been working for the client, as is often the case in this industry. Ideally, being hired by a provider should be a boon to employees who had been handling the same functions when they were direct employees of the client. No longer are these employees expensive support staff. Now they provide their employer's core competency and bottom-line results. The BPO provider delivers such people more opportunities for professional growth and a supportive environment while the client benefits from knowledgeable workers.

At least that's how this model should work. Companies hiring a BPO provider ought to be concerned that that's how it will work.

Small and midsize companies can benefit from business process outsourcing just as much as the giants. But they need to make sure they know how to take advantage of the opportunity. As more and more companies come to recognize the value in BPO, they should also come to recognize the critical issues.

Christine Kirk, CPA, is CEO of LeapSource, an emerging leader in the rapidly expanding business process outsourcing (BPO) market. Before co-founding LeapSource, she was a partner at Arthur Andersen, where she headed the BPO practice in the United States. LeapSource is based in Tempe, Ariz. You can contact them at info@leapsource.com.

Measurements for Business

Philip Stein

Measurements on the shop floor are essential to effective operations, but this article explores another set of measures for your business processes—the right measures executives can use to help assure efficiency and effectiveness in all aspects of the business. This article looks at what measures might be key in doing this and includes some ideas on how to select these measures. It takes a special look at measuring customer satisfaction.

As Thomas Pearson so eloquently demonstrates in his article "Measure for Six Sigma Success," measurements are the principal tool we use to manage our businesses. Six Sigma is the latest management philosophy to recognize the importance of measurement in its foundation, and it won't be the last. Engineers and scientists have been measuring ohms and centimeters for centuries and have developed a body of knowledge—a whole measurement science known as metrology.

But is any of this knowledge useful where business measurements are concerned? You bet! In fact, not only is it useful, but sometimes it's crucial. After all, every quality professional who supports process improvement must accept the responsibility of understanding the principles and processes behind the measurements he or she makes.

So, what measurements are made in support of business and in support of quality improvement efforts such as Six Sigma and others? One popular model for business measurements is known as the Balanced Scorecard. A paper announcing this approach, by Robert S. Kaplan and David P. Norton, first appeared in the *Harvard Business Review*, then as a Harvard business book.[1] This method is popular not only because of the esteem in which the Harvard Business School is held, but because it just makes good sense.

The Balanced Scorecard approach divides the need for business measurements into four quadrants: financial, operational, customer and research/learning. The term "balanced approach" means that these four measurement categories are given roughly equal weight in supporting management decisions. While this model can be effective, its biggest contribution is that it emphasizes, particularly to traditional managers, that financial measures (the bottom line) are not the only measurements needed to manage

From *Quality Progress*, February 2001. Copyright © 2001 by the American Society for Quality. Reprinted with permission.

effectively—there are other numbers of equal importance. This may seem obvious to quality professionals, but managing "by the numbers" is so strongly rooted in the realm of American business practices that, for many, it is a hard habit to break.

Let's see what metrology has to offer the business measurement practitioner. We will use scorecard quadrants as examples, but most of the principles here apply to any measurement.

Data Display

The purpose of a measurement, especially a business measurement, is to deliver the right information to the right person (or process) at the right time, displayed to the right degree of detail and aggregation. Both the CEO and the night shift supervisor need to know the efficiency of production for a new product line, but they need it at different times and in different degrees of detail, and they probably need it displayed differently as well. (See sidebar "Understanding Design Parameters in Business Measurements.")

Data display is one of the most important concepts in business measurements and one of the least understood. For trained scientists, engineers, statisticians and quality practitioners who use technical measurements every day, understanding and interpretation of measurement results come easily with practice, even when the presentation is not perfect. Business people at all levels will only rarely have the training and experience to understand data to their full depth and significance.

One relatively new idea is the business dashboard or instrument panel. Measurement data, results and information are collected in a single place and presented graphically in familiar displays such as a speedometer or gas gage. While it is tempting to think of this only as an executive tool, such a presentation method is useful at any level within an enterprise. Of course, the display must be tailored to the needs of each user. Assuring the data user that the data accurately represent what they are supposed to is equally important. This is one area where measurement science can help.

Any enterprise of medium to large size will have hundreds or thousands of measurements to characterize results not only from the four quadrants of a scorecard, but from areas such as employee satisfaction. No instrument panel can hope to make sense of such a large array of data, and perhaps it's not a good idea to try. For this reason, many models of management, including the Malcolm Baldrige National Quality Award criteria, suggest selecting a much smaller number of key measurements (note the similarity to Six Sigma's key process output or input variables).

Key measurements (or data, or information) are chosen to be elevated above the general masses because they are perceived to somehow carry information or messages that are exceptionally important. In fact, the choice of key parameters is frequently made incorrectly, often because it is done sub-

Both the CEO and the night shift supervisor need to know the efficiency of production for a new product line, but they need it at different times and in different degrees of detail.

> ## UNDERSTANDING DESIGN PARAMETERS IN BUSINESS MEASUREMENTS
>
> Every measurement has a set of design parameters, and we need to be clear about these if we are to use measurement data, analyses and information profitably. Parameters should take into account the following:
>
> - What underlying information are we trying to elucidate with this measurement? For example, in the learning/research quadrant, we may measure patents granted or papers published, but the underlying information desired is the extent to which we are enriching our intellectual capital in support of new products or new directions.
> - What is the unit of measure? Returning to the "papers published" example, it may be better to count papers per researcher per year so that one prolific group can't inadvertently cover up the fact that most staff members aren't publishing at all.
> - What is actually being used to make the measurement, and how good is it as a surrogate for or predictor of the underlying information desired? An ordinary voltmeter will measure voltage, for example, but it will also inadvertently measure temperature since its reading will vary with the temperature. You need to make sure that your measurement senses and records what you're actually looking for. A business measurement showing a commanding market share could be a disaster if you're losing a little on each sale. A better measure here might be something like return on capital employed.
> - Once you have documented exactly what is being used to make the measurement, you can decide how well you make the measurement. This is where you decide the accuracy, precision and resolution needed for the application, and what tools, techniques and processes will be used to achieve those results. If you are measuring electrical quantities, your tool might be a multimeter. If you are measuring customer satisfaction, your tool might be a survey. By exploiting these analogies between technical and business measurements, you can fine-tune your understanding of how the same underlying body of knowledge applies equally to both.
> - Once the measurement has been chosen, the tools acquired and installed, and the system declared operational, it's time for measurement process control. By exact analogy with statistical process control, using the same techniques (such as control charts), continually monitor the measurement processes to make sure that they are operating as intended.

jectively. Remember that information can seem to be important, and very well might be important, but if it gives uninformative or erroneous clues as to how the business is operating, it will do harm rather than good.

A common example of a key business measurement that is widely believed to be harmful is short-term profit. Wall Street is often blamed for reacting (or overreacting) to the bottom line of the most recent quarter; short-term profit is unlikely to be much of a measure of the future earnings potential of a company. Another such key measurement is machine utilization. As Eliyahu Goldratt demonstrates in his book *The Goal*,[2] keeping a machine or a worker busy at full capacity could be either the right thing to do or the completely wrong thing to do, depending on the context. Utilization is a measure that is often tracked, and that's fine, but if it is elevated to a key measure, it can drive undesired behaviors and suboptimized results.

Aggregated Measurements

Instead of choosing a few individual measurements from a cast of thousands, sometimes it's a good idea to use aggregate measures.

Let's segment our measurements into affinity groups—the four Balanced Scorecard quadrants, for example. Using the customer quadrant, we could have between five and 10 measurements of customer parameters:

- Customer satisfaction (by questionnaire).
- Customer dissatisfaction.
- Customer retention/loss.
- Call center hold time (or abandoned calls or service time).
- Customer value proposition acceptance (by survey).
- Customer loyalty (repeat business associated with brand).
- Brand recognition (by focus group).

An executive instrument panel might only have real-estate (dashboard share) for one or two of these customer measures, and what's worse is that many more measures could exist that aren't even listed. While a key measures approach would choose from among these, an aggregation approach would attempt to combine results from some or all of the measures to yield an overall customer measure. See the sidebar "Aggregating to Form a Single Customer Measure" for a simple approach to how this can be accomplished.

Aggregated measurements are very useful and are often more stable and less chancy than choosing single key variables. They do have their limitations though, and it's important to understand what they are. First, if the separate measurements that are aggregated are strongly correlated, aggregating them adds no value and may give a false sense of having created a widely representative tool.

Second, and more likely, an aggregated measurement will hide information that may be significant. Imagine a customer aggregate constructed from the measures in the bullet list and built as a weighted sum according to the instructions in the sidebar. Now suppose that the most important parameter, customer satisfaction, has been given a weight of 4, and call center hold time

> Utilization is a measure that is often tracked, and that's fine, but if it is elevated to a key measure, it can drive undesired behaviors and suboptimized results.

a weight of 1—not unreasonable choices.

On a dashboard, customer aggregate shows as 60.

Now, what happens if the customer satisfaction number goes up by one unit? This will make a nice little increase of four points in the total. Perhaps it is not an enormous improvement, but likely it can be seen as significant. If at the same time, however, the call center hold time number goes down by four units, the overall sum won't change. It's very possible that this is reasonable. If our weights and measurements were well chosen, we might want to display no change as a result of this combination of events. The problem, though, is that a worsening of four points, or 40%, in the call center hold time is almost certainly a signal of some kind of disaster—or at least something requiring investigation and corrective action. Yet, the aggregate has completely hidden the fact that anything has happened.

Measurement science and a bit of statistics to the rescue! Let's propose a slight change in our dashboard design. First, we need to know if the 40% change in hold time is significant or whether variation such as this is common. We need to ask the same question regarding a 10% change in customer satisfaction as well. The right tool for this job is the control chart. It will allow us to calculate whether these changes are routine or exceptional.

There's no need for the final user of the aggregated measure to interpret charts or even to see them. Computers have been used to store and analyze control chart data for many years and can even do so in real time. For our improved dashboard, we display the customer aggregate, but we add a simple additional indicator (an asterisk or a change in color, for example) to indicate that the aggregate is hiding a statistically significant datum below its summary-level information.

When this indicator is present, the dashboard should give its user an opportunity to investigate further by drilling down to a level of greater detail. If the user chooses, he or she could even view the control chart for the data that caused the indication. Troubleshooting and further action could then be decided.

The principle is that computer processing of considerable sophistication can be used to generate useful, informative, easy to understand displays without throwing away all of the supporting detail. Users are informed that further significant information is available in the hidden details. That information is completely accessible, but only when needed.

I've given you just a quick taste of how business metrics can be better understood and even enhanced by treating them as measurements. There's a whole world of opportunity waiting to be explored when the principles and people of the measurement and quality communities join efforts with their colleagues in the business end of an organization.

Aggregating to Form a Single Customer Measure

A simple aggregate is the weighted sum. These are the steps involved in forming a single customer measure:

1. Choose the measurements to aggregate.
2. Express each on the same scale (from 1 to 10, for example).
3. Make sure all of the scales run in the same direction (a rating of 1 is "poor" while a rating of 10 is the "best"). Sometimes you have to be especially careful in this regard—bigger does not always mean better. A large number for call center hold time is not a good thing. You may have to reverse the direction of that scale and rename it call center speed.
4. Choose a weight for each of the measurements based on a choice of which one is more important to your needs. Satisfaction may be deemed a more important component of customer results than is loyalty. The weights should be numbers that add up to 10, with larger numbers assigned to measurements that are more important.
5. Collect the data and place them on the appropriate scale.
6. Calculate the weighted data by multiplying each result by its assigned weight.
7. Add the weighted data. This will give an aggregated result between 0 and 100, where larger numbers are better.

Of course, this is only one of many ways to aggregate your data, but it's a very simple one.

References

1. Robert S. Kaplan and David P. Norton, *The Balanced Scorecard* (Watertown, MA: Harvard Business School Publishing, 1996).
2. Eliyahu M. Goldratt, *The Goal* (Great Barrington, MA: North River Press, 1992).

Philip Stein is a metrology and quality consultant in private practice in Pennington, NJ. He holds a master's degree in measurement science from The George Washington University in Washington, DC. For more information, go to www.measurement.com.

Improving In-Process Handling

Steve Parsley

As this article asserts, "delivery is the purpose of business." To do this, it's important to improve "in-process" work. The author of this article provides a methodology for doing this. The article examines the aspects of a process that are prime for improvement. These include too many handoffs, cycle time problems, fire-fighting rather than expediting, "end of the month syndrome," and more.

The information age has changed our lives and the way we do business forever. However, the dramatic leap in productivity and output that was forecast from such innovations as MRP, ERP, and the Internet have been largely lost due to the fact that our productive processes have not kept pace. Business redesign has focused on improving quality and reducing cost; improved delivery has received only secondary attention.

Even as information systems began to proliferate, the focus of business redesign centered on being the lowest-cost provider by eliminating labor embedded in the cost of sales and production or driving down the cost of inventory through zero-inventory production practices, standardization, and outsourced responsibilities for replenishment. Information systems played an important part in this effort by providing real-time reporting about activity-based costing, time-phased material requirements, and asset deployment effectiveness.

In many cases, however, the attention to improving consumer access to products has focused on rather traditional distribution models and on "burst-mode" planning to ensure that new products were available at roll-out. Too often, the ability to follow through with continued fulfillment has crippled or killed the potential of a new product—or at least opened it to the vulnerability of competition.

Delivery Is the Purpose of Business

Delivery is the fulfillment of consumer need. When consumers first develop a need for something, they may not yet know how that need will be satisfied. The use of information system tools may help shape consumers requirements for value and utility, but only when an actual product or service is located and recognized as *the* product sought by the consumer will the need become explicit, allowing the product to be sold.

Short or immediate delivery models can mitigate problems in meeting customer expectations. In complex cases in which unique product configurations are required, in-process material handling can dramatically affect the supplier's ability to satisfy the customer. In-process material handling refers to the normal flow of material among value-adding operations. Whether it is raw material from receiving or a finished good shipped from the dock, all activities in between operation points (minus the actual value-adding actions) are in-process handling steps that add only cost to the product. The cost that is added by in-process handling is a function of the time the material is in the system and the distance it travels.

Making reliable delivery commitments depends entirely on a predictable in-process handling system. This one truth will be more important and more influential to customer recruitment and retention than any other strategy of distribution.

> Making reliable delivery commitments depends entirely on a predictable in-process handling system.

The Improvement Process

In general, there are a few basic symptoms that will lead an observer to formulate a justification for change. These symptoms point to problems that complicate smooth flow through the process, inhibiting predictable delivery commitments:

Multiple stagings and hand-offs from receipt to consumption. This is often found in older operations in which additions have been made "temporarily" to accommodate a new process and then left in place permanently. Material handlers are used to move bulk quantities of materials from departmental output points to input staging locations. These moves would not be necessary except that the internal customer and supplier are not adjacent to each other.

For example, a manufacturer of customized awards was considering the addition of a new warehouse to store raw materials. The nature of this business meant that large volumes of material were kept in a generic inventory until orders were received. At that time, a custom plaque was created, attached to an award, packaged, and sent to the award recipient (Figure 1). The awards were diverse items such as watches, pins, television sets, canoes, golf clubs, and telescopes. Each award traveled nearly a mile through the process from launch to shipment. Material was retrieved from multiple sites, staged, and then moved to the next operation. The time from the order until the material was shipped was weeks. Labor was in short supply, and shipping errors were significant.

A plan was launched to re-engineer the process. Instead of adding another warehouse, the operations were combined to build the warehouse and factory

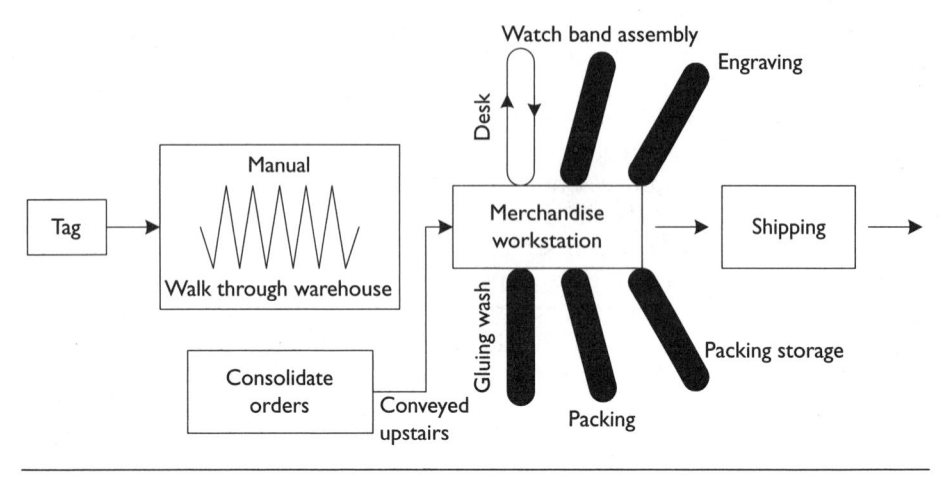

Figure 1.

> By acknowledging that the old process wouldn't work, the client was able to define the core processes his business was founded upon and develop a new operational plan.

as one integral process. Instead of workers fanning out and gathering the material, then taking it back to each workstation, material transport was automated to deliver material to the workstations. This allowed the value-adding operation to proceed uninterrupted by the need to handle or expedite material. Cycle times were reduced and labor efficiency increased dramatically.

By acknowledging that the old process wouldn't work, the client was able to define the core processes his business was founded upon and develop a new operational plan that eliminated all of the non-value-adding activities that had crept in over the years.

Actual cycle times are more than 10 times the direct labor content. If the labor standards are correct, then it should be simple to calculate the time between raw material entering and finished product leaving the facility. In fact, few labor standards address the hold time a material will spend in storage. Labor standards are just what the name implies—a standard for the direct, value-adding labor needed to complete the process. Everything else is non-value-adding and must be minimized to remove variance from the delivery projection.

Personnel with the official title or responsibility for expediting or supervisors who spend more than 40 percent of their time fighting fires. Expediting and daily fire-fighting point to a system in which the flow is so convoluted that to operate with some level of economy, large batches of product are routed through the process to minimize material handling. When batching is used to minimize handling, quality problems can hide in the shadows. This almost always causes major disruptions in the overall delivery cycle, especially when expeditors are dispatched to help the system recover from the discovered quality defect.

End-of-month syndrome. Compromises that are made to get the work out by a specific date are usually paid back during the first week or two of the next period. This, in turn, degrades performance that must be compensated for by the end of the next period. A never-ending pattern develops that over time becomes grudgingly accepted as the way things are, and few people pay attention to the actual impact on business profitability.

A television picture tube manufacturer recently completed an analysis of severe end-of-month syndrome. He concluded that the impact of not shipping uniformly through the month was the same as taping a $20 bill to each product as it left the dock.

Rising to the Challenge

The companies that have risen to the challenge of improving their ability to grow and capture market share have embraced several guiding principles:

The existing process may be beyond repair. Trying to make spot repairs to a system may be required due to timing or budget, but spot repairs to a bad overall process are never a successful strategy. While it may be human nature to address the overall system as a sum of its parts, it is a mistake.

The system must be viewed as a synergistic entity. Encouraging your analysis team to start with a clean sheet of paper doesn't mean you will scrap the plant and start over, but it almost always exposes issues that won't appear any other way. To emphasize this point, ask this question: If someone wanted to compete with you, would they do it by mirroring the process and facility layout you have in place?

Distance is the enemy of predictability. Moving a single component is more predictable than moving a batch the same distance. The time to create the batch is an accumulation of the variance required to create each individual item. But if the distance is great, the inclination to use batching seems to be a natural tendency despite the problems that batching can disguise. Furthermore, distances tend to be dealt with by passing the material from worker to handler to worker. Each of these transactions introduces a time variance to strict uniform processing. Shortening the distance reduces variance, which directly impacts the predictability of delivery.

Only touch material when you can add value to it. Discussion can go on all day about what is a value-adding activity vs. non-value-adding. In short, if it adds to the consumer's sense of quality, economy or utility it adds value. If not, the consumer doesn't care what type of fancy MRP system was used to schedule material for the product. The supplier with the first acceptable product on the shelf wins.

Eliminating non-value-adding touches may seem like a lofty goal, but that is the way zero-inventory manufacturing was viewed 20 years ago. The impact of eliminating non-value-adding touches is seen when one considers the most common complaint of manufacturers and distributors: the shortage of qualified labor.

A recent study of an appliance manufacturer focused on improving the deployment of a large fleet of lift trucks. In that project, a ratio-and-delay sampling analysis was used to find that for every move of raw material to the assembly lines, there were 3.5 moves of dunnage and 2.5 empty moves to go back and get more dunnage. Changing the process to de-trash material at a central point and move it to the line in kanban carts reduced fleet requirements by 40 percent. Eliminating non-value-adding activities frees up a tremendous source of labor. And eliminating the non-value-adding touches is the most direct way of decreasing overall process utilization.

High process utilization is not always productive. Early in the history of material and production control, algorithms were developed to compute the economic production lot sizes and predict the justifiable levels of safety stock. The algorithm included variables for order leadtime, the time value of money used to own the inventory, and the probability that the supplier would be late. The purpose of these algorithms was to keep processes busy. The first time a shortage of a critical item occurred, the affected party would see to it that safety stock levels increased. This created a cycle of inventory growth.

Using the single-arrival, single-server queuing model, the effects of variance and process utilization can be demonstrated.

Given:

λ = the rate at which work arrives to be serviced

μ = the rate at which work can be performed

L_q = number of items waiting to be worked upon

The value of L_q can be equated to the amount of work-in-process before the serving process. The value of λ can be equated to the rate at which a process consumes material, and the value of μ can be equated to the rate at which material is replenished to the process.

Novices in the design of just-in-time systems often make the mistake of assuming that L_q can be made to equal zero. They also assume that to accomplish this, they merely need to set $\lambda = \mu$. These are variable processes, however, that do not vary synchronously. Their variance is independent and causes WIP to grow.

The full equation for L_q is developed in most operations research textbooks. It conservatively notes that arrival and service rates vary exponentially:

$$L_q = (\lambda / \mu)^2 / (1 - \lambda/\mu)$$

The factor 1/m is also known, as the traffic intensity factor or the utilization factor. As the ratio approaches unity (utilization of 100 percent), the equation suggests that WIP levels will approach infinity (Figure 2). In fact, the

Improving In-Process Handling

waiting line begins growing exponentially as the utilization of the process approaches 85 percent.

The more highly loaded the process, the more variable the outcome will

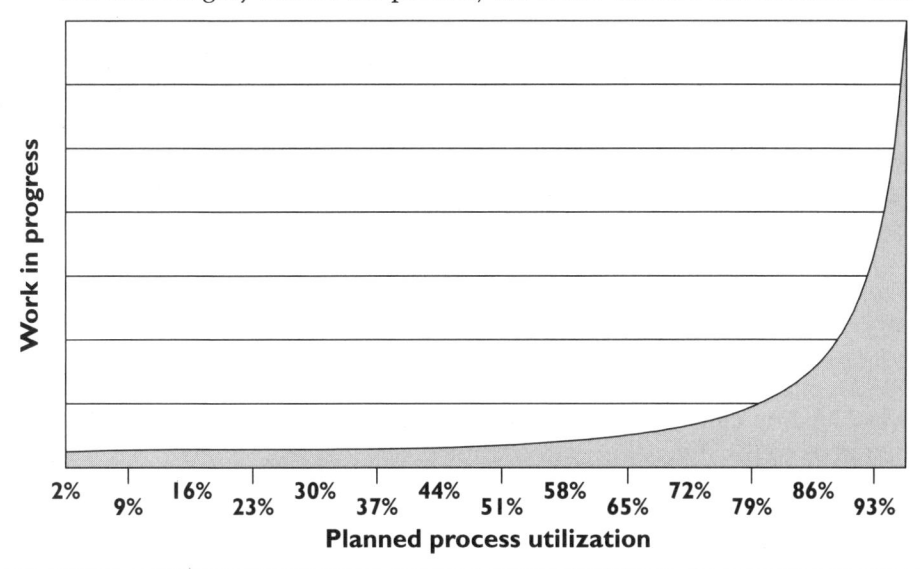

Figure 2. **WIP projections in simple processes**

be. Large WIP inventories suggest process overload that will result in missed delivery commitments and customer dissatisfaction.

Redesigning In-Process Handling Systems

Process re-engineering needs to follow a structured pattern to ensure that all options are considered and that all participants are fully on board. Following the process creates momentum that helps carry the project through implementation:

The walkthrough. The process begins with a walkthrough by a cross-functional team or an outsider to identify areas that exhibit the symptoms noted earlier. This tour should follow the flow of material from receiving through shipping, documenting such things as the distance material travels, the number of times it is handed off or staged, and the number of people who touch it. Other things to observe are handling methods and paths.

Gathering ideas. Following the tour, the team should brainstorm about what success would look and feel like if changes were made. In other words, what ideas were spawned during the tour, and what problems or flow inhibitors were observed that could expose areas for improvement?

Identify key processes. Identify and agree upon the key value-adding processes and the logistics requirements needed to conduct business smoothly and responsively. With delivery as the key focus, work backward from that transaction to define the ideal value-adding flow path that would allow your company to succeed. It is important that this definition be agreed to by the entire team or organization. From this definition will grow the tool to evaluate changes to the existing process.

Benchmarking. Perhaps the biggest mistake a process change team can make is formulating solutions too soon. Often, a team will take off on site-seeing missions before fully defining what they want to accomplish. Only after the key process definitions are complete should the team begin benchmarking. This effort should then be used to determine how the preferred key logistics processes are being done by others with similar logistics processes—not necessarily others in the same industry.

> Only after the key process definitions are complete should the team begin benchmarking.

An example of this occurred with a plastic manufacturer whose business was blending compounds of plastic for extrusion molding customers. Raw materials were delivered in gaylords and blended in large mixers. The finished products were reloaded into delivery gaylords and shipped to the customer for consumption. In observing the core logistics processes that were required for the company to produce plastic, several key techniques were listed as options for eliminating the non-value-adding labor associated with the operation. To benchmark the effectiveness of these options, the manufacturer was taken to a food plant that made pretzels. Gaylords of unseasoned pretzels, flavorings, salts, and other ingredients were taken to mixers, combined, and reloaded into gaylords for delivery to the packaging customer.

The reason for using benchmarks is not simply to get new ideas, but to gain confidence that a new idea for your facility will produce similar results as experienced by others who have applied the same solution to a similar problem. While it would be preferred to take a solution and detail all possible scenarios and arrive at a go/no-go answer, that is rarely practical. Nor would it be practical to engineer all solutions to final detail before determining the correct solution. Instead, confidence gained from seeing solutions to specific logistics processes in action is more beneficial than paper-based reasoning forgetting buy-in from people who must approve the change.

Prepare a preliminary design. A preliminary design that can be studied and discussed will assist in getting collaborative buy-in from all levels of the organization. This design should be modified as needed to absorb the input from team members and should include such information as an implementation strategy that addresses disruption and recovery during execution.

Develop an executive summary to sell the proposed change. Only when the plan is agreed upon by the team and thought out relative to need, justification, and implementation should the plan be brought forward for approval and implementation. When this occurs, the executive summary is the vehicle for proposing the change and for proposing support from management for the investment.

The content of the executive summary must be short, concise, and communicate the unanimous commitment of the team to making the change work as envisioned. Contents should address why the change is needed, how the proposed system works, how long will it take to make changes, the costs involved, return on this investment, potential impact of not making changes, and implementation.

The executive summary itemizes the decision process from which the recommendation for change has grown, and it provides the team with a list of steps to guide them through execution.

Develop the final project plan. Develop a strong project plan against which planning and assessment can be performed. It should clearly outline the roles and responsibilities of the team and the expected deliverables along the way.

In developing the plan, pay careful attention to training and human factors associated with what people will expect from the change. As mentioned earlier, because of the time between the definition of the need and the actual fulfillment, the plan is vulnerable to possible problems from people who don't fully understand what is going to happen or why the change was proposed. When this occurs, missed expectations result, causing less-than-desired outcomes from the project. Develop strong baseline measurements about what the plan should produce so that results can be measured and the end of the plan defined.

Execute the plan. If the process is followed as outlined, execution is not a decision but a natural event that follows preparation.

Plans that have failed to gain the momentum necessary to complete the execution almost always are the result of skipping or rushing through one of the steps outlined above. If the process is not followed, people may resist at the last minute, costing the project support. At the very least, skipping or incompletely doing one or more of the steps may cause the plan to miss opportunities.

The process of improving begins with a careful evaluation of what your operation must do to deliver products to customers. Delivery to the customer is the purpose of your business. The faster the delivery, the better your company's growth.

Steve Parsley, P.E, is the Northeast/Midwest regional manager for Eskay Corp., a supplier of integrated logistics solutions. A 30-plus-year veteran of the material handling industry, he has served the supply side of the industry, holding positions influencing the design, analysis, control, implementation and evolution of the technology.

QUALITY TOOLS AND TECHNIQUES

SIX SIGMA

Six Sigma on Business Processes: Common Organizational Issues

Doug Sanders and Cheryl Hild

Six Sigma is a way to formalize process improvement in an organization and it applies to any type of process, providing a methodology for identifying defects and taking action to eliminate them. Six Sigma is essentially an extension of quality management. In this article, the authors look at the use of Six Sigma as applied to business processes (as opposed to manufacturing processes), looking specifically at its ability to improve a loan packaging process.

As organizations face increasing global competitiveness and more stringent requirements on products and processes, greater attention is given to managing and improving processes that provide both products and services. As a result, more and more innovations or methods for improving processes and products have sprouted.

Recently, Six Sigma programs or similar quality initiatives have been credited with improving processes in many organizations. In such improvement approaches, process study has been defined as the acquisition of knowledge about process parameters to be able to manipulate process outputs in a predictable fashion with minimum variation (1). Typically, Six Sigma programs consist of a set of tools, including statistical methodologies, that are used in conjunction with engineering and process knowledge to discover the root causes of variation and to control and reduce that variation (2).

Reprinted by permission of the publisher from *Quality Engineering*, 12(4), 2000. Copyright © 2000 by Marcel Dekker, Inc. All rights reserved.

The documented success stories for statistical process improvement approaches are plentiful in the manufacturing arena. On the other hand, the applications are fewer with less quantitative results in the nonmanufacturing areas. Why are limited resources dedicated to the continual improvement of business processes? Even more puzzling is why, when resources are applied for process improvement efforts, efforts frequently meet with limited success. Are the methods just as applicable to business processes? Conceptually, the answer is a resounding "yes." The concepts of measuring process performance, making decisions via data, increasing efficiency, and improving quality are obviously much needed and logically applicable in the administrative and business areas of organizations. However, there are several organizational issues (in addition to the many local process issues) that frequently serve as barriers to the successful application of statistical improvement methods in business process areas.

Why is it that, when resources are applied for process improvement efforts, efforts frequently meet with limited success?

Issues with Business and Administrative Processes

These organizational issues are neither complex, difficult to understand, nor do they require sophisticated methods to overcome. However, they seem to be widespread in the business and administrative areas of organizations and they impact the ability to sustain improvement activities in business process areas.

1. Business functions are neither defined nor managed as processes. Many business and service processes are viewed as an "art"—highly dependent on individuals and their expertise. The sales process in many organizations is a classical example. There is hesitation to define many business functions as a series of activities used to achieve a set of specific requirements. As a result, specific measurements on process requirements are not used to assess process performance and determine appropriate change.

2. When a process is defined, it is usually defined in terms of the paper path, the inspection or auditing procedures, or the automated computerized version. Recently, a technical director was asked to draw out the flow for the process by which safety and environmental concerns were managed. Very quickly, he sketched the flows associated with the annual Environment, Safety, and Health (ES&H) auditing process (i.e., the decision-making process for determining compliance with regulatory requirements). When asked to relate the stages of the auditing process flow to the organizational requirement of fewer lost-time accidents, he was obviously not able to do so. The purpose of the annual audit is to document lack of compliance to government regulatory requirements.

3. Measurements are not in place to provide information on the performance of the business processes. The measurements taken in the business areas are typically to obtain periodic information on overall organizational (not process) performance. For example, in the auditing and examination division of an insurance company, typical metrics are hours per case and dollars assessed per case. Such management metrics do not necessarily allow for understanding the causes of inefficiency or ineffectiveness in the actual exam process.

4. Traditional cost accounting systems do not capture the true costs associated with many business processes. Not only have performance metrics (i.e., response variables) not been established for most of the business processes, neither have the costs of the processes been measured. What is the true cost to the organization of a past-due account going legal? What is the cost of the paperwork involved? The legal research? Very few organizations can provide specific answers to such questions. Typical financial measures only reflect the periodic costs of functional areas involved in the process, such as overtime hours and total payroll costs.

5. Many business processes are not aligned with external customer values. Even though any set of activities can be viewed as a process, an effective process must provide a critical competency that is tied to the strategic objectives of the organization. Otherwise, the reason for the existence of the process is questionable. Unfortunately, many administrative and business support processes have not been tied to the organizational goals and thereby do not enhance the organization's ability to meet customer requirements better. Even if the process does provide distinct outputs necessary for providing external customer requirements, those who work within the process are often unaware of the linkage.

6. Business processes are complex and cross-functional in nature. Even the most basic business processes are cross-functional in purpose. For instance, the mail delivery process affects every function in the organization. Thus, changes that are made in order to improve such processes require the involvement of multiple functions as well as different hierarchies of managerial support.

7. Large amounts of resources are spent to automate business functions and activities. Once activities are automated, people seem to define the activities or processes through the automated steps (or computer screens). Thus, innovation and new ideas for process change are often stifled. Additionally, organizations are reluctant to "unautomate" processes once the resources are expended, even if they have automated highly ineffective and inefficient ones.

8. The processes are managed in an inconsistent fashion. Frequently, business processes are required to meet multiple organizational objectives that are sometimes in conflict with one another. For instance, in a customer call center, one requirement is the effective processing of customer requests. This objective competes with the requirement or metric of reduced call times or increased number of calls per resource unit. Also, the managerial emphasis on which metric is most important changes across time. Such inconsistencies lead to cynicism among the process members regarding improvement efforts focused on any one of the objectives

This list of issues is not exhaustive; however, they do seem to complicate the ability to make fact-based business decisions that result in sustainable gains. Many business processes are constantly being considered for centralization or decentralization as well as for outsourcing to contract service entities. Such decisions lead to inconsistencies in focus and failures to work on systemic issues. Process study using approaches such as Six Sigma can provide important knowledge regarding process capability to meet requirements efficiently prior to such decisions being made.

After perusing these issues, a senior manager from a well-functioning, disciplined organization commented, "Even though I can see the reality of each of these, I find it amazing that organizations allow these issues to persist. Are conscious decisions made to ignore the inefficiencies and inconsistencies in business areas?" As previously stated, these issues are somewhat obvious. However, in order to address them, it is necessary for senior management to be willing to make fundamental changes to the way they manage business processes. *The* key to addressing such issues is the desire of the senior management to improve the situation.

Applying Six Sigma in a Business Process

At a manufacturer of prefabricated housing, Six Sigma improvement efforts in the manufacturing and design processes had been successful. Thus, a decision was made to use a similar approach to work on addressing business areas that were plagued with high processing costs and customer complaints. The initial attention was given to the Loan Processing Department located in a partially owned financial subsidiary. This department was selected for "Six Sigma" application due to the seemingly large number of complaints from major customer groups, including retail sales lots, credit managers, the controller, home buyers, and regulatory groups. The major classification of complaints were as follows:

- Long loan-processing times (by the retail lots and home buyers)
- Errors in processing (by credit managers, lots, and regulatory auditors)
- Excessive overtime hours (by the controller group)

A macro-level flow of the process and its major areas is provided in Figure 1. Loan packages are sent from retail centers (i.e., lots) to loan processing. Within the Loan Processing Department, information is logged and payment schedules are generated. Loan processing operates on a weekly schedule, with a weekly deadline, or close, for final approval and "booking" of loans. The main metrics that the department reports to senior management are total "deals" booked per week (along with total dollars lent) and payroll costs.

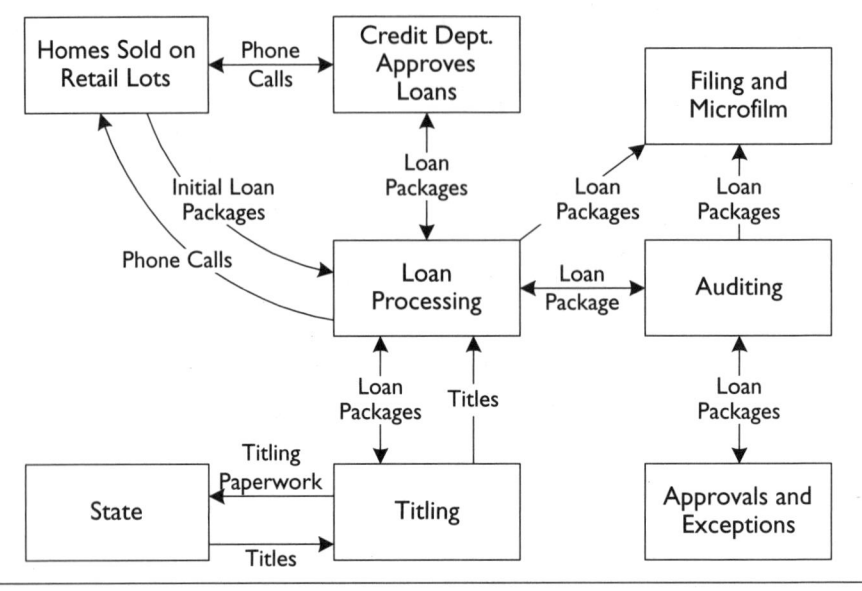

Figure 1. **Macro flow diagram of loan packages**

Payroll costs have been given much recent attention, as overtime hours are targeted as a part of a focused initiative to reduce business unit overhead costs.

Getting Started

Improvement efforts began with the identification of a process owner and a team of individuals representing various stages of the loan-processing area of the process. This group began by working to prioritize the key customers of the process and their requirements. Based on this understanding, they developed an initial process mission statement: *To process loan packages timely and accurately.* Simultaneously, key process inputs from suppliers and outputs were summarized. This work is summarized in the worksheet provided in Figure 2.

Issues faced during this stage of work were as follows:

1. Current metrics (and therefore behaviors) do not reflect the customer requirements identified.
2. No data are available to provide initial information on process performance or to identify where work should be directed with respect to cycle times or errors.
3. Loan packages are processed across multiple functional areas, as shown in Figure 1. The requirements identified in the process worksheet of Figure 2 indicate that work focused only within loan processing will not be capable of achieving expected reductions in cycle times and processing costs.

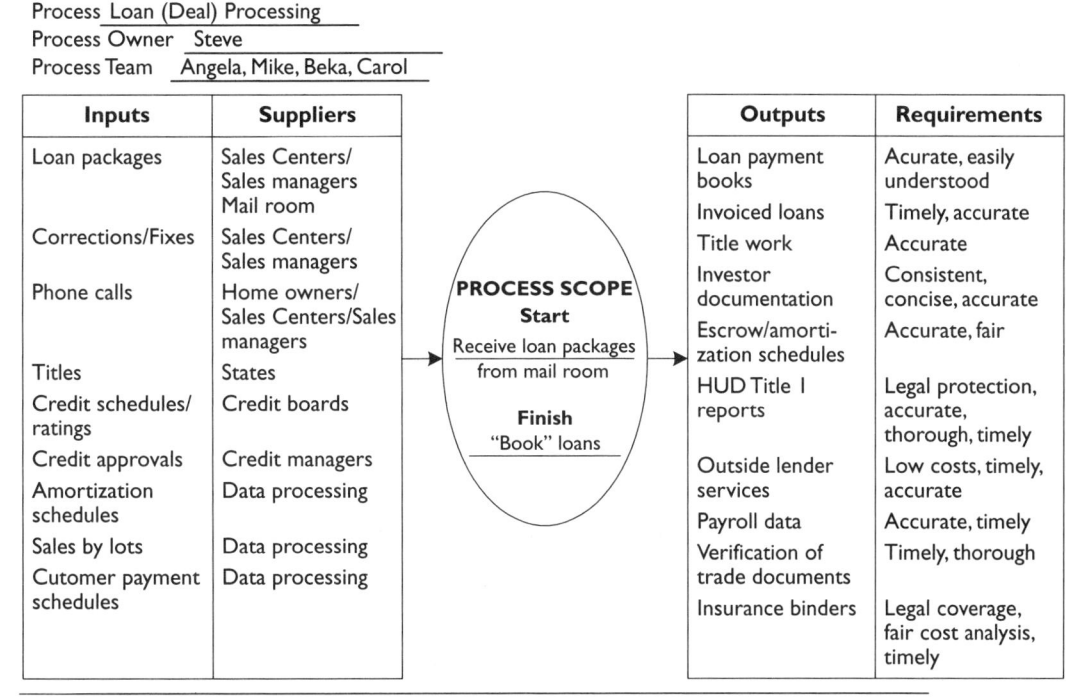

Six Sigma on Business Processes: Common Organizational Issues

Process **Loan (Deal) Processing**
Process Owner **Steve**
Process Team **Angela, Mike, Beka, Carol**

Inputs	Suppliers		Outputs	Requirements
Loan packages	Sales Centers/ Sales managers Mail room	**PROCESS SCOPE** **Start** Receive loan packages from mail room **Finish** "Book" loans	Loan payment books	Acurate, easily understood
Corrections/Fixes	Sales Centers/ Sales managers		Invoiced loans	Timely, accurate
Phone calls	Home owners/ Sales Centers/Sales managers		Title work	Accurate
			Investor documentation	Consistent, concise, accurate
Titles	States		Escrow/amortization schedules	Accurate, fair
Credit schedules/ ratings	Credit boards		HUD Title I reports	Legal protection, accurate, thorough, timely
Credit approvals	Credit managers		Outside lender services	Low costs, timely, accurate
Amortization schedules	Data processing		Payroll data	Accurate, timely
Sales by lots	Data processing		Verification of trade documents	Timely, thorough
Cutomer payment schedules	Data processing		Insurance binders	Legal coverage, fair cost analysis, timely

Figure 2. **Loan processing input/output worksheet**

Issues with Obtaining Process Data

In order to understand how well the process functioned currently and to highlight areas in which to focus work, the team began to identify possible response measures for the loan-processing area. The proposed measures include the following:

- Total cycle time of each loan with a breakdown of the cycle time into activity times at each work station and queue times
- Number of processing errors and the classification of those errors
- Total labor hours per week divided by number of loans processed

With each of these measures, there were barriers or dilemmas associated with the collection of the data. To discuss data on loan package errors, an auditor was included in the next team meeting. The discussion revealed that auditing did complete an auditing worksheet for each loan audited, but it did not record or track the errors by number or type. Therefore, the team sent a memo to the auditing manager requesting that the auditors collect data on the number and types of error. The manager refused the request, explaining his own pressure to reduce payroll costs. To resolve this barrier, it was necessary to involve the Vice President of Operations in a joint meeting between auditing and the loan-processing team.

In order to obtain data efficiently on cycle times and activity times, the team wanted the computer to log the time that each computer screen was entered. Unfortunately, the Information Systems (IS) Department had such a backlog of requests, a formal cost-benefit proposal with approval from senior management was required to get new programming requests into the short-term (60-90 days) IS schedule. In order to begin getting cycle time data, the team installed a temporary, manual data collection process via date/time stamping upon receipt of loan and upon placement of package in outgoing internal mail.

Finally, the team knew that past data on number of loans booked per closing and payroll hours existed in payroll. Upon obtaining and charting the data, there did not seem to be any correlation between the number of loans processed and payroll hours. The team was unable to suggest an alternate measure.

Issues faced during this stage of work were as follows:

1. The need for involvement by additional functional departments in order to obtain data on desired response measures.
2. The direct labor costs are not representative measures for understanding real processing costs and associated causes.
3. Historical data provided little information to help understanding of the variation in loans processed or causes for long cycle times.

Learnings from Initial Data Collection

Simultaneous to process mapping and flowcharting activities, data were obtained on cycle times and processing errors. The knowledge gained via data collected on errors, cycle times, and phone calls is summarized in Table 1. Some of the knowledge was obtained via the analysis of the data; however, several discoveries came from the attention given to processing conditions over the course of data collection.

Spurred by the information that a large percentage of total cycle time was being assigned to his process, the auditing manager requested the expansion of the team and mission to include the auditing process. He also suggested that the auditing error data should include not only errors made in loan processing but also mistakes made by lots in the initial compilation of data. Immediate work began to understand the frequent backlogs in auditing and the flows of information among auditing, retail lots, and loan processing. Subsequently, an additional measure, the number of phone calls (and faxes) per loan and associated reasons, was instituted.

When looking at the data on errors, possible causes for the differences by type of loan were understandable. As explained in Table 1 and shown in the Pareto of Figure 3, there were a few types of error that accounted for the majority of the mistakes made by the lots. With the permission of the VP of Operations, proposed changes to reduce these error types were presented to

Metric	Discoveries	Suspected Causes
Cycle times	• Majority of average total cycle time due to a small number of loan packages with extremely long cycle times	• Amount of time spent in auditing • Time to get fixes for errors made by lots • Multiple phone calls to and from lots often required for one "fix"
Errors (assigned to lots and loan processing)	• Majority of errors due to mistakes at lots • Number of errors differed by type of loan • Types of error did not differ by type of loan • Errors differed significantly across the different lots • Four types of errors accounted for approximately two-thirds of lot errors	• Complexity of loan packages, especially for FHA and HUD • Lack of training for retail center personnel • Poor communication to lots on requirement changes for loan applications • Poorly written and obtuse instructions
Phone calls and faxes per loan	• Multiple phone calls required to obtain a single piece of information • Majority of calls were "pleas" to obtain an exception to requirements or to process an incomplete loan package • A few lots accounted for a large number of the overall incoming phone calls	• Pressure to meet close deadline (i.e., to get the money) • The success of the pleas! • Certain sales managers requested exceptions repeatedly and consistently

Table 1. **Process discoveries from data collected**

senior management. For example, to deal with missing forms, the team proposed preassembling loan packages prior to sending the blank forms to the lots. In the past, the lots were merely sent boxes of individual forms. With the proposed change, the lots would receive completely assembled packages for each type of loan.

Although causes for the differences by loan type were fairly obvious, the reasons for differences between lots were much more difficult to explain. All lots received the same forms and the same instructions and processed the same types of loan. The team members obtained the necessary approvals to actually visit retail lots to understand the lot-to-lot differences they saw in their data.

The data on phone calls were difficult to collect due to the fact that many calls circumvented the process areas and went directly to managers. Still, the data confirmed that multiple phone calls were required frequently to obtain information to correct one error. Also observed was that the majority of calls were "pleas" to process an incomplete or incorrect loan in order to meet a close deadline (e.g., to receive the associated monies). It was further evident

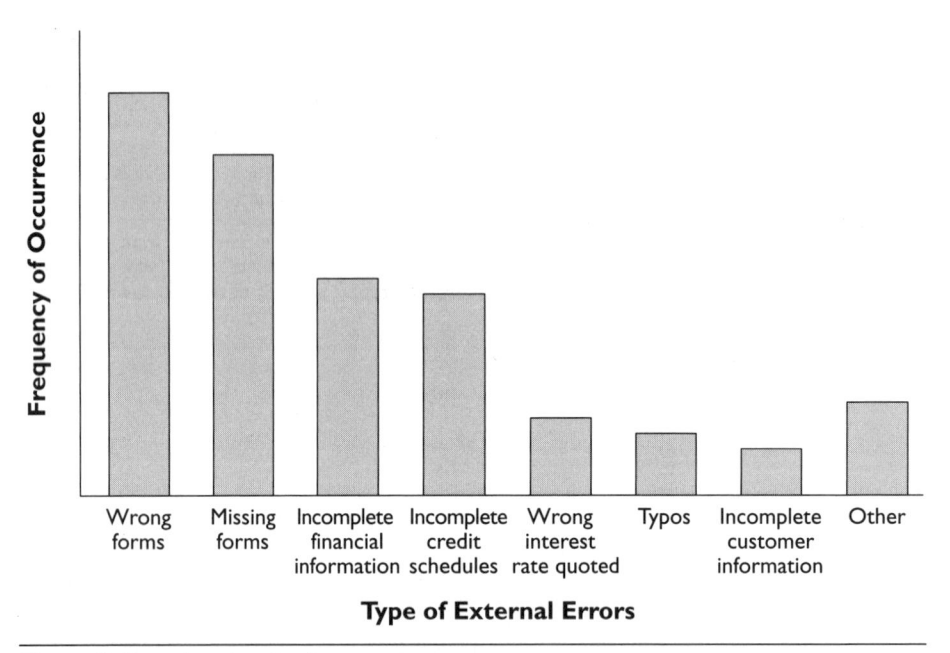

Figure 3. **Pareto chart of error types**

that for some of the retail lot managers who consistently made phone calls, the calls progressively went to higher levels in the organization. One manager made over 10 calls in a 24-hour period of time. The first one started with the loan-processing supervisor. The final call was to the president of the organization! As a result of these insights, frustration began to grow among the team members. As long as pleas from sales managers continued to work, sustaining any type of change in the process would be impossible. The lots had no incentives to cooperate. The team began to question the inconsistent adherence to approval criteria for bookings and the reason for the existence of the "Exceptions and Approvals" department (see Figure 1).

Issues faced during this stage of work were as follows:

1. Focus on process causal structures resulted in the examination of organizational and management practices.
2. Proposed changes and work to understand causes (e.g., travel to lots) cost time and money. The work was not free to the organization.
3. The retail lots, the suppliers to the process, were also the key customers of the organization.

Initial Results and Team Recommendations

The preassembly of loan packets and rewritten instructions for the lots were

Six Sigma on Business Processes: Common Organizational Issues 413

credited with a 55% reduction in external errors. As a result, phone calls for fixes were reduced by over 20% and overtime hours for the Loan Processing Department were reduced by over 15%. Obtaining these validated improvements allowed the team the opportunity to present the following ideas and challenges dealing with the larger, organizational issues to the senior management team.

1. The visits to the lots revealed that some lots had personnel dedicated to loan application preparation. Those who required their sales personnel to complete the loan packages all had a similar perception—it is their job to sell and loan processing's job to complete the loan packages. A quote from one sales representative was "I do my job. I'd like to know what you do. We all have to do our part."

Changing perceptions at the lots is the responsibility of management. As long as all communication to the lots is focused on "making sells" (via prizes and bonuses for most homes sold), perceptions and expectations will not change.

> The preassembly of loan packets and rewritten instructions for the lots were credited with a 55% reduction in external errors.

2. The pressure to process incomplete loan packages was partially due to the internal pressure to manage cash flows from investors. Managers increased "bookings" by the only means available to them—"Exceptions and Approvals." Thus, if weekly numbers were falling below the goal, managers allowed a certain number of incomplete loan packages to be processed. Those sales managers who had established relationships with internal managers often were granted exceptions.

Such practices needed to stop. Incentive structures needed to change. Without changing these behaviors, further reduction in overtime would be impossible. All data collected pointed to excess hours spent tracking down sales personnel to get additional critical information for already approved packages. Also, as long as these practices continued, the Auditing Department would continue to be a "holding" department for loans waiting for corrections and fixes.

3. The Loan Processing Department had *always* functioned as a batch process where the loan packages are passed between desks in batches of 20-25 loans. Each person hired is trained for one particular area of processing—a person to assign loan numbers, one to input information, one to obtain payment schedules, and so forth. Given this processing structure, those at the "end of the line" always incurred the heavy overtime hours. Those at the beginning frequently had idle time toward the end of the day.

Lean manufacturing principles were just as applicable to an administrative process as they were to the manufacturing areas. In fact, the team wanted to visit the manufacturing sites to explore lean manufacturing concepts, such as one-piece flow, cellular manufacturing, and balancing of workloads. However, managers who had been in the company for many years felt strongly that the current processing structure was the "right way" to process loans.

Without the support of senior management, continued efforts to explore such fundamental changes would be wasted.

Continued Efforts and Unresolved Issues

After much debate and discussion, the team was ordained to continue work to understand the applicability of lean principles to their own processes. Additionally, the team was provided the needed support to begin working with individuals from the retail lots to develop ideas for improving communications and relationships with the lots. The issues with respect to incentive structures and inconsistent managerial practices were left unresolved. Without a doubt, the continued work would continue to highlight these issues.

Conclusion

Even without proactive intent to address common implementation issues, the application of Six Sigma techniques still provided some gains in both process knowledge as well as reduction in costs. The ability to achieve improvements and to sustain gains is tied directly to the desire by the organization to change and the willingness to deal with issues and barriers as they are encountered. In this company, certain organizational behaviors demonstrated this desire. These included the following:

1. Senior management were involved throughout the improvement work. All new process questions, knowledge, and directions for work efforts were discussed with senior managers.
2. As a result of behavior 1, senior management supported the idea of making major, yet fundamental changes to functional responsibilities.
3. The improvement work was not confined by a sequential step-by-step approach to problem-solving. Thus, concepts from lean manufacturing, ideas from business process reengineering, and variation reduction techniques were utilized as needed to achieve the desired results.
4. Measurements were established that were relevant and representative of process performance. Functional metrics and managerial reporting metrics (e.g., monthly cash flows) were subordinated to the process measurements for the purpose of process management.
5. Due to the involvement from high-level managers, the improvement efforts did not stay within the boundaries of loan processing. Data were collected and changes were made across locations, functions, titles, and individuals.

These keys to successful implementation are relevant across all processes, especially business and administrative ones. If they are not in place, improvement efforts in business process areas cannot thrive. When they exist along with a decision to implement a data-driven improvement approach, such as Six Sigma, each and every issue faced is much easier to overcome.

References

1. Sanders, R., Leitnaker, M., and Sanders, D., The Analytic Examination of Time-Dependent Variance Components, *Quality Engineering*, 7(4), 315-336 (1995).
2. Sanders, D., and Hild, C., Discussions of Strategies for Implementation of Six Sigma, *Quality Engineering*, 12(3), 303-309 (2000).

Doug Sanders and Cheryl Hild are members of Six Sigma Associates, www.sigma-science.com. They have more than 12 years of experience in application of statistical methodologies in industry. Both authors obtained their Ph.D. in management sciences and industrial statistics from the University of Tennessee. Hild is co-author of The Power of Statistical Thinking: Improving Industrial Processes *(Prentice Hall, 1995).*

Reshaping Six Sigma at Honeywell

Robert Green

In this article we have a case study of the success of implementing Six Sigma at a large multinational corporation. It reports on what happened when Honeywell and AlliedSignal merged their divergent quality systems to form Six Sigma Plus. The bottom line is that the effort was successful enough that Honeywell International recently began offering its Six Sigma expertise to its suppliers and customers.

What happens when two companies with two distinct and effective quality management systems (QMSs) are merged? Ideally, the two systems are integrated to form a new system containing the most effective elements of each and shedding those that are redundant.

At the time of their 1999 merger, both AlliedSignal and Honeywell had years invested in their respective quality systems. Nevertheless, management would have to face the Herculean task of combining the two.

In 1994, Rick Schroeder, AlliedSignal's vice president of operations, brought his Six Sigma experience from Motorola to his new employer. By 1999, AlliedSignal was five years into its Six Sigma program, which headed the company's effort to capture growth and productivity opportunities more rapidly and efficiently by reducing defects and waste in all of its business processes—resulting in a $600 million annual savings.

Meanwhile, Honeywell had developed its own QMS—the Honeywell Quality Value (HQV) program—an assessment process based on the Malcolm Baldrige National Quality Award criteria.

AlliedSignal's Six Sigma efforts had developed a strong reputation, both internally and externally, for accelerating improvements in all of the company's processes, products and services and reducing the cost of poor quality through waste elimination and defect and variation reduction. Nevertheless, the merger between AlliedSignal and Honeywell—or more accurately, between the two companies' QMSs—would reshape that Six Sigma program. Its new name would be Six Sigma Plus.

The QMS of the melded companies, known as Honeywell International, is driven by Six Sigma Plus. The company now employs more than 120,000 peo-

Reprinted with permission from *Quality Digest*, December 2000. Copyright © 2000 QCI International. All rights reserved.

ple who work in 95 countries and offer aerospace products and services, electronic materials, home and building control, industrial control, performance polymers and chemicals, turbine technologies, and transportation products.

Whether flying on a plane, driving a car, heating or cooling a home, furnishing an apartment, taking medication for an illness, or playing a sport, most people use Honeywell International products in some way every day.

Integrating the Quality Management Systems

Following the merger, Honeywell International CEO Michael R. Bonsignore made clear the future of Six Sigma at the new company: "As a new organization, our challenge is to continue the performance improvements of our predecessors, delight customers and achieve aggressive growth. Six Sigma Plus will drive growth and productivity by energizing all of Honeywell International's 120,000 employees worldwide—providing the skills and tools to create more value for our customers, improve our processes and capitalize on the power of the Internet through e-business. I am determined to make it a way of life at Honeywell International."

Ray Stark, now Honeywell International's vice president of Six Sigma and productivity, led the effort to incorporate elements of both former companies' QMSs into a coherent and improved system.

"When we merged the two companies, Arnie Weimerskirch, the father of Honeywell's HQV, and I got together to discuss our respective quality management systems," says Stark. "We concluded that the new company would be served very well if we could take the best practices from these quality management approaches and bring them together. And that is how Six Sigma Plus was born."

> We concluded that the new company would be served very well if we could take the best practices from these quality management approaches and bring them together. And that is how Six Sigma Plus was born.

Six Sigma Plus Is Born

Key to making Six Sigma Plus universal in each of Honeywell International's businesses was committing to a strategy of approaching every improvement project with the same logical method, the DMAIC process:

- **D**efine the customer-critical parameters
- **M**easure how the process performs
- **A**nalyze the causes of the problems
- **I**mprove the process to reduce defects and variation
- **C**ontrol the process to ensure continued, improved performance

Six Sigma Plus combines the former AlliedSignal's formidable Six Sigma program and elements of the former Honeywell's HQV method; lean enterprise, a lean manufacturing component; and activity-based management (ABM), which aids in analyzing customer profitability and targeting future costs for new product development.

"One of our competitive advantages is our ability to integrate in a holistic way all of these tools and methodologies to bring greater value to our customers," explains Edward M. Romanoff, Honeywell International's communications director for Six Sigma Plus and productivity. "Lean helps us to reengineer a process to focus only on customer value-added elements. ABM helps us to understand the profitability of our products and services and to tailor our business models appropriately. The HQV process is being streamlined, timed to affect our annual operating plans, and geared to help our businesses prioritize remedial process improvements that affect customers and the financial well-being of the business.

"These two pieces—Six Sigma and HQV—come together nicely in that the latter provides the framework for how one should run a business in total, and Six Sigma gives you the quantitative specifics of what and how to improve."

But as well as HQV and Six Sigma may complement each other, their functions, goals and capabilities vary greatly. Responsible for developing and implementing Honeywell International's Six Sigma Plus strategy, Stark was charged with ensuring that both elements were understood and used to their maximum potential within the company.

"The Baldrige criteria might mandate that a company measure a given product's performance from a customer's perspective," explains Stark. "And if no such reporting mechanism existed, the Baldrige examiner would suggest that best-performing companies have this kind of system and that your company should put one in place. With a Six Sigma QMS, we would not only say you should put something in place, but we would give you the specific measurements that would help you understand the capability of the product. And it would be done in a way that would allow you to index its quality against a yardstick that we call Six Sigma."

Six Sigma Plus Training

Being able to effectively use that yardstick meant training. While employees of the former AlliedSignal needed to learn about the HQV elements added to their Six Sigma program to create Six Sigma Plus, the more formidable challenge was training employees of the former Honeywell in Six Sigma methodology, a program never developed or implemented there.

The first step was holding a series of leadership orientations aimed at teaching Six Sigma basics to the management. "Once they understood what it was and how it could be deployed, we then selected individuals out of each of these businesses that would be trained through application—they would learn how to apply these tools in particular projects," reports Stark. "They would then become the originators of process improvement and the experts of the application of these tools within their businesses."

Honeywell International uses Master Black Belts to guide those Six Sigma

GLOSSARY OF SIX SIGMA PLUS CERTIFICATIONS

Honeywell International employees who become skilled in Six Sigma Plus tools can earn certification in the following core areas of proficiency:

Green Belt—A person with working knowledge of Six Sigma Plus methodology and tools, who has completed training and a project to drive high-impact business results.

Black Belt—A highly skilled Six Sigma Plus expert who has completed four weeks of classroom learning and, over the course of four to six months, demonstrated mastery of the tools through the completion of a major process improvement project.

Master Black Belt—The Six Sigma Plus expert most highly skilled in the methodologies of variation reduction. After a year-long project-based certification program, Master Black Belts train and mentor Black Belts, help select and lead high-value projects, maintain the integrity of the sigma measurements, and develop and revise Six Sigma Plus learning materials.

Lean Expert—A person who has completed four weeks of lean training and one or more projects that have demonstrated significant, auditable business results and the appropriate application of Six Sigma Plus lean tools.

Lean Master—A person highly skilled in implementing lean principles and lean tool utilization in diverse business environments. Certification involves one year of intense study and practice in advanced lean tools, teaching and mentoring.

ABM Expert—A person who has demonstrated proficiency in activity-based management (ABM) through a business application involving product costing, process costing or customer profitability analysis. Certification involves attending an ABM training course, defining a meaningful project, displaying knowledge of the ABM tools and using the data for key decision making. ABM experts frequently link Six Sigma Plus tools to projected and actual financial results.

ABM Master—A person who has the skills of an expert plus the ability to develop and deliver ABM learning courses. Certification typically takes one year and involves demonstrating the use of ABM data for multiple purposes with repeatable and sustainable results. ABM Masters are proficient in the use of advanced cost management tools and have the ability to tailor cost data and analysis to a business's vision and strategy.

TPM Expert—A person who applies total productive maintenance (TPM) and reliability methodologies and tools to assist or lead teams in optimizing asset capacity-productivity at minimum life-cycle cost. A TPM Expert is responsible for determining critical equipment and measuring its overall

> effectiveness, thus enabling growth and productivity through optimum asset utilization.
>
> **TPM Master**—A highly skilled individual experienced in the use of TPM and reliability tools and methodologies. TPM Masters' responsibilities include assisting leadership in identifying high-leverage asset improvement opportunities; leading critical, high-leverage improvement projects in a business; and leading cultural paradigm shifts from reactive to proactive asset management.

Plus leaders. "Those individuals then go through their learning experience, guided by the Masters, with the objective of driving real results consistent with the goals and needs of their business," Stark continues. "Therefore, the result will be an improvement of some fashion, whether that be taking cost out of the process, avoiding extra cost, bringing a product to market faster or creating a new e-business channel."

But "training" doesn't accurately characterize Honeywell International's project-based educational system. "Our program is not about training, it's about learning," explains Romonoff. "You can put people in a classroom and give them statistical training. You can give them hypothetical examples to make your point and people do learn, some faster than others. But the part that's unique here is that people come into this mentored environment with a project beforehand. It's something that they or their business particularly needs done. And they're given that project and asked to go and learn about these tools and how they can apply them to get a desired result or outcome. It's very much results-orientated."

And management expects this newly gained knowledge to trickle down the corporate structure as soon as the training is completed. Employees who complete the program are expected to go back to their business and complete two to three Six Sigma projects per year. Additionally, they are to mentor as many as 10 groups of employees a year in their Six Sigma Plus learning curve.

"So if that's 10 teams at 10 people each, you've got 100 employees that can be potentially impacted by this one individual," explains Stark. "So it's very important that these people have the team-dynamic skills to deal with different types of people, behaviors and situations. At the end of the day, what we want is at least a simple understanding of the applications of these tools by every employee."

Also key to training employees in Six Sigma Plus is Honeywell International's Growth Green Belt program, which aims to bring Six Sigma quality to every aspect and department of the company—whether it be marketing, human resources or sales. As the company expands the reach of Six Sigma Plus methodology well beyond traditional manufacturing-based projects, several hundred teams led by its Growth Green Belts have engaged marketing and sales professionals, design engineers, and others in a quest to deliv-

> **SIX SIGMA PLUS LEADER CRITERIA**
>
> To bring Six Sigma Plus to every element of the company, Honeywell International first trains leaders from each of its businesses. Candidates for Six Sigma Plus leadership positions possess:
> - An aptitude for learning
> - The ability to lead
> - The ability to mentor others
> - The desire to continue to progress through the organization

er customer value by developing new products and services.

One of the first Growth Green Belt teams successfully boosted revenue at the Honeywell International Performance Polymers and Chemicals' Specialty Wax and Additives business by creating a product that expanded candle applications. Another helped extend the commercialization of a particular product to a new application.

"When we apply the DMAIC methodology to nontraditional projects, we see dramatic results that equal or exceed those we have seen in the manufacturing arena," notes Stark.

Six Sigma Plus' E-Business Component

One nontraditional element of Six Sigma Plus is e-business. Several Honeywell International businesses have a number of initiatives under way to take advantage of the power of the Internet's instant, convenient and global nature. MyPlant.com, MyAircraft.com and MyFacilities.com are the front-end portals, originating out of Six Sigma Plus projects, that customers are using to buy Honeywell International's services and products.

Additionally, Honeywell International's Aerospace Electronic Systems has a WebPlan tool to link customers and suppliers for a seamless sales and operating plan process. Honeywell International's Consumer Products Group has established an e-solution to speed response time to changing customer demands and reduce inventory assets across the entire supply chain. And Honeywell International's Global Business Services has also enabled online travel planning, which, in addition to increased accessibility and convenience, saves the company millions annually.

To gain the full benefit of these Internet applications requires a step-function focus from the Six Sigma Plus efforts to improve the integrity of the data used, reduce process defects and variation, and speed the flow of information and physical assets from customer to supplier across the supply chain.

Building on Success

Honeywell International's continuous performance improvement projects,

> ## Success Stories
>
> Using Six Sigma Plus methodology, an Industrial Control team developed a reliable, cost-effective family of chips and assembled components for the burgeoning data communications market. As a result, Industrial Control achieved a 500-percent increase in revenue growth, resulting in a year-over-year increase in operating profits of several million dollars. Cycle time was reduced 35 percent, and yields increased from 75 percent to 93 percent.
>
> More than 300 staff members, both in quality control and research and development laboratories across several Honeywell International businesses, participated in a customized Green Belt learning program to improve measurement systems. This sharing of best practices, resources and expertise has benefited the development of new products and the quality control of existing products. At the same time, it has helped save nearly $8 million.
>
> Aerospace Services, using Six Sigma Plus, merged activity-based management and lean manufacturing techniques at its Raunheim, Germany, facility. The site repairs auxiliary power units, propulsion engines and components that provide air conditioning and other power-related features aboard aircraft. The site impressed customers over the past two years with a 43-percent reduction in components repair time. It helped Honeywell International achieve a $47-million increase in revenue and was a major factor in $900,000 worth of productivity improvements.
>
> A turbocharging systems team in Mexicale, Mexico, part of the Transportation & Power Systems business, used Six Sigma Plus and lean tools in teardown and cleaning processes. This reduced cycle time by 92 percent and space by 51 percent, eliminated the use of chemical substances for cleaning operations, and saved $400,000. In addition, Six Sigma Plus has been useful in helping to reduce warranty expense and computer downtime and improving the integrity of an employee database.

dating back to AlliedSignal, have established an impressive track record of providing considerable payoffs in quality, on-time delivery, and competitively priced products and services. And Honeywell International management has put into place a system that continues to build on its successes, continuously striving for more improvement.

To this end, Honeywell International has committed to providing every employee with 40 hours of learning each year. The company has earmarked millions of dollars to give each of its 120,000 employees an opportunity to learn and embrace Six Sigma Plus fundamentals, which Honeywell International believes will result in concrete growth, improved productivity and increased efficiency.

In 1999, Honeywell savings related to Six Sigma amounted to more than

$600 million. Year 2000 cost savings provided by Six Sigma Plus are expected to save at least as much.

The Future

Honeywell International recently began offering its Six Sigma expertise exclusively to its current suppliers and customers. Services offered range from full deployment, where Honeywell International helps these partners develop and implement an entire customized Six Sigma Plus program, to simple advice.

Those customers and suppliers that choose to take advantage of the Six Sigma Plus commercialization can consult with a Honeywell International Six Sigma Plus expert about a particular problem, attend Honeywell International Six Sigma Plus training courses, participate in Honeywell International interactive online seminars, or have Honeywell International Master Black Belts deployed to their site to improve their processes and restructure their businesses.

However, recent news puts the state of many former programs very much up in the air. At the end of October, Honeywell International announced it had accepted a $45-billion acquisition offer by General Electric (GE). Pending only shareholder and regulatory approval, the leadership of the two companies will soon begin a process with which Honeywell International management is already very familiar.

While it's not clear what changes the pending GE acquisition will bring, it's likely that Stark, who will head the integration process for Honeywell International, will lobby to build on the success of his company's Six Sigma Plus program. And no company is better situated to make the most of Honeywell International's methodology, trained personnel and Six Sigma-based philosophy than General Electric.

Soon after a May 1995 address to GE executives by Lawrence Bossidy, former vice chairman of GE and then CEO of AlliedSignal, GE quickly became a leading supporter of and participant in the Six Sigma movement.

"One of the interesting aspects of the proposed GE acquisition is that we both speak the same language," comments Stark. "Both of our programs are rooted in the same philosophy. And this is one of the things that will be a real benefit in terms of the companies coming together. We are coming from exactly the same perspective when it comes to Six Sigma and its application, helping to drive growth and productivity and satisfying customer requirements."

Editorial Note: The GE-Honeywell merger did not go through because of antitrust concerns in the European Economic Community.

Robert Green is Quality Digest's assistant editor. E-mail him at rgreen@qualitydigest.com.

Six Sigma Beyond Manufacturing—a Concept for Robust Management

Mustafa R. Yilmaz and Sangit Chatterjee

This is a very nice review of Six Sigma and quality management concepts, including those of W. Edwards Deming. The authors explain exactly what Six Sigma is and demonstrate its value for process improvement using Deming's explanation of the organization as a system for their rationale. It includes an overview of the concept of failure modes and effects analysis and activity-based management. All in all, a good summary of several concepts.

An overarching objective for the top management of a modern-day business is the maximization of shareholder value as measured, for example, by the company's stock price. In today's global and highly competitive economy, stock price is strongly influenced by short-term financial performance. Although an acquisition or merger can sometimes produce a punctuated positive impact on shareholder value, long-term success of a company requires the creation of value in its core businesses in a sustained way. It is widely accepted that, in a manufacturing or product-oriented company, long-term performance ultimately depends on the quality and efficiency of production processes in delivering products that customers value. Thus, initiatives to improve quality and efficiency are usually focused on the product-related processes that are thought to have the highest impact on the bottom line.

In the 1980s, the vernacular of quality management was augmented by the addition of "six-sigma quality," originating in the highly successful quality improvement efforts at Motorola. The new term was used to describe a manufacturing process of highly robust quality, one that has very low variability compared with the tolerance limits specified for the product being manufactured. Development of this capability would ensure both dependable quality and efficiency of the manufacturing processes. With a real example at Motorola, this idea has motivated other companies to undertake similar efforts.

Reprinted with permission of the publisher from *Quality Management Journal*, Vol. 7, No. 3, July 2000. Copyright © 2000 by the American Society for Quality. All rights reserved.

The objective of this paper is to discuss six sigma as a concept that is applicable not only to goods and services, but also to the business processes that support production activities. Here, six sigma is used as a metaphor for excellence and managerial thought rather than a purely statistical concept. Even without technical details, six-sigma thinking can be a useful guide for robust management, one that is able to confront the challenges of a highly competitive and variable environment. These challenges include virtually instantaneous and worldwide availability of information to customers, ever-increasing efficiency of economic markets, competition approaching theoretical levels, and the resulting downward pressure on prices and profit margins.

Six-Sigma Quality

The term *sigma,* borrowed from statistics, is a measure indicating the typical deviation from the average of a measured quality characteristic. A six-sigma process has very low variability compared with the tolerance limits established for the quality characteristic. This is illustrated in Figure 1, where the bell-shaped curve in the middle represents the variability in the measured characteristic, with its average located at the center of the tolerance range. If the average varies by up to 1.5 standard deviations (dotted curves in Figure 1), then no more than 3.4 defects per million would be produced. If the average could be maintained exactly at the center, there would be only 2 defects per billion items. The notion of process capability combines the twin notions of process variability and a process shift depicted in Figure 1. A six-sigma process is capable of yielding virtually no defects, even though it is not entirely free of some inherent variability. (Note that these numbers are for a single process or quality characteristic. They would become larger as the number of processes required to finish the product is increased.)

> A six-sigma process has very low variability compared with the tolerance limits established for the quality characteristic.

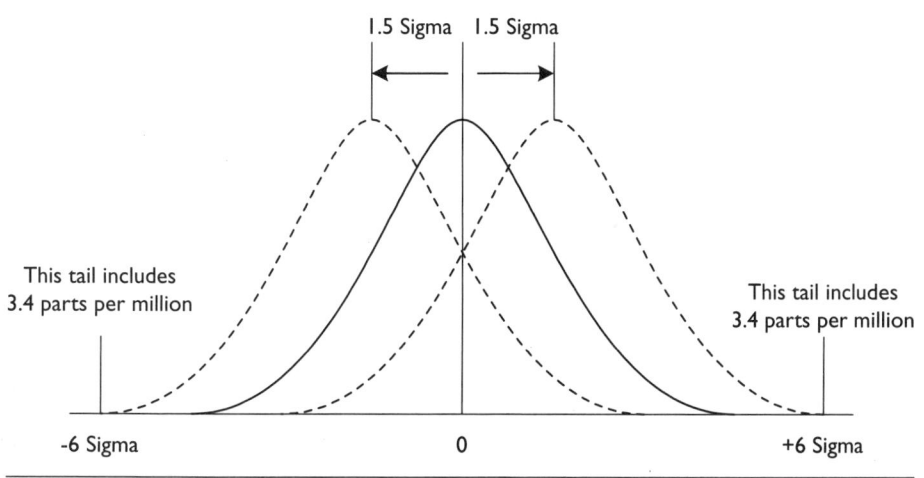

Figure 1. **Six-sigma quality for a measure with a bell-shaped distribution; tolerance limits are 6 sigma from the center**

The real success of the efforts at Motorola was not just in the fact that this level of quality can be achieved, but that it can be achieved without increasing the resources utilized, that is, by improving the capability and efficiency of production processes. Higher process capability would mean lower variability in quality, leading to improved efficiency. This would, in turn, lead to a reduction or elimination of waste, improved customer satisfaction, and ultimately, increased profitability. The challenge was in the development of manufacturing processes that operate at peak efficiency in using resources while ensuring high quality.

The primary means to achieving six-sigma quality is to eliminate the causes of quality problems before they lead to defects. Once a defect occurs, it consumes additional resources in trying to identify and repair it, or worse, it can be delivered to a customer without ever being discovered. Six-sigma quality essentially eliminates these problems, enhancing the company's quality image while reducing production line waste (which can consume as much as 15 percent or more of the resources). As new customers begin purchasing from a company known for its high-quality products, market share and revenues also increase (see Figure 2). Companies like Motorola, Texas Instruments, ABB, Allied Signal, and 3M have been striving to achieve six-sigma quality, and as a result, they have become known internationally as best-in-class companies that are successfully expanding their markets.

> The primary means to achieving six-sigma quality is to eliminate the causes of quality problems before they lead to defects.

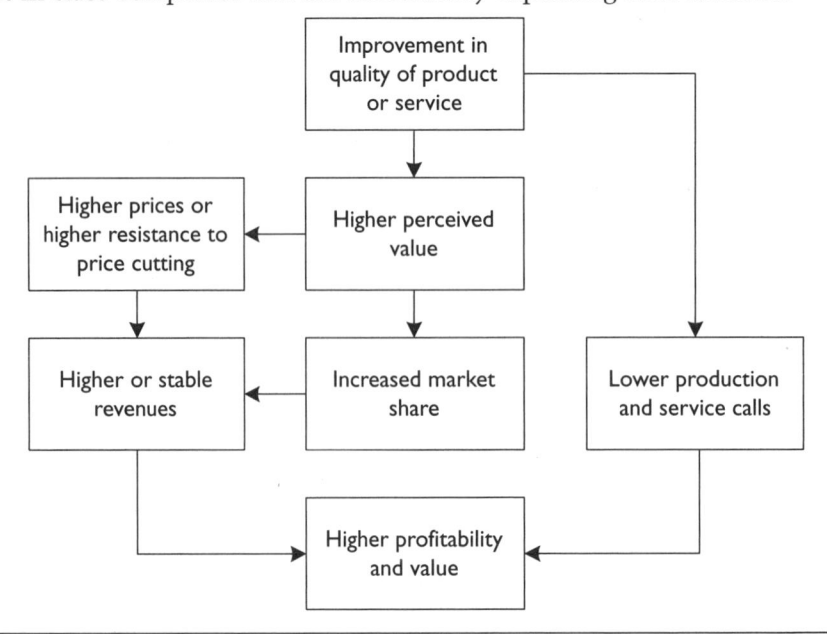

Figure 2. **Effect of quality on the creation of value (adapted from Evans and Lindsay, 1996)**

Business as a System for Value Creation

In his last book, *The New Economics* (1994), quality pioneer W. Edwards Deming emphatically argued that success in the world of modern business requires a management transformation to quality in all aspects of business. His term for the means to this transformation was "the system of profound knowledge," which must be acquired and adopted by management. This was composed of four interrelated parts.

1. Appreciation for a system
2. Knowledge about variation
3. Theory of knowledge
4. Psychology

Appreciation for a system. The first of these begins with the recognition that an organization is a system of interdependent components (subsystems) that work together to accomplish the aim of the system. The components are not necessarily organizational units that may appear in a traditional organization chart; they pertain to the accomplishment of functions and tasks that are necessary for achieving the system's purpose. In addition to major subsystems like production, logistics, marketing, customer service, and so on, they include administrative support subsystems such as accounting, finance, human resource management, and the like. Management of the entire system requires knowledge of the interrelationships among the components within the system, and in particular, the people who work in them.

Although it has ancient roots, a general study of systems was formalized by Bertalanffy (1968) and others in which the physical, mental, biological, psychological, cultural, and all other imaginable worlds are only components of the whole system. Of course, Forrester (1972, 1980) employed the systems view in many of his novel works, including a simulation of the energy resources of the world. Continued thinking in this view was brought into an organizational setting by Senge (1990) in his now famous *The Fifth Discipline*, which he called "organizational learning." Jung's *gestalt* is the psychological equivalent of the "whole." Deming's continued insistence on systems view was influenced not only by his knowledge of systems theory, but also an effective exposure to Taoist and Buddhist teachings during his visits to Japan.

> A consequence of the systems view is that optimization of the whole system does not mean each and every subsystem has to be optimized.

A consequence of the systems view is that optimization of the whole system does not mean each and every subsystem has to be optimized. An optimized whole system may have, or even necessitate, subsystems that are only suboptimal. On an assembly line for example, it is not desirable to optimize an operation that has some slack (by shortening its duration or devoting more resources to it). It may even be possible to increase the efficiency of the system by diverting excess resources from this operation to more critical ones. To use a biological analogy, a multicellular organism has various physiological, neurological, instinctual, and perceptual systems that may not be individually optimal, but the whole may be optimal in that the organs using the subsystems are in homeostasis, and this enables the species to survive in the long run. As a system, an organization that survives is equivalent to Deming's "jobs, more jobs." System perspective emphasizes the need for cooperation and coordination between subsystems, departments, and teams, for the system to thrive as a whole. Lack of cooperation (for example, suboptimization of each department separately or competition for monetary rewards) can destroy the system (Deming 1982).

The fact that an optimized system does not necessarily optimize all its subsystems presents a very interesting management challenge. Which systems or departments are allowed to have slack? How much of it? And how do other departments feel about that? In recent years, downsizing has largely been about eliminating any slack in all operations, but a systems view suggests this approach is fundamentally incorrect. It is necessary for management to identify and prioritize the activities that have the highest impact on the quality of what is delivered to the customers. Some tools that can help in meeting this challenge will be discussed later in the paper.

Knowledge about variation. The second part begins with the recognition that there is always some variability in any process, between people, in output, in service, in product. It is important for management to learn about the reasons for variability in a business process, develop measures to quantify variability when possible, use the measures to track performance, and take appropriate action. Strict deadlines, even if based on estimated averages of historical data, are not consistent with a thorough understanding of variation, and neither are numeric goals or quotas. It is more important to work on methods for improvement of the process than on reducing variability to produce the desired results. Deming strongly believed that rather than imposing numeric goals or quotas, management must provide workers with the methods and training that are needed to achieve those results. As he put it succinctly, "By what method?" At a departmental or business unit level, numeric goals can be replaced with less rigid (interval) goals such as "We would like to be within 10 percent of X."

A common pitfall for managers is to reward people (or perhaps, themselves) who performed much beyond a fixed goal, or to chastise people who fell short of a goal during a given period. This indicates a lack of understanding of variability as well as psychology. In the science of statistics, this would be considered as the incorrect use of a single observation to reach a general conclusion. A manager who is not conscious of this pitfall would be well advised to wait for several observations, when possible, before reaching any conclusions. Performance may go up one period and come down the next, all because of common factors that are at play. Attributing such changes to specific factors, and attaching rewards or penalties to them, is not good management practice.

There are, of course, numerous situations and decisions where repeated observations are not available, or they cannot be made within a reasonable time frame. In these cases, it is up to management to generate subjective estimates of variability that can be expected and of the risks associated with them. This is not an easy task, to be sure, but insight about the variability factors involved can only improve management's ability to generate these assessments.

Theory of knowledge. The third part provides the ability to make rational predictions of future observations based on information about the past, together with a theory that links the past and the future. Management requires prediction, which in turn requires a theory of knowledge. Information is not knowledge; a dictionary contains a lot of information but not knowledge. Knowledge requires a theory that can explain the past and allows predictions of the future, even though the predictions may not be very accurate (because of the variability arising from chance factors), or they can ultimately turn out to be wrong. This can be illustrated by the thinking of the Chaucer's proverbial rooster Chanticleer who observed that his daily crowing in early mornings provokes a sunrise, and thereby has a theory for sunrise. He had to revise his theory when the sun failed to rise one cloudy morning, but it is significant that he had a theory to revise and something to learn. The Kantian maxim that experience without theory is blind, and theory beyond experience is mere intellectual play, also stresses this point.

Clearly, knowledge about variation is an essential part of a theory of knowledge. For example, the use of a bell-shaped curve for the distribution of a measured qualify characteristic, as in Figure 1, represents a theory about the process that generates the characteristic. Such a curve allows the prediction of the proportion of defects that can be expected to occur if the factors influencing the system remain stable (though not at fixed levels). Theory requires management to study and learn about these factors also.

Psychology. The fourth part helps management understand people. As individuals, people are naturally different from one another. They learn in different ways, they have different sources of motivation, and they also work in different ways in doing a given task. Management must be aware of people's differences, and use this awareness to optimize their abilities and inclinations. Humans are not a mere society of ants carrying on a genetic program, in spite of B.F. Skinner's work on behaviorism, and more recently, E.O. Wilson's work on sociobiology. A more realistic view is that human society is based upon the achievements of the individuals, and is apt to end up in failure if the individual is made a cog in the organizational machine. Performance ratings of people according to fixed numeric targets are not consistent with psychology or knowledge about variation.

In the western culture of business, it is commonly thought that the primary responsibility of management is to create value for shareholders. Be that as it may, this should not be viewed as an objective unto itself since it cannot be achieved in a sustained way without a system view of the business. In the long run, the overall purpose of the system is to create value for everyone—shareholders, employees, customers, suppliers, community, and the environment. As Deming stated in the first of his 14 points, "constancy of purpose: to stay in business ever and forever ... to create jobs, and more jobs." Nonconstancy of purpose can spell doom for the organization in the long run.

The key to the creation of shareholder value rests most directly with continual creation of value for the customers. In return for the price charged for a product or service, a company must meet or exceed customers' expectations for that product or service. Delivering a quality product in terms of its design and manufacture is but one prerequisite for customer satisfaction. Other prerequisites include accessibility of the company to the customers before and after a sale, quality of order entry, tracking and billing, and timely and effective response to service requests. Quality can become a catalyst for value creation, and not merely a prerequisite, only if it is achieved as a whole rather than a few of its individual aspects.

> The key to the creation of shareholder value rests most directly with continual creation of value for the customers.

Examples

Six sigma is usually associated with the quality of manufacturing processes. One reason for this is the thought that basic quality characteristics of manufactured goods can be readily specified and measured. Traditionally, quality standards such as those of ANSI, ISO, or DIN originated in the production of physical goods. (Acronyms stand for American National Standards Institute (ANSI), International Organization for Standardization (ISO), and Deutsches Institut für Normung (DIN).) Yet, quality characteristics of most service products can also be identified and measured, albeit not quite as readily in some cases. A few examples are cited to emphasize this point

Retailing. There are a number of measures a retailer or reseller can utilize to track quality. These include the following. The quality of selection can be measured with the number of items and/or brands made available in each product category. Price competitiveness can be measured with the average deviation of its prices from its competitors by product. Accessibility of customer service can be measured with the number of customer calls received (via telephone, letters, e-mail, or through visits to its Internet site). Quality of customer service can be evaluated by the number of service requests processed, average time required for completion, and so on. Some of these data can be collected internally, but others must be gathered from external sources and through customer surveys. For example, price comparison data, which were difficult to obtain in the past, have become much more easily available from Internet-based sources. Some price reporting services on the Web routinely compare millions of prices each day, and make them immediately available to everyone, for free.

Insurance. An insurance company can measure the number of customizable policies it offers in each risk category, deviations of its prices from industry averages, average cycle times for claims settlement, number of disputed claims, and so on. It has become relatively easy to gather data on these and other measures in recent years.

Banking. A bank can measure the average processing time for different types of transactions, frequency of on-line account access by customers, number of processing errors, number of complaints received, number and duration of ATM breakdowns, and so on. The technology for handling banking transactions renders the collection of such data almost effortless today.

Health care. In the health care industry, it was long thought that the performance of providers (physicians, clinics, HMOs, hospitals) in delivering medical services was not readily amenable to quantifiable assessments of quality, but this is beginning to change. Recent efforts are producing specific criteria and measures for the quality of health care delivery processes and outcomes (Wilson and Goldschmidt 1995). These include technical criteria for assessing patients' health status improvement and patient satisfaction measures. With the increasing emphasis on controlling health care costs, without sacrificing quality, large health care providers are beginning to collect and track this kind of data on a regular basis.

These examples show that the measurement of quality includes service-based products, albeit the identification of specific quality measures for them may not be as obvious as those for manufactured goods. Development of useful metrics for quality of services offered by banking, insurance, communications, health care, and other organizations has been an important reason for enabling the quality revolution in the United States in recent years.

In addition to delivered products and services, a quality focus can also improve the internal administrative support systems in business and government organizations. As a case in point, consider the financial subsystem of a business organization. This subsystem aims to provide an accurate financial picture of the business, including the value created (for example, profitability) and the flow of funds over time or at any given instant. This subsystem was chosen not just because of its importance in the whole system, but also, it is not an area where six-sigma thinking has been commonly applied. As illustrated in Figure 3, the financial subsystem involves many functions and tasks that may not be apparent at first glance.

One interesting aspect of Figure 3 is that functions related to the creation of value in the top half of the picture are different from those related to keeping track of the flow of funds depicted in the bottom half. For example, accounting methods and procedures designed for accurate portrayal of costs (top) may not be the best methods for inventory valuation (bottom). Only recently has this basic observation led to the development of activity-based cost accounting (Cooper and Kaplan 1988), and its generalization, activity-based management (ABM).

A second interesting aspect of Figure 3 is the close connectivity between financial support functions and those that directly involve the production of

In the health care industry, it was long thought that the performance of providers in delivering medical services was not readily amenable to quantifiable assessments of quality, but this is beginning to change.

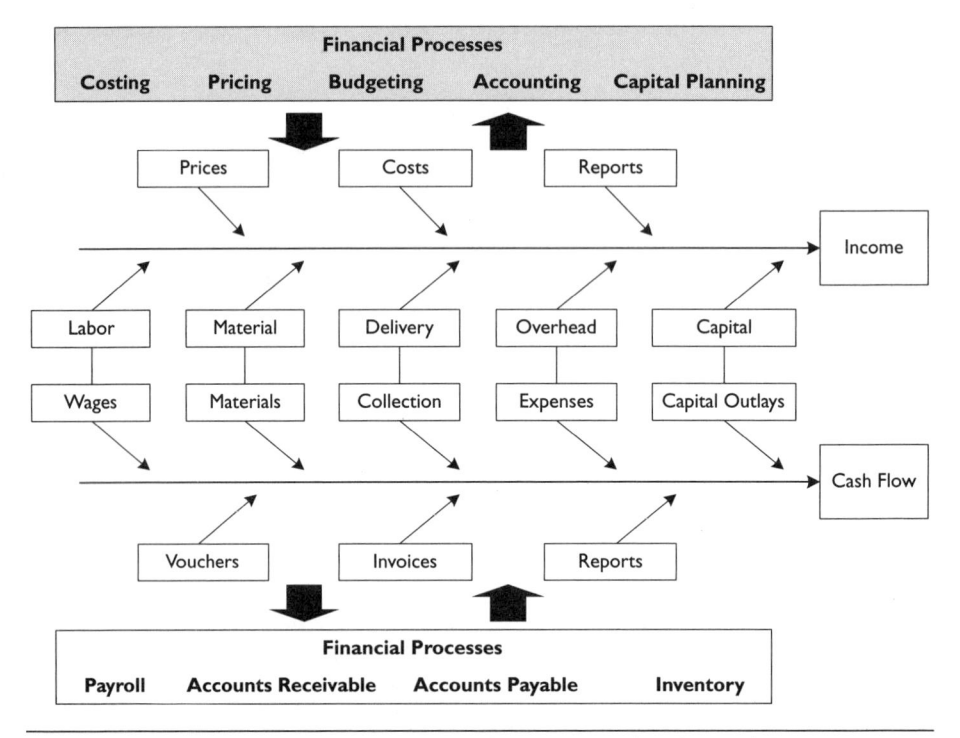

Figure 3. **Financial subsystem of a business organization, with processes that are closely connected to the production of goods and services**

goods or services, such as the use of labor and materials. Since the outputs of the subsystem (various financial statements and reports) are used internally as well as externally to judge operational performance, it is clear that quality of those outputs can have a major impact on the success of the overall system. Bad quality in financial processes can negate otherwise good quality in products or services. Robust financial processes can help focus improvement activities in the right areas, including customer- and supplier-related processes (for example, invoicing and logistics). Application of six-sigma thinking to financial processes can thus help in creating more value. It can also streamline the financial system, which will positively impact things such as more timely month-end closings, more accurate financial performance forecasts, less management of variances, improved working capital, and so on.

Quality Data and Data Quality

Quality management ideas and tools that are often associated with products are also applicable to services as well as internal administrative processes. Concepts such as quality of design and quality of conformance, and tools for attaining them, can be used to improve internal processes. For example, quality function deployment (QFD) techniques (Sullivan 1986; Hauser and Clausing 1988) can be employed in designing the outputs of financial processes, and six-sigma concept can help in maintaining a robust quality of conformance (Taguchi and Clausing 1990). Ultimate success in implementing these ideas rests with the capability to collect, track, and act upon high-quality data indicating the level and variability in quality.

Variability in business processes is caused by many factors involving people, methods, equipment, and software. These variability factors can be classified either as common (random, chance) factors that are uncontrollable or as specific factors that can be identified and controlled. Since six sigma requires the minimization of variability as much as possible, a reasonable (though not necessarily easy) approach is to try to identify and control the specific causes. This in turn requires the definition and documentation of processes, and subsequently, the quantification and tracking of important quality characteristics of the outputs (for example, frequency of errors and completion time needed).

It would be prudent to point out that the ability to describe and document a process does not guarantee an extraordinarily successful outcome. For example, it is not possible to ensure that an advertising campaign will be a huge winner, or that an R&D project will lead to a breakthrough product. As noted, uncontrollable chance factors preclude such guarantees. It is more important to ensure that processes are designed and implemented so that controllable factors are, in fact, controlled as much as possible. An advertising campaign can be effective without being a huge winner, or a new product can be successful without being a breakthrough product. Setting extraordinary success as a goal is not consistent with a thorough understanding of variability.

Failure modes and effects analysis (FMEA) is a technique that can be utilized to identify potentially high-risk failure mechanisms a process can experience, together with possible countermeasures to mitigate those risks in the future. To illustrate this, Table 1 shows some common failure modes and countermeasures for the nine major financial processes that were depicted in Figure 3. It is noted that a great majority of the countermeasures given in Table 1 involve the collection and tracking of accurate data about the process in each case. Along with the quality of performance in a process, this again brings forth the importance of the quality of data, and consequently, importance of an effective management information system.

Activity-based management (ABM) methods have been successfully utilized in numerous organizations for improved cost management by producing accurate cost data. ABM attempts to identify the specific activities that go into the production of goods or services, and allocates costs based on these activities. ABM techniques can also facilitate six-sigma quality efforts by identifying high-cost activities and help in setting priorities for process improvements. Some of the key actions associated with ABM and their outcomes are shown in Table 2. This diagram illustrates how the key items of information that emerge as a result of ABM studies can highlight the areas of focus for improve-

> Failure modes and effects analysis (FMEA) is a technique that can be utilized to identify potentially high-risk failure mechanisms a process can experience.

Process	Failure Modes	Effects	Countermeasures
Costing	• Inaccurate cost data • Inaccurate cost allocation • Lack of timeliness	• Inaccurate cost estimates • Cost information not available • Inaccurate report of income	• Collect and track accurate cost data • Activity-based cost allocation
Pricing	• Wrong pricing decisions • Wong timing	• Lost sales • Customer dissatisfaction	• Collect and track accurate cost data • Track market price trends
Budgeting	• Wrong budgets • Lack of timeliness	• Loss of control	• Collect and track budget data
Accounting	• Needed data not collected • Inaccuracies in data collected	• Inaccurate report of income • Inaccurate report of cash flow	• Establish criteria for capital decisions • Collect and analyze needs-related data (for example capacity usage)
Capital Planning	• Lack of need assessment • Lack of planning	• Impact on current profitability • Impact on current profitability	• Improved accuracy of data collection and entry • Improve accounting methods
Payroll	• Inaccurate payroll data • Mismatching of wages with work	• Employee dissatisfaction • Impact on shareholder concerns	• Wage/salary data collection • Trace and review wages and salaries
Accounts Receivable	• Invoicing errors • Lack of timeliness	• Customer dissatisfaction • Impact on cash flow	• Collect and track accuracy of invoicing data
Accounts Payable	• Payment errors • Lack of timeliness	• Supplier/vendor dissatisfaction	• Collect and track accuracy of voucher payments
Inventory	• Inaccurate data on inventory levels • Errots in inventory valuation	• Overstocks ot stockouts • Impact on profitability	• Collect and track inventory data

Table 1. **The use of failure mode and effects analysis (FMEA) in analyzing administrative financial support processes**

ment. It is seen that ABM can be helpful in prioritizing high-impact opportunities, and six-sigma tools could be used to improve those areas.

Of all quality-related data, ultimately the most important kinds come from the customers themselves. A simple questionnaire included with the delivery of a product or data gathered from customer service calls can provide a wealth of information about customer perceptions of quality. In order to provide truly useful data, however, questionnaires and other media must give the customers every opportunity to raise their concerns, problems, and suggestions. Questions can elicit apparently favorable responses without uncovering

ABM Action	Outcome	Benefits and Use
Execute detailed task analysis	• Tasks identified and clearly defined	• Eliminate redundant tasks • Better define required job skills • Better understand training needs • Eliminate nonvalue tasks • Task reengineering
Identify transactions that drive costs	• High-cost driver transactions identified • Source activities identified	
Determine costs associated with various activities	• High-cost activities identified • Better understandings of product cost	• Better pricing decisions
Identify areas of concentration	• High-cost areas identified • Priorities for improvement	• Efficiency improvement • Better investment/automation decisions • Cost reduction

Table 2. **Ways in which activity-based management (ABM) can help in quality and efficiency improvements**

serious problems. For example, asking a customer, "Were you treated courteously by our customer representative?" can elicit a positive response, but the customer may be thinking, "I should not have had to call in the first place!"

It is also important to get some feedback from potential customers who considered buying from a company, but chose to buy from competitors instead. This information is more difficult to obtain, and few companies make a serious attempt to get it. Since these customers comprise a large part of the market, it is well worth the effort to try to find out the reasons that made them buy elsewhere. Some Internet-based retailers, for example, ask the nonbuying visitors to their Web sites to write why they decided to shop elsewhere. This approach can also be used with shoppers at physical stores. To entice exiting shoppers to respond, reasonable incentives may be offered, such as a rebate coupon that can be redeemed with the next purchase. Even with a low response rate, this effort can produce extremely valuable information.

Conclusion

The main focus of this paper has been to show how six-sigma thinking can help improve the value-creation process, both in terms of products and services and administrative support processes. The paper has focused on two basic themes: (1) the connectivity of six-sigma thinking to the creation of value from a systems perspective, and (2) the importance of understanding variability and its sources in business processes.

The essence of six-sigma quality is the reduction of variability. To appreciate this, management must anticipate the inevitability of variability in all kinds of business processes, and make a long-term commitment to study, prioritize, and control it as much as possible. There are no magic tools that can guarantee the attainment of six-sigma quality, but it can be a useful guide to management even in situations where it is not entirely practical. Although different organizations can pursue it in different ways, its pursuit is indicative of a commitment to quality.

The fact that this paper did not focus on the cost of pursuing six-sigma quality is not to imply that the effort would be insignificant. It has been argued that the quality is free when the gains it provides and the losses it eliminates are taken into account (Crosby 1976). At least at the outset, however, the pursuit of six-sigma quality can amount to a significant investment whose payback period can be many years. Indeed, it would be more accurate to think of it as a long-run commitment—to customer satisfaction and the creation of value for all. In an era of unprecedented accessibility and nearly immediate availability of information in the marketplace, this kind of commitment is becoming a basic necessity for survival rather than a luxury or strategic advantage.

Paleontologists have observed an intriguing piece of evidence about the skull size of the early hominids: that their skull size stopped increasing about one hundred thousand years ago; the skull size had shown slow but continued growth in the prior quarter of a million years. A simple nonholistic linear theory would have suggested that this would be a disadvantage for the survival of the species; but the facts are precisely the opposite. In this period, Homo sapiens made their greatest strides—development of early languages, signs, paintings, culture, and socialization. The question is if information processing is so important and brain size is related to the ability of the amount of information processing, why are important advances not related to further increase in brain size? Though the answer is not clear, one possible answer goes like this (Mayr 1998, 240). Primitive humans lived in troops (just like chimpanzees do today), and troop size increased around this time. Once larger troops became the norm, reproductive advantages of the few (better endowed) members were lessened, gene flow among all members increased, and those with smaller brains enjoyed more protection, longer survival, and better reproductive success. Consequently, the increased social interaction of humans, while contributing greatly to cultural evolution, might have caused them to enter a period of stasis of the genome growth for skull size.

This scenario has much to offer in the discussion of systems in general. The system was better off when optimized for survival and growth even though the individuals within the system were not optimized for skull size and information processing ability. Although individuals could process less information (than if the brain size continued to increase), the group as a whole processed information more effectively, and as a result, increased its chances of further success (as if a serial computer was exchanged with a parallel computer). The Homo sapiens species became more robust through engaging all its members in its cause for survival, not just a few members, and so would a business organization.

References

Bertalanffy, L. von. 1968. *General system theory.* New York: George Braziller.

Cooper, R., and R.S. Kaplan. 1988. Measure costs right; make the right decisions. *Harvard Business Review 66,* 5: 96-103.

Crosby, R.B. 1976. *Quality is free.* New York: McGraw-Hill.

Deming, W.E. 1982. *Out of the crisis.* Cambridge, Mass.: Massachusetts Institute of Technology, Center for Advanced Engineering Study.

———. 1994. *The new economics.* Cambridge, Mass.: Massachusetts Institute of Technology, Center for Advanced Engineering Study.

Evans, J.R., and W.M. Lindsay. 1996. *The management and control of quality,* 3rd edition. St. Paul, Minn.: West Publishing.

Forrester, J.W. 1972. *Limits to growth.* Cambridge, Mass.: MIT Press.

———. 1980. *Systems dynamics.* Amsterdam: North Holland.

Hauser, J.R., and D. Clausing. 1988. The house of quality. *Harvard Business Review 66,* 3: 63-73.

Mayr, E. 1998. *This is biology.* Reprint edition. Cambridge, Mass.: Harvard University Press.

Senge, P.M. 1990. *The fifth discipline.* New York: Currency Doubleday.

Sullivan, L.R. 1986. Quality function deployment. *Quality Progress* 19, 6: 39-50.

Taguchi, G., and D. Clausing. 1990. Robust quality. *Harvard Business Review* 68, 1: 65-75.

Wilson, L., and P. Goldschmidt. 1995. *Quality management in health care.* New York: McGraw-Hill.

Mustafa R. Yilmaz is professor of management science in the College of Business Administration at Northeastern University, myilmaz@neu.edu.

Sangit Chatterjee is professor of management science in the College of Business Administration at Northeastern University, s.chatterjee@neu.edu.

Quality Tools and Techniques

E-COMMERCE

Catalyst for Collaboration

John Teresko

E-commerce, doing business using the Internet, has been widely adopted by nearly all businesses today. It is a tool for improving processes, communication, and connecting with customers. This article looks at e-commerce from the perspective of manufacturing exchanges, electronic marketplaces that simplify and reduce costs in the procurement of supplies. Such exchanges also have the potential of facilitating collaboration, as this article documents.

James Heppelmann thinks trading exchanges are the next big Internet opportunity. But it is not the buying or selling that has this executive at Parametric Technology Corp. (PTC) excited. It's the use of exchanges as a powerful strategic tool to improve product development and shorten time-to-market. "As exchanges develop new ways to link companies together, they are coming to represent the ideal platform to enable the B2B business processes that both precede and follow procurement, namely collaborative activities within the design and supply chain," says Heppelmann, executive vice president and general manager of Windchill Solutions, a unit of PTC.

He sees the procurement function, today's dominant exchange focus, as far short of its strategic potential. "I think that if you look at procurement and supply-chain management, and even ERP, to some extent these initiatives are all about improving the efficiency of a business—cutting costs, taking costs out of the business. That approach is good for the expense line, but it isn't actually doing much for the revenue line.

Reprinted with permission from *Industry Week*, February 12, 2001. Copyright © 2001 Penton Media. All rights reserved.

"Consider a company that invested in business-to-business exchanges for procurement and supply-chain management," Heppelmann continues. "Maybe in the last few years it finished a global ERP implementation. It should be in position to dominate, but if its products aren't competitive, all those implementations are sort of irrelevant. I think that people are realizing, even after they and their competitors have done the [exchange] procurement thing, that everyone is back at parity again. After all that effort, they missed the real question of 'whose products are better?'"

Heppelmann notes that manufacturing history is replete with competitive skirmishes where optimized business processes lose the market battle with those that compete with optimized products. He cites Motorola Inc. and its ongoing cellular phone battles as an example. "They once owned the business of analog phones, but lagged Nokia, Ericsson, and others in bringing digital models to market." The customer tends to "vote" on the tangibles of a product, he notes.

Of course, it is more than coincidence that this viewpoint comes from a firm that positions itself as a product-development company. But he's not alone in his thinking. "The major software-solution providers, whether in product development or enterprise resource planning, are seizing the opportunity to add value to the exchange phenomenon," says Arthur B. Sculley, partner, Sculley Brothers LLC, New York, and co-author with W. William A. Woods of *B2B Exchanges* (2000, ISI Publications Ltd.; 2001, HarperBusiness). Sculley says the future success of the exchange phenomenon depends on an evolution beyond providing an efficient means of buying or selling products or services. "The successful independent exchanges will have a whole series of other products and services."

But for most manufacturing companies, building a corporate strategy around exchange collaboration is not a priority. In a survey by AMR Research Inc., Boston, participants were asked to list 10 exchange capabilities in descending order of importance. "Collaboration was last on that list," says AMR's John Fontanella, service director, B2B marketplaces. But that may change. "I think when we take this survey again a year from now, product design will rise in the standings as people become more educated and more comfortable with the concept of an exchange. The other ingredient will be the emergence of supporting applications." At the top of the wish list is product search capability, followed by order status/tracking, product catalogs, vendor search capability, and supplier/buyer back-end integration.

Fontanella believes exchanges will be an especially cost-effective route to the benefits of collaboration. "Supporting technology can be expensive and the exchange [model] is a way to spread the cost. If you are a large company buying components from many different vendors, you can have one application to support many different component buyers and the component-engineering organization. And your suppliers can use the same application rather than having to go out and purchase it."

> I think that if you look at procurement and supply-chain management, and even ERP, to some extent these initiatives are all about improving the efficiency of a business—cutting costs, taking costs out of the business.

The challenge is today's relentless focus on the buyer-club kind of approach, says Joe Malloni, director of corporate strategic marketing, Structural Dynamics Research Corp. (SDRC), Milford, Ohio. The current fascination with procurement efficiencies is natural—it represents the "low-hanging fruit" of opportunity, says Stephen M. Ward Jr., general manager, global industry sector, IBM Corp., White Plains, N.Y. He says IBM, which buys $40 billion worth of goods annually, avoids $1 billion in expense by using the Internet. "But I think that the ultimate goal for exchanges is not to try to squeeze another nickel out of every supplier," Ward observes. "It's to find ways to use the phenomenon to increase the closeness of the supplier."

One example he emphasizes is design collaboration. Another is the simplification exchanges can put in place for suppliers. "Today suppliers have to contend with EDI transactions complicated by differing formats, numbering schemes, often requiring a lot of manual effort."

On design collaboration, SDRC's Malloni is hopeful. "The consensus on exchanges is starting to shift from seeking tactical benefits [procurement efficiencies alone] to setting revenue-producing strategies," he adds.

The trouble with focusing on pricing advantages is that it limits the benefits of exchanges to indirect goods such as office and factory supplies and other commodities, explains Heppelmann. In industries such as automotive, indirect goods account for a mere 14% of procurement expenditures, while direct commodity goods add only 20% more. The remaining 66% of total procurement dollars falls into yet another category beyond the reach of dynamic pricing: direct-engineered goods that are custom-designed through a collaborative-design-chain process involving both the buyer and the supplier (and potentially a network of others). Heppelmann wryly points out that it is difficult to hold a reverse auction to procure a part that has not yet been designed.

Enhancing the Design Process

The need for collaboration in what Waltham, Mass.-based PTC calls the design chain also is being driven by the ubiquitous trend toward outsourcing everything but a manufacturer's core competency. Volkswagen AG is an example cited by PTC's Bill Berutti, senior vice president, sales. "We learned that 80% of one VW model was designed in cooperation with suppliers. Our conclusion is that the whole idea of using exchanges to interact with suppliers has more to do with the design process, rather than just refreshing inventory. Design, the most important function of a manufacturing company, now becomes a B2B fundamental."

The development process is no longer a group of engineers inside a company designing a product completely by themselves, Berutti points out. It is now a chain of people in a multitiered supply chain that have the development responsibility. "In order to be competitive," he says, "such companies need to be able to comprehensively address the potential of that design process. The first reason is that the design process determines how quickly they bring products to market. The second is that the design chain determines whether they bring the right product to market. Last, but not least, is the fact that a tremendous amount of the cost of a finished good—some say as much as 80%—is committed in the design process." Another factor contributing to the design-chain imperative is the globalization of manufacturing, where companies around the world may contribute to a design concept on virtually a 24/7 basis.

With so much at stake, *Industry Week* asked Heppelmann's advice on how beginners should get involved with exchanges. "If you're looking for a breakthrough strategy, a significant advantage vis-à-vis your competition, look at the possibilities for collaboration via the design chain." (He defines the design chain as the early part of the supply chain where the focus is on intellectual property rather than physical property, which happens later.) "You can quickly get and incorporate the latest, greatest ideas of suppliers to maximize the most profitable part of the product's life cycle when the maker has a monopoly on unique features that result in a compelling product," he explains. "Would you rather chase expense reductions or revenue generation?"

PTC's ability to deliver its just-introduced design-chain solution—Windchill Netmarkets—can be traced to the company's acquisition of rival Computervision Corp. in 1997. At that time Heppelmann had started Windchill, with majority funding by Computervision. Today the Windchill initiative is a wholly owned business unit of PTC. At its genesis the product was positioned as a solution for Internet/intranet collaboration within enterprises, says Heppelmann. Today Windchill Netmarkets is focused on providing a collaborative solution for consortia, independent, and private exchange models. "Some companies will buy it for internal use, but the intent is to offer a collaborative capability that breaks down the enterprise, geographical, and system boundaries that exist among design-chain partners," he adds.

An early private-exchange adopter is SKF AB, Göteborg, Sweden, a global manufacturer of bearings and other products with more than 80 locations in 22 countries. The company is using Netmarkets to get closer to customers by participating in their design activity via the Internet. Heppelmann says Netmarkets makes it possible for SKF engineers to join the customer's design team. "Netmarkets is also making it possible for SKF customers to go online and collaborate on custom configurations." Adds Richard Olivecrona, group IT strategist at SKF: "Getting closer to our strategic customers and partners is critical to our transformation into a responsive, value-added solution provider. The creation of this private exchange is central to achieving this strategy."

Among independent exchanges, Conferos (originally BuyPlastics.com), Cambridge, Mass., is using Netmarkets to provide design-chain collaboration for the plastics industry. Heppelmann explains that bringing a plastic part to market generally requires collaboration among the company that designs the

If you're looking for a breakthrough strategy, a significant advantage vis-à-vis your competition, look at the possibilities for collaboration via the design chain.

part, another that designs the mold and production process, a third that provides the resin, and the customer. With Netmarkets the result is an e-community where the walls that separated partners no longer exist. "In yesterday's marketplace, OEMs were forced to select plastics processors and service providers from incongruent networks," says Chuck Hoar, president of Conferos.

Clearly the challenge for manufacturers is to understand how the collaborative potential of exchanges could add strategic revenue-producing value to the procurement benefits. The trick is to achieve that understanding in advance of competitors.

For solution and infrastructure providers, the race is on to provide new value and seamless integration for users. For example, PTC's Heppelmann says peer-to-peer (P2P) technology is beginning to impact exchanges. In the second quarter, Netmarkets will be both Web- and P2P-based (Web-based to collect, aggregate, and configure a repository of intellectual property, and P2P-based in the sense of co-authoring, reviewing, and actually generating that intellectual property in real time). PTC will implement the P2P platform from Groove Networks, Beverly, Mass., a start-up by Ray Ozzie, a founder of Lotus Notes.

Also in the P2P market space is start-up Oculus Technologies Corp., Boston. Born from the brain trust of the Massachusetts Institute of Technology's CADlab, Oculus is designed to do more for exchanges than simply facilitate collaboration, says Christopher Williams, president. The software permits the propagation of data changes rather than just notification of data changes. "For example, link with a supplier and when a change is made, the supplier sees that in real time as opposed to everyone receiving an e-mail at the same time." Williams stresses security. "To minimize the risk to intellectual property Oculus allows users to share only individual data points." He also emphasizes ease of use. "The software will be familiar to anyone who has used a Web browser. Current solutions require either more steps or a centralized architecture. Oculus offers the benefits of a decentralized system."

As manufacturing companies struggle to understand the evolving impact of trading exchanges, they ultimately must come to terms with a new business model that cannot be avoided. More than a technological phenomenon, exchanges should be viewed as the next step in the evolution of business. The result: a new way of sustaining competitiveness, profitability, and growth by collaborating to provide value to customers.

John Teresko is Senior Technology Editor for Industry Week. *E-mail him at jteresko@industryweek.com.*

Developing Your Company's New E-Business

Ava S. Butler

Every type of company has embraced the Internet to facilitate business processes, but getting started in some companies is problematic at best. This article examines ways to successfully launch an e-business initiative without making too many mistakes along the way. The author notes that those companies that excel at the basics of change management are most likely to successfully integrate e-initiatives.

Traditional change efforts simply don't work anymore. The speed of today's business environment means companies must replace sequential change processes with parallel processing. That is, organizations must create strategy, build business and technical architectures, and develop new cultures, skills, and measures simultaneously. Strategy requires experimentation rather than months of analysis.

But the move into a world of lightening-fast decision making, risk taking, and instant alliances is a difficult prospect, especially for traditional firms. They approach e-business with an existing corporate culture, a long history of how things are done, and, too often, with a "just do something" mentality.

E-business success is the new world order in business today. To ensure success, a company's commitment to an e-business initiative needs to be strong and clear in many vital respects—in its e-business leadership, roles and responsibilities, cross-functional interdependencies, budget matters, and management structure.

The need to manage corporate change is not a revolutionary concept. It's the speed of change on all levels and the possibilities that new technology provides that present new challenges and demands. Despite the challenges, however, there are ways to make an e-initiative work from within a well-established company.

Have a Clear, Well-Coordinated Starting Point

Because brick-and-mortar companies know they must "do something 'e' quickly"' they often adopt a scattershot approach. Well-intentioned initiatives are started on many levels of the organization, and in many divisions, departments, and regions. People with an interest in e-business do things on their own time. Unfortunately, these initiatives rarely add up to anything strategic, and often do not link together in the eyes of the customer in any way.

> Companies still fall into the trap of believing that knowing something is as good as doing something about it.

Companies still fall into the trap of believing that knowing something is as good as doing something about it. Now more than ever, clearly agreeing where to start, what results to expect, and in what timeframe is key to long-term success. Although head office, centralized efforts might be perceived as bureaucratic and bothersome, this is a time when a clear corporate plan is helpful.

Schneider Electric NA is one company that was early to embrace technology as a way to increase competitive advantage. Bob Ciurczak has been their Director of e-Business since 1997. "Time-box everything, and phase the work in no longer than 90-day increments," he advises. "Tight time-frames help decision makers set priorities, allow the team to focus on clear objectives, and prevent scope creep. New ideas are documented for prioritization in next steps."

Align and Educate Your Leadership and Management Teams

Some organizations have well-aligned executive teams. Many do not. A lack of alignment on strategic direction can be fatal to an e-initiative, because it heightens difficulties in making decisions, implementing change, and working across existing functional, geographical, and company boundaries. Therefore, leaders need to be "lead learners," challenging their own thinking and the thinking of those around them, looking for new business opportunities and new alliances, and learning about their business world outside traditional boundaries.

Bob Ciurczak points out that "e-business impacts everyone in the organization. We started by building Web sites, now 'e' is integrated into every part of our business. Executives need to be clear about why we are doing what we are doing, communicate the value throughout the organization, and follow up to ensure results. They need to have a solid understanding of the rapidly changing capabilities for technology. We have to be willing to 'burn the boats' in order to keep our competitive advantages. That doesn't happen without clear, aligned commitment from the top."

Establish a Cross-Functional Project Team

Most traditional companies that want to jumpstart their e-business find that creating a dedicated team of people produces the quickest success. Project teams consolidate new ideas, manage pilots and full implementation, and coordinate efforts between parts of the organization. As the organization becomes more sophisticated at managing success in the e-world, project teams may migrate to an entirely separate business unit or can become integrated into "business as usual."

Executive guidance and "air cover" for the team is essential. Most employees are politically astute enough to know when a project is perceived as "mission critical" and when it is perceived as a loser. Staying top of mind is the critical differentiator between the two, and executive steering teams to provide that differentiation.

Kevin Roper, General Manager for North America Systems, and Dave Davenport, V.P. Product Marketing, have both played a critical role in BancTec's e-initiatives. They suggest: "The quicker you can get a project team together, the better. Once the organization's leaders have made some initial decisions, you want to maximize momentum. Project teams are the most effective way to get things done. 100% dedication allows people to focus on a single objective without having to balance other daily activities."

Choose Project Leaders Carefully

Leaders chosen to launch e-initiatives must walk a tightrope between being entrepreneurs and "company men." They need an intimate understanding of how the business works, and they must constantly challenge the status quo.

They also need organizational credibility and an appreciation for the technical issues at hand. Think of your high flyers—the next generation of leaders—and get one of the best to lead your efforts. Look for the busiest person, not someone who has nothing to do. Choose someone who "gets it" and believes passionately in it. This is the person who will work most closely with the executives.

> It's important to select team members who are optimistic and enthusiastic about e-endeavors, people who naturally see the glass as half-full rather than half-empty.

Choose Team Members Wisely

Most traditional companies are understandably risk-averse. That can explain why change initiatives sometimes have under-performed or, even worse, been counterproductive. If they've experienced such failures in the past, project team members can feel there is a personal risk to their involvement. It's important, then, to select team members who are optimistic and enthusiastic about e-endeavors, people who naturally see the glass as half-full rather than half-empty. Like the project leader you choose, they must "get it" and believe passionately that the world is changing and they want to be part of it.

Ideal e-team members will exhibit leadership qualities, creativity, strong interpersonal skills, and an ability to influence co-workers and bosses. They have a passion for learning and can work in cross-functional teams. You want team members who have the ability and willingness to build upon their own skill sets by working with those who see the world differently than they do. The type of person who does not enjoy experimenting and working with ambiguity, challenging existing beliefs, and at a frenetic pace will not be comfortable.

Bob Ciurczak finds superior teamwork fundamental to Schneider Electric's success. "A strong e-business team is like a baseball team. You don't want a bunch of pitchers and no outfielders. You need a balanced team, with individuals whose unique skills combined can get the job done. The full-time team is with you all day, every day. However, you will also need strong part-time help from throughout the organization. Like the relief pitcher, they don't come to every meeting, don't play in every game, but they're there when you need them."

Often it's a good idea to seed the team with one or two people from the outside the firm—either new hires or consultants. Newcomers alone would find it difficult to work effectively. They won't know the existing organization well enough. But well-placed infusions of new perspectives and competencies will decrease the learning curve and accelerate results.

> Often it's a good idea to seed the team with one or two people from the outside the firm—either new hires or consultants.

Ensure That Communication on the Why, What, and How Is Clear

Alignment and clear communication of shared goals will go a long way to breaking through the inevitable barriers to success. Let managers know their role in overcoming functional barriers, such as freeing up resources and making quick decisions to address problems within their areas.

John Alexander, CIO with Aventis Pasteur USA, heads up their global e-commerce group. He believes: "Resistance comes not so much from leaders saying 'it's not my idea' as from the fact that everyone is very busy running their day-to-day businesses. One has to create a sense of urgency, from the chairman down. Our leaders see the potential, but it's hard to quantify. They know we have to be there, and they see e-business as a revenue generator, but we don't know what quantifiable results we can expect. Consequently, it's hard for them to see how technological solutions and new ways of working will help them meet their bottom-line deliverables in the short term. Face-to-face meetings are difficult when you work for a global firm, but the personal contact is key to success."

Communicating to the organization takes on special challenges too. Because today's e-business world is highly experimental, answering specific questions will be more difficult than ever. Employees have high expectations and often are more aware of the possibilities than their leaders. They know that speed is critical, and they expect fast action on the part of their employer. Before large-scale communications begin, make sure leaders agree on the way forward, have a common story to tell, and can answer likely questions consistently.

Knowing how changes are likely to affect individual groups will help you plan how to communicate with and involve each group:

- *Customer service representatives* usually see technological advances as a way to get rid of the mundane, a way to add more value to the customer. Most welcome the opportunity to have more interesting jobs and provide better service to their customers.
- *Traditional sales people* face radical changes. As technology becomes integral to the sales process, most will stop acting as order takers and will likely take on more of a consultant role. This requires new skills, new bonus structures, and new ways of working, none of which happen successfully without careful nurturing.
- *Distributors* are among the most threatened. Disintermediation scares them, and rightly so. Long-term partnerships along traditional channels are dissolving daily. Here communications need to be based on honesty and the focus of the company's future plans.
- *Customers* are usually excited about changes. They have everything to gain. Many traditional firms had little direct contact with their customers. John Alexander outlines a simple but powerful truth: "Don't think you're smarter than they are. Ask for their feedback regularly and then quickly do something about it."

Clarify Budgets

The budgets of e-initiatives at traditional companies are usually subsumed under someone else's existing budget, departmental or otherwise. Inevitably, questions arise about whether certain expenditures for e-projects are necessary, and the nimbleness of the e-team suffers tremendously as a result. This is most difficult when departments or functions do not already work together seamlessly.

Bob Ciurczak explains, "At Schneider Electric, we have a set amount of money set aside for innovations. The initial budget for innovations falls within the e-business unit, but as the idea moves from a test to a way of doing business, the budget moves to those responsible for ongoing success. When the value to the business is clear, who is going to pay for it quickly takes a back seat. We look for wins that will fund further initiatives."

Infrastructure costs are significant for those who have to update legacy systems. Executives often have sticker shock over the costs involved just to get and stay in the game. Anticipate the costs early. Plan how best to maximize value and use across the business. Once again, a centralized, integrated approach pays off. Independent decisions across functions and geographies rarely fit together seamlessly without careful planning.

Consciously Build a High-Performing Team

None of the foregoing will guarantee that your teams will achieve the high levels of performance necessary to get the quick and sustainable results. Ensure that each individual, as well as the team as a whole, has a clear sense of purpose and urgency.

Establish clear roles and responsibilities. Communicate these roles to the team and people throughout the organization who will be interacting with the team. Make it clear what level of decision making and communication is accepted and expected. Very bureaucratic or hierarchical organizations will have special obstacles to overcome in order to become nimble.

Don't assume that existing cultural values and norms will ensure success within your new group. In fact, existing cultures can inhibit success. Work together to consciously challenge existing ways of working and, where appropriate, establish new approaches and new monitoring systems.

People who have never worked together before need to take the time to build strong working relationships. Strong biases (IT people don't understand the business, the head office doesn't understand the customer, etc.) can run across traditional lines. A sure way to break through these traditional lines is to work side by side toward a common goal, in an environment that thrives on coming up with better solutions by understanding all aspects of the issue.

Jean Gonzales, Program Manager from US WEST Wireless Data Browse Now launch team, notes: "When we started designing our new product, customer service, marketing, and systems rarely met to agree a successful solution. We had to pave new ground, and it was painful at times. But within a few months, we understood the ramifications that a change in one area had on other areas. Now we check with each other before one department acts. The results are better for the customer and less aggravation for us."

When cross-functional teams work together, they learn from each other. Knowledge and skills are built daily, and in a "just-in-time" manner. When there is a passion for understanding the customer and exceeding customer expectations—both inside and outside the organization—people stretch beyond traditional boundaries.

Skeptics feel that team building takes too much time. When done properly, it saves time and creates an atmosphere of success. When team members take pride in their personal contribution to the organization's future, others sense it and want to be involved too. The word gets out that something important is happening.

Recognize and Reward Performance

Reward and recognition practices must support the e-initiative goals. Establish strong links to existing performance review processes. Make sure that measures of performance count in the larger picture of career planning, leadership development, bonus systems, and pay scales.

And don't forget the power of a "thank you" or recognition letter. Bob Ciurczak speaks to an example from Schneider Electric: "Every member of one of our initiative teams received a letter thanking them for their contribution both in the project and the company's overall success. It was signed by all 21 of our top executives. Most members of that team have the letter framed and displayed in their work area. That kind of recognition not only makes team members proud of their efforts, but it also helps get employees interested in participating in the next initiative involving their part of the organization."

Document Lessons Learned

Because of the highly experimental nature of the new e-world and the increasing importance of speed, learning becomes more important than ever. Learning means making mistakes and unexpected discoveries. Lessons are continually learned in many categories, including customer satisfaction, product and process innovations, and organizational change. Being able to access information from other projects and create links between them helps ensure you don't make the same mistakes twice.

The challenge is creating an easy-to-use format for documenting learnings. Company intranets work well, as long as they are accessible to the right alliance partners, and in a format people can understand. However, most team members do not rely only on technological formats. They want to talk to real people, who can guide and coach them. Establishing a network of coaches is an excellent augmentation to written materials. Determine which of these methods will work best in your organization.

BancTec's Roper and Davenport note: "Learning not only sparks new ideas, but we also find ourselves consistently refining our existing ideas. Our level of sophistication is much greater now, with a far more compelling solution for the customer. Initially we were deciding whether or not a solution was appropriate for electronic media—yes or no. Now we find ourselves refining the ideas in much greater detail, adding nuances and features we never considered—and value! We find that consistent team membership increases our learning as a group, helping drive new ideas to greater maturity faster. Right now, person-to-person interaction is the appropriate learning model for us. As we grow, we'll need more structure. Our learning models are growing alongside our e-initiatives."

> Because of the highly experimental nature of the new e-world and the increasing importance of speed, learning becomes more important than ever.

Learn from Previous Change Initiatives

Every established organization has been through several change initiatives. Quality improvement, re-engineering, downsizing, globalization, mergers and acquisitions, and ERP systems are just a few of the likely subjects of comparison.

If past change efforts have been handled well in your organization and are perceived as good, employees are likely to embrace the movement into this new era of innovation. Unfortunately, many organizations have handled change poorly: it hasn't lasted; it meant layoffs that were handled poorly; it meant hassles with little payback. It comes as no surprise that skepticism is high in such groups. The surprise is that organizations tend to make the same mistakes over and over.

Plan How to Ease Team Members Back into the Organization

When team members have completed their project work, they have new ways of working, capabilities, insights, and enthusiasm. Going back to their old jobs is difficult, and being left with no place to go, either mentally or physically, is even worse. The longer the project is, the more likely it is that the person could get lost in the system. Careful planning about team members' next career moves prevents your firm from losing newly developed talent.

Conclusion

These 12 tips can help your company successfully implement e-initiatives from within. Well-designed, strategic initiatives send a consistent and positive message to customers, alliance partners, and employees. They equip your organization to move with greater speed and agility than before. Relevant not only to your e-initiatives, these ideas will also support the implementation of all your corporate strategies. Remembering the fundamentals of working with people can make all the difference.

Ava S. Butler, M.A., is a principal with Cap Gemini Ernst & Young, specializing in addressing the leadership and organizational requirements for success in the e-world. She can be reached at abutler@usa.geminiconsulting.com.

Start Your Own Net Market

Anne Field

Net markets are relatively new to the business scene, yet they've changed a lot in two years. This article presents the essence of what an organization needs to know now to build a successful private electronic market, with lessons learned, advice, and warnings. In other words, nothing theoretical here, just practical advice on this new channel for connecting with customers.

Mother, please, I'd rather do it myself. Ever get that feeling when reading about Net markets? You understand your industry. You know what both sides of the transaction equation need. You're even somewhat conversant in the in's and out's of the various technologies. "Hey," you may think, "I could start one of these markets on my own."

There's just one catch: since Net markets first burst onto the scene two years ago, many of the rules of the game have changed. Here's what you need to know now to build a successful private electronic market.

1. Hot Spots and Services

The first step hasn't changed much since the early days. It's pretty straightforward. "Figure out where the weak points are in your industry and then how an electronic marketplace can improve the life of buyers and sellers," says David Yockelson, a director of the META Group, a market research firm in Stamford, Conn. First make sure your industry is actually ripe for a marketplace. That's usually true in cases where the purchasing process is highly inefficient or the industry is highly fragmented; but not too fragmented, of course. Otherwise, you'll have a hard time signing on the few influential buyers and sellers that are likely to bring the rest of the pack on board with them.

What's different these days is the matter of quantity. Most big industries, and even many niches, are already teeming with competitors. The result: your market needs to be appreciably different from what's out there already.

How do you stand out from the crowd? The answer lies in three little words: value-added services. Indeed, "it's not enough anymore just to give

Reprinted with permission of the author from *iSource Business*, March 2001. Copyright © 2001 Anne Field. All rights reserved.

someone the ability to locate and pay for goods or find something at a better price," says Ken Crafford, CTO of FutureNext Consulting, a McLean, Va.-based firm that advises Net markets. Instead, you have to offer lots of other features, anything from arranging credit to assisting with shipping. (That's also because companies are finding it harder to make money the old way—through transaction fees. By offering services you provide another, more effective approach.)

USBuild (www.usbuild.com) is a case in point. Aimed at buyers and sellers of materials for home construction, it focuses on a key aspect of the process: scheduling the shipping of products to make sure all the goods that are procured show up when a contractor really needs them, not a day earlier or later. Or consider Online Asset Exchange (www.onlineassetexchange.com), an exchange for buyers and sellers of used equipment. It does everything from inspecting the machinery and conducting appraisals for banks to arranging to get quotes from shippers and offering escrow services. "We're a one-stop shop," says Executive Vice President Norm Bastin.

In fact lots of existing companies are repositioning themselves, changing their focus away from being a vehicle for electronic procurement. Some don't even want to be called a Net market; the term of the moment is "enabler." Consider Chicago-based fob.com, which started out two years ago as a market for the chemical industry. What happened? The founders discovered that buyers weren't all that interested in an Internet-based way to buy materials, since 90 percent of chemicals are bought on contract. Instead what they needed was a method for managing such parts of the process as order entry and fulfillment. So, recently, they changed their business model to emphasize those features.

In addition, say the experts, there's another wrinkle: not just providing services, but making sure those services grab the customer "as early in the food chain as possible," says FutureNext's Crafford. That means you need to offer features that get buyers involved in the initial stages of the buying cycle. First, you'll reduce the likelihood that that they'll go to a competitor. Second, you'll reduce your expenses. "The cost of acquiring new customers goes up the further along they are in the purchasing cycle," says Crafford.

2. The Right Stuff

Your business will probably still be about hooking up buyers and sellers in some way. And, that's your next challenge—pinpointing just what structure, or market mechanism, you will implement. Should you, for example, build a catalog-like system through which buyers get easy access to an aggregation of catalogs from different suppliers? Or should you consider an exchange where buyers and sellers trade commodities, negotiating prices through a bid-and-ask system? Or an auction which lets buyers bid against each other for goods?

The answer, in part, hasn't changed. Catalogs are generally better suited to buyers who are looking for specific products that are hard to find in one fell swoop. Auctions tend to work with surplus goods, like industrial equipment for manufacturing, and exchanges for commodities where the decision about to whether to buy a product, like wheat, depends on just a few, straightforward factors.

It sounds simple enough, but what many Net market operators didn't realize at first was how important it would be to make the structure fit the actual behavior of the industry in question. In other words, you can't shoehorn buyers and sellers into accepting a system that runs counter to their usual *modus operandi*. "A lot of early marketplaces didn't understand how difficult it would be for an industry to adopt a different type of platform from the one they were using in the real world," says Dan Nissanoff, CEO of Free Trade Zone (www.freetradezone.com), a marketplace for electronic components. A company buying complex machinery, for example, won't take easily to an exchange system. Another unanticipated complication: suppliers' reactions. Sellers haven't responded favorably to certain market mechanisms, particularly reverse auctions, where, says META Group's Yockelson, "They've realized it doesn't behoove them in every case to allow prices to go down to their lowest level." The moral: think twice before plunging into a structure that might meet with a lot of supplier hesitation.

Perhaps the biggest lessons from which you can benefit have been those related to catalogs, where operators faced unexpected, technical challenges. With hundreds of sellers and constantly changing prices, offerings and availability, "There are a lot balls in the air to juggle—a lot more than anyone realized," says Tim Clark, senior analyst with Jupiter Research, a market research firm based in Los Altos, Calif. You'll not only have to devote a bigger chunk of your budget to coming up with the right technology, but you will also have to be prepared to make searching through the site easy. That means doing a lot of work upfront enhancing suppliers' catalogs—expanding product descriptions, organizing the structure of the information, and the like. "If it's cumbersome no one will use it," says Trey Simonton, executive vice-president of business development at ec-Content (now i2 Technologies, www.i2.com), a site aimed at construction, automotive after-market parts, and other manufacturing sectors, which also provides advice to other Net markets seeking help managing their content. Another challenge: convincing suppliers to come on board, and then to offer competitive pricing once they do. Simonton cites a fledgling company that hired ec-Content for advice after hitting a brick wall with important suppliers. Expecting to sign up hundreds of sellers in the first six months, they had only attracted about a dozen. Simonton's advice: start slow, cultivating a few, key relationships. "We advise that you start with three to five relationships, then build to 20, then to 100 in the first six months to a year," he says. He also helped them pinpoint the most important decision-makers in key suppliers' companies and the particular benefits to emphasize in their pitch. (For example the site would give them access to new customers, and the fact that the company, with $50 million in venture capi-

> It sounds simple enough, but what many Net market operators didn't realize at first was how important it would be to make the structure fit the actual behavior of the industry in question.

tal funding, was flush with cash.) The result: they were able to win a previously impenetrable key supplier.

3. The Backbone

Of course, your enterprise rests on a technological infrastructure. The big decision you'll face is whether or not to grow your own. Do you hire an expensive in-house IT staff to do the design, or do you outsource the job, possibly losing the critical element of control? It's a complex issue. These days it's possible to reduce internal development costs by using a wide assortment of off-the-shelf software that can be integrated and turned into a usable system. But by using the same stuff anyone else can buy, says the META Group's Yockelson, "You won't create a barrier to entry for competitors."

On the other hand, hiring outside developers and integrators can pose a lot of problems if you don't do it right. Consider SingleSource IT (www.ssit.com), which helps companies manage their IT assets. When the company first started a year ago, it hired outside consultants to do the development. In a hurry to get the system up and running, however, they didn't spend as much time planning out just what it was they wanted. As a result, their instructions to the developers weren't fully fleshed out—and the end result wasn't what Randy Wilcox, SingleSource IT's CEO, had in mind. "You have to spend time on the specs," says Wilcox. "If we'd done that, we might not have gotten up and running quicker, but the technology would have been better thought through."

4. Money Matters

Today paying for all this may be the biggest challenge. Before last April, venture capitalists were bending over backward to fund B2B companies—so much so that many Net markets were able to win $20 million infusions from just one firm. Since the stock market crash in Internet stocks, however, venture capital money for Net markets has slowed to a trickle. Still some venture capital is going to new Net markets. The big difference is that, if you can get any, you can expect them to go through a longer and more thorough due diligence—and to offer smaller chunks of money. Online Asset Exchange, for example, recently raised a second round of funding totaling $25 million, which was $60 million less than what they were expecting. What's more, although old-fashioned Net markets might be having a tough time, new-fangled "enablers" are in demand, and that is just one more reason why companies have recently started to rejigger their business models.

If you can't find venture funding, the likeliest alternative is to find a strategic partner—a supplier or buyer willing to make an equity stake. But tread carefully. Give away too much and you stand the chance of alienating your partner's competitors and, possibly, attracting the attention of the Federal Trade Commission. For that reason, when Bo Holland, CEO of Works.com, recently signed a deal with W.W. Grainger to make an equity investment in his company, he included in the contract steps that would keep it a minority stake. For example, their new investor can't buy shares in the company if it goes public. The bottom line: keep the total stake from suppliers to no more than 15 percent.

5. The Chicken and the Egg

Finally you'll have to face the basic conundrum of Net markets: Do you start by bringing in buyers hoping that they will lure sellers, or the other way around? The key is relatively simple: figure out where the power lies in your industry. Holland, for example, figured that for the small and midsize companies he wanted to serve, the influence lay with the sellers. So he made an effort to enlist big players like Dell Computer and W.W. Grainger. "They pulled in the customers," he says. At the same time, however, the answer also depends upon the particular relationships you have. Wilcox, for example, had started as a computer reseller and knew lots of suppliers. So he decided to concentrate on bringing in buyers. "I figured that if I had the customers, the suppliers would come," he says.

In an ever-evolving, nascent arena, you can expect the unexpected, but also the need to quickly change your focus. Customers so frequently told Wilcox what they really needed was help managing their computers and other IT assets that he realized that as the real opportunity. So he changed his focus. "The more you learn, the more you evolve your business model and end up doing something different," he says. And hopefully, you'll wind up making some money in the process.

Anne Field is a freelance writer based in Pelham, New York. She's written articles for such magazines and Web sites as Fast Company, Business Week, Newsweek, Inc., Worth, Context, *and* Fortunesmallbusiness.com. *Before becoming a full-time freelancer, she was an editor on the staff of* Business Week, Success, *and* Self. *You can e-mail her at annearf@aol.com.*

Creating a Customer-Friendly Website

Angelo M. Donofrio

Even the most attractive Web site won't guarantee that people will come back again and again. But, if you make your site customer-friendly by giving people what they really want, you can certainly improve your odds. This is yet another perspective on how to make sure a Web site, whether it's for internal or external customers, actually does what you want it to do—make visiting it a value-added experience.

You can't judge a website by its flashy graphics, any more than you can judge a book by its cover. It's not a matter of how good you *look*, it's how good you *are*. After viewers see the pretty home page, can they find useful information?

A website will survive and proper only if the total experience is a good one, states John Crowley, president of U.S. operations for VISION Consulting, an international Internet systems integration company with offices in the United States and Europe.

An attractive website will get you only so far. What users really want is a customer-friendly site that provides the information they need quickly, easily, in a readily digestible form, and in a format that is inviting and enjoyable.

Take a bank, for example. "The key tasks for a bank's website are to handle customers' financial transactions conveniently and securely," says Crowley. "On the other hand, a website for the entertainment industry should help visitors make use of leisure time in a satisfying way. After providing a positive experience, you need to tell site visitors where they can go to get more entertainment—by purchasing a CD, for example."

Coming Back for More

Since websites and e-businesses are based on satisfying customer concerns, Crowley points out, it's critical that the total business system be designed to support customer care. And just as banks differ from entertainment companies, there may be as many ways of achieving that goal as there are websites that strive to reach and grab the attention of the general public.

Reprinted with permission from *Beyond Computing* magazine, November/December 2000. Copyright © 2000 by IBM Corporation. All rights reserved.

As the World Wide Web becomes increasingly crowded, everyone from major corporations to start-ups to nonprofits is discovering that "sticky eyeballs" is what it's all about.

Providing Relevant News

Take CNNfn's Industry Watch, which is part of New York-based CNNfn's business and finance site, CNNfn.com. "Our aim is to provide busy professionals with quick, easy access to lots of *pertinent* information," explains managing editor Allen Wastler.

In addition to providing its users with a link to CNN.com, a sister site that covers domestic and international breaking news, CNNfn.com also taps into the resources of YellowBrix, a firm that combines artificial intelligence and Inxight software to provide personalized content on the web.

Wastler says the partnership with YellowBrix lets CNNfn.com provide its users with award-winning financial news coverage from its own reporters, as well as headlines from news sources around the world.

YellowBrix draws on approximately 800 resources — including wire service reports, specialized trade magazines and other websites—to collect news stories for a total of 120 categories, which range from banking to aerospace.

Every day, YellowBrix, which runs on Sun hardware using the Solaris operating system, serves up an organized list of news stories on CNNfn's Industry Watch to a busy and news-hungry public.

In February 1997, with the goal of enabling Internet users to quickly sort through all that news for stories relevant to them, YellowBrix turned to Inxight Software's Summarizer SDK technology. This allows viewers to obtain a three-sentence executive summary of any story simply by moving their cursor over the headline.

The key point is that this is an automatic process: no people are involved. The software automatically creates a summary in a few seconds and then sorts the stories into industry groups.

"Our goal is to provide breadth of news coverage all the time, while making it easy for our readers to find the information they want," Wastler says. "Our website and the technology it employs help us meet that objective."

> Our aim is to provide busy professionals with quick, easy access to lots of *pertinent* information.

Virtual Shopping

Clearly, technology can make an online experience useful and efficient, but it also can make it exciting and help customers get the best of two worlds: both real and virtual shopping.

Managers and traditional bricks-and-mortar retail stores have long understood the importance of a good-looking, interesting display to attract potential customers inside. Now entrepreneurs are transferring their retail knowledge and skills to an online shopping environment.

THE NON-PROFIT CUSTOMER

Turodrique Fuad, founder and CEO of San Francisco-based web design firm paper(media), caught a television news story one night about Médecins Sans Frontières (MSF or Doctors Without Borders), an organization that provides medical aid to disaster victims worldwide. The next day, Fuad called MSF, which won the Nobel Peace Prize in 1999, with an offer of help.

The result is a website (www.refugeecamp.org), launched in September, that gives viewers the opportunity to take a virtual tour through a refugee camp and gives them a dramatic look at the basics, such as developing a water supply and providing medical help for the refugees. "The intent is not to elicit sympathy," says Fuad, "but to get across the facts."

The MSF site was built using Macromedia Flash 4.0 and operates off a shared, hosted Microsoft Windows NT server running Apache Jserv. Flash provides streaming multimedia content. Rather than delivering the whole site in one big chunk, the site is delivered in small segments, distributing the load and making delivery easier on both the user and the server.

A key benefit has been the attention the site has garnered: in addition to a lot of positive feedback, the site has been profiled in *The Industry Standard, Fast Company* and *Yahoo! Internet Life*—important free publicity for its valuable work.

"Just as with our commercial websites," says Faud, "we want to communicate the message of the sponsor. The test of effectiveness for a site like this, where the goal is education, is time spent on the site and 'depth of clicking'—how deep the viewer or reader goes."

In its efforts to develop a visually stimulating website that can mimic a bricks-and-mortar shopping experience, ShopGoOnline.com, a Chico, Calif.-based Internet shopping mall, chose IBM's HotMedia software package. The software, which was installed in December 1999, enables ShopGoOnline.com to create interactive multimedia without adding special servers or plug-ins.

"Finding a niche in the competitive Internet marketplace is a continuing challenge," says Matthew Herman, vice president of the parent company, Go OnLine Networks. "IBM's HotMedia gives us a real advantage by bringing our products—which include everything from home and garden items to electronic devices and beauty aids—to life."

Viewers can quickly see that this is much more than just an online catalog. To illustrate, when site visitors click on "Vera's Retreat," they enter a room with a visual panorama of beauty aids, such as facial and hand creams, all in high-quality color images. It's almost a virtual reality experience, Herman reports.

But despite the lush visuals, visitors seldom wait more than 30 to 40 seconds to see content. Also, Herman points out that the wide variety of choices the software allows makes the viewer more likely to stay for a while—and buy.

> **KEEPING IT USEFUL**
>
> Immersant, an Internet consulting and development firm headquartered in New York, runs in-house usability labs to figure out what makes a site customer friendly. Using a hands-on testing process that evaluates the ease of use and effectiveness of a website, Immersant has come up with some guidelines that any smart company will follow in creating a customer-friendly website:
>
> - Respect the fine line between personalization and privacy. Build your customers' trust and ask for personal information only when absolutely necessary.
> - Don't shut out anyone who's unwilling to provide personal information—or you may lose that customer for good. Savvy consumers have learned to provide fake answers just to proceed.
> - Think simple. Don't jazz up your site with flashy graphics unless they really help you communicate with your customers.
> - Put your customers in the driver's seat. Let them decide whether they want to receive news from you by e-mail, hard copy or on the site. Use common sense to decide how often to contact a customer.
> - Hit the bull's-eye. Decide who your customers are and create a site that reflects their interests and needs. The better you understand the people you're targeting, the more effectively you'll serve them.
> - The customer knows best. If you're thinking of selling a new product, run the idea by your customer base first. If they're not visiting a particular area on your site, find out why.
>
> —Don Hameluck, senior usability analyst, Immersant

Personalizing Resources

Carefully applied technology can also help enable the web with that personal touch that well-run bricks-and-mortar outfits provide. This level of customer care lies at the heart of Chown Hardware, a five-generation Portland, Ore.-based business that distributes door hardware and plumbing fixtures. Company president Fred Chown was determined to use the web to serve the firm's customers even better and to expand sales opportunities—while sticking to a budget.

Chown has one AS/400e developer who maintains all business applications. Many of these are developed specifically for the residential and commercial door hardware business and provide a competitive edge over using generic business applications, without adding more programmers.

Ten years ago, Chown signed up with LANSA to provide its programmer with software tools that would help the growing company expand those AS/400 Operations. "The strategy has worked so well," explains Chown, "that two years ago, with LANSA's help, we were able to develop our website (www.chown.com) and get it up and running in less than three weeks."

LANSA software enabled Chown Hardware to create a business-to-business online product catalog containing about 10,000 items. The online version replaced many of Chown's expensive direct-mail flyers, catalogs and brochures which, combined, cost the company $50,000 a year.

"Still," says Chown, "the Internet can be very impersonal, so we try very hard to make our website customer-friendly." For example, the company will provide precise shipping costs as part of its website estimate and will track customer orders easily, thanks to UPS pricing and tracking software.

Efforts Are Ongoing

Chown Hardware is continuing its efforts to make its website more inviting. "We have been modifying our web applications—such as our catalog and our sales order entry process—to be individual-based as well as company-based," Chown reports.

The aim is to better serve companies that have a number of different buyers, each specializing in certain kinds of products.

"When it's complete by the end of this year, our new system will enable us to target the right people with special offers," Chown reports. The system currently allows each customer to build a custom web catalog and access his or her own B2B pricing, and will soon provide specific industry and job function catalogs online.

Other online catalogs will show specific brands and finishes, as well as specials and seasonal items. "We'll be able to track customer interest in each of these specific catalogs and the products within them," says Chown.

Currently, the website's hits are increasing at 40 percent per month, as the firm continues to make additional customer-friendly improvements.

"We firmly believe some of the product information and price quotes that we are providing to customers translate into sales when the calls come into our toll-free telephone lines," Chown reports.

In fact, the company is adding new products daily. In the past, the expensive print catalogs were updated only every three years. Like many of his fellow e-business entrepreneurs, Chown feels that the Internet has sharpened his company's focus on customer care. "That's the most important part of our business," he declares.

"We want to transfer to our website the goodwill and trust we've built up with customers over time. A site that caters to customer needs will help us achieve that goal."

Angie Donofrio, a freelance communications and marketing consultant based in Katonah, N.Y., helped design and develop content for user-friendly Web sites devoted to the Y2K issue and the 1998 Olympic Games in Nagano, Japan.

Functional Processes

SUPPLY CHAIN MANAGEMENT
The Value Added Information Chain

Susan L. Cisco and Karen V. Strong

This article pushes the definition of supply chain to include what the authors call the "value information chain," which is the successful linking of information from those who have it to those who need it to more effectively do their work. The author includes three case studies that show how different companies manage this chain. She explains the use of the Internet in all this and emphasizes the importance of managing the chain and not just information.

Michael Porter introduced the concept of a "value chain" in the 1980s to describe the nature of buyer and supplier relationships with organizations. Porter's Production Value Chain graphically depicted the discrete activities in the process of delivering products and services where costs occurred and identified where "value" was added. This marketing model set the stage for defining opportunities for differentiation in areas such as cost, production, and product development.

Many of the concepts from Porter's model can be applied to organizations today in another area—information management. "Value" defines usefulness or importance. "Value chain" is a model for depicting the increasing importance, or value-add, of activities in a process. An "information management value chain," therefore, focuses on the discrete activities that incur costs in order to add value to information. The value proposition is to improve the usefulness of information to the ultimate users, helping them make better decisions.

The underlying assumption for this application of the value chain model is that information management is a "process." In other words, the flow of information is a production line converting raw data into knowledge for decision making. Conversion of information into knowledge requires the input, capture, filtering, organization, sharing and use, and synthesis of many forms of information— data and documents.

If we take a holistic view of the value-added process of information management and compare that to the breakdown of responsibilities within organizations for these functions, do they necessarily add value? Many organizations have discrete activities for records management, document management, and knowledge management. Each of the information management activities are often thought of as separate disciplines that incur costs and are addressed through different business practices and technologies. All of these activities, however, play a role in managing and utilizing the "knowledge assets" of the organization.

The set of information management activities addressed by the Information Management Value Chain include:

- **Capture**—data and document based information and other "knowledge" is created and/or acquired.
- **Transform**—the information captured is filtered, structured, indexed, and organized.
- **Store**—the "information base" or "knowledge base" is maintained through a series of repositories and/or linkages.
- **Transfer**—the dissemination and/or presentation of the information.
- **Apply**—the information is used to support organizational decisions and actions.

This article takes an integrated look at the information management process, exploring the connection between records management, document management, integrated document management, and knowledge management. As "links" in a chain of interrelated information management activities within organizations, these activities can lay the foundation for differentiation in areas such as innovation, responsiveness, productivity, and competency. Supported by enabling technologies, these initiatives can facilitate organizational goals of process improvement and performance enhancement.

Link 1: Records Management: Strategies and Directions for the Future

Records management is a fundamental activity in the information management value chain. Records management professionals have always known that if records management practices and techniques are not integrated into electronic recordkeeping systems, the systems are doomed to eventual failure because of:

- Poor quality records which are inaccurate and/or incomplete.

- Records with no apparent owner and no known purpose for their existence.
- Records in unreadable formats.
- Too many records that are too old to be useful.

Now other business disciplines have realized the value of records management. At the 1997 Managing Electronic Records Conference sponsored by Cohasset Associates, Ted Smith, Chairman of FileNET, discussed the role of records management in document management systems. He made the case for the need to manage records because of legal regulations, tax laws, business requirements, and industry standards. In his model, document management technology supplies the physical storage, document production capabilities and access control. Smith sees records management supplying the essential components of document classification and filing system infrastructure, retention policies, and a migration strategy for stored documents.

Another compelling argument for records management was presented by Bruce Silver in a recent article. *(KM World*, 1998) He observed that records management is coming back as a strategic issue in business and as a technological challenge. He described a recent lawsuit at Prudential Insurance where the company was socked with a $1 million fine by an irate federal judge when it could not produce internal documents in a class action suit. In fact, it appeared that some documents had been willfully destroyed by a Prudential employee, but that did not cause the fine. What made the judge angry was that the company had no policy—not to mention a system—for managing internal electronic documents as corporate records, the principal records on the conduct of its business. Silver concluded by identifying three key features needed for records management:

- **Record Selection**—is it a record or a non-record?
- **Classification**—assigning the official category(ies) from the organizational filing system.
- **Retention**—how long does it need to be retained?

These two examples from thought leaders in the document management industry suggest that other business disciplines now appreciate the value of the records management discipline and its focus on records retention schedules and disposition, filing and information retrieval, protection and security of records, and storage and migration strategies.

The proliferation of records in electronic format is influencing the discipline of records management in at least three ways:

Single point of access. Electronic records are stored in "knowledge silos" designed for specific work groups or business processes. Knowledge silos usually are invisible to or unreachable by other employees in the organization. What employees need is a single point of access at the desktop where all electronic documents are available in one integrated system. Employees have only one place in which to look for documents regardless of whether they are scanned images, word processing documents, electronic forms, e-mail messages, digital voice mail messages, or spreadsheets. The same system can serve as pointer or catalog to hard copy/analog documents and provide a method for ordering copies.

Leveraging intranet/Internet technology. With all documents in one desktop system, employees need a simple, easy-to-use retrieval interface. The Internet provides such an interface—the standard Web browser (i.e., Netscape Navigator or Microsoft Internet Explorer)—to be used on a corporate intranet. For employees who use the Internet, the interface is already familiar, and access can be controlled by individual security profiles.

Transferring document indexing function to end users. Electronic documents must be indexed into the recordkeeping system so they can be retrieved at a later date. It is estimated that 70 percent to 80 percent of documents are now created electronically. Who will index the large volume of documents? For high value and/or vital documents, it is feasible that records management staff can assist in indexing. However, for the majority of electronic documents, the individuals who create and acquire the documents (end users) will be responsible for indexing them into the electronic record-keeping system. End users are not thrilled with the prospect of indexing all their electronic records! Therefore, the indexing system must be simple and easy to use. Over time, it is hoped that artificial intelligence technology can be applied to the indexing function so that the system can offer the most probable indexing for the end user to edit and/or approve.

Four issues have bubbled to the top as most critical in the management of electronic records:

Definition of a record. "Official" records are recorded information in any physical form or medium which are generated or received by a business enterprise as *evidence* of business decisions and transactions. Examples of documents that are not records are extra copies preserved only for convenience of reference and journal articles. Such "non- records" have their own destruction schedule based on usefulness, and their life cycle must not exceed that of official records of the same type. Educating end users on the distinction between records and non-records is confusing at best and bewildering at worst. The distinction is important for controlling the growth of recorded information.

Development of standard naming conventions. In order to classify and organize documents for retrieval across an organization, there needs to be an organizational information infrastructure that contains standard naming categories. Even the terminology for an infrastructure with naming conventions is not standardized. Dow Corning calls it "corporate taxonomy." Information scientists and librarians say "controlled vocabulary" or "thesaurus." Records managers tend to use the terms "file plan," "indexing system," or "uniform filing system." Information technology practitioners and archivists often refer to standard naming conventions as a "metadata system." Another popular term is "knowledge map," a directory that charts the existence and locations of knowledge resources. (Saffady, 1998) Regardless of the name, the principle of consistent and accurate naming of documents and their attributes is absolutely necessary for dependable retrieval over time.

Enforcing compliance with retention policy. Records managers ideally would be involved during the development of electronic recordkeeping systems so that retention management is integrated when a new system is being planned and implemented. In this scenario, the retention period usually is linked to the document type. Event-driven retention is more difficult. That is, an event happens (say a contract expires), then the retention clock starts. Many electronic recordkeeping systems are already implemented without consideration for retention management, and documents with various retention periods are commingled. These systems will require that retention policy be retrofitted. Hopefully, document type or retention code was captured for each document so that documents can be copied by document type to new media for appropriate disposition. Otherwise, documents will have to be re-indexed one by one.

Migration strategy for stored documents. Hardware and software upgrades occur frequently. Associated electronic documents will have to be upgraded along with the hardware and software to assure that documents will be readable for the entire retention period. It is essential that some entity within the organization is held accountable for the important responsibility of migrating records forward where retention periods exceed the life of the hardware, software, or storage media. The economic implications of migration are not insignificant. For 1 million electronic document images (30 gigabytes of optical disk storage) with a 50-year retention period, Saffady estimated that the cumulative conversion costs can exceed one-half million dollars if conversions are done at five year intervals.

In summary, the discipline of records management is evolving to include electronic records. Without conventional records management practices and techniques, a necessary link in the information value chain is absent and makes the feasibility of successful information capture and delivery unlikely.

Link 2: Document Management: Departmental and Enterprise Approaches

Successful document management is the ability to organize, access, and control document-based information—paper and electronic. Successful document management improves business performance. The improvements can be measured in terms of quality, customer service, productivity, and profitability. Managing documents, however, can be very complicated once an organization examines the complete process including authors, collaborators, editors, and consumers.

Documents are scattered throughout organizations on PCs, servers, mainframes, and in file rooms. Businesses manage the documents by maintaining arrays of hard drives, stacks of CDROMs, rows of filing cabinets, and vaults of paper. As a result, people must search for information and often end up making business decisions based on outdated and incomplete information.

Groups of workers and work teams generally resort to paper documents to transfer and share information even though they have access to sophisticated electronic communication tools such as e-mail. Often different departments throughout the organization who need to collaborate on business projects are slowed down by ineffective document storage, retrieval, and processing. As a result, productivity suffers, work quality suffers, and customer service suffers.

The document management challenge is characterized by common elements that are consistent across all organizations: (Strong, 1997)

- **Variety of document types**—organizations must define documents and understand their content, value, and use within the organization.
- **Variety of life cycle requirements**—organizations must understand the creation, use, storage, and disposition requirements of documents including legal and regulatory compliance.
- **Business process integration**—organizations must develop a model for describing document-based tasks and activities within business processes.
- **Access requirements**—organizations must define the access requirements for documents at the individual, work group, departmental, and organization-wide level.
- **Integration within the computing environment**—organizations must understand the technical implications of deploying the document information resource in the computing infrastructure.

Businesses that aggressively address the problem of managing documents can have a healthier bottom line and will continue to succeed in the years ahead. The historical view of documents as paper-based facts and figures used to support business recordkeeping must be expanded. Documents are collections of information—data, text, graphics, images, voice, and video—brought together for the purpose of communicating and supporting business decisions and transactions.

Most organizations face the challenge of accurately defining the value and use of documents within the business environment and utilizing the appropriate technologies and applications to leverage the corporate information asset of documents. Organizations that solve these problems typically experience increased lead time to market new products and services, improved customer satisfaction, increased worker productivity, and lower operating costs. Organizations with solutions to the document management problem create a competitive advantage.

Successful document management depends on two components: (1) an information management business discipline and (2) a set of information technology products and services. (Strong, 1997)

The first component, the business discipline, involves defining business needs for the assembly, control, reuse, distribution, and management of documents throughout their life cycle. To manage documents, it is critical to understand why documents are created, who uses them, and how they relate to a specific business process or decision activity. This process involves the management of the document content in addition to the media and location.

The second component—document information technologies—includes hardware, software, services, and applications to improve the ability to create, store, retrieve, and control document-based information. A broad range of information technologies fall into the document management arena, each with specific features and benefits designed to accomplish different business objectives. Document information technologies should become an integral part of the overall computing environment and should leverage investments made in PCs, servers, networks, communications, and other infrastructure technologies.

The business discipline and the document technologies to solve the document management challenge are available today. Addressing the challenge is not an issue of knowledge or technological capabilities, it is an issue of the complexity of the document information resource. Documents are tied to multiple business processes with many points of creation and many points of access. Documents are authored by employees with different work styles and processing requirements. Implementing document technologies will bring changes to employees and the work environment that must be properly defined and anticipated.

Information Management Business Discipline
FOCUS: Information Technology Products and Services

Process and Operational Improvement
FOCUS: Data and Document Resource Management

Figure 1. **Focus on information management business discipline and process and operational improvement**

Successful document management requires a structured approach to defining and then solving the business problems. The five major elements in the structured approach are as follows: (Strong, 1997)

1. Develop a document management strategy. The strategy will determine the actions necessary to achieve business goals; it will lay the foundation for success. Create a detailed list of activities to achieve the desired results and overcome any project-obstacles.

2. Define the document environment—the real world of work. Model and analyze the relationships between data, documents, processes and people and look for opportunities to use document technologies to enable business process redesign. Evaluate the documents in a document collection including location, users, access, format, and content. Develop a set of criteria for evaluating the value and usefulness of the documents within the collection.

3. Evaluate the document technologies. The document technologies are tools for automating business processes to achieve the desired business results. Some of the key document technologies include document imaging, document management, workflow, text retrieval, and computer output to laser disk (COLD). Each of these technologies offers specific features and functions designed to solve different types of document management problems.

4. Build the business case, which is a decision making process. It addresses how to define the opportunity for improvement to ensure top management support.

5. Implement a course of action. The course of action for implementing a document management solution includes the use of document technologies within the work environment.

At the work group or departmental level, each of these elements can be analyzed within a specific target group of users and applications. "Enterprise-wide" means taking into consideration an entire organization's needs rather than the needs of a single application or business unit. At the enterprise-wide level, each of these elements takes on additional complexity as the focus becomes all users, processes, applications, and documents in the organization. The benefits of an enterprise-wide approach to document management are clear and include:

- Searching multiple repositories
- Sharing documents across the organization
- Reusing document information from other work groups
- Controlling organizationwide document information

The goal is to achieve the benefits of enterprise-wide document while designing the project initiative so that it can be managed and successfully implemented. A core project team must be formed to drive the enterprise-wide initiative. The team will address the two components of successful document management described above: the information management business discipline and the information technology products and services. The focus of the core team's efforts in each area is shown above. (Strong, 1997)

Successful enterprise-wide document management depends on defining the shared elements in each of these components; in other words, addressing only the factors common to all document management solutions at the enterprise level. Examples of shared elements include standard naming conventions, analysis methodologies, and computing infrastructures.

In today's work environment, however, the enterprise-wide document management initiative should go beyond the enterprise. Document creation and delivery options go beyond in-house networks and systems to the World Wide Web for global access and mass distribution. Document information delivery and exchange should be expanded to include customers, suppliers, and business. The opportunity to leverage the potential of the electronic document in the intranet/Internet environment opens up new opportunities for improving business performance and adding value to customers. Each of the policies, standards, and guidelines developed using the enterprise-wide document management framework can be extended to include the intranet/Internet.

The benefits of improved document management at both the departmental and enterprise level include strategic and operational benefits. These initiatives can—and should—move an organization closer to its overall business goals and objectives.

Document creation and delivery options go beyond in-house networks and systems to the World Wide Web for global access and mass distribution.

Link 3: Integrated Document Management: Desktop Access and Control

Integral document management (IDM) is an extension of document management technology to every desktop. IDM solutions are designed to become core enterprise technologies offering universal client software and a "suite" of desktop document management functions. IDM overcomes many of the problems associated with process/application or departmental solutions approaches such as:

- Different vendors
- High integration costs
- Multiple procurement processes
- Different release dates
- Training difficulties
- No common support

The IDM infrastructure is generally messaging-driven, leveraging current investments in groupware (i.e., Lotus Notes, Microsoft Exchange, Novell GroupWise) and intranet solutions currently in place or under development. A baseline comparison of characteristics of document management and integrated document management are shown below. (Puccinelli 1998)

Deployment of IDM tools raises many of the challenges addressed earlier regarding enterprise-wide implementations including the definition of standard naming conventions, development of a shared document access model, and development of a data/document repository strategy. In addition, successful deployment requires an organizationwide strategy for awareness and education to ensure the product suite is leveraged in each of the various business applications/departments where it is deployed.

IDM links underlying business processes to the many types of documents required to perform production, collaboration, and desktop work activities. Fully implemented, IDM provides desktop access and control for virtually any document in the organization.

IDM supports business models such as integrated work management whereby organizations can define the business rules and policies of an application or process and invoke them using the most suitable document management tools and technologies. In this work model, it is possible to automate the delivery of tasks to the right people with the right information to complete the tasks. An integrated "work packet" can contain scanned images, PC application files (i.e., word processing, spreadsheets), data information, or other forms of digital information. Workflows can be defined using visual tools to specify the delivery of work packets based on decision requirements.

Document Management	Integrated Document Management (IDM)
Application Specific	Business Specific
Address Specific Problems	Address Organization Infrastructure
Enterprise—Issue of Scalability	Enterprise—Issue of Deployment
Focus: Application	Focus: Tool

Figure 2. **Comparing document management and integrated document management**

Some of the strategic benefits realized by organizations that have deployed IDM on an enterprise level include productivity improvements, enhanced management and control of work activities, and improved customer service. In order to realize these benefits, it is critical to know the business processes and design/redesign processes to produce the desired end result.

Link 4: Knowledge Management: Strategic Applications and Experiences

Knowledge management refers to the practice and technologies that facilitate the efficient creation and exchange of knowledge on an organizationwide level to enhance the quality of decision making. (The Delphi Group, 1998) In order to understand the concept of "knowledge management," the authors surveyed three organizations, in diverse industries, that have already implemented or are planning to implement a knowledge management system: Booz-Allen & Hamilton (Booz-Allen), a consulting firm; PeopleSoft, a producer of business software; and Dow Corning, a world leader in silicon technology. At each organization, the person interviewed was an individual who was closely involved with the knowledge management system. They were all asked the following open-ended questions:

- How do you define knowledge management?
- How do you distinguish it from records management and document management?
- Describe the system your company has for knowledge management including equipment and staff.
- Does your knowledge management system contribute to your strategic business objective? If yes, how?
- What lessons did you learn in implementing your knowledge management system that you could pass to other organizations thinking of establishing one?
- What are your organization's future plans for knowledge management?

Booz-Allen and Hamilton

Management consulting firms were among the first organizations to realize the value of knowledge management and address its capture using Web-based information technologies. For Booz-Allen, one of the world's largest management and technology consulting firms, knowledge management is a strategic point of view and includes the company's best thinking, frameworks, tools, and approaches. (Remeikis, 1998) First implemented in 1994 as a simple bulletin board application, the knowledge management system was switched in late 1995 to a corporate intranet using Netscape as the Web browser and Oracle as the database. (Tristram 1998)

At Booz-Allen, records management and document management are considered tools and techniques to be used with confidential work done for clients. Knowledge management tools maintain reusable knowledge such as training material, marketing documents, best practices, case studies, and Booz-Allen resumes.

Fourteen Booz-Allen & Hamilton knowledge managers are authorized to enter knowledge into the system. Half of the knowledge managers have master's degrees in library and information science while the other half have master's degrees in other varied areas. Certain clerical employees may also enter knowledge into the system. There are between 30 and 40 employees globally who can refine, edit, structure content, and enter knowledge into the system. However, any Booz-Allen employee can retrieve knowledge.

Booz-Allen used "controlled vocabularies" to maintain consistency in capturing knowledge. Under development since 1994, the abstracting and indexing team (two employees) maintains the controlled vocabularies. As of February 1998, approximately 3500 pieces of intellectual capital had been captured, amounting to 1.5 gigabytes of text-only data. (Tristram, 1998)

Some of the lessons learned by Booz-Allen from implementing this sys-

Management consulting firms were among the first organizations to realize the value of knowledge management and address its capture using Web-based information technologies.

tem are as follows: (Remeikis, 1998)

1. **The knowledge management system must be part of an overall strategic plan** for the company, and it must have strong leadership from the top. If knowledge management is not treated as a strategic effort, it is a waste of resources to attempt deployment.
2. **"If you just build it, they won't come."** End users will use a knowledge management system because they believe it has a purpose for them, both contributing value and receiving value from the system.
3. **A knowledge management system must be able to demonstrate bottom line impact, that is measurable.**
4. **There has to be real content in the system that is relevant and timely.** It is the responsibility of the knowledge managers to keep the information on the system current and accurate.

PeopleSoft

PeopleSoft builds enterprise-wide software solutions for the following applications: human resources, financial, distribution, materials management, manufacturing, supply chain management, and student administration. Tracy Leighton, Manager of Knowledge Development at PeopleSoft, defined knowledge management as providing an answer to an end user's question without his/her knowing exactly what piece of information is needed or where it is located. She distinguished it from records management and document management because they take lots of bits of data and put them in order so people can scroll through them. End users usually need to know exactly what they are looking for to extract useful information from a records or document management system.

PeopleSoft's knowledge management system is geared toward help desk applications—troubleshooting and solving problems that employees experience with their computers and telephones. The backbone of the system is a CasePoint Web server (Inference in Novato, Calif.) deployed over PeopleSoft's network to internal help desk call center representatives. "Eureka" is a scaled down version of CasePoint and is accessed by PeopleSoft employees via a corporate intranet. CasePoint! Eureka is a collection of databases organized with a question hierarchy and a natural language front end. This means that end users can type in a query in their own words and enter it into the system. The system asks additional questions and eventually leads them to a solution.

Implemented in 1996, CasePoint/Eureka structures knowledge into cases; as of February 1998, the system contained about 2500 cases. A case is defined as a problem solution set where multiple problems may have the same solution and there may be multiple solutions to the same problem. Leighton and a staff of five employees are responsible for the creation, development, and maintenance of all databases as well as acquisition of new information.

According to Leighton, "Eureka allows our employees to be more productive instead of spending time trying to solve problems by asking a person down the hall. Necessary information is at their fingertips. There are immeasurable savings in employee productivity."

Eureka gets an average of 2700 user sessions per month. In addition, the knowledge management system provides PeopleSoft with an approach for showing customers that knowledge management systems do work internally. Leighton added, "We've become an example for how this works in our industry, which gives us competitive advantage."

Lessons learned from the implementation include:

1. **The system must have end user buy-in.** While it may seem that getting top management support is the biggest challenge, getting user buy-in is more important.
2. **Marketing and promotional campaigns can encourage knowledge contributions.** Locating experts from whom to get knowledge is also challenging. PeopleSoft designed t-shirts to give employees who made knowledge contributions. Whenever an employee shared knowledge, he/she received a shirt. When others saw the shirt, they wanted one, too.
3. **Continuing commitment from senior management is critical.** It takes from one to five years to be successful with a knowledge management system. Continued buy-in from top management is essential for long-term success.
4. **The design and implementation of a knowledge management system requires a creative, innovative, and dedicated team.**

Leighton indicated that PeopleSoft plans to expand its knowledge management system to informational cases such as reserving conference rooms, ordering office supplies, human resources, and a "Yellow Pages" of in-house experts. They also plan to use the newest Web-based technologies to make the system even more user friendly.

Dow Corning

According to Karen Biskup, Dow Coming's Information Assets Specialist, knowledge management is a combination of expertise, document management technology, and information asset management (formerly records management). Many of Dow Corning's most valued employees are retiring and the company wants to capture their knowledge before they leave.

Biskup defined records management as the function that sets and enforces policies such as the records retention schedule. Document management enables the implementation of policies through technology; knowledge management is more of a business practice than a technology.

Dow Corning started planning for enterprise-wide information and knowledge management by developing a corporate taxonomy, which provides a path for classifying any document for retrieval consistently across the organization.

Biskup offered the following insight to organizations considering a knowledge management system:

1. **People think they have to keep all records to preserve knowledge.** What is needed is an approach for extracting valuable information in a meaningful way.
2. **Manage the politics.** Some people will think they will lose part of their power by sharing knowledge. That is, "if you take my knowledge, you won't need me anymore."
3. **Find ways to capture knowledge.** One of Dow Corning's ideas was to turn veteran employees into mentors for newer employees who harvest the veteran's knowledge.

Dow Corning expects that the knowledge management system will be embedded in office technology tools that have already been selected as organization standards (i.e., SAP and Documentum). Implementation is expected to begin as early as 2000.

The Common Thread

As defined by the three organizations in the study, knowledge is mostly in people's heads (usually called "tacit" information as distinguished from "explicit" information, which is recorded). At Booz-Allen & Hamilton, knowledge is their employees' best thinking, frameworks, tools, and approaches. At PeopleSoft, knowledge is defined as best practices based upon experience. And at Dow Corning, it is the experience and expertise that resides in employees who will retire; there is a need to capture the valuable information before people leave.

Knowledge management needs cooperation to work most effectively, and yet employees tend to be reluctant to share their knowledge. Recent trends of downsizing in organizations nationwide has resulted in a loss of organizational loyalty among employees. Thus, employees have to trust that their donations will not undermine their jobs or competitiveness. In some organizations, financial incentives may be necessary.

Organizations need a system for classifying knowledge into the system (usually a database). Booz-Allen called the classification system "controlled vocabularies." PeopleSoft structures knowledge into cases, and Dow Coming established a "corporate taxonomy." Each approach allows for consistent classification and organization of documents for retrieval across the organization over time.

Knowledge management does not come in a box. As yet, there is no end-to-end knowledge management solution. There are many tool sets that apply, including records management software, document management software, document imaging systems, search engines, and data mining tools.

It is unclear whether the concept of knowledge management is the latest business management trend or a critical link in the information management value chain. Certainly, the information stored in employees' heads about business processes and customers, employees' experience and skills, and their intuition has value. Capturing and maintaining this valuable information is what knowledge management is all about.

Defining Your Role in the Value Chain

Each of these disciplines—records management, document management, integrated document management, and knowledge management—can be addressed as discrete activities within an organization. This perspective, however, limits the potential benefits of viewing them as interrelated information management activities that build on each other and add value throughout the information management value chain.

As discussed earlier, the set of information management activities addressed by the Information Management Value Chain include capture, transform, store, transfer, and apply. In each of these discrete activities, costs are incurred in order to add value throughout the process. Sound business practices from each of the major information management disciplines, and an integrated approach to technology use is required to succeed. Improving the usefulness of information to the ultimate users helping them make better decisions is derived from added value in two major areas—leveraging shared access and leveraging shared learning.

People with various skills and responsibilities must come together to design, develop, and deliver fully integrated information management systems based on the value chain concept presented here. The matrix in Figure 3 highlights the key skills required for information management professionals in each of the value chain activities.

The shared role of information management experts in the initiatives is required in three major areas:

- Developing assessments regarding the "value" of information.
- Addressing risk management (protection, security, controls, and legality).
- Understanding the relationships between people, processes, information, and technology.

Successful initiatives in each of these areas require top management commitment of resources to support and direct the activities ensuring alignment with the organization's vision, strategy, and business objectives. To be successful they also must be based on a thorough understanding of business processes, apply "best" practices from all information management disciplines, integrate the appropriate technologies, and measure the results.

For many organizations, the result is that information management systems become valuable— even vital—to the functioning of the organization.

Improving the usefulness of information to the ultimate users helping them make better decisions is derived from added value in two major areas—leveraging shared access and leveraging shared learning.

Value Chain Activity	Records Management	Document Management /IDM	Knowledge Management
Capture	Provide Service Control Costs Selected Sources	Acquire Create Production Process	Tacit to Explicit Integrated Process Forms/Formats
Transform	Filter for Value Classify/Index Organize	Work Management Profile Summarize	Categorization Format/Aggregate
Store	Inventory Media/Protection Retain/Dispose	Control/Security Metadata Infrastructure	Meta "Levels" Relationships Media/Formats
Transfer	Access/Navigate	Share/Collaborate Push/Pull Delivery Content/Context	Presentation Modeling Tools Decision Tools
Apply	Human and Automated Decisions and Actions Integrated Feedback Process		

Figure 3. **Five steps of value chain activities**

Bibliography

1. Biskup, Karen, Information Assets Specialist, Dow Corning. Telephone interview. February 26, 1998.
2. Leighton, Tracy, Manager of Knowledge Development, PeopleSoft. Telephone interview. February 27, 1998.
3. Porter, Michael. *Competitive Advantage.* 1985.
4. Puccinelli, Bob. "Messaging is the Medium," *Inform.* January 1998.
5. Remeikis, Lois. Booz-Allen & Hamilton. Telephone interview. February 27, 1998.
6. Saffady, William. *The Document Life Cycle: A White Paper.* 1996.
7. Saffady, William. *Knowledge Management: A Manager's Briefing.* 1998.
8. Silver, Bruce. "Records Management Rides Again." *KM World.* February 23, 1998 www.kmworld.com/newestLibrary/1998/february_23/recmgmtridesagain.cfm.
9. Smith, Ted, Presentation at Managing Electronic Records. Cohasset Associates. November 1997.
10. Strong, Karen. "Enterprise Document Management: Fact or Fiction." AIIM White Paper. 1997 www.aiim.org/publications/infoshop/info_isr.htm.

11. Strong, Karen. "Successful Document Management: A Structured Approach." Volume I of the Clarity DMI Video Consulting Series. 1997 *www.claritydmi.com/prodinfo.htm*.
12. The Delphi Group. Home page. July 26, 1998. <*http://www.delphi-group.com*>.
13. Tristram, Claire. "Common Knowledge." *CIO Web Business.* September 1, 1998.

Susan L. Cisco is chairperson of the Management and Supervision Department at Oakton Community College.

Karen V. Strong is president of Clarity, Inc. and the Clarity Document Management Institute (Clarity DMI), an Austin-based consulting and education firm specializing in innovative approaches to enterprise document content management.

Dock-to-Shop Is Just-in-Time

Maranda McBride, Sheilah Harrison, and Brian Clark

Just-in-time delivery of supplies is not a new concept, but technology is making it easier to implement and even more efficient. This article looks at how companies are setting up systems that bring in needed materials direct from dock-to-shop without ever going to the warehouse. The systems are a refinement on the kanban approach to supply management, using barcodes and special computer programs. Learn more here.

Dock-to-shop (DTS) is the process by which material is received from a supplier onto a customer's receiving dock and is sent directly to the shop floor, bypassing the storeroom. It is a just-in-time process that allows organizations to maintain less storeroom inventory and thereby save storage costs.

Lucent Technologies implemented a DTS process in its Columbus, Ohio, facility in 1994. The transition was a challenge due to the variable demands in the telecommunications industry as well as the history of the company. There was a time when Lucent (formerly a part of AT&T) was the forerunner in the communications business, which allowed the company to take its time building quality products and not worry much about cycle times or production costs. However, the deregulation of the telecommunications industry caused increased competition, and it became evident that Lucent had to decrease the production interval and costs.

DTS is intended to increase the amount of consigned inventory. This means that the material is not owned by Lucent until it is about to be consumed in the production process. By doing this, Lucent decreases the amount of material on the books and is not liable for the taxes incurred on that material until it is consumed on the assembly line. A second benefit is recognized because the material usually flows straight from the receiving dock to the shop floor without being stocked in the storeroom, eliminating a large portion of the cost associated with stocking and picking operations.

The process by which DTS operates in Columbus is that the supplier keeps a certain amount of material on hand at its facility or at a local warehouse based upon forecast requirements. Along with a weekly forecast from

From *IIE Solutions*, September 2000. Reprinted with the permission of the Institute of Industrial Engineers, 25 Technology Park, Norcross, GA 30092, 770-449-0461. Copyright © 2000.

Lucent, suppliers receive a daily report that specifies what material was consumed the previous day showing them the daily usage. Lucent sends an electronic pull signal via electronic data interchange (EDI) that triggers the supplier to ship a certain amount of material to the facility. The pull signal includes a unique identification number for each shipment (known as the request ID), the component identification number or part number (known as the comcode), the standard predetermined quantity to be shipped, and the delivery location for the material once it arrives on Lucent's receiving dock. The supplier creates a barcode label with this information and applies it to packaged material. When the material arrives on the receiving dock, a "locate" scan makes use of the request ID, which designates the material as being in-house even though it still belongs to the supplier. The material is then sent to the appropriate shop floor assembly line, where it is staged until it is ready to be used.

When the assembly line is ready to use the material, a worker performs a "consume" scan using the request ID. This designates the material as Lucent's investment, making it the owner of the material. The consume scan can send a pull signal automatically to the supplier or the shop operator can place an order manually to request a desired quantity. The latter method is preferred when customer demand for a part is variable. While the process described so far has been a great success, by saving Lucent a substantial amount in inventory and labor costs, there are always areas for the industrial engineering team to tackle improvements.

Replenishment Methods

When the DTS process was first implemented at the Columbus factory, material was set up using the kanban method of replenishment, which requires a set pipeline number consisting of the total amount of material that is on order, in transit, and on the floor.

Material is sent in fixed package sizes—kanbans—according to specifications designated by the supply line engineer. When the material is consumed, the request ID on the kanban is scanned, and the shop floor maintenance system creates a new replenishment request to be sent to the supplier. But his may not be the best method of bringing in material for the parts with variable demand. First, if the shop floor neglects to scan the request ID before using the material, the material will not be reordered and the potential for shortage is increased. Second, sometimes the product on the line is not going to be built for an extended period of time, and if the consume scan is performed, more material is requested even though it may not be needed. If production picks up, the amount of material in the pipeline may not be adequate to sustain production. If demand fluctuates, material planners must put in additional requests for material or the supply line engineer must increase or decrease the pipeline size for each component on DTS to accommodate production.

This method can be very time consuming and labor intensive unless demand is steady. Therefore, to accommodate those assembly lines where demand is not constant, the timeline method of replenishment was implemented. With the timeline method, each assembly line is responsible for placing orders for its DTS components. The operator enters his assembly line number in the shop floor maintenance system and sees all of the timeline parts listed. The operator selects components from this list and can place an order up to seven days before receipt of the materials is desired (see Figure 1).

Timeline Scheduling

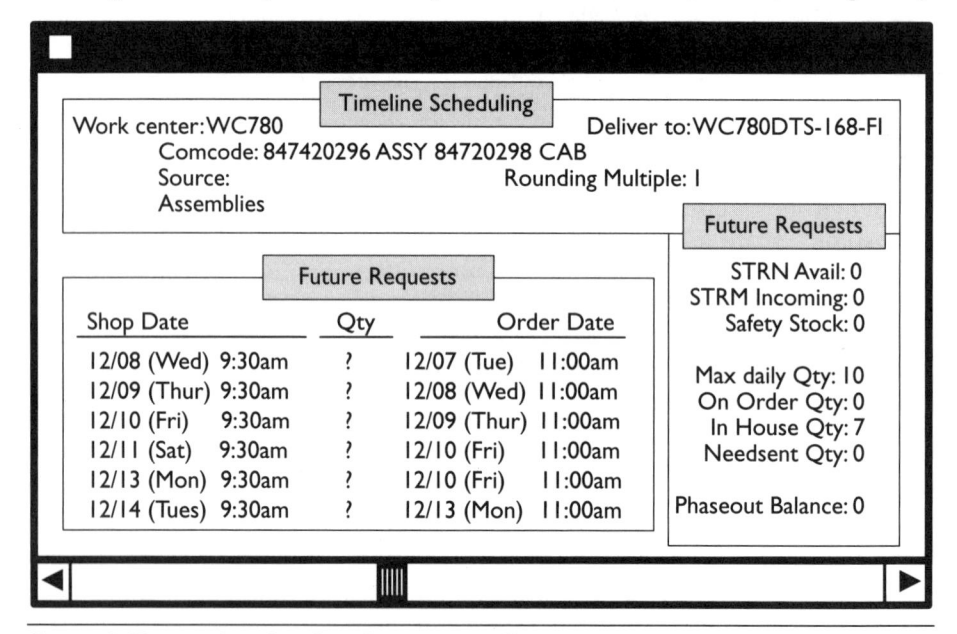

Work center: WC780 Deliver to: WC780DTS-168-Fl
Comcode: 847420296 ASSY 84720298 CAB
Source: Rounding Multiple: 1
Assemblies

Future Requests

STRN Avail: 0
STRM Incoming: 0
Safety Stock: 0

Max daily Qty: 10
On Order Qty: 0
In House Qty: 7
Needsent Qty: 0

Phaseout Balance: 0

Future Requests

Shop Date	Qty	Order Date
12/08 (Wed) 9:30am	?	12/07 (Tue) 11:00am
12/09 (Thur) 9:30am	?	12/08 (Wed) 11:00am
12/10 (Fri) 9:30am	?	12/09 (Thur) 11:00am
12/11 (Sat) 9:30am	?	12/10 (Fri) 11:00am
12/13 (Mon) 9:30am	?	12/10 (Fri) 11:00am
12/14 (Tues) 9:30am	?	12/13 (Mon) 11:00am

Figure 1. **Example of a timeline scheduling screen**

This method empowers operators by giving them more control over shop floor inventory. When space requirements demand it, operators can reduce the amount of material driven in, and when demand increases, they can specify the amount of material that comes in each day to minimize the amount of material on the shop floor.

For cases in which Lucent manufactures material only if an order is placed, the reorder point replenishment method is used. In this scenario, the system requests material only if it is needed for a customer order (as opposed to being needed as stock). Each morning a program subtracts the total amount of material on hand and in transit from the total amount of material needed for kits and for customer orders over a predetermined time period (usually five days). If the amount is less than or equal to zero, no requests are generated. If the amount is greater than zero, the quantity is rounded up to the nearest package quantity multiple, and requests are sent to suppliers at the next EDI batch run. An example is illustrated in Figure 2.

> Customer order #ABC123 requires 40 parts;
> Customer order #DEF456 requires 17 parts; and
> Customer order GHI789 requires 82 parts.
> The package quantity is 32 pieces for one Request ID.
> There are 64 pieces in transit.
> There are 13 pieces on hand.
> The amount needed would be [(40+17+82) + 62 pieces.
> Since the orders have to be in multiples of 32, the order quantity would be 64, or 2 request IDs.

Figure 2. **Example of reorder point replenishment**

Barcode Changes for Storeroom Inventory

Before sending DTS requests for a component to a supplier, all in-house inventory must be depleted. In the past, the actual conversion could be postponed for months at a time if the inventory was high. When the part was identified to be converted to DTS, no more orders would be placed. This inventory had to be monitored closely in order to ensure that the conversion was completed at the right time.

This challenge has been combatted by putting a process in place that checks storeroom on-hand balances before sending EDI pulls to suppliers. If a part being requested has an on-hand balance, a storeroom pick ticket is generated. Using a "check excess" flag in the shop floor maintenance system, all material in a storeroom will be pulled before a request is sent to a supplier. The transactions were working well; however, since the storeroom treated the material like any other material by putting only a pick ticket on the box, the shop did not know the material was on DTS. Therefore, operators did not know to perform the consume scan. Because of these difficulties, on-hand quantities had to be monitored during the change period in order to determine when to let the shop know that the material was officially on DTS and being sent directly from the supplier.

It was decided that the storeroom should print and attach to the DTS material a 3S barcode label—like the one suppliers are required to put on DTS deliveries—when the material is picked so that it is transparent to the shop whether it comes from the supplier or the storeroom. The 3S barcode label serves as a flag to alert operators to do a consume scan. This allows a component to be moved to DTS at any time regardless of the in-house balance.

This storeroom 3S barcode contains a "check excess" flag that tells the system to check the storeroom balance of a component before sending requests to the supplier. If material is present in the storeroom, a barcode much like the

3S barcode used for DTS is printed in the storeroom along with the pick ticket. The barcode is populated with a work order number, which is scanned before consumption just like the request ID number. The material is replenished the same way by either the kanban or timeline method, which makes it transparent to the shop. When all the material in the storeroom has been depleted, requests go out to the supplier for replenishment.

The check excess and 3S barcode processes have provided seamless transitions from stocked material arrangements to the DTS program. The new arrangement is transparent to the shop and allows arrangements to be modified quickly as business needs change.

Supplier and Shop Training

Although some of the suppliers have been on the DTS program from the beginning, they have demonstrated the need for a refresher course. Some employees have rotated assignments; some have not performed the daily DTS responsibilities; and others have left the company altogether.

Two to three people from each supplying company were invited to an on-site visit. It was requested that they send only the people handling the daily EDI or material transaction to ensure that the right people received the right training.

The current process was described from the beginning to the end, via both a slide presentation and a tour of the factory. The suppliers were updated on some of the new process improvements that were being made internally. The training was concluded with a description of external improvements being considered.

Internally, there were only a handful of supply line engineers working this process, and it was very difficult to convey changes to the entire factory. It was agreed that if we trained the process engineer of each assembly line to troubleshoot and suggest improvements, there would be more time for improving the process and it would help everyone in the factory see DTS as the best choice for procuring material.

Process Improvement Metrics

The supply line engineering team has established metrics to track how well everyone is executing the process:

ASN (advanced ship notice) performance: When a request for material is sent to DTS suppliers, they are expected to respond with an ASN via EDI. The ASN contains the request ID, the carrier code, the carrier tracking number, the expected quantity, and the expected arrival date. Some suppliers have difficulty sending the ASN due to manual processes or insufficient training at the supplier's location. Some faithfully send the ASN, but it may not contain the correct information. Figure 3 represents the data being collected.

Dock-to-Shop Is Just-in-Time

EDI 856 - ASN

Received by Lucent	91%
On-Time	71%
No Pro #	5%
No SCAC Code	0%
Incorrect SCAC Code	13%
Wrong Request ID	2%

Figure 3. **The ASN metric**

The first section captures the frequency with which ASNs are received and the percentage of those that arrive on time. The second category helps specify the errors within the ASN. Sometimes the carrier neglects to put in the correct carrier code or tracking number. Occasionally, there are suppliers who mis-key or use old request IDs in the ASN. The previous week is automatically displayed, but the metric user may opt to view the data by supplier or as the overall performance during the previous 13 weeks.

Consumption velocity: This metric measures the amount of time it takes the factory to use the material. It is measured from the time the material arrives on the receiving dock to the time the consume scan is performed. As discussed briefly above, there are two ways of ordering material: kanban and timeline. Due to the way each process is designed, the numbers reflected in Figure 4 are generally different.

This metric can also be displayed by supplier or assembly line or a historical account can be generated. This allows the supply line engineering group to narrow the area that is experiencing issues in order to address and correct problems.

Consumption Velocity

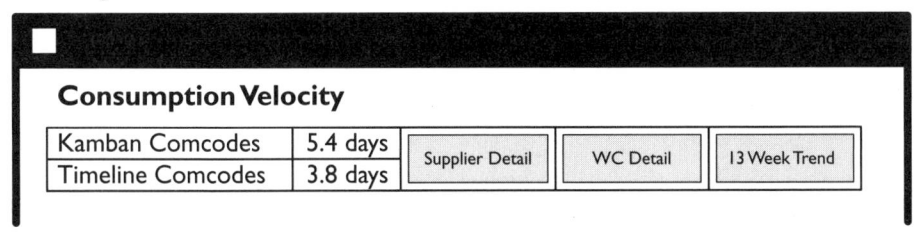

Kamban Comcodes	5.4 days
Timeline Comcodes	3.8 days

Figure 4. **Consumption velocity metric**

Conclusion

The improvements that have been made to the DTS program have made the process more beneficial and user friendly. The process steps are continuously improved. However, DTS has not only benefitted Lucent by creating a more

JIT material flow environment, it has helped suppliers by giving them visibility of the forecasts and daily use of their components. As more parts are put up on the DTS program, process improvements will continue. This program has helped Lucent Columbus attain its mission of high quality products, lowest possible cost, and on-time delivery.

Maranda McBride has worked at Lucent Technologies since January 1998. Prior to her current position as a supply line engineer, she worked as a process engineer in the material planning department.

Sheilah Harrison has been with Lucent Technologies for three and a half years. Before moving into supply line engineering, she was a process engineer at the distribution center where assembled and ancillary material is consolidated for shipment to customers.

Brian Clark has worked at Lucent Technologies for two years. Prior to his current position in supply line engineering, he was a manufacturing process engineer in circuit pack manufacturing.

Optimizing Economic Order Quantity (EOQ)

Dave Piasecki

Economic order quantity is an accounting formula that determines the point at which the combination of order costs and inventory carrying costs are lowest. The author of this article contends that most organizations can benefit from using EOQ to determine the most cost-effective quantity to order in at least some area of their operation. He explains how to calculate EOQ, he provides guidance in using the formula, and he outlines two ways to implement EOQ.

Inventory models for calculating optimal order quantities and reorder points existed long before the arrival of the computer. When the first Model T Fords were rolling off the assembly line, manufacturers were already reaping the financial benefits of inventory management by determining the most cost-effective answers to the questions of when and how much. Long before acronyms such as JIT, TQM, TOC, and MRP rolled off the tongues of industrial engineers, companies were using those same (then unnamed) concepts to manage production and inventory.

I recently read *Purchasing and Storing*, a textbook that was part of a "Modern Business Course" at the Alexander Hamilton Institute in New York. The textbook, published in 1931, was essentially a how-to manual on inventory management in a manufacturing environment. The core concepts of managing a business have changed very little with time and reading about these concepts in a vintage text is a great way to reinforce the value of the fundamentals. The occasional references to "The War" (World War I) keep it interesting and the complete absence of acronyms is refreshing.

This 70-year-old book contained a section on minimum cost quantity, which is what we now refer to as economic order quantity (EOQ). I can imagine that in the 1930s an accountant—or more likely a room full of accountants—would have calculated EOQ or other inventory-related formulas one item at a time in a dimly lit office using the inventory books, a mechanical adding machine, and a slide rule. Time-consuming as this was, some manufacturers of the time recognized the financial benefits of taking a scientific approach to making these inventory decisions.

So why is it that, in these days of advanced information technology, many

From *IIE Solutions*, January 2001. Reprinted with the permission of the Institute of Industrial Engineers, 25 Technology Park, Norcross, GA 30092, 770-449-0461. Copyright © 2001.

companies are still not taking advantage of these fundamental inventory models? Part of the answer lies in poor results they may have received due to inaccurate data inputs. Accurate product costs, activity costs, forecasts, history, and lead times are crucial in making inventory models work. Ironically, software advancements may also be to blame, in part: many ERP packages have built-in calculations for EOQ that work automatically, so the users do not know how it is calculated and therefore do not understand the data inputs and system setup that control the output. When the output appears to be out of whack, it is simply ignored. This can create a situation in which the executives who purchased the software incorrectly assume that the material planners and purchasing clerks are placing orders based upon the system's recommendations. In addition, many organizations find these built-in EOQ calculations inadequate and in need of modification to deal with the diversity of their product groups and processes.

Corporate goals and strategies can sometimes conflict with EOQ. Measuring performance by inventory turns is one of the most prolific mistakes made in the name of inventory management. Many companies have achieved aggressive goals in increasing inventory turns only to find their bottom line has shrunk due to increased operational costs.

EOQ is essentially an accounting formula that determines the point at which the combination of order costs and inventory carrying costs are the least. The result is the most cost-effective quantity to order. In purchasing this is known as the *order quantity*; in manufacturing it is known as the *production lot size*.

While EOQ may not apply to every inventory situation, most organizations will find it beneficial in at least some aspect of their operation. Any time there is repetitive purchasing or planning of an item, EOQ should be considered. Obvious applications for EOQ are purchase-to-stock distributors and make-to-stock manufacturers; however, make-to-order manufacturers should also consider EOQ when they have multiple orders or release dates for the same items and when they plan components and sub-assemblies. Repetitive-buy maintenance, repair, and operating (MRO) inventory is also a good application for EOQ. Though EOQ is generally recommended in operations where demand is relatively steady, items with demand variability such as seasonality can still use the model by going to shorter time periods for the EOQ calculation. (Just make sure the usage and carrying costs are based on the same time period.)

Doesn't EOQ conflict with just-in-time? While I don't want to get into a long discussion on the misconceptions of what JIT really is, I will address the most common misunderstanding: that JIT means all components should arrive in the exact quantities "just in time" for the production run. JIT is actually a quality initiative with the goal of eliminating wasted steps, wasted labor, and wasted cost; EOQ should be one of the tools used to achieve this. EOQ is used to determine which components fit into this JIT model and what

Optimizing Economic Order Quantity

level of JIT is economically advantageous for an operation.

As an example, let us assume you are a lawn equipment manufacturer and you produce 100 units per day of a specific model of lawn mower. While it may be cost-effective to have 100 engines arrive on the dock each day, it would certainly not be cost-effective to have 500 screws (a one-day supply) used to mount a plastic housing on the lawn mower shipped daily. To determine the most cost-effective quantities of screws or other components, you need to use the EOQ formula (Figure 1).

$$EOQ = \sqrt{\frac{2(\text{Annual usage in units})(\text{Order cost})}{(\text{Annual carrying cost per unit})}}$$

Figure 1. **The standard economic order quantity formula**

While the calculation itself is fairly simple, the task of determining the correct data inputs to accurately represent your inventory and operation is a bit of a project. Exaggerated order costs and carrying costs are common mistakes made in EOQ calculations. Using all costs associated with purchasing and receiving to calculate order cost or using all costs associated with storage

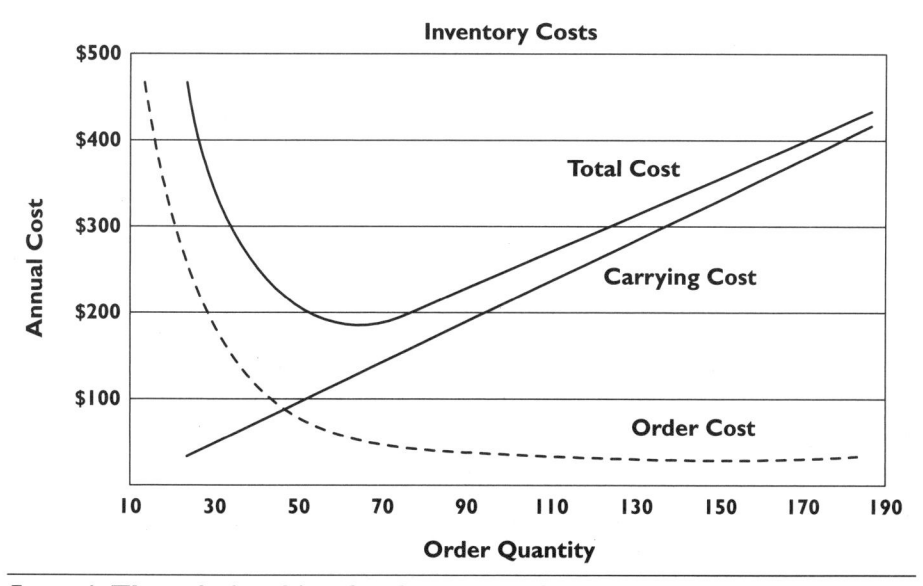

Figure 1. **The relationship of order cost and carrying cost to total cost.**
This example shows an itme with an order cost of $15, a carrying cost of 20 percent, a unit cost of $20, and annual usage of units. The result is EOQ of 47 units with a total annual operational cost of $190. (This cost does not include the product cost itself.) Note that the total cost changes very little from 40 to 55 units and is dramatically higher below 20 and above 100 units.

and material handling to calculate carrying cost will give you highly inflated costs and therefore inaccurate results from the EOQ calculation. I also caution against using benchmarks or published industry standards in calculations. I have seen references in magazine articles and product brochures to average purchase order costs of $100 to $150. Often, these references trace back to studies performed by advocacy agencies working for business that directly benefit from these exaggerated costs used in return-on-investment calculations. I am not denying that some operations may have costs in this range, especially if there is frequent re-sourcing, re-quoting, or buying from overseas vendors. However, if an operation is primarily involved with repetitive buying from domestic vendors, which is more common, you'll likely see purchase order costs in the substantially lower $10 to $30 range.

As you prepare to undertake this project keep in mind that even though accuracy is crucial, small variances in the data inputs generally have very little effect on the outputs. The following explanations of the data inputs will give added insight into each.

Annual Usage

Expressed in units, this is generally the easiest part of the equation. You simply input your forecasted annual usage.

Order Cost

Also known as purchase cost or set-up cost, order cost is the sum of the fixed costs that are incurred each time an item is ordered. These costs are not associated with the quantity ordered but primarily with physical activities required to process the order.

For *purchased items* these would include the cost to enter the purchase order and requisition, any approval steps, processing the receipt, incoming inspection, invoice processing, and vendor payment. In some cases a portion of the inbound freight may also be included in order cost.

It is important to note that these are costs associated with the frequency of the orders, not the quantities ordered. For example, the time spent checking in the receipt, entering the receipt, and doing other related paperwork in the receiving department would be included; the time spent repacking materials, unloading trucks, and making deliveries to other departments should likely not be included. If there is inbound quality inspection in which a percentage of the quantity received is inspected, the time to get the specs and process the paperwork should be included. On the other hand, if a fixed quantity per receipt is inspected, include the entire time for inspecting, repacking, etc. In the purchasing department, include all time associated with creating the purchase order, the approval process, contacting the vendor, expediting, and reviewing order reports; do not include time spent reviewing forecasts, sourcing, getting quotes (unless quotes are obtained each time you order), and setting up new items. All time spent dealing with vendor invoices would be included in order cost.

Associating actual costs to the activities surrounding order cost is where many an EOQ formula runs afoul. Do not make a list of all of the activities and then ask the people performing the activities how long it takes them to accomplish each one. The results of this type of measurement are rarely even close to accurate. It is more accurate to determine the percentage of time that is consumed performing specific activities in the department, multiplying that number by the total labor costs for a given time period (usually a month) and then dividing by the line items processed during that same period.

It is extremely difficult to associate inbound freight costs with order costs in an automated EOQ program and I suggest it only if the inbound freight cost has a significant effect on unit cost *and* its effect on unit cost varies significantly based upon the order quantity.

In *manufacturing*, the order cost should include the time to initiate the work order, the time associated with picking and issuing components (excluding time associated with counting and handling specific quantities), all production scheduling time, machine set-up time, and inspection time. Production scrap directly associated with the machine set-up should also be included in order cost, as should any tooling that is discarded after each production run.

There may be times when you want to inflate or deflate set-up costs. If you lack the capacity to meet the production schedule using the EOQ, you may want to increase set-up costs artificially to increase lot sizes and reduce overall set-up time. If you have excess capacity, you may want to decrease set-up costs artificially, which will increase overall set-up time and reduce inventory investment. The idea is that if you are paying for the labor and machine overhead anyway, it makes sense to take advantage of the savings in reduced inventories.

For the most part, order cost is primarily the labor associated with processing the order; however, costs for such things as phone calls, faxes, postage, and envelopes can be included as well.

Carrying Cost

Also called holding cost, carrying cost is the cost of having inventory on hand. It is primarily made up of the costs associated with the costs associated with inventory investment and storage. For the purpose of the EOQ calculation, if the cost does not change based upon the quantity of inventory on hand, it should not be included in carrying cost. In the EOQ formula, carrying cost is represented as the annual cost per average on-hand inventory unit. The primary components of carrying cost include:

Interest. If you had to borrow money to pay for inventory, the interest rate would be part of the carrying cost. If you did not borrow for the inventory but have loans on other capital items, the interest rate on those loans can be used since a reduction in inventory would free up money that could be used to pay the loans. If by some miracle you are debt-free, you need to determine how much you could make if the money were invested.

Insurance. Since insurance costs are directly related to the total value of the inventory, they are included as part of carrying cost.

Taxes. If you are required to pay any taxes on the value of inventory, include that amount.

Storage. Mistakes in calculating storage costs are common in EOQ implementations. Generally, companies take all costs associated with the warehouse and divide the total by the average inventory to determine a storage cost percentage for the EOQ calculation. This tends to include costs that are not directly affected by the inventory levels and does not compensate for storage characteristics. Carrying costs for the purpose of the EOQ calculation should only include costs that are variable based upon inventory levels.

For pick/pack operations in which there are fixed picking locations assigned to each item and the locations are sized for picking efficiency (not designed to hold the entire inventory), that portion of the warehouse should not be included in carrying cost since changes to inventory levels do not affect costs here. However, the overflow storage areas would be included in carrying cost. Operations that use purely random storage for their product should include the entire storage area in the calculation. Areas such as shipping/receiving and staging areas are usually not included in the storage calculations; however, if an additional warehouse has to be added to house overflow inventory, all areas of the second warehouse should be included, as should freight and labor costs associated with moving the material between warehouses.

Since storage costs are generally applied as a percentage of the inventory value, you may need to classify your inventory based upon a ratio of storage space requirements to value in order to assess storage costs accurately. Let's say you're opening a new e-business called BobsWeSellEverything.com. You calculated overall annual storage costs at 5% of the average inventory value and applied this to your entire inventory in the EOQ calculation. The average inventory on a particular piece of software and on 80-lb. bags of concrete mix both came to $10,000. The EOQ formula applied a $500 storage cost to the average quantity of each of these items, even though the software took up only one pallet position while the concrete mix consumed 75 pallet positions. Categorizing these items would place the software in a category with minimal storage costs (1% or less) and the concrete in a category with extreme storage costs (50%), which allows the EOQ formula to work correctly.

There are situations in which you may not want to include any storage costs in the EOQ calculation. If your operation has excess storage space for which it has no other uses, you may decide not to include storage costs, since reducing the inventory will not provide any savings in storage costs. As your

Optimizing Economic Order Quantity

> ## Variations on a Model
>
> There are many variations on the basic EOQ model, the most useful ones being:
> - Quantity discount logic can be programmed to work in conjunction with the EOQ formula to determine optimum order quantities. Most systems will require this additional programming.
> - Additional logic can be programmed to determine maximum quantities for items subject to spoilage or to prevent obsolescence on items reaching the end of their product life cycle.
> - When used in manufacturing to determine lot sizes where production runs are very long (weeks or months) and finished product is released to stock and consumed or sold throughout the production run, you may need to take into account the ratio of production to consumption to represent the average inventory level more accurately.
> - The safety stock calculation may take into account the order cycle time that is driven by the EOQ. If so, you may need to tie the cost of the change in safety stock levels into the formula.

operation grows near a point at which the physical operations require expansion, you would then start including storage in the calculation.

Time. A portion of the time spent on cycle counting should also be included in carrying cost. Remember to apply costs that change based on changes to the average inventory level. So in cycle counting, include the time spent physically counting but not the time spent filling out paperwork, doing data entry, and traveling between locations.

Order cost	$13.50
Carrying cost	20%
Annual usage	750
Price break qty.	**Unit cost**
0	$3.75
EOQ	**164**

Order cost	$13.50
Carrying cost	20%
Annual usage	750
Price break qty.	**Unit cost**
0	$500
50	$475
250	$465
500	$460
EOQ	**50**

Order cost	$22.75
Carrying cost	14%
Annual usage	1,500
Price break qty.	**Unit cost**
0	$0.79
250	$0.68
500	$0.65
1,000	$0.63
5,000	$0.60
EOQ	**1,000**

Figure 3. **Examples of EOQ calculations**
The first shows a simple calculation with no price breaks, the second and third with price breaks. Inventory turns based on average inventory investment on the three examples are 9, 30, and 3, respectively. This shows why inventory turns are not a good metric of cost savings in inventory management.

Other costs. These include risk factors associated with obsolescence, damage, and theft. Do not factor in these costs unless they are a direct result of the inventory levels and are significant enough to change the results of the EOQ equation.

Implementing EOQ

There are primarily two ways to implement EOQ, both of which require that the associated costs are predetermined. The simplest method is to set up the calculation in a spreadsheet program, manually calculate EOQ one item at a time, and then manually enter the order quantity into your inventory system. If the inventory has fairly steady demand and costs and there are less than a couple thousand SKUs, you can probably get by using this method once per year. If there are more than a couple thousand SKUs and/or higher variability in demand and costs, you will need to program the EOQ formula into the existing inventory system. This allows you to recalculate EOQ quickly and automatically as often as needed. A hybrid of the two systems can be used by downloading data to a spreadsheet or database program, performing the calculations, and then updating the inventory system manually or with a batch program. Whichever method you use, follow these steps:

Test the formula. Prior to final implementation, test the programming and set-up. Run the EOQ program and manually check the results using sample items that are representative of the variations of your inventory base.

Project results. Run a simulation or use a representative sampling of items to determine the overall short-term and long-term effects the EOQ calculation will have on warehouse space, cash flow, and operations. Dramatic increases in inventory levels may not be immediately feasible. If this is the case, you may temporarily adjust the formula until arrangements can be made to handle the additional storage requirements and compensate for the effects on cash flow. If the projection shows inventory levels dropping and order frequency increasing, you may need to evaluate staffing, equipment, and process changes to handle the increased activity.

Maintain EOQ. The values for order cost and carrying cost should be evaluated at least once per year taking into account any changes in interest rates, storage costs, and operational costs. The *total annual cost* calculation can be used to prove the EOQ calculation:

Total Annual Cost =
[(annual usage in units)/(order quantity)(order cost)]+{[.5(order quantity)+(safety stock)]*(annual carrying cost per unit)}

This formula is also very useful when comparing quotes from vendors that offer different minimum order quantities, price breaks, lead times, transportation costs.

Use it! The EOQ calculation is "hard science": if you have accurate inputs, the output is absolutely the most cost-effective quantity to order based on current operational costs. To further increase inventory turns, you will need to reduce the order costs. E-procurement, vendor-managed inventories, bar coding, and vendor certification programs can reduce the costs associated with processing an order. Equipment enhancements and process changes can reduce costs associated with manufacturing set-up. Increasing forecast accuracy and reducing lead times, which result in the ability to operate with reduced safety stock, can also reduce inventory levels.

For Further Reading

J. David Viale and Christopher Carrigan (Editor), *Basics of Inventory Management*, Crisp Publications, 1997.

James H. Greene, *Production and Inventory Control Handbook*, 3rd edition, McGraw-Hill, 1997.

Richard J. Tersine, *Principles of Inventory and Materials Management*, 4th edition, PTR Prentice Hall, 1993.

David R. Anderson, Dennis J. Sweeney, Thomas A. Williams, and John S. Loucks, *An Introduction to Management Science: Quantitative Approaches to Decision Making*, 9th edition, South-Western (International Thomson Publishing), 1999.

Dave Piasecki is owner/operator of Inventory Operations Consulting LLC, a consulting firm providing services related to inventory management, material handling, and warehouse operations to manufacturers and distributors in Southeast Wisconsin. He has more than 15 years' experience in warehousing and inventory management and can be reached through his Web site (www.inventoryops.com), where he maintains additional relevant information and links.

Corporate Change and the Logistics Model

Jim Coker

Logistics, the management of the entire process of product movement, is becoming increasingly critical to businesses as e-commerce and the global economy evolve. This is the theme of this short article on how change across the organization affects the physical delivery of products. It lays out a basic model for logistics changes today.

A little understood yet far-reaching example of continuous change in today's corporate world is the way businesses are addressing their logistics challenges. To better understand this shift in corporate focus, we must define two terms that many people mistakenly use interchangeably. These are distribution and logistics.

Distribution encompasses the planning and controlling of the physical movement of goods from the operation to the end user. This very focused area of control involves picking, packing and shipping a product to a customer from a stocking warehouse. Logistics involves managing the entire process of product movement, from acquisition of the components from outside vendors, through the operation in which value added steps are performed, and finally to the end user where the demand originated.

To better understand logistics, let's look at the various components that combine to build a basic logistics model, and the role each plays in the process.

Business Planning

As with any good business model, our logistics model begins on a foundation of planning. Before we start the first step toward product acquisition, we need a business forecast of what and how much we hope to sell. This plan is then broken down by market and region, two keys for use in the next phase of our model.

As we develop our sales forecast, certain elements other than desired sales goals must also be considered. Does the plan meet the business's financial goals? What resources are necessary to achieve the plan?

Reprinted by permission of the author. Copyright © 2000 by Jim Coker, Vice President of Logistics for interBiz, the e-Business applications division of Computer Associates. All rights reserved.

Corporate Change and the Logistics Model   495

Factors such as sufficient capacity in-house or from outside vendors to deliver the quantity of product to hit the forecast must also be taken into account. It would be hard to proceed to the next component of our model with a business plan built on an unobtainable forecast.

Logistics Planning

The next step in our corporate logistics model is to combine a logistics-planning phase with our business plan. Here we begin to match the projected demand from our forecast to our ability to deliver the product in a designated time frame. While taking into consideration the various elements of product cost and overhead, we use this plan to align our acquisition of product to the optimal destination sites based on the demand profiles from our market and regional forecast.

Execution

Our logistics model now moves from the planning phase to the execution phase. Here we match actual demand to projected demand from the earlier phase of our model. Much as we matched our acquisition of product to its relative destination sites, we now align actual demand and delivery point to its optimal supply point within our logistics network. Of key importance to this step is maintaining a focus on our customers' required lead-time demands. This effort can often be critical in gaining a competitive edge over those corporations who don't properly emphasize it.

Market Influences

While there are many market influences causing this shift to business based on our logistics model, let's take a look at two of them. Over the past several years we've seen rapid changes in how customers communicate with suppliers. First came mail, then the phone, then the fax and EDI.

Now the Internet has emerged as a new channel in the corporate world. This new way of doing business, called electronic commerce or e-commerce, has tightened up planning and delivery time frames across the supply chain. Consumers can now go online, shop for whatever product they need, compare price and delivery, and enter their orders. Buyer loyalty is contested based on ease of finding information, quality of the product, price, and the ability to deliver when the consumer wants.

A second market influence can he seen today in the manner and speed with which corporations are growing and changing. Growth no longer means simply an increase in sales, but also a combination of new business partnerships, acquisitions and mergers. While we've seen this in the past with companies in the same market, the current trend has a whole new twist to it.

It's not uncommon to find two operations in totally different markets coming together. This forces the new combined entity to handle an increasingly varied range of products, many times in a manner new to the operation. Often, a restructuring of the business is necessary to make the transition efficiently.

Cost control and planning become increasingly more and more important, in both cases mentioned above, for capital as well as operational needs. It's not sufficient to simply react to supply and demand changes. Trends such as these are good examples of the types of pressures pushing corporations toward a new manner of running their businesses based on the logistics model.

Forecasting Change Rather Than Reacting to It

As warehouse operations see the products they handle diversify, they're forced to react to changes to their traditional way of doing business, possibly by creating a new distribution center or consolidating one or more centers. New technology is often introduced to address this change, such as new warehousing systems, automated material handling equipment and radio frequency devices. Each changes daily operations in its own way.

In markets where product quality is consistent among vendors, reducing time-to-market is often key toward gaining a competitive edge in the market. Achieving this goal also helps businesses become more pro-active to customers' needs, in contrast to the reactive mode many operate in today.

The basis of this new approach is a system built on an accurate market forecast. Our ability to consider historic sales and the impact of external factors will have a direct influence on the accuracy of product mix and positioning in repeating markets.

The corporations that can achieve their operational goals and reduce overhead and expenses will be the ones that come out on top in the new millennium. This means focusing on resource efficiency, supply chain management, improved control systems throughout the office and plant, and the final stage of supply chain execution. Regardless of an operation's size, its objective is the same—to become centers for excellence in all areas of operation.

Having a Quality Product Isn't Enough

To succeed in today's economy, a company must offer a quality product when and where the customer wants it.

Consequently, the drive to enhance profitability is opening all areas of the supply chain to ever-closer scrutiny. Savings across the board, from increased efficiencies from product acquisition to movement through the network and reduced obsolescence, all contribute to the bottom line. With every logistics move corporations make today, there is one primary objective: improved customer service.

Those businesses that can shift to a pro-active customer service approach will be the ones that grow and prosper in the global market today, tomorrow, and in the future.

Jim Coker is vice president of logistics for interBiz, the e-business applications division of Computer Associates International. Coker has over 31 years of experience in information systems, with the last 21 focused in the manufacturing and distribution, commercial application industry.

Functional Processes

INFORMATION TECHNOLOGY

Fast Friends: Virtuality and Social Capital

Eric Lesser and Joseph Cothrel

This article looks at the idea of social interaction in the organizational setting and its importance in moving projects forward as well as coming up with new ideas and working together in all the ways that help get things done. Using technology to facilitate this interaction, such as e-mail and bulletin boards, works to some degree, but in this article the authors explain how the company Ace Hardware has taken technology to a whole new level to make online interaction nearly as good as face-to-face, and in some cases, better.

The new currency won't be intellectual capital. It will be social capital—the collective value of whom we know and what we'll do for each other. When social connections are strong and numerous, there is more trust, reciprocity, information flow, collective action, happiness, and by the way, greater wealth.

Social capital—the bonds between individuals in a group, organization, or society that constitute a valuable asset—has been getting increasing attention in today's business world. Once the province of sociologists, political scientists and economic development specialists, social capital has emerged as an important discipline in management studies and organizational development. Management scholars have embraced social capital as a way of understanding and interpreting a variety of management phenomena, ranging from the development of high technology industry in Silicon Valley to the differentials in managerial pay and promotion rates. Recently published books by Wayne Baker, a professor at the University of Michigan, and Don Cohen and Laurence Prusak at the IBM Institute for Knowledge Management have further advanced

Reprinted from *Knowledge Directions*, Spring/Summer 2001, the journal of the IBM Institute for Knowledge Management, copyright © 2001, IBM.

the notion that both individual and organizational social capital can have a significant influence on enterprise performance.

One contributor to the growing importance of understanding and supporting social capital is the spread of computer-based communication technologies. These technologies have made companies more aware that social networks support formal organizational structures. As they put global networks in place, companies have learned that establishing an electronic connection does not ensure that a productive working relationship will result. The connections between virtual interaction and social capital in business organizations are just beginning to be explored. Will virtual interaction enhance—or endanger—the ties that bind us? In many ways, this argument parallels the debate about the impact of the Internet on communities and neighborhoods, about which Barry Wellman and Milena Gulia have written:

> The Manicheans on either side of this debate assert that the Internet either wilt create wonderful new forms of community, or will destroy community altogether... The statements of enthusiasm and criticism leave little room for the moderate, mixed situations that may be the reality.[1]

In organizations, too, new communications technology will neither destroy nor ensure healthy social capital. How can businesses achieve a balanced approach to these new media?

We survey the current thinking on social capital here, with an eye to the challenges organizations face in promoting its creation and preservation. We explore the ways virtual communication technologies help address these challenges, while introducing new challenges of their own. Finally, we examine a case from Ace Hardware Company as an example of how companies are using virtual technologies to create, maintain, and exploit their social capital.

We explore the ways virtual communication technologies help address these challenges, while introducing new challenges of their own.

Social Capital: A Key Ingredient in Today's Economy

What is social capital? Janine Nahapiet of Oxford University and Sumantra Ghoshal of the London Business School propose the following definition: Social capital is "the sum of the actual and potential resources embedded within, available through, and derived from the network of relationships possessed by an individual or social unit."[2]

Emerging trends in the business world have pushed social capital to the forefront of management thinking.[3] High on the list of trends is the migration towards a knowledge-based economy. As knowledge begins to supplant land, labor, and capital as the primary source of competitive advantage in the marketplace, the ability to create new knowledge, share existing knowledge, and apply organizational knowledge to new situations becomes critical. The presence (or absence) of social capital can affect an organization's capacity to replicate best practices, develop and maintain explicit knowledge repositories, or simply provide guidance and mentoring to less experienced staff. All of these capabilities relate directly to an organization's ability to exploit its knowledge.

Social capital also plays a critical role in an environment that is increasingly marked by mergers, strategic alliances and joint ventures. As more and more resources that are critical to success lie outside organizational boundaries, establishing the right connections and relationships between relevant parties becomes both more important and more difficult. Identifying relevant subject matter experts, ensuring coordination between different firms, and building a sense of coherence among strangers (or even competitors) can all be daunting tasks, but accomplishing them is critical to successful collaboration. In the absence of social capital between alliance members, the likelihood of knowledge mismanagement increases. When knowledge critical to the success of the alliance becomes misused, misappropriated, misinterpreted, or is just plain missing, huge investments in resources, physical capital, and brand image may be jeopardized. One has only to look at the grim example of the Ford-Firestone tire situation to understand some of the problems that can result when knowledge breakdowns occur between companies that are dependent on one another.

As we have noted, increased reliance on computer-based communication as a tool to improve organizational effectiveness also makes understanding, developing and using social capital important. As organizations try to tap into the knowledge and experience of individuals separated by time zones, geographies and cultures, they have learned that there is more to building productive relationships than giving people the means of communication. They are also concerned, with some reason, about the potential negative impact of virtual tools on social capital, particularly in instances where face-to-face interactions are being replaced by virtual ones.

Challenges of Social Capital in Business Organizations

Nahapiet and Ghoshal further define social capital as having three dimensions:

- Individuals must perceive themselves to be part of a network (the structural dimension).
- A sense of trust and mutual obligation must be developed across this network (the relational dimension).
- The members of the network must have a common interest or share a common understanding of issues facing the organization (the cognitive dimension).

Challenges exist in each of these dimensions for organizations seeking to create, maintain, and exploit their social capital.

Structural Challenges

Connections made through face-to-face interactions are the best foundation for the development of social capital. A recent study showed that the level of trust that exists in virtual workgroups could be measurably improved by even a single face-to-face interaction at the beginning of the project.[4] But barriers of time, distance, and physical setting can make such interactions difficult to achieve. First, the number of connections an individual can create and maintain via face-to-face interaction is limited to the number of people at the physical locations he or she frequents. Further, tangible barriers including different floors or buildings, the absence of shared spaces where individuals can spontaneously interact, and common inhibitions associated with going outside of one's general sphere of influence can limit interaction among individuals. While examples of work environments specifically designed for collaboration and social connection exist—Alcoa's corporate offices and Oticon are examples—many of the buildings and spaces that people work in do not facilitate serendipitous encounters between co-workers.[5] Even where chance encounters can occur, the opportunity to have non-work-related conversations—a key element in building personal relationships—may be squeezed out by the time demands of the work day.[6]

Relational Challenges

In addition to these barriers to connection, other barriers get in the way of turning those connections into relationships of trust and mutual obligation. Corporate culture strongly influences an individual's ability to form trusting relationships with co-workers. A highly competitive, individualistic culture, for example, may actively discourage bonds of mutual obligation. Work processes and incentive programs that are excessively individualistic can create barriers as formidable as any wall or floor.

There may also be natural limits to the size of an individual's personal network. British anthropologist Robin Dunbar, whose work is highlighted in Malcolm Gladwell's popular book *The Tipping Point*, has argued that there is a natural limit to the number of people with whom a single individual can form stable relationships by means of direct personal contact. This number, 150, recurs so often in society—from the basic unit of military forces to the size of tribes and villages—that Dunbar's hypothesis merits serious attention.[7]

Cognitive Challenges

One of the biggest frustrations encountered in large organizations is the difficulty of ensuring that everyone is "reading off the same page." Varying interpretations of formal corporate communications and informal hints, tips and messages make it dangerous to assume that any communication is received and understood with its core properties intact. Shared understanding is not guaranteed even when people are physically together, observing and discussing the same environment. But a shared environment and the opportunity to talk together go a long way toward building mutual understanding. For example, if two people simultaneously look at a defective part in a machine and can see, hear, smell and feel the surrounding conditions, then the likelihood of their being able to identify a possible solution to the problem increases. Similarly, two people looking at the same spreadsheet can interact with one another to question assumptions, identify root causes implications, and determine alternative courses of action in ways that isolated individuals can not.

Written materials and, to some extent, the telephone, are not particularly useful in capturing environmental conditions and fostering the interaction that can make it easier to develop an accurate and shared understanding of the root causes of a particular situation. Xerox copier repair personnel found that standard manuals did little to help them diagnose problems. The complexity of the copiers and the influence of local environmental factors like temperature and humidity demanded a richer, more context-dependent approach than any manual could provide. Successful repair depended on being there and on sharing knowledge with other experienced repair people. Ultimately, the technicians discovered that discussion with their peers—not formal procedures—was most likely to produce the solutions required for repairing equipment in the field.[8]

How Virtual Interactions Address Social Capital Challenges

Face-to-face interactions are clearly vital for building social capital. Given the fact that face-to-face interactions are not always practical or possible, however, we must look for ways to build and leverage social capital virtually. Over the last several years, a number of technologies have emerged to help extend the reach of our relationships. A range of technologies relevant to each of the three dimensions of social capital can help sustain and perhaps increase the value that can be extracted from the development of relationships within an organization.

Over the last several years, a number of technologies have emerged to help extend the reach of our relationships.

Structural Challenges

The chief benefit of computer-based communication is clearly the ability to help people make connections. In 1968, ARPANET pioneers J.C.R. Licklider and Robert Taylor predicted that computer networks would help individuals overcome the tyranny of location and the limitations imposed by the happenstance groupings in which human beings found themselves. Licklider and Taylor foresaw a day when these networks could foster "communities not of common location, but of common interest."[9] Although we sometimes debate the impact of these technologies in crossing boundaries, particularly with regard to hierarchy, the debate always focuses on the magnitude of the impact; there is no disagreement that an impact exists.[10]

Researchers who have explored virtual collaboration at Lucent Technologies note that:

> ...Evolution of an affective bond often occurs through gradual escalation across opportunistic conversations, not necessarily related to work. Occasions for such encounters at a distance are limited by the intentional and formal nature of long distance communication. That is, a conference call with colleagues and superiors is not the ideal environment to probe for similarities with others that may form the basis for a deeper relationship.[11]

The findings suggest that the ease of use and relative informality of such tools as e-mail help break down the formal nature of long distance communication, making communication more frequent and therefore more conducive to development of relationships. But while "opportunistic conversations" can occur, e-mail, bulletin boards, and other traditional online tools do not support the chance encounters that some say spark real creativity in organizations.[12] Such capability has only recently appeared with instant messaging applications. Because these applications indicate when other members of the group or company are online, ad hoc interactions are possible among hundreds of people instead of the handful that might be encountered in the hallway of the typical office building on a given workday.

One of the biggest challenges for people in enterprises that extend across multiple locations is how to make connections with others having a specific expertise. Initial attempts to address this problem focused on the development of electronic "yellow pages" and the development of dedicated skill directories where individuals could provide data regarding their level of expertise on a variety of topics. While some of these initial efforts proved useful, many of them clearly did not achieve their desired results. Many of these systems relied upon generalized categories that were not relevant to those who were either classifying their skills or trying to locate a specific subject matter expert. Also, many systems were self-populating, relying on end users to make judgments about their own proficiency. Experience has shown that individuals are often poor judges of their own abilities. Further, many of these repositories required users to manually update their expertise profiles on a regular basis, which individuals often failed to do. As a result, the systems lost currency and value.

A new generation of expertise technologies incorporates "passive profiling" technologies that help address these issues. These systems use text-mining technologies to analyze the content in e-mail and other repositories to develop profiles of individual interests. Individuals can then review and modify these profiles and allow the system to update the profiles dynamically, based on additional content. These profiles allow individuals to query others in the organization and identify those willing and able to provide insight on a range of topics.

Other systems locate expertise through a question-and-answer format, rating systems, and a process for experts to "opt in" in specific topic areas. The software facilitates question routing and ensures that experts are not overwhelmed by requests for help. Like passive profiling systems, these technologies also refine themselves over time, since individuals have the opportunity to rate the responses they receive, and all users can view these ratings and can address questions specifically to an individual based upon them.

Relational Challenges

Connections are easy; relationships are hard. The problem of how best to foster relationships in virtual environments has attracted a significant amount of interest among both academics and business practitioners.

Connections are easy; relationships are hard. The problem of how best to foster relationships in virtual environments has attracted a significant amount of interest among both academics and business practitioners. The Internet age has given rise to a whole range of questions about how we evaluate the trustworthiness of others that we cannot see, and perhaps have never met. As Tim Berners-Lee, one of the founders of the modern-day Web, argues, "these (issues) have to do with information quality, bias, endorsement, privacy and trust—fundamental values of society, much misunderstood on the Web, and also highly susceptible to exploitation by those who can find a way."[13] Given the ease with which individuals can misrepresent themselves and their intentions to others in a virtual environment and the difficulty in ensuring compliance without traditional social reinforcement mechanisms, it would be only natural to expect individuals to surround themselves with barriers to guard against exploitation. Further, the public nature of many virtual conversations, such as discussion databases, can leave individuals exposed to attacks by others, many of them anonymous and not constrained by the norms and responsibilities of traditional social interactions. This form of attack, known as "flaming," can lower the level of social trust within a virtual environment and can inhibit the participation of individuals seeking more forthright relationships.[14]

In some respects, though, virtual technology provides new ways of communicating relationship-building social cues. We use situations where we can witness an individual's behavior in a public environment to evaluate the trustworthiness of another individual. In physical environments, this can sometimes be difficult. While we sometimes can see if an individual has adequately prepared for a team meeting, or if he or she has provided a helpful piece of information to a colleague who is struggling with a difficult problem, often these transactions occur away from the view of a larger audience. People may be hesitant, or unwilling to broadcast their altruism, or conversely, may actively try to conceal distrustful behavior. In a virtual environment, however, these transactions can be made visible by collaborative technologies. The most common of these are discussion forums or databases, and groupware. In these environments, everyone can see who contributed to threaded discussions, and can identify who has made explicit knowledge available for others to use.

Cognitive Challenges

Virtual communications compound the problems of ensuring that everyone has a common understanding of the background and context of a given situation. In the virtual world, a number of barriers make it difficult to ensure that each participant in a conversation has appropriate contextual clues necessary to developing mutual understanding and share knowledge. First, communicating across time and space often introduces cultural and linguistic differences that can hamper the best-intended discussions. Communicating with someone who is less familiar with your language can be difficult in a face-to-face setting; trying to do so without the benefit of facial expressions, gestures, and shared objects is harder. In addition, building common context in a virtual environment is made more difficult because the most commonly used forms of communication, the telephone and e-mail, primarily focus on using and isolating either our visual or auditory senses. These media are not particularly effective in sharing other sensory inputs that could provide additional assistance in transferring knowledge and developing common understanding.

Perhaps the biggest problem facing the development of social capital in a virtual environment is the difficulty associated with building a common set of assumptions and understandings. In physical settings, the interaction around common artifacts, or tools of the trade, makes it easier to develop reference points that everyone m a conversation can share. For example, when attempting to fix a broken piece of equipment, technicians working face-to-face all see the setting in which the equipment exists, sense the environmental conditions that could potentially affect the operation of the machine, and point to potential tools that they could use to solve the problem.

In a virtual world, building the common context necessary for effective knowledge sharing is significantly more difficult. The lack of environmental clues, compounded by the variety of assumptions that can be associated with cultural differences and language barriers, can significantly hinder the knowledge transfer process. A number of technologies can help overcome this barrier, however. Videoconferencing offers enough "face-to-face" interaction and environmental information to help build a joint view of a given situation. The classic example of the Virtual Teamworking project at British Petroleum underscores the importance of being able to visualize situations to improve decision-making in a remote environment.[15] Videoconferencing technology allowed members of globally dispersed teams to understand and solve problems together. Another important component of the Virtual Teamworking project was the use of shared "whiteboarding" technology, which allowed geographically separate individuals to jointly view and comment on a specific document. This ability to see changes made to a report or a presentation simultaneously can help ensure that everyone is literally "reading off the same page." While some of these technologies are considered difficult to use, increases in the availability of bandwidth within organizations and future refinements will make it easier for individuals to collaborate in real time shared environments.

Ace Hardware: Building and Exploiting Social Capital with Virtual Community

Leave it to a 75-year-old company to show how virtual interaction can help a company build and exploit its store of social capital. Ace Hardware's Commercial and Industrial Supply Community (ACIS) helps more than 300 dealers learn, problem-solve, and serve their large customer accounts better.

Social Capital in a Member Cooperative

Ace Hardware sells building materials, tools, paint, garden supplies, and a full range of other hardware products from more than 5,000 locations in the U.S. and 62 other countries. Ace is a member cooperative, unusual among retailers, though far from unique among hardware chains. Dealers voluntarily affiliate with the co-op to take advantage of Ace's volume pricing, and to benefit from Ace's national advertising, insurance policies and training programs. The co-op distributes to its retailers from more than 20 wholesale warehouses. Dealers also receive dividends from the co-op's profits. Because they are part of a co-op, the relationship among members is a commercial one that is also characterized by bonds of trust and loyalty. Many members are second or third-generation Ace dealers, whose relationship with the co-op is therefore personal and familial as well as commercial.

> Ace Hardware's Commercial and Industrial Supply Community (ACIS) helps more than 300 dealers learn, problem-solve, and serve their large customer accounts better.

The neighborhood Ace hardware store is a familiar icon in America's cities and towns. Though most of these stores sell primarily to do-it-yourselfers, Ace also does a significant business selling to commercial and industrial (C&I) accounts like home improvement companies, hospitals, schools, and the like. In fact, many of those neighborhood stores serve C&I accounts out of "the back of the store" while also meeting the needs of residential customers.

In the competitive U.S. hardware market, C&I accounts have become increasingly important for local dealers, who can often serve these accounts more effectively than "big box" retailers like Home Depot. Serving these accounts requires its own set of knowledge and expertise, however, as well as different product lines. To build rapidly on its base of commercial and industrial expertise, Ace needed to exploit its best asset: the social capital that existed in its dealer network. The virtual community was built on already established ties of common experience, common aims, and personal acquaintance.

Building the ACIS Community

Some Ace dealers have served C&I accounts for decades. Others are new to the segment and are eager to climb the learning curve as quickly as possible. Helping these dealers connect and learn from one another is the primary objective of the ACIS community.

The heart of the ACIS program is an extranet site, ACENET 2000, an integrated set of message boards, online seminars, newsletters and program materials relevant to the C&I hardware business. The message boards serve several purposes: one board, Merchandise Mart, allows dealers to discuss their experiences with different vendors and products. Another, Ask Tina, allows Tina Lopotko, the manager of the ACIS program, to answer dealer questions in a way that allows everyone to benefit from her answers. The Sourcing board enables dealers to ask for help in locating hard-to-find merchandise.

Online seminars are part of a program called "Coach's Corner." Anyone with expertise to share can be a "coach": a dealer, an Ace employee, even a vendor. In addition to sharing some prepared material, the coach is available to answer any questions the dealers might have.

A popular feature is the "Store of the Month." The home page of the ACIS site features the picture of a store being highlighted, along with whatever history the dealer wants to share. Because of the nature of the hardware store as a family-run business, the histories shared online combine births and deaths, natural disasters, and the normal vicissitudes of life along with business events. Building trust and connection, the feature helps anchor business concerns in the similar and shared life experiences of the hardware dealers. In addition to being highlighted on the home page, the Store of the Month also has a message board where other dealers can share their common experiences or ask questions of the dealer being profiled.

The Role of Social Capital

The ACIS community is at once an effort to *build* social capital and to exploit it. It is an effort to exploit the social capital that exists in the organizations to enable it to learn more quickly and evolve to meet the demands of the marketplace. This social capital wasn't created this year or this month: it has developed among members over many years, and has long been fostered and renewed in four face-to-face meetings every year. Yet, the ACIS on-line community is an effort to build that capital as well.

To understand how the ACIS builds social capital, it is necessary to examine the elements that constitute it. In his examination of the impacts of technology on social capital, Paul Resnick focuses on seven "productive resources" that develop in a social network over time:

- Communication paths
- Common knowledge
- Shared values
- Collective identity
- Roles and norms
- Obligations
- Trust[16]

These resources address the challenges of our three critical social capital dimensions. The first, communications paths, is structural, the next four mainly cognitive, and obligations and trust clearly relational. Online interac-

The heart of the ACIS program is an extranet site, ACENET 2000, an integrated set of message boards, online seminars, newsletters and program materials relevant to the C&I hardware business.

tion in the ACIS community has an observable impact on each of these resources. As with any other networking initiative, the effort has expanded the communication paths that exist between dealers in the network. Not every dealer can attend face-to-face meetings. Interaction between meetings via telephone tends to occur among dealers who are already acquainted. Today, one third of the dealers in the ACIS community log on once a week, and virtually all of them visit at least once a month. The online community has enabled connections that would otherwise not have occurred.

Knowledge exchange is one of the stated goals of the ACIS effort, and the impacts are evident both in the conversations visible on the site, and the stories that dealers tell about problem-solving with their peers. A dealer in Bullhead, Arizona, for example, tells of his experience selling Ace brand paint to a casino operator. The casino operator said another vendor's product had a "direct-to-metal" ratio that indicated superior adhesion to metal surfaces. Unaware of such a ratio, the Ace dealer turned to the community for advice. Another dealer saw his question on the message board and suggested that he send a sample of the competitor's product to Ace's lab for analysis. The analysis showed that the competitors "direct-to-metal" rating was a marketing gimmick—the chemical composition of Ace's product actually made it a better choice for metal. The dealer won the contract, but the entire community benefited from the learning that resulted.

> Unlike other forms of collaboration, online interactions in a community setting are public and very visible. They therefore serve as a continual reminder of the values that the community shares.

Unlike other forms of collaboration, online interactions in a community setting are public and very visible. They therefore serve as a continual reminder of the values that the community shares. On the "Merchandise Mart" board, dealers talk candidly about their experience with vendors and products. They compare notes with each other and in the process help Ace understand their needs better. By creating this forum, Ace shows it respects its dealers and takes their problems seriously. By using the forum, dealers demonstrate that Ace is a place where problems can be surfaced and resolved.

Ace understood that one of its challenges in expanding the C&I business was one of identity. Even today, any dealer can sell to C&I customers. There is no requirement to identify yourself as belonging to this group. In an organization like a co-op. where independence is a first principle, this is as it should be. Yet Ace recognized that much can be gained by forging a shared identity among C&I dealers with common goals. The C&I community has made that possible on a national scale.

What about mutual obligations? Though prizing their independence, dealers understand that support networks are a powerful asset. Yet communities become truly effective when a generalized trust prevails: that is, when members help other members without the expectation that the recipient will personally return the favor, expecting instead that someone will be there when the helper needs help. The "Sourcing Board" on the ACIS site provides a good example. Using the Sourcing Board, dealers ask for help when a customer requests an item that the dealer has never purchased before. With C&I accounts, good service often means going out of your way to find something your customer wants. The sourcing board helps dealers do this without expending extraordinary effort. A dealer in New York who helps a dealer in San Francisco is not necessarily looking for a response in kind, yet both dealers benefit from the community of generalized trust and generalized mutual assistance.

Long-time virtual community expert Lisa Kimball often points out that most groups—online or offline—are more productive when roles and norms are explicitly defined. It is a virtue of virtual groups, she says, that people accept that fact more readily in a virtual setting than a face-to-face gathering. For example, few hardware dealers would think of themselves as capable of "coaching" other dealers, no matter how experienced they might be. But through forums like "Coach's Corner," in which individual dealers and Ace personnel host discussions on topics in which they have expertise, the community recognizes that all of us have something to learn, and something to teach.

Finally, trust. Daniel McAllister has made a useful distinction between affect-based trust, which represents an emotional bond between people, and cognition-based trust, which represents a trust that an individual is reliable.[17] Both kinds of trust are clearly critical to organizations. While the conditions and interactions that foster affect-based trust are not clear, it does seem obvious that the shared history made visible in an online setting—a history of interactions among people that reveal, in different ways, expertise, responsiveness, reliability, and other aspects—provides a basis for cognition-based trust to grow.

The success of the ACIS community demonstrates how virtual interactions can build on and enhance the social capital that is so important for cooperation and knowledge exchange. We will continue to learn more about social capital and virtual interactions as we observe the progress of this and other on-line communities.

Endnotes

1. Barry Wellman and Milena Gulia, "Virtual Communities as Communities: Net Surfers Don't Ride Alone," in Marc Smith and Peter Kollock, *Communities in Cyberspace: Perspectives on New Forms of Social Organization* (London: Routledge, 2001), pp. 167-194.
2. Janine Nahapiet and Sumantra Ghoshal, "Social Capital, Intellectual Capital, and the Organizational Advantage," *Academy of Management Review*, Vol. 23, No. 2, 1998, p. 243.
3. See Chapter 1 of Eric Lesser (ed.), *Knowledge and Social Capital* (Woburn, MA: Butterworth-Heinemann, 2000).
4. Elena Rocco, "Trust Breaks Down in Electronic Contexts But Can Be Repaired by Some Initial Face-to-Face Contact," *Proceedings of CHI '98* (New York: ACM Press, 1998).

5. For a more extensive description of the Alcoa and Oticon examples, see Don Cohen and Laurence Prusak, *In Good Company: How Social Capital Makes Organizations Work*, (Cambridge, Massachusetts: Harvard Business School Press, 2001).
6. Elena Rocco, Thomas Finholt, Erik Hofer, and James Herbsleb, "Designing as if Trust Mattered," Collaboratory for Research on Electronic Work (CREW) technical report, University of Michigan, Ann Arbor, 2000.
7. Dunbar's argument is laid out in *Grooming, Gossip, and the Evolution of Language* (Cambridge, Massachusetts: Harvard University Press, 1996).
8. Julian Orr, *Talking About Machines: An Ethnography of a Modern Job* (Ithaca, New York: ILR Press, 1994).
9. J.C.R. Licklider and Robert W. Taylor, "The Computer and Communication Device," *Science and Technology* (April 1968), pp. 21-31.
10. David A. Owens, Margaret A. Neale, and Robert I. Sutton, "Technologies of Status Management: Status Dynamics in E-Mail Communications," *Research on Managing Groups and Teams*, Volume 3, 2000, pp. 205-230.
11. Rocco, et al.
12. Cohen and Prusak, p. 143.
13. Tim Berners-Lee, *Weaving the Web: The Original Design and Ultimate Destiny of the World Wide Web* (New York: Harperbusiness, 2000), p. 206.
14. Anita Blanchard and Tom Horan, "Virtual Communities and Social Capital," in Eric Lesser (ed.), *Knowledge and Social Capital* (Woburn, MA: Butterworth-Heinemann, 2000), p. 299.
15. Thomas H. Davenport and Laurence Prusak, *Working Knowledge* (Cambridge, Massachusetts: Harvard Business Review Press, 1997), p. 19.
16. Paul Resnick, "Beyond Bowling Together: SocioTechnical Capital," to appear in *HCI in the New Millenium*, John Carroll (ed.)(Reading, MA: Addison-Wesley).
17. D.J. McAllister, "Affect- and Cognition-Based Trust as Foundations for Interpersonal Cooperation in Organizations," *Academy of Management Journal*, 38: 24-59, 1995.

Eric Lesser is Executive Consultant at the IBM Institute for Knowledge Management. Joseph Cothrel is Vice President of research at Participate.com.

Through the Looking Glass: A Progress Report on the Enterprise Portal

The Editors of Knowledge Management Magazine

Is the enterprise information portal still the "killer app" for knowledge management, as Knowledge Management *proclaimed a few years ago? Yes—although still more in theory than in practice. The authors of this article assert that "the need for an EIP has in no way diminished," but cite research that suggests "this is another case in which implementing 'the next great technology' lags behind the buzz about it." Many companies are just not ready to put EIPs to work yet.*

In July 1999, *Knowledge Management* published its first cover story on the enterprise information portal, declaring, "Knowledge management has found its killer app." Nineteen months later, this is still an accurate statement, borne out by our own investigations and the research of industry analysts. But the newness of portal tools and the business-critical nature of EIP deployment have led large corporations to move forward with caution on their portal implementations.

"The portal market is in an embryonic state, and there are few if any enterprise deployments," says Peter J. Auditore, vice president for U.S. marketing at Hummingbird Ltd., a portal vendor in Toronto. A survey of 1,000 IT executives and managers in small, medium-size and large organizations, done last year for Hummingbird, indicated that most companies plan to have portals, but 60 percent of them were only in the "conceptual phase" of EIP deployment; a mere 7 percent had pilots under way, and only 8 percent had completed deployment. To some extent, this slow movement may be related to company size and readiness to invest the time and money that a portal project requires. Among the 52 companies in the survey that have revenues of more than $15 billion, the "conceptual" statistic dropped to 40 percent, while 11.5 percent were piloting portal projects and 23 percent had deployed them.

"Large organizations are still early in their deployment efforts," says Linda Clark, head of the EIP initiative at the PricewaterhouseCoopers consultancy in Bethesda, Md. "Many are still experimenting with multiple pilot solutions and trying to understand all the issues critical to a broad and deep

---

Reprinted by permission of the publisher from *Knowledge Management* magazine, February 2001. Copyright © 2001 by Freedom Technology Media Group. All rights reserved.

enterprise-wide portal implementation."

The need for an EIP has in no way diminished. Corporate knowledge workers continue to struggle to find information on crowded desktops and to master the idiosyncratic interfaces of various IT platforms. In contrast, portals offer a single, personalized point of access to relevant business knowledge no matter where it resides. By their nature, they centralize knowledge and can shorten paths between data and business processes. In sum, a properly deployed portal can streamline decision-making and thus a company's costs and time to market for new products.

Why then are there relatively few portal deployments to date? Research appears to confirm that this is another case in which implementing "the next great technology" lags behind the buzz about it. The Delphi Group of Boston reported in September that in its own survey of more than 1,000 businesspeople, only one-fourth of respondents said they had already invested in portal technology, but more than half indicated that they'd make a significant investment in it within the next year (see Figure 1).

A second reason for the delay in implementation is that for virtually all strategic business process projects, companies must be ready to do more than simply install technology—and in this area many of them are not. "It may be that portals were somewhat oversold, at least initially," says Henry Morris, vice president for data warehousing and knowledge management at International Data Corp. in Framingham, Mass. "People led with the technology rather than looking at the state of organizational readiness for a portal."

> Research appears to confirm that this is another case in which implementing "the next great technology" lags behind the buzz about it.

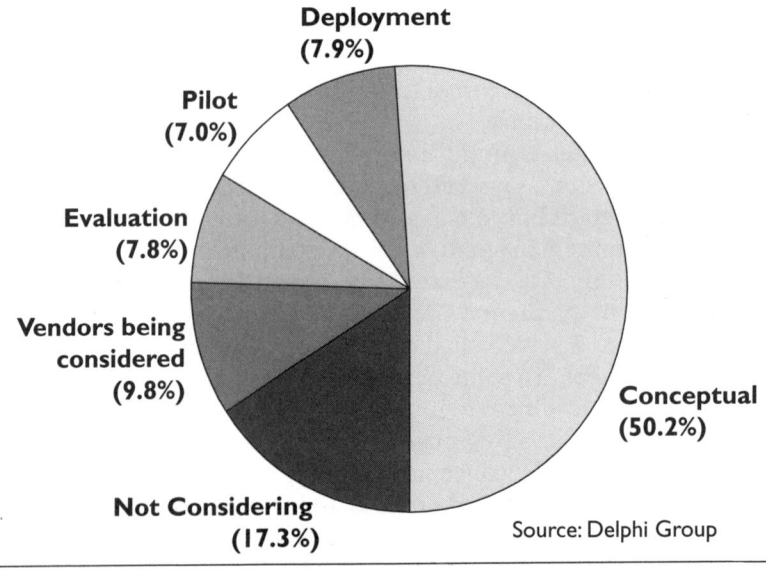

Deployment (7.9%)
Pilot (7.0%)
Evaluation (7.8%)
Vendors being considered (9.8%)
Not Considering (17.3%)
Conceptual (50.2%)

Source: Delphi Group

Figure 1. **A recent survey showed that half of corporations are only in the conceptual phase of portal projects and less than 15 percent have reached the pilot phase or deployment.**

Like any other knowledge management project, deploying an EIP involves technology tools but cannot be driven by them. "Portals need a purpose," says Madan Sheina, senior analyst for analytical applications and business intelligence portals with the Aberdeen Group of Boston, "a business roadmap that leads from deployment to strategic business value in the form of decision support, faster time to market, lower overhead and better competitive positioning." Making such a business case involves more than buying products and should include input from various business units that will use the portal, not just IT specialists.

Generation Gap

Finally, beyond the expense, complexity and organizational issues of getting an EIP up and running, there's the likelihood that early generations of portals didn't deliver enough of what enterprises wanted to make them an immediate necessity. Among the promises only now being fulfilled are improved collaboration among all parties involved and delivery of information to support business-to-business (B2B) transactions both within the enterprise and with partners and suppliers.

The initial releases of portals were basically data aggregation tools, what Tad W. Piper, a research analyst at U.S. Bancorp Piper Jaffray in Palo Alto, Calif., characterizes as "My Yahoo for the enterprise." The information to be aggregated typically included massive amounts of unstructured data in e-mail or on Web pages as well as structured data organized in proprietary software applications, relational databases and mainframe-based legacy files.

But the first generation portal had limits, often derived from the market niche of the vendor that built it. Some products, based on search or document management technology, focused on access to a business's store of unstructured information. Others, oriented toward enterprise data management and business intelligence, were honed for reporting against structured data. As time passed, it became evident that the initial iterations of EIPs were too static, needed to do a better job of integrating the knowledge and workflow information they presented and didn't scale upward well enough to be easily extended throughout an enterprise.

First-generation portals have delivered some business value in the form of speeding access to knowledge, but speed alone has limited strategic worth. "Aggregation is not a valuable business tool. It's a fun thing to do for IT, but it is not a business driver," says Ron Bienvenu, president and CEO of portal vendor SageMaker Inc. in Fairfield, Conn. "If Amazon.com disappeared tomorrow, it's not going to affect the world economy. But if a trading room floor goes down for one minute during the trading day, you will see violence because that is real business."

The history of portal products from Plumtree Software Inc. of San Francisco illustrates the evolution of the technology. The first Plumtree

> First-generation portals have delivered some business value in the form of speeding access to knowledge, but speed alone has limited strategic worth.

> **BEST PRACTICES FOR PORTALS**
>
> Linda Clark, who leads the enterprise information portals initiative at consultant PricewaterhouseCoopers in Bethesda, Md., offers the following suggestions as best practices for a portal implementation project:
>
> 1. Start with a prototype—not just a demonstration from the vendor—to begin pilot deployments and the development of an implementation strategy.
> 2. Identify and involve a variety of stakeholders, but choose an initial focus for the prototyping that addresses real business problems.
> 3. Use a phased approach that delivers near-term value but increasingly supports a broader vision. Don't try to attack the whole project at once, but don't miss out on greater benefits by not continuing to improve and expand the deployment.
> 4. Be selective about the information you expose through the portal. Be sure that each source has good-quality data and is well maintained. Clearly identify ownership of each source.
> 5. Have a security plan that is robust enough to meet your requirements and is expandable.
> 6. Be aware that as data stores and application services are made available to employees beyond the organization's power users, additional context or metadata may be required. this will create more demand for knowledge management processes and service, so be prepared to provide them.
> 7. Find a strong leader who has the status and diplomacy to champion the EIP. A coalition of leaders and stakeholders is even better.

Corporate Portal, introduced three years ago, offered a hierarchical, searchable directory of documents, Web pages and messages. It allowed customers to plug in components that could scan new types of repositories and content. The second version offered users a personalized view of content from the directory and some interactive application services. This revision also introduced a class of components called "gadgets" for the integration of application services. Last fall Plumtree released its third major iteration of the product, Plumtree Corporate Portal 4.0, which allows communities of interest, workgroups and project teams to share information and has an architectural approach that enables simultaneous processing of input from multiple gadgets.

Now, as most companies are getting serious about EIP deployment, leading vendors are moving on from first-generation Web server-based portals that aggregate information modules in a desktop window. Vendors and analysts say that the next-generation portals now in development will deliver more of what was promised for their predecessors: integrated environments that provide enterprise-wide information access, support collaborative work and com-

B2B Portal Provides Self-Service

Despite the relative immaturity of the portal market and the challenges companies face in integrating existing heterogeneous systems and managing disparate content streams, some are creating business value by deploying them. In mid-1999 Herman Miller Inc., a 77-year-old office furniture manufacturer in Zeeland, Mich., rolled out MySIGN, which stands for Supplier Information Global Network. Working with TopTier Software Inc., Herman Miller has implemented what Mike Brunsting, electronic commerce team leader, calls a "supplier self-service portal"; MySIGN is a secure Web site that offers access to inventory, pricing and shipping information through a single interface. Tied to Miller's Baan Co. enterprise resource planning (ERP) system, the portal provides real-time access to business data.

"We are trying to replace what we used to do via phone calls, automated faxes and mailed reports by giving the suppliers that information directly through the portal," Brunsting says. "Things like our detailed demand schedules go out every day. In the past, suppliers would receive a fax; now they can access and download that information through the portal. They can see receipt information. If they have a question about whether or not a shipment was received, they can see that in real time on our back-end ERP system, as well as inventory, planning information, quality data and pricing payments—basically, anything that has to do with the supplier relationship they have access to."

A sort of hybrid portal, MySIGN incorporates a pricing system for the parts it uses to build its office furniture; parts and supplies vendors can update their prices through the portal, which then triggers notifications to the appropriate company personnel. That employee simply approves the changes, and the data is updated automatically in Herman Miller's ERP system. According to Brunsting, the company also would like to establish "voucher-on-receipt," price synchronization and interactive quality monitoring through the portal.

Integrating systems has been a focus point for Miller's e-commerce group. "We've had to spend most of our time on the back end," says Brunsting. "For instance, we're aggregating demand from multiple systems, including the Baan ERP; we also have a mainframe legacy system. In certain situations we've decided to extract data from those systems and consolidate them into an Oracle database. We still use the portal to present that and give users access to it, but on the back end we are doing some things with ActiveWorks, which is now owned by WebMethods—that's more of a middleware. And we're doing some Java programming to serve as the middleware for moving and consolidating data and then using the portal to present it."

Herman Miller chose TopTier Software as its supplier originally because it sold a Web-enabled Baan ERP system that fit with the company's

> existing technology. "We didn't want to build something ourselves, we wanted to use technology that was out there," says Brunsting. "At the time, their product really wasn't meant to be an extranet system, but they worked closely with us to develop that functionality."

plete transactions.

"Portal software must allow for straightforward access to relevant facts," says Larry Bowden, vice president of portal solutions at IBM's Silicon Valley Laboratory in San Jose, Calif. "Users need to collaborate with others around these facts for opinion and insight, and they need to take action quickly once a decision has been reached. A well-designed second-generation enterprise portal reduces the friction associated with these tasks."

Observers sometimes differ as to what is new about new portals. For example, many vendors are promoting the ability to provide a centralized view of all resources, including back-end enterprise resource planning (ERP) systems, as a core knowledge management function of second-generation portals. But according to Gene Phifer, an analyst at the Gartner Group in Plano, Texas, that capability is already found in first-generation portals, as are tools for developing taxonomies to categorize content.

In the collaboration realm, next-generation portals generally include features such as instant text and voice messaging, audio and video conferencing, shared calendaring and, perhaps most important, dynamic document sharing.

Scaling on up

The farthest-reaching characteristic of the new generation of portals, however, is that many are being developed on Web application server platforms to deliver the scaleability, robustness and interactivity that businesses need. "From a pure technology perspective, a number of issues need to be addressed for portals to really support the next generation of sites that some organizations are looking to build—things like tying the portal more closely to a transaction-processing environment, as opposed to having a portal running solely on a Web server," says Kathleen Hall, a Boston-based industry analyst with Giga Information Group. "If you are talking about an external-facing portal, you also need more kinds of advanced transaction processing."

Such an application-centric focus should enable greater integration of individual components. "Users don't live in applications any more; they use application services instead," says Aberdeen's Sheina. "IT as yet has been unable to provide an effective organizing principle at the desktop that coordinates multiple data sources." A superior portal implementation will realize that principle by offering an integrated desktop that delivers workflow functions. It is no accident that vendors are embracing the "dashboard" metaphor when referring to these portals.

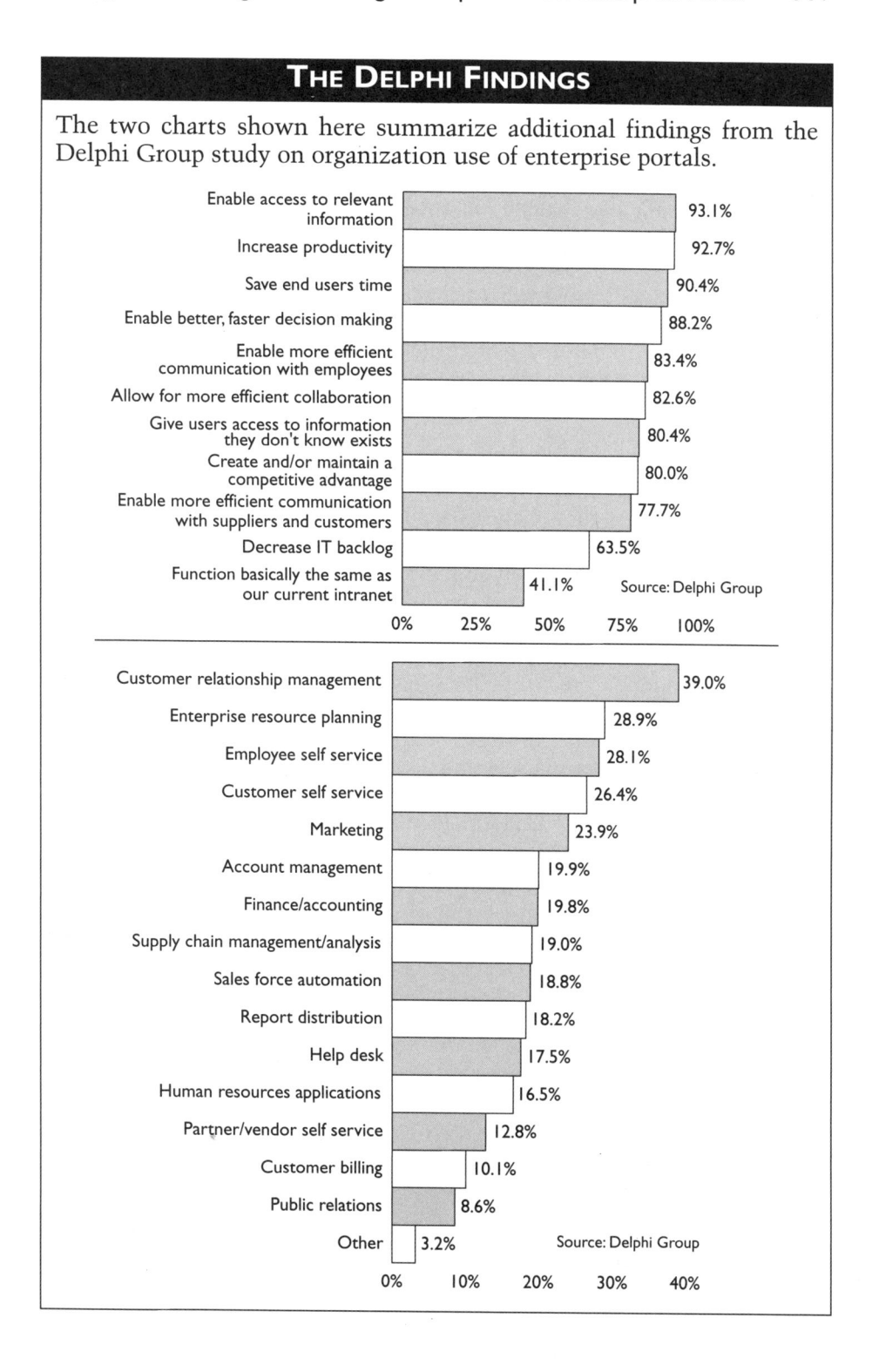

THE DELPHI FINDINGS

The two charts shown here summarize additional findings from the Delphi Group study on organization use of enterprise portals.

Benefit	Percentage
Enable access to relevant information	93.1%
Increase productivity	92.7%
Save end users time	90.4%
Enable better, faster decision making	88.2%
Enable more efficient communication with employees	83.4%
Allow for more efficient collaboration	82.6%
Give users access to information they don't know exists	80.4%
Create and/or maintain a competitive advantage	80.0%
Enable more efficient communication with suppliers and customers	77.7%
Decrease IT backlog	63.5%
Function basically the same as our current intranet	41.1%

Source: Delphi Group

Application	Percentage
Customer relationship management	39.0%
Enterprise resource planning	28.9%
Employee self service	28.1%
Customer self service	26.4%
Marketing	23.9%
Account management	19.9%
Finance/accounting	19.8%
Supply chain management/analysis	19.0%
Sales force automation	18.8%
Report distribution	18.2%
Help desk	17.5%
Human resources applications	16.5%
Partner/vendor self service	12.8%
Customer billing	10.1%
Public relations	8.6%
Other	3.2%

Source: Delphi Group

Unplugged Portals Planned

Many EIP vendors are working to extend the capabilities of their products beyond the walls of the office through wireless connectivity. The Delphi Group of Boston reports that more than half the enterprises it surveyed recently are planning to deploy mobile devices for access to portals within the next year.

The enterprise wireless space illustrates the confusion that competitive pressures for rapid deployment can create. Transmission technology still hobbles the speed of data throughput; if 56kbps for dial-up connectivity tries the patience of desktop users, imagine how accessing a portal at the average wireless data throughput of 9.6kbps will feel. And competing carrier systems and protocols—such as the Wireless Application Protocol (WAP), the WML extension of the eXtended Markup Language (XML) and NTT DoCoMo Inc.'s i-mode—hinder standardization. Early adopters will have to make a leap of faith to deploy wireless portal access tools.

Madan Sheina, senior analyst for analytical applications and business intelligence portals with the Aberdeen Group of Boston, suggests that this lack of market clarity will be an obstacle to the use of mobile devices as primary portal interfaces for at least two more years. Nonetheless, widespread support for mobile devices will increasingly be one of the yardsticks by which the vendors of portal tools will be judged. That message has gotten through to vendors; Corechange Inc., IBM Corp., Oracle Corp. and Sybase Inc., for example, promote mobile access as a core element of their portal solutions. Mobile access is central also to Microsoft Corp.'s .Net initiative.

However, not all portal users find it necessary to take on this added burden. "We are not even considering mobile," says Mike Brunsting, electronic commerce team leader at Herman Miller Inc., a manufacturer of office furniture in Zeeland, Mich. He notes that the company's new portal already taxes the bandwidth capacity of some of its suppliers.

Enterprises that do want to take the plunge should plan thoroughly, advises Larry Bowden, vice president of portal solutions at IBM's Silicon Valley Laboratory in San Jose, Calif. "The first thing to do is get organized," he says. "Get the portal, the access, the controls, personalization and collaboration set. Then you just say, 'I've got that running on my PC and want to expand it. I want to go through different dial tones to different types of devices.'"

IBM's Bowden describes a portal environment in which individual applications—which he calls "portlets," similar to Plumtree's gadgets—are dynamically aware of activities in the others and can respond to them with displays of relevant data. "The differentiator, not in the next nine months but up to two years from now, will be portals that can provide this dynamic nature of having peer awareness and using contextual relationships—essentially bringing knowledge management and collaboration into the fold," he says.

In a white paper last year, Delphi Group noted that many desktop environments mimic the process of an executive gathering information by phone—a process in which the only real source of continuity is the paper notepad being written on. Delphi suggested that what is needed to replace the islands of information of early portals is a single, integrated decision-support package. Second-generation portals can be expected to integrate information feeds and workflow options at the user interface and tie together back-end processes for information sharing among applications, as part of an architecture built on a Web application server.

Sheina argues that back-end integration of data sources, not the interface or delivery mechanism, will become the real differentiator among portal products. IDC's Morris goes one step farther, calling for portals to incorporate a "process manager": an engine that learns and then manages business processes. "Take a sales rep and how you qualify a lead," he says. "These processes involve a number of different steps and the collaboration of many different individuals. After you define the process, a process manager would monitor all the different steps that need to happen." In this model, the portal would know what role each individual plays in each part of the process and present the person with current information applicable to it.

"What I actually will see as I go into the portal will [change and] be different, not just for me versus someone else but for me today versus yesterday," Morris adds. "Having this kind of context is going to make portals much more dynamic. It's a logical extension to the idea of enabling collaboration, defining and managing a business process that requires multiple people to be involved together and requires the interoperation of many different applications." He adds, though, that in terms of both available technology and sophistication of business processes, the realization of this vision will be a long-term project.

These advanced functions may sound a bit futuristic, but out on the leading edge are user companies that already need them. For example, Science Applications International Corp. (SAIC), a San Diego-based IT systems integrator, provides information systems and services for government agencies as well as private-sector companies. According to Tracy Bair, an SAIC vice president, the company wants to build just such a next-generation portal. "We are looking toward a complete process-oriented portal that includes workflow components," she says. "Our focus is how you integrate workflow components—the business process within the portal itself—so that you have a single point of view for not only looking for and assessing data, but also doing traditional business processes of coordination, review and approval."

Bair says that products with these capabilities are just now coming to market. As an example she cites Integic Corp.'s Enterprise Process Portal, which integrates that company's e.Power platform (a process management engine that provides links to business transaction systems) with

> Delphi suggested that what is needed to replace the islands of information of early portals is a single, integrated decision-support package.

Hummingbird's Enterprise Information Portal. SAIC hasn't implemented this type of tool yet, but she foresees the adoption of a browser or portal framework that becomes the primary place where daily business gets done.

The Knowledge Imperative

Many knowledge management practitioners and analysts have identified the corporate portal as a killer app because it offers a single way in to disparate knowledge sources. Moreover, it can be used to organize content in appropriate taxonomies to satisfy the needs of internal and external communities. "The knowledge portal is a key component of many intranet-based KM systems, providing an interface for knowledge work that KM has lacked," says Sheina. "It also provides an interface to facilitate collaboration, without which KM would be impossible."

Product advances should allow next-generation portals to play more fully to the strengths and needs of knowledge management projects. According to Bair, SAIC's motivation is to realize the benefits of a KM approach. "How do you take advantage of the information that's in an enterprise?" she says. "It might be gathered and obtained by another functional area, but if you had insight into it, you could improve your business operations." Cutting-edge EIPs, she suggests, can enable enterprises to effectively flow lessons learned and business decision support capabilities across functional areas.

Potentially, these are matters not merely of convenience and incremental improvement but of survival. "One of the determining factors for corporate growth is how quickly it can respond to change and identify and exploit new opportunities," says Sheina. "But companies struggle to make intellectual capital more visible, accessible and manageable. Successful enterprises will be those that can take full advantage of their corporate information."

Another determining factor for success in this new market environment is the emergence of the virtual enterprise and the concomitant need to extend knowledge access and transactional capabilities to suppliers, partners and customers as well as to a company's own employees, wherever they may be. To serve them all, companies need a single, consolidated point of access to the enterprise knowledge flow, which is likely to be centered on a company's supply chain or value chain but reaches out in many directions. One vision of the future of the portal is Lotus Development Corp.'s Raven project. The first fruit of that development effort is the new Lotus Discovery Server, which incorporates the K-station knowledge portal that Lotus released late last year. Discovery Server is supposed to enable the user to pull together various documents relevant to a topic or query and help to locate the tacit knowledge held by individuals with expertise in that topic.

"The portal to date has been talked about as an interface," says Glenn Kelly, general manager for K-station marketing at Lotus in Cambridge, Mass. "K-station is more than an interface; it's the ability to take action, to work almost as a knowledge repository. That enables people to interface into data or knowledge sources that are out there but also to interact with people in higher levels of collaboration."

As EIPs become integrated with analytical, reporting and document or text filtering tools, knowledge workers will get better access to higher-quality information, and that will improve the decision-making process. In the end, says PwC's Clark, the knowledge worker will gain status in the enterprise because he or she will be focused on more valuable activities such as problem analysis, root cause identification, creative solution development, innovation, decision making and action taking.

The biggest challenge facing developers of portal technology, according to IDC's Morris, is facilitating business processes. "How do your best sales reps qualify a lead? They use information about the account to know what the next steps are," he says. "Those types of things are expertise. Capturing a process and guiding people through that process is a great way to mentor them. That's a dynamic aspect beyond where portals are today."

The bottom line is that employees need to be able to make better, more informed decisions, in consultation with all stakeholders, in less time. An effective portal of any generation will support the entire process of making a business decision. The enterprise portal is a door to the future that many companies will choose to open, because stronger competitiveness, lower costs and improved financial performance lie through it.

Functional Processes

FINANCE AND ACCOUNTING

Improving Financial Performance Through Benchmarking and Best Practices

Susan J. Leandri

Technology has freed CPAs from many traditional responsibilities and opened the door to a broader, more strategic role in their client's or employer's business. CPAs can leverage their expertise in analyzing quantitative information while contributing to decision-making. The techniques of benchmarking and best practices allow CPAs to move beyond presenting financial data "as it is" and take a more active role in shaping financial performance "as it should be."

Technological advances and business process improvements have been a mixed blessing for CPAs. On one hand, these advances have streamlined much of the practitioner's work: no longer are CPAs up to their elbows in financial statements and reports. On the other hand, technology has usurped many traditional duties and left the CPA's role more open to discussion. In the past, accountants often found themselves in the role of corporate cop: detecting and correcting problems and enforcing proper procedures. But this is not enough. CPAs can—and must—take on broader roles as business analysts, consultants, and change agents. They are expected to be more proactive participants on the front end, keeping problems at bay and creating an atmosphere for continuous improvement.

Reprinted with permission from *The CPA Journal*, January 2001. Copyright © 2001 The CPA Journal, 530 Fifth Avenue, New York, NY 10036, U.S.A. All rights reserved.

Moving to this next level means that CPAs cannot just evaluate their client's or employer's balance sheets and operations "as is." The focus needs to shift to the "should be," steering organizations to improve performance and results. Determining this ideal calls for a broader understanding of a company's underlying business processes and strategic goals.

Because CPAs are skilled in detecting problems, they're a natural choice to spearhead comprehensive financial initiatives. Two effective tools for unearthing the bigger picture are benchmarking and best practices. By adding these business improvement tools to their toolbox, CPAs can increase their value to clients and employers and broaden their professional opportunities.

What Are Benchmarking and Best Practices?

The terms benchmarking and best practices are established in today's business lexicon, but CPAs may not be sure what they really involve and what role they really play.

Benchmarking is a means of comparing operations—usually a specific business process—with the performance of others. These comparisons can be both quantitative and qualitative. Benchmarking projects can also have different focuses: universal, competitive, or internal.

Universal benchmarking compares a company's results with high performers, regardless of their industry, size, geography, or products. Companies frequently stumble across breakthrough ideas for business improvement through venturing outside of their industry in search of insight. *Competitive* benchmarking assesses a company's performance against that of competitors or similar companies. Comparisons are typically made by industry, size (e.g., revenues or employees), or geography. *Internal* benchmarking entails measuring one part of a company against another. All benchmarking approaches have the end goal of identifying problem areas, establishing ideal performance levels, and creating an improvement plan.

Best practices enter the picture in the improvement plan. They are simply the best ways to perform a business process. In the process of gathering quantitative benchmark data, project leaders also seek to identify best practices and, as a result, the two techniques complement each other. For example, if a company discovered that a benchmark peer could close its books in two rather than 12 days, then it would make sense to investigate and document the best practices that enable the peer to close its books quicker. Similarly, if a company is benchmarking its performance internally (e.g., among business divisions), the benchmarking project leaders should identify the best practices a division or manager uses to achieve such results.

Benchmarking and Best Practices in Action

When used as a one-two punch, benchmarking and best practices reveal the "why" behind the numbers. Together, they can transform data into actionable knowledge.

> Because CPAs are skilled in detecting problems, they're a natural choice to spearhead comprehensive financial initiatives.

To undertake a benchmarking project, companies often need some form of outside assistance. External consultants or professional or trade organizations are good sources for benchmarking data and expertise. Quality off-the-shelf surveys and benchmark data are often reasonably priced and are adequate for the baseline stages of a benchmarking project. Depending on a project's goals, it may be worthwhile to seek out competitors and encourage them to participate in a cooperative benchmarking project.

Whether a company participates in a prepackaged benchmarking exercise or performs a customized project, key performance indicators for a business process must be determined. Performance measures enable companies to express the results of a business process in precise quantitative terms. Instead of using subjective terms like good, fast, or low cost, performance measures translate those judgments into precise metrics. For example, the following approaches would be ways to analyze the accounts payable process:

- Instead of saying that the accounts payable process is good, a company reports that 100% of invoices were processed without error.
- Instead of saying that the accounts payable process is fast, a company reports that it takes an average of two days to edit and review an invoice.
- Instead of saying that the accounts payable process is low cost, a company reports that the total cost to finance accounts payable is 5% of total revenue.

By identifying performance levels and understanding what drives them, CPAs take the first step toward acting as change catalysts. The following cases illustrate different approaches to benchmarking and best practices projects.

A Universal Approach to Process Improvement

A small subsidiary of a large conglomerate wanted to improve its accounts receivable process. An audit team noted that the company had high bad-debt expense and declining accounts receivable turnover. The company's controller wanted to reverse this trend by uncovering the root cause of the problem and suggesting ways to improve the situation.

The controller used qualitative and quantitative surveys from a business information provider to collect key data and develop a picture of the accounts receivable process. After explaining the project goals, the controller worked with staff members to gather the necessary quantitative and qualitative information and compile a list of process strengths and weaknesses.

After gathering the data, the controller compared the quantitative data to existing universal benchmarks. Qualitative information was compared with best practices in the areas of billing, credit, and collections. A report discussing the findings from the benchmarking survey and best practices review identified improvement opportunities as well as areas of good performance.

One critical problem highlighted by the report was staff turnover (stemming from cost concerns), which caused ongoing problems with the quality and timeliness of credit and collection work. Specific improvement opportunities were identified, categorized as either immediate or longer-term initiatives, and incorporated into an action plan for improvement.

CPAs can employ similar approaches to isolate and tackle problem areas. Once aware of an obvious negative trend, most companies are eager to reverse it. Sometimes all they need is a trusted advisor to point the way.

Learning from Internal Benchmarking

In another case, a new liaison to the CFO at a multinational construction aggregate company undertook an internal benchmarking project to determine how well the decentralized finance units were operating. The liaison saw the project as an opportunity for the various units to learn from one another and share best practices.

The company used a survey designed to benchmark its global finance and accounting functions. A project team of members from each division convened to collect quantitative data. Following the data collection, team members received reports that illustrated their division's performance relative to others. A consultant then visited each division to collect qualitative process information. Upon completion of the site visits, all team members received a summary of qualitative responses from each division and templates for preparing action plans to submit to management. The templates included guidance in identifying next steps for wider implementation of best practices uncovered by the benchmarking survey.

Although this example involves a large company with multiple operations, internal benchmarking also benefits smaller companies. Even on a small scale, companies can achieve greater operational consistency and improve their processes by sharing best practices internally.

Looking to Peers

Business processes that are particularly critical to operations are obvious benchmarking targets for CPAs looking to enhance the bottom line. Consider the example of an international transportation provider that wanted to improve its contract administration process. The process was critical for several reasons: It consumed significant cash flow and involved people in multiple functions, thousands of contracts were outstanding at any given time, and risks were high if the process broke down. Yet the company was unsure whether this key process was functioning at peak performance.

The company decided it could improve through competitive benchmarking. First, internal auditors assessed the company's contract administration process. Then, site visits were conducted at six companies of similar size in

Success Factors for Benchmarking and Best Practices Reviews

With any benchmarking or best practices initiative, the primary goal is simple: avoid pitfalls and maximize the benefits of the project. The following factors increase the likelihood of completing a meaningful study:

- Involve management by communicating the visions, values, goals, and strategies behind initiatives.
- Involve process owners and staff at all points in the process.
- Understand the business process under review before comparing it with other organizations'.
- Keep the project as focused and simple as possible; break a large project into phases.
- Provide sufficient time for planning and training staff.
- Prepare data collection tools to minimize complexity and maximize consistency.
- Provide sufficient time to collect data and analyze results.
- Prepare adequately for site visits with benchmarking partners.
- Be willing to give benchmarking partners something in return for their participation.
- Consider the culture changes necessary in making any changes to business processes.
- Never lose sight of the project's original scope and intent.
- Do not get caught up in numbers and exactness.
- Keep a best practices mind-set at all times.

the same industry. The company also wanted to compare its process with best practices in contract administration and identify performance gaps, so it turned to external knowledge bases of best practices research. The findings highlighted trends in contract management that pointed to improvement ideas. These opportunities were organized into strategy, structure, people, process, and technology. From there, the company was able to set priorities for improving its process.

A Learning Process

Benchmarking surveys and best practices reviews are useful tools for uncovering problems, discovering ways to improve, and stimulating positive change. But a word of caution is in order.

"Benchmarking and best practices are tools for business improvement, but they will not solve everything that is ailing a company," cautions Jeffrey Berk, manager of benchmark development and services for Arthur Andersen Global Best Practices. "Benchmarking and best practices initiatives are most successful when they're approached with an open mind and the belief that they represent a learning process."

As trusted advisors that already have a keen understanding of the ebbs and flows of a client's or employer's business, CPAs are in an ideal position to collect benchmark data and study best practices. Many companies are eager to participate in benchmarking surveys and best practices reviews—especially once they see the results.

A FRAMEWORK FOR BENCHMARKING AND BEST PRACTICES REVIEWS

Step One: Determine What to Benchmark

The first step for any benchmarking initiative or best practices review is determining what to benchmark. This is often more complex than it seems; hasty decisions can lead to problems during the project.

- Determine which processes or issues are most important or in need of improvement.
- Determine whether a benchmarking and best practices approach is appropriate for the proposed project.

Step Two: Build Buy-in and Plan the Project

Project buy-in ensures the team is fully committed to the project and has management support and the necessary resources. Planning ensures a well-organized project that can be completed on time and on budget.

- Obtain a commitment to the project from management, process owners, and staff.
- Develop an action plan or framework to focus efforts.
- Establish the project team and define members' roles and responsibilities.

Step Three: Understand the Existing Process ("As Is")

The purpose of this step is to gain a thorough understanding of the process "as is." If the existing process is misunderstood, it is nearly impossible to compare it to the results of a benchmarking or best practices review.

- Determine the appropriate tools to study the process.
- Review and analyze activities related to the process.
- Determine the key performance indicators for the process.

Step Four: Research the Process and Potential Partners ("Should Be")

For a company to make a meaningful contribution to its peers, it must be familiar with other perspectives and approaches. External research helps refine what a company knows about its own processes and encourage out-of-the-box thinking in the pursuit of creative insights. External research also helps determine the most appropriate benchmark partners.

- Understand more about the process from an external perspective.
- Determine criteria for appropriate benchmark partners.
- Invite potential benchmark partners to participate in the project.

Step Five: Gather Data and Identify Best Practices

Once the appropriate benchmark partners have been determined, the CPA will want to help the client or employer explore ways of making the interaction with partners a valuable and rewarding experience for both partners. A successful outcome will depend upon how information is elicited and performance attributes identified.

- Prepare for meeting with the benchmark partner.
- Determine appropriate data collection methods.
- Design a questionnaire (based on project scope, if appropriate).
- Gather data by conducting site visits or disseminating surveys.
- Recognize superior performance in the data analysis.

Step Six: Pinpoint Improvement Areas

As best practices are identified, it is important to funnel differences between a company and benchmark partners into an organized set of conclusions so that appropriate follow-up can take place.

- Identify performance gaps in the business process.
- Explain the gaps in a manner that identifies root causes.

Step Seven: Conclude and Communicate

After preparing, analyzing, and collecting the necessary information, the benchmarking project team must draw some conclusions and communicate them to project sponsors, process owners, and staff.

- Organize conclusions in a thoughtful, cohesive manner.
- Select a communication method that fits the company's needs.

Step Eight: Create an Action Plan for the Future

Benchmarking projects and best practices reviews uncover the creative insights needed to improve performance. Although they are not tools for implementation, the insights they bring to light enable companies to develop tools for transforming ideas into actions.

- Develop an action plan to institute change.
- Develop a program to manage change.
- Monitor results over time to ensure the process improves.

Susan J. Leandri is the managing director of Arthur Andersen Global Best Practices, a group dedicated to capturing, analyzing, and sharing critical business knowledge. She can be reached at susan.j.leandri@us.arthurandersen.com.

Standards and Assessments

ISO 9000 AND BALDRIGE

ISO Quality Management Principles

ISO and Quality Systems Update Editors

The following document was developed by the International Organization for Standardization (ISO) to ease the transition of thousands of companies around the world to the year 2000 revision. It is reprinted here with permission of ISO. Copies of this document are also available on ISO's Web site www.iso.ch. This is the third in a four-part series of ISO guidance documents on the new standard to appear in Quality Systems Update.

This document introduces the eight quality management principles on which the quality management system standards of the revised ISO 9000:2000 series are based. These principles can be used by senior management as a framework to guide their organizations towards improved performance. The principles are derived from the collective experience and knowledge of the international experts who participate in ISO Technical Committee ISO/TC 176, *Quality Management and Quality Assurance,* which is responsible for developing and maintaining the ISO 9000 standards.

The eight quality management principles are defined in ISO 9000:2000, *Quality Management Systems—Fundamentals and Vocabulary,* and in ISO 9004:2000, *Quality Management Systems—Guidelines for Performance Improvements.*

This document gives the standardized descriptions of the principles as they appear in ISO 9000:2000 and ISO 9004:2000. In addition, it provides examples of the benefits derived from their use and of actions that managers typically take in applying the principles to improve their organizations' performance.

Reprinted by permission of the publisher from *Quality Systems Update*, January 2001. Copyright © 2001 by McGraw-Hill, Inc. All rights reserved.

- Principle 1—Customer focus
- Principle 2—Leadership
- Principle 3—Involvement of people
- Principle 4—Process approach
- Principle 5—System approach to management
- Principle 6—Continual improvement
- Principle 7—Factual approach to decision making
- Principle 8—Mutually beneficial supplier relationships
- The next step

Principle 1—Customer Focus

Organizations depend on their customers and therefore should understand current and future customer needs, should meet customer requirements and strive to exceed customer expectations.

Key benefits:
- Increased revenue and market share obtained through flexible and fast responses to market opportunities.
- Increased effectiveness in the use of the organization's resources to enhance customer satisfaction.
- Improved customer loyalty leading to repeat business.

Applying the principle of customer focus typically leads to:
- Researching and understanding customer needs and expectations.
- Ensuring that the objectives of the organization are linked to customer needs and expectations.
- Communicating customer needs and expectations throughout the organization.
- Measuring customer satisfaction and acting on the results.
- Systematically managing customer relationships.
- Ensuring a balanced approach between satisfying customers and other interested parties (such as owners, employees, suppliers, financiers, local communities and society as a whole).

Principle 2—Leadership

Leaders establish unity of purpose and direction of the organization. They should create and maintain the internal environment in which people can become fully involved in achieving the organization's objectives.

Key benefits:
- People will understand and be motivated towards the organization's goals and objectives.
- Activities are evaluated, aligned and implemented in a unified way.

ISO Quality Management Principles

- Miscommunication between levels of an organization will be minimized.

Applying the principle of leadership typically leads to:
- Considering the needs of all interested parties including customers, owners, employees, suppliers, financiers, local communities and society as a whole.
- Establishing a clear vision of the organization's future.
- Setting challenging goals and targets.
- Creating and sustaining shared values, fairness and ethical role models at all levels of the organization.
- Establishing trust and eliminating fear.
- Providing people with the required resources, training and freedom to act with responsibility and accountability.
- Inspiring, encouraging and recognizing people's contributions.

Principle 3—Involvement of People

People at all levels are the essence of an organization and their full involvement enables their abilities to be used for the organization's benefit.

Key benefits:
- Motivated, committed and involved people within the organization.
- Innovation and creativity in furthering the organization's objectives.
- People being accountable for their own performance.
- People eager to participate in and contribute to continual improvement.

Applying the principle of involvement of people typically leads to:
- People understanding the importance of their contribution and role in the organization.
- People identifying constraints to their performance.
- People accepting ownership of problems and their responsibility for solving them.
- People evaluating their performance against their personal goals and objectives.
- People actively seeking opportunities to enhance their competence, knowledge and experience.
- People freely sharing knowledge and experience.
- People openly discussing problems and issues.

Principle 4—Process Approach

A desired result is achieved more efficiently when activities and related resources are managed as a process.

Key benefits:
- Lower costs and shorter cycle times through effective use of resources.
- Improved, consistent and predictable results
- Focused and prioritized improvement opportunities.

Applying the principle of process approach typically leads to:
- Systematically defining the activities necessary to obtain a desired result.
- Establishing clear responsibility and accountability for managing key activities.
- Analysing and measuring of the capability of key activities.
- Identifying the interfaces of key activities within and between the functions of the organization.
- Focusing on the factors—such as resources, methods, and materials—that will improve key activities of the organization.
- Evaluating risks, consequences and impacts of activities on customers, suppliers and other interested parties.

Principle 5—System Approach to Management

Identifying, understanding and managing interrelated processes as a system contributes to the organization's effectiveness and efficiency in achieving its objectives.

Key benefits:
- Integration and alignment of the processes that will best achieve the desired results.
- Ability to focus effort on the key processes.
- Providing confidence to interested parties as to the consistency, effectiveness and efficiency of the organization.

Applying the principle of system approach to management typically leads to:
- Structuring a system to achieve the organization's objectives in the most effective and efficient way.
- Understanding the interdependencies between the processes of the system.
- Structured approaches that harmonize and integrate processes.
- Providing a better understanding of the roles and responsibilities necessary for achieving common objectives and thereby reducing cross-functional barriers.
- Understanding organizational capabilities and establishing resource constraints prior to action.
- Targeting and defining how specific activities within a system should operate.

- Continually improving the system through measurement and evaluation.

Principle 6—Continual Improvement

Continual improvement of the organization's overall performance should be a permanent objective of the organization.

Key benefits:
- Performance advantage through improved organizational capabilities.
- Alignment of improvement activities at all levels to an organization's strategic intent.
- Flexibility to react quickly to opportunities.

Applying the principle of continual improvement typically leads to:
- Employing a consistent organization-wide approach to continual improvement of the organization's performance.
- Providing people with training in the methods and tools of continual improvement.
- Making continual improvement of products, processes and systems an objective for every individual in the organization.
- Establishing goals to guide, and measures to track, continual improvement.
- Recognizing and acknowledging improvements.

Principle 7—Factual Approach to Decision Making

Effective decisions are based on the analysis of data and information.

Key benefits:
- Informed decisions.
- An increased ability to demonstrate the effectiveness of past decisions through reference to factual records.
- Increased ability to review, challenge and change opinions and decisions.

Applying the principle of factual approach to decision making typically leads to:
- Ensuring that data and information are sufficiently accurate and reliable.
- Making data accessible to those who need it.
- Analysing data and information using valid methods.
- Making decisions and taking action based on factual analysis, balanced with experience and intuition.

Principle 8—Mutually Beneficial Supplier Relationships

An organization and its suppliers are interdependent and a mutually beneficial relationship enhances the ability of both to create value.

Key benefits:
- Increased ability to create value for both parties.
- Flexibility and speed of joint responses to changing market or customer needs and expectations.
- Optimization of costs and resources.

Applying the principles of mutually beneficial supplier relationships typically leads to:
- Establishing relationships that balance short-term gains with long-term considerations.
- Pooling of expertise and resources with partners.
- Identifying and selecting key suppliers.
- Clear and open communication.
- Sharing information and future plans.
- Establishing joint development and improvement activities.
- Inspiring, encouraging and recognizing improvements and achievements by suppliers.

The Next Step

This document provides a general perspective on the quality management principles underlying the ISO 9000:2000 series. It gives an overview of these principles and shows how, collectively, they can form a basis for performance improvement and organizational excellence.

There are many different ways of applying these quality management principles. The nature of the organization and the specific challenges it faces will determine how to implement them. Many organizations will find it beneficial to set up quality management systems based on these principles.

The requirements of quality management systems and supporting guidelines are given in the ISO 9000 family.

Further information on the ISO 9000 standards is available from ISO's national member institutes or from the ISO Central Secretariat ISO 9000 enquiry service. Sales enquiries should also be directed to the ISO members or to the ISO Central Secretariat sales department.

ISO publishes the bimonthly *ISO 9000 + 150 14000 News**, which provides updates on these families of standards and news on their implementation around the world. A Spanish-language edition is published by the Spanish national standards institute, AENOR.

*Editorial Note: In October 2001 *ISO 9000 + 150 14000 News* was replaced by *ISO Management Systems*.

Does ISO 9000 Give a Quality Emphasis Advantage?
A Comparison of Large Service and Manufacturing Organizations

Gavin Dick, Kevin Gallimore, and Jane C. Brown

This is an interesting study of whether ISO certification makes a difference in quality in service and manufacturing organizations. It describes, in traditional academic article fashion, the nature of the study and its results. It's a useful review of the value of ISO certification, and ultimately it shows it does make a difference, though in this study it was services more than manufacturing that raised customers' perceptions of the quality of the outputs.

Since 1987, when the International Organization for Standardization first published the ISO 9000 series of quality standards, the worldwide take-up of quality certification to the ISO 9000 standard (QCert) has increased rapidly. At the end of 1998, more than 270,000 firms, in over 143 countries, were certified to the standard, an increase of 48,000 on the previous year (ISO 1999). In the third quarter of 1999 in North America (Canada, Mexico, and the United States), over 40,000 firms were registered as certified to an ISO 9000 standard. This North American total represents a real growth of 32 percent from the total a year earlier and indicates the rapidly growing number of companies in the region that perceived value in adopting ISO 9000 quality management systems. The progressive increase in applications from manufacturing firms in the United States for approval to standards such as ISO 9000 suggests that QCert is viewed as important to competitive position by manufacturing organizations.

Recently, in Europe, the popularity of QCert has spread into service industries. No doubt, the increasing globalization of the service sector will see this trend spread to North America, where only 13 percent of registered firms are from the service sector (Anderson 2000).

Implied in the pursuit of quality certification is the assumption that quality certification is associated with improved quality. However, although it is

Reprinted with permission of the publisher from *Quality Management Journal*, Vol. 8, No. 1. Copyright © 2001 by the American Society for Quality. All rights reserved.

clear from the research reviewed on business performance factors that quality does have a consistent positive relationship with better performance, the research reviewed on the link between quality certification and business performance suggests that no link is proven. Combining these findings leads to the inference that quality certification is not consistently associated with a greater emphasis on quality. Given the growth in ISO 9000 applications, it is clearly important to explore the relationship between quality certification and quality emphasis.

The research data analyzed in this article were obtained by questionnaire survey of 500 of the United Kingdom's largest service and manufacturing companies. The survey examines the relative importance attached by chief executives to internal and external dimensions of quality. The relationship between these quality dimensions and the importance placed on the possession of QCert is analyzed.

The survey findings indicate that ISO 9000 quality management systems can give a significant quality emphasis differential to service firms. In contrast, there is less to be gained in manufacturing. The lack of such a marked quality differential in manufacturing firms suggests that any competitive advantages gained will be much weaker than for service firms.

Literature Review

Quality and Business Performance

The contribution of quality to business performance has consistently been claimed by the quality gurus (Crosby 1979; Juran 1982; Deming 1986). Empirical research such as the PIMS studies (Schoefler, Buzzel, and Heany 1974; Buzzel and Wiersema 1981; Craig and Douglas 1982; Phillips, Chang, and Buzzel 1983) and more recent findings (Maani, Putterill, and Sluti 1994; Jacobson and Aaker 1987; Flynn, Schroeder, and Sakakibara 1995; Flynn et al. 1997; Forker, Vickery, and Droge 1996; Adam et al. 1997) all support the proposition that better quality has a positive relationship with business performance. This is also true for the service sector. Capon, Farley, and Hoening (1990) identify 20 service studies that find a positive relationship between quality and business performance. Rust, Zahorik, and Keiningham (1994), who review the marketing literature on service quality and performance, come to the conclusion that a link exists between quality and financial returns. Caruana and Pitt's (1997) study of 131 UK service firms suggests that better quality does have a positive effect on the overall performance of the firm, relative to its competitors.

The factors that relate to business performance can be summarized into two categories: first, those that improve the product or service quality differential against competitors and, second, those factors that reduce the cost of quality. An effective quality assurance system will have product and service quality conformance as its primary goal. The research reviewed found that better conformance quality was associated with sales growth and better sales margins. It was also found that good quality control was related to competitive advantage. An effective quality assurance system will have process control as an essential activity. Better process control will, the research suggests, be consistently associated with less rework and hence lower costs. These lower costs will lead to better comparative business performance. This is in line with Deming (1986), who reasons that as quality improves, waste is eliminated, costs are reduced, and financial performance improves.

Quality Certification and Business Performance

Implied in the pursuit of quality certification is the assumption that quality certification is associated with improved quality systems, leading to better quality and hence to better business performance. However, the research reviewed for this study, on the link between quality certification and business performance, reveals contradictory results. To provide an understanding of this contradiction, the intermediate links between quality certification and business performance variables are also explored.

Many studies report expectations of increased market share and improved quality from ISO 9000 implementation (for example, Ebrahimpour, Withers, and Hikmet 1997). The UK research of Mann and Kehoe (1994) noted that QCert was associated with improved business performance at the operational level. Buttle's (1996) survey of 1220 certified UK companies, which included 415 service sector firms, found that improving operations and marketing gains were claimed by most of the firms following QCert. However, the large-scale descriptive studies of Lloyd's Register of Quality Assurance (1993), The Institute of Quality Assurance (1993), and Brecka (1994) report that the greatest gain from quality certification is widening market opportunities rather than improvements in quality itself.

In contrast to the studies reporting business benefits, Batchelor's (1992) study of more than 600 registered UK firms found that only 15 percent of firms achieved gains from quality certification. These benefits were largely internal, such as reduction in error rates and procedural efficiency, rather than external dimensions such as market share. This is supported by a recent rigorous empirical study (Terziovski, Samson, and Dow 1997) of 1000 firms in Australia and New Zealand, which found that QCert had no significant, positive relationship with business performance. They noted that the principal motivation for pursuing QCert was the ability of the certificate to open customers' doors that were previously closed, or would close if QCert were not achieved. Seddon's (1997) case study research in the United Kingdom goes further to suggest that if ISO 9000 has any effect on performance, then it is negative.

Insights into the reasons for pursuing QCert, and the effect this has on subsequent business performance, are provided by the Science and

The research reviewed for this study, on the link between quality certification and business performance, reveals contradictory results.

Engineering Policy Studies Unit (1994) study, which reviewed 28 surveys relating to ISO 9000. It concluded that there appears to be a relationship between managers' motives for adopting certification and gains achieved in business performance. Companies that cited customer pressure as their reason for pursuing certification were less likely to report improvements than those that gave other reasons for adopting QCert. Other studies (for instance, Gore 1994) have suggested that organizations reacting to external pressure may see QCert registration as the prime objective and adopt a minimalist approach to achieve. These firms may possess QCert but they do not value the quality assurance system that QCert requires.

These studies suggest that the motive for seeking certification is an important predictor of performance. Insights into this motivation variable are provided by a recent empirical study of 272 Australian firms by Jones, Arndt, and Kustin (1997). It found evidence that firms that sought QCert because of externally imposed perceptions of the necessity to "obtain a certificate" were found to experience fewer beneficial outcomes of QCert than firms that had a "developmental" view of quality improvement. These developmental firms' motives included a desire to use QCert to improve the company's internal processes and/or help lower quality costs and increase customer focus. Unfortunately, differences between service and manufacturing sectors were not reported.

An insight into the importance of having a developmental orientation toward quality is provided by the study by Chapman, Murray, and Mellor (1997) of large service and manufacturing firms in Australia. These authors found that improved financial performance (sales per employee) was linked to greater integration of quality plans into strategic business plans. This relationship was found to be stronger in service firms than in manufacturing ones.

In contrast to Jones, Arndt, and Kustin's (1997) and Chapman, Murray, and Mellor's (1997) findings indicating that a developmental or strategic orientation is a moderating variable, Terziovski, Samson, and Dow (1997) found that their variable "TQM environment" (indicative of a developmental view of quality) had no significant influence on the relationship between QCert and business performance. However, the quality staircase model of Kim, Miller, and Heineke (1997) provides an argument against the similarity of a "developmental orientation" and TQM. In firms with a strong TQM environment, QCert may not make much difference to business performance, because it is focused on mastering conformance to specification, which is at the bottom of the staircase, so QCert may do little more than document what are already good quality attitudes and systems. Conversely, firms with a weak TQM environment, who have a "developmental orientation," may improve their business performance through adoption of QCert because of the need to establish the foundation step of mastering conformance quality before moving up the staircase to TQM.

Overall, it would seem that possession of QCert has little or no explanatory power in terms of organizational performance, unless complex variables such as motives or orientations are taken into account.

A more direct variable that captures whether the ISO 9000 quality management system is embedded in the firm's thinking could have the potential to avoid these measurement problems. If a firm has an embedded quality system and has QCert, then it could be expected that the firm would rate QCert as important to the way it defines quality. Therefore, in this research, the intent is to measure the "value" placed on QCert's contribution to an organization's definition of quality. How this is operationalized will be detailed in the methodology section.

Differences Between Manufacturing and Services

Other research suggests that the perception of service and manufacturing sector managers of the link between quality dimensions and business performance are different. Madu, Kuei, and Jacob (1996) and Gowen and Tallon (1999) found that manufacturing firms tend to perceive a positive correlation between quality improvement and business performance but service firms do not. Does this suggest that the correlation between quality certification and quality emphasis will be greater in service firms than in manufacturing ones? Service firms that see no value in quality certification are unlikely to put much emphasis on quality as they perceive no business advantage in doing so. In contrast, manufacturing firms will tend to emphasize quality whether they value quality certification or not, because they recognize the contribution of quality to business performance.

From this, it could be theorized that the quality dimension differential due to quality certification will be greater among service firms than manufacturing firms.

Research Question and Methodology

Quality Dimensions

The literature suggests that there are significant quality similarities between service and manufacturing sectors (Ghobadian, Speller, and Jones 1994; Dotchin and Oakland 1994). This view has guided the authors to propose quality dimensions that combine those of Garvin (1987) and the SERVQUAL ones of Parasuraman, Zeithaml, and Berry (1988). Since Garvin's dimensions are focused on an operations/internal perspective, while Parasuraman, Zeithaml, and Berry's are rooted in a marketing/external one, then any set of quality dimensions used across manufacturing and services must include both perspectives.

The findings on the relative importance of the SERVQUAL dimensions (Parasuraman, Zeithaml, and Berry 1988 and 1991; Zeithaml, Parasuraman, and Berry 1990) consistently found their reliability dimension (the ability to perform the promised service dependably and accurately) to be the most critical driver of service quality. This service dimension equates to the conformance dimension of Garvin (1987). Naturally, Garvin's terminology for this dimension is used. Other intangible dimensions of SERVQUAL, assurance, and empathy, all relate to the way in which the customer interface is managed, and are combined in this research under a quality dimension named "interactive." This dimension equates to the interactive quality dimension suggested by Lehtinen and Lehtinen (1991) and the core attributes dimension of Phillip and Hazlett (1996). It is intended to cover all the aspects of quality that originate in the interaction between the consumer and the service organization. (See Chandon, Leo, and Philippe 1997 for how interactive quality can be broken down into components.)

The final dimension is less clear cut in its equivalence. Garvin's reliability (dependability) dimensions are combined with the service failure/recovery elements of Parasuraman, Zeithaml, and Berry's responsiveness dimensions. To avoid ambiguity the term "post-sale" is used to describe this dimension.

The proposed quality dimension may be criticized for not adequately emphasizing the range of quality dimensions in services found by Parasuraman, Zeithaml, and Berry (1988). While customer contact itself has a strong bearing on perceived quality, the views of a growing body of literature criticizing the five-dimension conceptualization of service quality (for instance, Carman 1990; Babakus and Boller 1992; Dabholkar, Thorpe, and Rentz 1996; Caruana and Pitt 1997; Mels, Boshoff, and Nel 1997) are reflected in this research. All these critiques agree that the five dimensions of quality are not immutable, while some suggest the need for an internally focused quality measure.

Therefore, in this research, only three dimensions that reflect the dominant quality focus in the post-design quality cycle are used. They are defined as follows:

1. Conformance—Meeting specifications, tolerances, or standards
2. Interactive—Quality at the customer interface; the customer's satisfaction with the service encounter
3. Post-sale—After-sales performance; meeting and maintaining the performance expectations of customers

Research Question

From the literature reviewed, it is deduced that QCert will only be associated with a greater emphasis on quality where firms value the quality assurance system that QCert requires. This understanding is used to frame the research questions used in the survey so as to distinguish respondents by their rating of the importance of QCert in contributing to their definition of quality, rather than by their possession of QCert. This variable is termed "QCert value." Firms with a minimum QCert value may or may not have QCert.

Does ISO 9000 Give a Quality Emphasis Advantage?   541

Higher ratings indicate degrees of importance of QCert in contributing to the firm's definition of quality. Where QCert value is high, firms are implying that their certified quality assurance system is making a valuable difference to the way in which they define and achieve good quality.

Derived from the literature, the following two hypotheses are defined for testing.

1. The importance of the quality dimensions will be greater in firms with higher QCert values.
2. The quality dimension differential (between firms with high versus low QCert values) will be greater among service firms than manufacturing firms.

Methodology

The research data were obtained by a questionnaire survey of the United Kingdom's largest companies *(The Times 1000* 1996). The organizations were selected to give a systematic sample across the major industry classifications and to represent, equally, manufacturing and service industries. This framework limited the population to be sampled to 500 firms. A review of Cohen's (1988) sampling size planning tables showed that for correlation above 0.2, at a significance level of 0.05, nearly 200 cases would have to be returned to achieve a power of 0.8. Fortunately, 205 usable responses were received (93 service and 112 manufacturing) with a response profile that reflected the sample frame.

The cover letter requested completion of the questionnaire by the chief executive. Three reasons determined this decision. First, the chief executives are more likely to provide objective responses because they are free from the functional bias of quality professionals. Second, the chief executive's views on QCert and quality are likely to pervade the organization. Finally, Hambrick (1981) strongly advises the use of only the CEO, should the researcher have no option but to access only a unique respondent. The questionnaire was addressed by name to the chief executive of each organization surveyed. A consideration was how many questionnaires would actually be completed by the named individuals. The majority of the returns were either signed or had accompanying compliment slips, the latter often containing a handwritten note. In most cases the signature on these documents was that of the chief executive, although in a few cases, the questionnaire had been passed on to quality managers/directors or company secretaries.

To improve internal reliability, each quality dimension was measured as a composite of the responses to three questions that rate in importance.

1. The dimension's contribution to competitive position
2. The dimension's contribution to the firm's definition of quality
3. The dimension as a quality measurement

Reliability testing of the internal consistency of the components of the additive scales for each quality dimension using Cronbach's alpha resulted in coefficients meeting the minimum level of 0.7 suggested by Nunnaly (1978).

All of the questions could be answered on a four-point Likert-type scale, ranging from "important" to "unimportant." The questions of relevance to this paper can be found in the appendix.

Discussion of Findings

Manufacturing and Services QCert Value Differences

As expected, the findings in Figure 1 indicate that the importance placed on QCert is higher in manufacturing firms than in service organizations. The most substantial difference is that three times more service firms consider QCert unimportant (24 percent) than manufacturing firms (8 percent).

QCert	Manufacturing	Service
Unimportant	8%	24%
Minor	29%	31%
Moderate	37%	26%
Important	26%	19%
Number of cases	112	93

Figure 1. **The importance of quality certification to a firm's definition of quality**

The growing importance of QCert in services is clear; only a minority (24 percent) of firms consider it unimportant to their definition of quality. No doubt customer pressures for quality certification have played a part in this growth, but the increased production orientation (Ritzer 1995) in services must also be considered a factor. This increased production orientation leads to an increased emphasis on the conformance dimension in many service firms, an appreciation of the relevance of formal quality assurance systems, and efforts to introduce quality assurance systems to meet internal needs. Firms that have been unaffected by these factors are likely to take a more limited view of the importance of quality.

Hypothesis 1

The importance of the quality dimensions will be greater in firms with higher QCert values.

This is supported if a significant positive correlation exists between the quality dimensions and QCert value. Correlation analysis uses Spearman's

Does ISO 9000 Give a Quality Emphasis Advantage? 543

rho with two-tail significance testing.

The analysis (Figure 2) found that for manufacturing firms there was no significant correlation with QCert value except for the conformance dimension, with a 0.22 correlation ($p = 0.022$). In contrast the service firms had significant correlations on all dimensions, conformance (0.41, $p = 0.000$), interface (0.30, $p = 0.004$), and post-sale (0.22, $p = 0.038$). The results provide support for the hypothesis that the importance of the quality dimensions will be greater in firms with higher QCert values, but only for service firms. In manufacturing firms, the relationship is limited to conformance quality. This suggests that ISO 9000 standards are interpreted in a profound way by services firms. It appears that manufacturing firms find it easy to relate to conformance quality and concentrate on it, while service firms are inclined to seek the application of their quality system to external dimensions of quality.

QCert Dimension	Manufacturing Firms	Service Firms
Number of cases	112	93
Conformance		
Correlation	0.22*	0.41***
Signficance	.022	.000
Interactive		
Correlation	0.06	0.30**
Signficance	.560	.004
Post-sale		
Correlation	.11	0.22*
Signficance	.267	.038

Spearman's Rho two-tail significance: *** <0.001, **<0.01, *<0.05

Figure 2. **Quality dimensions relationship to QCert value by service/manufacturing classification**

Hypothesis 2

The quality dimension differential (between firms with high versus low QCert values) will be greater among service firms than manufacturing firms.

This is supported if the differences between the means of firms that have high QCert and low QCert value are greater in services than manufacturing, with a significant *t*-test value. Lower QCert value is defined by firms scoring on the two points on the unimportant end of the scale (not important and minor importance). High QCert value is defined by firms scoring on the two points on the important end of the scale (important and moderately important).

An examination of Figure 3 shows that the hypothesis is supported strongly for the conformance dimension. The difference between the means for service firms with high QCert value and low QCert value is significant (*t*-value 2.78, *p* = 0.007), while the difference between those for the manufacturing firms is lower and not statistically significant (*t*-value 1.89, *p* = 0.061). A similar but weaker differential is found on the external quality dimension interface and post-sale. The interface dimensions means have a significant *t*-test value (*t*-value 2.31, *p* = 0.023), while the manufacturing firms are less, and not significant (*t*-value 1.70, *p* = 0.092). The post-sale dimension has a significant t-value of 2.04 *(p* = 0.044), while the manufacturing firms have a *t*-value of 1.93 that is not significant *(p* = 0.057).

Quality Dimensions	Manufacturing Mean	Service Mean
Number of cases	112 (71 high, 41 low)	93 (42 high, 51 low)
Conformance		
QCert value high	11.07	10.33
QCert value low	10.56	8.82
t-value	**1.89**	**2.78****
Significance	.061	.007
Interactive		
QCert value high	11.16	11.36
QCert value low	10.66	10.75
t-value	**1.70**	**2.31***
Significance	.092	.023
Post-sale		
QCert value high	11.07	10.86
QCert value low	10.56	10.14
t-value	**1.93**	**2.04***
Significance	.057	.044

Two-tail significance: **<0.01, *<0.05

Figure 3. **Quality dimension mean scores**

The findings show that the service firms that have higher QCert values rate the quality dimensions significantly higher than those service firms with lower QCert values. This differential is greater than that found in manufacturing firms. These findings support the hypothesis that the quality dimension differential (between firms with high versus low QCert values) is greater among service firms than manufacturing firms. This is in line with the predictions made from the research of Madu, Kuei, and Jacob (1996) and Gowen and Tallon (1999), which highlighted the different perceptions of service and manufacturing sector managers. It was predicted that service firms with lower QCert values are unlikely to put much emphasis on quality, as they perceive no business advantage in doing so. In contrast, manufacturing firms will tend to emphasize quality whether they have high or low QCert values, because they recognize the contribution of quality to business performance.

A complementary explanation is provided by considering the mature nature of quality in manufacturing firms relative to service firms. It has been the norm for many years in large manufacturing organizations to have quality professionals, quality assurance systems, and often, functional representation at board level. All these are indicative of maturity and the acceptance of the importance of quality. In service firms, this has not been the case. It is only recently that quality has started to receive similar recognition. This leads to the conclusion that, relative to manufacturing, service firms are much lower on Kim, Miller, and Heineke's (1997) quality staircase, where the first step is mastering conformance to specification. Therefore, service firms moving up the steps have more scope to achieve a large quality gain from QCert than manufacturers.

> The findings show that the importance of all the quality dimensions is significantly greater in service firms that consider QCert value to be important.

Conclusions

In this research, firms have been analyzed by their rating of the importance of QCert in contributing to their definition of quality rather than by their possession of QCert. This QCert value has been found to be a significant variable. The variable is more a direct measure of a firm's view of QCert than those used previously, which have considered the firms' motives (Jones, Arndt, and Kustin 1997), strategic integration (Chapman, Murray, and Mellor 1997), or TQM environment (Terziovski, Samson, and Dow 1997). Although it has proved to be a significant variable, the limitation of a direct variable such as the one used here is that it provides no explanation for why firms consider QCert important or not. Additional insights likely could be gained by using a combination of explanatory and direct variables in future research into ISO 9000 and performance improvement

The findings show that the importance of all the quality dimensions is significantly greater in service firms that consider QCert value to be important. In contrast, in manufacturing firms the increase only applies to conformance quality. This suggests that ISO 9000 standards are applied in a deeper way by service firms than manufacturers. Manufacturing firms find it easy to relate to conformance quality, and concentrate on it, while service firms are inclined to extend the application of their quality system to external dimensions of quality. These findings are confirmed by the greater differential found in service firms than in manufacturers. It was found that the service firms that value quality certification place much more emphasis on quality than other service firms do. In contrast, there is not such an extreme differential in manufacturing firms. This is in line with the predictions made from the research of Madu, Kuei, and Jacob (1996) and Gowen and Tallon (1999). The differential between service firms with high and low QCert values was large, since service firms with lower QCert values perceive no business advantage in emphasizing quality. In contrast, manufacturing firms tend to emphasize quality whether they have high or low QCert values, because they recognize the contribution of quality to business performance.

Thus, it can be concluded that ISO 9000 quality management systems can give a significant quality emphasis differential to service firms. In contrast, there is less to be gained in manufacturing. The lack of such a marked quality differential in manufacturing firms suggests that any competitive advantages gained will be much weaker than for service firms. These conclusions support those of Chapman, Murray, and Mellor (1997), who found greater performance gains in services than manufacturing firms from the adoption of QCert.

QUESTIONNAIRE TO THE CHIEF EXECUTIVE

All questionnaires were pre-coded with the respondent's firm's industrial sector. All questions were answered on a Likert four-point scale with polar labels "unimportant" and "important."

Please rate in importance the following quality measurements:
1. Failure rate in meeting specifications, tolerances, or standards
2. Levels of customer satisfaction with the customer supplier interface
3. Failure rates in meeting customer performance expectations

Please rate in importance the following in contributing to your definition of quality:
1. Conformance to specifications, tolerances, or standards
2. Customer perception of the customer supplier interface
3. The ability of a product/service to maintain initial performance expectations
4. Possession of a recognized quality certificate (for example, BS5750, ISO 9000)

Please rate in importance the following in contributing to competitive position:
1. Quality of product/service
2. Quality of customer supplier interface
3. Quality of after-sale performance

References

Adam, E.E., Jr., L.M. Corbett, B.E. Flores, N.J. Harrison, T.S. Lee, B. Rho, J. Ribera, D. Samson, and R. Westbrook. 1997. An international study of quality improvement approach and firm performance. *International Journal of Operations and Production Management* 17, no. 9:842-873.

Anderson, S. 2000. Business thrives in North America for ISO management system standards. *ISO 9000 + ISO 14000 News 9*, no. 2:20-21.

Babakus, E., and G.W. Boller. 1992. An empirical assessment of the SERVQUAL scale. *Journal of Business Research* 24, no. 3:253-268.

Batchelor, C. 1992. Badge of quality, *Financial Times*, 1 September.

Brecka, J. 1994. Study finds gains with ISO 9000 registration increase over time. *Quality Progress* (May): 18-20.

Buttle, F. 1996. ISO 9000: marketing motivations and benefits. *International Journal of Quality and Reliability Management* 14, no. 9:939-947.

Buzzel, R.D., and F.D. Wiersema. 1981. Modeling changes in market share: A cross sectional analysis. *Strategic Management Journal* 2, no. 1:27-42.

Capon, N., J.U. Farley, and S. Hoening. 1990. Determinates of financial performance: A meta analysis. *Management Science* (October): 114-1159.

Carman, J.M. 1990. Consumer perceptions of service quality: an assessment of the SERVQUAL dimensions. *Journal of Retailing* 6, no.1:33-55.

Caruana, A., and L. Pitt. 1997. INTQUAL—An internal measure for service quality and the link between service quality and business performance. *European Journal of Marketing* 31, no. 8:604-617.

Chandon, J., P. Leo, and J. Philippe. 1997. Service encounter dimensions—A dyadic perspective: measuring the dimensions of service encounters as perceived by customers and personnel. *International Journal of Service Industry Management* 8, no. 1:65-86.

Chapman, R.L., P.C. Murray, and R. Mellor. 1997. Strategic quality management and financial performance indicators. *International Journal of Quality and Reliability Management* 14, no. 4:432-448.

Cohen, J., 1988. *Statistical power analysis for the behavioral sciences.* Mahwah, N.J.: Lawrence Erlbaum Associates.

Craig, C.S., and S.P. Douglas. 1982. Strategic factors associated with market share and financial performance. *Quarterly Review of Economics and Business* (summer): 101-111.

Crosby, P.B. 1979. *Quality is free.* New York: New American Library.

Dabholkar, P.A., D.I. Thorpe, and J.O. Rentz. 1996. A measure of service quality for retail stores: Scale development and validation. *Journal of the Academy of Marketing Science* 24, no. 1:36-44.

Deming, W.E. 1986. *Out of the crisis.* Cambridge, Mass.: Center for Advanced Engineering Study.

Dotchin, J.A., and J.S. Oakland. 1994. Total quality management in services part 1: Understanding and classifying services. *International Journal of Quality and Reliability Management* 1, no. 3:9-26.

Ebrahimpour, M., B.E. Withers, and N. Hikmet. 1997. Experiences of U.S.- and foreign-owned firms: A new perspective on ISO 9000 implementation. *International Journal of Production Research* 35, no. 2:569-576.

Flynn, B.B., R.G. Schroeder, and S. Sakakibara. 1995. The impact of quality management practices on performance and competitive advantage. *Decision Sciences* 26, no. 5:659-692.

Flynn, B.B., R.G. Schroeder, F.J. Flynn, S. Sakakibara, and K.A. Bates. 1997. World-class manufacturing project: Overview and selected results. *International Journal of Operations and Production Management* 17, no. 7:671-685.

Forker, L.B., S.K. Vickery, and C.L. Droge. 1996. The contribution of quality to business performance. *International Journal of Operations and Production Management* 16, no. 8:44-62.

Garvin, D.A. 1987. Competing on the eight dimensions of quality. 1987. *Harvard Business Review* 65, no. 6:101-109.

Ghobadian, A., S. Speller, and M. Jones. 1994. Service quality concepts and models. *International Journal of Quality and Reliability Management* 11, no. 9:43-66.

Gore, M. 1994. The quality infrastructure. *Purchasing and Supply Management* (February): 41-43.

Gowen, C.R., and W.J. Tallon. 1999. Quality management practices in manufacturing and service corporations: How are they different? *Mid-American Journal of Business* 14, no. 1:33-40.

Hambrick, D.C. 1981. Strategic awareness within the top management team. *Strategic Management Journal* 2, no. 3:263-279.

Institute of Quality Assurance. 1993. *Survey on the use and implementation of BS5750.* London: Institute of Quality Assurance.

International Organization for Standardization. 1999. *The ISO survey of ISO 9000 and ISO 14000 certificates (eighth cycle).* Geneva, Switzerland: International Organization for Standardization.

Jacobson, R., and D. Aaker. 1987. The strategic role of product quality. *Journal of Marketing* 51, no. 4:31-44.

Jones, R., G. Arndt, and R. Kustin. 1997. ISO 9000 among Australian companies: Impact of time and reasons for seeking certification on perceptions of benefits received. *International Journal of Quality and Reliability Management* 14, no. 7:650-660.

Juran, J.M. 1982. *Juran on quality improvement.* New York: Juran Institute.

Kim, K.Y., J.G. Miller, and J. Heineke. 1997. Mastering the quality staircase, step by step. *Business Horizons* (January-February): 17-21.

Lehtinen, U., and J.R. Lehtinen. 1991. Two approaches to service quality dimensions. *The Service Industries Journal* (July): 287-303.

Lloyd's Register of Quality Assurance. 1993. *Setting standards for better business. Report of Survey Findings.* London: Lloyd's.

Maani, K.E., M.S. Putterill, and D.G. Sluti. 1994. Empirical analysis of quality improvement in manufacturing. *International Journal of Quality and Reliability Management* 11, no. 7:19-37.

Madu, C.N., C.H. Kuei, and R.A. Jacob. 1996. An empirical assessment of the influence of quality dimensions on organizational performance. *International Journal of Production Research* 34, no. 7:43-62.

Mann, R., and D. Kehoe. 1994. An evaluation of the effects of quality improvement activity on business performance. *International Journal of Quality and Reliability Management* 11, no. 4:29-44.

Mels, G., C. Boshoff, and D. Nel. 1997. The dimensions of service quality: The original European perspective revisited. *Service Industries Journal* 17, no. 1:173-189.

Nunnaly, J.C. 1978. *Psychometric theory.* 2nd edition. New York: McGraw-Hill.

Parasuraman, A., V.A. Zeithaml, and L.L. Berry. 1988. SERVQUAL: A multiple-item scale for measuring customer perceptions of service quality. *Journal of Retailing* 64, no. 1:12-40.

——.1991. Refinement and reassessment of the SERVQUAL scale. *Journal of Retailing* 67, no. 4:420-450.

Phillip, G., and S. Hazlett. 1996. The measurement of service quality: A new P-C-P attributes model. *International Journal of Quality and Reliability Management* 14, no. 3:260-286.

Phillips, L.W., D.R. Chang, and R.D. Buzzel. 1983. Product quality, cost position, and business performance: a test of key hypotheses. *Journal of Marketing* 37, no. 1:26-43.

Ritzer, G. 1995. *The McDonaldization of society.* London: Pine Forge.

Rust, R.T., A.J. Zahorik, and T.I. Keiningham. 1994. Return on quality (ROQ): Making service quality financially accountable. *Journal of Marketing* 59, no. 2:58-70.

Schoefler, S., R.D. Buzzel, and D.F. Heany. 1974. Impact of strategic planning on profit performance. *Harvard Business Review* (March-April): 137-145.

Science and Engineering Policy Studies Unit. 1994. *UK quality management-policy options. SEPSU Policy Study 10.* London: Royal Society and Royal Academy of Engineering.

Seddon, J. 1997. *In pursuit of quality: the case against ISO 9000.* London: Oak Tree Press.

Terziovski, M., D. Samson, and D. Dow. 1997. The business value of quality management systems certification: Evidence from Australia and New Zealand. *Journal of Operations Management* 15, no. 1:1-18.

The Times 1000. 1996. [A ranking of the UK's 1000 largest companies by capital employed.] London: Times Books.

Zeithaml, V.A., A. Parasuraman, and L.L. Berry. 1990. *Delivering quality service: Balancing customer perceptions and expectations.* New York: Free Press.

Gavin Dick is a senior lecturer in operations management at Staffordshire University Business School. He joined the university in 1990 from the electronics industry, where he was a factory manager. Dick has been involved in the accreditation of quality management systems from their defense procurement origins through to today's ISO 9000 standards. He may be contacted as follows: Staffordshire University Business School, Stoke on Trent, Staffordshire, ST4 2DF, UK; 44-1782-294000; e-mail: G.P.M.Dick@staffs.ac.uk.

Kevin Gallimore is a senior lecturer in strategic management at Manchester Metropolitan University. Prior to his career in higher education, he worked in the chemicals industry in roles covering technical, sales, operations, and quality management.

Jane Brown is a senior nurse manager with North Staffordshire Combined Healthcare NHS Trust, with responsibility for all nursing quality issues, including clinical audit, clinical governance, and risk management. She holds posts as a specialist lecturer in quality and health care at Staffordshire University and public sector strategy at Manchester Metropolitan University.

Fourteen Years of ISO 9000: Impact, Criticisms, Costs, and Benefits

Thomas H. Stevenson and Frank C. Barnes

This article offers a sober look at ISO 9000 certification, in terms of its benefits, proposed versus actual. The authors are frank about the criticisms they have discovered with regard to certification: for perhaps too many it involves compliance with rules to get business rather than improve quality. However, the authors also point out that the newly revised ISO standards will make it easier for companies both to become certified and to seek quality.

The ISO 9000 certification process has existed for more than a decade. Originating in 1987 with a bulletin from the International Organization for Standardization, its purpose was to provide a series of worldwide standards for quality systems that could be used for external quality assurance purposes. Administered in the United States by the American National Standards Institute (ANSI), ISO 9000 registration has been sought and obtained by thousands of businesses seeking to demonstrate that their procedures meet global quality standards.

Now the ISO 9000 standards have undergone revision. New standards were published in December 2000, and despite criticism of the process, there are few signs that interest in certification is waning. Indeed, the number of registrations is growing. By the end of 1999, there were 343,643 certifications in 150 countries—a 26.4 percent increase over the previous year. The greatest number of new registrations in 1998 was in the United States, where 6,406 certificates were issued—a 34.5 percent increase from the previous year. Moreover, the number of new registrations had increased annually every year over the previous five years. Thus, by the end of 1998, a total of 24,987 ISO 9000 certificates had been issued in the United States.

Nevertheless, despite continued growth in the number of ISO 9000 certifications in the U.S., the country trails other regions in total registrations. There are several likely reasons for this, but a major factor is that misunderstandings have grown up around the certification process. Some believe it is merely the latest quality fad. Others are convinced that no real benefits can be attained from it, or that the process generates excessive costs and paperwork. Still others do not understand the process, or believe it applies only to companies doing business in Europe. As a result, the U.S. represents only 9.6 percent of companies registered worldwide, and total North American registrations represent only 13.1 percent. In comparison, European registrations represent more than 55 percent of the worldwide total, with 16 percent in the Far East. And the numbers are still rising in these regions. If U.S. registrations are to increase to the levels of other regions, thousands more American companies will at least need to consider whether they should join the ranks of those already certified. And they will need up-to-date information to help them make their decision.

So it is timely to clarify what ISO 9000 certification is and is not, what it offers, and what it costs in terms of dollars and man-hours. In that light, we will briefly review the registration process and year 2000 changes, review the criticisms of the process, identify the costs, and document the payoffs to companies achieving ISO 9000 certification.

ISO 9000: History, Framework, Revisions

The International Standards Organization (ISO) was founded in Europe in 1947. Its purpose was to facilitate worldwide trade through the development of international quality standards for products and services. Among the activities of this organization—and perhaps the most influential and far-reaching—was the issuance of the 1987 bulletin that devised "a series of international standards dealing with quality systems that can be used for external quality assurance purposes." The standards provided companies with a series of guidelines on how to establish systems for managing quality products and services. Businesses were given standards to use to document practices that affected the quality of their offerings. They could then follow ISO guidelines to become certified.

The underlying premise of ISO 9000 certification is that the creation of products and services is the result of a system, the inputs and outputs of which can be measured at various points as the system adds value. ISO 9000 registration documents the procedures in the system and measures how well they conform to such documentation. In short, ISO 9000 sets system standards—for paperwork, not products—by setting guidelines for establishing corporate systems. (As we will discuss later, the focus on paperwork is one of the major criticisms of the registration process.)

ISO 9000 actually comprises several standards, which were simplified in December 2000. Figure 1 outlines the previous series as well as these recent revisions. Before last December, ISO 9000 was the general standard that served as a guide to the others. ISO 9001 was the most comprehensive, covering research, design, development, production, shipping, and installation. ISO 9002 was less comprehensive; omitting design and development, it was

Previous Standard	
Standard	**Focus**
ISO 9000	Quality management and assurance standards for selection and use
ISO 9001	Quality systems model for quality assurance in design, development, production, installation, and servicing
ISO 9002	Quality systems model for quality assurance in production and installation
ISO 9003	Quality systems model for quality assurance in final inspection and testing
ISO 9004	Quality management and quality system element guidelines
Year 2000 Revisions	
Standard	**Focus**
ISO 9000	Quality fundamentals and vocabulary
ISO 9001	Quality management systems (consolidates the previous ISO 9001/9002/9003 standards into a single document)
ISO 9004	Quality management system guidelines for performance improvement

Source: *Year 2000 revisions adapted and updated from International Organization for Standardization, press release, ref 757, 1999-03-05.*

Figure 1. **The ISO 9000 Series**

for companies that produce, install, and service only existing products. ISO 9003 was for companies that perform even fewer functions, such as final inspection and testing. ISO 9004 was a document to guide further internal quality development.

The standards are updated periodically. New programs, such as QS-9000 and ISO 14000, have been added over the years. The former was developed by the automotive industry because it needed a more specific and prescriptive system of standards. Reports Mullin (1998), "QS-9000 includes stipulation for 100 percent on-time delivery, supplier development programs, and statistical record keeping far beyond what is required in ISO 9000." ISO 14000 was introduced in 1996 to provide a series of global standards for environmental management that deal with environmental audits, labeling, performance evaluations, life-cycle assessment, and terms and definitions.

Now the ISO 9000 series has undergone a major revision that results in a simplified version of the original standards. According to the International Organization for Standardization, the basic thrust of the recent revisions includes stake-holder orientation, continual improvement, and greater user-friendliness. These changes are expected to mollify those who believe the current standards promote merely consistency rather than quality. Instead, says Zuckerman (1999), the revised standards are patterned "on national quality standards such as the Malcolm Baldrige Awards in the U.S. There is supposed to be more emphasis on continuous improvement and process."

Currently, companies seeking to become ISO 9000 certified must be audited by an independent "registrar," a basic process that should not be materially affected by the proposed revisions. The process is daunting and lengthy. However, several books and articles have been written to facilitate an understanding of it, providing step-by-step instructions for certification procedures. Davies (1997) developed a manual in the form of a workbook to guide the process. Peach (1997) edited *The ISO 9000 Handbook,* a collection of independent papers that cover all aspects of certification. Johnson (1997) provided thorough coverage in *ISO 9000: Meeting the New International Standards,* as did Zuckerman in her 1995 *ISO 9000 Made Easy.* Ferguson (1996) described an eight-step implementation procedure using a computerized system designed by Wilson (1994). Common to most such guides is a stepwise procedure similar to that shown in the sidebar "ISO 9000 Certification Process," which demonstrates that achieving certification is complex as well as expensive, both in terms of dollars and man-hours. As a result, certification itself is the main source of criticism of ISO 9000, though other issues have surfaced over the 14 years since its inception.

> Many experts believe certification is too costly and consists of a pursuit of quality certificates rather than a pursuit of quality.

Criticisms of ISO 9000 Certification

One recurring criticism of ISO 9000 registration concerns the formal certification process. The process that has developed was not envisioned when ISO 9000 was established. Many experts believe certification is too costly and consists of a pursuit of quality certificates rather than a pursuit of quality. As Richard Brown (1994) stated,

> While rooted in good intentions, once dissected, it is painfully obvious that ISO certifications are merely more expensive and elaborate schemes that promise high quality and a competitive edge.... [C]ertification costs are astronomical and growing, and an ISO certification means little in Europe. When the smoke clears, the only organizations guaranteed to profit from this experience will be those deemed to be qualified to do the audits and issue the certificates.

In retrospect, this was probably an oversimplification. Some recent studies have indicated that many companies have experienced benefits in terms

> ## ISO 9000 Certification Process
>
> **1. ISO 9000 Assessment.** The initial assessment is a detailed review of the company's quality systems and procedures compared to ISO 9000 requirements. This process defines the scope of the ISO 9000 project.
>
> **2. Training.** All employees must be trained in two areas. First, they must have an overall understanding of ISO 9000 vocabulary requirements, the role of the quality manual, and the benefits that will be derived from the system. Second, they must understand the actual day-to-day process of upgrading and improving procedures.
>
> **3. Documentation of Work Instructions.** All procedures must be described and documented so that they can be understood prior to approval. Once completed, this documentation should outline every process a company undertakes that affects the quality of its finished products.
>
> **4. Quality Assurance Manual.** While ISO 9000 standards do not require a quality assurance and policy manual, they do require that a company document everything it does and every system that affects the quality of the finished product. The manual is often used to assemble all documentation in one place.
>
> **5. Registration Audit.** The final step in certification is an audit by an organization chosen as external registrar to see that the system is working as described in the quality manual and that it meets ISO 9000 requirements.

of profitability, communications, operations, and market expansion (to be discussed later). Nevertheless, many businesses have taken a wait-and-see approach because some of the companies that have achieved ISO 9000 certification have found that actual results did not equal those anticipated. Further, there is no question that ISO 9000 registration requires a mountain of paperwork and adds so much structure that some believe it interferes with new and better ways of operating. The International Organization for Standardization has been sensitive to this criticism; its 2000 revisions are patterned on well-known national quality standards.

Beyond the discussion of the overall purpose and value of ISO 9000 certification, other criticisms have been raised as well. For example, the regulation and implementation of the standards was left up to the participating countries' individual standards organizations, which select the agencies qualified to issue ISO 9000 certifications. Once registrars become accredited, there is no single set of guidelines for them to follow, and the amount of work a company is required to do for certification can vary according to the registrar. In the past, not all companies or countries would acknowledge certification from all registrars because the standards had been interpreted somewhat variably in different countries. One result of this was that companies such as Hewlett-Packard, Motorola, Novell, Microsoft, and others led a self-certification movement, which provided greater flexibility in meeting objectives, reduced costs, and heightened customer understanding of the quality management systems. Similarly, the National Tooling & Machinery Association asked its 3,000 members to conform to ISO 9000 standards rather than pursue actual certification. Thus, some companies view self-paced compliance as a viable option to ISO 9000.

Another issue that has emerged over the past 14 years is that ISO 9000 is not industry-specific. Some critics claim it is too general and fails to address the unique problems and issues inherent in some industries. Worldwide, ISO 9000 registration is strongest in the transportation, chemical, oil, electronics, and computer industries. Facing tough international competition, the chemical processing industry has embraced the standards. In fact, DuPont created its own ISO 9000 service for use both inside and outside the industry. On the other hand, tool manufacturers, automakers, steelmakers, and some woodworking machine manufacturers are among those who say that ISO 9000 registration primarily benefits consultants.

One result of this attitude could be seen in the auto industry in the late 1980s, when ISO 9000 was deemed inadequate for the industry's needs. Suppliers voiced concern about the duplication of efforts in the documentation required by the Big Three automakers. So the industry developed QS-9000 and, with the permission of the International Organization for Standardization, included ISO 9001 verbatim. Although this did not eliminate concerns about competing standards, there were some interesting results. In 1994, Chrysler and GM mandated that their first-tier suppliers be certified by the end of 1997. However, by the summer of 1997 the Auto Industry Action Group reported only 2,791 locations certified, leaving roughly 7,000 uncertified. So Chrysler and GM issued an ultimatum that suppliers become certified or cease doing business with them. Fifteen months later, say Zuckerman and Daniels (1998), 8,645 suppliers were registered.

Beyond the issues of complexity, irrelevance to quality, and generality, the most overarching concerns and criticisms are the costs of achieving ISO 9000 certification and the somewhat dubious benefits of certification. These issues will be discussed more fully in the sections that follow.

Costs of ISO Certification

Four major factors generate costs in achieving ISO certification: time, training, consultants, and the registration itself. The amount of time needed to become certified ranges from less than a year to more than two years, but usually takes from about a year to 18 months. It depends on many factors, including a company's size and complexity, current level of work quality, extent of current documentation, and degree of management commitment (see Figure 2). Typically, a 6- to 12-month training and preparation period is followed by an intensive yearlong effort to adapt company procedures to the ISO standard.

Time Frame	Condition of Organization to Start
3 to 6 months	Company is in full compliance with a military or nuclear standard.
6 to 10 months	Company has fairly current procedures, job descriptions, and a working quality organization.
10 to 16 months	Company is very large, or has sketchy procedures and haphazard records.
16 to 24 months	Quality systems model for quality assurance in final inspection and testing. The quality function is responsible for final inspection.
ISO 9004	Company has no commitment from senior management.

Source: *Rabbit and Bergh, 1993*

Figure 2. **Certification time requirements**

In the early 1990s, about 35 percent of companies failed to achieve certification on the first attempt, but more recently the failure rate has dropped below 30 percent. About half the failures are due to a lack of documentation. Once a company has been certified, it faces follow-up visits by auditors every six months to make sure it is following its own procedures. After three years, it must undergo another full assessment.

In the early 1990s, about 35 percent of companies failed to achieve certification on the first attempt, but more recently the failure rate has dropped below 30 percent.

Training, a second major cost factor, usually costs $4,000 to $5,000 for a single site. A core group of employees, usually consisting of the ISO coordinator, senior managers, and team leaders, receives a formal overview in a one-day introductory class that typically costs about $500 per person. The coordinator also takes another two-day advanced seminar generally costing about $1,000. Additional expense factors are the internal cost of preparing documents, document control, and retraining of employees.

Hiring consultants to facilitate the process also contributes to costs. Consultants can be retained to assist with any part of the certification procedure, or they can be employed to take a company from start to finish, virtually assuring passage of the ISO audit. Their fees generally range from $800 to $1,600 per day.

The actual registration fees themselves are also high. To illustrate, the National ISO Support Group asked a sample of registrars to submit a quote for a 250-employee automotive supplier with a single manufacturing site. The average cost for registration fees was $11,300, ranging from $4,000 to $20,000. Half of the registrars said they had special pricing packages for businesses with fewer than 75 employees. For a large business site, the fee could reach $40,000. Surveillance costs over the three-year period could run another $3,000 to $4,000, plus travel.

It is apparent, then, that when the costs of time, training, consultants, and registration are totaled, certification can represent a major expenditure. According to Weston (1995), the *Quality Systems Update* reported that the average total certification cost, including training and implementation, was $245,000. Factors influencing final total costs, beyond those already identified, are company size, number and type of products, and the existing state of the company's quality control system. A survey of equipment manufacturers showed large corporations spending more than $1 million for certification, and smaller firms (with annual sales of about $25 million) spending an average of $250,000, plus annual maintenance costs of more than $70,000. These costs, reports Zuckerman (1994), included registration fees of about $35,000 for a three-year cycle, employee time, and, in some cases, additional employees.

Nevertheless, such cost claims should be taken with some skepticism. A Colorado study, reports Weston (1995), revealed that 70 percent of companies did not keep track of time expenditures. Weston also found that 58 percent of ISO 9000 registered companies indicated they did not keep track of costs because the decision to seek registration was strategic, customer-driven, or in the long-term interests of the company. Fully 93 percent reported that they did not attempt to justify the costs of the registration procedure because "registration was strategic and ... tracking costs had no purpose since [the companies] were obligated for business reasons to pursue registration." In short, some companies have spent quite a bit of money on ISO 9000 registration, while others have chosen to proceed with no attention to costs. This suggests that there are payoffs associated with ISO 9000 certification.

Payoffs of ISO 9000 Certification

Companies seek to become ISO 9000 certified in anticipation of significant benefits that will offset, or at least mitigate, the high costs. Among the reasons researchers have identified for pursuing registration is gaining greater market share, meeting customer requirements, and improving process efficiency. Others mention lower operating costs or achieving external benefits of higher quality and competitive advantage, as well as internal benefits of improved documentation and quality awareness. An overview of the top ten anticipated benefits is shown in Table 1. These findings suggest four primary benefits associated with ISO 9000: cost savings and/or higher profitability, better communication, improved operations, and market expansion.

With regard to cost savings and profitability, research findings have generally been positive. A survey by Lloyd's Register Quality Assurance ("Study Finds ..." 1994) indicated that ISO 9000 registration increased net profits. Simmons and White (1999) found that, after controlling for size, ISO 9000-registered companies were more profitable than non-registered companies. A joint study by Deloitte-Touche and Quality Systems Update (Johns 1994) reported that companies claimed average annual savings of $179,000 from registration. Wolak (1994) reported that the costs of registration were recovered in three years. According to the British Standards Institution, says Stanley Brown (1994), firms that achieve ISO 9000 certification reduce their annual operating costs by an average of 10 percent.

Improved communication has also been cited as a benefit. In a survey of ISO 9000 certified manufacturing companies in New Zealand, Lee and Palmer (1999) reported that both large (more than 100 employees) and small companies experienced better communication after ISO implementation. Zuckerman and Hurwitz (1996) listed six ways in which communication would be enhanced via ISO 9000 registration:

- it builds interpersonal communication between employees and managers;
- it helps resolve political conflicts, work procedure inconsistencies, and conflict between formal and informal communication flows;
- it trains management and employees in communication skills, such as interviewing, writing, and editing;
- it creates a documentation system and a system for disseminating information companywide and to all customers;
- it provides the basis for a networked communication system; and
- it lays a foundation for using employees as sophisticated information gatherers and sorters.

Perhaps as a result of improved internal communications, some companies achieving ISO 9000 certification also report improvements in their operations. This was the case with Clark-Reliance Corporation. A manufacturer of liquid processing equipment, Clark-Reliance scheduled joint meetings between its sales and production departments during the ISO implementation. The result was an improvement of its on-time delivery from 30 to 90 percent.

Nevertheless, company operations do not always improve to the level anticipated prior to ISO 9000 certification (see Table 1). When Simmons and White (1999) studied U.S. and Canadian firms in the electronic/electrical equipment and components industry and compared certified and non-certified firms, they found no difference in operational performance between the two groups. Despite this finding, Simmons and White were reluctant to conclude that registration does not affect business performance, recommending instead that longitudinal analyses be conducted on a larger sample of companies across a broader spectrum of industries. Similarly, Lee and Palmer (1999) called for more studies of ISO 9000 certification-related performance improvements, especially with regard to firm size. However, their study of registered companies concluded that corporate performance improves significantly after the company becomes certified.

Market expansion is also thought to be facilitated by ISO 9000 certification, but, as in the case of several of the other anticipated benefits, not to the level expected prior to certification (again, see Table 1). Yet even though ISO

	Percent Agreeing	
Benefit	**Anticipated**	**Achieved**
1. Improvement in documentation	73.8	84.5
2. Improvement in operating standards	68.4	74.5
3. Improvement in quality awareness	71.6	77.4
4. Ability to sustain market share	67.3	57.4
5. Improvement in perception of product quality	65.1	64.7
6. Ability to increase market share	62.9	45.1
7. Reduction in cases of nonconformity	60.7	54.6
8. Improvement in customer satisfaction	58.6	52.8
9. Improvement in competitive advantage	57.8	44.8
10. Reduction in quality audits	50.2	48.0

Source: Skrabec et al. (1997)

Table 1. **Top ten anticipated benefits of ISO certification**

9000 certification does not always yield the expected impetus to market growth, and even though it is not governmentally mandated, large certified corporations are requiring certification of their suppliers. (ISO 9000 requires that certified firms qualify their vendors, and many meet this requirement by mandating that their suppliers be certified as well.) Thus, businesses seeking to expand or maintain their markets by serving as suppliers to ISO 9000-registered companies must seek registration themselves. Indeed, maintains Ferguson (1996), it has been asserted that "industrial buyers often use the list of ISO registered suppliers as their only source for identifying potential suppliers." This can place non-certified companies at a competitive disadvantage in relation to certified competitors. Juran (1995) posited this as the major reason for seeking certification. Struebing's (1996) study of 48 certified firms in the New York area supported this assertion. She found that one of the top two reasons for seeking registration was that customers required it.

It appears, then, that certification gives sellers credibility. Buyers know that a certified company has had to demonstrate and document adherence to worldwide standards for quality systems, and are assured that a potential supplier can provide products of a consistent quality. A further benefit to buyers is that they can reduce the number of supplier audits. If the supplier base, including first-, second-, and third-tier suppliers, is ISO 9000 certified, then the final products, which may consist of thousands of parts and components from registered suppliers, should have superior quality, performance, and reliability. This in turn could support buyers' market expansion aspirations.

Fourteen years after the debut of the ISO 9000 standards, it is apparent that they have had a major impact on worldwide commerce. Despite criticisms of the costs and complexity of the process, and in the face of doubts about the benefits of becoming certified, the rate of increase in registrations remains high as more and more companies seek to certify their quality systems. In the United States, where the adoption rate of companies seeking ISO 9000 certification once lagged behind that of other regions of the world, the total number of new domestic registrations now exceeds that of most other countries. Thus, for those in the U.S. who have adopted a wait-and-see approach, this may be the time for another look at the process.

The ISO 9000 registration process has undergone changes that promise to simplify the system and tie it more closely to quality initiatives. Evidence is building that real benefits can result from achieving certification. However, these do not come cheap, either in dollars or man-hours. ISO 9000 is not for everyone. Some industries have adopted other quality standards that serve them well. Others serve limited markets in which the payoff would be too little to justify the cost. Still others lack the basic infrastructure to support such a system. In these cases, where formal certification is unrealistic, the ISO model could still be used as a benchmark to assess the adequacy of quality programs. Those responsible for the quality function should become familiar with ISO 9000 and align their systems with that model. Such an alignment should contribute to the systematic improvement of overall quality and profit throughout the business world.

On the other hand, where ISO 9000 registration is feasible, careful consideration is needed before seeking certification. An important early step is to determine the role ISO 9000 plays in one's industry and markets. If it becomes apparent that certification is necessary to support competitive and marketing initiatives, then the company should begin the process. But it should proceed with the knowledge that, in the short run, becoming certified will be costly, time-consuming, and disruptive. Benefits can be realized, but a long-term view is required.

References

American Society for Quality Control Standards Committee, *Quality Systems for Quality Assurance in Production, Installation, and Servicing* (Milwaukee, WI: ASQC Quality Press, 1994).

R. Brown, "Does America Need ISO 9000?" *Machine Design,* June 6, 1994, pp. 70-74.

S. Brown, "Now It Can Be Told," *Sales and Marketing Management,* November 1994, pp. 34-35.

J.S. Davies, *ISO 9000 Management Systems Manual* (New York: McGraw-Hill, 1997).

M. Ebrahimpour, B.E. Withers, and N. Hikmet, "Experiences of U.S. and Foreign-Owned Firms: A New Perspective on ISO 9000 Implementation," *International Journal of Production Research*, February 1997, pp. 569-576.

W. Ferguson, "Impact of the ISO 9000 Series Standards on Industrial Marketing," *Industrial Marketing Management,* July 1996, pp. 305-310.

International Organization for Standardization, *ISO 9000 Revisions: Draft International Standards Expected in 4Q 1999,* press release ref. 757, Geneva, Switzerland, 1999.

International Organization for Standardization, *ISO 9000 Revisions Progress to FDIS Status,* press release ref. 779, Geneva, Switzerland, 2000.

The ISO Survey of ISO 9000 and ISO 14000 Certificates: Eight Cycle 1998 (Geneva, Switzerland: International Organization for Standardization, 1998).

V. Johns, "Beyond the Myths: The ISO 9000 Certification Process Is Still Hampered by a Number of Misunderstandings," *Chemical Marketing Reporter,* April 11, 1994, pp. 8-10.

P.L. Johnson, *ISO 9000: Meeting the New International Standards* (New York: McGraw-Hill, 1993).

J.M. Juran, *A History of Managing for Quality: The Evolution, Trends, and Future Directions of Managing for Quality* (Milwaukee, WI: ASQC Quality Press, 1995).

K.S. Lee and E. Palmer, "An Empirical Examination of ISO 9000-Registered Companies in New Zealand," *Total Quality Management,* August 1999, pp. 887-899.

T.Y. Lee, "The Experience of Implementing ISO 9000 in Hong Kong," *Asia Pacific Journal of Quality Management, 4,* 4 (1995): 6-16.

S. Lorge and A. Cohen, "Can ISO Certification Boost Sales?" *Sales and Marketing Management,* April 1998, p. 19.

R. Mullin, "Rewrite Aims for 'Elegant Simplicity,'" *Chemical Week,* April 8, 1998, pp. 42-43.

R.W. Peach, *The ISO 9000 Handbook* (Chicago: Irwin Professional Publishing, 1997).

J.T. Rabbit and P.A. Bergh, *The ISO 9000 Book: A Global Competitor's Guide to Compliance and Certification* (New York: Quality Resources, 1993).

B.L. Simmons and M.A. White, "The Relationship Between ISO 9000 and Business Performance: Does Registration Really Matter?" *Journal of Managerial Issues,* Fall 1999, pp. 330-343.

Q.R. Skrabec, T.S. Ragu-Nathan, S.S. Rao, and B.T. Bhatt, "ISO 9000: Do the Benefits Outweigh the Costs?" *Industrial Management,* November-December 1997, pp. 26-30.

L. Struebing, "Survey Finds ISO 9000 Is Market Driven," *Quality Progress,* March 1996, p. 23.

"Study Finds that Gains with ISO 9000 Registration Increase Over Time," *Quality Progress,* May 1994, pp. 18-20.

M. Terziovski, A. Samson, and D. Dow, "The Impact of ISO 9000 Certification on Customer Satisfaction," *Asia Pacific Journal of Quality*

Management, 4, 2 (1995): 66-68.

F.C. Weston, "What Do Managers Really Think of the ISO 9000 Registration Process?" *Quality Progress*, October 1995, pp. 67-73.

L.A. Wilson, *How to Implement ISO 9000* (New York: Learner First, Inc., 1994).

J. Wolak, "ISO 9000—A Software Market," *Quality*, March 1994, pp. 44-45.

A. Zuckerman and S. Daniels, "Big Three Are Serious About QS-9000 Certification," *Quality Progress*, January 1998, pp. 17-18.

A. Zuckerman, "The High Price of Admission," *Appliance Manufacturer*, May 1994, p. 8.

A. Zuckerman and A. Hurwitz, "How Companies Miss the Boat on ISO 9000," *Quality Progress*, July 1996, pp. 23-25.

A. Zuckerman, *ISO 9000 Made Easy: A Cost-Saving Guide to Documentation and Registration* (New York: AMACOM, 1995).

A. Zuckerman, "ISO 9000 Revision Might Miss Year-2000 Deadline," *Purchasing*, April 8, 1999, p. 35.

Thomas H. Stevenson is the Charles E. Cullen Professor of Marketing at the University of North Carolina at Charlotte. E-mail him at thsteven@email.uncc.edu.

Frank C. Barnes is a professor of operations management at the University of North Carolina at Charlotte. E-mail him at fcbarnes@email.uncc.edu.

The State of Quality Auditing

Greg Hutchins

This article looks at what's going in the auditing function in organizations and which types of audits add value and which types do not. It looks at the redundancies between internal auditors and what the future holds. The author suggests that "At the simplest level, the term 'quality audit' is fading from ISO 9000 vocabulary. We're simply going to become business auditors much like our counterparts in internal auditing."

Recently, a *Fortune* 500 company was on the financial ropes. Upper management looked at its operations and asked, "What doesn't add value?" This question was eventually posed to every senior manager.

The vice president of quality got together with the vice president of internal auditing to discuss redundancies. ISO 9000 first-party audits and other internal audits were soon on the table for discussion because they were considered redundant. One had to go. What do you think happened? Internal audits won. ISO 9000 first-party audits were outsourced, while the internal auditing department became the dominant auditing function—overseeing financial, operational, process, customer-supplier and the ISO 9000 first-party audit function.

Think this scenario can't happen in your company? Guess again. I think internal, quality (including first-party ISO 9000), operational, safety, environmental, compliance and customer-supplier auditing are all going to converge. This is going to become the dominant model for many organizations, particularly publicly held ones. It is something that all quality auditors, consultants, registrars and other quality professionals must be ready for.

Some Recent History

First a little history lesson may help. In the 1970s, a number of financial firms went belly up due to illegal payments, embezzlements, fraud and other criminal practices. Then in 1979, the U.S. Congress passed the Foreign Corrupt Practices Act (FCPA), which requires publicly held companies to maintain an appropriate system of internal control. Thus internal auditing departments were established. The professional association for this group is the Institute of Internal Auditors (IIA). Think of this group as the equivalent of ASQ except that it represents internal auditors.

Internal control focuses on:

- Safeguarding assets.
- Ensuring accurate and reliable accounting records.
- Encouraging compliance to company policies, procedures and other standards.

Internal control is usually divided into administrative and accounting controls. Administrative controls include plans, policies and procedures to help managers achieve operational efficiency and effectiveness. Accounting controls are plans, policies and procedures to safeguard internal assets and ensure the accuracy of financial records. The overall goal of both types of internal controls is to eliminate redundancies and waste.

Do these compliance audits of accounting and financial policies and procedures conducted by internal audits sound familiar? In much the same way, internal quality auditors do the same thing to ensure compliance with ISO 9001 requirements.

Internal auditing developed assessment tools and technologies around the concept of internal control, and these tools and technologies became institutionalized in many companies. Internal auditors became the owners of internal operational assessments and internal compliance audits of financial controls.

The good thing is that the widespread acceptance and adoption of the concept of internal control was a major driver to the wide penetration of ISO 9000.

The ISO 9000 family of quality management standards was adopted in 1987, and sector specific derivatives followed in the automotive, aviation and telecommunications industries. Thousands of organizations have become registered or certified to these standards.

> The good thing is that the widespread acceptance and adoption of the concept of internal control was a major driver to the wide penetration of ISO 9000.

Power and Visibility

As you can see from the preceding, many of the concepts of internal control predated ISO 9000 by almost 10 years. Since the idea of internal control was firmly established in many companies, ISO 9000's existence as a parallel quality control system was easily and quickly adopted.

In the quality arena, quality auditors were the owners of the ISO 9000 assessments. Because these were sometimes considered redundant, the question of who had the most power and visibility—internal auditors or quality auditors—became very significant. The reliance of external financial auditors on internal auditors explains why internal auditors are winning the influence battle.

External financial auditors used internal auditing findings to report on the financial compliance to generally accepted accounting principles (GAAP). In fact, they relied so strongly on the internal auditors that the influence of internal auditors is readily apparent in most *Fortune* 500 financial statements. The concept of internal control is prevalent throughout these statements. Here's an example that is typical of what's included in most:

> Management is responsible for maintaining a system of internal accounting controls to provide reasonable assurance that the records reflect the transactions of the company and that the established policies and procedures are carefully followed. Perhaps the most important feature in the system of control is that it is continually reviewed for its effectiveness and is augmented by written policies and guidelines, the careful selection and training of qualified personnel and a strong program of internal audit.
>
> The Board of Directors, through the audit committee, is responsible for assuring that management fulfills its responsibilities in the preparation of financial statements.
>
> *Signed by the chairman of the board of directors, the CEO, and the chief financial officer*

The continuing importance of internal auditing is reflected in its high corporate profile and position. In most organizations, the head of internal auditing is a senior vice president, vice president or at least a director level person. He or she usually reports to the chief financial officer in a solid line relationship and to the board of directors in a dotted line relationship (see Figure 1).

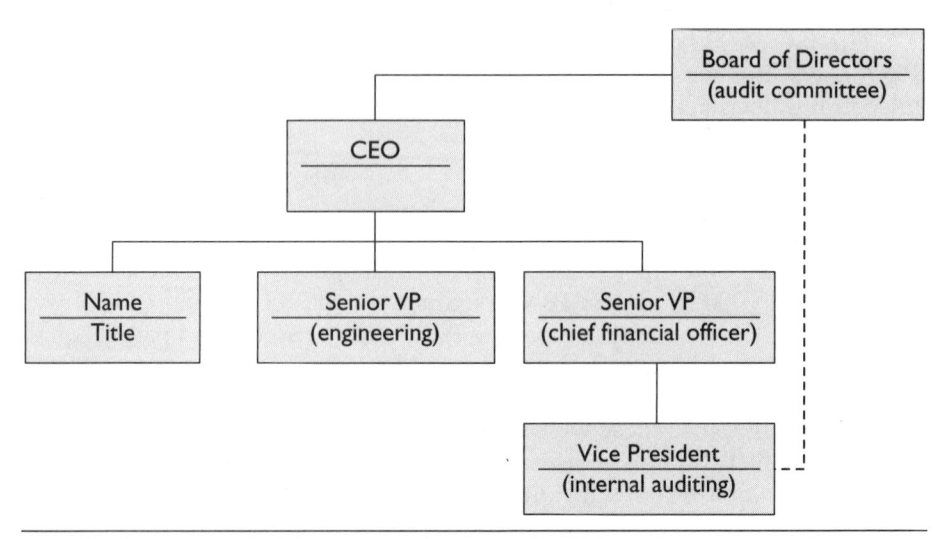

Figure 1. **Internal auditing reporting relationship**

The State of Quality Auditing

So, who had the most power and visibility? The answer lies in another question: When have you ever seen quality and ISO 9000 get the type of attention indicated in the preceding paragraph?

What Stakeholders Want

Internal control was initially viewed as an auditing consideration to get a favorable report from the external financial auditor. But over the years the concept of internal control matured.

As internal control matured, so did internal auditing, which now is at a crossroads. In the early days, internal auditing was stunningly successful in adding credibility to financial statements. The concepts of internal control have been institutionalized in many organizations and are fundamental to most management decision making. The responsibility for the integrity of financial reports has shifted to the company senior management and board of directors.

But critical stakeholders now aren't happy with the value they are receiving from financial statements. Why? These statements often reflect a situation that is three months or a year old. This seems like an eternity in today's rapidly changing market.

Financial analysts, investors and shareholders want more current, reliable and accurate financial information and, more importantly, operational data. They want to know that overall business risks are controlled and that there will be no major surprises.

Senior management wants to know that processes are stable and safe. They want to know that risks are identified and mitigated. Customers want a safe, consistent and value priced product.

More often than not, compliance audits, whether internal audits or first-party quality audits, don't deliver critical decision making information quickly enough to satisfy critical organizational stakeholders.

> Today "value added audits" is the preferred term for management, internal and performance audits because the critical question management wants answered is: "Do all of these audits add value?"

Value Added Audits

So how do these stakeholders get the information they need from financial statements? The term that we'll be hearing a lot about in the future is "value added audits."[1]

Today "value added audits" is the preferred term for management, internal and performance audits because the critical question management wants answered is: "Do all of these audits add value?"

As what adds and detracts from value is looked at ever more closely, value detracting activities are being eliminated, and in the process, internal auditing is being reinvented. In much the same way, the quality world is reinventing itself by developing new standards such as ISO 9000:2000 and ISO/CD2 19011: 2001 Guidelines on Quality and Environmental Management Systems Auditing.

We're seeing the integration of internal auditing with operational and quality auditing. The term "quality auditing" is going away and is being replaced by "auditing." The Institute of Internal Auditors (IIA) and the American Institute of Certified Public Accountants are developing new auditing standards and processes.[2]

In fact, in 1999 the IIA Board of Directors adopted the following expanded definition of internal auditing:

> Internal auditing is an independent, objective assurance and consulting activity designed to add value and improve an organization's operations. It helps an organization accomplish its objectives by bringing a systematic, disciplined approach to evaluate and improve the effectiveness of risk management, control and governance processes.[3]

Let's look at the latest definition of quality auditing. The Committee Draft of ISO 19011 doesn't even define "quality audit." The term has been eliminated in favor of just "audit," simply defined as a "systematic, independent and documented process for obtaining audit evidence and evaluating it objectively to determine the extent to which audit criteria are fulfilled."[4]

Audit criteria are further described by ISO 19011 as a "set of policies, procedures or other requirements against which collected audit evidence is compared." Audit evidence consists of "records, statements of fact or other information, relevant to the audit and which are verified."

We're going to see a convergence of internal auditing and quality auditing over the next three years.

What strikes you when you read the two preceding definitions of auditing? My impression is that the CD/ISO 19011 definition is compliance based while the internal auditing definition is more business driven. The internal auditing definition seems to be the definition that more closely reflects the intent of the ISO 9000:2000 standard with its emphasis on effectiveness.

When you read IIA's definition of internal auditing, do you hear a lot of quality related language, such as the words "assurance, adding value, risk management, systematic, disciplined, control and process orientation"? We're beginning to see the integration of quality auditing and internal accounting auditing into a generic value added model of partnering, assessment and business process improvement.

In much the same way, the terms "accounting controls" or "financial controls" are disappearing in favor of simply "internal control." The term "internal control" can be applied to both financial control and adherence to ISO 9000.

We're going to see a convergence of internal auditing and quality auditing over the next three years. Most of us know what the new ISO 9000:2000 standard looks like. It is more process oriented, customer focused and business driven. The first, most popular word in the standard is "shall." The second, most critical word in the standard is "effectiveness." An ISO 9000 registered company can't rest on its quality laurels anymore; it must demonstrate quality system effectiveness.

The State of Quality Auditing

The name or label of these audits is still up in the air. IIA and AICPA currently favor the term "value added audits." There's nothing new here since we've already been hearing much about the concepts of management audits and performance audits from Allan Sayle, an early proponent of value added auditing.

New IIA Standards

All quality auditors and consultants should become familiar with the new IIA standards. The exposure draft of level one standards consists of three documents:

- Attribute standards.
- Performance standards.
- Assurance standards.

The level one IIA standards and code of ethics are the core standards of internal auditing. You can find a discussion draft of the level one standards at www.theiia.org/ecm/guide-stand.cfm.

Level two IIA practice advisories are authoritative guidance documents. While not mandatory, they are formally endorsed by the IIA and are used by internal auditors. The practice advisories help to implement the level one standards and to apply them in specific internal auditing environments.

Level three IIA development and practice aids include research studies, books, seminars and conferences that promote the professional development of internal auditing.

> We're going to add value through conducting compliance audits and value added assessments.

What Does This Mean to Quality and Internal Auditors?

At the simplest level, the term "quality audit" is fading from ISO 9000 vocabulary. We're simply going to become business auditors much like our counterparts in internal auditing. So, this begs the questions, how are we going to add value and how are we going to differentiate ourselves from our internal auditing counterparts? We're going to add value through conducting compliance audits and value added assessments.

The changes the IIA are advocating are critical to functional management including quality management. Under the old definition, internal auditors provided arm's-length, compliance appraisals focusing on internal controls. Under the new definition, internal auditing has a larger scope, providing assurance, risk management, control and internal performance improvement consulting services.

The changes mean that internal auditing will provide services that were often the purview of industrial engineering, manufacturing engineering, quality assurance/control, purchasing and other functional departments. How the new IIA standards will be operationalized will be interesting in light of these competing interests of other departments.

Let's Join up with Internal Auditing

As previously mentioned, internal auditing, quality auditing and other internal assurance/control functions are being reinvented. We're seeing more cross functionality, where perceived operational redundancies are being eliminated and functions are being integrated.

Many assurance functions, including security, safety, environment, quality, customer-supplier evaluations and internal auditing, may be subsumed into a risk management, risk assurance or internal auditing organization. It will consist of a multidisciplinary group that provides best practice guidance, internal consulting and regulatory auditing. And over the course of three years or so, we're going to integrate our value adding services under an assurance and risk mitigation organization.

Instead of fighting these developments, quality professionals and auditors should understand what's occurring with internal auditing standards and be prepared. If we resist or fight the integration of quality assessments into internal auditing or some other organization, we'll lose the war. The smart option is to lend our operational expertise and problem solving skills to internal auditing. In the process, quality will get senior management and board level exposure, and everyone will win.

Takeaways

All too often, I hear the refrains of "this too shall pass" or "this doesn't have anything to do with me." But the situation I described in this article is real.

I'm not reading tea leaves. We've had a great franchise with ISO 9000 and quality auditing for over 13 years, but things are changing. Companies are in the process of reviewing internal operations and reinventing themselves.

Why? We've had 10 years of a robust economy. We are preparing for a soft landing or what could be a harder landing. Earnings are soft. Stock prices are plummeting in company after company. Companies are downsizing to bolster their financial reports. The scenario spelled out in this article is all too real, so ISO 9000 auditors, registrars and consultants had better be prepared.

References

1. There is much discussion on who coined the term "value added auditing." Allan Sayle, a quality consultant, was one of the early adopters and popularized this concept.
2. "About Internal Auditing," IIA Web site, 2000, at www.theiia.org.

3. Ibid.

4. *ISO CD2/ISO 19011* (Milwaukee: ASQ Quality Press, 2000).

Greg Hutchins is principal of Work It LLC and of Quality Plus Engineering, a project and process management company in Portland, OR. He is the author of the Standard Manual of Quality Auditing *published by Prentice Hall and several ISO 9000 books published by John Wiley & Sons. He is currently writing* Standard Manual of Value Added Auditing *and* Checklists for Value Added Auditing, *from which the material in this article is derived.*

Journey to the Baldrige

Debbie Phillips-Donaldson

Is the Baldrige Award still relevant? As far as we are concerned, the answer is an unqualified yes. The reason: the Baldrige is about managing for excellence in every aspect of your operations, and it provides sound direction for doing this. This article describes the quality journey at some Baldrige recipient companies. They are role models for doing the right things at all levels and in all functions.

"Quality is a journey with no finish line." That statement by Roger Quayle, vice president of quality and technology for Operations Management International Inc. (OMI), during the 13th Quest for Excellence conference earlier this year, sums up the commitment to quality of all winners of the Malcolm Baldrige National Quality Award. The 43 organizations that have won the award since its inception in 1988 have not only engaged in continuous improvement programs to earn the honor; typically, they see the award as just one milestone in their ongoing mission to achieve performance excellence.

The Baldrige National Quality Program, managed by the National Institute of Standards and Technology, has only one requirement of award recipients: that they share nonproprietary information from their application summaries to help foster U.S. competitiveness and the pursuit of performance excellence. This includes participating in the Quest conference.

Another way OMI, one of four winners for 2000, has chosen to impart its best practices is by submitting an article to *Quality Progress* ("Quality Makes a Splash," September 2001). The other three 2000 recipients—Dana Corp.-Spicer Driveshaft Division, Karlee Co. Inc. and Los Alamos National Bank—have been equally generous and forthcoming in sharing information that showcases their quality journeys at the conference and for this article.

Driving for Quality: Spicer Driveshaft

An operating unit of Dana Corp., Spicer Driveshaft (SD) takes its name from Dana's founder, Clarence Spicer, who introduced the first universal joint to

From *Quality Progress*, September 2001. Copyright © 2001 American Society for Quality. Reprinted with permission.

the automotive industry in 1904. SD currently bills itself as the largest independent supplier of driveshafts and related components to North American original equipment manufacturers and aftermarket customers. Consisting of 17 facilities with headquarters in Holland, OH, SD employs more than 3,000.

How does such a large, far-flung organization align its goals and get so many people on the same quality page—enough so that it could win a Baldrige Award in the manufacturing category? While an emphasis on "doing things right" can be traced all the way back to Spicer himself, SD began its quality journey in earnest in 1981 by deploying statistical process control. In 1985 it instituted a program called excellence in manufacturing, which focused on problem solving, problem analysis and root cause analysis.

In 1990, seeing this program was not sufficient to drive excellence at all levels, SD's senior management decided to implement a Six Sigma quality challenge. "This program was based on Baldrige Award criteria, but the objective at first was not to win a Baldrige," says Vince Morgillo, SD's director of quality. "Rather, it was to become a Six Sigma company."

This plan also failed, in this case because management did not get complete buy-in from all employees. The chief complaints were that following the program took too much time and created too much paperwork.

Standards, Closed Loops and Hellweek

Starting in 1992, SD joined a corporate program, the Dana quality leadership process (DQLP), based on Baldrige Award criteria. The program requires every Dana operating unit to submit an application annually to an internal board of examiners, who review all applications, provide written feedback and issue awards to deserving units. SD won a DQLP award in 1995.

But as with the Baldrige program, the key to DQLP is not winning awards but using the application process and the examiners' feedback to identify opportunities for improvement. "Cross functional DQLP teams are a primary vehicle for analyzing and improving our business processes," states SD's Baldrige application summary.

In 1995 SD also became certified to QS-9000 to align with its customers and suppliers in the automotive industry. SD still uses the management review element of the standard to continually evaluate and improve its leadership system.

Another element adapted from the standard, a corrective action report system, ensures all customer complaints are communicated throughout an operating unit and each complaint results in follow-up and resolution to the customer's satisfaction. The system functions as a closed loop, so the only person who can close out a report is the employee who initiated it.

DQLP is also supplemented by a quality council, comprised of SD's senior leaders and supported by manufacturing and strategic business councils centering on operational and strategic issues, respectively. In addition, SD uses market strategy teams to maintain a consistent customer focus and customer platform teams to address specific markets and customers.

SD first applied for the Baldrige in 1999 and used the feedback report from the examiners to drive further quality improvements—as the company is doing now with the 2000 feedback report. It also uses feedback from the internal DQLP assessment, funneling all this information into its strategic planning.

The planning involves aligning objectives with Dana corporate goals as well as with the objectives of Dana's automotive systems strategic business unit, to which SD belongs. The package consists of a long-term (three to five years) strategic business plan plus a detailed one-year plan to drive short-term progress. The one-year plan is created in just one week throughout all SD facilities, departments and levels, a process so intense that the official name for it is Hellweek.

Performance against the strategic plan is measured by SD's total quality management (TQM) control plan, which breaks down the mission statement into five segments and assigns a key business driver (KBD) to each. Each KBD, in turn, has measures called TQM indicators, and performance targets, frequencies and areas of responsibility are attached to those.

Most Important Asset

Back in 1969, Dana had numerous corporate policies—enough to create a stack of paper more than 30 inches thick. "Those documents represented a rigid structure that prevented people from making their own decisions," says Joe Sober, vice president and general manager of SD.

Dana CEO Ren McPhearson boiled all those documents down into brief brochures that define the culture for employees of all Dana operating units. A brochure added 20 years later details a management system known as the Dana style, which, in short, says, "People are our most important asset."

Key components of the style are:

- A complete training and education system, including an internal program called Dana University, resulting in an average of 42 hours of training per employee each year. To become a supervisor at SD, an employee has to pass six rigorous courses through the university.
- An employee idea generation system, with an 86% implementation rate.
- A strong promote-from-within policy.
- A quality culture survey to measure staff satisfaction.
- Complete employee involvement in the DQLP system, from volunteering for teams to training to become internal examiners to visiting other SD and Dana facilities for benchmarking and learning opportunities.

These measures obviously work—SD's employee attendance rate is 98.3%, while turnover is less than 1%.

Next Stop on the Journey

Besides accomplishments on the human resources side, SD's drive for quality has resulted in noteworthy business successes, too, including:

- A return on net assets of more than 25% in 2000. (As recently as 1997, the return was less than 20%.)
- A decrease in internal defect rates of more than 75% from 1996 to 2000. Defect rates for key suppliers have also decreased significantly.
- An average of 80% or better in overall customer satisfaction for the past three years, as measured by a third-party survey.
- A decrease in customer complaints from 6.8 per million units shipped in 1995 to about 2.8 per million in 2000. Since 1996, SD has not lost a customer.

By the end of this year, SD plans for all its facilities to become certified to ISO 14001 to help improve the company's environmental management systems. And it will keep using its core quality programs to foster continuous improvement. After all, the short version of its vision statement reads, "Committed to the pursuit of excellence as a way of life."

Racing Toward Its Goals: Karlee

Like a few other highly successful companies (think Hewlett-Packard), Karlee Co. Inc. got its start in a garage. Since that point in 1974, the 550-person company in Garland, TX, has come a long way to win a 2000 Baldrige Award in the manufacturing category.

Founded by Lee Brumit (the "lee" in the company name), an avid racing fan who wanted to build race car engines (the "Kar" in the name), Karlee is now a contract manufacturer offering vertically integrated services, precision sheet metal and machined components to the telecommunications, semiconductor and medical equipment industries.

The company incorporated in 1977 and, since 1979, has grown exponentially, from sales of $1 million to $79 million in 2000. Its number of employees, called team members, has also increased dramatically, from 13 in 1979 to the current level. Since 1996 the company has achieved an annual growth rate exceeding 25%.

A highly visible component of Karlee's success is its CEO and chairman, Jo Ann Brumit, who has been the main visionary and driver behind the company's quality journey. In 1990 she initiated formal strategic planning, use of the Baldrige criteria as a business model and creation of the Karlee steering committee, comprised of senior executives, management team leaders and key support area representatives. Karlee added ISO 9002 certification in 1996 to complement its quality program.

At first, Brumit the founder was skeptical of the new quality efforts, according to CEO Brumit and other Karlee team members. "We had to convince Lee, but once we showed him the results, he was on board," the CEO says.

Karlee didn't stop its quest for performance excellence at certification. Since 1997 it has created a senior executive leader team to review and refine the company's mission, vision and values each year. In addition, it has added contract manufacturing integration, just-in-time manufacturing with key suppliers and an e-manufacturing system.

Karlee was a 1999 regional winner of the Texas Business of the Year Award from the Texas Association of Business and Chamber of Commerce. In 2000 the company became certified to TL 9000 to better meet the needs of its telecommunications clients.

More than Just Partners

That Karlee would take extra measures to stay in step with—and ahead of—customer needs is not unusual; its mission statement is "to exceed our stakeholders' expectations."

The company's fundamental business strategy revolves around building long-term relationships with a few primary customers. "We limit the number of customers so we can build two-way, win-win relationships, not just partnerships," Jo Ann Brumit says.

"We've actually turned down business from some potential customers and resigned from others," adds Rick Cherry, president of Karlee.

In fact, a crucial part of the company's customer and market focus is its customer selection process. Karlee looks for customers that support the same values (including its systematic approach to business and performance management), desire long-term relationships and are global leaders in their markets. Then the company keeps those customers by following a process it calls "building partnerships by providing solutions" in areas such as customers' business challenges, schedule changes, communication and cost reduction.

These steps, combined with dedicated cross functional teams for each account and a proactive problem resolution process, have led to Karlee receiving a 2000 customer satisfaction rating of 1.36 on a 1 to 5 scale, with 1 being the best. This compares favorably with both its 2000 goal (1.5) and the rating of a local competitor (2.0).

Hoshins: Not Large Bodies of Water

In late 1997 David Briggs joined Karlee as director of performance excellence. He became vice president in 2000. With experience as an examiner for both the Baldrige and the Texas Award for Performance Excellence, Briggs was the logical choice to write the application and prepare the company for trying to win the Texas award, a goal it achieved in 1999. One year later, he followed the same routine for the Baldrige.

Briggs and Karlee in general are such believers in the Baldrige program

> Karlee looks for customers that support the same values (including its systematic approach to business and performance management), desire long-term relationships and are global leaders in their markets.

that they use it as the basis for their strategic planning process. "It mirrors the Baldrige criteria in terms of format and order," Briggs says.

Karlee's major planning activity occurs in August or September, with directors and managers meeting for about two days. Deployment through the Karlee steering committee follows about a week later. If leaders see a need for revisions, they hold a mid-year planning meeting in May.

The process includes updating key business drivers, which align with five stakeholders: customers, team members, suppliers, owners and community. All objectives, goals and strategies must also align with the mission, vision ("to be a continuing improving leader in performance excellence") and core values:

- Team member growth and development.
- Encouragement and recognition.
- A clean and safe environment.
- Mutual trust, honesty and respect.
- Social responsibilities.

Another key element of the planning process is selecting one or more *hoshins*. This word does not, as Briggs jokes, mean large bodies of saltwater. ("That's what some of us Texans thought at first," he says.) The Japanese term refers to breakthrough planning: identifying areas of performance for making significant improvement. For Karlee the *hoshin* for 2000 and 2001 is lean manufacturing.

Performance against the key objectives and *hoshin* is carefully and continuously measured and monitored according to a variety of data, with much of the information posted for all team members to see.

> If you refer to the Karlee core values and read the first letter of each value going down the list, you'll discern an acronym: TEAMS.

All in the Family

If you refer to the Karlee core values and read the first letter of each value going down the list, you'll discern an acronym: TEAMS. Given the company's team based culture, this is obviously no accident. As Briggs says, "Teams 'R' Us."

Jo Ann Brumit and other Karlee leaders are not shy about stating the culture is based on Christian ethics and family values. The company focuses on hiring people with the same values, which often means bringing aboard several members of the same extended family.

The Karlee work force is also quite diverse: 47% Hispanic, 34% white, 12% African American and 7% Asian American. All important company documents and information are printed in Spanish and Vietnamese in addition to English.

As part of its quality foundation, Karlee affords its team members a large dose of empowerment. Most members have the authority to help set performance targets, monitor daily performance, stop production, improve processes, request new metrics and perform monthly self-audits.

The company also provides formal training to the annual tune of a minimum of 25 hours per team member and 40 hours per team leader. And it reimburses for education pursued by a team member outside the company, as long as the course or seminar has some relation to business or the person's career.

Karlee takes to heart its pledge to share its best practices and does all it can to spread the Baldrige philosophy. Perhaps Brumit best expresses her company's commitment to the philosophy: "Do you want to make money? Do you want to make your company better? Do you want to make a difference? If you can say yes to any of those questions, you have a good reason to get involved with the Baldrige program."

Small and Strong: Los Alamos National Bank

The first bank to win a Baldrige Award, Los Alamo National Bank (LANB) started its journey in 1963 as an independent community bank, a status it still holds today. Then, it served a rather unique community: the people working on the Manhattan Project, which gave rise to the city of Los Alamos itself. Today, the Los Alamos National Laboratory, which the project evolved into, remains the city's largest employer.

In 1963 the bank had five employees and $1 million in capital. Those figures today are 184 employees (which placed the bank in the small business category when it won the Baldrige) and $77 million in capital, with more than $700 million in assets. This growth makes LANB the largest independent bank in New Mexico. Besides the main office in Los Alamos, LANB also has branches in Santa Fe and White Rock.

Perhaps even more noteworthy is how LANB's numbers compare with those of its competitors, which are now mainly regional and national banks. Mergers have led to the demise of many mid-size banks, which has created a niche that LANB now dominates. Its efforts to fill this gap in the market and position itself directly opposite its competitors translate into its key business factors:

- **Service**—LANB's personal, friendly service is guided by 11 service standards and supported by telephone, Internet and extensive ATM banking.
- **Efficiency**—thanks to technology and personnel development, only 49 cents of every revenue dollar go to overhead, compared with 64 cents for the nearest competitor.
- **Competitive pricing**—LANB makes less than one-eighth of its income from service charges. Most banks earn at least one-third of their income from this source.
- **Net interest margin management**—this is the spread between the interest the bank pays on deposits and what it charges on loans. For LANB, the spread is less than 4%, compared with more than 5% for most banks (with some as high as 35%).

How Do You Celebrate a Baldrige Award?

Your organization just won the Baldrige—what are you going to do next?

After months of hard work writing an application and preparing for a site visit by examiners, most Baldrige Award winners celebrate by letting their hair down a little, and the 2000 winners are no exception. But just as their companies have unique cultures and ways of handling their quality initiatives, so do their celebrations reflect their own styles.

Spicer Driveshaft (SD), according to its leaders, has been celebrating for months. Shortly after the award was announced, each of its 17 facilities held a luncheon for all staff. Subsequently, each of its 3,000-plus employees received a commemorative Baldrige pin, a $500 savings bond and a personal letter, mailed to their homes, from Joe Sober, SD's vice president and general manager, thanking them for their contributions to the company's success. In addition, SD launched a publicity campaign in each facility's area so the local communities could share in congratulating all SD employees.

For **Karlee Co. Inc.**, based in Texas, the only logical choice for a celebration was a huge hoedown for all team members, plus any family or friends they wanted to bring. The company also invited local and state dignitaries to share in the celebration. Every team member received recognition pins, special T-shirts and other memorabilia. Because the Karlee culture includes regular social events, celebration of the Baldrige has been ongoing.

At the first announcement of **Los Alamos National Bank's** (LANB) Baldrige Award, the quality council broke out the champagne. Next, the company held a lottery for the 50 spots allotted for the trip to Washington, DC, in early April, when President George W. Bush presented the 2000 awards at a White House ceremony. For those employees left behind, the bank set up a closed-circuit television in the lobby so everyone—including customers—could watch. In addition, when employees arrived at the bank that morning, they each found on their desks a gift accompanied by a thank-you card from the CEO and president. Later that day, they enjoyed a catered lunch.

When the ceremony delegation returned from DC, the bank held another celebration that included dance lessons, piñatas and another gift for each person: a Baldrige picture frame with the LANB mission statement on one side and space for a personal photo on the other. The bank held yet another ceremony when the award itself arrived.

Operations Management International Inc. (OMI) had to find a way to celebrate across more than 170 sites. Like LANB, OMI held a lottery to determine who would attend the White House ceremony. For the rest of the 1,400 OMI associates who did not attend, the ceremony was broadcast over satellite to all facilities, with local media invited to each site to view the broadcast, too. OMI had mini-Baldrige Awards created so each facility would have a replica, and each associate received a decorative Baldrige Award cube and a commemorative badge for his or her uniform.

- **Employee ownership and empowerment**—all LANB employees are fully trained and then empowered, and share directly in the bank's success. In many banks, decision making and the opportunity for profit sharing or bonuses reside solely within top management.
- **Community support and reinvestment**—LANB invests almost exclusively in northern and central New Mexico.
- **Financial security and sustainability**—LANB's return on equity to shareholders (mainly employees and area residents) averaged 15% in 1999, and its net income has increased by more than 60% over the past five years.

Quality in Small Pockets

Thanks to the focus on these key factors, LANB has captured much of the local market. In Los Alamos County, 80% of mortgages are through LANB, and 66% of residents use it as their primary bank. In Santa Fe County, LANB is one of the top three mortgage lenders.

What led LANB to its current strength? In the 1980s management began implementing some of the quality principles and methods of W. Edwards Deming. The bank then tried quality circles, which helped spur progress but lacked commitment throughout the organization and suffered from insufficient communication. Later that decade, LANB joined the Los Alamos Quality Network, whose members visited Motorola Inc. to study its quality program.

During all these initiatives, the bank's management "tried quality in small pockets in individual departments, hoping it would take over," says Steve Wells, LANB president. "But it was a big failure."

In 1993 LANB became a charter member of Quality New Mexico. The networking that alliance provided, along with the adoption of Baldrige principles, started the bank on its way up the quality curve. First it chucked its old mission statement of 30 words for this succinct, direct version: "Exceed the expectations of our customers, employees and investors."

Next the bank defined its core values, which include customer service, people, efficiency, flexibility and innovation. The last item not only helps LANB offer the same value as larger banks and with better service, but it also pays homage to the technological advances Los Alamos is known for.

LANB then established three key corporate objectives: individual achievement, service excellence and financial performance. In all internal bank documents, these objectives are displayed as interlocking circles. The area in the middle where the three circles overlap is what Tim Doyle, vice president and COO, refers to as the "sweet spot": the high-performance area that all employees are always striving to achieve.

Along its quality journey, LANB learned many lessons, including the measures that were most important to ensuring success. "First we measured

> First it chucked its old mission statement of 30 words for this succinct, direct version: "Exceed the expectations of our customers, employees and investors."

nothing, then everything," Wells explains. "Finally we settled on three key measures: net interest margin, efficiency and mortgage loan servicing."

Evolution of Improvement

As its quality program evolved, the bank added strategic planning to the mix. While this operates as a continuous cycle, it culminates in an annual planning meeting, during which the board of directors and executive management review the vision, mission and corporate objectives. Based on their assessments, they may amend or redirect any of those items and add new corporate objectives. Quarterly follow-up meetings allow them to review and recommend changes in strategic direction.

The corporate objectives provide a framework in which departmental leaders develop their own objectives. The leaders do not work alone; this level of planning involves every employee and results in action plans that directly address one or more corporate objectives. The action plans, which often encompass several departments, are deployed down into individual goals for each employee. In 2000 LANB had about 90 action plans under way.

Because LANB practices management by fact, every area of performance is tracked using specific measures. The bank refers to its measurement system as its "brain center" for aligning organizational performance with strategic direction and objectives. And because LANB is committed to technology, it uses state-of-the-art data gathering and analysis tools—in essence, a relational database and balanced scorecard software on a client-server system—to run that center.

> Because LANB practices management by fact, every area of performance is tracked using specific measures.

A variety of forms and frequencies of communication—including regular meetings, a monthly newsletter and daily e-mail and intranet updates—ensure each employee is always aware of his or her goals and how they fit into and support the organization in reaching its vision.

Since 1998 LANB has used another communication vehicle, the quality council, which meets biweekly and is comprised of representatives from every area and level of the bank. Meetings are open to all employees.

The council's charter is to focus on continuous improvement: establish criteria, prioritize opportunities, train employees on process improvement, coordinate and oversee improvement projects and distribute information throughout the organization. Employee suggestions are funneled through this program, as is information such as the Baldrige examiners' feedback report.

All these improvement efforts have paid off. As a precursor to its Baldrige win, LANB won New Mexico's highest quality award, the Zia, in 1999. In 1996 it was named one of *Inc.* magazine's 26 "Banks We Love" and, in 1995, *Money* magazine's "best bank in New Mexico."

Incentives and Perks

In concert with their role in the planning and performance of the bank, employees have a chance to reap the rewards of its success, too. Individual performance at a high level leads to incentives such as profit sharing and employee stock ownership, which can amount to more than 21% of an employee's annual salary.

Such incentives, combined with training, support the full empowerment of employees to handle all customer interactions. Employees are completely authorized to resolve customer complaints on the spot. "If they make a mistake, we tell them they're even more valuable because the organization has more invested in them now," Doyle says.

Training, which thoroughly covers the bank's mission, vision, core values and other vital areas, also includes leadership training at almost every level. In 1999 more than 90% of LANB employees received leadership training. That compares with only 8% of bank employees nationwide. For employees who seek additional education, the bank reimburses tuition and materials costs for business classes and awards raises to those who earn an A or B.

For employees with 10 or more years of service, a perk that's becoming popular is the opportunity to take a four-week sabbatical. During a sabbatical (which is open to only one person at a time), the employee is allowed to have absolutely no contact with the bank. In fact, most people who take the sabbatical are highly encouraged to tack on two weeks of vacation to extend the leave to six weeks.

In 2000 LANB had an unfortunate opportunity to show its deep commitment to its employees and the community. The Cerro Grande fire that May forced the evacuation of 12,000 LANB customers as well as the bank's main office and one branch. More than 400 families—including some LANB employees—saw their homes destroyed by the fire.

The bank responded by offering affected employees monetary assistance (cash and zero interest loans), counseling and paid time off, plus double time to employees who worked during the evacuation. For customers, the bank issued a moratorium on mortgage payments, offered zero interest loans and grants to rebuild, doubled ATM withdrawal limits and extended its hours of service to accommodate schedules hampered by the disaster.

Take It to the Bank

LANB's leaders say its pursuit of excellence has just begun. "In response to a 50-page application for the Baldrige, we received 66 pages of feedback from the examiners," Wells points out. "So we still have a lot of work to do."

What's inspiring about this attitude—and indeed, that of all Baldrige winners—is that they relish the chance to improve and are truly passionate about the quest for excellence. In addition, they all show a profound capacity for hard work and boundless determination.

As Doyle says about the quality journey: "Don't let up. Keep at it, no matter what the hurdles."

For all organizations aspiring to the Baldrige or at least to the next level of performance, that is advice you can take to the bank.

Bibliography

"Criteria for Performance Excellence," Baldrige National Quality Program, 2000.

"Quest for Excellence XIII Application Summaries," Baldrige National Quality Program, 2001.

"Quest for Excellence XIII Conference Program," Baldrige National Quality Program, 2001.

"2000 Award Winner: Dana Corp.-Spicer Driveshaft," Baldrige National Quality Program, 2001.

"2000 Award Winner: Karlee," Baldrige National Quality Program, 2001.

"2000 Award Winner: Los Alamos National Bank," Baldrige National Quality Program, 2001.

Debbie Phillips-Donaldson is editor of Quality Progress. Contact her at ddonaldson@asq.org.

PART FOUR

Quality References

We have created *The Quality Yearbook* for your use as an anthology and reference to the principles, practices, and practitioners of this approach to managing. Parts One to Three are the anthology section of the book. Part Four is the reference section. There are four items that make up this reference. Specifically, you'll find:

- **Quality Resource Organizations.** This is a directory of associations and organizations primarily in the United States and Canada that are directly or indirectly related to the study and support of quality and quality-related practices. It includes contact information and a brief description of each organization's activities. This has been completely updated from 2001.
- **Quality Resources Online 2002.** This serves as a starting point for getting on the Web and locating sites dedicated to quality practices. We provide you with a directory of discussion groups and World Wide Web sites. Included also is the article, "A Quality Manager's Guide to the Internet."
- **Directory of Magazines, Newsletters, and Journals.** This section lists over 70 publications that focus on or regularly include articles on quality and management excellence. This directory provides information on subscribing and annotations that describe the focus of each publication.
- **Calendar of Major Events, 2002.** This lists many conferences that will occur during the year 2001, with dates and locations of the conferences, along with Web site addresses where you can find additional information.

We've prepared a detailed index to supplement the table of contents. This should be valuable in helping you find topics, organizations, and people covered in our anthology. If you've purchased earlier editions of the yearbook, you will note that we previously included an overview of the Baldrige Award winners, which were traditionally announced in October. Because the awards now include educational institutions, and schools start only in August or September, the Baldrige committee changed its announcement date to late November. Therefore, we are unable to include the award recipients in this yearbook. However, we urge you to watch for the announcement and visit the Baldrige Award Web site to learn more about the 2001 award-winning organizations (www.quality.nist.gov/Award_Recipients.htm).

Directory of Quality Resource Organizations

There are many organizations dedicated to providing information on quality practices, conferences, seminars, and publications. While interest in quality management in the U.S. may be on the decline or at least yielding to other approaches to improving business, it is growing throughout the rest of the world, particularly in the movement to establish, promote, and enforce standards and the trend of companies and nations to form partnerships for economic strength. Quality is truly a global concern: it's become the standard for success, required to survive and thrive in the 2000s.

In recent years, the number of organizations founded to promote quality has grown dramatically around the world. Also, more and more organizations have gone international, although that term varies greatly in meaning. With these trends in mind, we have had to make some tough decisions for our yearbook.

We have combined listings for organizations in the U.S. and Canada with listings for global or truly international organizations. We have not included many national or regional organizations outside the U.S. and Canada, because they are too numerous and most are members of such bodies as the International Organization for Standardization (ISO), the European Organization for Quality, the European Committee for Standardization, the European Foundation for Quality Management, European Accreditation, the Mercosul Committee for Standardization, the Inter-American Metrology System, IQNet—the International Certification Network, the International Accreditation Forum, the Comunidad Andina (Andean Community), and INSTA (Internordiske Standardiseringssa-marbejde). Readers interested in national or regional organizations outside the U.S. and Canada should check with these international organizations or consult the 2000 edition of *The Quality Yearbook*.

We have included only organizations that are primarily concerned with quality process improvement, standards, and certification. Because of space limitations, we have not included the many hundreds of small local organizations. Check the section "Quality Resources Online 2002" for other organizations. If there are any organizations that we should include in our next edition, please e-mail jwoods@cwlpub.com. To improve the quality of this yearbook, we depend on input from you, our customers.

Agency for Healthcare Research and Quality
2101 E. Jefferson St., Suite 501
Rockville, MD 20852
Phone: 301 594-1364
Fax: NA
E-mail: info@ahrq.gov
Web: www.ahrq.gov
AHRQ, formerly known as the Agency for Health Care Policy and Research, conducts research that provides evidence-based information on health care outcomes; quality; and cost, use, and access. Information from AHRQ's research helps people make more informed decisions and improve the quality of health care services.

American College of Medical Quality
4334 Montgomery Avenue
Bethesda, MD 20814
Phone: 301 913-9149, 800 924-2149
Fax: 301 913-9142
E-mail: acmq@acmq.org
Web: www.acmq.org
ACMQ is the medical specialty society for physicians and other healthcare professionals in the many fields of medical quality management. Its mission is to provide leadership in creating, sustaining, and applying a scientifically based infrastructure for the practice of clinical quality improvement. It publishes the *American Journal of Medical Quality*.

American Health Quality Association
1140 Connecticut Avenue, NW, Suite 1050
Washington, DC 20036
Phone: 202 331-5790
Fax: 202 331-9334
E-mail: ahqa@ahqa.org
Web: www.ahqa.org
AHQA is a national, not-for-profit membership association of independent, community-based Quality Improvement Organizations (QIOs) representing the 50 states, the District of Columbia, and the U.S. territories. QIOs work collaboratively with health care practitioners, health plans, and hospitals to analyze health care patterns, identify opportunities for improvement, and interpret and share information about current science and best practices with physicians, hospitals, and health plans.

American Management Association
1601 Broadway
New York, NY 10019-7420
Phone: 800 262-9699, 212 586-8100
Fax: 212 903-8168
E-mail: cust_serv@amanet.org
Web: www.amanet.org
The AMA has increasingly taken note of quality practices over the past several years, incorporating these new management methods into its seminars.

American National Standards Institute
1819 L Street, NW, 6th Floor
Washington, DC 20036
Phone: 202 293-8020
Fax: 202 293-9287
E-mail: ansionline@ansi.org
Web: www.ansi.org
ANSI is a private, nonprofit membership organization supported by private and public sector organizations. It has administered and coordinated the private sector voluntary standardization system in the U.S. since 1918. ANSI facilitates development of national standards by establishing consensus among qualified groups. ANSI is an ISO member body.

American Productivity and Quality Center
123 N. Post Oak Lane, 3rd Floor
Houston, TX 77024
Phone: 800 776-9676, 713 681-4020
Fax: 713 681-1182
E-mail: apqcinfo@apqc.org
Web: www.apqc.org
APQC is a quality research center that accumulates information on best practices for all processes. It does research on best practices, supplies copies of articles on processes, conducts seminars, and sells publications. It formed the International Benchmarking Clearinghouse in 1992, to improve learning from best practices.

American Society for Engineering
Member Support Department
P.O. Box 820
Rolla, MO 65402-0820
Phone: 573 341-2101
Fax: 573 364-3500
E-mail: asemmsd@rollanet.org
Web: www.asem.com

ASEM was founded in 1979 by engineering managers from industry, education, and government who recognized that managing and administering large technical engineering and research projects and budgets requires special skills and improved management processes and that a career path that places engineers in management must be supported by engineering management education and organizations that strive to develop and enhance management skills. ASEM holds an annual conference and publishes *Engineering Management Journal*.

American Society for Nondestructive Testing, Inc.
Sandi Thomas, Executive Assistant
P.O. Box 28518
1711 Arlingate Lane
Columbus, OH 43228-0518
Phone: 800 222-2768, 614 274-6003
Fax: 614 274-6899
E-mail: sthomas@asnt.org
Web: www.asnt.org

ASNT is the world's largest technical society for nondestructive testing (NDT) professionals. It provides a forum for exchange of NDT technical information, NDT educational materials and programs, and standards and services for the qualification and certification of NDT personnel and facilitates NDT research and technology applications.

American Society for Quality
600 North Plankinton Avenue
Milwaukee, WI 53202
P.O. Box 3005
Milwaukee, WI 53201-3005
Phone: 800 248-1946, 414 272-8575
Fax: 414 272-1734
E-mail: cs@asq.org
Web: www.asq.org

This is the most important quality association in the world, with the largest membership. It co-administers the Malcolm Baldrige National Quality Award, publishes journals (*Quality Progress*, *Journal of Quality Technology*, *Technometrics*, *Quality Engineering*, *Quality Management Journal*, *Six Sigma Forum Magazine*, and *Software Quality Professional*), conducts seminars on quality-related issues, and publishes books on quality themes. It offers a certification program for quality assurance and other related topics.

American Society for Testing and Materials
100 Barr Harbor Drive
West Conshohocken, PA 19428-2959
Phone: 610 832-9585
Fax: 610 832-9555
E-mail: infoctr@astm.org
Web: www.astm.org

The mission of this organization is "to be the foremost developer and provider of voluntary consensus standards, related technical information, and services having internationally recognized quality and applicability that promote public health and safety, and the overall quality of life; contribute to the reliability of materials, products, systems and services; and facilitate national, regional, and international commerce."

American Society for Training and Development
1640 King Street
P.O. Box 1443
Alexandria VA 22313-2043
Phone: 800 NAT-ASTD (628-2783), 703 683-8100
Fax: 703 683-1523
E-mail: astd@astd.org, info@astd.org
Web: www.astd.org

This is the major American association for those developing training programs. Increasingly in the last several years, it has concentrated efforts on quality training. It hosts annual conferences in the spring and fall and publishes *T&D*, and *Info-*

Line. It's also produced the *National Report on Human Resources*, *Who's Who in Training and Development*, and *ASTD's Buyer's Guide and Consultant Directory*.

American Society of Safety Engineers
1800 E. Oakton Street
Des Plaines, IL 60018-2187
Phone: 847 699-2929
Fax: 847 768-3434
E-mail: customerservice@asse.org
Web: www.asse.org
Founded in 1911, ASSE is the world's oldest and largest professional safety organization. Its 33,000 members manage, supervise, and consult on safety, health, and environmental issues in industry, insurance, government, and education. ASSE publishes a monthly journal, *Professional Safety*.

American Statistical Association
1429 Duke Street
Alexandria, VA 22314-3415
Phone: 703 684-1221, 888 231-3473
Fax: 703 684-2037
E-mail: asainfo@amstat.org
Web: www.amstat.org
The ASA is a scientific and educational society founded in 1839 to promote excellence in the application of statistical science across the wealth of human endeavor. It publishes a dozen periodicals, including *The American Statistician* (quarterly) and the *Journal of the American Statistical Association* (quarterly). Of particular interest is the Quality & Productivity Section.

American Supplier Institute
38701 Seven Mile Road, Suite #355
Livonia, MI 48152-0109
Phone: 800 462-4500, 734 464-1395
Fax: 734 464-1399
E-mail: asi@amsup.com
Web: www.amsup.com
ASI is a nonprofit, employee-owned company with the mission of helping organizations meet the needs of customers through research, training, implementation, and publications on quality improvement techniques. Since 1981, ASI has worked with business and industry to bring the latest in management and quality improvement techniques, methods, and philosophies to companies worldwide. It pioneered the implementation of QFD and Taguchi methods in the U.S.

APICS—The Educational Society for Resource Management
5301 Shawnee Road
Alexandria, VA 22312-2317
Phone: 800 444-APICS (2742), 703 354-8851
Fax: 703 354-8106
E-mail: j_battin@apics-hq.org, international@apics-hq.org
Web: www.apics.org
Founded in 1957 as the American Production and Inventory Control Society, this organization has expanded its focus to include programs and materials on individual and organizational education, standards of excellence, and integrated resource management. This not-for-profit organization is now international, with nearly 70,000 individual and corporate members in 20,000 companies worldwide. APICS publishes *APICS—The Performance Advantage* and holds an annual international conference and exposition.

Asia-Pacific Quality Organization
Secretariat
P.O. Box 116
U.P. Campus, Diliman
Quezon City, Philippines D-1101
Phone: 632.931.9696
Fax: 632.932.4148
E-mail: apqo@mydestiny.net
Web: www.qil.com/apqo
The APQO is an autonomous, non-political, non-profit, scientific and technical organization. Member organizations represent the U.S. (American Society for Quality), Mexico, Australia, China, Korea, India, Indonesia, Malaysia, New Zealand, The Philippines, Singapore, Sri Lanka, and Vietnam.

Directory of Quality Resource Organizations

ASME International
3 Park Avenue
New York, NY 10016-5990
Phone: 800 843-2763, 973 882-1167
Fax: 973 882-1717
E-mail: infocentral@asme.org
Web: www.asme.org
ASME International was founded in 1880 as the American Society of Mechanical Engineers. It is now a nonprofit educational and technical organization serving 125,000 members around the world and promoting "the art, science, and practice of mechanical engineering." It publishes books and other materials, holds some 30 technical conferences and 200 professional development courses each year, and sets many industrial and manufacturing standards.

Association for Manufacturing Excellence, Inc.
380 West Palatine Road, Suite 7
Wheeling, IL 60090-5863
Phone: 847 520-3282
Fax: 847 520-0163
E-mail: info@ame.org
Web: www.ame.org
AME is a not-for-profit group of manufacturing professionals who share their experiences so that North American manufacturing may become more competitive. AME publishes a quarterly magazine, *Target*.

Association for Quality and Participation
Executive Building #200
2368 Victory Parkway
Cincinnati, OH 45206
Phone: 800 733-3310
Fax: 513 381-0070
E-mail: aqp@aqp.org
Web: www.aqp.org
AQP is an international not-for-profit membership association dedicated to improving workplaces through quality and participation practices. Founded in 1977 as the International Association of Quality Circles, AQP sponsors conferences, maintains a library and research service on quality and employee issues, publishes a journal (*The Journal for Quality and Participation*) and a newsletter, grants organizational team excellence awards, and sells resource materials.

Association for Work Process Improvement
185 Devonshire Street, Suite 770
Boston, MA 02110
Phone: 617 426-1167
Fax: 617 521-8675
E-mail: info@tawpi.org
Web: www.tawpi.org
The mission of TAWPI is to enhance the performance of organizations and strengthen the value of professionals that employ emerging technologies in mail, remittance, document, and forms processing.

Baldrige National Quality Program
National Institute of Standards and Technology
100 Bureau Drive Stop 1020
Gaithersburg, MD 20899-1020
Phone: 301 975-2036
Fax: 301 948-3716
E-mail: nqp@nist.gov
Web: www.quality.nist.gov
NQP manages the Malcolm Baldrige National Quality Award.

Canadian Environmental Auditing Association
1-6820 Kitimat Road
Mississauga, ON L5N 5M3
Canada
Phone: 905 567-4705
Fax: 905 814-1158
E-mail: administration.ceaa@sympatico.ca
Web: www.ceaa-acve.ca
The Canadian Environmental Auditing Association was founded in 1991. It is a multidisciplinary organization open to all individuals directly or indirectly involved with environmental auditing. Its mission is to encourage the development and discipline of environmental auditing and the improvement of environmental management of public and private organizations through environmental audi-

tor certification and the application of environmental auditing ethics, principles, and standards.

Canadian General Standards Board
222 Queen Street, Suite 1501
Ottawa, ON K1A 1G6
Canada
Phone: 819 956-0894
Fax: 819 956-1634
E-mail: ncr.cgsb-ongc@pwgsc.gc.ca
Web: w3.pwgsc.gc.ca/cgsb
The Canadian General Standards Board, part of the federal government (Public Works and Government Services Canada), is one of Canada's largest standards development organizations. Since 1934 it has been developing standards for products and services. CGBS also offers accredited quality system registration services (including ISO 9000) and environmental management systems services (ISO 14000). It also maintains extensive certified and qualified product lists, which are used widely by governments and business as a tool for procurement.

Center for Quality and Productivity Improvement
University of Wisconsin-Madison
610 Walnut Street, 575 WARF Building
Madison, WI 53705
Phone: 608 263-2520
Fax: 608 263-1425
E-mail: quality@engr.wisc.edu
Web: www.engr.wisc.edu/centers/cqpi
CQPI is a research center founded in 1985 to develop techniques for improving the quality of products, product designs, manufacturing processes, and service. Specific advances have included statistical approaches to the development of robust products and processes, the design of experiments, advanced statistical process control techniques, and critiques and improvements of quality techniques coming from Japan.

Center for Quality of Management, Inc.
1 Alewife Center, Suite 450
Cambridge, MA 02140
Phone: 617 873-8950
Fax: 617 873-8980
E-mail: CQM_Mail@cqm.org
Web: www.cqm.org
The Center is a non-profit organization founded by senior executives to promote mutual learning through educational programs, advising services, research initiatives, and networking events.

The Conference Board, Inc.
845 Third Avenue
New York, NY 10022-6678
Phone: 212 759-0900
Fax: 212 980-7014
E-mail: info@conference-board.org
Web: www.conference-board.org
This nationally recognized council of American businesses is best known for its research on business trends. It publishes its research, some of which is related to quality practices.

Decision Sciences Institute
35 Broad Street
Atlanta, GA 30303
Phone: 404 651-4073
Fax: 404 651-2804
E-mail: dsi@gsu.edu
Web: www.decisionsciences.org
The DSI is "an interdisciplinary, international organization dedicated to the advancement of the science and practice of education and research about business decisions." The DSI "promotes excellence in teaching and scholarship, and seeks to serve current and future developmental needs of doctoral students, faculty, and academic administrators."

Environmental Auditors Registration Association
Welton House
Limekiln Way
Lincoln, Lincolnshire LN2 4US
United Kingdom
Phone: +44 (0) 1522 540 069
Fax: +44 (0) 1522 540 090
E-mail: eara@dial.pipex.com
Web: www.greenchannel.com/iea/eara-home.htm

EARA is an independent register of environmental auditors and environmental management system auditors. In its first five years of operation, EARA registered over 1900 auditors from 46 countries. The registration criteria meet or exceed the requirements of ISO 14012.

European Federation for Non-Destructive Testing
Secretariat
Confédération Française pour les Essais Non Destructifs (COFREND)
1 rue Gaston Boissier
75724 Paris Cedex 15
France
Phone: 01.44.19.76.18
Fax: 01.44.19.75.04
E-mail: cofrend@worldnet.fr
Web: www.efndt.org
The European Federation for Non-Destructive Testing (EFNDT) was founded in May 1998 in Copenhagen at the 7th European Conference for Non-Destructive Testing, by 27 national NDT societies. Full membership is open to national NDT societies, one per country.

Federal Consulting Group
Office of Thrift Supervision Building
Anne Kelly, Director
1700 G Street, NW, Lower Level
Washington, DC 20552
Phone: 202 906-6287
Fax: 202 906-6162
E-mail: anne.kelly@ots.treas.gov
Web: NA
The FCG, formerly the Federal Quality Consulting Group, was formed by consultants from the former Federal Quality Institute when it died. The FCG is a fee-for-service franchise; its mission is "to consult with senior leaders to accelerate the change to customer-focused, high-performing, results-oriented government organizations; import and share best practices from both the public and private sectors; and provide developmental opportunities for senior executives to learn new ideas and concepts."

Health Care Quality Alliance
4938 Hampden Lane, #201
Bethesda, MD 20814
Phone: 202 905-3535
Fax: 301 263-0245
E-mail: info@healthquality.org
Web: www.healthquality.org
HCQA was founded in 1987 to ensure that quality is the core value of the nation's health care agenda. HCQA brings together 97 national health care consumer, provider, and industry organizations committed to promoting quality health care for all, by increasing public awareness, sharing perspectives and information, and fostering consensus on critical policy issues. The Alliance publishes *HCQA Quality Forum*.

Independent Association of Accredited Registrars, Inc.
E-mail: info@iaar.org
Web: www.iaar.org
The IAAR, a non-profit organization, is an association of accredited management system registrars operating in North America. Its main purpose is to facilitate the registration of companies throughout North America in a consistent manner to promote the integrity and credibility of the registration process.

Independent International Organization for Certification
c/o Sandy Sutherland (chair)
Lloyd Register Quality Assurance Ltd.
LRQA Centre, Carolyn House
Dingwall Road
GB-Croydon CRO 9XF
United Kingdom
Phone: + 44 181 688 6882
Fax: + 44 181 681 8146
E-mail: sandy.sutherland@lrqa.com
Web: NA
The primary objectives of IIOC are to support the concept of accredited certification in accordance with European and international standards, provide a forum for the discussion of matters of mutual interest with the users of certification, and work toward eliminating the need for multi-

ple accreditation. IIOC participates in the meetings and working groups of the European Accreditation of Certification, International Accreditation Forum, Pacific Accreditation Forum, and the International Auditor Training Certification Association.

Indy Quality, Productivity and Involvement Council, Inc.
c/o Ray Becker
Walker Information
3939 Priority Way South Drive
Indianapolis, IN 46240-0972
Phone: 800 334-3939, 317 843-3939
Fax: 317 843-8897
E-mail: iqpic@nuvo.net
Web: www.iqpic.org
The mission of IQPIC is to facilitate continuous improvement of individuals and organizations by providing a forum to nurture the theory and principles of W. Edwards Deming. IQPIC provides a resource network for practitioners to share, cooperate, and study innovative management techniques for improving quality and customer satisfaction.

Institute for Healthcare Improvement
375 Longwood Avenue, 4th Floor
Boston, MA 02215
Phone: 617 754-4800
Fax: 617 754-4848
E-mail: info@ihi.org
Web: www.ihi.org
IHI is an independent, non-profit organization working since 1991 to accelerate improvement in health care systems in the United States, Canada, and Europe by fostering collaboration among health care organizations.

Institute for National Measurement Standards
Montreal Road, Building M-36
Ottawa, ON K1A 0R6
Canada
Phone: 613 990-7049
Fax: 613 952-1394
E-mail: inms.questions@nrc.ca
Web: www.cisti.nrc.ca/inms
The Institute for National Measurement Standards draws together activities at Canada's National Research Council related to metrology to provide the foundation for Canada's National Measurement System.

Institute of Electrical and Electronics Engineers, Inc.
3 Park Avenue, 17th Floor
New York, NY 10016-5997
Phone: 212 419-7900
Fax: 212 752-4929
E-mail: customer-service@ieee.org
Web: www.ieee.org
"The IEEE helps advance global prosperity by promoting the engineering process of creating, developing, integrating, sharing, and applying knowledge about electrical and information technologies and sciences for the benefit of humanity and the profession."

Institute of Industrial Engineers
25 Technology Park
Norcross, GA 30092-2988
Phone: 800 494-0460, 770 449-0460
Fax: 770 441-3295
E-mail: cs@iienet.org
Web: www.iienet.org
The only international, non-profit professional society dedicated to advancing the technical and managerial excellence of industrial engineers, the IIE provides its members with current information on improving productivity and quality in the workplace. Through periodicals and professional journals, continuing education, seminars and conferences, professional books, and services, IIE promotes the exchange of ideas among industrial engineers around the world.

Instrumentation, Systems, and Automation Society
67 Alexander Drive
P.O. Box 12277
Research Triangle Park, NC 27709
Phone: 919 549-8411
Fax: 919 549-8288

E-mail: info@isa.org
Web: www.isa.org
ISA, the international society for measurement and control, is an organization dedicated to technicians and engineers in measurement and control technology. It publishes *InTech Magazine*, a monthly magazine for ISA members.

Inter-American Accreditation Cooperation
Rua Santa Alexandrina n° 416 - 9° Andar
Sala 905 - CEP: 20261-232
Rio Comprido - Rio de Janeiro RJ
Brazil
Phone: ++55-21 563-2824
Fax: ++55-21 502-6542
E-mail: iaac@inmetro.gov.br
Web: www.ibpinetsp.com.br/iaac
IAAC is a collaborative of accreditation, certification, inspection, testing, and calibrating bodies and other interested parties. The objective is to facilitate commercial exchange among their nations or blocs of nations in the Americas through a system of conformity assessment bodies. IAAC was created in November 1996 by delegates from 17 countries, who committed to work toward a Multilateral Recognition Agreement. Members in the U.S. are the American National Standards Institute and the American Association for Laboratory Accreditation.

International Accreditation Forum, Inc.
IAF Secretariat
#1801 - 2 Marcus Clarke Street
Canberra City ACT 2601
Australia
Phone: +612 6257 1962
Fax: +612 6257 1965, +612 6222 2761
E-mail: iafsecr@email.com
Web: www.iaf.nu
IAF is the world association of conformity assessment accreditation bodies and other bodies interested in conformity assessment. Its primary function is to develop a worldwide program of conformity assessment that will promote the elimination of non-tariff barriers to trade.

International Auditor Training and Certification Association
Secretariat
P.O. Box 363
Toronto NSW 2283
Australia
Phone: +61 2 4959 8388
Fax: +61 2 4959 8399
E-mail: iatca@itaca.com
Web: iatca.com
IATCA is a voluntary international organization established in 1995 to create and operate programs for uniform international training and certification / registration of auditors, with the objective of achieving single programs recognized worldwide. Member organizations in the U.S. and Canada include the Registrar Accreditation Board, the Standards Council of Canada, the National Quality Institute Canada, and the Canadian Environmental Auditing Association.

International Center for Standards Research
Secretariat
Interdisciplinary Telecommunications Program
Engineering Center
ECOT 317
Campus Box 530
University of Colorado-Boulder
Boulder, CO 80309
Phone: 303 492-3653
Fax: 303 492-1112
E-mail: icsr@standardsresearch.org
Web: www.standardsresearch.org
The motto for the ICSR is "advancing interdisciplinary research and education for the global standards community."

International Certification Network
IQNet Association
Bernstrasse 103
P.O. Box
CH-3052 Zollikofen
Switzerland
Phone: +41 31 910 35 90

Fax: +41 31 910 35 99
E-mail: headoffice@iqnet.ch
Web: www.iqnet-certification.com
IQNet is a network of nonprofit certification bodies that operate in accordance with the IQNet Code of Conduct and Ethics, the IQNet Multilateral Agreement, and its internal rules. The main aims of IQNet, established in 1990 (as EQNet), are to recognize and promote management system certificates issued by its members and to coordinate the work to be performed for certification of organizations operating in several countries.

International Committee for Nondestructive Testing
Via Foresti, 5
25127 Brescia
Italy
Phone: +39 030 24 15 252
Fax: +39 030 32 19 18
E-mail: icndt@icndt.org
Web: www.icndt.org
The ICNDT is a nonprofit organization devoted to the international development of nondestructive testing, in conjunction with individual NDT societies. The ICNDT organizes world conferences on nondestructive testing and encourages the formulation of international standards for nondestructive testing in collaboration with the International Organization for Standardization and national standards bodies.

International Council for Quality Function Deployment
Glenn Mazur, Executive Director
1140 Morehead Court
Ann Arbor, MI 48103-6181
Phone: 734 995-0847
Fax: 734 995-3810
E-mail: info@icqfd.org
Web: www.icqfd.org
The ICQFD was established in 1997 to encourage a united effort by national QFD organizations to promote QFD as a "best practices" method of producing products and services that satisfy customers. The ICQFD convenes an annual International Symposium of QFD.

International Council on Systems Engineering
2150 N. 107th Street, Suite 205
Seattle, WA 98133-9009
Phone: 206 361-6607 or 800 366-1164
Fax: 206 367-8777
E-mail: incose@halcyon.com
Web: www.incose.org
A not-for-profit membership organization founded in 1990, INCOSE is an international authoritative body promoting systems engineering, "an interdisciplinary approach and means to enable the realization of successful systems. It focuses on defining customer needs and required functionality early in the development cycle, documenting requirements, then proceeding with design synthesis and system validation while considering the complete problem."

International Customer Service Association
401 N. Michigan Avenue
Chicago, IL 60611-4267
Phone: 800 360-4272, 312 321-6800
Fax: 312 245-1084
E-mail: icsa@sba.com
Web: www.icsa.com
ICSA recognizes excellence in customer service through annual conferences, competitions, publications, and other programs. It publishes *Customer Service: A Journal of Theory, Research and Practice* (biannual).

International Electrotechnical Commission
3, rue de Varembé
P.O. Box 131
CH-1211 Geneva 20
Switzerland
Phone: +41 22 919 02 11
Fax: +41 22 919 03 00
E-mail: info@iec.ch
Web: www.iec.ch
Founded in 1906, the IEC is the global organization that prepares and publishes international standards for all electrical, electronic and related technologies. Membership consists of more than

60 participating countries, including all the world's major trading nations and a growing number of industrializing countries.

International Federation of Standards Users
c/o ISO Central Secretariat
Case Postale 56
1, rue de Varembé
CH-1211 Geneva 20
Switzerland
Phone: + 41 22 749 01 11
Fax: + 41 22 749 01 55
E-mail: ifan@iso.ch
Web: www.ifan-online.org
IFSU is a non-profit international association of national organizations for the application of standards, companies, professional and trade associations, and governmental agencies concerned with the use of standards.

International Foundation for Customer Focus
c/o Jan Eklöf, Secretary General
HHS
Box 6501
SE-113 83 Stockholm
Sweden
Phone: NA
Fax: +46-8-348161
E-mail: office@ifcf.org
Web: www.ifcf.org
The IFCF was initiated December 15, 1999 by a small group of researchers from Århus Business School (Denmark), Sheffield Hallam University (United Kingdom), and Stockholm School of Economics (Sweden). The aim of this non-profit foundation is to "enhance the comparative international measurement and analysis of customer orientation and focus."

International Institute of Concurrent Engineering (CETEAM)
Biren (Brian) Prasad, Director
P.O. Box 3882
Tustin, CA 92782
Phone/Fax: 714 389-2662
E-mail: Prasadb1@home.com
Web: www.ceteam.com
The CETEAM was founded in May 1992 as the CERA Institute, to advance the Concurrent Engineering (CE) methodologies and state-of-the-art applications in concurrent product development, concurrent processes, and concurrent design practices. CETEAM publishes *Concurrent Engineering: Research & Application (CERA Journal)* and sponsors an annual conference with the International Society for Productivity Enhancement.

International Laboratory Accreditation Cooperation
ILAC Secretariat
c/o National Association of Testing Authorities
7 Leeds Street
Rhodes NSW 2138
Australia
Phone: +61 2 9736 8222
Fax: +61 2 9743 5311
E-mail: info@ilac.org, ilac@nata.asn.au
Web: www.ilac.org
ILAC is an international cooperation among the various laboratory accreditation schemes operated throughout the world.

International Organization for Standardization (ISO)
1, rue de Varembé
Case Postale 56
CH-1211 Geneva 20
Switzerland
Phone: + 41 22 749 01 11
Fax: + 41 22 733 34 30
E-mail: central@iso.ch
Web: www.iso.org
ISO is a worldwide federation of national standards bodies from some 130 countries, one from each country. Established in 1947, ISO promotes the development of standardization and related activities in the world in order to facilitate the international exchange of goods and services and develops cooperation in the spheres of intellectual, scientific, technological, and economic activi-

ty. ISO's work results in international agreements that are published as International Standards.

International Quality Federation
Thomas Pyzdek, President
Pyzdek Consulting, Inc.
2405 N. Avenida Sorgo
Tucson, AZ 85749-9305
Phone: 520 749-9113
Fax: 240 255-2395
E-mail: comments@iqfnet.org,
tom@pyzdek.com
Web: www.iqfnet.org

Founded in January 2000, the IQF provides a forum for people involved in quality to share their knowledge and experience. Its mission is to promote quality improvement throughout the world.

International Register of Certificated Auditors
P.O. Box 25120
12 Grosvenor Crescent
London SW1X 7ZL
United Kingdom
Phone: +44 (0)20 7245 6833
Fax: +44 (0)20 7245 6755
E-mail: irca@irca.org
Web: www.irca.org

IRCA has two major activities: certification of auditors of management systems and approval of training organizations that deliver auditor training courses. IRCA currently certifies around 11,500 management system auditors from 100 countries and approves some 90 training organizations to present certificated auditor training courses.

International Society for Performance Improvement
1400 Spring Street, Suite 260
Silver Spring, MD 20910
Phone: 301 587-8570
Fax: 301 587-8573
E-mail: info@ispi.org
Web: www.ispi.org

ISPI is dedicated to improving productivity and performance in the workplace. Founded in 1962, it has over 10,000 members throughout the U.S., Canada, and 40 other countries. Most of its members are performance technologists, training directors, HR managers, instructional technologists, change agents, human factors practitioners, and organizational development consultants. ISPI publishes the *Performance Improvement Journal* and *Performance Improvement Quarterly*, plus books and *News & Notes*, a society newsletter. It also sponsors a yearly international conference and exposition.

International Society for Productivity Enhancement
Biren (Brian) Prasad, Director
P.O. Box 3882
Tustin, CA 92782
Phone/Fax: 714 389-2662
E-mail: Prasadb1@home.com
Web: www.ceteam.com/ISPE.htm

ISPE was founded in 1984 "to accelerate the international exchange of ideas and scientific knowledge with absolutely no barriers of disciplines or field of technological application." The main objective is "to foster cross-fertilization of technology, strategy and 4M resources (manpower, machine, money and management) to enhance productivity, competitiveness and thereby improve the quality of life." ISPE publishes the *International Journal of Concurrent Engineering: Research & Applications* and sponsors an annual international conference with the International Institute of Concurrent Engineering.

International Society for Quality in Health Care Inc.
Level 9, Aikenhead Centre
St Vincent's Hospital
41 Victoria Parade
Fitzroy Victoria 3055
Australia
Phone: + 61 3 9417 6971
Fax: + 61 3 9417 6851
E-mail: isqua@isqua.org.au
Web: www.isqua.org.au

ISQua offers the opportunity for individuals and organizations interested in quality in health care to share expertise and experience through an international, multidisciplinary forum. The primary objective is "to promote quality improvement on a continual basis in health care internationally in both the public and private sectors, among politicians, senior government officials, industry, representatives of the media, health institution managers, educators, health care providers and consumers and other purchasers of health care." ISQua publishes the *International Journal for Quality in Health Care*.

International Society of Agile Manufacturing
Suren N. Dwivedi
2851 Johnston Street, #325
Lafayette, LA 70503
Phone/Fax: 337 989-7262
E-mail: suren@louisiana.edu
Web: www.ucs.louisiana.edu/~snd7483/ISAM2.html

IASM was founded by Dr. Suren N. Dwivedi, Endowed Chair of Manufacturing at the University of Louisiana at Lafayette, "to enhance state-of-the-art research and development." ISAM "concentrates on all the areas which contribute to Agile Manufacturing like product development, novel applications, and tools in the areas related to agile manufacturing."

International Society of Six Sigma Professionals
7678 East Greenway Road, Suite 100
Scottsdale, AZ 85260
Phone: 877 9-ISSSP-1 (877 947-7771), 480 368-7083
Fax: 480 585-0640
E-mail: info@isssp.org
Web: www.isssp.org

The ISSSP is "an organization dedicated to promoting the advancement of the Six Sigma methodology and its practitioners."

ISO Support Group
Division of Intelex Corporation
165 Spadina Avenue, 3rd Floor
Toronto, ON M5T 2C3
Canada
Phone: 416 599-6009
Fax: 416 599-6867
E-mail: isogroup@isogroup.net
Web: www.isogroup.net

This support group is a network of companies already registered or seeking registration sharing experiences and suggestions about obtaining compliance with ISO 9000, QS-9000 (including the Tooling and Equipment Supplement), or ISO 14000. It provides a forum for discussion about how to implement a standard, where to get further information or help, and how to become registered at the lowest cost.

Maintenance and Reliability Center
506 East Stadium Hall
University of Tennessee
Knoxville, TN 37996-0750
Phone: 865 974-9625
Fax: 865 974-4995
E-mail: mrc@utk.edu
Web: www.engr.utk.edu/mrc

The Maintenance and Reliability Center is a resource for industry, using research and cutting-edge technology to help its member companies reduce losses caused by equipment downtime. Its vision is to become the international focus for education, research, development, information, and application of advanced maintenance and reliability engineering.

Manufacturers Alliance/MAPI
1525 Wilson Boulevard, Suite 900
Arlington, VA 22209-2411
Phone: 703 841-9000
Fax: 703 841-9514
E-mail: info@mapi.net
Web: www.mapi.net

MAPI is a non-profit policy research organization that promotes policies that stimulate technological advancement and economic growth for the benefit of U.S. industry and a public interest.

Metrology Automation Association
900 Victors Way
P.O. Box 3724
Ann Arbor, MI 48106

Phone: 734 994-6088
Fax: 734 994-3338
E-mail: info@metrologyautomation.org
Web: www.metrologyautomation.org
MAA is "dedicated to improving the competitiveness of the North American manufacturing sector through promotion and enhancement of metrology automation equipment and technology."

Mouvement Québécois de la Qualité (Quebec Quality Movement)
455, rue Saint-Antoine Ouest, bureau 404
Montréal, QC H2Z 1J1
Canada
Phone: 514 874-9933 x 228 or 888 874-9933 x 228
Fax: 514 866-4600
E-mail: mqq@qualite.qc.ca
Web: www.qualite.qc.ca
MQQ is a non-profit organization formed in 1995 to support organizations in Quebec in their efforts to improve quality management and be more competitive locally, nationally, and internationally. MQQ publishes a membership magazine, *Forum Qualité*, and bestows the Grands Prix Québécois de la Qualité.

National Association for Healthcare Quality
4700 W. Lake Avenue
Glenview, IL 60025-1485
Phone: 800 966-9392
Fax: 877 218-7939
E-mail: info@nahq.org
Web: www.nahq.org
The mission of NAHQ is to improve the quality of healthcare by advancing the theory and practice of quality management in healthcare organizations and by promoting the professional growth and development of healthcare professionals. It publishes the *Journal for Healthcare Quality*.

National Association of Industrial Technology
3300 Washtenaw Avenue, Suite 220
Ann Arbor, MI 48104-4200
Phone: 734 677-0720
Fax: 734 677-2407
E-mail: nait@nait.org
Web: www.nait.org
NAIT is a professional association responsible for promoting industrial technology in business, industry, education, and government; accrediting industrial technology programs in colleges, universities, and technical institutes; and certifying industrial technologists and the recognizing their continued professional development. NAIT publishes the *Journal of Industrial Technology*.

National Association of Service Managers
P.O. Box 536
Lake Zurich, IL 60047-0536
Phone: 262 857-7227 or 888 562-7004
Fax: 262 857-1127
E-mail: vince@nasm.com
Web: www.nasm.com
This is the oldest association of product service managers in North America, founded in 1955. It promotes service quality by businesses, improved practices by service industry organizations, and provides educational programs. It hosts an annual conference and publishes a newsletter for members, *Service Management*.

National Committee for Quality Assurance
2000 L Street, NW, Suite 500
Washington, DC 20036
Phone: 202 955-3500
Fax: 202 955-3599
E-mail: customersupport@ncqa.org
Web: www.ncqa.org
NCQA is a private, not-for-profit organization dedicated to assessing and reporting on the quality of managed care plans. It is governed by a board of directors that includes employers, consumer and labor representatives, health plans, quality experts, policymakers, and representatives from organized medicine. NCQA's mission is to provide information that enables purchasers and consumers of managed health care to distinguish among plans based on quality, thereby allowing them to make more informed health care purchasing decisions.

National Conference of Standards

Directory of Quality Resource Organizations

Laboratories International
1800 30th Street, Suite 305B
Boulder, CO 80301-1026
Phone: 303 440-3339
Fax: 303 440-3384
E-mail: info@ncslinternational.org
Web: www.ncslinternational.org
NCSL is a nonprofit organization formed in 1961 to promote cooperative efforts for solving the common problems faced by measurement laboratories. NCSL has over 1500 member organizations from academic, scientific, industrial, commercial, and government facilities around the world. Membership is open to any organization with an interest in the science of measurement and its application in research, development, education, or commerce.

National Conference on Weights and Measures, Inc.
15245 Shady Grove Road, Suite 130
Rockville, MD 20850
Phone: 240 632-9454
Fax: 301 990-9771
E-mail: owm@nist.gov
Web: ncwm@mgmtsol.com
The NCWM is a standards development organization for weights and measures regulatory agencies, representatives of business, industry, trade associations, and consumer organizations. A major objective of the NCWM is to foster understanding and cooperation among weights and measures regulatory officials and all industrial, business, and consumer interests.

National Center for Standards and Certification Information
Office of Standards Services
National Institute of Standards and Technology
U.S. Department of Commerce
100 Bureau Drive, MS 2150
Gaithersburg, MD 20899-2150
Phone: 301 975-4040
Fax: 301 926-1559
E-mail: ncsci@nist.gov
Web: www.ts.nist.gov/ncsci
Established in 1965, NCSCI provides information on U.S., foreign, and international voluntary standards; government regulations; and rules of conformity assessment for non-agricultural products. The Center serves as a referral service and focal point in the U.S. for information about standards and standards-related information.

National Forum for Health Care Quality Measurement and Reporting
601 13th Street, NW, Suite 500 North
Washington, DC 20005
Phone: 202 783-1300
Fax: 202 783-3434
E-mail: info@qualityforum.org
Web: www.qualityforum.org
The National Forum is a not-for-profit membership organization created to develop and implement a national strategy for health care quality measurement and reporting.

National Institute of Standards and Technology
100 Bureau Drive, MS 3460
Gaithersburg, MD 20899-3460
Phone: 301 975-6478, TTY 301 975-8295
Fax: 301 926-1630
E-mail: inquiries@nist.gov
Web: www.nist.gov
NIST was established by Congress "to assist industry in the development of technology ... needed to improve product quality, to modernize manufacturing processes, to ensure product reliability ... and to facilitate rapid commercialization ... of products based on new scientific discoveries." NIST, through its Baldrige National Quality Program (separate entry), manages the Malcolm Baldrige National Quality Award. It is responsible for defining the criteria and point values and for the judging process.

National Quality Institute / Institut National de la Qualité
2275 Lake Shore Boulevard West, Suite 307
Toronto, ON M8V 3Y3
Canada

Phone: 800 263-9648, 416 251-7600
Fax: 416 251-9131
E-mail: info@nqi.ca
Web: www.nqi.ca

NQI is an independent not-for-profit organization established in 1992 to make Canadians more competitive in the global marketplace. NQI works with strategic partners and supporters to promote, encourage, and support the understanding of total quality principles and practices in all sectors and to recognize outstanding achievement through the Canada Awards for Excellence Program, which bestows the Quality Award and the Healthy Workplace Award. NQI is responsible for certifying Quality Management System Auditors in Canada.

National Safety Council
1121 Spring Lake Drive
Itasca, IL 60143-3201
Phone: 630 285-1121
Fax: 630 285-1315
E-mail: customerservice@nsc.org
Web: www.nsc.org

The mission of NSC is "to educate and influence society to adopt safety, health and environmental policies, practices and procedures that prevent and mitigate human suffering and economic losses arising from preventable causes." NSC is a nonprofit, international public service organization dedicated to improving the safety, health, and environmental well-being of all people.

National Society of Professional Engineers
1420 King Street
Alexandria, VA 22314-2794
Phone: 703 684-2800
Fax: 703 836-4875
E-mail: customer.service@nspe.org
Web: www.nspe.org

NSPE represents engineering professionals and licensed engineers across all disciplines. Founded in 1934, NSPE promotes engineering licensure and ethics, advocates for and protects legal rights of engineers at the national and state levels, publishes news of the profession, and provides continuing education opportunities. NSPE serves some 60,000 members and the public through 54 state and territorial societies and more than 500 chapters.

QCI International
17055 Quailridge Road
Cottonwood, CA 96022
Phone: 888 215-4697, 530 893-4095
Fax: 530 893-0395
E-mail: ttt@qci-intl.com
Web: www.qci-intl.com

QCI International, in business since 1978, is a consulting, training, and publishing firm providing products and services that fall under the umbrella of Total Quality Management. QCI offers seminars, in-house training, books, and videos and publishes a monthly magazine, *Quality Digest*.

Quality Assurance Institute
7575 Dr. Phillips Boulevard, Suite 350
Orlando, FL 32819
Phone: 407 363-1111
Fax: 407 363-1112
E-mail: qaiadmin@qaiusa.com
Web: www.qaiusa.com

QAI is an international organization dedicated to partnering with the enterprise-wide information quality profession in search of effective methods for detection-software quality control and prevention-software quality assurance. QAI provides leadership and solutions in the form of consulting, education services, and assessments.

Quality, Engineering, and Manufacturing Association
1001 E. Georgia Avenue
Phoenix, AZ 85014
Phone: 602 264-3772
Fax: 602 264-9941
E-mail: info@tqm.com
Web: www.tqm.com

QEMA is a member organization dedicated to aerospace, military, automotive, and commercial companies.

QFD Institute
Glenn Mazur, Executive Director
1140 Morehead Court

Directory of Quality Resource Organizations

Ann Arbor, MI 48103-6181
Phone: 734 995-0847
Fax: 775 307-4637
E-mail: information@qfdi.org
Web: www.qfdi.org
This institute was founded to advance quality function deployment. It provides information about QFD events, application case studies, bibliographies, and QFDI forums and master classes.

Quality Methods Association
Administrator
QMA
P.O. Box 486
Derby DE22 2ZS
United Kingdom
Phone/Fax: +44 (0)1332 557900
E-mail: qma@globalnet.co.uk
Web: www.qma.co.uk
QMA was established in 1991 to hold meetings and other events to encourage the sharing of knowledge and best practice related to all aspects of quality improvement and quality management.

Reengineering Forum
P.O. Box 400
Burlington, MA 01803
Phone: 781 272-0049
Fax: 781 272-8464
E-mail: forum@reengineer.org
Web: www.reengineer.org
The Forum is a non-profit industry association established to encourage combined industry/research review of the state of the art and the state of the practice in reengineering of software, systems, and business processes. It is a meeting place for developers, researchers, and users in the reengineering and reverse engineering fields.

Registrar Accreditation Board
600 N. Plankinton Avenue, Suite 300
Milwaukee, WI 53203
P.O. Box 3005
Milwaukee, WI 53201-3005
Phone: 888 722-2440, 414 272-3937
Fax: 414 765-8661
E-mail: rab@rabnet.com
Web: www.rabnet.com
RAB is a not-for-profit organization that exists to serve the conformity assessment needs of business and industry, registrars, course providers, and individual auditors. It operates accreditation programs for ISO 9000 and ISO 14001 registrars and auditor training course providers through the ANSI-RAB National Accreditation Program and independently operates certification programs for quality and environmental management systems auditors.

SAVE International
60 Revere Drive, Suite 500
Northbrook, IL 60062
Phone: 847 480-1730
Fax: 847 480-9282
E-mail: value@value-eng.org
Web: www.value-eng.org
Formerly known as the Society of American Value Engineers, SAVE is the only professional society in the U.S. devoted totally to advancing and promoting the Value Methodology (VM). Members strive to improve quality and increase functions of products and services, while reducing project costs. SAVE offers many educational programs, symposia, and publications in the field of value engineering and value management and offers a certification program for qualified value management professionals.

Society for Human Resource Management
1800 Duke Street
Alexandria, VA 22314
Phone: 703 548-3440
Fax: 703 535-6490
E-mail: shrm@shrm.org
Web: www.shrm.org
SHRM represents human resource professionals, with more than 90,000 members around the world. SHRM provides its members with education and information services, conferences and seminars, government and media representation, and publications, including *HRMagazine*.

Society for Industrial and Applied

Mathematics
3600 University City Science Center
Philadelphia, PA 19104-2688
Phone: 215 382-9800
Fax: 215 386-7999
E-mail: service@siam.org
Web: www.siam.org
SIAM was founded in 1951 to advance the application of mathematics to science and industry, promote mathematical research that could lead to effective new methods and techniques for science and industry, and provide media for the exchange of information and ideas among mathematicians, engineers, and scientists. SIAM publishes nine peer-reviewed research journals and about 25 books per year and conducts an annual meeting and specialized conferences, short courses, and workshops.

Society for Maintenance and Reliability Professionals
401 N. Michigan Avenue
Chicago, IL 60611-4267
Phone: 800 950-7354, 312 321-5190
Fax: 312 527-6658
E-mail: smrp@sba.com
Web: www.smrp.org
SMRP is an independent, non-profit society with nearly 2,000 members. It hosts an annual conference.

Society of Consumer Affairs Professionals in Business
675 North Washington Street, Suite 200
Alexandria, VA 22314
Phone: 703 519-3700
Fax: 703 549-4886
E-mail: socap@socap.org
Web: www.socap.org
Founded in 1973, SOCAP is open to "all professionals who are in some way responsible for creating and maintaining customer loyalty." It publishes *Customer Relationship Management* and holds several annual conferences.

Standards Council of Canada/Conseil Canadien des Normes
270 Albert Street, Suite 200
Ottawa, ON K1P 6N7
Canada
Phone: 613 238-3222
Fax: 613 569-7808
E-mail: info@scc.ca
Web: www.scc.ca
SCC is a federal crown corporation with the mandate to promote efficient and effective standardization. An ISO member body, SCC accredits quality certification associations and companies and it coordinates the activities of Canada's ISO Technical Committee responsible for ISO certification activities.

Standards Engineering Society
13340 SW 96th Avenue
Miami, FL 33176
Phone: 305 971-4798
Fax: 305 971-4799
E-mail: director@ses-standards.org
Web: www.ses-standards.org
SES was established in 1947 to promote the use of standards and standardization. Its members are in industry, commerce, academia, service organizations, government, and standards development organizations.

Union Internationale des Laboratoires Indépendants/International Union of Independent Laboratories
Beverly Adams, Assistant to the Executive Director, ACIL
1629 K Street, NW, Suite 400
Washington, DC 20006
Phone: 202 887-5504
Fax: 202 887-0021
E-mail: badams@uili.org
Web: www.uili.org
UILI is the worldwide organization for independent testing and calibration laboratories and for independent consulting organizations.

W. Edwards Deming Institute

P.O. Box 59511
Potomac, MD 20859-9511
Phone: 301 294-8405
Fax: 301 294-8406
E-mail: staff@deming.org
Web: www.deming.org
The Institute is a nonprofit organization founded in 1993 by W. Edwards Deming. The aim of the Institute is to foster understanding of the Deming System of Profound Knowledge to advance commerce, prosperity, and peace.

Water Quality Association
4151 Naperville Road
Lisle, IL 60532-1088
Phone: 630 505-0160
Fax: 630 505-9637
E-mail: info@mail.wqa.org
Web: www.wqa.org
WQA is the international trade association representing the household, commercial, and industrial water quality improvement industry. Its 2,600 corporate member companies manufacture and sell point-of-use/point-of-entry equipment, package water treatment plants, and customized water treatment systems.

Work in America Institute
700 White Plains Road
Scarsdale, NY 10583
Phone: 914 472-9600, 800 787-0707
Fax: 914 472-9606
E-mail: info@workinamerica.org
Web: www.workinamerica.org
Founded in 1975, Work in America Institute works to advance productivity and the quality of working life through the principles of sound human resource practices that are applicable in all industries. Through its policy studies, education and training programs, technical assistance, and publications, the not-for-profit research organization serves as a resource and clearinghouse, a network of practical know-how for thousands of organizations.

Workflow and Reengineering International Association
3116 North Federal Highway, #374
Lighthouse Point, FL 33064
Phone: 800 74-WARIA, 954 782-3376
Fax: 954 782-6365
E-mail: waria@waria.com
Web: www.waria.com
WARIA is a non-profit organization whose mission is to identify and clarify issues that are common to users of workflow, electronic commerce, and those who are in the process of reengineering their organizations.

Workforce Excellence Network
200 Constitution Avenue, NW, Suite C-4318
Washington, DC 20210
Phone: 202 693-2990
Fax: 202 693-2768
E-mail: WENwebpage@doleta.gov
Web: www.workforce-excellence.net
This organization "represents the next generation of quality efforts for the workforce development system to foster unparalleled levels of quality services to its customers—job-seekers, workers, and employers." Its purpose is "to engage state and local workforce development organizations in a voluntary process of pursuing performance excellence."

World Confederation of Productivity Science
500, Sherbrooke West, Suite 900
Montreal, QC
Canada, H31 3C6
Phone: 514 282-3838
Fax: 514 844-7556
E-mail: wcps@affaires.com
Web: www.affaires.com/wcps
WCPS was set up in 1969 as an association of individuals and organizations throughout the world concerned with the improvement of productivity and the quality of working life. It provides a network of international contacts and runs periodic international conferences.

World Standards Services Network
Address: NA
E-mail: NA (through Web site)
Web: www.wssn.net
WSSN is a decentralized network of publicly accessible World Wide Web servers of standards organizations around the world. Through the Web sites of its members, WSSN provides information on international, regional, and national standardization and related activities and services.

Quality Resources Online 2002

The Internet is an essential source of information on virtually everything, including quality. We started this section of *The Quality Yearbook* in 1995; since then, the amount of material on quality management has increased exponentially.

The Internet has something for everybody and information to meet every need—if you can find it. That's why we provide this list of 'Net resources ... and some reminders.

Discussion lists are like any other communities: the value to any member depends on what the other members are contributing at any given time. Web sites are like any other resources: they vary greatly in quality, they may suffer from age, and they may be moved to another location or just disappear.

We've tried to provide a good sampling of online resources, a representative snapshot of what was on the 'Net when we compiled this section. In addition to the sites listed here, most of the organizations and periodicals listed in our Directory of Quality Resource Organizations and Directory of Magazines, Journals, and Newsletters have Web sites that may provide resources.

Since most World Wide Web sites have links to other sites, with the sites listed below you're just a few clicks away from many more sites. The same is true of discussion lists: you're often just a query away from other lists, since list members are generally very willing and able to suggest lists for you to join. At the end of these lists, we provide more help to get you what you need from the 'Net.

What You'll Find Here

Our directory of online resources is divided into three categories:

- **Internet Discussion Lists**. These are free mailing lists. Most allow members (subscribers) to send e-mail messages to a central location, which then copies the messages to all members of that group. Some mailing lists are for distribution only: they send members information (usually publications or other resources), but don't allow members to post messages.

- **World Wide Web Sites**. These are sites hosted by associations, companies, and other organizations that cover a variety of quality topics, including standards, particularly ISO.

- **Other Internet Resources**. These Web sites can direct you to more discussion lists and Web sites.

This is just a sampling of 'Net resources. We've simply tried to mention some of the best lists and sites and to show the variety. We offer them as suggestions for you to explore the opportunities out there ... and wish you good luck.

If you'd like to recommend a list or a site that we haven't included here, please e-mail us at jwoods@cwlpub.com.

Internet Discussion Lists

There are two ways to join discussion lists—through a Web site or by e-mail. If you join through a Web site, the site generally provides easy instructions, although you may be required to register. If you join by e-mail, you send a message to the computer that maintains the list. (It may then pass to the list owner.) The message varies according to the computer program used to administer the list (usually listserv, majordomo, mailbase, or listproc) and the wishes of the list owner/moderator. For each of the groups below, we give the Web site URL and/or the e-mail address and specific message to send.

When you subscribe to a list, you should receive an introductory message. This message should tell you how to post messages and how to leave the list if you don't find it of value. Save this message: it can help you avoid embarrassment and frustration.

ASQC-CSD (Customer-Supplier Division of ASQ)
Address: majordomo@quality.org
Message: subscribe asqc-csd

ASQC-DCD (Design and Construction Division of ASQ)
Address: majordomo@quality.org
Message: subscribe asqc-dcd

ASQC-HCD (Health Care Division of ASQ)
Address: majordomo@quality.org
Message: subscribe asqc-hcd

ASQC-MQD (Measurement Quality Division of ASQ)
Address: majordomo@quality.org
Message: subscribe asqc-mqd

Baldrige (quality awards: state, local, and national)

Address: majordomo@quality.org
Message: subscribe baldrige

BPR-IAC (business process reengineering in government)
Address: majordomo@quality.org
Message: subscribe bpr-iac

BPReengineering (business process reengineering)
Web site: groups.yahoo.com/group/BPReengineering
E-mail—
Address: BPReengineering-subscribe@yahoogroups.com
Message: (blank)

Change (challenge of navigating major organizational transformation)
Web site: www.topica.com/lists/change
E-mail—
Address: change-subscribe@topica.com
Message: (blank)

CImprovement (continuous improvement for business)
Web site: groups.yahoo.com/group/CImprovement
E-mail—
Address: CImprovement-subscribe@yahoogroups.com
Message: (blank)

CM SIG (Constraints Management Special Interest Group: improving performance through the theory of constraints)
Address: join-CMSIG@lists.apics.org
Message: (blank)

Consulting (for consultants in all areas, focusing on the consulting process)
Address: majordomo@quality.org
Message: subscribe consulting

Crea-CPS (creativity and creative problem solving)
E-mail—
Address: listserv@nic.surfnet.nl
Message: subscribe crea-cps
or
Address: crea-cps-subscribe@topica.com
Message: (blank)

DEN (Deming Electronic Network)
Address: den.list-request@deming.eng.clemson.edu

Subject line: subscribe
Message: (blank)

Dotcom-quality (developing quality benchmarks, processes, etc. for dot-com companies)
Address: majordomo@quality.org
Message: subscribe dotcom-quality

Downsizing
Address: majordomo@quality.org
Subject line: subscribe downsizing
Message: (blank)

EPSS (planning, designing, and developing electronic performance support systems)
Web site: groups.yahoo.com/group/EPSS
E-mail—
Address: EPSS-subscribe@yahoogroups.com
Message: (blank)

Food-qual (quality issues and concerns related to food processing industry)
Address: majordomo@quality.org
Subject line: subscribe food-qual
Message: (blank)

HC-CON (consultants in health care fields)
Address: majordomo@quality.org
Message: subscribe hc-con

HHSQUA-L (quality, team, and empowerment topics in the Department of Health and Human Services)
Address: listserv@list.nih.gov
Message: subscribe hhsqua-l

Hoshin-Kanri (development and practice of hoshin kanri)
Address: mailbase@mailbase.ac.uk
Message: join hoshin-kanri firstname lastname

HumPerf (human performance in workplace settings)
Web site: groups.yahoo.com/group/humperf
E-mail—
Address: humperf-subscribe@yahoogroups.com
Message: (blank)

ISO 25 (ISO Guide 25)
Address: majordomo@quality.org
Message: subscribe iso25

ISO 9000 (ISO 9000 standards)
Address: listserv@listserv.nodak.edu
Message: subscribe iso9000

ISO 9000-3 (ISO 9000-3 standards)
Address: majordomo@quality.org
Message: subscribe iso9000-3

ISO 14000 (ISO 14000 standards)
Address: majordomo@quality.org
Message: subscribe iso14000

Knowledge Management ("share information about knowledge management through building a community of professionals in the field")
Web site: groups.yahoo.com/group/Knowledge_Management
E-mail—
Address: Knowledge_Management-subscribe@yahoogroups.com
Message: (blank)

Learning-Org (discussion of the concept of the learning organization)
Address: majordomo@world.std.com
Message: subscribe learning-org

Mentor-Center (development, implementation, maintenance, and improvement of mentoring programs)
Web site: groups.yahoo.com/group/mentor-center
E-mail—
Address: mentor-center-subscribe@yahoogroups.com
Message: (blank)

MgtDev-L (management and executive development)
Address: listserv@listserv.muohio.edu
Message: subscribe mgtdev-l firstname lastname

MOP-Group (measuring organizational performance)
E-mail—
Address: majordomo@quality.org
Message: subscribe mop-group

NEA-QualityEd (application of quality principles to public education)
Web site: ist.nea.org

NoCows (all aspects of quality, "with no sacred cows")
Address: majordomo@quality.org
Message: subscribe nocows

OrgDyne (group and organizational dynamics, as supported by systemic and psychodynamic thinking)
Web site: groups.yahoo.com/group/orgdyne
E-mail—
Address: orgdyne-subscribe@yahoogroups.com
Message: (blank)

PerfMgt (performance management, appraisal, and improvement)
Web site: groups.yahoo.com/group/perfmgt
E-mail—
Address: perfmgt-subscribe@yahoogroups.com
Message: (blank)

Performance-Management (performance management)
Web site: groups.yahoo.com/group/performance-management
E-mail—
Address: performance-management-subscribe@yahoogroups.com
Message: (blank)

QFD (researchers and practitioners in Quality Function Deployment)
Web site: www.jiscmail.ac.uk/lists/qfd.html

QFD-L (Quality Function Deployment)
Address: majordomo@quality.org
Message: subscribe qfd-l

QP-Health (quality issues for professionals in health care)
Address: majordomo@quality.org
Message: subscribe qp-health

Quality (TQM in manufacturing and service industries)
Address: listserv@pucc.princeton.edu
Message: subscribe quality

Quality Management (all aspects of business and manufacturing improvements)
Web site: www.jiscmail.ac.uk/lists/quality-management.html

QUEST ("for research and information exchange encompassing the emerging national and international trend to combine quality, environmental, safety

structures and system assessments")
Address: listserv@listserv.nodak.edu
Message: subscribe quest

REGO-ORG (Reinventing Government: transforming organizational structures)
Address: listproc@gmu.edu
Message: subscribe rego-org firstname lastname

REGO-QUAL (Reinventing Government: creating quality leadership and management)
Address: listproc@gmu.edu
Message: subscribe rego-qual firstname lastname

RPM-Info (Recursive Process Management)
Address: majordomo@oosix.icce.rug.nl
Message: subscribe rpm-info

TeamNet-L (teamwork and topics related to collaborative systems)
E-mail—
Address: majordomo@mail.cas.unt.edu
Message: subscribe teamnet-L

Total-Quality-AsiaPac (total quality in Asia Pacific)
Address: mailbase@mailbase.ac.uk
Message: join total-quality-asiapac firstname lastname

Total-Quality-Construction (total quality in construction)
Address: mailbase@mailbase.ac.uk
Message: join total-quality-construction firstname lastname

Total-Quality-Culture (total quality and organizational and national cultures)
Address: mailbase@mailbase.ac.uk
Message: join total-quality-culture firstname lastname

Total-Quality-EcoSys (environmental systems)
Address: mailbase@mailbase.ac.uk
Message: join total-quality-ecosys firstname lastname

Total-Quality-5S (5-S technique as first step toward TQM)
Address: mailbase@mailbase.ac.uk
Message: join total-quality-5S firstname lastname

Total-Quality-Healthcare (total quality in health care)

Address: mailbase@mailbase.ac.uk
Message: join total-quality-healthcare firstname lastname

Total-Quality-InfoTech (total quality in information technology)
Address: mailbase@mailbase.ac.uk
Message: join total-quality-infotech firstname lastname

Total-Quality-ISOStds (ISO standards)
Address: mailbase@mailbase.ac.uk
Message: join total-quality-isostds firstname lastname

Total-Quality-Statistics (statistical concepts and techniques for continuous improvement)
Address: mailbase@mailbase.ac.uk
Message: join total-quality-statistics firstname lastname

TQM (TQM, other continuous improvement issues, quality in general)
Address: tqm.list-request@deming.eng.clemson.edu
Subject line: subscribe
Message: (blank)

TQM-D (TQM in industry)
Web site: groups.yahoo.com/group/tqm-d
E-mail—
Address: tqm-d-subscribe@yahoogroups.com
Message: (blank)

TQMEDU-L (TQM in education)
Address: listserv@admin.humberc.on.ca
Message: subscribe tqmedu-l

TRDEV (training and development)
Web site: groups.yahoo.com/group/trdev
E-mail—
Address: trdev-subscribe@yahoogroups.com
Message: (blank)

WARIA-L (Workflow and Reengineering International Association)
Address: majordomo@quality.org
Message: subscribe waria-l

WorkComm (communication in the workplace)
Web site: groups.yahoo.com/group/workcomm
E-mail—

Address: workcomm-subscribe@yahoogroups.com
Message: (blank)

WorkCon (prevention, management, and resolution of conflict in the workplace)
Web site: groups.yahoo.com/group/workcon
E-mail—
Address: workcon-subscribe@yahoogroups.com
Message: (blank)

World Wide Web Sites

Agile Manufacturing Resources
www.quality.org/html/agile.html
This page on the Quality Resources Online site consists of more than a dozen links to sites relevant to agile manufacturing. It's a good place to start.

American National Standards Institute
web.ansi.org
The purpose of ANSI Online is to provide "convenient access to timely and relevant information on the ANSI Federation and the latest national international standards-related activities." ANSI offers to help organizations develop and implement standards for measuring and maintaining consistency in processes and quality in outputs.

American Quality Mall
www.americanquality.com
Created by the American Quality Institute, this site for quality management professionals provides a variety of resources—articles, discussion, lists of quality job opportunities, and links.

American Society for Quality, Health Care Division
www.healthcare.org
The mission of this ASQ division is "to facilitate continuous improvement of health and health care in communities worldwide by providing leadership in the use of quality principles, concepts and technologies."

American Society for Quality, Measurement Quality Division
www.metrology.org
This division of ASQ sets as its goal "to improve measurement-based decisions in laboratory, calibration, manufacturing, and management processes at all levels of accuracy."

APICS
www.apics.org

This is the site of APICS—The Educational Society for Resource Management. It includes information on the organization and, of special interest, archived articles from *APICS—The Performance Advantage* magazine.

Association for Manufacturing Excellence
www.ame.org

This site features succinct explanations of key concepts in manufacturing, links to resources, archives of *Target*, and discussion lists and groups (including Total Quality Management, lean manufacturing, and ISO 14000).

Baldrige National Quality Award
www.quality.nist.gov

The premier source for information about the Malcolm Baldrige National Quality Award, this site includes the Criteria for Performance Excellence in business, health care, and education that can be used to conduct internal audits.

Baldrige Plus
www.baldrigeplus.com

The purpose of this site is "to be a Baldrige Award resource site, ... to publish and support a world-class collection of performance excellence case studies and exhibits, ... to put the Baldrige approach to performance excellence in a real-world, everyday-workplace context."

Business 2.0
www.business2.com

This is the site of *Business 2.0* magazine, a new magazine covering dot-coms and modern business practices. It includes daily updates on news items and an archive of articles.

Business and the Environment's ISO 14000 Update
www.cutter.com/iso14000

This site presents "global news and analysis" on ISO 14000 issues or related matters.

Business Process Reengineering Online Learning Center
www.prosci.com

The learning center offers an index of BPR articles from around the world, an online tutorial series, benchmarking studies, yellow pages for BPR resources, and information on reengineering toolkits and document templates for project teams.

Crazy About Constraints!
www.rogo.com/cac
This site is "dedicated to providing resources and information about the Theory of Constraints, the Thinking Processes, Synchronous Manufacturing, and other techniques developed by Dr. Eliyahu Goldratt."

Critical Linkages II
www.carolsager.com
The purpose of this site and the newsletter is to support and promote the growth and continuous improvement of learning by building *Critical Linkages* across traditional academic, professional, and occupational boundaries.

CWL Publishing Enterprises
www.cwlpub.com
This site is maintained by John Woods, co-editor of this book. It features books, a directory of links to quality sites and information on discussion lists, articles, quotes on quality, and much more.

The Deming Cooperative
www.deming.edu
There's a little of everything at this site: users groups, conferences, seminars, workshops, information on books by or about Deming, videos and training materials, and contacts and consultants.

Deming Electronic Network
deming.ces.clemson.edu/pub/den
The site was established "to foster understanding of the Deming System of Profound Knowledge to advance commerce, prosperity, and peace." It includes lots of articles and essays related to Deming's approach to management.

Fast Company
www.fastcompany.com
This magazine site includes an archive of all articles published in this magazine.

InsideQuality
www.insidequality.com
This site features information on all aspects of the quality industry, including quality standards, metrology, and quality management issues. The site features experts on discussion boards, a marketplace network of more than 2,000 vendors, article archives. and a career center for quality industry jobs.

Institute of Management and Administration
www.ioma.com
IOMA publishes several dozen newsletters that include articles on quality issues. This site features articles from those newsletters.

Intelligent Enterprise
www.iemagazine.com
This magazine site features articles and information on knowledge management and e-commerce.

iSixSigma
www.isixsigma.com
The mission of iSixSigma is "providing the resources you need to successfully implement Six Sigma Quality."

ISO 9000:2000
www.iso-9000-2000.com
This site is intended to be "The ISO 9000:2000 Journal and Resource Center."

ISO 9000, ISO 14000, and QS-9000 Support Group
www.isogroup.simplenet.com
The purpose of this site is to help with implementation of ISO 9000, QS-9000, and ISO 14000. Access to some content is free; paid membership includes newsletter, discussion, access to restricted web site, and unlimited e-mail ISO support.

The ISO 14000 Information Center
www.iso14000.com
This is a good place to find publications, discussion lists, educational and training resources, organizations, and links to a variety of sites focusing on ISO 14000 and related subjects.

ISO Center
www.isocenter.com
This site, hosted by SCS Engineers, features a selection of material on ISO 14000, including certification requirements, specific information on ISO standards, and recommendations for implementing environmental management systems (EMS).

ISO Easy
www.isoeasy.org
This site is dedicated to helping organizations understand and implement the ISO 9000 and ISO 9001 standards. The approach is straightforward but lighthearted; there are even a few jokes.

ISO Online
www.iso.ch

If you want to know about the organization that sets and administers ISO 9000 standards and certification, this is a good place to get information and find out about resources offered.

Metrology World
www.metrologyworld.com

This site is intended as an information resource for the metrology industry. It features news and links to suppliers and products.

National Institute of Standards and Technology
www.nist.gov

This site provides information on NIST resources for improving manufacturing processes and on NIST-sponsored conferences, training programs, and publications. NIST also administers the Malcolm Baldrige National Quality Award, so there's a link to information on the award program.

National Standards Systems Network
nssn.org

"A National Resource for Global Standards," NSSN is committed to "promulgating standards information to a broad constituency." A cooperative partnership of the American National Standards Institute, U.S. private-sector standards organizations, government agencies, and international standards organizations, NSSN aims to be the Web's most comprehensive data network on developing and approved national, foreign, regional, and international standards and regulatory documents.

Online Quality Resource Guide
deming.eng.clemson.edu/onlineq.html

This is an eclectic collection of resources maintained by John Hunter.

QFD Institute
www.qfdi.org

This site exists to advance quality function deployment. It provides information about QFD events, forums, and training.

Quality Digest
www.qualitydigest.com

This site features access to articles from the magazine, news, a list of state quality awards, and a good collection of links categorized by topic.

Quality Homepage
home.wxs.nl/~cbon/home.html

This page by Kees de Bondt, a quality consultant, includes information on discussion groups and links to Web sites for TQM, BPR, QFD, ISO 9000, BPR, kaizen, balanced scorecard, and other approaches to quality improvement.

Quality Management Principles
qmp.wineasy.se
This simple site, created by Krister Forsberg, is devoted to eight basic quality management principles—a good place to start.

Quality Network
www.qualitynetwork.org
The Quality Network is a subscription service "for school leaders involved in systemic reform and continuous improvements of their classrooms, buildings, and district." It provides "information on how to translate quality management principles to systemic improvement of schools" through a newsletter and Web conferences.

The Quality Portal
thequalityportal.com
This is a good resource, covering everything, more or less.

Quality Resources Online
www.quality.org
Hosted by Bill Casti, this site has it all: information, groups, discussion lists, and other resources. It's overwhelming by content, simple by design. If you try only one Web site, this might a good bet.

Quality Tools Cookbook
www.sytsma.com/tqmtools/tqmtoolmenu.html
"The aim of the Quality Tools Cookbook is to provide a free, comprehensive, reference to the quality tools for students, faculty, or anyone on the Internet who may find it useful." It covers a wide range of traditional tools, with graphics and examples.

Quality University On-Line
www.quniversity.com
Quality University On-Line claims to be the first Web-based learning environment for on-line study of the quality management process.

SAVE International
www.value-eng.org
Formerly known as the Society of American Value Engineers, SAVE is "devoted to the advancement and promotion of the value methodology." The site provides information about VM and ways to find out more.

Second Moment
www.secondmoment.org
This site is intended to be "a dynamic meeting place for academia and industry in the fields of applied statistics and analytics."

Six Sigma Forum
www.sixsigmaforum.com
The American Society for Quality offers information and resources for all levels of Six Sigma experience; some content is free and some is accessible only to paid members.

Software Quality Assurance Resources
www1.ics.uci.edu/~cliu1/sqa
This site offers resources related to software quality assurance research and practice.

Standards Bodies and Services
www.ses-standards.org/links.html
This page by the Standards Engineering Society provides links to standards organizations of all types, in the U.S. and Canada and around the world.

Superfactory Project
www.superfactory.com
"Resources for global manufacturing excellence," this site is intended to be "a globally interconnected manufacturing community creating incredible excellence and productivity worldwide."

TQM Terms
www-personal.engin.umich.edu/~gmazur/tqm/tqmterms.htm
This site by Glenn Mazur is likely the best online glossary for quality terms (and beyond!), with links to other sites for charts and examples. You'll want to bookmark this one.

The W. Edwards Deming Institute
www.deming.org
The W. Edwards Deming Institute features teachings, publications, and events.

Other Internet Resources

The 'Net is so huge and growing so fast that even the most comprehensive directory would be inadequate as soon as it's compiled. Consequently, any listing of Internet resources in a yearbook should include some instructions so you can find other discussion lists and Web sites to meet your specific needs.

To find other *discussion lists*, you can use the search functions of the following Web sites:

groups.yahoo.com
www.topica.com
paml.net
tile.net/lists
www.lsoft.com/lists/listref.html

To find other *Web sites*, you can use any of dozens of search engines. Search engines use varying protocols, but are basically similar, at least for less complex searches. The following search sites are among the best at this time:

www.google.com
www.altavista.com
www.alltheweb.com
hotbot.lycos.com
www.yahoo.com
www.dogpile.com
www.search.com
www.all4one.com
www.excite.com
www.lycos.com
www.webcrawler.com
www.thebighub.com

A Quality Manager's Guide to the Internet

Vanessa R. Franco

Since 1995, The Quality Yearbook has listed Internet resources of interest to people involved in quality. This article reviews a variety of Web sites "that can help quality managers do their jobs more easily, efficiently and effectively." Any list of sites is necessarily incomplete, of course, but these will help those with less Web experience make a good start in exploring the quality resources on the Internet. We include it as a supplement and extension to our collection of online quality sites.

Ever-busy quality managers must keep an eye on many facets of their businesses, including process management, personnel training, efficiency-boosting software, tool maintenance and the standards certifications necessary to compete. One ability all efficient managers hone is maximizing every available resource, and perhaps no resource is more affordable and easily accessible today than the Internet.

Although technophobes are finding their numbers dropping, many managers still don't utilize the Internet to its full capacity. This is understandable, because despite the existence of some excellent search engines such as Google and Yahoo!, it still takes time to ride through the links to sort the good from the outdated, the no-longer-existent and the irrelevant. With this in mind, *Quality Digest* has done some of the work for you to find the sites that can help quality managers do their jobs more easily, efficiently and effectively.

General Quality Resources

The American Society for Quality's (ASQ) Web site, *www.asq.org*, offers five categories of information: "About Quality," which includes a glossary, quality forum, news archive, and links to quality-related sites; "Standards and Certification," with information on QS-9000, ISO 9000, TL 9000 and ISO 14000; "Membership"; "ASQ Products," including publications, conferences, education, and reward and recognition products; and "Research and Information Service," offering the "Quality Information Center" (consisting of a research library, referral to subject matter experts for technical assistance, customized research and document delivery services) and the "Quality

---

Reprinted with permission from *Quality Digest*, February 2001. Copyright © 2001 QCI International. All rights reserved.

> ### OPTIMIZING YOUR CONNECTION
>
> Unless you've got a whole lot of free time and even more patience, the faster your Internet connection, the more satisfied you'll be with your system. InsideQuality's Web Editor Dirk Dusharme identifies the three most important factors in getting the most out of your time online:
>
> **1. Modem**—If you are using a modem to connect to the Internet, get the fastest modem you can find, probably a 56K. A fast modem is crucial to rapid page loading. Also, check into DSL. This high-speed, low-cost connection is becoming more widely available.
>
> **2. Browser software**—If you haven't already sworn allegiance to one, check out both Internet Explorer and Netscape Navigator. Although both will get you to your favorite sites, the user interface, overall feel and performance is a little different for each. You'll likely develop a clear preference, but whichever you choose, make sure to get the most recent version.
>
> **3. Computer**—As with modems, faster is better. Get a computer with the fastest processor and the most memory you can afford, but keep in mind that computer speed is nowhere near as critical as modem speed it comes to navigating the Internet.

InfoSearch," which allows visitors to search for articles on specific topics or browse through a number of journals.

Another source of general quality leads is Quality Resources Online (*www.quality.org*), which provides not only a tremendous number of quality-related links, but also an online marketplace for Internet services, e-mail discussion lists, job listings, recruitment and headhunter resources, and Internet warnings and virus hoax notices.

Finally, if *Quality Digest*'s new "everything quality" portal, InsideQuality, doesn't have the answers to your quality questions, it can help you find out who does. The site, *www.insidequality.com*, has product and service showrooms spotlighting the goods of nearly 2,000 vendors; an "Ask the Experts" question-and-answer forum; a career center; daily quality news; weekly polls; online tools, including demos, downloads, tools for interactive SPC; classifieds; publications; and much more.

Standards

If you're considering registration to any of the International Organization for Standardization (ISO) standards, want updates or news about standards development, could use some guidance on making the transition from ISO 9000:1994 to ISO 9000:2000, or just need more information about the standards, the first site to visit is ISO's *www.iso.ch*. The site also presents ISO's catalog, FAQs, ISO contacts, products for your business, standards and world trade workshops and seminars, and explanations of World Trade Organization agreements.

If you still have questions about the ISO standards or are looking for information about QS-9000 or the TE Supplement, a must-visit is *www.iso9000commerce.com*, a Web portal devoted to these standards and their related issues. The site offers full coverage of ISO 9000:2000; a "Magical Demystifying Tour of ISO 9000 and ISO 14000"; and a comprehensive Resource Center broken down into the categories of certified companies, compliant companies, consultants, registrars, books, software, seminars/workshops/conferences and discussion forums. Finally, it also provides links to associations, publications, government organizations, government quality awards and more.

Looking for your own copy of a standard? The American National Standards Institute (ANSI) Web site, *www.ansi.org*, sells electronic copies of many standards from the online ANSI Electronic Standards Store. The ANSI site also offers online versions of ANSI's bi-weekly publication, *Standards Action*, to keep you up to date as new standards are shaped; information and services about ISO 14000; links to regional and international standardization organization; and a great deal more information about standards development.

If you'd rather have a paper copy of your standard of choice, head to Global Engineering Documents' site, *www.global.ihs.com*, where you'll find U.S. and international standards, specifications and publications for industry, government and military. If this site doesn't have it, it may not exist: Global Engineering Documents' holdings include more than 1 million documents from more than 460 organizations worldwide. You can also go to the site to sign up for Global's free industry-specific e-newsletters, which update subscribers on new standards development and availability in their field.

The National Institute of Standards and Technology (NIST) is home to the Malcolm Baldrige National Quality Award Program (please see the more detailed description under "Awards"), but *www.nist.gov* also offers a wealth of information on the organization's other programs and services, all nicely organized into sections. The Measurement and Standards Laboratories section includes information, contacts, services, products, projects and programs, and publications from NIST's electronics and electrical engineering laboratory, information technology laboratory, manufacturing engineering laboratory, and four more laboratories. The other two sections are the Advanced Technology Program and the Manufacturing Extension Partnership. The NIST site also provides useful information on weights and measures, such as conversions and tables of equivalents.

The Registrar Accreditation Board's (RAB) Web site, *www.rabnet.com*, supplies ISO 9000:2000 transition tips, a list of authorized registrars and an approved transition training course list. Also available is general information about quality management systems (QMS) and environmental management systems (EMS) as well as accreditation steps, criteria and procedures, directories, and much more for QMS and EMS auditors, course providers and registrars. Finally, the site has a page of links to searchable databases of certified companies.

The International Electrotechnical Commission (IEC), the standards and conformity assessment body for electrotechnology fields, sells its publications in electronic and paper form on its Web site, *www.iec.ch*. The site also provides information about the IEC and the importance of international standards, newsletters and news releases, a resource area to provide support tools and documents for IEC process participants, a customer service center, and a searchable publications and documents database. Additionally, it links to *www.iecq.org*, which provides details about the IEC's quality assessment system for approving and certifying electronic components and provides contact information for the National Authorized Institutions of 18 countries.

Finally, if you're looking for companies that have been registered to ISO 9000 or QS-9000, you can find them on *Quality Digest*'s free, searchable database at *www.qualitydigest.com*.

Awards

Think your U.S. organization is ready to try for a Malcolm Baldrige Quality Award? If so, make your way to NIST's *www.quality.nist.gov*. The site, which you can also access through a link from NIST's main Web site, offers details about the award process and criteria, case studies and info sheets, a winners showcase, conference schedules, news, and information about the current recipients.

If you'd like to nominate someone for one of the ASQ's various awards, first visit *www.asq.org/abtquality/awards/asqawards.html*. There you'll find a brief synopsis for each prize and downloadable nomination forms for the Deming, Edwards, Feigenbaum, Freund-Marquardt, E.L. Grant, Ishikawa, E. Jack Lancaster and Shewhart Medals.

Most U.S. states also offer quality awards for various types of organizations with operations in those states. *Quality Digest*'s Web site, *www.qualitydigest.com*, offers a free database of individual state quality awards, with contact information for the agencies that administer them. Canadian award information is also provided in the database.

Canadian managers considering applying for national quality awards for their companies should head to *www.nqi.ca*. In addition to the award criteria, profiles of last year's winners, application process details and a downloadable entry guide for the Canada Awards for Excellence Quality Award and the Healthy Workplace Award, Canada's National Quality Institute (NQI) site has an online store and provides information on certification programs, NQI membership, news and events, and courses.

Managers of European businesses and organizations that demonstrate their commitment to continuous improvement through their quality processes might want to apply for the European Quality Award. Information brochures, application forms, press releases on winners from the last three years, ordering information for award-winning applications, and details on how to become an award assessor are all available at *www.efqm.org/award.htm*.

Training

The quality section of ScheduleEarth's professional development portal, *www.scheduleearth.com*, is an excellent place to start if anyone in your organization could use some training. It offers course and seminar listings, complete with dates and times and "register/more information" links to the companies offering them. Past seminar topics, highly relevant to many aspects of the quality profession, have included benchmarking, SPC, balanced scorecard, auditing and more. The site also hosts a quality discussion group.

The American Society for Training and Development (ASTD) has compiled a buyer's guide of more than 500 companies providing training and consulting, indexed by industry, location and more than 400 subject headings. To use the guide, shop at ASTD's online store or join one of its online learning communities, direct your browser to *www.astd.org*.

Software

If you're looking for free statistical software or want to try out some limited-use demos, you'll want to check out *members.aol.com/johnp71/javasta2.html*. The site offers links to free downloads in the categories of general statistical analysis, subset packages, curve fitting and modeling, and more, all handily labeled under the headings "completely free" and—for restricted-use demos or student packages—"free, but...." Another feature is the Lycos-powered Internetwide "find software" search engine, useful if you're unable to find the particular application you're looking for.

Managing Automation Software Guides' *www.masg.com* is designed to help you find the right software to automate your critical enterprisewide processes. The site's extensive database of enterprise-application and manufacturing-point solutions and services provides sophisticated search tools that will assist you in generating a list of potential suppliers, from which you can follow the links to vendor profiles and online brochures and catalogs. Additionally, the Software Evaluation Tool can simplify and shorten the task of defining specifications, qualifying and ranking vendors, and writing proposal requests, while the Resource Center offers a free e-mail newsletter, industry trend reports, case studies, tip sheets, calculators and white papers. The site's glossary provides pertinent definitions of terms arranged into functional categories, including SCM/ERP, Plant/Shop Floor, Engineering and E-Business.

Calibration

If your plant uses even one piece of equipment that requires calibration, check out *www.ecalibration.com*, Blue Mountain Quality Resources Inc.'s site offering current industry and product news, a career center, a free weekly calibration e-newsletter, a discussion board and more. One of the site's most useful features is its well-organized, user-friendly directories, which provide information on calibration services, training, instrumentation, consulting, software, organizations and supplies.

Another helpful calibration site is *www.calibrationclub.com*, which offers a free calibration tracking and reminder service. The service allows users to create custom profiles for all instruments requiring regular calibration.

The Internet and You

Although the aim of this article is to help you easily find some of the sites that make the Internet so useful as a quality tool, this list is by no means exhaustive. One of the Internet's most exciting—and most frustrating—qualities is that it changes constantly, with two new sites emerging for every old site that folds. Your browser's "bookmark" or "favorites" feature can be one of your greatest time-saving devices for sites you return to frequently, but it's definitely worth your time to periodically peruse the Web for new sites of interest or to search it every now and again using words you haven't tried before. Don't assume that closely related words in your field will yield identical results as search terms; slight variations in wording can make all the difference with a search engine. Above all, though, don't be afraid to try anything: the Internet is an amazing resource, but as with any resource, you'll come closest to being able to utilize it to its full potential when you've taken the time to experiment and find out how best to get the results you're seeking.

Vanessa R. Franco is Quality Digest's *managing editor. If you have any comments about this article, please e-mail them to vfranco@qualitydigest.com.*

Directory of Magazines, Journals, and Newsletters That Cover Quality

This section of *The Quality Yearbook* provides a comprehensive (though not exhaustive) listing of publications that regularly cover issues on quality. Some of them are dedicated to quality issues and some of them include quality as part of their regular coverage. Many quality organizations publish newsletters of interest to their members, depending on area of specialization. Those publications are generally not listed here, as they are available only to members. Nearly all industry associations also publish newsletters and/or magazines.

We have organized this listing into three categories:

1. Magazines, journals, and newsletters dedicated to quality
2. General business magazines, journals, and newsletters that often include articles on quality
3. Industry and special-interest magazines, journals, and newsletters that cover quality issues

For each listing, you'll find the publisher's mailing address, phone number, fax number, e-mail address, and Web site URL. You'll also find subscription information (in US$ and for an annual hard-copy subscription, unless indicated otherwise) and a brief description to give you a sense of the usefulness of this publication to your work. Check the Web site for changes.

We're committed to improving the quality of the resources we provide in *The Quality Yearbook*. If you have any corrections or any recommendations for publications we should list in the next edition of this annual, please contact us through McGraw-Hill or e-mail us at jwoods@cwlpub.com.

Magazines, Journals, and Newsletters Dedicated to Quality

Accreditation and Quality Assurance
Published monthly by Springer-Verlag New York, Inc., Journal Fulfillment Services Dept., P.O. Box 2485, Secaucus, NJ 07096-2485, phone: 800 SPRINGER (777-4643), fax: 201 348-4505, e-mail: custserv@springer-ny.com, Web: link.springer.de/link/service/journals/00769/index.htm.

Subscriptions: U.S., $423; for all other rates, check the Web site.

This practice-oriented journal is devoted to quality, comparability, and reliability in chemical measurements, with special attention to transnational problems and to problem solving for practitioners. It publishes scientific and technical contributions, short communications, and discussion and position papers. The focus is on accreditation, certification, EN 45 000 standards, the ISO 9000 series, GLP, measurement, calibration, and validation.

American Journal of Medical Quality
Published bimonthly by the American College of Medical Quality. Editorial: 4334 Montgomery Avenue, Bethesda, MD 20814, phone: 301 913-9149 or 800 924-2149, fax: 301 913-9142, e-mail: ACMQ@acmq.org, Web: www.acmq.org. Subscriptions: Allen Press, Inc., 810 East 10th Street, Lawrence, KS 66044, phone: 800 627-0326 or 785 843-1234, fax: 785 843-1244, e-mail: info@allenpress.com, Web: www.allenpress.com.

Subscriptions: U.S., $189; other countries, $219.

This journal features original, peer-reviewed articles of interest to professionals in clinical quality improvement, including reports on empirical studies related to quality improvement. The editorial objective is to balance the theoretical and the applied by publishing material of interest to both academicians and practitioners.

Benchmarking: An International Journal
Published in five issues (five dispatches) by MCB University Press Ltd., 60/62 Toller Lane, Bradford, West Yorkshire, England BD8 9BY, phone: +44 (0) 1274 777700, fax: +44 (0) 1274 785200, e-mail: customerservices@mcb.co.uk, Web: www.emeraldinsight.com/bij.htm.

Subscriptions: North America, $1549; Australasia, AUS$1999; Europe, Euro 1599 plus VAT Euro 139.91; UK and elsewhere, £979 plus VAT £85.66.

This journal covers such topics as the theory of benchmarking, benchmarking as part of total quality, tools and techniques, international benchmarking, test scenarios, benchmarking as part of organizational change, case histories and practical applications, working with multiple benchmarking partners, process innovation, and using benchmarking to improve project management skills.

Directory of Magazines, Journals, and Newsletters That Cover Quality

BioQuality

Published monthly by I2I Corporation, P.O. Box 1137, Idyllwild, CA 92549, phone: 909 659-1957, fax: 909 659-3233, e-mail: info@i2icorp.com, Web: www.i2icorp.com/newsletter.htm.

Subscriptions: $395.

The purpose of this publication is to promote current awareness for quality and regulatory professionals in the biopharmaceutical industry. It provides short, quickly read, easy-to-understand bites covering the latest meetings, Federal Register notices, and new FDA guidances. It lists recent, relevant articles with one-sentence summaries. Each issue also provides bullet-point summaries of FDA 483 observations.

Business Process Management Journal

Published in five issues (five dispatches) by MCB University Press Ltd., 60/62 Toller Lane, Bradford, West Yorkshire, England BD8 9BY, phone: +44 (0) 1274 777700, fax: +44 (0) 1274 785200, e-mail: customerservices@mcb.co.uk, Web: www.mcb.co.uk/bpmj.htm.

Subscriptions: North America, $1399; Australasia, AUS$1699; Europe, euro 1449 plus VAT euro 126.79; UK and elsewhere, £869 plus VAT £76.04.

This journal covers all aspects of business process management, including its place within an organization, advantages and disadvantages, benchmarking performance, choosing software for BPM projects, developing corporate strategies that work with BPM, and putting together process improvement teams.

CAL LAB Magazine

Published quarterly by 6136 Mission Gorge Road, Suite 224, San Diego, CA 92120, phone: 619 281-6250, fax: 619 281-6279, e-mail: office@callabmag.com, Web: www.callabmag.com.

Subscriptions: U.S., $45; Canada and Mexico, $50; all other countries, $60.

"The International Journal of Metrology," this publication covers "the field of metrology and calibration in any discipline area."

Concurrent Engineering: Research & Applications

Published quarterly by the CERA Institute and Sage Publications, Inc. Editorial: CETEAM International, P.O. Box 3882, Tustin, CA 92781-3882, phone: 714 952-5562, fax: 714 505-0663, e-mail: prasadb1@home.com (Biren Prasad, Managing Editor), Web: www.ceraj.com. Subscriptions: Sage Publications, Inc., 2455 Teller Road, Thousand Oaks, CA 91320, phone: 805 499-0721, fax: 805 499-0871, e-mail: info@sagepub.com, Web: www.sagepub.com.

Subscriptions: U.S, $550. UK, Europe, Middle East, and Africa, £393. Elsewhere, $550.

The official journal of the Institute of Concurrent Engineering of the International Society for Productivity Enhancement, this multidisciplinary journal provides information on computer-aided product design, engineering and manufacturing, and product life-cycle management.

Control
Published monthly by Putman Publishing Company, 555 Pierce Road, Suite 301, Itasca, IL 60143, phone: 630 467-1300, fax: 630 467-1124, e-mail: pstudebaker@putman.net (Paul Studebaker, Editor in Chief), Web: www.controlmagazine.com.

Subscriptions: Free to qualified applicants.

The focus of this magazine is "horizontal process industry application and integration of control, instrumentation, and automation systems and components" in all industries.

COR Clinical Excellence
Published monthly by COR Health LLC, P.O. Box 50507, Santa Barbara, CA 93150-0507, phone: 805 564-2177, fax: 805 564-2146, e-mail: corinfo@corhealth.com, Web: www.corhealth.com.

Subscriptions: $248.

This newsletter provides a broad overview of clinical management information from more than 150 publications and original articles, research, and commentary on clinical management issues. It's complemented by an online information service.

Critical Linkages II Newsletter
Published five times a year by Sager Educational Enterprises, 21 Wallis Road, Chestnut Hill, MA 02467-3110, phone: 617 469-9644, fax: 617 469-9639, e-mail: cs@carolsager.com, Web: www.carolsager.com.

Subscriptions: U.S., $40; other countries, $46.

This newsletter is based on two beliefs: the key to productivity is learning and success in any field depends on building partnerships that cross over traditional academic, professional, and occupational boundaries. Its mission is to support and promote the growth and continuous improvement of learning by building "critical linkages" across traditional boundaries.

Customer Service: A Journal of Theory, Research and Practice
Published biannually by the International Customer Service Association, 401 N. Michigan Avenue, Chicago, IL 60611-4267, phone: 800 360-ICSA (4272) or 312 321-6800, fax: 312 245-1084, e-mail: icsa@sba.com, Web: www.icsa.com.

Subscriptions: Free to ICSA members.

This journal features in-depth articles written by customer service professionals with first-hand experience dealing with the complexities and nuances of customer service. Each issue focuses on a particular area of interest, such as outsourcing or technology.

Customer Service Manager's Letter
Published 24 times per year by Aspen Publishers, 200 Orchard Ridge Drive, Gaithersburg, MD 20878, phone: 301 417-7500, fax: 301 695-7931, e-mail: customer.service@aspen-publ.com, Web: www.aspenpub.com.

Subscriptions: U.S., $179.80; elsewhere, contact the publisher.

This is an eight-page newsletter intended to help customer service managers develop highly proficient reps, reduce turnover (both employee and customer), ensure consistent customer satisfaction, and maximize profits. It covers technology; hiring, training, coaching, and motivating reps; measuring service performance and customer satisfaction; and building customer loyalty.

Engineering Management Journal
Published quarterly by the American Society for Engineering Management, Ted Eschenbach, Editor, School of Engineering, University of Alaska-Anchorage, 3211 Providence Drive, Anchorage, AK 99508, phone: NA, fax: (907) 786-1079, e-mail: aftge@uaa.alaska.ed, Web: www.asem.com.

Subscriptions: Free to members of ASEM, the Engineering Institute of Canada's Canadian Society for Engineering Management, and the Society for Engineering Management, Australia.

This journal publishes articles and features related to the management of engineering and technical professionals and of the organizations that rely on them to meet the challenges of coordinating the design, integration, and use of new technology in the workplace. It focuses on new theories and tools, insightful and innovative applications, and well-known engineering management principles. Articles encompass all engineering disciplines. Special issues have dealt with themes such as TQM and systems engineering.

Environmental Quality Management
Published quarterly by John Wiley & Sons, Inc., 605 Third Avenue, New York, NY 10158-0012, phone: 212 850-6000 or 212 850-6645 (subscriptions), fax: 212 850-6088 or 212 850-6021(subscriptions), e-mail: subinfo@jwiley.com, Web: www.interscience.wiley.com/jpages/1088-1913.

Subscriptions: U.S., Canada, and Mexico, $530 (Canada, add 7% GST); other countries, $554.

While aimed at managers and, to some degree, engineers in the environmental area, with practical articles and case studies, this journal (formerly *Total Quality Environmental Management*) covers a broad spectrum in the application of TQM principles, showing how to go beyond compliance.

European Journal of Innovation Management
Published quarterly by MCB University Press Ltd., 60/62 Toller Lane, Bradford, West Yorkshire, England BD8 9BY, phone: +44 (0) 1274 777700, fax: +44 (0) 1274 785200, e-mail: customerservices@mcb.co.uk, Web: www.emeraldinsight.com/ejim.htm.

Subscriptions: North America, $549; Australasia, AUS$939; Europe, euro 599 plus VAT euro 52.41; UK and elsewhere, £349 plus VAT £30.54.

This journal focuses on the phenomenon of innovation in a modern context, taking a holistic approach and presenting innovation management as an all-encompassing integrated process, with discussion papers, case studies, and reports on breakthroughs and the philosophy behind the theory and the practice of continuous improvement in innovation.

European Quality
Published bimonthly by the European Organization for Quality and European Quality Publications Ltd., John Kelly, Managing Editor, 9 St. Albans Place, N1, London, United Kingdom, phone: (020) 7704 2000 or (020) 7704 9534, fax: (020) 7704 2700, e-mail: jk@european-quality.co.uk, Web: www.european-quality.co.uk.

Subscriptions: £96.

This is the official journal of the EOQ. It is intended for high-level management and focuses on all aspects of quality. The journal supports the European business excellence model as a holistic management tool while offering detailed analysis of other strands of quality management such as the ISO series, benchmarking, Baldrige Award, Deming Prize, and various national and company initiatives.

Eye on Improvement
Published electronically twice monthly by the Institute for Healthcare Improvement, Institute for Healthcare Improvement, Institute for Healthcare Improvement, 375 Longwood Avenue, 4th Floor, Boston, MA 02215, phone: 617 754-4800, fax: 617 754-4848, e-mail: info@ihi.org, Web: www.ihi.org/resources/eyeoi.

Subscriptions: Free on Web site.

This newsletter, formerly a print publication, publishes abstracts of recently published literature on improvement and in-depth reports on quality improvement projects that are making a significant difference at health institutions.

HCQA Quality Forum
Published quarterly by the Health Care Quality Alliance, 4938 Hampden Lane, #201, Bethesda, MD 20814, phone: 202 955-3535, fax: 301 263-0245, e-mail: info@healthquality.org, Web: www.healthquality.org/newsletter.

Subscriptions: Free.

This is the official publication of the Health Care Quality Alliance, a non-profit, 501(c)3 public benefit organization dedicated to preserving and improving health care quality.

Homecare Quality Management

Published monthly by American Health Consultants, Inc., 3525 Piedmont Road NE, Building #6, Suite 400, Atlanta, GA 30305-0056, phone: 404 262-7436 or 800 688-2421 (customer service), fax: 404 262-7837 or 800 284-3291 (customer service), e-mail: customerservice@ahcpub.com, Web: www.ahcpub.com/ahc_root_html/products/newsletters/hqm.html.

Subscriptions: $339.

This newsletter is intended to help health professionals prepare for a joint commission survey and keep current on such vital issues as risk management, outcomes, and quality improvement.

IEEE Engineering Management Review

Published quarterly by the Engineering Management Society, Institute of Electrical and Electronics Engineers, IEEE Customer Service Center, 445 Hoes Lane, P.O. Box 1331, Piscataway, NJ 08855-1331, phone: 800 678-4333 (U.S. and Canada) or 732 981-0060, fax: 732 981-9667, e-mail: storehelp@ieee.org, Web: www.ieee.org.

Subscriptions: IEEE Engineering Society members, $24. Nonmembers: U.S., Canada, and Mexico, $150; elsewhere, add $25 for shipping and handling or $43 for airmail.

Each issue of this journal covers a certain theme, often related to quality management issues, with articles by leading writers, researchers, and practitioners reprinted from other journals over the past few years.

The Informed Outlook

Published monthly by the International Forum for Management Systems, 15913 Edgewood Drive, Montclair, VA 22026-1723, phone: 703 680-1436, fax: 703 680-1356, e-mail: theinformedoutlook@home.com, Web: www.informintl.com/outlook.

Subscriptions: U.S., $325; Canada, $350; other countries, $400. Discount for members of the American Society for Quality.

This newsletter provides readers with the latest news on standards, such as ISO 9000, QS-9000, and ISO 14000. It features regular reports on developments and interpretations, conferences and meetings, relevant new technologies, and other standards-related information.

InTech

Published monthly by the Instrumentation, Systems, and Automation

Society, 67 Alexander Drive, P.O. Box 12277, Research Triangle Park, NC 27709, phone: 919 549-8411, fax: 919 549-8288, e-mail: info@isa.org, Web: www.isa.org/journals/intech.

Subscriptions: Free to ISA members and qualified applicants.

This publication covers the measurement and control field, providing information about technical developments, trends, and standards, and industry, economic, and business news important to measurement and control practitioners and the organizations that employ them.

International Journal for Quality in Health Care

Published bimonthly by Oxford University Press Journals. Subscriptions (Americas): Journals Marketing, 2001 Evans Road, Cary NC 27513, phone: 800 852-7323 or 919 677-0977, fax: 919 677-1714, e-mail: jnlorders@oup-usa.org, Web: www3.oup.co.uk/intqhc.

Subscriptions: Individuals, £59 or $96; institutions, £315 or $540.

This is the official journal of the International Society for Quality in Health Care. A peer-reviewed journal, it publishes papers in all disciplines involved in health care quality and provides a forum for the exchange of news and information about quality-related activities and the society.

International Journal of Advanced Manufacturing Systems

Published semiannually by the International Society of Agile Manufacturing, Rougeou Hall, #223, Lafayette, LA 70504, phone: 337 482-5361, fax: 337 482-1129, e-mail: suren@louisiana.edu (Suren N. Dwivedi, Chief Editor), Web: www.ucs.louisiana.edu/~snd7483/IJAMS.html. Subscriptions: Agility Research Institute, Subscription Department, 2851 Johnston Street, #325, Lafayette, LA 70503.

Subscriptions: $300.

This journal addresses the use of advanced manufacturing systems, including areas of information modeling, distribution, planning and scheduling, collaborative decision-making, and the organization and management of advanced manufacturing systems.

International Journal of Agile Manufacturing

Published semiannually by the International Society of Agile Manufacturing, Rougeou Hall, #223, Lafayette, LA 70504, phone: 337 482-5361, fax: 337 482-1129, e-mail: suren@louisiana.edu (Suren N. Dwivedi, Chief Editor), Web: www.ucs.louisiana.edu/~snd7483/IJAM.html. Subscriptions: Agility Research Institute, Subscription Department, 2851 Johnston Street, #325, Lafayette, LA 70503.

Subscriptions: $300.

The journal addresses the use of agility, including areas of information modeling, distribution, planning and scheduling, collaborative decision-making, and organization and management. Emphasis is on agile technologies that result in faster productivity and better customer value.

International Journal of Health Care Quality Assurance
Published in seven issues (four dispatches) by MCB University Press Ltd., 60/62 Toller Lane, Bradford, West Yorkshire, England BD8 9BY, phone: +44 (0) 1274 777700, fax: +44 (0) 1274 785200, e-mail: customerservices@mcb.co.uk, Web: www.emeraldinsight.com/ijhcqa.htm.

Subscriptions: North America, $3549; Australasia, AUS$4299; Europe, euro 3699 plus VAT euro 323.66; UK and elsewhere, £2229 plus VAT £195.04.

This journal targets anybody involved in developing, initiating, and monitoring quality assurance programs in the health care industry.

International Journal of Process Management and Benchmarking
Published quarterly by Inderscience Enterprises Ltd. Editorial: Abby Ghobadian, Executive Editor, Middlesex University Business School, The Burroughs, London NW4 4BT, United Kingdom, phone +44 (0) 208 411 5827, fax: +44 (0) 208 411 5758, e-mail: A.Ghobadian@mdx.ac.uk, Web: www.inderscience.com. Subscriptions: Order Department, World Trade Center Building, 29 route de Pré-Bois, Case Postale 896, CH-1215 Geneva 15, Switzerland, phone: NA, fax: +41 (22) 791 0885 or +44 (0) 1234-240515, e-mail: subs@inderscience.com.

Subscriptions: $340 plus $30 shipping and handling outside Great Britain.

This journal, launched in 1999, provides a refereed reference in process management, TQM, and benchmarking, covering private and public sectors, manufacturing and services industries.

International Journal of Quality & Reliability Management
Published in nine issues (five dispatches) a year by MCB University Press Ltd., 60/62 Toller Lane, Bradford, West Yorkshire, England BD8 9BY, phone: +44 (0) 1274 777700, fax: +44 (0) 1274 785200, e-mail: customerservices@mcb.co.uk, Web: www.emeraldinsight.com/ijqrm.htm.

Subscriptions: North America, $6599; Australasia, AUS$7499; Europe, euro 6799 plus VAT euro 594.91; UK and elsewhere, £4129 plus VAT £361.29.

This journal covers worldwide trends in quality assurance and management; quality costing, management, systems, practices, and policies; equipment maintenance and availability, gauging, calibration, and measurement; life cycle costing; marketing aspects of quality; product liability; product testing techniques and systems; quality function deployment; reliability and quality education and training; productivity and adjusting; and assessment and certification.

International Journal of Reliability, Quality and Safety Engineering
Published quarterly by World Scientific Publishing Co., Inc., U.S. Office, 1060 Main Street, River Edge, NJ 07661, phone: 800 227-7562 or 201 487-9655, fax: 888 977-2665 or 201 487-9656, e-mail: sales@wspc.com, Web: ejournals.wspc.com.sg/journals.html.

Subscriptions: $374 (institutions) or $136 (individuals), plus $25 for airmail.

This is a refereed technical journal focusing on both the theoretical and the practical aspects of reliability, quality, and safety in engineering. It covers a broad spectrum of issues in manufacturing, computing, software, aerospace, control, nuclear systems, power systems, communication systems, and electronics.

ISO 14000 Update
Published monthly by Cutter Information Corporation, 37 Broadway, Arlington, MA 02474-5552, phone: 800 964-5118 or 781 641-5118, fax: 800 888-1816 or 781 648-1950, e-mail: info@cutter.com, Web: www.cutter.com/iso14000.

Subscriptions: North America, $200; outside North America, $240.

This newsletter, which began as a supplement to the newsletter *Business and the Environment*, reports on the status of the entire ISO 14000 series—from ISO 14001, the environmental management system standard, to ISO 14040, the lifecycle assessment standard.

Joint Commission Journal on Quality Improvement
Published monthly by the Joint Commission on Accreditation of Healthcare Organizations, 1 Renaissance Boulevard, Oakbrook Terrace, IL 60181, phone: 630 792-5000, fax: 630 792-5005, e-mail: info@jcrinc.com, Web: www.jcaho.org.

Subscriptions: U.S., $175; Canada, $200; other countries, $215.

The goal of this refereed journal is to publish articles that emphasize practical approaches to improving health care quality, which includes the measurement, assessment, and/or improvement of performance in health care quality and delivery.

Journal for Healthcare Quality
Published bimonthly by the National Association for Healthcare Quality, 4700 W. Lake Avenue, Glenview, IL 60025-1485, phone: 800 966-9392 or 847 375-4720, fax: 847 375-4777, e-mail: jhq@nahq.org, Web: www.nahq.org/pubsjhq.htm.

Subscriptions: Free to NAHQ members; nonmembers, $105; institutions, $150. Other countries, $175.

The official journal of the National Association for Healthcare Quality, this publication is aimed at professionals responsible for promoting and monitoring quality, safe, cost-effective healthcare, with articles that focus on improvement, risk management, utilization review, and the latest regulations from the Joint Commission, PROs, and payment systems. It also reviews publications in the field and provides updates on pertinent legislation.

Journal for Quality and Participation
Published bimonthly by the Association for Quality and Participation, Executive Building #200, 2368 Victoria Parkway, Cincinnati, OH 45206, phone: 800 733-3310 or 513 381-1979, fax: 513 381-0070, e-mail: journal@aqp.org, Web: www.aqp.org.

Subscriptions: Available only to AQP members.

This journal presents practical, detailed articles on implementing quality in different industries and organizations—employee involvement, quality circle programs, self-managing teams, SPC, TQI, employee ownership, gainsharing, and labor-management cooperation. It often includes articles by well-known quality practitioners and consultants. This is one of the best periodicals on quality for managers.

Journal of Consumer Satisfaction, Dissatisfaction and Complaining Behavior
Published annually by Consumer Satisfaction, Dissatisfaction and Complaining Behavior, Inc., H. Keith Hunt (editor), 632 TNRB, Marriott School of Management, Brigham Young University, Provo, UT 84602, phone: 801 378-2080, 801 378-3113, or 801 224-2867, fax: 801 226-7650, e-mail: hkhunt@byu.edu or hkh@itsnet.com, Web: NA.

Subscriptions: U.S., $15; other countries, $18.

This journal publishes articles solely on the topics indicated in the title of the journal, primarily for academic and industry researchers specializing in the topics.

Journal of Industrial Technology
Published electronically quarterly by the National Association of Industrial Technology, 3300 Washtenaw Avenue, Suite 220, Ann Arbor, MI 48104-4200, phone: 734 677-0720, fax: 734 677-2407, e-mail: nait@nait.org, Web: www.nait.org.

Subscriptions: Free.

The articles in this journal cover all areas of industrial technology, aimed at "educators, students, graduates, industrial representatives, and others interested in Industrial Technology."

Journal of Organizational Excellence
Published quarterly by John Wiley & Sons, Inc., Customer Service (Americas),

605 Third Avenue, New York, NY 10158-0012, phone: 212 850-6000 or 212 850-6645 (subscriptions), fax: 212 850-6088 or 212 850-6021 (subscriptions), e-mail: subinfo@jwiley.com, Web: www.interscience.wiley.com/jpages/1531-1864.

Subscriptions: U.S., Canada, and Mexico, $399 (in Canada, add 7% GST); other countries, $423.

Formerly *National Productivity Review*, this journal includes practical articles focusing on implementing quality in all types of organizations. It delivers in-depth articles and current case studies detailing quality programs that work, written by and for leaders of quality and productivity improvement efforts in the both private and public sectors.

Journal of Product Innovation Management

Published bimonthly by Elsevier Science, Regional Sales Office, Customer Support Department, P.O. Box 945, New York, NY 10159-0945, phone: 212 633-3730 or 888 4ES-INFO (437-4636), fax: 212 633-3680, e-mail: usinfo-f@elsevier.com, Web: www.elsevier.com/inca/publications/store/5/0/5/7/2/4/index.htt.

Subscriptions: All countries outside of Europe except Japan, $453; Europe, euro 405; Japan, yen 53,700.

This journal, a publication of the Product Development & Management Association, is dedicated to advancing management practice in all of the functions involved in product innovation. Its purpose is to provide managers with theoretical structures and practical techniques that will help them manage more effectively. The scope is broad, taking account of those issues that are crucial to successful product innovation in external and internal environments.

Journal of Quality Technology

Published quarterly by the American Society for Quality, 600 North Plankinton Avenue, Milwaukee, WI 53203, P.O. Box 3005, Milwaukee, WI 53201-3005, phone: 800 248-1946 or 414 272-8575, fax: 414 272-1734, e-mail: cs@asq.org, Web: www.asq.org/pub/jqt.

Subscriptions: Individuals: ASQ members, $26 in the U.S., $47 in Canada (includes 7% GST), and $44.50 in other countries; nonmembers, $37 in the U.S., $49 in Canada (includes 7% GST), and $56.50 in other countries. Institutions: $100.

Technically oriented with heavy use of statistics, this journal emphasizes the practical applicability of new techniques, instructive examples of the operation of existing techniques, and results of historical researches. Useful only to those involved in quality control technology.

Knowledge and Process Management: The Journal of Corporate Transformation

Published quarterly by John Wiley & Sons, Ltd., Customer Service (Americas), 605 Third Avenue, New York, NY 10158-0012, phone: 212 850-6645, fax: 212 850-6021, e-mail: subinfo@wiley.com, Web: www.interscience.wiley.com/jpages /1092-4604.

Subscriptions: $500 (in Canada, add 7% GST); United Kingdom, £300.

This journal, which incorporates *Business Change and Re-engineering*, is the official journal of the Institute of Business Process Re-Engineering. It is intended to provide information to executives responsible for driving performance improvement in their business or for introducing new ideas to business through thought leadership.

Managing Service Quality

Published in six issues (six dispatches) a year by MCB University Press Ltd., 60/62 Toller Lane, Bradford, West Yorkshire, England BD8 9BY, phone: +44 (0) 1274 777700, fax: +44 (0) 1274 785200, e-mail: customerservices@mcb.co.uk, Web: www.emeraldinsight.com/msq.htm.

Subscriptions: North America, $1549; Australasia, AUS$1899; Europe, euro 1599 plus VAT euro 139.91; UK and elsewhere, £979 plus VAT £85.66.

This journal covers such topics as measuring customer satisfaction, empowering staff to handle customer complaints, creating and managing a comprehensive customer loyalty program, managing the relationship between service quality and customer expectations, and building an effective customer retention strategy.

Manufacturing Engineer

Published bimonthly by the Institution of Electrical Engineers, P.O. Box 96, Michael Faraday House, Stevenage, Hertsforshire SG1 2SD, United Kingdom, phone: +44 (0) 1438 313311, fax: +44 (0) 1438 742792, e-mail: mfgeng@iee.org.uk or sales@iee.uk.org, Web: www.iee.org.uk.

Subscriptions: in Americas, $260 (add $35 for airmail); elsewhere, £150 (add £20 for airmail).

This publication for manufacturing engineers covers manufacturing methods, quality and processes from initial specification to final product.

Measuring Business Excellence

Published in four issues (four dispatches) by MCB University Press Ltd., 60/62 Toller Lane, Bradford, West Yorkshire, England BD8 9BY, phone: +44 (0) 1274 777700, fax: +44 (0) 1274 785200, e-mail: customerservices@mcb.co.uk, Web: www.emeraldinsight.com/mbe.htm.

Subscriptions: North America, $229; Australasia, AUS$379; Europe, euro 249 plus VAT euro 21.79; UK and elsewhere, £149 plus VAT £13.04.

The focus of this journal is to show you how businesses are measuring their performance, through case notes and case studies. As of September 2000, this publication contains a section formerly published as *Quality Focus*.

Momentum: The Quality Magazine

Published bimonthly by the Quality Society of Australasia Limited, P.O. Box 742, Crows Nest, NSW 1585, Australia, phone: +61 2 9901 9938, fax: +61 2 9901 4677, e-mail: magazine@qsanet.com, Web: www.qsanet.com.

Subscriptions: Free to QSA members. Nonmembers: Australia, AU$44; New Zealand, AU$60; elsewhere, AU$80.

This magazine, formerly *The Quality Magazine*, covers the latest developments in quality in a broad range of areas, including customer focus, empowerment, management of change, quality assurance, and accreditation and certification.

NCSL Newsletter

Published quarterly by the National Conference of Standards Laboratories International, 1800 30th Street, Suite 305B, Boulder, CO 80301-1026, phone: 303 440-3339, fax: 303 440-3384, e-mail: info@ncslinternational.org, Web: www.ncslinternational.org/publications/pubs-list.cfm.

Subscriptions: Members, $15; nonmembers, $40.

The newsletter contains articles of interest to the measurement community, reports on recent regional meetings, and information about upcoming meetings and conferences.

Process Control and Quality

Published bimonthly by VSP, P.O. Box 346, 3700 AH Zeist, The Netherlands, phone: +31 30 692 5790, fax: +31 30 693 2081, e-mail: vsppub@compuserve.com, Web: www.vsppub.com/journals/jn-ProConQua.html.

Subscriptions: $486 or euro 418.

This international journal is dedicated to the science and technology of process quality measurement systems. It provides a multidisciplinary forum for scientists and engineers involved in research, plant design, process quality control, and environmental monitoring.

QEHSzine

Published electronically three times a year by the American Society for Quality, Energy and Environmental Division, through WPI, 2000 Kraft Drive, Suite 2100, Blacksburg, VA 24060-6373, phone: 540 557-6000, fax: 540 557-6043, e-mail: steve_grieco@wpi.org (Steve Grieco, Editor), Web: www.asq-eed.org.

Subscriptions: Free.

The subtitle says it all: "The Electronic Magazine for Quality, Environmental, Health, and Safety Professionals."

QI/TQM
Published monthly by American Health Consultants, Inc., 3525 Piedmont Road NE, Building 6, Suite 400, Atlanta, GA 30305-0056, phone: 404 262-7436 or 800 688-2421 (customer service), fax: 404 262-7837 or 800 284-3291 (customer service), e-mail: customerservice@ahcpub.com, Web: www.ahcpub.com/ahc_root_html/products/newsletters/qit.html.

Subscriptions: $527.

This newsletter provides detailed strategies and case studies for implementing continuous quality improvement and total quality improvement in health care facilities. It covers benchmarking, data collection, clinical improvement strategies, and outcomes management.

Quality
Published monthly by Business News Publishing Co., 1050 IL Route 83, Suite 200, Bensenville, IL 60106-1096, phone: 630 616-0200 or 847 291-5224 (customer service), fax: 630 227-0204 or 847 291-4816 (customer service), e-mail: babiczg@bnp.com (Gillian Babicz, associate editor), Web: qualitymag.com.

Subscriptions: Free, through the Web site.

This magazine covers quality assurance and process improvement in manufacturing. It reports on the use of metrology methods, statistical analysis, and process improvement techniques to improve quality.

Quality 1st
Published biweekly by The Dartnell Corporation, 360 Hiatt Drive, Palm Beach Gardens, FL 33418, phone: 800 621-5463, fax: 561 622-2423, e-mail: quality@dartnellcorp.com, Web: www.dartnellcorp.com.

Subscriptions: $245.70 (five copies), plus $41 shipping and handling.

This is a four-page newsletter mainly aimed at supervisors and employees. It includes a variety of suggestions and ideas for helping employees understand that quality work improves job satisfaction, job security, and professional development.

Quality and Reliability Engineering International
Published bimonthly by John Wiley & Sons Ltd., Customer Service (Americas), 605 Third Avenue, New York, NY 10158-0012, phone: 212 850-6000 or 212 850-6645 (subscriptions), fax: 212 850-6088 or 212 850-6021(subscriptions), e-mail: subinfo@jwiley.com, Web: www.interscience.wiley.com/jpages/0748-8017.

Subscriptions: Individuals: $940. Institutions: $1255. (In Canada, add 7% GST.)

This is a technical journal with articles designed to fill the gap between theoretical methods and scientific research on one hand and current industrial practices on the other. Highly specialized and mathematical, this journal is recommended only for engineers in this area.

Quality Assurance: Good Practice, Regulation, and Law
Published quarterly by Taylor & Francis Ltd. Subscriptions: Taylor & Francis Group, U.S. Customer Service, 325 Chestnut Street, Suite 800, Philadelphia, PA 19106, phone: 800 354-1420, fax: 215 625-8914, e-mail: info@taylorandfrancis.com, Web: www.tandf.co.uk/journals/tf/10529411.html.

Subscriptions: $172 or £104 (individual) and $395 or £239 (institutional).

This international, peer-reviewed journal publishes original papers on quality principles and procedures in all fields of science, especially the biological, physical, environmental, and engineering sciences, with particular attention to scientific, regulatory, legal, and international harmonization issues.

Quality Assurance in Education
Published in four issues (four dispatches) by MCB University Press Ltd., 60/62 Toller Lane, Bradford, West Yorkshire, England BD8 9BY, phone: +44 (0) 1274 777700, fax: +44 (0) 1274 785200, e-mail: customerservices@mcb.co.uk, Web: www.emeraldinsight.com/qae.htm.

Subscriptions: North America, $1899; Australasia, AUS$2369; Europe, euro 1999 plus VAT euro 174.91; UK and elsewhere, £1199 plus VAT £104.91.

This journal is intended to be a resource for anyone concerned with raising quality standards in higher and continuing education. It evaluates innovative ideas for teaching and development and assesses new approaches to help meet demands for increased output, better quality standards, and more effective cost management.

Quality Assurance Journal
Published quarterly by John Wiley & Sons Ltd., Office for the Americas, 605 Third Avenue, New York, NY 10158-0012, phone: 212 850-6000 or 212 850-6645 (subscriptions), fax: 212 850-6088 or 212 850-6021 (subscriptions), e-mail: subinfo@jwiley.com, Web: www.interscience.wiley.com/jpages/1087-8378.

Subscriptions: Individual, NA; institutional, $390 or £235. (In Canada, add 7% GST.)

Published in association with the Society of Quality Assurance, this journal, subtitled "The Quality Assurance Journal for Pharmaceutical, Health and Environmental Professionals," provides an international forum for quality assurance professionals, particularly in the life sciences.

Quality Digest
Published monthly by QCI International, 40 Declaration Drive, Suite 100, Chico, CA 95973, phone: 530 893-4095, fax: 530 893-0395, e-mail: editorial@qualitydigest.com or circulation@qualitydigest.com, Web: www.qualitydigest.com.

Subscriptions: Free in U.S., Canada, and Mexico through the Web site. Elsewhere, contact the publisher.

This magazine covers quality-related activities in manufacturing, financial services, communications, utilities, transportation, government and military services. There are also monthly columnists, software reviews, and book reviews.

Quality Engineering
Published quarterly by the American Society for Quality and Marcel Dekker, Inc. Editorial: American Society for Quality, 600 North Plankinton Avenue, Milwaukee, WI 53203, P.O. Box 3005, Milwaukee, WI 53201-3005, phone: 800 248-1946 or 414 272-8575, fax: 414 272-1734, Web: www.asq.org/pub/qe. Subscriptions: Marcel Dekker, Inc., Customer Service, Cimarron Road, P.O. Box 5005, Monticello, NY 12701, phone: 800 228-1160 or 845 796-1919, fax: 845 796-1772, e-mail: jrnlorders@dekker.com, Web: www.dekker.com.

Subscriptions: ASQ members: $30.25 U.S. and $46.25 elsewhere (rate in Canada includes 7% GST). Nonmembers $49.75 and institutions: $550, through Marcel Dekker.

This journal is a forum for the exchange of quality problem-solving stories and results. The articles provide in-depth examples concerning technical applications to the manufacturing process. Each issue examines inspection and test equipment.

Quality in Manufacturing
Published bimonthly by Nelson Publishing, 6001 Cochran Rd., Suite 104 Solon, OH 44139, phone: 440 248-1125, fax: 440 248-0187, e-mail: qm@aip.com, Web: www.qualityinmfg.com.

Subscriptions: Free to qualified applicants in the U.S.; otherwise, contact publisher.

This magazine promises "strategies, tools, solutions."

Quality Letter for Healthcare Leaders
Published 11 times a year by Aspen Publishers, Inc., 200 Orchard Ridge Drive, Gaithersburg, MD 20878, phone: 800 234-1660 or 301 417-7500, fax: 800 901-9075 or 301 417-7550, e-mail: customer.service@aspenpubl.com, Web: www.aspenpublishers.com.

Subscriptions: $375.

This newsletter provides information on quality control for "everyone involved in measuring and improving quality in hospitals, health systems, HMOs, group practices, and other health facilities."

Quality Management in Health Care
Published quarterly by Aspen Publishers, Inc., 200 Orchard Ridge Drive, Gaithersburg, MD 20878, phone: 800 234-1660 or 301 417-7500, fax: 800 901-9075 or 301 417-7550, e-mail: customer.service@aspenpubl.com, Web: www.aspenpublishers.com.

Subscriptions: $165.

This peer-reviewed journal provides a forum to explore the theoretical, technical, and strategic elements of total quality management in health care.

Quality Management Journal
Published quarterly by the American Society for Quality, 600 North Plankinton Avenue, Milwaukee, WI 53203, P.O. Box 3005, Milwaukee, WI 53201-3005, phone: 800 248-1946 or 414 272-8575, fax: 414 272-1734, e-mail: cs@asq.org, Web: www.asq.org/pub/qmj.

Subscriptions: Individual: U.S., $60, Canada, $90 (includes 7% GST), other countries, $84. ASQ members: $10 discount. Institutional: U.S., $130, Canada, $160 (includes 7% GST), other countries, $150.

The mission of this peer-reviewed journal is to publish significant research that is relevant to quality management practice and to provide a forum for discussion of such research for both academics and practitioners.

Quality Matters
Published three times a year by the National Committee for Quality Assurance, 2000 L Street, NW, Suite 500, Washington, DC 20036, phone: 888 275-7585, fax: 202 955-3531, e-mail: Customersupport@ncqa.org, Web: www.ncqa.org/pages/communications/publications/qmpub.htm.

Subscriptions: $90.

This newsletter reports on quality-related activities in the managed care industry and at NCQA. It provides statistics and information on NCQA's accreditation program, updates readers on the development and promulgation of performance measures, and discusses NCQA's role in an ever-evolving health care system.

Quality Progress
Published monthly by the American Society for Quality, 600 North Plankinton Avenue, Milwaukee, WI 53203, P.O. Box 3005, Milwaukee, WI 53201-3005, phone: 800 248-1946 or 414 272-8575, fax: 414 272-1734, e-mail: cs@asq.org, Web: www.asq.org/pub/qualityprogress.

Subscriptions: Free to ASQ members. Nonmembers: U.S., $60; elsewhere, $95 (in Canada, includes 7% GST). Institutions: U.S., $120; elsewhere, $130 (in Canada, includes 7% GST).

This is the foremost magazine dealing with quality management topics and the source of many articles in *The Quality Yearbook*. Every issue has a theme, but also includes several other articles dealing with a broad spectrum of issues. The articles are nearly always practical and provide perspectives that anyone interested in quality management will find valuable. Regular features include event calendars and reviews.

Quality Systems Update
Published monthly by QSU Publishing Company, 3975 University Drive, Suite 230, Fairfax, VA 22030, Editorial: Paul Scicchitano, Publisher, phone: 703 359-8466, fax: 703 359-8462, e-mail: isoeditor@aol.com. Customer service: Sabrina Eugenio, phone: 703 359-8460 or 866 225-3122, fax: 703 359-8462, e-mail: seugenio@qsuonline.com, Web: www.qsuonline.com.

Subscriptions: $375. Canada, $405; other countries, add $425.

This newsletter focuses on ISO 9000 and QS-9000—registration, implementation, and developments.

Quality World
Published monthly by the Institute of Quality Assurance, 12 Grosvenor Crescent, London SW1X 7EE, United Kingdom, phone: +44 (0) 20 7245 6722, fax: +44 (0) 20 7245 6755, e-mail: iqa@iqa.org, Web: www.iqa.org.

Subscriptions: Free to IQA members. Nonmembers: UK, £49; Europe, £63; elsewhere, £78 or £83 (check Web site).

The magazine covers "quality theory from the traditional to the radical," as well as environment issues and information technology.

Reliability Magazine
Published bimonthly by Reliability Magazine, 1704 Natalie Nehs Drive, Knoxville, TN 37931-4554, phone: 865 531-2193 or 865 531-2194, fax: 865 531-2459, e-mail: info@reliability-magazine.com, Web: www.reliability-magazine.com.

Subscriptions: U.S., $49; outside U.S., $73.

"The Magazine for Improved Plant Productivity," this is "the first trade journal dedicated specifically to machinery reliability, the predictive maintenance industry, root cause failure analysis, reliability-centered maintenance, and CMMS."

Six Sigma Forum Magazine
Published quarterly by the American Society for Quality, 600 North Plankinton Avenue, Milwaukee, WI 53203, P.O. Box 3005, Milwaukee, WI

53201-3005, phone: 800 248-1946 or 414 272-8575, fax: 414 272-1734, e-mail: cs@asq.org, Web: www.asq.org/pub/sixsigma.

Subscriptions: Available only to Six Sigma Forum members: U.S., $40; other countries, $50 (in Canada, includes GST).

Launched in fall 2001 as the "first and only magazine tailored for Six Sigma Executives, Champions, Master Black Belts, Black Belts, and Green Belts" and the "flagship magazine of Six Sigma Forum."

Software Quality Professional

Published quarterly by the American Society for Quality, 600 North Plankinton Avenue, Milwaukee, WI 53203, P.O. Box 3005, Milwaukee, WI 53201-3005, phone: 800 248-1946 or 414 272-8575, fax: 414 272-1734, e-mail: cs@asq.org, Web: www.asq.org/products/journals/sqp.html.

Subscriptions: ASQ members: U.S., $40; other countries, $60. Nonmembers: U.S., $70; other countries, $95. Institutions: U.S., $120; other countries, $150. (Rates for Canada include 7% GST.)

Focusing on the practical needs of professionals including engineers and managers, this journal, launched in December 1998, provide readers with information that will contribute to their personal development and success in the field of software quality.

Standardization News

Published monthly by the American Society for Testing and Materials, International Headquarters, 100 Barr Harbor Drive, West Conshohocken, PA 19428-2959, phone: 610 832-9585, fax: 610 832-9555, e-mail: service@astm.org, Web: www.astm.org.

Subscriptions: Free to ASTM members. Nonmembers: North America, $18; elsewhere, $20.

This is the official magazine of the American Society for Testing and Materials. It publishes feature articles, commentary, news briefs, and updates on ASTM technical committee activity.

Supervisor's Guide to Quality & Excellence®

Published biweekly by Clement Communications, Inc., 10 LaCrue Avenue, Concordville, PA 19331, phone: 888 358-5858, fax: 800 459-1933, e-mail: customerservice@clement.com, Web: www.clement.com.

Subscriptions: $195.

This newsletter provides news and information for supervisors and managers on improving quality and promoting excellence in the workplace.

The Systems Thinker

Published 10 times a year by Pegasus Communications, Inc. Editorial: 1

Moody Street, Waltham, MA 02453, phone: 781 398-9700, fax: 781 894-7175, e-mail: editorial@pegasus.com, Web: www.pegasuscom.com/tstpage.html. Subscriptions: P.O. Box 2241, Williston, VT 05495, phone: 800 272-0945 or 802 862-0095, fax: 802 864-7626, e-mail: customerservice@pegasuscom.com.

Subscriptions: North America, $89; elsewhere, $119.

This newsletter helps managers and leaders put systems thinking to work in their organizations. It carefully introduces readers to the basic tools and concepts of systems thinking, then builds expertise in this essential component of management literacy through a variety of approaches.

Technometrics
Published quarterly by the American Society for Quality, 600 North Plankinton Avenue, Milwaukee, WI 53203, P.O. Box 3005, Milwaukee, WI 53201-3005, phone: 800 248-1946 or 414 272-8575, fax: 414 272-1734, e-mail: cs@asq.org, Web: www.asq.org/pub/techno. Subscriptions (nonmembers): American Statistical Association, 1429 Duke Street, Alexandria, VA 22314-3402, phone: 703 684-1221 or 888 231-3473, fax: 703 684-2037, e-mail: asainfo@amstat.org, Web: www.amstat.org/publications/technometrics.

Subscriptions: ASQ or ASA members: $24. Nonmembers: $36. Institutions: $60. (Canadian rates include 7% GST.)

Published in conjunction with the American Statistical Association, this journal is subtitled "A Journal of Statistics for the Physical, Chemical, and Engineering Sciences." Articles describe new techniques and applications for research, development, design, and performance improvement.

Test & Measurement World
Published 15 times a year by Cahners Business Information. Editorial: 275 Washington Street, Newton, MA 02158-1630, phone: 617 558-4671, fax: 617 558-4470, e-mail: tmw@cahners.com, Web: www.tmworld.com. Subscriptions: Cahners Business Information, 8878 S. Barrons Boulevard, Highlands Ranch, CO 80129-2345, phone: 303 470-4445, fax: 303 470-4280, e-mail: cahners.subs@denver.cahners.com.

Subscriptions: Free to "to electronics engineers who specify, recommend, authorize, or buy test, measurement, inspection, or QC equipment, software, or services."

This magazine covers the electronics testing industry, providing how-to information for engineers who test, measure, and inspect electronic devices, components, and systems.

Total Quality Management
Published eight times a year by Taylor & Francis Ltd. Subscriptions: Taylor & Francis Group, U.S. Customer Service, 325 Chestnut Street, Suite 800, Philadelphia, PA 19106, phone: 800 354-1420, fax: 215 625-8914, e-mail:

info@taylorandfrancis.com, Web: www.tandf.co.uk/journals/routledge/09544127.html.

Subscriptions: Individual, $292 or £177; institutional, $859 or £499.

This journal aims to stimulate thought and research in all aspects of total quality management and to provide a natural forum for discussion and dissemination of research results. The journal is intended to encourage interest in all matters relating to total quality management and to appeal to both the academic and professional community working in this area.

The TQM Magazine
Published in six issues (six dispatches) by MCB University Press Ltd., 60/62 Toller Lane, Bradford, West Yorkshire, England BD8 9BY, phone: +44 (0) 1274 777700, fax: +44 (0) 1274 785200, e-mail: customerservices@mcb.co.uk, Web: www.emeraldinsight.com/tqm.htm.

Subscriptions: North America, $1799; Australasia, AUS$1999; Europe, euro 1849 plus VAT euro 161.79; UK and elsewhere, £1129 plus VAT £98.79.

This journal covers the quality gamut, including leadership and its importance in implementing a quality strategy, measuring quality and ROI, customer satisfaction and its link to profitability, getting management commitment to quality, preparing and launching a quality improvement program, integrating benchmarking and re-engineering with TQM, training for quality, people management, empowerment, and employee satisfaction.

Value Engineering and Management Digest
Published monthly by Tufty Communications Co., Hal Tufty, 3812 Livingston Street, NW, Washington, DC 20015, phone: 202 347-8998, fax: 202 543-6776, e-mail: htufty@capaccess.org, Web: NA.

Subscriptions: $180. Outside the U.S., add $15 for shipping.

Published since 1960, this publication is devoted primarily to Value Engineering—"the problem identifying and solving technique that achieves the required function at the best value"—and such spinoffs as Value Analysis and Value Management.

Value World
Published semiannually by SAVE International, 60 Revere Drive, Suite 500, Northbrook, IL 60062, phone: 847 480-1730, fax: 847 480-9282; e-mail: value@value-eng.org, Web: www.value-eng.org.

Subscriptions: Free to members (U.S., $63; Canada and Mexico, $75; other countries, $88).

This is the technical journal of this society, devoted to advancing and promoting the Value Methodology to improve quality and increase functions of products and services, while reducing project costs. It "provides a medium for contributors to express themselves professionally on advances in the state of the art."

General Business Periodicals That Include Coverage of Quality

Across the Board
Published bimonthly by The Conference Board, Inc., 845 Third Avenue, New York, NY 10022-6679, phone: 212 759-0900, fax: 212 980-7014, e-mail: atb@conference-board.org, Web: www.conference-board.org.

Subscriptions: Conference Board associates, $39; others, $59.

This general interest business magazine for all managers—"a magazine of ideas and opinion"—includes columns, commentaries, how-to and company profiles, and issue-related articles. Articles occasionally directly related to quality, but nearly all are indirectly related.

Business Ethics
Published bimonthly by Business Ethics Magazine, P.O. Box 8439, Minneapolis, MN 55408, phone: 612 879-0695, fax: 612 879-0699, e-mail: bizethics@aol.com, Web: www.business-ethics.com.

Subscriptions: U.S., $49; other countries, $59. (Discount for orders through Web site.)

The "Corporate Social Responsibility Report" focuses on topics of ethical and social concern to business, all of which are related to quality in one way or another. The articles go beyond theory and show how ethics and social responsibility play vital roles in business. There are occasionally articles specifically on quality management and its implementation in socially responsible organizations.

Business Horizons
Published bimonthly by Elsevier Science, Regional Sales Office, Customer Support Department, P.O. Box 945, New York, NY 10159-0945, phone: 212 633-3730 or 888 4ES-INFO (437-4636), fax: 212 633-3680, e-mail: usinfo-f@elsevier.com, Web: www.elsevier.com/inca/publications/store/6/2/0/2/1/4/index.htt.

Subscriptions: Individual: all countries outside of Europe except Japan, $96; Europe, euro 86; Japan, yen 11,400. Institutional: all countries outside of Europe except Japan, $269; Europe, euro 240; Japan, yen 31,800.

Produced by the Indiana University Graduate School of Business, this journal publishes articles of interest to academicians and practitioners of business. The articles range widely over many areas and emphasize significant issues and subjects, often with broad economic, social, or political implications. The articles regularly relate directly or indirectly to quality management.

California Management Review

Published quarterly by the University of California, F 501 Haas School of Business #1900, University of California, Berkeley, CA 94720-1900, phone: 510 642-7159, fax: 510 642-1318, e-mail: cmr@haas.berkeley.edu, Web: haas.berkeley.edu/cmr.

Subscriptions: U.S., Canada, and Mexico, $65 (individual) or $90 (institutional); elsewhere, $105.

This is a serious journal, but with a practical orientation, often including in-depth articles on management that are related directly or indirectly to TQM. It's intended to serve as "a vehicle of communication between those who study management and those who practice it."

Executive Excellence Magazine

Published monthly by Executive Excellence Publishing, 1366 East 1120 South, Provo, UT 84606-0637, phone: 800 304-9782 or 801 375-4060, fax: 801 377-5960, e-mail: info@eep.com, Web: www.eep.com/Merchant/executive.htm.

Subscriptions: U.S. and Canada, $129.

This publication is billed as "the leading monthly digest of the world's best value-centered, principle-based ideas and strategies for organizational and executive development." The articles are usually by well-known consultants and executives.

Harvard Business Review

Published monthly by the Harvard Business School Publishing, 60 Harvard Way, Box 230-5C, Boston, MA 02163, phone: 800 274-3214 or 617 495-6800, fax: 617 496-8145, e-mail: hbr_editorial@hbsp.harvard.edu or corpcustserv@hbsp.harvard.edu, Web: www.hbsp.harvard.edu/products/hbr/index.html.

Subscriptions: U.S., $118; Canada and Mexico, $128 (in Canada, includes 7% GST); all other countries, $165.

This journal presents in-depth articles on management techniques in all functional areas by "the leading business thinkers around the world." It often includes articles of direct or indirect relevance to those interested in quality.

Industry Week

Published 23 times a year by Penton Media, Inc. Editorial: Penton Media Building, 1300 E 9th Street, Cleveland, OH 44114, phone: 800 326-4146 or 216 696-7000, fax: 216 696-7670, e-mail: iwinfo@industryweek.com, Web: www.industryweek.com. Subscriptions: P.O. Box 901979, Cleveland, OH 44190-1979, phone: 216 931-9188, fax: 216 696-6413, e-mail: subscriptions@penton.com.

Subscriptions: Free to qualified applicants in the U.S. and Canada. Otherwise: U.S., $65; Canada, $85 (add 7% GST); all other countries, $105.

This magazine publishes articles, columns, and reviews of timely interest to managers, although the emphasis has recently been less on topics directly relating to quality management. It also tends to feature profiles of individual managers.

Organizational Dynamics

Published quarterly by Elsevier Science, Regional Sales Office, Customer Support Department, P.O. Box 945, New York, NY 10159-0945, phone: 212 633-3730 or 888 4ES-INFO (437-4636), fax: 212 633-3680, e-mail: usinfo-f@elsevier.com, Web: www.elsevier.com/inca/publications/store/6/2/1/0/4/5/index.htt.

Subscriptions: U.S., Canada, and Mexico, $74 (individual) or $85 (institutional). Other countries: check Web site.

This publication covers primarily organizational behavior and development and secondarily HRM and strategic management. The objective is to link research with management practice, to show how research findings can help deal more effectively with the dynamics of organizational life.

Sloan Management Review

Published quarterly by the MIT Sloan School of Management, Room E60-100, 77 Massachusetts Avenue, Cambridge, MA 02139-4307, phone: 617 253-7170, fax: 617 258-9739, e-mail: smr@mit.edu, Web: mitsloan.mit.edu/smr/index.html.

Subscriptions: U.S.: $89 (individual) or $148 (institutional). Canada: $99 (individual) or $192 (institutional). Elsewhere: $125 (individual) or $214 (institutional).

"The intellectual resource for the professional manager," this journal includes practical, yet thoughtful articles on a variety of issues of direct interest to managers. Articles often directly or indirectly relate to quality issues. There's a good book review section.

strategy+business

Published quarterly by Booz-Allen & Hamilton. Editorial: 101 Park Avenue, New York, NY 10178, phone: 888 557-5550 or 212 551-6673, fax: 212 551-6008, e-mail: editors@strategy-business.com, Web: www.strategy-busi-ness.com. Subscriptions: Subscriber Services Center, P.O. Box 548, Lewiston, NY 14092-0548, phone: 877 280-3001, 888 557-5550, or 203 341-7450, e-mail: service@SBsubscriber.com, Web: www.sbsubscriber.com/Services/Welcome.cfm.

Subscriptions: U.S., $38; elsewhere, $48.

The goal of this magazine is to present new ideas about the most important topics in business—such as knowledge management, brand-building, corporate structure, supply chain strategies, and complexity theory—and illustrate how all of these ideas can be used by today's global corporate leadership. The magazine features thoughtful articles and book reviews. The authors are prominent researchers, executives, and Booz-Allen consultants. It's done well and relevant to quality practitioners.

Strategy & Leadership
Published bimonthly by MCB University Press Ltd., 60/62 Toller Lane, Bradford, West Yorkshire, England BD8 9BY, phone: +44 (0) 1274 777700, fax: +44 (0) 1274 785200, e-mail: customerservices@mcb.co.uk, Web: www.emeraldinsight.com/sl.htm.

Subscriptions: North America, $239; Australasia, AUS$699; Europe, euro 449 plus VAT euro 39.29; UK and elsewhere, £269 plus VAT £23.54.

This magazine, formerly published by The Strategic Leadership Forum, focuses on strategies, long-range planning, and leadership.

Industry and Special-Interest Periodicals That Sometimes Cover Quality

Advanced Manufacturing
Published bimonthly by Clifford/Elliot Ltd., 209-3228 South Service Road, Burlington, ON, Canada L7N 3H8, phone: 905 634-2100, fax: 905 634-2238, e-mail: ew@advancedmanufacturing.com, Web: www.advancedmanufacturing.com.

Subscriptions: Free to qualified applicants in Canada.

This newsletter provides knowledge and insights about advanced manufacturing practices, techniques, and technologies, covering manufacturing theory, design engineering, automation systems, robotics, applied technology, research and development, quality control, supply chain management, and exporting and marketing.

APICS—The Performance Advantage
Published monthly by APICS—The Educational Society for Resource Management. Editorial: 5301 Shawnee Road, Alexandria, VA 22312-2317, phone: 800 444-APICS (2742) or 703 354-8851, fax: 703 354-8106, e-mail: editorial@apics-hq.org, Web: www.apics.org/magazine. Subscriptions: Group West Systems Ltd., 400 Franklin Street, Braintree, MA 02184-5535, phone: 781 380-0945, fax: 781 356-8577.

Subscriptions: Free to APICS members. Nonmembers: U.S., $65; Canada and Mexico, $77; elsewhere, $93.

This journal covers the latest manufacturing principles and practices, case studies, columns, and news. Articles are sometimes technical, as is appropriate for the target readers. The focus is on MRP/MRPO II, scheduling, warehousing, MES, inventory control, auto ID, supply chain management, materials management and handling, and production control. It often includes articles on quality management in its field.

Change: The Magazine of Higher Learning
Published bimonthly for the American Association for Higher Education by Heldref Publications, 1319 18th Street, NW, Washington, DC 20036-1802, phone: 202 296-6267 or 800 365-9753 (subscriptions), fax: 202 293-6130, e-mail: ch@heldref.org (managing editor) or subscribe@heldref.org, Web: www.heldref.org/html/body_chg.html.

Subscriptions: Free to AAHE members. Nonmembers: U.S., $48 (individual) and $97 (institutional); outside the U.S., add $15 for postage.

This publication addresses issues of interest to the administration of colleges and universities. It occasionally carries articles on quality management topics.

Data Strategies & Benchmarks
Published monthly by National Health Information, L.L.C., P.O. Box 15429, Atlanta, GA 30333-0429, phone: 800 597-6300 or 404 607-9500, fax: 404 607-0095, e-mail: nhinfo@aol.com, Web: www.nhionline.net/products/products.htm.

Subscriptions: $329.

Subtitled "The Monthly Advisory for Health Care Executives," this newsletter shows how to collect, analyze, format, distribute, and use data to compete under managed care.

Educational Leadership
Published eight times a year by the Association for Supervision and Curriculum Development, 1703 N. Beauregard Street, Alexandria, VA 22311-1714, phone: 800 933-ASCD (2723) or 703 578-9600, fax: 703 575-5400, e-mail: info@ascd.org, Web: www.ascd.org.

Subscriptions: Free to ASCD members. Nonmembers: $36.

This is a journal for educators and administrators that occasionally includes articles covering quality principles in teaching and administration.

Health Care Management Review
Published quarterly by Aspen Publishers, Inc., 200 Orchard Ridge Drive, Gaithersburg, MD 20878, phone: 800 234-1660 or 301 417-7500, fax: 800 901-9075 or 301 417-7550, e-mail: customer.service@aspenpubl.com, Web: www.aspenpublishers.com.

Subscriptions: $185.

This refereed journal addresses challenges and concerns facing health care managers—finance, marketing, labor relations, cost containment, antitrust laws, quality assurance, planning, technology, staff recruitment, and pay and benefits.

Health Forum Journal

Published bimonthly by Health Forum, Inc., 180 Montgomery Street, Suite 1520, San Francisco, CA 94104, phone: 415 248-8400, 800 821-2039, or 800 AHA-2626 (subscriptions), fax: 415 248-0400, e-mail: hfcustsvc@healthforum.com, Web: www.healthforum.com/hfj.

Subscriptions: U.S., $58; other countries, $78 ($110 by airmail).

This journal focuses on quality, innovation, and ethics and features editorial themes on topics like health promotion and prevention, integrated systems, and creating healthier communities.

Healthcare Executive

Published bimonthly by the American College of Healthcare Executives, 1 N. Franklin Street, Suite 1700, Chicago, IL 60606-3491, phone: 312 424-2800 or 312 424-9456 (subscriptions), fax: 312 424-0023, e-mail: HE-Editor@ache.org, Web: www.ache.org/PUBS/HCEXEC/overview.html.

Subscriptions: Free to ACHE members. Nonmembers: $70. (Outside the U.S., add $15 for postage.)

This is the official magazine of the American College of Healthcare Executives, aimed at health care managers. This journal regularly covers quality management issues. Each issue is devoted to a single, critical health care topic.

Hospitals & Health Networks

Published twice monthly by Health Forum, Inc., 180 Montgomery Street, Suite 1520, San Francisco, CA 94104, phone: 415 248-8400, 800 821-2039, or 800 AHA-2626 (subscriptions), fax: 415 248-0400, e-mail: hfcustsvc@healthforum.com, Web: www.hhnmag.com.

Subscriptions: Free to AHA members. Nonmembers: U.S., $80; other countries, $140.

"The management magazine for health care executives," this publication occasionally includes articles on quality management.

HR Focus

Published monthly by the Institute of Management and Administration, Subscription Department, 29 W. 35th Street, 5th Floor, New York, NY 10001-2299, phone: 800 401-5937 or 212 244-0360, fax: 212 564-0465, e-mail: subserv@ioma.com, Web: www.ioma.com.

Subscriptions: $259 (discount through Web site).

This periodical covers a variety of issues and news items of interest to HR managers, with occasional articles on quality subjects.

HRMagazine
Published monthly by the Society for Human Resource Management, 1800 Duke Street, Alexandria, VA 22314-3499, phone: 703 548-3440, fax: 703 535-6490, e-mail: hrmag@shrm.org, Web: www.shrm.org/hrmagazine.

Subscriptions: Free to members. Nonmembers: U.S., $70; other countries, $125.

Dedicated to human resource issues, this magazine carries articles related to quality management topics, such as training and teamwork on a fairly regular basis.

IIE Solutions
Published monthly by the Institute of Industrial Engineers, 25 Technology Park, Norcross, GA 30092-2988, phone: 800 494-0460 or 770 449-0460, fax: 770 441-3295, e-mail: cs@www.iienet.org, Web: 128.241.229.5/magazine.

Subscriptions: Free to IIE members. Nonmembers: U.S., $73; elsewhere, $94 (for airmail, add $72).

This is the official member publication of the IIE. While aimed at its members, it regularly includes articles that deal with issues related to quality management. It's written for engineers and managers responsible for reducing costs, increasing efficiencies, and boosting productivity.

Industrial Management
Published bimonthly by the Society for Engineering and Management Systems, Institute of Industrial Engineers, 25 Technology Park, Norcross, GA 30092-2988, phone: 800 494-0460 or 770 449-0460, fax: 770 441-3295, e-mail: cs@www.iienet.org, Web: www.iienet.org.

Subscriptions: Society for Engineering and Management Systems members: free. IIE members: $30.

This is a serious journal, with an academic bent. The articles cover management issues for engineers and sometimes include quality-oriented topics, such as worker motivation, work culture, strategic planning, and quality management systems.

Manufacturing Engineering
Published monthly by the Society of Manufacturing Engineers, 1 SME Drive, P.O. Box 930, Dearborn, MI 48121-0930, phone: 313 271-1500 or 800 733-4763 (subscriptions), fax: 313 271-2861, e-mail: service@sme.org, Web: www.sme.org.

Subscriptions: Free to SME members; articles available on the Web site.

This magazine provides some coverage of quality issues.

Performance Improvement
Published 10 times a year by the International Society for Performance

Improvement. Subscriptions: ISPI Online Book Store, 1400 Spring Street, Suite 260, Silver Spring, MD 20910, phone: 301 587-8570, fax: 301 587-8573, e-mail: info@ispi.org, Web: www.ispi.org.

Subscriptions: ISPI members: free. Nonmembers: $69.

    This journal is aimed at practitioners of human performance technology in the workplace. The articles are almost always practical and often directly or indirectly related to quality.

Performance Improvement Quarterly

Published quarterly by the International Society for Performance Improvement. Subscriptions: ISPI Online Book Store, 1400 Spring Street, Suite 260, Silver Spring, MD 20910, phone: 301 587-8570, fax: 301 587-8573, e-mail: info@ispi.org, Web: www.ispi.org.

Subscriptions: ISPI members: $40. Nonmembers: $50.

    This is a peer-reviewed journal created to stimulate professional discussion in the field and to advance the discipline of human performance technology through publishing scholarly works, literature reviews, and experimental studies with a scholarly base, and some case studies.

Real Healthcare

Published quarterly by the National Healthcare Cost and Quality Association, 11313 Weddington Street, First Floor, North Hollywood, CA 91601, phone: 888 761-3600, fax: 877 792-2329, e-mail: contact@realhealthcare.com, Web: www.realhealthcare.com.

Subscriptions: Free to members ($29).

    The official publication of the NHCQA (*CQ—The Quarterly Journal of Cost & Quality* until July 2001), this journal covers the legal, financial, and clinical issues that affect healthcare cost and healthcare quality.

Sales & Marketing Management

Published monthly by Bill Communications, Inc., 770 Broadway, New York, NY 10003-9595, phone: 646 654-7323 (editorial) or 646 654-7259 (customer service), fax: 646 654-7616 (editorial), e-mail: edit@salesandmarketing.com or service@salesandmarketing.com, Web: www.salesandmarketing.com/smmnew.

Subscriptions: U.S., $48; Canada, $67; elsewhere, $105.

    This magazine covers marketing and sales management issues, with an emphasis on technique, as well as on executive and company profiles. There are sometimes articles about developing and improving customer satisfaction.

The School Administrator

Published monthly by the American Association of School Administrators, 1801 N. Moore Street, Arlington, VA 22209-1813, phone: 703 528-0700, fax:

703 841-1543, e-mail: info@aasa.org, Web: www.aasa.org.

Subscriptions: Free to AASA members ($228).

Dedicated to the problems and opportunities of school administrators, this publication occasionally includes articles on quality in schools.

T+D

Published monthly by the American Society for Training and Development, 1640 King Street, Box 1443, Alexandria, VA 22313-2043, phone: 800 628-2783 or 703 683-8100, fax: 703 683-1523, e-mail: customercare@astd.org, Web: www.astd.org/virtual_community/td_magazine.

Subscriptions: ASTD members, $60. Nonmembers: U.S., $85; other countries, $165.

The focus of this magazine—formerly *Training & Development*—is training, human resources, performance, and management issues, with frequent coverage of quality management topics. It's a good resource for all areas of HR and people management, with lots of practical features, including book reviews and learning tools.

Target

Published quarterly by the Association for Manufacturing Excellence, 380 W. Palatine Road, Suite 7, Wheeling, IL 60090-5863, phone: 847 520-3282, fax: 847 520-0163, e-mail: info@ame.org, Web: www.ame.org.

Subscriptions: Free to AME members ($125).

This magazine includes many practical articles on quality initiatives in manufacturing and management to increase productivity. It also includes reports from regional chapters, book reviews, and an events calendar.

Training

Published monthly by Bill Communications, Inc., Human Resource Group, 50 S. Ninth Street, Minneapolis, MN 55402, phone: 800 707-7749 or 612 333-0471, fax: 612 333-6526, e-mail: edit@trainingmag.com or circwork@bill-com.com, Web: www.trainingmag.com.

Subscriptions: U.S., $78; Canada, $88 plus 7% GST *or* 15% HST; all other countries, $99.

This magazine includes articles on issues of interest to corporate trainers and managers in general, with frequent articles on quality management and training. The articles are practical, well-written, and of interest to all involved in quality management.

Calendar of Major Events, 2002

To help you plan for 2002, the following list provides information about some events of interest to professionals in areas of quality, with Web sites that you can check for details. Since we cannot include every event and since our publishing schedule requires that we gather information far in advance of the events, you might also want to visit the Web sites listed in our Directory of Quality Resource Organizations.

January

Workforce Excellence Network
4th Annual Journey to Performance Excellence
January 13-16, 2002
Orlando, FL
www.journey2002.net

The Conference Board
2002 Strategic Management Conference: "Ways to Improve Profits, Growth and Innovation in This Changing and Connected Economy"
January 16-17, 2002
New York, NY
www.conference-board.org

McMaster University, Michael G. DeGroote School of Business
23 Annual McMaster World Congress:
5th World Congress on the Management of Intellectual Capital
3rd World Congress on the Management of Electronic Commerce
January 16-18, 2002
Hamilton, ON, Canada
worldcongress.mcmaster.ca

Calendar of Major Events, 2002

Worldwide Quality Management Network (UK)
Institute of Directors (India)
12th World Congress on Total Quality (WCTQ 2002): "Business Excellence Models for Success in the 21st Century"
January 19-21, 2002
Mumbai, India
www.wwquality.com/wctq.htm

Measurement Science Conference Organization
2002 Measurement Science Conference: "Turning Measurement Science Information into Knowledge"
January 24-25, 2002
Anaheim, CA
www.msc-conf.com

American Society for Quality
2nd Six Sigma Conference: "Delivering Organizational Value"
January 27-29, 2002
Tampa, FL
sixsigma.asq.org

American Institute of Aeronautics and Astronautics
ASQ Electronics and Communications Division
ASQ Reliability Division
IEEE Reliability Society
IEST Quality Control, Evaluation and Product Reliability Divisions
IIE Quality Control and Reliability Engineering Division
Society of Automotive Engineers—Reliability Division
Society of Logistics Engineers
Society of Reliability Engineers
Systems Safety Society
48th Annual Reliability and Maintainability Symposium: "Beyond 2001—The Reliability and Maintainability Odyssey Continues"
January 28-31, 2002
Seattle, WA
www.rams.org

International Quality & Productivity Center
HR Measurement 2002: "Defining, Measuring, and Improving Human Resources Management"
January 29-February 1, 2002
Orlando, FL
www.iqpc.com

American Health Quality Association
2002 Technical Conference: "The Changing Face of Health Care"
January 29-February 3, 2002
Dallas, TX
www.ahqa.org

February

American Society for Training and Development
TechKnowledge® 2002 Conference and Exposition
February 4-7, 2002
Las Vegas, NV
www.astd.org

Institute for International Research, USA
Braintrust 2002: The Fourth Annual Knowledge Management World
    Summit: "Putting Knowledge to Work"
February 10-13, 2002
San Francisco, CA
www.iirusa.com/braintrust

Freeman International
Customer Care 2002
February 11-13, 2002
Ottawa, ON, Canada
www.execcongress.com/customercare

ASQ Quality Audit Division
11th Annual Quality Auditor Conference
February 11-14, 2002
St. Louis, MO
www.asqquality.org/Divisions/qad/qad.html

Software Quality Engineering
Applications of Software Measurement Conference (ASM 2002): "Measuring
    and Improving Software Quality and Productivity"
February 11-15, 2002
Anaheim, CA
www.sqe.com/asm

The International Society of Agile Manufacturing
The International Society for Productivity Enhancement
International Conference on Supply Chain Management
February 13-15, 2002

Lafayette, LA
www.ucs.louisiana.edu/~snd7483/ISAM2.html

American Society for Quality, Quality Audit Division
11th Annual Quality Audit Conference: "2001 Audit Odyssey"
February 14-15, 2002
St. Louis, MO
www.asqquality.org/Divisions/qad/qad.html

VNU Business Media
Training 2002 Conference and Expo
February 18-20, 2002
Atlanta, GA
www.vnulearning.com

Monash University, Faculty of Business and Economics, Department of Management
6th International Research Conference on Quality, Innovation and Knowledge Management: "Convergence in the Digital Economy"
February 18-20, 2002
Kuala Lumpur, Malaysia
www.monash.edu.au/oce/qikconference

The W. Edwards Deming Institute
Research Seminar
February 19-20, 2002
New York, NY
www.deming.org/calendar

Society for Consumer Psychology
9th Annual Winter Conference 2002
February 21-23, 2002
Austin, TX
fisher.osu.edu/marketing/scp

European Quality Institute, Inc.
10th Annual International Conference on ISO 9000 and Related Standards
February 25-27, 2002
Las Vegas, NV
www.iso9000directory.com

American Society for Quality, Quality Management Division
14th Annual Quality Management Conference: "The Changing Face of Quality"

February 25-March 1, 2002
New Orleans, LA
www.asq-qmd.org

The Conference Board
2002 Strategic Management Conference: "Ways to Improve Profits, Growth and Innovation in This Changing and Connected Economy"
February 27-28, 2002
Marina Del Rey, CA
www.conference-board.org

The Conference Board
2002 Customer Relationship Management Conference: "Gaining Competitive Advantage Through an Integrated Enterprise-Wide Customer Focus"
February 27-28, 2002
New York, NY
www.conference-board.org

The Conference Board
2002 Organization of the Future Conference: "From Ownership to Strategic Purpose"
February 28-March 1, 2002
New York, NY
www.conference-board.org

March

American Society for Quality, Aviation/Space and Defense Division
Conference on Quality in the Space and Defense Industries (COSDI 2002)
March 4-5, 2002
Cape Canaveral, FL
www.asdnet.org/cqsdi

Software Dimensions
International Institute for Software Testing
10th International Conference on Practical Software Quality Techniques
4th International Conference on Practical Software Testing Techniques (PSQT/PSTT 2002 South)
March 4-8, 2002
New Orleans, LA
www.softdim.com/psqt2002South

Water Quality Association
Convention and Exhibition
March 5-9, 2002

New Orleans, LA
www.wqa.org

International Association for Management of Technology
11th International Conference on Management of Technology
March 10-14, 2002
Miami Beach, FL
www.iamot.org/IAMOT2002

Association for Quality and Participation
24th Annual Spring Conference on Teams in the Workplace: "Thriving Through Teamwork"
March 11-13, 2002
Las Vegas, NV
www.aqp.org

Italian National Research Council
University Consortium in Quality Engineering
5th International Conference on "Achieving Quality In Software" (AQuIS 2002)
March 11-13, 2002
Venice, Italy
www.iei.pi.cnr.it/AQUIS2002/index.html

Institute of Electrical and Electronics Engineers, Inc., Computer Society
University of Szeged
The Case Consult Group
6th European Conference on Software Maintenance and Reengineering
March 11-13, 2002
Budapest, Hungary
rgai.inf.u-szeged.hu/CSMR2002

Institute of Industrial Engineers
5th Annual Applied Ergonomics Conference
March 11-14, 2002
Baltimore, MD
www.iienet.org

Software Research Institute
Quality Week Europe (QWE2002): 5th International Internet & Software Quality Week Europe Conference
March 11-15, 2002
Brussels, Belgium
www.soft.com/QualWeek/QWE2002

American Society for Quality
American Society for Quality, Energy and Environmental Division
9th Annual ISO 9000/ISO 14000 Conference: "Standards for Business Results"
March 12-15, 2002
Indianapolis, IN
www.asq.org/ed/conferences/iso9000_iso14000

Society of Consumer Affairs Professionals in Business
2002 SOCAP Symposium
March 17-20, 2002
New York, NY
www.socap.org

Institute of Electrical and Electronics Engineers, Inc.
3rd International Symposium on Quality Electronic Design (IEEE 2002)
March 18-20, 2002
San Jose, CA
www.isqed.org

American Society for Nondestructive Testing, Inc.
Spring Conference and 11th Annual Research Symposium
March 18-22, 2002
Portland, OR
www.asnt.org

Institut de Sûreté de Fonctionnement, Nanterre, France
European Safety and Reliability Association
European Safety and Reliability Conference (ESREL 2002): "Safety and Reliability: Facilitating Decision Making and Risk Management"
March 19-21, 2002
Lyon, France
www-assoc.frec.bull.fr/isdf/lm13/index-a.htm

Institute for Healthcare Improvement
British Medical Journal
7th Annual European Forum on Quality Improvement in Health Care
March 21-23, 2002
Edinburgh, Scotland
www.quality.bmjpg.com

April

Centre for Management Quality Research at RMIT University
7th International Conference on ISO 9000 and TQM (7-ICIT): "Change Management"
April 2-4, 2002
Melbourne, Australia
www.hkbu.edu.hk/~samho/7icit.htm

Natural and Artificial Intelligence Systems Organization
3rd World Manufacturing Congress
April 2-5, 2002
Rochester, NY
www.icsc.ab.ca

Imark Communications
Collaborative Commerce and Integration Conference and Expo: Leveraging the Value Chain
April 3-5, 2002
Chicago, IL
www.cciexpo.com/cci/index.htm

Athens Laboratory of Business Administration
3rd European Conference on Organizational Knowledge, Learning, and Capabilities (OKLC 2002)
April 5-6, 2002
Athens, Greece
www.alba.edu.gr/2002OKLC

National Institute of Standards and Technology
Quest for Excellence XIV Conference (Malcolm Baldrige National Quality Award)
April 7-10, 2002
Washington, DC
www.quality.nist.gov/Quest_for_Excellence.htm

Institute of Industrial Engineers
Simulation Solutions 2002 Conference
April 7-10, 2002
San Diego, CA
www.iienet.org

Utah State University, College of Business
14th Annual Conference and Awards Ceremony: Shingo Prize for Excellence in Manufacturing

April 8-12, 2002
Covington, KY
www.shingoprize.org

Penton Media, Inc.
Supply Chain Expo 2002
April 16-18, 2002
Rosemont, IL
www.supplychainexpo.com

North American QFD Institute
International Council for QFD
1st National Symposium on Quality Function Deployment
April 17-19, 2002
Izmir, Turkey
tusec.deu.edu.tr/qfd2002

European Association of Research and Technology Organisations
2002 Annual Conference
April 18-19, 2002
Graz, Austria
www.earto.org

American Society for Quality
13th Annual Koalaty Kid International Conference
April 20-23, 2002
Schaumburg, IL
www.koalatykid.org/conference.asp

International Society for Performance Improvement
40th Annual International Performance Improvement Conference & Expo: "Pathways to Performance"
April 21-25, 2002
Dallas, TX
www.ispi.org

Quality Assurance Institute
International Conference on Effective Methods for IT Quality
April 22-26, 2002
Orlando, FL
www.qaiusa.com/conferences/april2002/index.html

Society of Manufacturing Engineers
Rapid Prototyping & Manufacturing 2002 Exposition

Cincinnati, OH
April 29-May 2, 2002
www.sme.org

May

SAVE International
42nd Annual Conference: "Engineer Change to Elevate Value"
May 5-8, 2002
Denver, CO
www.value-eng.org/conference/conference.htm

Maintenance and Reliability Center
MARCON 2002: "Moving Forward Toward Excellence"
May 5-8, 2002
Knoxville, TN
www.engr.utk.edu/mrc/marcon.html

National Association of Purchasing Management
87th Annual International Supply Management Conference and Educational Exhibit
May 5-8, 2002
San Francisco, CA
www.napm.org/conferences/conferences.cfm

Centre for Research on Transportation
Optimization Days 2002
May 6-8, 2002
Montreal, QC, Canada
www.crt.umontreal.ca/jopt2002

Oak Ridge Metrology Center
Oak Ridge Centers for Manufacturing Technology
Quality Magazine
NCSL—International
Metrology Automation Association
4th Annual International Dimensional Workshop and Exhibition: "Dimensional Metrology—Standards and Accreditation—Their Impact" (IDW2002)
May 6-9, 2002
Knoxville, TN
www.qualitymag.com/idw

American Automatic Control Council
2002 American Control Conference

May 8-10, 2002
Anchorage, AK
www.ent.ohiou.edu/~acc2002

Technical Committee on Communications Quality & Reliability, IEEE Communications Society
2002 International Workshop (CQR 2002)
May 14-16, 2002
Okinawa, Japan
www.ieice.org/cs/cq/CQR2002

Institute of Electrical and Electronics Engineers, Inc., Instrumentation and Measurement Society
International Symposium on Virtual and Intelligent Measurement Systems (VIMS 2002)
May 19-20, 2002
Anchorage, AK
www.ewh.ieee.org/soc/im/vims/vimscur/index.html

Institute of Industrial Engineers
IIE Annual Conference 2002
May 19-22, 2002
Orlando, FL
www.iienet.org

American Society for Quality
56th Annual Quality Congress and Exposition
May 20-22, 2002
Denver, CO
www.asq.org/ed/conferences/aqc

Institute of Electrical and Electronics Engineers, Inc., Instrumentation and Measurement Society
Instrumentation and Measurement Technology Conference (IMTC 2002)
May 21-23, 2002
Anchorage, AK
www.ewh.ieee.org/soc/im/imtc

Center for the Study of Work Teams
10th Annual Symposium on Collaborative Work Systems
May 22-24, 2002
Denton, TX
www.workteams.unt.edu

Allgemeine Unfallversicherungsanstalt (Austrian Workers' Compensation Board)
Hauptverband der österreichischen Sozialversicherungsträger (Federation of Austrian Social Security Institutions)
International Social Security Association
International Labour Office
XVIth World Congress on Safety and Health at Work
May 26-31, 2002
Vienna, Austria
www.safety2002.at/page.asp/index.htm

June

Society of Consumer Affairs Professionals in Business
7th Annual Technology Forum
June 2002
Minneapolis, MN
www.socap.org

European Operations Management Association
9th International Annual Conference: "Operations Management and the New Economy"
June 2-4, 2002
Copenhagen, Denmark
www.cbs.dk/euroma2002

American Society for Training and Development
International Conference and Exposition
June 2-6, 2002
New Orleans, LA
www.astd.org/virtual_community

European Federation of National Maintenance Societies
Euromaintenance: 16th International Maintenance Congress
June 3-5, 2002
Helsinki, Finland
www.kunnossapito.fi/em2002/em-home.htm

International Project Management Association
16th World Congress on Project Management
June 4-6, 2002
Berlin, Germany
www.worldcongress.de

Institute of Electrical and Electronics Engineers, Inc., Computer Society
Metrics 2002: 8th International Software Metrics Symposium
June 4-7, 2002
Ottawa, ON, Canada
www.software-metrics.org

American Management Association
Top Management Forum
June 6-7, 2002
London, United Kingdom
www.amanet.org

American Society of Safety Engineers
Professional Development Conference and Exposition: Advancing the EH&S Profession
June 9-12, 2002
Nashville, TN
www.asse.org

Center for Excellence Finland
European Organization for Quality—Software Group
Quality Connection: 7th European Conference on Software Quality
June 9-12, 2002
Helsinki, Finland
www.qualityconnection.org

Reed Exhibition Companies
Quality Detroit Expo
June 12-13, 2002
Novi, MI
www.quality.reedexpo.com

American Statistical Association, Quality and Productivity Section
2002 Quality and Productivity Research Conference
June 12-14, 2002
Morristown, NJ
web.utk.edu/~asaqp

Bureau International des Poids et Mesures
IEEE Instrumentation and Measurement Society
National Institute of Standards and Technology (USA)
National Research Council of Canada
Union Radio Scientifique Internationale
2002 Conference on Precision Electromagnetic Measurements (CPEM 2002)
June 16-21, 2002

Ottawa, ON, Canada
www.nrc.ca/confserv/cpem02

International Statistical Institute, Committee for Statistics in Business and Industry
3rd International Conference on Mathematical Methods in Reliability: Methodology and Practice (MMR 2002)
June 17-20, 2002
Trondheim, Norway
www.math.ntnu.no/mmr2002

Asociación Española de Ensayos Non Destructivos (Spanish Association for Nondestructive Tests)
European Federation for Non-Destructive Testing
8th European Conference for Nondestructive Testing
June 17-21, 2002
Barcelona, Spain
www.aend.org/congresos/ingles.html

PMI France Sud
Marlow Events
PMI Europe 2002: The Project Management Festival (5th European Project Management Conference)
June 19-20, 2002
Cannes, France
www.pmieurope2002.com

International Institute of Forecasters
22nd International Symposium on Forecasting (ISF 2002)
June 23-26, 2002
Dublin, Ireland
www.isf2002.org

Society for Human Resource Management
54th Annual Conference and Exposition
June 23-26, 2002
Philadelphia, PA
www.shrm.org/conferences/annual

Air & Waste Management Association
95th Annual Conference and Exhibition
June 23-27, 2002
Baltimore, MD
www.awma.org/ACE2002

University of Verona, Faculty of Economics, Department of Financial, Industrial and Technological Studies
7th World Congress for Total Quality Management
June 25-27, 2002
Verona, Italy
www.tqmworldcongress.org

Gaziantep University
Nottingham University
2nd International Conference on Responsive Manufacturing
June 26-28, 2002
Gaziantep, Turkey
www1.gantep.edu.tr/~rmc2002

July

Business Information Systems, University College Cork
Laboratoire d'Informatique de Paris 6 (Université Pierre et Marie Curie and CNRS)
International Federation for Information Processing
International Conference on Decision Making and Decision Support in the Internet Age (DSI-Age 2002)
July 4-7, 2002
Cork, Ireland
afis.ucc.ie/DSIAge2002

National Society of Professional Engineers
Annual Convention & Exposition: NSPE 2002
July 11-16, 2002
Orlando, FL
www.nspe.org

National Contract Management Association
World Congress 2002
July 22-24, 2002
Long Beach, CA
www.ncmahq.org/calendar/WC02/WC02.html

Association for Computing Machinery, Special Interest Group on Software Engineering (SIGSOFT)
International Symposium on Software Testing and Analysis (ISSTA 2002)
July 22-24, 2002
Rome, Italy
galileo.iei.pi.cnr.it/issta2002

Association for Computing Machinery, Sigmetrics and Special Interest Group on Software Engineering (SIGSOFT)
3rd International Workshop on Software and Performance (WOSP 2002)
July 24-26, 2002
Rome, Italy
univaq.it/~wosp02

International Society for Productivity Enhancement
International Institute of Concurrent Engineering
9th ISPE International Conference on Concurrent Engineering: Research and Applications (ISPE/CE2002)
July 27-31, 2002
Cranfield, Bedford, United Kingdom
www.ceconf.com/ce2002/home.htm

International Council on Systems Engineering
12th International Symposium (INCOSE 2002): "Engineering 21st Century Systems: Problem Solving Through Structured Thinking"
July 28-August 1, 2002
Las Vegas, NV
www.incose.org/symp2002

Atlas Conferences, Inc.
5th International Conference on Managing Innovative Manufacturing (MIM 2002): "e-Manufacturing and e-Business Integration"
July 29-31, 2002
Milwaukee, WI
www.uwm.edu/CEAS/ims/MIM2002/index.htm

College of Engineering, Nanyang Technological University, Singapore
Society of Project Management, Japan
International Conference on Project Management (ProMAC 2002): "Breakthrough with Project Management
July 31-August 2, 2002
Singapore
www.ntu.edu.sg/MPE/ProMAC2002

August
Association for Work Process Improvement
TAWPI Work Process 2002: 32nd Annual Forum and Exposition
August 4-7, 2002
Chicago, IL
www.tawpi.org

NCSL international (National Conference of Standards Laboratories)
Annual Workshop and Symposium
August 4-8, 2002
San Diego, CA
www.ncslinternational.org/conference

International Society of Science and Applied Technologies
International Conference on Quality and Reliability in Design
August 7-9, 2002
Anaheim, CA
www.rci.rutgers.edu/~hopham/ISSAT/opening.htm

Standards Engineering Society
Annual Conference
August 12-13, 2002
Pittsburgh, PA
www.ses-standards.org

September

QFD Institut Deutschland (German QFD Institute)
8th International Symposium on Quality Function Deployment
September 4-6, 2002
Munich, Germany
www.qfd-id.de/veranstaltungen/international/isqfd02_e.html

Society for Manufacturing Engineers
Association for Manufacturing Technology
International Manufacturing Technology Show 2002
September 4-11, 2002
Chicago, IL
www.sme.org

Penton Media, Inc.
Supply Chain and Logistics Conference and Exhibition
September 10-12, 2002
Atlanta, GA
www.SupplyChainLogistics.com

Asia Pacific Quality Organization
8th APQO Conference
September 2002
Beijing, China
www.qil.com/apqo

International Accreditation Forum, Inc.
Annual Meeting
September 15-21, 2002
Berlin, Germany
www.iaf.nu

ERP Environment
Business Strategy and the Environment Conference
September 16-17, 2002
location TBD
www.erpenvironment.org/conferences/conferences.html

American Health Quality Association
2002 Annual Session and House of Delegates Meeting
September 18-21, 2002
New York, NY
www.ahqa.org

National Association for Healthcare Quality
27th Annual Educational Conference Information
September 22-25, 2002
Nashville, TN
www.nahq.org/conference

International Customer Service Association
ICSAnet 2002: Customer Service Networking, Education and Technology
September 22-25, 2002
Chicago, IL
www.icsa.com/public/conference

American Society for Quality, Aviation/Space and Defense Division
Conference on Quality in Commercial Aviation
September 22-25, 2002
Dallas, TX
www.asdnet.org/cqca

American Society for Quality, Service Quality Division
11th Annual Service Quality Conference
September 23-24, 2002
Las Vegas, NV
www.asq-sqd.com

Center for the Study of Work Teams
13th Annual International Conference on Work Teams: "Theme: Leveraging Team Performance for Business Results"

September 23-25, 2002
Dallas, TX
www.workteams.unt.edu

VNU Business Media
Performance Support 2002 Conference and Expo
September 23-25, 2002
Anaheim, CA
www.vnulearning.com

Human Factors and Ergonomics Society
46th Annual Meeting
September 23-27, 2002
Pittsburgh, PA
hfes.org

Institute of Quality Assurance
46th European Organization for Quality Congress: "New Times, New Horizons, New Business"
September 29-October 2, 2002
Harrogate, Yorkshire, United Kingdom
www.iqa.org/q2002

October

American Society for Quality, Software Division
12th International Conference on Software Quality: "Managing for Software Quality and Service Quality"
October 2002
Ottawa, ON, Canada
www.icsq.org or www.asq-software.org

National Safety Council
90th Annual Congress & Expo
October 7-9, 2002
San Diego, CA
www.nsc.org

The W. Edwards Deming Institute
Fall Conference 2002
October 12-13, 2002
Washington DC
www.deming.org/calendar

Australian Organisation for Quality
QUALCON 2002: "Quality Beyond the Enterprise"
October 13-16, 2002
Perth, Australia
www.qualcon.com.au

Institute of Electrical and Electronics Engineers, Inc., Industry Applications Society
37th Annual Meeting
October 13-18, 2002
Pittsburgh, PA
www.ewh.ieee.org/soc/ias/ias2002

Hungarian Chemical Society
Hungarian Scientific Society of Measurements, Automation and Informatics
1st International Conference on Environmental Measurements
October 14-18, 2002
Budapest, Hungary
www.imeko2002.mtesz.hu

BetterManagement.com
2002 BetterManagement LIVE Conference: Performance Management and Business Analytic Solutions
October 16-18, 2002
Las Vegas, NV
www.bettermanagement.com/events

ISA—Instrumentation, Systems, and Automation Society
ISA 2002: Instrumentation, Systems, and Automation Conference and Exhibition
October 21-24, 2002
Chicago, IL
www.isa.org/events

Quality Assurance Institute
22nd Annual Software Testing Conference
October 21-25, 2002
Orlando, FL
www.qaiusa.com/conferences/index.html

Society for Maintenance & Reliability Professionals
10th Annual SMRP Conference
October 27-30, 2002
Nashville, TN
www.smrp.org/events

APICS—The Educational Society for Resource Management
International Conference and Exposition
October 27-30, 2002
Nashville, TN
www.apics.org

IEEE Technical Council on Software Engineering
Reengineering Forum
9th Working Conference on Reverse Engineering (WCRE 2002)
October 28, 2002 (tentative)
Richmond, VA
reengineer.org

Korean Standards Association, Korea
Linköping University, Sweden
Pusan International Conference on Quality Management and Organizational Development (QMOD 2002)
October 29-31, 2002
Pusan, Korea
www.ksa.or.kr/english/aboard/ekongji1.htm

November

American Society for Nondestructive Testing, Inc.
Fall Conference and Quality Testing Show
November 4-8, 2002
San Diego, CA
www.asnt.org

Association for Manufacturing Excellence
18th Annual Conference
November 4-8, 2002
Chicago, IL
www.ame.org

National Association of Industrial Technology
2002 Convention
November 6-9, 2002
Panama City, FL
www.nait.org

MIT Total Data Quality Management Program
7th International Conference on Information Quality (IQ-2002)
November 8-10, 2002

Cambridge, MA
web.mit.edu/tdqm/www/iqc/02.html

Decision Sciences Institute
33rd Annual Meeting
November 23-26, 2002
San Diego, CA
www.decisionsciences.org

December

Institute for Healthcare Improvement
13th Annual National Forum on Quality Improvement in Health Care
December 8-11, 2002
Orlando, FL
www.ihi.org

Institute of Electrical and Electronics Engineers, Inc., Control Systems Society
41st IEEE Conference on Decision and Control
December 10-13, 2002
Las Vegas, NV
www.eecs.tulane.edu/cdc02

Index

A
ABB Industry, 76-77
Aberdeen Group, 518
Abraham, May, quoted, 372
Accounting, cases and practices, 522-528
Ace Hardware, social capital and virtual communities in, 506-507
Acree, Dee, quoted, 16, 17, 18, 19
Activity-based costing, 361-363
Alexander, John, quoted, 446
AlliedSignal, Six Sigma at, 416-423
American Greetings, 232, 233
Anderson, Kristin, on customer relationship management, 151-159
Argyris, Chris, ideas of, 215-216
ARPANET, 502
Arthur Andersen, leadership training at, 198-199
Auditore, Peter J., quoted, 511
Automotive industry, role of quality in, 96-102

B
Babicz, Gillian, on gages, 378-382
Bainbridge, Alan, on intellectual capital, 171-181
Bair, Tracy, quoted, 519
Baker, Wayne, 498-499
Balanced scorecard, as fad, 22-23
Balanced scorecards, 390-391
Baldrige Award
  cases and practices, 529-583
  relevance of, 572-583
Barnes, Frank C., on ISO 9000, 551-563
Barnett, Shirley, role of discount cards, 293-307
Bartholomew, Doug, on cost vs. quality, 96-102
Bastin, Norm, quoted, 452
Bell Atlantic, value of teams to, 329-338
Bellman, Geoffrey, quoted, 15, 17, 18, 20, 21, 22
Benchmarking;
  customer satisfaction, 266-268, 274-275
  general, 402, 522-528
Bender, David, quoted, 256, 257
Berutti, Bill, quoted, 440-441
Best practices, 198, 522-528
Bibliography
  customer expectations, 147-150
  service quality, 128-129
Bienvenue, Ron, quoted, 513
Bilger, Mike, quoted, 289
Blanchard, Ken, and *One Minute Manager*, 17-18
Blue Cross Blue Shield of North Carolina (BCBSNC), knowledge management at, 370-377
Bogaski, Linda, quoted, 379, 380, 381-382
Bonner, Dede, quoted, 311
Bonsignore, Michael R., quoted, 417
Booze-Allen & Hamilton, knowledge management at, 470-472
Bowden, Larry, quoted, 516, 518
Bridgestone/Firestone, Ford and, 96-102
Brown, Jane C., on ISO 9000, 535-550
Brown, Richard, quoted, 554
Brunsting, Mike, quoted, 518
Buckman Laboratories, teaming at, 309
Bukowitz, Wendi, quoted, 310
Bullinger, Nick, building solutions-based organizations, 280-288
Butler, Ava S., on developing e-business, 443-450

C

Calhoun, David, 196
Calibration, gages and, 378-382
Capital projects, on managing, 67-73
Capone, Russ, quoted, 372
Capshaw, Stacie, quoted, 256, 258, 259, 260-261
Caterpillar, Inc., invests in Six Sigma training, 100
Cavanagh, Dan, 100
Chatterjee, Sangit, on Six Sigma, 424-437
Chemical industry, managing capital projects in, 67-73
Cherry, Rick, quote, 576
Christiansen, Chris, on data security, 289
Cisco, Susan L., on value added information chains, 461-477
Ciurczak, Bob, quoted, 444, 446, 447
Clark, Brian, on just-in-time delivery, 478-484
Clark, Linda
    quoted, 511-512
    ideas of, 514
Clark, Tim, quoted, 453
Cohen, Don, 498-499
Coker, Jim, on logistics, 494-497
Cook, Robin, how to change cultures, 231-234
Conferences and events 2002, 660-681
Costello, Daniel, on role of infomediaries, 256-261
Cothrel, Joseph, virtuality and social capital, 498-510
Covey, Stephen, ideas of, 19-20
CQI, case study, 38-54
Crafford, Ken, quoted, 452
Crosby, Philip B., on Quality Management Maturity Grid, 3-13
Cross, Rob, alternatives to teams, 315-328
Crowley, John, quoted, 456
Cultural transformation, cases and practices, 213-234
Culture
    empowerment in, 213-230
    how to change, 231-234
Customer expectations, managing, 130-150
Customer knowledge communities (CKC), described, 247
Customers
    expectations of, managing, 130-150
    keeping confidential data about, 289-292
    managing relationships with, 151-159
    retention of, 298
    satisfaction programs, 262-279, 346-349
    voice of, cases and practices, 262-307
    Web sites for, 456-460

D

DaimlerChrysler AG, cost of quality, 96-102
Dale, B.G., on resistance to quality, 26-37
Davenport, Dave, quoted, 445
Davis, Mark, how to define an organization, 163-170
Dell Computer, 233
Delivery, just-in-time, 478-484
Deming, W. Edwards
    role in quality, 15-16
    Six Sigma and, 424-437
Dick, Gavin, on ISO 9000, 535-550
Dingell, John, 97
Discount cards, effect on customer relations, 293-307
Dock-to-shop, described, 478-484
Dominguez, Linda, quoted, 17, 23, 25
Donofrio, Angelo M., on creating Web sites, 456-460
Dorfman, Peter, on negative knowledge management practices, 249-255
Dow Corning, knowledge management at, 473-474
Downing, Carole, quoted, 23
Doyle, Tim, quoted, 580, 582
Drucker, Peter, quoted, 151
Dutch Shell, 201-202
Duvall, Steve, partnering in manufacturing, 103-115

E

Eastern Corporate Federal Credit Union, case study, 292
e-Commerce, cases and practices, 438-460
Economic order quantity (EOQ), optimizing, 485-493
Edvardsson, Bo., on satisfaction and loyalty, 116-130
eLab, 232

INDEX

Ellis, Kristine, KM and teamwork, 308-314; on managerial fads, 14-25
Emotional intelligence, as fad, 24-25
Employees, role in customer satisfaction programs, 268-269
Empowerment, why hard to achieve, 213-230
Enterprise portal, status of, 511-521
Enterprise Rent-A-Car, knowledge management at, 252-254
Events 2002, calendar of, 660-681
Expectations, customer, how to manage, 130-150

F
Fads, managerial, 14-25
Feist, Hollace A., value of teams, 329-338
Field, Anne, on starting net markets, 451-455
Finance, cases and practices, 522-528
Fiorina, Carly, 199
Fisher, Larry, quoted, 17, 18, 20, 21, 22, 23
Focus groups, limits of, 339-341
Fontanella, John, quoted, 439
Ford, Jr., William, quoted, 186
Ford Motor Company
    cost of quality, 96-102
    leadership development in, 185-195
Forecasting, 496
Franco, Vanessa R., on quality manager's guide to the Internet, 623-628
Friedman, Stewart D., on leadership development at Ford Motor Co., 185-195
Fuad, Turodrique, quoted, 458
Fulmer, Robert M., on developing leaders, 196-212
Functional processes, cases and practices, 461-528

G
Gages, knowing what they measure, 378-382
Gallimore, Kevin, on ISO 9000, 535-550
Gardner, Robert A., resolving process paradox, 355-369
General Electric, sources of leaders, 196, 204-205, 206-207, 210
General Motors, has loyalty program, 126
Ghoshal, Sumantra, on social capital, 499-500
Gibbs, Philip A., on developing leaders, 196-212
Gilmore, James H., on limits of focus groups, 339-341
Goldsmith, Marshall, on developing leaders, 196-212
Goleman, Daniel, on emotional intelligence, 24-25
Gonzales, Jean, quoted, 448
Grant, Tom, 194
Gray, Van, improving production line performance, 85-95
Green, Robert, on Six Sigma at Honeywell, 416-423
Growth, effects of satisfaction and loyalty on, 116-130
Gryna, Frank M., on market research, 342-354
GSD&M, 232, 233
Gulia, Milena, quoted, 499
Gustafsson, Anders, satisfaction and loyalty, 116-130

G
Hall, Kathleen, quoted, 516
Hall, Robert W., on Toyota production system, 57-66
Handling, within processes, 396-403
Happelmann, James, Quoted, 438, 439
Harley-Davidson,
    and CRM success factors 158-159
    self-managed teams at, 103-115
    work performance processes at, 103-115
Harrison, John, clock maker's story, 313
Harrison, Sheilah, on just-in-time delivery, 478-484
Hauschild, Susanne, on creating knowledge culture, 235-243
Herman, Matthew, quoted, 458
Herman Miller, Inc., 515-516
Herkstrater, Cor, 201
Hewlett-Packard, 199-200, 207
Hild, Cheryl, on using process improvement and Six Sigma, 404-415
Hoare, Rohan, on managing capital projects, 67-73
Hogan, Joseph, 196
Honeywell, Six Sigma at, 416-423
Horner, Ralph, quoted, 373
Horvath, Joseph, quoted, 257, 258
Hutchins, Greg, on quality auditing, 564-571

I

IBM, knowledge management, 247
Immelt, Jeffrey, 196
Infomediaries, role of, 256-261
Information,
    role in employee empowerment, 223-224
    on shop floors, 74-84
    value chains of, 461-477
Information Technology, cases and practices, 498-521
Integral Document Management (IDM), described, 469-470
Intellectual capital, as strategic tool, 171-181
Internet
    cases and practices, 438-460
    manager's guide to, 623-628
    quality resources, directory, 607-622
ISO 9000, cases and practices, 529-583

J

Jackson, Jr., Donald W., on implementing customer satisfaction programs, 262-279
Jackson, Michael, and auto safety, 97, 99
Jacobsen, Kristine, on intellectual capital, 171-181
Johnson & Johnson, 205
Johnson, Darrell, on knowledge management, 252
Johnson, Michael D., on satisfaction and loyalty, 116-130
Johnson, Spencer, role of, 17-18
Jones, Lee, on perceptions of quality, 38-54
Journals focusing on quality, directory of, 629-659

K

Kaplan, Robert, on balanced scorecards, 22-23
Kasvi, Jyrki J.J., on performance support on shop floor, 74-84
Kay, Emily, how people operate, 370-377
Kelly, Glenn, quoted, 520-521
Kenmar Corporation, customer feedback at, 265-266
Kerr, Carol, on customer relationship management, 151-159
Kimball, Lisa, 509
Kirk, Christine, on outsourcing processes, 383-389

Knowledge management (KM)
    bad practices, 249-255
    building culture of, 235-243
    cases and practices, 235-261
    enterprise portal and, 511-521
    how people operate and, 370-377
    social capital and, 498-510
    value added information chains, 461-477
    voice of the customer, 244-248

L

Larsen, Ralph, 198
Leadership, cases and practices, 182-212; development of, 196-212
Lean manufacturing, Toyota production system, 57-66
Learning organization
    as fad, 20-22
    cases and practices, 339-354
Leandri, Susan J., on benchmarking and best practices, 522-528
Leighton, Tracy, quoted, 472
Lesser, Eric
    on managing customer knowledge, 244-248
    virtuality and social capital, 498-510
Licht, Thomas, on creating knowledge culture, 235-243
Logistics, effect of corporate changes on, 494-497
Loofbourrow, Tod, quoted, 371
Loyalty, customer
    effects on profits and growth, 116-130
    programs described, 295-296
Lucent Technologies
    on collaboration at, 503
    just-in-time delivery at, 478-479

M

Magazines focusing on quality, directory of, 629-659
Malloni, Joe, quoted, 440
Managerial fads, described, 14-25
Mantey, Ed, quoted, 101-102
Manufacturing, cases and practices, 57-115
Maor, Shlomo, quoted, 19, 25
Market research, for small businesses, 342-354
McBride, Maranda, on just-in-time delivery, 478-484

INDEX

McClintock, Colleen, quoted, 372, 373, 374
McIlroy, Andrea, role of discount clubs, 293-307
McNerney, James, 196
McNerney, Jr., J. Jana, quoted, 16
Measurements
    and gages, 378-382
    Quality Management Maturity Grid and, 3-13
    on shop floor, 390-395
Merlin Exercise, 203
Midwest Community Hospital, treats patients as customers, 152
Miller, Brad, quoted, 102
Moore, Geoffrey, quoted, 384
Multimedia, use on shop floor, 75-76
Mundel, David, on managing customer knowledge, 244-248
Murphy, David, quoted, 195

N

Nahapiet, Janine, on social capital, 499-500
Nardelli, Robert, 196
Nasser, Jacques, quoted, 97, 186, 193
Naumann, Earl, on implementing customer satisfaction programs, 262-279
Net markets, on starting, 451-455
Newell, Chris, quoted, 258, 26
Newsletters focusing on quality, directory of, 629-659
Nortel, 233, 234
Norton, David, on balanced scorecards, 22-23

O

O'Connell, Jean, quoted, 16
Oil production, managing capital projects in, 67-73
Ojasalo, Jukka, on managing customer expectations, 130-150
Olivecrona, Richard, quoted, 441
One Minute Manager, as fad, 17-18
Outsourcing, of processes, 383-389
Owens, David, quoted, 312
Owens, Jim, quoted, 100

P

Parsley, Steve, on improving in-process handling, 396-403

PDA, uses of, 156
Pedersen, Kaj, quoted, 290, 291
PeopleSoft, knowledge management, 472-473
Peters, Doug, quoted, 16, 21, 23
Peters, Tom, on service excellence, 18-19
Phillips-Donaldson, Debbie, on value of Baldrige Award, 572-583
Piasecki, Dave, on optimizing economic order quantity (EOQ), 485-493
Pine II, B. Joseph, on limits of focus groups, 339-341
Piper, Tad W., quoted, 513
Pirret, Richard, quoted, 378
Piszczalski, Martin, quoted, 99
Planning, cases and practices, 163-181
Platt, Lewis E., 200
Porter, Michael, knowledge management, 461-477
Process improvement, use of Six Sigma for, 404-415
Process management, cases and practices, 355-403
Process maturity continuum, 362-363
Procter & Gamble, 169
Profits
    customers and, 297-298
    effects of loyalty and satisfaction, 116-130
Production line improvements, 85-95
Prusak, Laurence, 498-499

Q

Quality
    classic in, 3-13
    conferences and events 2002, calendar of, 660-681
    cost of, in automotive industry, 96-102
    how to reverse problems with, 35-37
    journals, magazines, and newsletters focusing on, 629-659
    online resources, directory of, 607-622
    on perceptions of commitment to, 38-54
    on resistance to, 26-37
    transformation cases and practices, 163-338
Quality auditing, 564-571
Quality Management Maturity Grid, described, 3-13
Quality organizations, directory of, 587-606
Quality of Work Life, movement, 165

Quality perspectives, various, 14-54
Quantum Idea Project (QIP), described, 188-189
Quote.com, case study, 290-291

R

Randolph, W. Alan, on empowerment, 213-230
Reagan, Ronald, 196
Records management, 461-477
Relationship marketing, role of, 294-295
Rhey, William L., on market research, 342-354
Rice, John, 196
Roberts Express, 233
Robinson, Dana, quoted, 22
Romanoff, Edward M., quoted, 418
Roos, Goran, on intellectual capital, 171-181
Roper, Kevin, quoted, 445
Rosenbaum, Mark S., on implementing customer satisfaction programs, 262-279
Ross, Ron, quoted, 371-372
Ruesch International, case study, 290
Rumizen, Melissie, quoted, 309
Ryan, Sue, quoted, 371

S

St. Paul Companies, case study, 312
Sanders, Doug, on using process improvement and Six Sigma, 404-415
Satisfaction customer
  programs and, 296-297
  effects on profits and growth, 116-130
Schroeder, Rich, role, 417
Seiler, Gerhard, on managing capital projects, 67-73
Semler, Ricardo, on self-managed teams, 23-24
Senge, Peter, ideas of, 20-22
Seven Habits, as fad, 19-20
Service excellence, as fad, 18-19
Services, cases and practices, 116-159
Sheina, Madan, quoted, 513
Sheridan, Steve, building solutions-based organization, 280-288
Shop floor production
  measurements for, 390-395
  performance support, 74-84
  role of information and, 74-84

Silver, Bruce, on record keeping, 463
Simonton, Trey, quoted, 453
Singer, Joe, partnering in manufacturing, 103-115
Singer, Peter, on customer data confidentiality, 289-292
Six Sigma, cases and practices, 404-437
Smith, Alice E., quoted, 102
Smith, Chris, quoted, 292
Smith, Kevin, quoted, 97
Smith, Ted, on record keeping, 463
Snowden, David, quoted, 308, 309, 313, 314
Social capital, IT and, 498-510
Solutions-based organizations, described, 280-288
Southwest Airlines, 233
Standards and assessments, cases and practices, 529-583
Stark, Ray, quoted, 417, 418, 423
Stein, Philip, on shop floor measurements, 390-395
Stein, Wolfram, on creating knowledge culture, 235-243
Sterling Consulting, 233
Stevenson, Thomas H., on ISO 9000, 551-563
Strandvik, Tore, satisfaction and loyalty, 116-130
Strategy, intellectual capital as, 171-181
Strong, Karen V., on value added information chains, 461-477
Sudbury Valley School, 169
Supply chain management, cases and practices, 461-497
Survey, on knowledge management, 255
Szoc, Ron, quoted, 290

T

Teams
  cases and practices, 308-338
  cost of, 319-324
  as fad, 23-24
  at Harley-Davidson, 103-115
  need to build e-commerce, 448
  value of, 316-319
Technology, CRM and, 154-156
Teresko, John, on e-commerce, 438-442
Theory of Constraints, production line improvements case, 85-95

INDEX

3M, Baldrige winner, 16
Tools and techniques, cases and practices, 355-460
Total Quality Management (TQM), as fad, 15-16
Toyota production system (TPS), described, 57-66
Toyota, quality at, 96-102
Trading exchanges, role of, 438-442
Trust, teaming and, 313-314

U

Umble, Elisabeth, on improving production line performance, 85-95
Umble, Michael, on improving production line performance, 85-95
Unions, teaming case, 103-115
Universities, quality case of, 38-54

V

Value creation process matrix, described, 360-362
Vartiainen, Matti, on performance support on shop floor, 74-84
Von Krogh, Georg, ideas of, 241-242

W

Wastler, Allen, quoted, 457
Waterman, Bob, on service excellence, 18-19
Wayman, Bob, 200
Web sites, on creating, 456-460
Welch, Jack, 196, 204; quoted, 197, 205
Wellman, Barry, quoted, 499
Weyerhauser Company, knowledge management at, 373-374
Wilcox, Randy, quoted, 454
Wiecha, Charles, on managing customer knowledge, 244-248
Wiele, A. van der, on resistance to quality, 26-37
Williams, A.R.T., on resistance to quality, 26-37
Williams, Ruth, quoted, 310
Wing, Kennard T., on being better leader, 182-184
Wisner, Priscilla S., on value of teams, 329-338
Wolfensohn, James, 201
World Bank, 210

X

Xerox, 502

Y

Yates, Don, how to define an organization, 163-170
Yilmaz, Mustafa R., on Six Sigma, 424-437
Yockelson, David, quoted, 451, 454
Yong, Karen, quoted, 21, 22, 25

Z

Zobell, Greg, quoted, 19, 20